GLOBALISATION AND T
IN IMPERIAL GERI

The process of globalisation in the late nineteenth century had a profound effect on the trajectories of German nationalism. While the existing literature on the subject has largely remained within the confines of national history, Sebastian Conrad uses the example of mobility and labour migration to show to what extent German nationalism was transformed under the auspices of global integration. Among the effects of cross-border circulation were the emergence of diasporic nationalism, the racialisation of the nation, the implementation of new border regimes and the hegemony of ideological templates that connected nationalist discourse to global geopolitics. Ranging from the African colonies, China and Brazil to the Polish-speaking territories in eastern Europe, this ground-breaking book demonstrates that the dynamics of German nationalism were not only negotiated in the Kaiserreich but also need to be situated in the broader context of globalisation before the First World War.

SEBASTIAN CONRAD is Professor of Modern History at the Freie Universität Berlin.

NEW STUDIES IN EUROPEAN HISTORY

Edited by

PETER BALDWIN, University of California, Los Angeles
CHRISTOPHER CLARK, University of Cambridge
JAMES B. COLLINS, Georgetown University
MIA RODRÍGUEZ-SALGADO, London School of Economics and
Political Science
LYNDAL ROPER, University of Oxford
TIMOTHY SNYDER, Yale University

The aim of this series in early modern and modern European history is to publish outstanding works of research, addressed to important themes across a wide geographical range, from southern and central Europe, to Scandinavia and Russia, from the time of the Renaissance to the Second World War. As it develops the series will comprise focused works of wide contextual range and intellectual ambition.

A full list of titles published in the series can be found at:
www.cambridge.org/newstudiesineuropeanhistory

GLOBALISATION AND THE NATION IN IMPERIAL GERMANY

SEBASTIAN CONRAD

Freie Universität Berlin

TRANSLATED BY
SORCHA O'HAGAN

CAMBRIDGE
UNIVERSITY PRESS

CAMBRIDGE UNIVERSITY PRESS
Cambridge, New York, Melbourne, Madrid, Cape Town, Singapore,
São Paulo, Delhi, Dubai, Tokyo, Mexico City

Cambridge University Press
The Edinburgh Building, Cambridge CB2 8RU, UK

Published in the United States of America by Cambridge University Press, New York

www.cambridge.org
Information on this title: www.cambridge.org/9780521177306

Originally published in German as *Globalisierung und Nation im Deutschen Kaiserreich* by
Verlag C. H. Beck oHG, Munich 2006

© Verlag C. H. Beck oHG, Munich 2006

First published in English as *Globalisation and the Nation in Imperial Germany* by
Cambridge University Press 2010

English edition © Cambridge University Press 2010

Printed in the United Kingdom at the University Press, Cambridge

A catalogue record for this publication is available from the British Library

Library of Congress Cataloguing in Publication data
Conrad, Sebastian.
[Globalisierung und Nation im deutschen Kaiserreich. English]
Globalisation and the nation in imperial Germany / Sebastian Conrad ; translated by
Sorcha O'Hagan.
p.   cm. – (New studies in European history)
Includes bibliographical references and index.
ISBN 978-0-521-76307-3 – ISBN 978-0-521-17730-6 (pbk.)
1. Germany–History–1871–1918.   2. Nationalism–Germany–History.
3. Germany–Emigration and immigration–History.   4. Germans–Foreign
countries–History.   5. Foreign workers, German–History.   6. Germans–Ethnic
identity.   I. Title.   II. Series.
DD220.C6613 2010
943.08′4–dc22
2010021897

ISBN 978-0-521-76307-3 Hardback
ISBN 978-0-521-17730-6 Paperback

Contents

v

Illustrations

Maps

vii

Introduction

The nineteenth century is generally regarded as the century of the nation state. Inspired by the example of the *Grande Nation* (and the challenge it presented), western Europe, so the grand narrative of modernisation runs, transformed itself from a patchwork of minor states into a landscape of nations. 'Blood and iron' (Bismarck), internal nation-building and the 'invention of traditions' turned highly varied political units into imagined communities that all saw themselves as nations: large and small ones, late developers, oppressed and incomplete ones. During the nineteenth century this model was exported around the world, and from then onward, national states were seen as the only possible subjects of international law, the only political actors. In historiography, too, this has long remained the privileged perspective. The past was usually narrated in the form of national histories.

But at the same time, the late nineteenth century was an era of worldwide interaction and exchange. This fact is returning to historical consciousness only now, in the context of the current wave of globalisation. Individual nation states entered into relationships with each other to an increasing extent. International relations and diplomacy emerged as the incarnation of politics. States were economically interlinked to a high degree, as symbolised in the World Exhibitions; in many ways, this level of interlinkage was only reattained in the 1970s. Trade in consumer goods increased to a previously unknown degree and influenced reading habits, tastes in art and trends in fashion. Many of the main aspects of the current globalisation process were already in existence in 1900.

The present volume is a contribution to the attempt to return attention to some of the global dimensions of German history. German history did not unfold solely within the boundaries of the nation state. Nor did the world remain outside; external events had far-reaching effects on German society. The Kaiserreich formed an integral part of the political, economic and cultural interrelationships that characterised the world before 1914. Pre-First World War German history is and has always been part of the history of the process of globalisation around 1900.

The chapters below examine the question of how the dominance of perspectives based on the nation state can be reconciled with the formation of a globalised world. After all, contemporaries were well aware of the global context in which German society was located. Terms such as 'world politics' (*Weltpolitik*) and 'world economy' became ubiquitous, and there was intense debate about emigration laws, protectionism, Americanisation and the 'yellow peril'; all this is evidence of the global consciousness that emerged around 1900. If we take a closer look at how contemporaries interpreted this globalising process, it is striking to see that they typically saw it more or less as a natural stage of development. First, it was generally assumed, nations developed into modern nation states; then they would gradually enter into contact with each other, begin to become international, and start to engage in global trade and world politics. 'The family became the clan [*Stamm*]; a combination of clans became the state and the nation', August Bebel assured the public, 'and finally, the close links between nations developed into internationality. That is the historical process.'[1] First the nation, then the interconnections: we may call this the paradigm of consecutivity, a model of stages of global development.

But is this idea not a 'national inversion', an attempt to make transnational and systemic contexts comprehensible and, where possible, controllable?[2] Nationalisation and globalisation, I will argue, are

---

[1] Bebel, *Commune*, p. 29. This viewpoint was by no means limited to Germany. 'The Nineteenth Century was the Century of Nationalism', the British journalist W. T. Stead declared in 1907, 'the Twentieth Century is the Century of Internationalism' (quoted in Herren, 'Internationalism', p. 121).

[2] I have borrowed the term 'national inversion' from Hill, *National History*, Chapter 1.

not two stages of a consecutive process of development, but rather were dependent on each other. This book suggests that the dynamics of nationalisation and nationalism must always be understood as, in part, a product of the globalisation of the turn-of-the-century era and not merely as its prerequisite. This idea aims to complement prior research on the nation, which focused mainly on the internal history of the Kaiserreich. The present volume argues, in contrast, that the transformation of the idea of the nation and of nationalism in the Wilhelmine era can also be seen as an effect of global interlinkages: as a partly exogenous formation of the nation in the context of globalisation.[3]

This link will be investigated using the example of the debates about labour mobility and the effects these debates had on the idea of the German nation. The explorations below start from the observation that transnational interlinkages of work reached a peak at around 1900, while, paradoxically, the idea of the specific national character of 'German work' became most widely held during the same period. The trope of 'German work' (*deutsche Arbeit*) emerged as an important element of the way the nation was conceived during the Wilhelmine period.[4] It continued to be of importance, in different guises, in the decades to follow. The concept played a fatal role in the ideology of National Socialism and the latter's 'soldiers of labour'. The term was revisited during the years of the West German 'economic miracle', when work functioned as a surrogate for coming to terms with

---

[3] The chapters that follow thus also contribute to the attempt to elucidate the relationship between globalisation and modernisation. Globalisation is often understood as a continuation or extension of modernisation, a modernisation that includes the process of nationalisation. This viewpoint picks up on the contemporary idea of 'world politics' (*Weltpolitik*), which was seen in industrial circles as linked to the (desirable) further modernisation of German society. In contrast, the process of globalisation is here viewed as the constitutive framework within which strategies and practices of modernisation and nationalisation can be explained – and, it is suggested, which formed the framework within which it was determined what should be regarded as modern and national. For a discussion of these two perspectives see Smith, 'Weltpolitik'.

[4] Other subjects could also be used to exemplify this tension between the universal and the particular – for example, the idea of 'German science'; see Jessen and Vogel (eds.), *Wissenschaft und Nation*, which also gives further references.

the recent past (Hannah Arendt has spoken of a 'weapon against the claims made by reality'), and when the term 'German quality work' (*deutsche Wertarbeit*) had its second coming; it was also reincarnated in the East German moniker of a 'country of work' (*Staat der Arbeit*).

How can we explain the fact that the idea of the ahistoric, unchangeable and nationally specific character of 'German work' became established at a moment in history that was characterised by mobility, exchange and circulation? In this book I aim to unravel this paradox. Globalisation contributed, around 1900, to the popularity of ideas about distinct national characteristics because of and not in spite of the fact that it was creating upheavals in the political, economic and discursive orders of this world of nations. Instead of dissolving national borders, mass mobility in the late nineteenth century could 'actually help to explain the intensity of nationalist movements and the focus of national states on ideological nation-building in the years prior to World War I', as Donna Gabaccia claims.[5] The search for particularity and for the elements of an unchangeable national identity, I suggest below, was not a threatened relic of a pre-global world order, but rather an actual effect of processes of cross-border circulation.

This perspective is supported by new approaches taken in the theoretical literature on globalisation. For some time, the sociological theory of globalisation assumed that increases in exchange, in inter-relationships and in circulation would lead to a gradual homogenisation of the world. During the nineteenth century, European expansion across the globe was accompanied by optimistic expectations of a common, assimilated (in the contemporary rhetoric: 'civilised') world, that were supported by the euphoria of free-trade propaganda, or later by the visions of the League of Nations. This hope, or rather fear, which still pervades current discourse about the 'Coca-colonization' of the world and the development of a 'McWorld',[6] has given way, over recent years, to a more differentiated understanding of global interlinkages. The consequences of interactions include not only homogenisation and assimilation (under asymmetric conditions)

---

[5] Gabaccia, 'Juggling Jargons', p. 54.
[6] An example of this point of view can be found in Barber, *Jihad*.

but also delimitation and fragmentation. As such, the process of globalisation was characterised not only by cross-border interactions; it also contributed to the creation and consolidation of these borders.[7] The increase in transnational interrelationships can thus be seen as one of the most important factors contributing to the consolidation of national categories. As Craig Calhoun phrases it: 'No era placed greater emphasis on the autonomy of the nation state or the capacity of the idea of nation to define large-scale collective identities. But it did so precisely when and partly because the world was becoming pronouncedly international.'[8]

Any transnational history of globalisation has to investigate a complex web of 'shared histories' (*geteilte Geschichten*; Shalina Randeria) of the modern era. The German term *geteilte Geschichten* combines two opposing connotations in English, both 'shared' and 'divided', and thus expresses the ambivalences of a history of exchange and interaction. On the one hand, the formation and development of the modern world can be read as a 'shared history' in which a variety of cultures and societies interacted and interrelated, thus jointly constituting the modern world, and in which processes of mutual appropriation led to homogenising effects. On the other, the increasing circulation of goods, people and ideas did not only create commonalities – it also resulted in delimitations, difference and a need for particularity. This applies both to a large number of differences and inequalities within societies and to the policies of delimitation between nation states.[9]

As such, the arguments below form part of the project of transnational historiography. These debates are the result of processes of increasing European integration and of discussion on globalisation. The main goal of the concept is to overcome the tunnel vision

---

[7] For examples of the literature on globalisation theory see Appadurai, *Disjuncture*; Robertson, *Globalization*; Bauman, *Globalization*; Dirlik, 'Is There History'; Dirlik, *Global Modernity*; and Scholte, *Globalization*. See also, with a slightly different area of investigation, Bayart, *Gouvernement*.

[8] Calhoun, 'Nationalism', p. 463.

[9] On this concept see Conrad and Randeria, 'Geteilte Geschichten'; and Randeria, 'Geteilte Geschichte'.

that focuses on national societies alone, excluding their regional and global interlinkages. The concept picks up on approaches from comparative history and the history of transfers that, since the 1980s in particular, have helped to place national narratives in context and to relativise them.[10] Transnational history is understood here primarily as a perspective that allows us to go beyond the sharp division between 'internal' and 'external', and the question of which has primacy. Historical processes are seen as relational, and the focus is on the constitutive role played by the interactions between regions and nations in the development of modern societies. Transnational history is critical of the idea that national developments took place autonomously and that they can be understood on the basis of the nation's own traditions. Instead, the links between the European and non-European worlds, inextricably bound up since the nineteenth century at the very latest, form the point of departure for a historiography that does not limit itself to national teleologies.[11]

Such discussions are not restricted to Germany. In Britain, in particular, recent studies on imperial history, often focusing on the 'new imperialism' from the 1890s onward, have examined the question of the importance of the empire for Great Britain. Peter Cain and Anthony Hopkins brought the empire back to the metropole with their concept of 'gentlemanly capitalism'.[12] The 'Manchester School' of social history around John MacKenzie focused in particular on the effects of imperial expansion on everyday life in Britain.[13]

---

[10] On comparative history and the history of transfers, see Haupt and Kocka, *Geschichte*; Kaelble, *Vergleich*; Espagne, 'Limites'; and Paulmann, 'Vergleich', which gives further references. See also Middell, 'Kulturtransfer'.

[11] See, for example, the discussions in Osterhammel, 'Transnationale Gesellschaftsgeschichte'; Spiliotis, 'Transterritorialität'; Wirz, 'Gesellschaftsgeschichte'; Conrad, 'Doppelte Marginalisierung'; Werner and Zimmermann, 'Histoire croisée'; Werner and Zimmermann, 'Vergleich'; Patel, 'Transatlantische Perspektiven'; and Patel, *Nationalfixiertheit*. Transnational approaches can in many cases link in to the history of international politics: Loth and Osterhammel, *Internationale Geschichte*. See also Subrahmanyam, 'Connected Histories'; and Gruzinski, 'Mondes'.

[12] See Cain and Hopkins, *British Imperialism*; and Dumett, *Gentlemanly Capitalism*. See also Hopkins' influential essay 'Back to the Future'.

[13] Among a large number of studies see MacKenzie, *Propaganda*; *Imperialism*; and *Empire of Nature*.

Many studies in the areas of postcolonial and cultural studies have looked at the effects of the colonial experience on the home country and have argued that 'British "nationhood" was built up through empire'.[14] For the history of Britain, with its long-lasting and extensive colonial empire, this remains an important perspective, all sceptical voices notwithstanding.[15] In the USA, too, the national past is increasingly placed in transnational contexts. Here, it is not so much a formal empire that is under examination but rather the country's place in global history.[16]

In a similar spirit, the following pages focus on the non-European dimensions of German history as an attempt to complement a historiography that has to date looked mainly at Germany in its European context. But around the turn of the century, Europe had expanded to every corner of the globe, and had been altered and shaped by the experience of this expansion. In the course of colonialism and – of even greater importance for the Kaiserreich – of global interlinkages that went beyond formal territorial claims, the world had increasingly become a single area of action and its systemic constraints had effects on Europe and on the German empire. For that reason, the goal is not so much to play off European, colonial and global references against each other, but rather to recognise that European – and German – history around 1900 took place in a global context.[17]

MOBILITY

In 1900, Germany was on the move. Wanderers and travelling journeymen walked the highways as they had in the previous decades. Railways, the tourism industry and the seaside resorts were evidence of the mobility of the bourgeoisie. Population growth, the increasing

---

[14] Marks, 'History', p. 117. See also Burton, 'Civilising Subjects'; and Kumar, 'Nation'.

[15] See for example Cannadine, *Ornamentalism*; and Porter, *Absent-Minded Imperialists*.

[16] See in particular the landmark volume edited by Bender: *Rethinking*; as well as Bender, *Nation among Nations*.

[17] On this subject see the contributions to Conrad and Osterhammel, *Kaiserreich*.

pull of the cities, and the economic opportunities that the industrial centres presented all led to a flight of people from rural areas. But migration from the countryside to the urban centres was often just the first stage of a longer journey that brought many Germans abroad (and frequently back again). Between 1880 and 1893, approximately 2 million left the country. In addition, German ports were points of departure for large numbers of emigrants from eastern Europe. By the eve of the First World War, around 7 million people had passed through Bremerhaven alone on their way across the Atlantic. But Germany was not merely a point of departure for migrants; it was also the destination of many immigrants, from Holland, Poland and Italy, for example, seeking either permanent or temporary work. Many of these movements were by no means final – they were just the first stage of further movements. During harvest periods, many seasonal workers and *Sachsengänger* (travellers to Saxony) supplied the seasonal demand for labour in agriculture. The national economist Werner Sombart compared Germany to an ant-heap into which a passer-by had pushed his walking-stick.[18] Between 1890 and 1914, mobility within, out of and into Germany became 'a mass phenomenon which was without precedent in Europe'.[19]

Mass mobility was one of the main characteristics of globalisation in the nineteenth century. A series of profound changes, mainly linked to the global expansion of capitalist methods of production, led to a considerable increase in mobility and in the distances that people travelled. Industrial production and the expansion of plantation agriculture, combined with the interlinking of markets around the world, meant that the demand for labour was increasingly met outside national boundaries. The creation of global labour markets was greatly facilitated by revolutionary changes in transport and in information technology, but also by the imperial penetration of large

---

[18] Sombart, *Volkswirtschaft*, p. 408.
[19] Wehler, *Gesellschaftsgeschichte*, Vol. III, p. 503. See, especially on domestic migration, Köllmann, *Bevölkerung*; and Langewiesche, 'Wanderungsbewegungen'. On emigration and immigration see Bade, *Europa*; Bade, 'Massenauswanderung'; Herbert, *Ausländerbeschäftigung*; and Hoerder and Nagel, *People*. On the transit migration movements from eastern Europe see Just, *Amerikawanderung*.

areas of the planet from 1882 onward.[20] During the nineteenth century, some 60 million people emigrated from Europe alone, mainly to the New World. Germany was one of the centres of this mass exodus. But European migration was merely part of a global process of mobility that was frequently organised by colonial governments and that was further intensified by the abolition of slavery. The numbers involved were enormous. From 1834 to 1937, between thirty and 45 million people left the Indian subcontinent; almost 50 million moved from Russia and north-eastern Asia to Siberia and Manchuria; over 19 million Chinese emigrated to south-eastern Asia; Japanese workers moved to Hawaii, California and Brazil; Java provided workers for the European colonies in Asia; and in Africa, worker mobility also continued to increase, often under conditions not far removed from slavery. Often, imported workers were preferred to natives because they were assumed to be easier to discipline (and to fire).[21]

Contemporaries, too, saw mobility as one of the central characteristics of the era. Around 1900, there was an 'almost neurotic consciousness of the process of mobility', as Geoffrey Barraclough has noted, which culminated in a global fear of the 'Yellow Peril'.[22] In Germany, too, this level of mobility led to intense and controversial debate about movement and stability, restrictions on access and restricted periods (*Karenzzeiten*), the freedom of movement and boundaries, segregation and alterity, amalgamation and identity. These debates did not take place in isolation. Close attention was paid in Germany to debates in other countries about limiting immigration, in particular in the USA, Australia and South Africa. The debate on migration reveals how a global consciousness developed among German political actors – especially when restrictions elsewhere created a risk that migratory flows would be redirected to Germany.[23] Hopes and fears linked to mobility, to transport or to the arrival of 'population

[20] See O'Rourke and Williamson, *Globalization*; and Williamson, 'Globalization'.
[21] See McKeown, 'Global Migration'. See also McNeill and Adams, *Human Migration*; Nugent, *Crossings*; Segal, *Atlas;* Wang, *Global History*; van der Linden, 'Geschichte'; and Hoerder, *Cultures*, esp. pp. 331–404.
[22] Barraclough, *Introduction*, p. 80.
[23] See Zolberg, 'Global Movements'.

masses' were among the ingredients of discourses on the nation. The way the nation viewed itself was permanently affected by the debates about Germans abroad (*Auslandsdeutsche*) and the 'loss of national energies', about overseas settlers and colonial 'New Germany', and about seasonal workers and the threat of 'Polonisation'. Nationalism in the Wilhelmine era was always influenced by issues of mobility, circulation and globalisation.[24]

Of course, mobility was not a phenomenon that was new to Germany. In fact, it had a long history. During the pre-modern age, migration for work (most famously by the 'Holland-goers') and the movements of travelling merchants were the most important forms of employment migration, along with the wanderings of travelling journeymen. Proletarian mass migration began during the 'great transformation', the crisis-ridden period during which Germany changed from an agricultural to an industrial society, especially from the 1840s. These migratory trends were reinforced by the growth in population during the nineteenth century. During the peak of pauperism, around the middle of the century, large numbers of impoverished people could be found on the country's highways. Emigration also took off in the early nineteenth century, mainly to the United States. It reached its first peak in 1846/47 as a result of the agricultural and trade crises of those years, with 1.3 million people leaving the German states. (The second major wave was from 1864 to 1873.)[25]

Thus, the transition to mass mobility was a gradual process without any abrupt shifts. However, mobility did become even more important in Germany from the 1880s onward, both in terms of the numbers involved and in terms of public perception. It was only during this period that the country as a whole became industrialised, and this was also the time of the largest wave of emigration: almost 2 million people left the country in the years after 1880. There were even higher levels of through-migration from eastern Europe, mainly

---

[24] Bade, *Deutsche im Ausland*; and O'Donnell, Bridenthal and Reagin, *Heimat Abroad*.

[25] See, as an introduction to the extensive literature, Moch, *Moving Europeans*; Bade, *Europa*, pp. 17–120; Köllmann, *Bevölkerung*; and Küther, *Menschen*. See the overview given in Kocka, *19. Jahrhundert*, pp. 61–79.

via Berlin (Ruhleben) and the ports of Hamburg and Bremerhaven. The introduction of steamships facilitated the increase in transatlantic mobility, and also contributed to the high numbers of emigrants who returned. In addition – and this was a new development – from the 1890s onward, there was considerable migration into Germany, which quickly became the 'country with the highest level of labour imports in the world' after the United States.[26] This led to intense debates on domestic policy; the immigration of Polish workers, in particular, was treated as an issue where the nation itself was at stake. But emigration, too, was now seen as a problem of national importance. One of the main arguments for Germany acquiring its own colonial empire after 1884 was that this would allow emigration flows to be redirected to German-controlled lands. Without doubt, in the three decades before the First World War migration had a significant impact on German history.

When, during the Wilhelmine era, the opportunities and, especially, the risks of mobility and migration were under discussion, what was of interest was not so much the development of tourism or the first 'globetrotters' – a term that became established in Germany after 1900 – nor the movements of economic elites, diplomats or artists. The main concern was the mobility of the petit bourgeois, peasant and proletarian masses, and the circulation of labour. The scale of this mobility was seen as new and, in many ways, threatening; it was also at the centre of the transformation of feudal and agricultural societies into modern industrial states. Labour flexibility was both a precondition for, and an effect of, the industrial transformation of production; and mobility – both social and spatial – was the sign of the times.

WORK IN AN AGE OF GLOBALISATION

The nineteenth century saw itself as the 'century of work' – or at least was, around 1900, frequently described in retrospect in these terms. 'If we aim to describe the nineteenth century with a single phrase

---

[26] Ferenczi, *Kontinentale Wanderungen*, cited in Bade, *Europa*, p. 67.

that describes its inmost character in contrast to all other ages', Willy Wygodzinski stated in 1907, summarising a commonly held opinion, 'we may term it, in brief, "The Century of Work"'.[27] Of course, this was a stylisation; work was done in earlier eras too and the nineteenth century is by no means alone in its claim to have been industrious. However, three developments came together after 1800 that made the privileging of work plausible for a broader public, both bourgeois and proletarian.

Firstly, people around 1900 could look back on a long period during which work had gradually been assigned increasing value. Of course this did not apply across the board, and philosophical and popular hymns to work went hand-in-hand with the hard and relentless nature of actual work experiences. But many studies have shown us that, influenced partly by Christian ideas, partly by the way of life in European cities since the Middle Ages, by the Reformation, by the Enlightenment and, last but not least, by capitalism, the significance of and value placed on work in people's lives and by politics and society in general had been gradually increasing. The order of the industrial society was based explicitly on work – performance, careers, success – and no longer on ascriptive status criteria, on ancestry and estate. Work was seen as the 'source of all riches and of all culture', as the Gotha Programme of the Socialist Workers' Party stated. This process of valorisation found expression in the idea of the 'occupation' (*Beruf*), with its emphatic loading, and in the 'Gospels of Work' compiled by authors such as Thomas Carlyle or Samuel Smiles.[28]

Secondly, gainful employment had undergone far-reaching changes during industrialisation. This affected mainly waged employment in industrial plants, which was characterised by the division of labour and 'alienation', by anonymity in large-scale factories, and also by new forms of social integration.[29] It was accompanied by the introduction of rigid work disciplines, in fact by a process of making the

---

[27] Wygodzinski, *Wandlungen*, p. 32.
[28] For introductions to this subject see Zorn, 'Arbeit'; Conze, 'Arbeit'; Ehmer and Gutschner, 'Befreiung'; and Kocka and Offe, *Geschichte*.
[29] See Kocka, *Arbeitsverhältnisse*.

employed population more 'diligent'.[30] But the effects of industrialised work extended beyond the area of manufacturing plants and factories. The separation of work and the family; the increase in gender-specific divisions of labour; and, more generally, the differentiation of work as a discrete realm in both spatial and biographical terms, were all characteristics of the work regime of the nineteenth century.

Thirdly, toward the end of the century, in particular from the 1880s onward, there was an increasing tendency to define social participation through work. The establishment of the welfare state institutionalised work as a key category, since social welfare was now linked to waged work. Instead of the individual or the family, the social insurance system of the Bismarck era took work (male, industrial work) as its point of reference. Exclusion, too, was defined by means of work performed and the willingness to work. This affected marginalised groups such as the Sinti and Roma, and also the Jews; discrimination against these groups was justified in part by their supposed lack of a work ethic. Finally, the 1912 'Work-Shy Act' codified the boundaries that the bourgeois work ethic placed on social participation. Josef Ehmer has stated that, at the turn of the century, 'work became a major factor in political inclusion and exclusion'.[31]

The central role of work is also reflected in contemporary social theories. The most influential, and the theory that had the most sustained effect on the development of historiography, was Max Weber's 1905 text on the Protestant work ethic. This text is a manifesto of the importance of work for defining modern subjectivity and, as such, is itself a product of the centuries-long process of valorisation of the idea of work. In the late nineteenth century, work was at the core of the modern concept of the individual, defined nations (and their national economies) and was the motor of (dialectic-materialistic) history. Michel Foucault has described 'labour' (along with language and life) as one of the 'transcendental principles' that structured the episteme of the modern age.[32]

---

[30] See Schenda, 'Verfleißigung'; Dreßen, *Pädagogische Maschine*; Helmstetter, 'Austreibung'; Flohr, *Arbeiter*; and Steinert and Treiber, *Fabrikation*.

[31] Ehmer, 'Geschichte'.

[32] See Foucault, *Order*, esp. pp. 272–329.

Most of the changes discussed above were initiated and shaped by the triumph of industrialised work. Factory work was usually at the centre of any discussion of the idea of work. But when the mobility of labour was being discussed, the main focus of attention was on agricultural workers. Discussion of the effects that the interconnectedness of labour markets would have on the nation paid special attention to agricultural activities. This does not mean that industrial work did not play any role in debates about mobility – one example is the conflict between international solidarity and the goal of protecting the national labour force that was played out in the unions and the socialist parties. When, during the late nineteenth century, 'work' was being discussed, the term could be used to refer to a variety of different things – industrial work, but also craftwork, housework or 'intellectual work'.[33] If, in the paragraphs below, the focus is often on agricultural work, that is because the topic dominated discussions on global labour mobility and its effect on nationalist discourse.

Why did agriculture gain this privileged status in discussion of the significance of labour mobility? One reason is that mobility in the Kaiserreich was seen mainly as something that affected the rural population – even if, of course, most people were moving into the urban industrial regions, eliciting debates about social upheaval, and about poverty in the 'Moloch' of the city. But contemporaries saw mobility primarily as a 'flight from the land'. This can be seen in the popular concern for agriculture that was reflected in repeated discussions about whether 'freedom of movement' should be limited. Most experts (including Max Weber) even believed that the 'flight from the land' in the eastern provinces of Prussia had not been caused by industrialisation, but should in fact be seen as displacement of the rural population by mobile Polish agricultural workers.[34]

Another reason is that agricultural work played a central role in discussions about the future of the nation. This was not so much a

[33] On the competing interpretations of the science of work see for example Rabinbach, *Human Motor*. On the central role the ideal of skilled craftwork played for the working class see Welskopp, *Banner*.

[34] See the overview given in Nichtweiß, *Saisonarbeiter*.

direct result of the increase in agricultural productivity, related to the introduction of machinery. It had more to do with the falling proportion of the working population engaged in agriculture (by 1913 this had fallen to 35 per cent) and the 'endangerment' of rural regions through mass immigration (of non-German nationals) from the 1890s onward. In Wilhelmine Germany, agriculture came to be seen – especially in conservative and nationally minded circles – as a symbol of the fatherland and a nursery of national strength and energy: not least, as a source from which soldiers could be recruited to defend the common good. 'The rural population', as the *Konservative Korrespondenz* wrote at the turn of the century, 'forms an irreplaceable basis not only for our German army but for the entire national power of the *Volk*'.[35] In addition, agricultural work featured in debates about social renewal and in the life-reform movement, in which it was seen as the basis of an idealised society that would be free from the supposedly devastating effects of industrialisation and globalised labour markets.[36] Finally, agricultural work was also at the centre of discussions on 'German work', the popular expression of the nationalisation of work. My focus on this process of nationalisation means that in the following account, other dimensions of work – for example, work as the locus of social conflicts, or changes in views of work in the context of industrialised capitalism – must take a back seat.

THE GLOBAL NATION

In this book, the topos of 'German work' is used as an example of the nationalising effects of global circulation. The three decades before the First World War were, I suggest, marked by a change in form of the idea of the nation, under the conditions of intensified globality. This perspective requires a rethinking of the standard historiography of nationalism. What is at stake here, then, is a revision of common

[35] *Konservative Korrespondenz* (27 February 1900). On the role played by army recruits from rural areas (who, in 1911, still made up two-thirds of conscripts) see in particular Förster, *Militarismus*.

[36] See Rohkrämer, *Andere Moderne*; Bergmann, *Agrarromantik*; Barlösius, *Lebensführung*; and Buchholz *et al.*, *Lebensreform*.

assumptions concerning the history of nationalism. My argument is intended as a contribution to a 'spatial turn' in the historiography of nationalism. For the most part, the dynamics of nationalism have been located within the nation states at issue: as long traditions and continuities of a national 'essence', as 'imagined communities', as reactions to the disruptive effects of modernisation, as 'invented traditions' or as new departures by social groups that aimed at a different kind of modernity. What I will suggest, however, is that the particular form that nationalism and the representation of the nation took around 1900 need to be read in the context of interactions and entanglements on a global scale. The shifts and changes in the discourse of nationalism thus appear as effects not only of internal trajectories, as the familiar picture would suggest, but just as much of the larger process we retrospectively call globalisation.

This not only refers to the obvious fact that the nation state concept, in many countries, was the result of cultural transfers. This is well recognised in many (if not all) theories of nationalism. Benedict Anderson and others have stressed the degree to which the nation was a product of relationships.[37] In particular in the colonial world the nation state was thus an import that superseded traditional forms of belonging and loyalty – and remained, as Partha Chatterjee has phrased it, a 'derivative discourse'.[38] It is thus widely recognised that the institution of the nation state has travelled. However, the specific meanings and dynamics of nationalism are generally seen as emanating from local conditions. The spread of the 'nation form' (Etienne Balibar), in other words, may be the product of systemic conditions of world order, while the particular ideological contents of nationalism are assumed to derive from cultural traditions and to draw on legacies entirely from within.[39] What I will argue, instead, is that the way the nation was defined, understood and practised – the particular contents of nationalism – owed more to the global context in which it was constituted than has hitherto been recognised.[40] The logic and

---

[37] See Anderson, *Imagined Communities*. See also Cubitt, *Imagining Nations*.
[38] Chatterjee, *Nationalist Thought*.
[39] Balibar, 'The Nation Form'.
[40] I have greatly benefited from the powerful argument in Hill, *National History*.

dynamics of nationalism, as Rebecca Karl has argued for late Qing China, were not only shaped by diachronic 'stages of development', but equally by a synchronic 'staging of the world'.[41]

This does not mean, to be sure, that the history of nationalism and the creation of the nation in Germany began only with the intensification of global interlinkages from the 1880s onward. The national idea had a long tradition, stretching back at least to the time of the Napoleonic wars. Romanticism, the 1848 revolutions and the national movement, and the unification of the empire all effected transformations and changes of focus for nationalism in Germany. By 1880, nationalism was not a new phenomenon. In other words, the argument is not that nationalism and nation state parameters developed only in the course of intensified processes of globalisation from the 1880s onward. But there can be no doubt that from this period, if not earlier, the internal formations of the nation state and also of nationalism were strongly influenced by global events, and any reconstruction of their dynamics must take that context into account.

This interest in the transformations in the idea of the nation that occurred around the turn of the century follows on from approaches previously taken by research on the nation. German national imagination and the development of new forms of social integration were in no sense monolithic; they always cooperated and/or competed with regional, religious, gender-specific, social and political identities. For this reason, the history of nationalism is by no means unilinear and teleologic. However, most historians agree that there was a definite change in the self-understanding of the German nation around 1890.

Two main dimensions of this change have been discussed. Firstly, during the Wilhelmine era, nationalism was popularised and began to reach far beyond the educated elites that formed its original constituency. The growing importance of state institutions that inculcated nationalism – above all the military and the schools – was an important factor in creating a mass base for nationalism, as were the press and the emergence of a spate of national associations. The Navy League (*Flottenverein*) was arguably the most powerful and influential

---

[41] Karl, *Staging the World.*

agent of such nationalisation, which was always complemented, however, by many institutions that nurtured grass-roots nationalism 'from below'.[42]

Secondly, nationalism changed in terms of its contents and structure. For a long time, this change has been seen mainly as a political change, a move from 'left-wing' nationalism to 'right-wing' nationalism.[43] However, more recent research has made it clear that aggressive and exclusionary aspects had been constituent parts of German nationalism at least since the beginning of the nineteenth century.[44] The aspect that was new was the way that nationalism became loaded with ethnic categories and social-hygienic or eugenic technologies. This led to the creation of new ideas about 'enemies' of the nation, which increasingly focused on 'foreign' populations both inside and outside the boundaries of the state. This superimposition of a discourse of race onto the idea of the nation – of which modern anti-Semitism is a typical example – must be seen as the main characteristic of the radicalisation of nationalism around 1900; in fact it is sometimes even seen as a 'radical re-interpretation of the nation as a biopolitical agenda'.[45]

A third dimension should be added: one which has not previously taken centre stage in the literature on nationalism. It has less to do with the idea of the nation as such than with the legal and material consolidation of national borders. At the end of the nineteenth century, increased attention was being paid, around the world, to border security and to controlling cross-border mobility. Biometric data were being recorded and perfected, citizenship laws were being

---

[42] On the *Flottenverein* see for example Deist, *Flottenpolitik*; see also Chickering, *We Men*; and Doerry, *Übergangsmenschen*. On nationalism 'from below' see for example Rohrkrämer, *Militarismus*; and Kunz, *Verortete Geschichte*.

[43] For a typical example see Winkler, 'Nationalismus'. For a criticism of this approach see Langewiesche, *Nationalismus im 19. und 20. Jahrhundert*.

[44] See in particular Jeismann, *Vaterland*. For an overview see Wehler, *Nationalismus*; Langewiesche, 'Forschungsstand'; Langewiesche, *Nation, Nationalismus, Nationalstaat*; and Haupt and Tacke, 'Kultur'.

[45] Geulen, *Wahlverwandte*, p. 30. See also Weindling, *Health*. On anti-Semitism see for example Berding, *Moderner Antisemitismus*; Katz, *Vorurteil*; Volkov, 'Antisemitismus'; Zumbini, *Wurzeln*; and Benz and Bergmann, *Vorurteil*.

cemented and were becoming increasingly exclusive, passports and personal documents were becoming more common, and travel restrictions and immigration quotas were being introduced. This all meant that national borders became tighter and were more rigidly controlled, and that they became more and more important in structuring social processes.[46] In addition, the physical form of the borders themselves was changing. The erection of thirty-nine border posts by the *Deutsche Feldarbeiterzentralstelle* (the 'German Central Office for Field Workers'; for national, identity-based and hygiene-policing controls on mobility) was just one example of how boundaries and their material forms in space were reinforced.[47]

For a long time, the transformation of nationalism was explained mainly in terms of internal forces. Typically, the emergence of mass nationalist associations and the more strident tone of nationalism in the 1890s have been explained as wholly the result of internal conflicts in the developing industrial society. The more serious the tensions created by the process of transformation, it has been argued, the more aggressive the reaction in the form of extreme nationalism. Radical nationalism has thus been seen merely as a veiling superstructure, 'as a compensatory ideology of development'.[48] This view has been challenged by Geoff Eley and others, who did not dismiss nationalism as retrograde ideology, but rather stressed the forms of social and political contestation that were specific to the dynamic forms of capitalist modernity being generated between the 1890s and 1914. While the focus here, too, is on the fields of conflict inside German society, the thrust of the argument is closer to what I will argue as it takes

---

[46] See Cole, *Suspect Identities*; Fahrmeir, 'German Citizenships'; Fahrmeir, Faron and Weil, *Migration Control*; Gosewinkel, *Einbürgern*; Vec, *Spur*; Torpey, *Invention*; and Caplan and Torpey, *Documenting*. See also Bashford, *Medicine at the Border*. On the Indian context, which was an important setting for trying out new identification procedures, see Singha, 'Settle, Mobilize, Verify'; and Sengoopta, *Imprint*. For historical points of reference see also Groebner, *Schein*.

[47] This material dimension of borders has not yet been systematically analysed, in contrast to the history of the locations of the borders themselves or indeed changes in mental maps. An investigation would be worthwhile.

[48] Wehler, 'Verbandsforschung'. For an overview of research on German nationalism see Wehler, *Nationalismus*, pp. 62–89; and Langewiesche, *Nation, Nationalismus, Nationalstaat*, pp. 190–236.

Wilhelmine nationalism as a point of departure rather than a mere continuation of older traditions.[49]

More recent work by cultural historians has modified this internalist perspective and has shown that the dynamics of nationalism in Germany cannot be understood without reference to other societies. France in particular, the 'fatherland of the enemies', was a perennial point of reference;[50] and so was the examination of the 'enemies at home' (especially the Jews),[51] while other points of reference – for example, Poland – have been little explored.[52] German nationalism has, from its beginnings, not just from 1890 onward, always been a transnational nationalism.[53]

The explorations below follow on from these ideas, by extending the focus to the global dimensions of German history. Limiting explorations to European points of reference risks overlooking the extent to which important debates about the role and the future development of the Kaiserreich were framed within a global consciousness. Examples include the discussions about protective import duties, about the alternative of an agricultural or an industrial state, about naval policy and about the citizenship law of 1913. Here, too, there is an extensive literature that can be built upon. The history of international relations, of foreign policy in the Wilhelmine era, of imperialism and of colonialism examines the increasing global interconnectedness of the Kaiserreich.[54] The present volume takes these

---

[49] Eley, *Reshaping the German Right*; and Chickering, *We Men*.

[50] See in particular Jeismann, *Vaterland*. See also Tacke, *Denkmal*; and Nolan, *Mirror*. This perspective can be found mainly in the literature on the Napoleonic wars; see for example Luys, *Anfänge*, esp. pp. 29ff.; Weber, *Lyrik*, esp. pp. 156ff.; and Düding, *Organisierter gesellschaftlicher Nationalismus*, esp. pp. 28ff.; but see also Buschmann, *Einkreisung*. For a general account, see Bielefeld, *Nation und Gesellschaft*.

[51] In addition to the extensive literature on anti-Semitism see for example Alter, Berghoff and Bärsch, *Konstruktion*.

[52] See for example Hagen, *Germans*; and Pletzing, *Völkerfrühling*.

[53] A groundbreaking study for this perspective was Colley's *Britons*; see also Bayly, *Birth*, esp. pp. 112–14, 199–245. On the importance of war and the experience of war for nationalism see Langewiesche, *Nation, Nationalismus, Nationalstaat*, esp. pp. 193ff. See also Bloom, *Personal Identity*; and Hoffmann, 'Konstruktion'.

[54] See Wehler, *Bismarck*; Baumgart, *Deutschland*; Schöllgen, *Imperialismus*; and Hildebrand, *Vergangene Reich*. Of the rapidly expanding more recent literature see

approaches as a basis for investigating the role this interconnectedness played in Wilhelmine nationalism.[55] While previous research has generally seen the radicalisation of nationalism as a precondition for the change toward imperialistic policies or 'world politics' (*Weltpolitik*), this volume asks the opposite question: what effects did globalisation have on national parameters?[56]

Many levels of interaction were involved: trade, global markets and production based on the division of labour; political scope in the context of *Weltpolitik*; the transfer of ideas, institutions and cultural goods. Of particular importance, I will argue, was human mobility: both emigration from Germany and, increasingly from 1890 onward, immigration into Germany. Emigration and immigration linked the Kaiserreich both mentally and physically with a world that had been fundamentally restructured by modern colonialism. The colonial order was not limited to overseas peripheries; it also had effects on European societies. One of the central categories permeating this order was that of race, and this also had effects on nationalism during the Wilhelmine era. If, around 1800, German nationalism needed to be situated mainly in a European context, then around 1900, it developed in a context of global interconnectedness.

OVERVIEW

This book examines German history between 1880 and 1910 as part of a history of globalisation. The transnational perspective means that the individual chapters deal with different locations, beyond the spatial confines of the Kaiserreich. Focusing on issues of mobility (and

---

inter alia Chickering, *We Men*; Epkenhans, *Flottenrüstung*; Fröhlich, *Imperialismus*; Etges, *Wirtschaftsnationalismus*; Paulmann, *Pomp*; Hering, *Konstruierte Nation*; Neitzel, *Weltmacht*; and Neitzel, *Zukunftsvisionen*.

[55] See Gollwitzer's enlightening essay, 'Weltgedanken', in which he argues that 'national identity … can never be separated from overriding international structures' (p. 87). See also Gollwitzer, *Geschichte*.

[56] See, for example, discussions on situating Wilhelmine society in global history in Grosse, *Kolonialismus*; Smith, *Ideological Origins*; Smith, *Politics*; Geulen, *Wahlverwandte*; Hoffmann, *Politik der Geselligkeit*, pp. 283–95, 310–25; Wildenthal, *German Women*; van Laak, *Infrastruktur*; and Schröder and Höhler, *Welt-Räume*.

the limits placed on it) means that the areas under investigation are not limited to eastern Prussia, Berlin or the Ruhrgebiet, but include eastern Asia, the Pacific, South America and Africa. By the end of the nineteenth century, cultures and social actors were already becoming moving targets. The Swedish social anthropologist Ulf Hannerz has described the reality of globalisation by stating that 'geographical spaces cannot really contain or limit culture'. In certain sections of this book, then, the Kaiserreich is only one of a number of locations under investigation, and in some instances is not even to the forefront. Borrowing concepts from cultural anthropology, one could speak here of a form of 'multi-sited historiography' that does not limit itself to a territory defined by state boundaries but follows the trail left by its objects, depending on the issue and question at hand.[57]

The intensification of mobility and circulation in the late nineteenth century suggests that an interpretation of German history must not be confined to the nation state itself, but must also investigate vectorial factors – 'routes' as well as 'roots', as the ethnologist James Clifford has called it.[58] In this way, a transnational approach could both undermine the category of 'German history' and place the consolidation of this category in its context, a context that has always transcended the borders of Germany (and of Europe).

The Kaiserreich does remain the starting point and the point of reference. The book does not claim to be a global history of migration or a study of Brazilian or Polish nationalism, for example, but a contribution to German history. There are essentially two reasons for retaining a German perspective. *Firstly*, globalisation around 1900 did not take place in a vacuum; it manifested itself at different locations in very different ways. In order to take account of this positionality of global processes, the viewpoint here is in the first instance the view from Germany. It is not, therefore, a 'subaltern' perspective, as owing

---

[57] Hannerz, 'Kultur', p. 68; see also Hannerz, *Transnational Connections*. On the concept of moving targets see also Breckenridge and Appadurai, 'Moving Targets'; Clifford, 'Introduction'; and Welz, 'Moving Targets'. On the concept of multi-sited ethnography see Marcus, 'Ethnography'; and *Ethnography through Thick and Thin*.

[58] See Clifford, 'Mixed Feelings'; 'Travelling Cultures'; and *Routes*.

to the broad geographical reach of the study, the agency and the share that the 'others' had in this history will have to be given relatively short shrift. A full account would be a different book, with a different goal. *Secondly*, even its embeddedness in a history of globalisation, as we shall see, did not make the nation obsolete; it did not lead to the dissolution of borders or to the utopia of a post-national history. Quite the reverse – the stabilisation and territorialisation of the nation state were two of the main effects of pre-First World War global interconnectedness. Thus, the approach taken here, in the form of a history of globalisation, is not to lift an ideological veil and reveal nations as a 'false consciousness'; rather, it focuses attention on the very real formation of nation states within the discursive order and social practice that were shaped by globalisation.

Chapter 1 attempts to place German history in the decades before the First World War in the context of turn-of-the century globalisation. The focus is on the Kaiserreich's political, economic and cultural connections with the rest of the world in the age of world trade, '*Weltpolitik*' and imperialism. This synthesis of the different levels of global interaction will also make clear the central role of migratory processes and labour mobility (the topic of this book) in this phase of globalisation. The overview of structures of global interconnectedness then leads into a general discussion of the link between globalisation and the nation. At its centre are the changes in how time and space were perceived, and the ambivalent relationship between homogenisation and differentiation that characterised this phase of global interconnectedness. It will be argued, here in a relatively abstract form, that one of the central characteristics of turn-of-the-century globalisation was the strengthening of national demarcation.

The next four chapters are empirical in nature. All of them examine the importance assigned to mobility and mobile labour in contemporary debates about the link between globalisation and nation. Agricultural work played a particularly important role in these processes of self-confirmation and is therefore to the forefront of all four chapters. Chapters 2 to 4, concerned with Africa, Poland and China, investigate the way in which German identity was called into question in the course of mobility and migration. Chapters 3 and 4 do so expressly in relation to immigration – whether actual or proposed. Chapter 5, however, dealing with Brazil, focuses on emigration and investigates the mechanisms by which Germanness was consolidated in the context of global mobility. All four case studies explore the colonial structures in which labour mobility took place and that found expression, not least, in the overlapping of national topoi with the contemporary discourse on race. While these sections are set mainly outside Germany, Chapter 6 then looks at the discussions about 'German work' in the Kaiserreich itself – which I interpret as an effect of global labour mobility.

Chapter 2 focuses explicitly on the colonial dimension of labour mobility at the turn of the century. From the mid 1890s onward, the most urgent problem that German colonial policy faced was the 'labour issue'. A variety of strategies were used in attempts to create native workforces. However, the attempt to transplant 'German work' to Africa was not merely a question of cultural export. 'Native policy' was not restricted to the colonies. Rather, as will be made clear, the colony and the metropolis were much more closely linked than the rigid separation of the two spheres in contemporary discourse would indicate. The project of 'educating to work' (*Erziehung zur Arbeit*) was not merely a colonial project. It was also targeted at the vagabonds and 'work-shy' who walked the roads of the German Reich. This attempt to connect these seemingly separate phenomena turns attention to the interlinkages between two forms of practice that converted a policy of social reform into a practice of exclusion. This discussion also reveals both the inclusive (expansive) and exclusive aspects of the term 'labour'. I will return to this discussion in Chapter 6.

Chapter 3 turns to Europe and looks at the immigration of seasonal labourers who were employed in agriculture in Prussia after 1890. Despite the economic conditions that seemed to make it necessary to attract agricultural workers from abroad, there was intense debate around the turn of the century about labour mobility and the related risk to German identity. In particular, the influx of Polish workers from Russia and Galicia triggered fears of the Polonisation of the German countryside. Migration into the eastern provinces of Prussia contributed to the intensification of strategies of national exclusion.

Guarded border crossings, the segregation of nationalities, and the construction of a colonial difference between Germans, Poles and Ruthenes were some of the technologies used in this politics of difference. The chapter also makes it clear that 'Poland' increasingly took on the role of an ersatz colony – in fact almost an actual colony – for the German empire. As German–Polish relationships were reshaped by colonial associations and practices, so the strategies of national exclusion at Germany's eastern border were radicalised.

Around the turn of the century, serious consideration was given to the idea of attracting 'coolies' from China for agricultural work instead of Polish workers. Chapter 4 discusses the (virtually unknown) initiatives taken by large landowners, the discussions held on the subject in the Reichstag, and the analyses submitted to Berlin by the embassies in China, in which the opportunities and dangers presented by such an 'import of labour' were debated. Through these debates, the Kaiserreich was participating in one of the most significant global processes of the second half of the nineteenth century – the wave of Chinese emigration that saw millions of Chinese workers leave China for every continent on the planet. Although resistance of various kinds led to the failure of the plan to attract Chinese workers to Germany, the debate about Chinese labour influenced the development of reactions to mobility and practices of exclusion in Germany as elsewhere. These debates led to the erection of barriers around the world to limit uncontrolled migration. The example of Chinese emigration and the topos of the 'yellow peril' can be used as an example to show how the phenomenon of mobility around 1900 was overlaid by the concept of 'race'.

In contrast to the previous chapters, the focus of Chapter 5 is on mobility out of Germany. Between 1880 and 1893, almost 2 million people left Germany for the Americas. This period of emigration led to an intense debate about the consequences and dangers of demographic decline, about 'the loss of national energy' and the effects of centrifugal mobility. At the same time, the overseas diasporas were championed as idealised outposts of 'Germanness', unaffected by the detrimental effects of industrialisation and class conflicts. It is important to note that these utopias were not confined to Brazil. Rather, they were geared toward an audience in Germany, mainly to the educated and bourgeois classes. More importantly, the project of rejuvenation itself was not only directed at the emigrant community, but rather targeted German society as well. The diaspora communities in Southern Brazil, in particular, were interpreted as a privileged site for the transformation of 'Germanness'. The rhetoric of the 'renewal' of the nation at the periphery was related to fears about the durability of the 'German' under conditions of global mobility.

While Chapters 2 to 5 concentrate on the mobility of labour and its global interlinkages, Chapter 6 focuses on the idea of 'German work'. In spite of all the circulation and interlinkages that characterised the age, there was a popular idea, in the decades before the First World War, that the German way of working was unique – and that this German work tradition was an unchangeable and ahistoric resource. The chapter will show that this seemingly paradoxical idea – a belief in cultural constancy at a time of intense interlinkages and hybridisation – must be understood as an effect of the contemporary process of globalisation. The topos of 'German work' will also be used as an example of the close relationships, around 1900, between mobility and consolidation, circulation and delimitation, globalisation and the nation state. This global context of nation and nationalism has long been neglected by the paradigm of historiography that focuses on internal developments – a paradigm that can itself be read, as an analysis of Max Weber's Protestantism study will show, as an effect of global interconnectedness.

In Chapter 7, some of the results of the case studies will be briefly summarised. However, the focus will be on initial steps toward a global perspective of the role of the nation, nationalism and the nation state before the First World War. The nationalism of the Wilhelmine period formed part of a global reconfiguration of the idea of the national that took place around 1900. In concluding, I suggest that the concept of the 're-territorialisation of the national' can be a useful point of departure for interpreting this transformation.

CHAPTER ONE

German globalisation around 1900

Globalisation has its own history. Although newspaper articles and the sociological literature, with their focus on the supposed novelty of the phenomenon, may give a different impression, globalisation (in the general meaning of increasing interlinkages around the world) is not a deus ex machina. In fact, the processes of world interconnections can be traced back far into the past. Even global consciousness, the knowledge that each local situation is embedded in a global context, is by no means unique to the late twentieth century. Also our understanding of the post-1980s globalisation shaped by transnational capitalism, and of the oppositional movements it has spawned, can benefit from a historical viewpoint.

To date, historiography has investigated questions about global interlinkages, transnational contacts and the creation of global structures within a number of different paradigms. Specifically, they have been examined in the context of the world systems theory, based on Immanuel Wallerstein's ideas, in the context of the return to world history after the Second World War and, more recently, in the context of global history.[1] These approaches have made great contributions to our understanding of the interdependencies of the modern world, and a perspective focusing on the history of globalisation can build on the results and insights gained through this research. In particular, it can build on the interest in interactions and interlinkages that characterises some work in the area of world history (and especially, more recently,

---

[1] For an initial overview see Osterhammel, 'Höherer Wahnsinn'. See also Stokes, 'Fates'; and Wolfe, 'History'.

in global history).[2] One of the legacies of world systems theory, crucial for any reconstruction of earlier epochs of globalisation, is that attention is now paid to the systemic and structural aspects of modern world orders.[3]

In addition, the present volume picks up on recent work on the history of globalisation that builds on these approaches. What makes this recent work different is, firstly, its rejection of the paradigm of diffusion that can still be found in many studies on world history.[4] In the present volume, too, globalisation is *not* understood simply as the spread of western standards and institutions, nor as the gradual integration of Asia, Africa and South America into a western-dominated order.[5] Secondly, a history of globalisation aims to transcend the focus on economics that usually characterises world-systems approaches. Although the requirements of capitalist production and distribution played a major role in structuring the modern world, interactions and interlinkages were also shaped by political, social and cultural developments whose dynamics did not follow the logic of global capitalism. Thirdly, in recent years historians have often pointed to the long pre-history of global interlinkages. There is debate about when this development commenced and when the world became one coherent unit.[6] Among historians, the early sixteenth century, with the beginnings of colonialism and the capitalist structures dominated by Europe, is often regarded as one possible starting-point for a history of globalisation. The late eighteenth century is another important turning-point.[7]

---

[2] On world history see Pomper, Elphick and Vann, *World History*. On the global history approach see Mazlish and Buultjens, *Conceptualizing*; and Geyer and Bright, 'World History'. For an overview see also Manning, *Navigating*.

[3] For an initial overview of world-systems theory, see Frank and Gills, *World System*; but primarily Wallerstein, *Modern World System*.

[4] See the polemical criticism by Blaut in *Colonizer's Model*.

[5] The paradigm of the 'rise of the West' was classically put forward by McNeill, *Rise*. For an account with a similar direction see Landes, *Wealth and Poverty*. For a contrary view see Hodgson, *Rethinking*; or the more polemical view in Frank, *ReOrient*.

[6] See Frank and Gills, *World System*.

[7] See the discussion in Hopkins, 'History', esp. pp. 21–24. On the later turning-point see Bayly, *Birth*.

In contrast to the issue of the starting-point and 'origins' of global-isation, a widespread consensus has already emerged in the literature concerning the time around 1900. There is general agreement that the period between 1850 and the First World War was a time during which the development of global interlinkages and structures reached a zenith.[8] Even in economic terms – price convergence, trade, direct investments – global connectedness had advanced to a degree that was only reached again around 1980.[9] In comparison with the level of interconnectedness that characterised the world in this era, some historians would view the time between 1914 and 1950 as an era of 'deglobalisation'.[10]

It is important, however, not to subject world history to a new meta-narrative, as some of the approaches outlined above are in dan-ger of doing. The explorations below are based less on an under-standing of globalisation as a uniform process. Rather, the point of departure is the variation of forms of entanglement, and the plurality of global perspectives. The perspective on the history of globalisa-tion suggested here does not assume a global totality; it needs to be situated in space and 'glocalised', to use Roland Robertson's term.[11] In addition, the development of globalisation was by no means a law of nature, even if it has been, and is still, treated as such. A history of globalisation is not a linear narrative of the increasing consolidation of the world. Processes of economic interlinkage could coincide with political conflict; cultural openness was not always synchronous with phases of political and economic exchange. Thus, the history of glo-balisation is not merely an adapted theory of modernisation in which 'tradition' is replaced by 'isolation' and 'modernity' by interconnec-tion. Rather, this history of globalisation is a perspective, a specific

---

[8] Of the growing historical literature on the history of globalisation see for example Hopkins, 'History'; Harper, 'Empire'; Tilly, *Globalisierung*; and Osterhammel and Petersson, *Geschichte*.

[9] See Bairoch, 'Globalization'.

[10] See for example Hopkins, 'History', esp. pp. 28–33. See also James, *End*. However, this view neglects the fact that protectionism and separation can also be interpreted as part of globalisation.

[11] See Robertson, 'Glokalisierung'.

way of seeing that may allow German history at the turn of the century to be viewed in a new light. Rather than presenting a teleology of globalisation, the account below focuses on the contradictions, ambivalences and counter-reactions that have always been provoked by mobility and cross-border processes.

The rest of this chapter attempts to situate German society in the Wilhelmine era in the context of this surge in globalisation around 1900. The chapter has two objectives. First, it attempts to identify the main dimensions of this era of global interconnectedness, and to place German society in this context. The first part focuses mainly on political, economic and infrastructural aspects of global interconnectedness. However, these processes were – as the second part of the chapter attempts to show – mediated by a particular form of cultural adaptation, a global consciousness that developed as the result of political and economic entanglements. The cultural history of globalisation was marked by a fundamental transformation in ideas about space and time, and by both increasing similarity and difference. These themes will then be used as the basis to develop an argument about the link between globalisation and the transformation of the idea of the nation around 1900.

THE GERMAN *REICH* AS PART OF THE PROCESS OF GLOBALISATION AROUND 1900

Free trade imperialism and British hegemony

'In place of the old local and national seclusion and self-sufficiency', two early commentators noted, 'we have intercourse in every direction, universal inter-dependence of nations'.[12] A revolution of intercourse and political–economic interdependency: in 1848, when this statement was made, it was still largely a prediction for the future. But by the end of the nineteenth century this vision had become a reality, and the political, economic and cultural interconnectedness of the

[12] Marx and Engels, *Manifesto*, p. 139.

world had become a cliché of journalism and public debate in Europe. 'If we examine the economic movement of Europe', the Prague-based political scientist Karl Thomas Richter enthused, 'we see that the borders between countries and peoples in economic terms are increasingly disappearing; the individual industrial regions are pursuing one and the same goal in increasingly similar ways'.[13] In 1901, the British historian James Bryce noted optimistically that 'a new kind of unity [was being created] among mankind'.[14]

But the development of a worldwide system was not a chaotic or unstructured process, even if it appeared so to some of its contemporaries. Long before attempts began to create a 'rational' world order by means of conventions, agreements, and international organisations such as the Hague Convention or, later, the League of Nations, world interlinkages were embedded in the hierarchies of a developing world order. Until well into the nineteenth century, this order was dominated by Great Britain, though not exclusively so – think for example of the so-called 'great game', the rivalry between Britain and Russia, or of the competition Britain experienced at the end of the century from the new industrial powers of Germany and the USA. But the development of economic interlinkages, which were increasing rapidly as a result of the industrial revolution and of developments in transport and communication, and which were facilitated by the gold standard and by the developing international division of labour, did take place under British leadership. British hegemony was based in the first instance on industrial production, but in the face of the challenge posed by the USA and Germany it increasingly concentrated on its supremacy in trade, capital investment, and information and transport.[15]

This does not mean that during the period up to the First World War the entire planet had become interconnected. The effects of globalisation were not felt everywhere to the same extent, and even outside Europe globalisation built upon existing traditional structures. The large empires such as the Ottoman empire and the Qing dynasty

[13] Richter, *Fortschritte*, p. 25.
[14] Cited in Harper, 'Empire', p. 143.
[15] See Metzler, *Großbritannien*. See also Hobsbawm, *Industry and Empire*; Foreman-Peck, *History*; Foreman-Peck, *Historical Foundations*; and Pohl, *Aufbruch*.

in China were still very important. In many regions, political activities reinforced existing structures and were barely shaped by changes in Europe.[16] But during this period, the pressure to adapt that emanated from western 'civilisation' onto other cultures had effects even on regions that were not subjected to direct interventions from the West. Japanese attempts at modernisation and the effect that these had on other nations in the region can only be understood in this context. These systemic pressures increased and societies were forced to adapt, although they retained some scope to adopt their own strategies.[17]

John Gallagher and Ronald Robinson have coined the influential term 'free-trade imperialism' for the economic world system of the nineteenth century.[18] The term alludes to the central role that the free-trade regime played in nineteenth-century economic development. The free-trade regime was not a formally institutionalised system, or, at most, was only such between 1860 and 1879, between the date of the Anglo-French Trade Agreement and the return to protectionism in Germany. Rather, Great Britain opened its markets unilaterally and, through its economic superiority, created global dependencies that few countries were able to resist. Together with the City of London as the world's financial capital, the British empire thus dominated world trade.[19]

However, this economic domination was not the result of deliberate market liberalism. Rather, as the term 'free-trade imperialism' suggests, it was based on territorial expansion. The nineteenth century was characterised by a colonisation of the planet by European powers that was without precedent in human history. In 1800, some 35 per cent of the earth's surface had been controlled by western European nations. By the First World War this had increased to over 85 per cent.

---

[16] See Harper, 'Empire', pp. 143–45.
[17] See Osterhammel and Petersson, *Geschichte*, pp. 57–59. Westney, *Imitation and Innovation* provides an account of the scope of appropriation for the example of Japan. For a general account see Rothermund, *Aneignung*.
[18] Gallagher and Robinson, 'Imperialism'. For a case study see Owen, *Cotton*. See also the critical view in Nye, 'Myth'.
[19] Kindleberger, 'Rise'; Cain, *Free Trade*; Howe, *Free Trade*; Marrison, *Free Trade*; and Trentmann, *Free Trade Nation*.

At the height of imperialism, from the 1880s onward, those areas not yet colonised, especially Africa, were divided up among the major powers. The British empire was at the forefront of this development. No empire in history had ever controlled so many, so geographically disperse and so densely inhabited regions as Great Britain did in the nineteenth century. In 1800, the British empire was made up of some 20 million people, but a century later this figure had reached almost 400 million. This empire, on which 'the sun never set', formed the basis for the country's dominance of world trade and accumulation of capital. British colonies – India first and foremost – provided the raw materials, labour and tax revenue that secured British hegemony until the late nineteenth century.[20]

Thus, political and economic hegemony was the result of British policy. The instruments of this policy included its colonial armies, but especially its navy. Britain's almost unlimited supremacy at sea was the basis for its expansion, an expansion that – at least from the time of the Indian Mutiny in 1857 onward – was based not only on capitalist interlinkages but also on territorial conquest. But Britain's strength was not merely the result of the open exercise of power; it was also underpinned by ideology. We could argue, following Giovanni Arrighi, that this dimension is a form of hegemony as defined by Gramsci: i.e. as the supremacy of a cultural idea that is not secured by force. In this sense, British expansion was seen not as a selfish act, but as being in the interest of mankind. Great Britain's economic and political goals could be represented both by British elites and others as an expression of universal interests. Sir Eyre Crowe stated that British supremacy was a special expression of the 'general desires and ideals common to all mankind'.[21] Free-trade imperialism was regarded by its champions as the realisation of higher laws that regulated political and economic exchange between states. The abandonment of protective tariffs and the system of international law on which the rise of Britain in the nineteenth century was based could be represented as

---

[20] Of the extensive literature see Davis and Huttenback, *Mammon*; Cain, *Economic Foundations*; Cain and Hopkins, *British Imperialism*; Edelstein, *Overseas Investment*; and Fieldhouse, *Economics*. On Germany, see Hentschel, *Freihändler*.

[21] Crowe, 'Memorandum'.

an almost metaphysical authority that was independent of any individual interests.[22]

Transport and mobility

The desire for political and economic expansion that, as in other countries, increasingly characterised politics in Germany around the turn of the century was made possible by a revolution in communications. The rapid development of transport and communication technologies was one of the basic conditions that made possible the interlinking of people, goods and ideas. The leaps forward in transport and information technology corresponded closely with Britain's interest in integrating its empire, which itself was made possible only by innovations in these areas. Great Britain created the first global information infrastructure and in doing so put itself in a hegemonial position. The information revolution had its own geopolitics, one which centred on England.[23]

Railways, in particular, made it much easier to move raw materials and industrial goods, people and also information rapidly from place to place. From the mid century onward, railways increasingly altered goods transportation in the industrialised countries of Europe. During the latter half of the century they then became established as a common, everyday means of transport for people.[24] They were not just a technical and economic project. Railways also carried cultural meanings and symbolized the progress that the modern age was to bring. By 1914, a functioning railway network had also been developed in some countries outside Europe, notably in India, Japan and Argentina. After the turn of the century, the process of territorial consolidation undertaken in many colonies brought railways to the colonial states of Africa (most successfully in South Africa).[25]

---

[22] See Arrighi, *Long Twentieth Century*, p. 56.
[23] For a general account of the transport revolution see Vance, *Capturing*.
[24] On the development of the railways see Mitchell, *Train Race*; Treue, *Eisenbahnen*; O'Brien, *Railways*; Ziegler, *Eisenbahnen*; and Gall and Pohl, *Eisenbahn*.
[25] On the German colonies see for example Schmidt, *Eisenbahnpolitik*; and Biermann, *Tanganyika Railways*. For a more general account see also Davis, Wilburn and

An even more important factor for transnational connections and trade flows was the development of the steamship.[26] The first steamships were employed on inland waterways before 1850, but they gradually became dominant on the seas and superseded sailing ships between 1860 and 1880. The growth in the use of steamships had dramatic effects on sea transport. Increasingly, unskilled staff were used to run the new steamships, and these were recruited from around the globe. The main effect of steamships, however, was to change transport routes and travel times.[27] The duration of an Atlantic crossing fell from three weeks (in 1870) to around ten days in 1900. The opening of the Suez Canal in 1869 also helped to speed up sea transport, reducing the travel time between England and India by half.[28] These developments reduced the cost of freight and changed the geography of the world economy irrevocably. By the turn of the century, transporting a ton of wheat from New York to Mannheim cost no more than from Berlin to Kassel.[29]

The transport revolution was accompanied by a revolution in communication and information technologies.[30] The telegraph, in particular, made information about prices, supply and demand rapidly available around the globe. The first transatlantic cable was completed in 1866. By 1880, at the latest, the most important trading centres and markets in the world were linked by a dense telegraphic network. The importance of the telegraph for the development of the world economy can scarcely be overemphasised; in particular, it made planning much easier, enabled rapid decision-making and created the trust that is essential for carrying on transnational

---

Robinson, *Railway Imperialism*. On this prestige project of the 'informal German empire', see Mejcher, 'Bagdadbahn'; Pohl, *Stambul*; and van Laak, *Infrastruktur*, pp. 150–64.

[26] Fisher and Nordvik, 'Maritime Transport'. See also Knick-Harley, 'Transportation'.

[27] See Gerstenberger and Welke, *Wind*; Giese, *Geschichte*; and Moltmann, *Geschichte*.

[28] Headrick, *Tools*, p. 155.

[29] See O'Rourke, 'European Grain Invasion'.

[30] On this subject see Mattelart, *Mapping*; Mattelart, *Networking*; Hugill, *Global Communications*; and Headrick, *Information*.

business.[31] Communications were made even easier when the wireless telegraph was introduced. The first transatlantic message was sent in 1901 and from then onward it allowed the hubs of information exchange to be multiplied with no need for cables. An international conference was held in Berlin in 1903 to lay down the rules for the use of wireless telegraphy.[32] From 1906 onward, Nauen, near Berlin, became the German 'centre of the universe', transmitting wireless signals around the world – not least to the colonies, which could thus, it was hoped, be even more closely linked to the 'mother country'.[33]

Other developments also helped to speed up the transmission of information. These included the geographical and quantitative expansion of postal services, which profited from the modernisation of transport. *Reichspost* steamship lines were set up to link the German Reich with eastern and south-eastern Asia, allowing the newly acquired colonies to be integrated into the postal system.[34] The telephone, invented in 1876, rapidly became established and – even more so than the telegraph – allowed large sections of the population access to the new technology. Bismarck had a line laid between Berlin and his estate in Varzin as early as 1877.[35] By 1885, eighty-five German cities had direct telephone links to Berlin. The first international line was created between Paris and Brussels in 1887. Germany adopted the new technology comparatively quickly, and there were already 1.3 million telephone connections in the country by the outbreak of the First World War.[36]

The importance of these changes in transport and information technologies is obvious. In economic terms, they contributed to creating an integrated world market that was characterised by mechanisms for

---

[31] See Neutsch, 'Nervenstränge des Erdballs'; Fortner, *International Communication*; Headrick, *Tentacles*; and Headrick, *Invisible Weapon*.
[32] See Wedlake, *SOS*; Standage, *Internet*; and Friedewald, *'Tönenden Funken'*.
[33] On this subject see Sebald, 'Funkstrategie'; Klein-Arendt, *'Kamina ruft Nauen!'*; and van Laak, *Infrastruktur*, pp. 91–93.
[34] See Reinke-Kunze, *Geschichte*; Achilles, 'Infrastruktur'; and Gerlach, *Deutsche Kolonisation*.
[35] See Kern, *Culture*, p. 214.
[36] See Wessel, 'Rolle'; and 'Verbreitung'.

communicating supply and demand and also showed the first signs that price structures were becoming standardised. Considerable evidence has now been presented showing that price convergence did take place and that it led indirectly to the convergence of living standards.[37] At the same time, a global labour market developed, which extended even to transatlantic seasonal migration (the best-known example being the *golondrinas* who travelled from Spain and Italy to Argentina and back), and which also led to the eventual convergence of wage levels.[38]

By far the most important factor contributing to the convergence of wage levels was human mobility.[39] In the nineteenth century migration became global (rather than regional) and increased vastly in terms of the numbers involved. Between 1824 and 1942, some 60 million people emigrated from Europe alone to North and South America. Other major migratory flows included (to name only the most important) those from Europe to the African and Asian colonies (especially to Australia); the forced migration of African slaves, which continued throughout the nineteenth century despite the anti-slavery movement and the bans on slavery introduced successively in different places; labour migration by Indians to East Africa and south-east Asia; and the exodus of around 50 million Chinese people, mainly to Manchuria, Singapore and Malaysia, but also to South and North America, South Africa, and Australia.[40]

Along with individual local causes, a number of common factors contributed to these mass migrations. One was the explosion in population experienced by many societies from the early nineteenth century onward. Emigration was facilitated by the new methods of transport, and industrial manufacturing and its concentration in industrial areas created a demand for flexible waged labour. Finally, the migratory flows were also linked to the political and economic

---

[37] See Williamson, 'Globalization'; and Dowrick and DeLong, 'Globalization'.
[38] See Williamson, 'Evolution'; O'Rourke and Williamson, *Globalization*; Potts, *Weltmarkt*; and Chiswick and Hatton, 'International Migration'.
[39] See O'Rourke and Williamson, *Globalization*, pp. 145–66.
[40] Of the extensive literature see Moch, *Moving Europeans*; Segal, *Atlas*; Wang, *Global History*; Hoerder, *Cultures*; and McKeown, 'Global Migration'.

structures of the age of imperialism, including the growth in plantation economies. Mass labour mobility was a central feature of this
phase of globalisation. It represented a major life upheaval for those
directly involved. But in addition, family connections, personal contact and an – often emotional – public debate about the process meant
that labour mobility was one of the most important ways in which
much of the population experienced the increasing interconnectedness of the world. The specific characteristics of globalisation around
1900 thus include, along with political economic integration under
British hegemony and the technological revolution, the large-scale,
and often permanent, migration of usually impoverished classes.

Colonial globality

For Germany in particular, the desire to steer emigration flows to
overseas locations was one of the most powerful arguments for the
country establishing its own colonial empire. From 1884 onward, the
German Reich began to acquire territories in Africa, making it a colonial power. This was also part of a more general push by a number of
countries to acquire colonial territories. The early 1880s were marked
by a major change in the long history of colonialism. The most noticeable feature of this era was the competition between European powers
to subjugate the last 'available' regions of the planet. In particular, the
'Scramble for Africa', which occurred mainly over a few short years
between 1882 and 1900, meant that inter-European conflicts could
now be fought out around the globe – and vice versa.[41]

But the effects of this era of high imperialism were not limited
to the redrawing of maps. The differences between this and earlier
periods of colonialism were, rather, the specific ways in which the
colonies were integrated into world politics, long British-dominated,
and their linkages with an increasingly interconnected world economy. European economies became increasingly focused on the

---

[41] On the history of colonialism between 1880 and 1914 see Osterhammel,
Kolonialismus; von Albertini, *Europäische Kolonialherrschaft*; and Wirz and Eckert,
'Scramble'.

resources – raw materials, but also labour – and the markets of the colonial periphery. In addition, colonial expansion played an important role in the 'social-imperialistic' management of social tensions in Europe. The consequences for the areas colonised included not only political rule from abroad, which had also taken place in earlier forms of colonisation, but also deliberate attempts to 'modernise' local societies. This policy was based on a change in the way colonial exploitation was understood and on the discovery by the European metropoles of the colonial 'population'. The change in colonial policy from around the turn of the century onward toward 'native policy' (*Eingeborenenpolitik*), as it was termed at the time, and extensive infrastructural projects was itself part of a modern trend towards 'biopolitics'.[42]

But colonialism was not just an economic and societal regime. It was accompanied by a specific discourse. The colonial expansion by western Europe and the United States was not based simply on weapons, technical superiority, economic penetration and political power: it was also a cultural project, and colonial fantasies played an important role in the expansion by the European powers. One of the fundamental operations of imperialism was the defining and maintaining of the cultural difference between the colonisers and the colonised. At the same time, taking control of foreign territories was just the first stage in the internalisation of the empire's outlook and its promise of progress, and in making colonisation seem a self-evidently natural process for both sides.[43]

Undoubtedly, colonialism's most far-reaching effects were those on the colonies themselves. But the effects were by no means limited to the colonies, as older colonial history would make it appear; colonialism was not a one-way street. Recent research has illuminated the extent to which European societies were also changed by colonial

---

[42] On the concept of imperialism see Mommsen, *Imperialismustheorien*; and Wolfe, 'History'. On the move to 'biopolitics' see, for Britain and India, Scott, 'Colonial Governmentality', among others. See also the discussion in Prakash, *Another Reason*, pp. 123–226. On Germany see van Laak, *Infrastruktur*, pp. 130–49.

[43] For an introduction to post-colonial studies see Gandhi, *Postcolonial Theory*; and Young, *Postcolonialism*.

interaction. This interest in the effects on the colonising country or, more precisely, on the common development of the modern world within a colonial context, is one of the main topics of post-colonial studies.[44] German history, too, bears the traces of the colonial experience, as many different areas of society were influenced by the effects of the colonial project.[45]

To come to terms with the reciprocity of the modern experience, some authors in the field of post-colonial studies have coined the term 'colonial modernity'. By this they mean that the development of modern categories, structures and institutions was fundamentally embedded in colonialism. It has been suggested in this context that the colonies were assigned the role of 'laboratories of modernity'. In many ways, it is argued, the colonies were spaces in which European bureaucracies could experiment, where they could test major interventions and social reforms. For example, it is argued, measures related to the infrastructural modernisation of society – whether urban planning, medical and hygiene-related projects, or land reform – were often tested in the colonies before they were applied in the western metropolises. These authors suggest that the colonies should not be seen merely as objects of imperialist intervention, but rather as laboratories for European modernity.[46]

Similarly, one could suggest that the globalisation of the late nineteenth century cannot be conceived outside the colonial structures that shaped it. The mobility of objects, people, ideas and institutions – the interlinking of the world – took place, before the First World War, under the conditions of colonialism. The world economy was based on the asymmetric use of the raw materials, labour and demand of non-European societies. Colonialism was a condition and a central

---

[44] On this perspective, with further literature, see Conrad and Randeria, *Eurozentrismus*.

[45] Of the growing literature on this subject see Kundrus, *Imperialisten*; and, *Phantasiereiche*; van der Heyden and Zeller, *Kolonialmetropole*; Honold and Simons, *Kolonialismus*; Eckert and Wirz, 'Wir nicht'; Conrad, 'Doppelte Marginalisierung'; and Conrad and Osterhammel, *Kaiserreich*.

[46] On the term 'colonial modernity', see for example Barlow, *Formations*. On the idea of 'laboratories of modernity' see Stoler and Cooper, 'Between Metropole and Colony', p. 5; and the critical analysis of the concept in van Laak, 'Kolonien'.

ingredient of the political world order – but also of the legal and ideological legitimation of that order. 'Modernisation' in both colonies
and metropolises was shaped by colonialism, as was the process of
mutual cultural acquisition. To some extent these patterns are still in
place and are still structuring the current phase of globalisation. For
example, the concept of 'development', which even at the start of the
twenty-first century remains the dominant interpretive framework
for global interaction, bears the traces of its colonial heritage.[47] The
popularity of post-colonial studies in the 1990s can itself be seen as a
sign of increasing awareness of the fact that even after formal colonialism has ended, the effects of colonial structures and arrangements
can still be very much felt. In any case, globalisation around 1900
was directly shaped by the asymmetrical relationships of the colonial
situation even outside the effects of formal colonial empires. For that
reason the specific character of global interactions before the First
World War can be described as 'colonial globality'.

German globalisation around 1900

To what extent was the German Kaiserreich part of this turn-of-the-
century globalisation? How strongly was it influenced by the processes of global interaction, and to what extent was Germany itself an
agent in this development? Both of these issues are important if we
wish to evaluate the importance of globalisation for German society.
In very general terms, both Germany's colonial links and its wider
global interlinkages increased between 1880 and the First World War.
These interlinkages were supported by a number of different groups,
first and foremost by the vociferous proponents of *Weltpolitik* such
as Bülow, Tirpitz and the representatives of the numerous nationalistic groups. They were supported by broad swathes of the educated
bourgeoisie, the most important propagators of a global consciousness around 1900. *Weltpolitik*, as Woodruff Smith has shown, was
also a private capitalist programme for global market acquisition, and

---

[47] On this subject see Escobar, *Encountering*; and Cooper and Packard, *International Development*.

for that reason was supported by entrepreneurs and industrialists.[48] Agricultural groups were much more reticent, although their business decisions were influenced greatly by the development of a world market, and peasants had a high share in the migratory movement. Those least affected by the global interlinkages of the Kaiserreich were probably the petit bourgeois and sub-proletarian classes. The working class experienced the effects caused by industry's dependence on the world market; and trade unions debated the internationalisation of the labour market. It is important to take these different actors and interests into account. Engagement with the world was always of a contested nature; some benefited from late-nineteenth-century globalization, while others clearly did not.

To assess the place of global interlinkages in German history, we need to differentiate between different areas of society. Firstly, in economic terms, Germany was highly involved in the process of globalisation – in many areas, its involvement was exceeded only by that of Great Britain.[49] The use of the term 'world economy' and the setting-up of the Kiel Institute for the World Economy in 1911 are indications that contemporaries were well aware of this. By 1914, foreign trade made up 34 per cent of national income – a level that was attained again only in the 1960s. In the years leading up to 1914, the German empire became 'the most dynamic, and soon, in many markets, the most important exporting power'.[50] This had effects on the foreign-trade balance and also helped to determine which areas of manufacturing in Germany grew most strongly.[51] The chemicals industry, in particular, was focused heavily on export business. Before the First World War it exported 35 per cent of its production (transported mainly on British ships).[52] The electrical and metal industries and consumer manufacturing also produced large amounts for export.[53] As a

---

[48] See Smith, *Ideological Origins*.
[49] On the subject in general see Torp, *Herausforderung*.
[50] Petersson, 'Kaiserreich', p. 55.
[51] See Spohn, *Weltmarktkonkurrenz*.
[52] See Schröter, 'Auslandsinvestitionen'; Wetzel, *Naturwissenschaften*; Plumpe, *IG Farbenindustrie*, esp. pp. 40–99; and Teltschik, *Geschichte*.
[53] On this subject see Hagen, *Direktinvestitionen*; and Buchheim, 'Deutschland'.

result of the country's transition to an industrial economy, imports of raw materials became more and more important. This also had effects on agricultural regions. While new industries often focused their activities on the world market, many in agriculture, especially from East Prussia, saw themselves as victims of globalisation who were seemingly at the mercy of the process rather than as agents of it. Wool was imported from Australia and South Africa, and wheat from the USA, Russia, and also Argentina and Canada. Germany's links with the world market had a major impact on the structure of agriculture in East Prussia, which reacted to the crisis in the cereals market by increasing production of the lucrative sugar beet, with great success. In 1880, the value of sugar exports already exceeded that of machinery exports or exports of chemical products.[54]

Almost three-quarters of German exports went to Europe, mostly to Britain. A large proportion also went to the United States. Smaller markets such as Argentina, Egypt, Morocco, China and Japan all became increasingly important but never reached the level of Germany's European trading partners. Most capital investment, however, took place within Germany, and in France and Austria; projects such as the Baghdad Railway were mainly designed to gain international prestige.[55] There was very little capital investment in the colonies, and in fact more was invested in the British empire than in 'New Germany'.[56] Britain remained central to Germany's international economic interlinkages, not merely as its most important, favoured market for industrial goods, but also because it was at the centre of world trade flows. The accumulation of capital through these trade flows would not have been possible without British free trade, its high import rates and its integration of colonial economies.[57]

Secondly, foreign policy in the Wilhelmine period was marked by the broadening of fields of political activity. Many political decision-makers regarded it as an established fact that the system of European

[54] See Fischer, *Expansion*, esp. pp. 101–122.
[55] See Barth, *Hochfinanz*.
[56] See Schinzinger, *Kolonien*.
[57] See Petersson, 'Kaiserreich'. See also Fischer, 'Ordnung'. On the integration of the capital markets see Obstfeld and Taylor, 'Globalization'.

equilibrium had been superseded by one of world equilibrium.[58] Here, too, the British example, or rather concern about the political and economic dominance of London, played a role.[59] The phenomenon of *Weltpolitik* was to a large extent an attempt to break British hegemony and make Germany a 'world empire' that would, according to widely held hopes, play its part in determining world events.[60] Territorial expansion was on the agenda, as even Britain recognised: Sir Eyre Crow in the British Foreign Office stated that the German Reich had a 'natural right' to expand. Naval policy, which occupied much of the Reich's internal and foreign policy debate from 1897 onward, was the result of the competition with Great Britain with which the Kaiserreich felt it was faced in the new area of *Weltpolitik*.[61] Burning foreign policy issues now often involved locations outside Europe – the Chinese Taku forts, Venezuela, Agadir and Samoa. All these conflicts also had local causes and are evidence of the expansion of German politics around the turn of the century. But they always also need to be situated within the European power politics that remained the Kaiserreich's primary concern. This is even true of Germany's actual colonial policy, which was both directed against Britain and France and at the same time part of a collective European project (and later an American and Japanese one) despite the national rivalries involved.

Thirdly, the effects of this expansion were not limited to conflicts in the area of foreign policy. There were also effects on domestic politics. One example is the protectionism introduced by Bismarck in 1879, ending the liberal phase of his early years of government, as a result of pressure from agricultural and conservative groups. From the very start, protectionism had an anti-British dimension – just

---

[58] See Gollwitzer, *Geschichte*, pp. 243–53.
[59] On the general subject see Kennedy, *Rise*.
[60] On this subject see Neitzel, *Weltmacht*; and *Zukunftsvisionen*. On *Weltpolitik* in general see Winzen, *Bülows Weltmachtkonzept*; and 'Genesis'; Mommsen, *Großmachtstellung*; and Hildebrand, *Vergangene Reich*, pp. 173–442.
[61] See Berghahn, *Tirpitz-Plan*; Plagemann, *Übersee*; Epkenhans, *Flottenrüstung*; and Lambi, *Navy*. Of the contemporary literature see for example Eisenhart, *Abrechnung*; and Erdmann, *Seeherrschaft*.

as debates on protective tariffs in Great Britain had an anti-German thrust. German free traders were discredited in Germany and described as 'champions of English interests'. By contrast, the protectionism that became established in Europe during the 1880s was usually presented as an alternative to the British market-liberal economic order.[62] At the same time, this policy was a direct reaction to the economic depression of the time and to the pressure of the world market. Thus, protective tariffs cannot be interpreted unilaterally as a retreat from globalisation, as is often done. Rather, they must be read as one specific reaction to the challenges posed by increasing interaction.[63] The end of the 'liberal era', then, was linked to global contexts, and also the development of mass support for conservative politics and the resistance of the resurgent conservative parties to reform can be understood against the background of the agricultural crisis caused by globalisation. This formed the basis for rallying large-scale industry and agriculturalists into a national bloc (*Sammlungspolitik*) on which 'the politics of the Kaiserreich was to rest until 1918'.[64] Debates about protectionist measures, which continued throughout the entire Wilhelmine era, were just one example of discussions about ostensibly domestic issues in which the impacts of global integration were negotiated: others include the 'Hottentot elections', naval policy and citizenship. The issue of whether Germany should change from being an agricultural state to an 'industrial state', thus making itself dependent on the world market, was debated intensely right up until the First World War, but the debate always focused on the consequences for German domestic policy.[65] From the 1880s, at the latest,

---

[62] Quoted in Etges, *Wirtschaftsnationalismus*, p. 262; see also Lambi, *Free Trade*; Böhme, *Deutschlands Weg*; Kaelble, *Interessenpolitik*; and Hornbogen, *Travail*.

[63] The theory of deglobalisation is posited by, among others, Osterhammel and Petersson, *Geschichte*, pp. 69–80; and James, *End*. In contrast, Borchardt, *Globalisierung*, interprets protectionism as an unavoidable reaction to the redistributional effects of globalisation. For a similar point of view see also Aldenhoff-Hübinger, *Agrarpolitik*, esp. pp. 16–21, which argues that in the context of the *Sonderweg* literature, the world economic situation is given relatively little weight in triggering a basically internal debate on democratisation and social influence.

[64] Wehler, *Gesellschaftsgeschichte*, Vol. III, p. 642.

[65] On this subject see Barkin, *Controversy*; Steinkühler, *Agrar- oder Industriestaat*; Harnisch, 'Agrarstaat'; and Etges, *Wirtschaftsnationalismus*, pp. 287–293.

the development of German society must be interpreted in the context of the globalisation processes taking place.

Fourthly, migration was one of the main ways in which large sections of the population experienced globalisation. Domestic migration, mainly from rural areas to the developing industrial centres, had been one of the most significant social phenomena of the nineteenth century and had made a major contribution to transforming society. This internal migration, the 'largest mass movement in German history' (Köllmann), was linked to an increase in mobility that did not stop at national borders. German collective memory associates with the Wilhelmine era mainly the third, and largest, wave of emigration: that between 1880 and 1893, during which almost 2 million people emigrated, primarily to the United States. One of the objectives behind the acquisition of overseas colonies was to redirect this 'loss of national energies' to the prospective territories of 'New Germany'. In this context, the Malthusian topos of overpopulation and worry about German *Lebensraum* (Friedrich Ratzel) were both *en vogue*. The fact that Wilhelmine Germany experienced very little emigration from 1893 onward was almost completely overlooked. In fact, the country imported labour and de facto became a country of immigration.[66]

Finally, the general impression of expansion had its effects culturally and ideologically, too. References to the 'world' became almost all-pervasive: *Weltpolitik*, world economy, world powers, world empires. Woodruff Smith has described the competing, but also complementary, concepts of *Weltpolitik* and *Lebensraum* as ideological components of German modernism that developed under the conditions of globalisation at around 1900, and has traced the effects of these components into the 1930s.[67] Not much research has been done on the effect this broadening of horizons during the Wilhelmine era had on 'high culture' in the narrow sense. Germany took part in the broader, (western) European development of modern art, which

---

[66] See Bade, *Europa*; Hoerder and Nagel, *People*; Herbert, *Ausländerbeschäftigung*; and Wenning, *Migration*. On the development of the means of transport that made this migration possible, see Kludas, *Geschichte*; and Seiler, *Hapag–Lloyd*.

[67] See Smith, *Ideological Origins*.

incorporated influences from abroad, primarily from Japanese art and African sculpture.[68] However, the country's global points of reference can also be identified in popular culture – in board games with a colonial theme, the Liebig *Sammelbilder* (pictures distributed with the company's meat extract product), advertising, the novels of Karl May, travel literature and popular science fiction. The effects on popular culture were probably even greater than on 'high culture'.[69]

As well as being an exporter of industrial goods, the Kaiserreich was certainly global in terms of its cultural and social effects abroad. In many countries, Germans took over institutions, translated them and appropriated them. For the sciences especially, the Kaiserreich was the starting-point for a process of vigorous intellectual transfer that brought the Humboldt model of a university to Europe and also to the USA and Japan (although not without modifications). The ideas covered both organisation and institutional structure as well as the development of disciplines and areas of study.[70] German medicine, oriental studies, language studies, sociology and historical studies were among the most successful exports of German universities, where many members of modernising elites spent time.[71] But German influence was not limited to research and teaching. After Prussia defeated France, Prussian military advisers were in demand around the world. The best known was Otto Liman von Sanders in the Ottoman empire, but such advisers could also be found in Chile, in China and in Japan, where Jacob Meckel prepared the Japanese army for its victory over China in 1895. The Reich constitution, which was seen as a 'third way' between absolutism and egalitarian democratisation, was used as a model for the Meiji constitution of

---

[68] For an overview see Osterhammel and Petersson, 'Jahrhundertwende'. See also Lloyd, *Expressionism*; Rubin, *Primitivismus*; Brugger *et al.*, *Emil Nolde*; and Berger, *Japonismus*.

[69] See for example Berman, *Orientalismus*; Schuster, *China*; Ciarlo, 'Rasse'; and Scholz-Hänsel, *Plakat*. See also a number of interesting vignettes in Honold and Scherpe, *Deutschland*. On the World Exhibitions see Fuchs, 'Weltausstellungen', which gives additional references.

[70] See Schalenberg, *Humboldt*; and *Kulturtransfer*.

[71] Of the extensive literature see for example Lingelbach, *Klio*; Schwentker, *Max Weber*; and Mehl, *Vergangenheit*.

1889. For latecomers such as Japan, mainly from the 1880s onward, and Turkey, after 1908, Germany was seen as a model for modernising society as a whole, as a pattern for development that promised to reconcile modernity and autochthonous traditions.[72]

Germany was part of a globalizing world, as this short synthesis suggests, but at the same time the world reached deep into turn-of-the-century Germany. Taking different parameters into account, the Kaiserreich was hardly less involved in late-nineteenth-century globalisation than France and the United States; only Britain played in a different league. German industry exported to Europe and well beyond; migration from, through and into Germany increased throughout the 1890s; and global relations have left their traces particularly in the realm of popular and even high culture. The colonial empire was less important for Germany than for France, the Netherlands, and even Japan – not to mention Britain. But repercussions of the colonial encounter, as recent scholarship has shown, were more important than an older historiography has made us believe. Moreover, colonialism and globalisation cannot be meaningfully separated: the global integration of the world around 1900 was inconceivable apart from the colonial structures that permeated economic and political exchange, migration, and cultural interactions. The experience of the world was one of colonial globality.

To be sure, not everything in the Kaiserreich was globally entangled, and domestic issues continued to be of prior importance to many social milieux. Moreover, transnational relations may have increased, but they connected Germany to Britain and Austria, France and Russia, more than to Chile, Egypt and Siam. For the Kaiserreich, western Europe remained the privileged point of reference. It is clear, however, that the neat separation of the 'domestic' from the 'European' and 'global' is an analytical tool that only imperfectly renders the multiple forms of overlap and interdependency in social practice. Germany's European relations, in other words, themselves were often part of larger circuits. Polish immigration, to give

---

[72] See for example Martin, *Japans Weg*; Ando, *Entstehung*; and Howland, *Translating*. On Turkish modernity see for example Gencer, *Bildungspolitik*.

an obvious example, was also an effect of transatlantic migration that depopulated the Prussian countryside. The impact of Cubism went beyond transfers between Munich, Berlin and Paris. Europe itself had changed in the course of events, and it is not helpful to discuss European history detached from the process of global integration within which it evolved. Finally, it should be recognized that the apex of global and colonial entanglements of Wilhelmine Germany coincided with a fundamental transformation of German society and the formation of European high modernity. Around the turn of the century, central structures and conflicts emerged in social, political, economic and cultural relations that were to characterize western industrial societies well into the twentieth century. For this reason, the effects and repercussions of global/colonial interactions in this period seem to be of particular importance.[73]

GLOBAL CONSCIOUSNESS AND THE RECONFIGURATION OF TIME AND SPACE

The compression of space and time

Late-nineteenth-century globalisation was not solely – not even primarily – a political and economic process, even if it was mainly the diplomatic, military and economic interactions that led contemporaries to speak of 'world politics' and a 'world economy'. The global interconnectedness that had been made possible by technological development was accompanied by changes in cultural patterns. Globalisation around 1900 was characterised by the movement of goods and a search for possible 'places in the sun', but also by a fundamental reconfiguration of ideas about space and time.[74]

The paragraphs below will give a rough outline of these developments. Numerous comments were made at the time reflecting the changes in thinking about space and time. They mainly came from

---

[73] See Nolte, '1900'; and Nitschke *et al.*, *Jahrhundertwende*. For a European perspective see Barraclough, *Introduction*, pp. 9–42.

[74] On the changes in ideas about time and space see, in the context of an analysis of modernisation, the discussion in Giddens, *Consequences*.

the bourgeoisie and did not usually reflect the everyday realities experienced by the mass of the population. In fact, even the statements made by bourgeois commentators were based less on their own experiences than on projections, hopes and fears. Opinions on the importance of the changes were by no means uniform: there were always contrasting views, both euphoric and sceptical reactions. The paragraphs below do, however, focus on the overall tendencies of these reflections on time and space, on similarity and difference. The aim is to develop some theoretical ideas on the link between globalisation and the nation.

Even before the First World War, global interconnectedness had become a subject for debate. What shaped the character of globalisation around 1900 was not merely the expansion of exchange and interaction, but also the *awareness* that the world was an interlinked place and the new perception that those involved had about the world.[75] Far-distant events were taken as a model and an example, and often used as a warning of potential local or national problems. In addition, the belief that even distant events could affect the local situation was widespread among the educated classes and political and economic decision-makers.[76]

This awareness was the result of the technological innovations discussed above, but it also contributed to making them possible. Changes in technology and mentality did not yet turn the world into McLuhan's 'global village', but they allowed bourgeois commentators to develop a feeling of simultaneity and the bridging of spatial distances that had previously seemed utopian. In a different context, the geographer David Harvey has coined the term 'time–space compression' to explain these processes. As distances became 'compressed' by technical means, the world became a unit in which the different regions seemed to enter into an era of synchronicity.[77] In 1892,

---

[75] On the general duality of the globalisation process see Robertson, *Globalization*, pp. 8ff.

[76] But the statement that before the First World War more people consciously thought or acted in a global context 'than at any time since' (Harper, 'Empire', p. 158) is certainly an exaggeration.

[77] See Harvey, *Condition*.

Max Nordau warned of the damage, not least to people's health, that would be caused by progress in communications such as daily newspapers. 'The last villager', he believed, 'is taking part … in a thousand events that are happening at every point on the earth, following and receiving them with curiosity'.[78] The 'shrinking' of space was perceived as taking place even faster than it actually was; imaginings of global interlinkages became separated from real developments. The 1890 edition of the encyclopaedia *Meyers Konversationslexikon* stated that a 'journey around the whole globe' was now 'an everyday occurrence'.[79]

Stephen Kern has described how, during the decades leading up to the First World War, western European societies and the United States experienced a far-reaching revolution in their understanding of space and time. One important symbol of these changes was the introduction of world time, which was agreed upon, after intensive efforts by a number of pioneers, at the Prime Meridian Conference in Washington in 1884. Even before this, several railway companies had begun to force the standardisation of clock times within nation states by using uniform timetables to bridge the numerous regional time differences. World time was based on the convention of a prime meridian and the introduction of time zones. But the concept was only accepted gradually. It was adopted in Germany in 1893; other countries such as France insisted on retaining their 'national' timekeeping for longer. The introduction of world time was an important turning point for the development of economic relationships – for the capital markets in particular but also for politics and for military logistics (as Helmuth von Moltke, who lobbied the Reichstag in 1891 for its introduction, was well aware).[80]

The effects of this standardisation of time were not limited to international events; they could be felt in everyday life, too. The use of clocks in public areas and of pocket-watches became widespread, reaching a peak in the years leading up to 1914. This was part of a discourse

[78] Nordau, *Entartung*, pp. 62–63.
[79] Quoted in Bausinger, *Reisekultur*, p. 343.
[80] See Kern, *Culture*, pp. 10–14. On the introduction of world time see the (slightly disappointing) account in Blaise, *Zähmung*. See also Howse, *Greenwich*.

of punctuality that had set in long beforehand and had become commonplace through the establishment of factory discipline, but now became universal. In many societies – in Europe and beyond – clocks were treated as symbols of modernity and were installed in parliament buildings, courthouses and schools.[81] They were also linked to increasingly strict work disciplines.[82] An even more important factor in the development of simultaneity was the establishment of the Gregorian calendar as the world standard at the end of the nineteenth century. This double 'fixing'– an orientation based on the sun and on the 'zero meridian' of the birth of Jesus Christ – made the Gregorian calendar one of the most important agents in this process of cultural adaptation and temporal standardisation. The calendar changed the naming of years and the number of leap years. But by neutralising time – holidays as well as dates that were seen as lucky or unlucky – it had a far-reaching effect on people's everyday lives. Clocks, timetables, the calendar and fixed working hours were all components of the 'metronomic society' that developed in many places at the end of the nineteenth century.[83] However, the victory of the western calendar was not so complete that it eradicated all traces of alternative ways of marking time. In many societies, a plurality of time regimes remained social practice for a considerable period.[84]

The changing notion of time was also based, in part, on a revolution in speed. Railways, trams (introduced in Berlin in 1879) and, later, cars, made 'acceleration the absolute defining category', one which had dramatic effects on long-existing patterns of experience.[85] The gradual way in which these patterns of perception changed in everyday consciousness can be seen, for example, in the English

---

[81] On the role of time and clocks in general see Landes, *Revolution*; Dohrn van Rossum, *Geschichte*; and Aveni, *Empires*.
[82] See for example Eckert, 'Zeit', with the relevant literature.
[83] See Young, *Metronomic Society*. See also Thompson, 'Time'.
[84] For accounts of how the Gregorian calendar became established see, for Japan, Coulmas, *Japanische Zeiten*; Okada, *Meiji kaireki*; and Shimada, *Grenzgänge*, pp. 70–122. For other examples of the plurality of time regimes see van Schendel, 'Modern Times'; Zerubavel, *Rhythms*; and Hoskins, *Play*.
[85] Berghoff, 'Ziele', p. 50.

Highways and Locomotives Act of 1878. It stipulated that every vehicle on public roads must be preceded by someone on foot, and laid down a speed limit of four miles per hour. In the years that followed, these regulations were repeatedly amended; by 1904 the speed limit had been increased to twenty miles per hour.[86] Wireless telegraphy and the telephone speeded up communications and traffic, while the introduction of assembly lines and Taylorism resulted in ever-faster production processes. Every new speed record seemed to be broken again almost immediately; cinema and futurism gave cultural expression to the obsession with speed. But this acceleration-of-acceleration also led to resistance and negative reactions. 'Our era is nervous and hasty enough already', warned Oberbaurat Stambke, one of the leading German authorities on railways. 'We should not foster that even further by continually increasing speeds.' The 'discovery' and epidemic spread of neurasthenia from the 1890s onward was seen as a characteristic feature of this era of speed.[87]

But the increased mobility and circulation of goods and information was not merely related to time. It also formed part of the 'spatial revolution' (Carl Schmitt) of the nineteenth century. The acceleration of traffic and information created the impression that distances were being reduced and that the world was shrinking – although this did not yet actually apply to the lives of the vast majority of people, even in western Europe. But in the perception of the educated classes, spatial distances were being overcome, almost eliminated. Charles Richet, the doctor, later Nobel Prize winner and for many years editor of the *Revue scientifique*, wrote as early as 1891 that '[t]o say that there are no longer any distances is a banal truth'.[88] The vision of a journey *Around the World in Eighty Days*, predicted and described in Jules Verne's novel of 1873, was a symbol of this compression of time and space. The project of a voyage around the earth acquired mythical qualities; when, in 1889, the American journalist Nellie Bly

[86] See Kern, *Culture*, pp. 113ff. See also Schivelbusch, *Geschichte*.
[87] See Kern, *Culture*, pp. 109–30. See also Virilio, *Revolutionen*; Eichberg, 'Schneller'; and Borscheid, *Tempo-Virus*. On the development of neurasthenia in Germany see Radkau, *Zeitalter*, esp. pp. 190–214 (p. 204 for the quotation).
[88] Richet, 'Cent ans', p. 780.

set out to reproduce Phileas Fogg's fictional journey for real, a large audience followed her attempt with great interest. The newspaper carrying her reports, Joseph Pulitzer's *New York World*, received over a million responses to its call for predictions of the length of time the journey would take her. In fact Bly made it back home from her journey, which had included a ceremonious meeting with Jules Verne in France, after only seventy-two days. During the years that followed, Bly's time was reduced several times; by the turn of the century, a journey lasting just half the length of Fogg's seemed possible.[89] The synchronisation of experience and the continual increase in speeds corresponded, for bourgeois observers, to the idea that distance was being eliminated.

Homogenisation

The European view of globalisation before the First World War was deeply affected by the possibility of bridging huge distances and creating a feeling of simultaneity between different regions and continents. This change in ways of seeing, closely linked to contemporary technological developments, formed an integral part of a world-view that it also helped to create, and that dominated the cultural world order around 1900. The impression that time and space were being compressed overlapped with the idea that different cultures were gradually becoming the same, as a result of the diffusion of the achievements of western modernity – in other words, with the paradigm of 'civilisation'.[90]

 The prevailing view of how the world would develop in the future was that the increase in exchange and interaction would gradually lead to living conditions around the world becoming similar. 'Transport', the geographer Friedrich Ratzel reasoned, 'cancels out differences and dampens down contrasts'. International mobility allowed people to get to know different cultures and regions, he argued, creating a

---

[89] See Costello, *Jules Verne*, esp. pp. 118–21; see also Zimmermann, *Technikverständnis*. Popular accounts include Kroeger, *Nelly Bly*; Rittenhouse, *Nelly Bly*.

[90] Robertson, *Globalization*, p. 115 describes the discourse of civilisation as 'a, perhaps the, central ingredient in the globalization process' around 1900.

better understanding of difference and thus breaking down cultural barriers.[91] To a certain extent this corresponded to the concept of modernisation, which also promised to lead to conformity and equality – of individuals, genders and classes – without eliminating all difference. In an age of globalisation, this process also took place at an international level. 'The needs of the peoples of the earth', the Prague lawyer Karl Thomas Richter believed, 'are becoming more and more similar and balanced, as are the means of meeting them'.[92] However, cultural assimilation was not seen as the result of mutual influence and interdependency but, in the main, as a centrifugal process. In pre-1914 Europe, the understanding of cultural globalisation was based on the mechanism of diffusion.

This world-view found popular expression in the concept of the civilising mission. The term was used mainly in the context of imperialism from 1880 onward and suggested that the political dominance of the West was in the public interest (and in particular in the interest of the colonised). The interconnectedness of the world under the conditions of political asymmetry would lead, it was believed, to the gradual 'elevation' of the 'natives' and to the increasing similarity of political and cultural standards. This understanding of colonialism, as a benevolent guardianship of colonial subjects, corresponded with the prevailing liberal world-view and its trust in forms of educational paternalism. In the logic of this ideology, the colonial powers were selflessly taking upon themselves the onerous task of modernising backward societies: 'the white man's burden'.[93]

The concept of the civilising mission was – like the world order of cultural globalisation in general – part of a discourse of homogenisation. Its remit extended far beyond colonial relationships with the non-European world. The interactions of 'civilised' nations, too, were usually interpreted within this paradigm of adjustment and assimilation. The paradigm found institutional expression in the broad

[91] Ratzel, *Geographie*, p. 380.
[92] Richter, *Fortschritte*, p. 25.
[93] See vom Bruch, *Weltpolitik*; Conklin, *Mission*; Fischer-Tiné and Mann, *Colonialism*; and Gong, *Standard*. On the compatability of colonialism and the liberal world-view see Mehta, *Liberalism*.

movement of 'internationalisation', one of the main facets of turn-of-the-century globalisation. From the end of the nineteenth century onward, many organisations and social movements that had previously been organised mainly at a national level began to make contact with others and to create cross-border 'internationals'. They included workers' internationals, but also internationals in the women's movement, the peace movement, and even a 'Racists' International'. Internationalism, however, was not only pursued by oppositional movements. There was also cooperation at official level: examples include international scientific conferences, the revival of the Olympic Games, the Red Cross and attempts to create a military 'International of the Sword'. Alongside these numerous non-governmental organisations, multilateral governmental contacts focusing on cooperation in matters relating to urban planning and hygiene, education, environmental protection or criminal prosecution, also formed part of pre-First World War internationalisation.[94]

The 'mechanics' (Geyer and Paulmann) of this process of internationalisation were based mainly on national associations entering into negotiations with each other on an international stage. Those involved in the internationality of the late nineteenth century felt that it linked national units that were entering into increasing, and increasingly close, contact, and in this way contributed to the interconnectedness of the world. Contemporaries thus believed that processes of globalisation required the prior existence of nations or nation states. Increasing contact between them, in the form of social-reform conferences and scientific conferences, but also by other means, would, it was believed, lead to national entities becoming increasingly homogeneous.

One eloquent symbol of this interpretation of internationalisation as homogenisation was the movement toward standardisation, which reached a peak during this era and reflected the hopes shared

---

[94] On this rapidly growing area of research see Lyons, *Internationalism*; Gollwitzer, *Internationale*; Ritterberger, *Organisationen*; Murphy, *Organization*; Ishay, *Internationalism*; Iriye, *Internationalism*; Rupp, *Worlds*; Kühl, *Internationale*; Boli and Thomas, *Constructing*; and Geyer and Paulmann, *Mechanics*. On the history of the term see also Friedemann and Hölscher, 'Internationale'.

by many contemporaries for peaceful ways to arrange and order the world. The process of standardisation was seen by its protagonists as the logical consequence of the transformation of traditional societies into industrialised states and their increasing international interconnectedness. For that reason, most of the rules devised had to do with simplifying the international division of manufacturing labour or trade in industrial products. Railway gauges were unified and the first steps were made toward codifying industrial standards. Standardisation of weights and measures was a central issue. The determination of the standard metre was the best known example of a process that extended to ohms, volts, coulombs, amperes, watts and joules. The gold standard, the basis for trade and exchange, was also the result of negotiation and international agreements. But this trend toward standardising human interaction went beyond commercial issues. Although those arguing for the introduction of world time, for example, highlighted economic and infrastructural reasons, the trend had effects far outside these areas. Culture, too, was affected by standardisation, as evidenced by attempts to institutionalise a 'world language' or to standardise rules for sporting events. But above all, cultural standardisation involved processes by which standardisation took place without any formal agreements to that effect – for example, the spread of the naturalist novel, or the gradual standardisation of fashions in clothing. Standardisation also included conventions that were not simply negotiated between national associations but regulated the interaction of states themselves – such as the establishment of international law. This example once again makes it clear that legal, technical, economic and cultural standardisation was part of power politics and often represented particular interests as 'universal'.[95]

Difference

These processes of standardisation were an expression of the predominant view of globalisation as homogenisation. It was based on

---

[95] On this subject see Geyer, 'Language'; de Cecco, *Gold Standard*; Gallarotti, *Anatomy*; Wilson, *Battles*; Greenaway, *Science*; Herren, *Hintertüren*; Fanizadeh, Hödl and Manzenreiter, *Global Players*; and Koskenniemi, *Gentle Civilizer*.

the widespread belief that a dramatic change was taking place in the way time and space were experienced, even though many contemporaries did not actually experience global interlinkages for themselves. This belief can be described as the dominant paradigm of globalisation at around 1900. The paradigm suggested that the world had become smaller and distances could be covered more quickly; speed had begun to eliminate space. To overstate the case slightly, one could argue that the nineteenth century was, in general terms, shaped by the supremacy of time. Reinhard Koselleck has suggested that during the period flanking the French revolution – the so-called *Sattelzeit* – a new understanding of time developed that was based on a fundamental difference between the past, the present and the future. Michel Foucault, too, has described how representational space was replaced during the nineteenth century by the dynamics of time, and how European culture, from then onward, gave privileged treatment to origins, causality and history. The idea of 'development' that progressed in a linear manner, dividing the past from the present in qualitative terms and thus making it possible to narrate history as progress, was characteristic of nineteenth-century European thought and contributed to the formation of the 'sciences of the successive' (in sociology, history and biological development theory), as Simmel termed it.[96]

The victory of the idea of progress was not an inherent event in European intellectual history; rather, it played a constitutive part in the growing asymmetry of the relationships between Europe and the non-European world. Johannes Fabian has shown that, since the nineteenth century, travel to remote places has also been seen as travelling in time; foreign cultures seemed to European observers to be earlier stages in human history. Europe and its Other could thus be seen as two worlds in different times. This 'denial of coevalness' also formed the basis for the construction of the idea of progress from 'primitive' societies to the pinnacle of European civilisation. The

---

[96] Simmel, 'Problem'. On the same subject see also Koselleck, *Zukunft*; Koselleck, 'Fortschritt'; Wieland, 'Entwicklung'; Sternberger, 'Zauberwort'; Hölscher, *Entdeckung*; Lepenies, *Ende*; and Foucault, *Order*, esp. Chapter 8.

expansionary reordering of space during the nineteenth century itself required a fundamental reorganisation of time. The colonisation of the planet and the transformation of the past into histories of progress were co-determined.[97]

Thus, the nineteenth century was shaped by the logic of a 'simultaneity of the non-simultaneous'. Differences between regions and cultures were to a large extent perceived as temporal gaps, as differences between progressive, stagnating and backward societies. As an evolutionary world-view became established, this perspective became ubiquitous; Social Darwinism helped to ensure that the metaphors of the survival of the fittest and of selection were transferred to societal issues, including the relationships between nations and cultures. This view of time was firmly anchored in influential nineteenth-century trends and it operated within a modus of the temporalisation of difference.[98]

Yet some trends can be discerned at the end of the nineteenth century that would seem to undermine this paradigm. On the one hand, pre-1914 globalisation took place in the name of progress and the civilising mission (in particular from the European and American point of view). Internationalisation, standardisation and 'civilisation' were sold as processes that would homogenise the world and reduce cultural differences between societies to mere differences in time, i.e. different stages of evolution. But around the turn of the century, this concept began to be undermined and, paradoxical as it may seem, this was a direct result of the increases in interlinkage and integration. Globalisation around 1900, then, also marked the beginning of the end of the universalist idea of progress and, at the same time, was accompanied by a 'return of space'.[99]

---

[97] See Fabian, *Time*. See also the discussion on the eighteenth century in Albrecht, *Geopolitik*.

[98] See also, though with a slightly different chronology, Mignolo, 'Globalization'. On the spread of Darwinism see for example Pusey, *China*; and Schwartz, *Search*.

[99] Schlögel, *Raume*. On the recent debate on the category of space, on the spatialisation of historiography and on the link between globalisation and the return of space, see Harvey, *Condition*; Smith, *Uneven Development*; Soja, *Geographies*; and Wigen and Lewis, *Myth*.

This does not mean that spatial categories had been of no importance in the preceding decades. An obsession with spatial expansion and the colonial conquest of the planet had long existed, as we can see from the German reception of Alexander von Humboldt's travels, or the colonial fantasies of the 'armchair conquerors' of the early nineteenth century.[100] Cartography, which was institutionalised during the Napoleonic wars, was an important instrument for statistical offices and for the policy of integration in the German territorial states (although the popular use of maps, which was facilitated not least by falling production and printing costs, was mainly a late-nineteenth-century phenomenon).[101] As Charles Maier, and Charles Bright and Michael Geyer have argued, cartographic mapping of a country was part of a process of territorialisation that the United States and the countries of western Europe experienced around 1850. Thus, the nineteenth century had already witnessed booms in spatial awareness and 'growth spurts' in territorialisation.[102]

However, it is safe to say that in the broader public consciousness we can identify a gradual separation of historical thinking from geographical categories. During the Enlightenment these two categories had belonged together. One of the last major figures to combine these two ideas and, in particular, to emphasise the historicity of geography was Carl Ritter. It is typical that the professorial chair he held in Berlin until 1859 was in *Länder- und Völkerkunde und Geschichte* (roughly: regional geography, ethnology and history).[103] But by that time such a close link between historical and geographical interests was already unusual. After 1800, geography and historical studies became increasingly separate. The 1830s marked a major change in

---

[100] On the colonial imagination see Zantop, *Colonial Fantasies*.

[101] On this topic see the interesting study by Gugerli and Speich, *Topographien*. The key accounts of early cartography in German-speaking areas are still Scharfe, *Abriß*; and Dörflinger, *Kartographie*. See also, with a very similar chronology, the excellent study by Edney, *Mapping*.

[102] See Maier, 'Consigning'; Geyer and Bright, 'World History'; Geyer and Bright, 'Where in the World'. On the same topic see also Black, *Maps*, esp. pp. 27–80.

[103] On Ritter see introductory accounts in Beck, *Carl Ritter*; Büttner, *Carl Ritter*; and Lenz, *Carl Ritter*. On Ritter as a historian see Osterhammel, 'Geschichte'.

this regard.[104] During the growth of historicism, geography became successively marginalised. Space became, as Karl Schlögel has written, a neutral and 'passive stage for historical actors'.[105] The rise of geography as a separate university discipline began only after the German Reich was established and during the period of colonial agitation and expansion.[106] Thus it has been said that, to a large extent, space ceased to be an analytic category during the nineteenth century, and only regained a dominant role in the final decades of the century.[107]

One of the pioneers of this new awareness of space during the era of the *Neuer Kurs* and Wilhelmine *Weltpolitik* was Friedrich Ratzel. A trained zoologist and geologist, Ratzel was – at least from the point of view of his successors – one of the founders of the geopolitical thinking that became more and more dominant in German public life around the turn of the century. Ratzel wanted to examine space as an objective and incontrovertible factor in politics. His view of geography as a science based on natural laws contrasted with the predominant hermeneutic paradigm in the discipline, but also rejected the assumption that racial factors had determining effects. Instead, he emphasised the role of the environment and of geography.[108]

But Ratzel was a child of his own time. His understanding of space was shaped by the colonial globality of high imperialism. He championed colonial claims, and in doing so was very influential in academic circles. His expansionism was based on a Darwinist world view. In his work – he was a co-founder of the *Flottenverein* and of the *Alldeutscher Verband* (Pan-German League) – the 'struggle for survival' was first and foremost a 'struggle for space'. It was in this context that he shaped the term *Lebensraum*, which came into widespread use from

---

[104] See Osterhammel, 'Peoples'.

[105] Schlögel, *Raume*, p. 44.

[106] On the institutional history of German geography see Schultz, *Deutschsprachige Geographie*; Schultz, *Geographie*; and Sandner, 'Search'.

[107] On this topic see Soja, *Geographies*. See also Schlögel, *Raume*, esp. the chapter 'Die Wiederkehr des Raumes', and therein esp. pp. 36–47.

[108] On Ratzel see Müller, *Ratzel*; Osterhammel, 'Raumerfassung'; Gollwitzer, *Geschichte*, pp. 58–62; Schultz, 'Geographie im 19. Jahrhundert'; and Buttmann, *Ratzel*.

the 1920s onward.[109] Ratzel attempted to develop a scientific basis for the concept and tried to establish the 'laws governing the spatial growth of states'. Peoples at a lower cultural level, he assumed, would only control small political spaces. Cultural progress corresponded with the transition from small areas to large ones: the amount of space required increased with increasing cultural sophistication. The *Weltpolitik* for which he was here providing the scientific legitimation was nothing more, he believed, than a general (and advanced) stage of national development.[110]

German geography and geopolitics at the turn of the century contributed to the rehabilitation of the concept of space. But in doing so geography and geopolitics were operating within a paradigm of cultural diffusion. The idea had been propagated by Ratzel in opposition to the common paradigm of evolutionism. Ratzel postulated that cultural innovations were, in many cases, created only once, and then spread to other societies.[111] This supposition was the basis for the political accusations made against him by writers such as the Frenchman Camille Vallaux. Vallaux believed that Ratzel's theory of space was simply a scientific camouflage for German imperialism.[112] But the issue of the role of space in the discourse of globalisation goes beyond the issue of political instrumentalisation or ideology. The question is, rather, whether the interlinkage of the world around 1900 was accompanied by a 'spatial turn', as has been identified for globalisation a century later. Or was the revival of the category of space limited, as would seem to be the case for Ratzel, to a derived function within a discourse of progress, diffusion and development: i.e. of time?

Some recent contributions to current theories of globalisation have identified precisely this feature as the specific characteristic of the pre-First World War era. Arif Dirlik, for example, has described

---

[109] Ratzel, 'Lebensraum'. On Ratzel's role in the history of geopolitics see Diekmann, Krüger and Schoeps, *Geopolitik*; Kost, *Einflüsse*; Schulte-Althoff, *Studien*; Faber, 'Vorgeschichte'; and Korinman, *Allemagne*.

[110] Ratzel, 'Gesetze'. See also Smith, *Ideological Origins*, esp. pp. 146–52.

[111] See Smith, *Politics*, pp. 140–61.

[112] See Vallaux, *Géographie*. On the debate on geopolitics see Osterhammel, 'Wiederkehr'; and 'Raumbeziehungen'.

the growing connectedness of the nineteenth-century world as a process that took place within a Eurocentric paradigm of modernisation based on the western model. By contrast, late-twentieth-century globalisation has emancipated itself, he argues, from such universalistic ambitions: 'Globalization as paradigm is enabled by its divorce from the universalist aspirations that marked it earlier in its history.' The key difference between globalisation around 1900 and globalisation around 2000 is, he believes, the way in which difference is negotiated. The pre-First World War temporalisation of differences (and colonialism as the political expression of that discourse) has, he suggests, given way a century later to the idea of 'multiple modernities'. The analysis in terms of hierarchy that characterised the older theories has currently been supplanted by the paradigm of cultural difference, ranging from a culturally relativistic multiculturalism to the diagnosis of a 'clash of civilisations'.[113]

This striking observation is an interesting attempt to put the European–American intellectual debate about globalisation in an analytic nutshell. Dirlik's idea also explains why the term 'globalisation' has only been used since the 1980s even though the history of global interlinkage can be traced back to the sixteenth century and the start of the capitalist penetration of the world. What is new in twentieth-century globalisation, he argues, is not integration, but the awareness of particularisation – in political terms, the questioning of the hegemony of the West and the formulation of alternative claims to modernity, and, in cultural terms, the undermining of Eurocentric hierarchies. Dirlik sees globalisation around the millennium as the product, even the triumph, of a capitalist (and thus, for Dirlik, Eurocentric) world order, yet paradoxically also of its collapse and its spatial fragmentation.[114]

However, when we look more closely we can see that this development began even before the First World War. It is true that in Europe it was assumed that exchange and transport would have a homogenising, 'civilising' effect – and not just in Europe: the idea

---

[113] See Dirlik, 'Globalization'.
[114] See also Dirlik, 'Is There History'; and 'Modernity'.

of modernisation was often readily accepted by modernising elites even outside Europe. In some cases this appropriation went so far that we can speak of the indigenisation of modern institutions. Modernisation was not seen as 'westernisation' but as the result of the society's own traditions and cultural resources.[115] At the same time, however, oppositional movements developed outside Europe and the United States that questioned the linearity of historical progress and modernisation. Pan-Asiatic and pan-Islamic movements, in particular, gave expression to anti-western sentiments from about the 1880s onward. Such movements were opposed to the marginalisation of indigenous traditions in the course of modernisation. They opposed imperialism as a form of rule, and also opposed imperialistic ideologies that were based on the ideas of 'race', the 'Orient', and empire. The spread of biologistic ideas about race was one of the main reasons behind the disillusionment with the project of modernisation based on a European model that can be identified in the thinking of many intellectuals, ranging from the Ottoman empire to eastern Asia. The idea of race also formed the basis for a number of alternative visions put forward against the imperialist order.[116] However, it would not be correct to argue that most of these 'pan-movements' put forward anti-modern ideas. In fact, the attractiveness of modernising concepts remained in force even after 1880, even after 1905 (and probably even after the First World War, which some authors have prematurely identified as the end of the lure of western 'civilisation').[117] But during that period, and especially after the Japanese victory over Russia, alternative concepts to that of western modernism and the political and cultural homogenisation of the world were explicitly formulated. The core of these movements was their insistence on a cultural difference that could not be subsumed by the paradigm of development with its linear understanding of time. Thus, they sought alternative routes toward modernisation, the dynamics of which could not be

---

[115] On the appropriation of the logic of the cultural mission see Schäbler, 'Globale Moderne'. See also Aydin, 'Conception'.

[116] On this subject see Dikötter, *Construction*; and Oguma, *Genealogy*.

[117] See for example Adas, 'Hegemony'.

calculated on the basis of their difference from the western European blueprint.[118]

These alternative visions were more than simply expressions of anti-western fundamentalism or a retreat from the globalised world. Rather, they must be seen both as part of and as a reaction to the process of globalisation around 1900. The goal of politically reorganising the world into regional blocs and the cultural scepticism toward the project of 'westernisation' were also the product of alternative ways of conceiving space that took global interconnectedness under asymmetric power relationships into account. Thus, ideas of 'Asia' developed – in both the Ottoman empire and in China and Japan – that were both trans-religious and transnational. At the turn of the century, pan-Asianists such as Okakura Tenshin who were attempting to bring together the Asian nations had emphasised their common Buddhist tradition. But increasingly, voices could be heard for whom 'Asia' did not primarily mean the ideal of a common civilisation defined by cultural heritage, but was the expression of a geopolitically informed global consciousness. Their common (although differing) historical experience of subaltern integration into an imperialist world order became more important for the formation of cross-regional identities than their religious and cultural heritage.[119]

As these dynamic conceptions of space and strategies of political and cultural demarcation make clear, pre-1900 globalisation was also accompanied by processes of fragmentation. Even before the First World War, the intensification of global and imperial

[118] On this topic see Aydin, *Politics*. On the 'pan-movements' in general, see Snyder, *Macro-Nationalisms*. On pan-Asianism, see for example Duara, 'Discourse'; Najita and Harootunian, 'Japan's Revolt'; Saaler, 'Pan-Asianismus'; and Esenbel, 'Japan's Global Claim'. On pan-Islamisim, see for example Kayali, *Arabs*. On pan-Africanism, which, until well into the 1940s, was much more of an ideology of modernisation, see Geiss, *Panafrikanismus*; Langley, *Pan-Africanism*; and Esedebe, *Pan-Africanism*. See also Gilroy, *Black Atlantic*.

[119] See Aydin, *Politics*, esp. the chapter 'Awakening of the East/equality with the West (1905–1912)'. See also Karl, *Staging the World*, esp. pp. 151–76. On the changing understanding of 'Asia', see also Lee, 'Asien'; Osterhammel, 'Spatial Ordering'; Shimada, 'Überlegungen'; and Furuya, *Gendai*. See also Wigen and Lewis, *Myth*.

interconnectedness was accompanied by oppositional movements that one could read as the beginnings of a 'spatial turn'. This change can best be illustrated through a key European concept of the era: that of 'civilisation'. In eighteenth-century universal histories, the term was usually used in a relativistic manner, and the idea that civilisations and religions might be of equal value was accepted in principle. China, in particular, was often used as an alternative model, held up as a mirror to European societies. During the nineteenth century, this changed. From 1830 onward, it became common to differentiate clearly between civilised peoples and uncivilised peoples; in addition, the temporal dimension that the concept had acquired during the Enlightenment became dominant. The word 'civilisation' was now usually used in the singular. It was measured on a uniform scale, the units of which were the degree of historical progress. The process of civilisation as a historical development from hunter-gatherer societies to the cultural heights of modern societies characterised by the division of labour was seen as a universal phenomenon. Cultural differences were thus seen more as a question of 'earlier' or 'later' than as 'here' and 'there'. This universalist (and temporalised) idea of civilisation was now, at the start of the twentieth century, gradually challenged by a spatial concept of civilisations (now in the plural). The pan-Asian and pan-Islamic movements are evidence of this proliferation of concepts of civilisation. The spatial component had never been completely eliminated from the concept but this dimension once again became more important when exchange and mobility expanded. Globalisation around 1900 was a process not merely of homogenisation (as the time paradigm suggested) but also of the constitution of difference and the return of spatially understood 'cultural circles' (*Kulturkreise*). This conceptual change was also reflected in Europe – for example, in the ideas of *Mitteleuropa*, in the *fin de siècle* critique of civilisation and, after 1918, in the favourable reception given to Oswald Spengler's *Untergang des Abendlandes*.[120]

---

[120] See Fisch, 'Zivilisation'; Febvre, 'Entwicklung'; Osterhammel, *Entzauberung*, esp. pp. 394–403; Lüsebrink, 'Civilization'; and Duara, 'Discourse'. On the plans for *Mitteleuropa* see Theiner, '"Mitteleuropa"-Pläne'. On the critique of civilisation in

NATION

A similar relationship between interconnectedness and spatial separation can also be identified at a smaller scale than the relationships between 'civilisations'. During the late nineteenth century the
demarcation of nation states accompanied the process of globalisation and was indeed a reaction to it. In fact, the increase in interconnectedness, in the literal sense, was accompanied in many regions,
especially Asia, by the creation of new nation states. As global legal
standards developed and international law became established, many
nation states (or national movements working toward establishing a
state) were created, as only such states could hope to be respected as
independent actors.

Of course, this does not mean that nations and nationalisms only
developed as a reaction to globalisation.[121] For western Europe it is
possible to identify peaks of territorialisation of national rule during
the Napoleonic era, and again in the 1840s and 1850s. The reconfiguration of the idea of the nation around 1900 could thus be understood as a new wave within a range of transformations: one that had
a reinforcing effect where national identities and forms of organisation had already gained ground. For Britain, as Anthony Hopkins has
argued, imperialism, overseas expansion and the development of the
empire were 'part cause and part consequence of the growth of the
nation state'. Global interconnectedness did not so much contribute to
the dissolution of nation states, as some contemporary commentators
believed, but rather was instrumental in constituting them and making them permanent.[122]

This impression is confirmed when we look at the European mainland. We can observe a wave of nationalisation at about the same

Germany see Rohkrämer, *Andere Moderne* (although with a narrow national focus
and taking only bourgeois thinkers into account). A literary-studies approach,
focusing completely on national history, is taken by Beßlich, *Wege*. Finally, see
Spengler, *Untergang*.

[121] This view is taken in the systems-theory literature, in which national borders are
seen as the result of globalisation. See for example Nassehi, '"Welt"-Fremdheit';
Stichweh, *Weltgesellschaft*; and Meyer *et al.*, 'World Society'.

[122] Hopkins, 'History', p. 30. See also his 'Back to the Future'.

time for all the industrialised countries that turned to protectionism to reduce the effects of the Great Depression and their dependence on the global market. France, for example, had abolished the requirement for citizens of western European countries to carry passports in 1874. In doing so it was simply giving legal recognition to existing practice. For much of the nineteenth century, nationality was of little importance for mobility (and for labour markets) and its impact was less than that of social status. From the 1880s onward, this changed. This process of nationalisation was related not only to well-known internal factors such as school education and symbolic representation, but also to worries about the mobility of goods and of people – a worry about 'infiltration'.[123]

Fear of the consequences of unchecked circulation soon led, in the industrialised countries of Europe and in the United States, to the development of a whole range of technologies of inclusion and exclusion.[124] These technologies became established alongside the process of globalisation; in fact they were an integral part of it. This view is not universal. One influential interpretation of the history of the twentieth century sees the interruption of global interconnectedness during the era of the two World Wars as a kind of 'original sin', the beginning of an era of nationalisms, xenophobia and separation. In contrast, the pre-1914 world is seen as a utopia of peaceful interaction and cultural interchange. As long as the spirit of bourgeois cosmopolitanism remained strong enough, there was no interruption to the unchecked mobility of people, goods and ideas. In this view, it was only the First World War, the *ur*-catastrophe of the century, followed as it was by the world economic crisis and totalitarian nationalism, that put an end to this happy era of globalisation, of free trade and of borderless circulation.[125] The economic historian Jeffrey Williamson

---

[123] On this topic see the stimulating discussion in Noiriel, *Tyrannei*.

[124] On the topic in general see Zolberg, 'Global Movements'; Zolberg, 'Great Wall'; Böcker, Groenendijk, Havinga and Minderhoud, *Regulation*; Jones, *Boundaries*; Fahrmeir, Faron and Weil, *Migration Control*.

[125] See for example Hopkins, 'History', esp. p. 29. Harper, 'Empire', p. 158 speaks of the 'closing of global possibilities'. See also James, *End*. Of the literature on

even speaks of a pre-1914 *belle époque*, which was followed by 'dark middle years' until 1950 before a 'renaissance' brought globalisation back on course.[126]

Stefan Zweig's nostalgic memories of the 'world of yesterday' gave expression to this widespread emotion: 'Before 1914, the planet had belonged to everyone. Everyone could go where he wanted and stay as long as he wanted.' There had been no borders that were more than 'symbolic lines that one could cross in as carefree a manner as the meridian in Greenwich'. This ideal world had, Zweig suggested, been destroyed after 1914. He then depicted the era that some authors now describe as deglobalisation as the 'terrible relapse … which the world has suffered since the First World War', as the end of cosmopolitan hopes. 'It was only after the war that the destruction of the world by National Socialism began', Zweig summarised; only after the war did 'hatred of foreigners' begin, 'or at least fear of foreigners'.[127]

But Zweig's experience was not necessarily representative. As a respected and wealthy writer and as an educated white man from western Europe he was subject to different conditions than those that applied to Chinese 'coolies', to the average immigrant to the USA or to Polish seasonal workers in eastern Prussia. Zweig's impression that mobility knew no boundaries – 'one got on and got off without asking or being asked' – cannot simply be applied to the mass migration that was one of the key characteristics of turn-of-the-century globalisation. By this time, travellers did not just include Englishmen on their 'grand tour' or the first modern globetrotters (a contemporary neologism) but a large number of members of lower social classes who were not travelling for visits, but to stay. Concerns about immigration and invasion were not focused on people like Stefan Zweig.

---

the theory of present-day globalisation, Ohmae, *Borderless World* and Levitt, 'Globalization' emphasise the integrative and 'civilising' aspects of globalisation. For an overview of the different positions in the theoretical debate, see Guillén, 'Globalization'.

[126] Williamson, 'Globalization', quoted in McKeown, 'Global Migration', n. 48. Economic historians are particularly given to suggesting that 1914 marked a complete change: see O'Rourke and Williamson, *Globalization*, esp. Chapter 1.

[127] Zweig, *Welt*, p. 465.

They were based on the perception of immigration as a 'flood' of many nameless individuals from outside the borders.

Thus, the interconnectedness of the world was accompanied not only by cosmopolitan visions but also by laws on immigration and by the perfecting of controls. 'The more trade and communication develop', Gérard Noiriel said of this mechanism, 'the more important become identificatory techniques of protection'.[128] These included instruments to make identification easier, such as bertillonage, which was presented at the World Exhibition in 1889. When Bertillon was creating his catalogue of biometric characteristics for identification, he had intended it mainly for use in identifying criminals. But his technique was also aimed at identifying foreigners without residence permits who had entered France under false names after the requirement for passports was abolished.[129] Further technologies of demarcation included fixed border posts such as the thirty-nine posts set up by the German *Feldarbeiterzentralstelle* (the 'German Central Office for Field Workers') to control immigration from Russia and Austria. Other components of modern technologies for monitoring mobility included increasingly rigid rules on nationality and asylum, and the issuing of passports. In effect, between 1890 and 1914, imagined lines in Europe became national borders.[130]

This fixing of the external boundaries of nation can be understood, partly, as the result of external, even systemic contexts of interactive flows and patterns of circulation. The production of spaces of national specificity, then, was a universal process. This runs counter to contemporary discussions, which focused mainly on the peculiarities of each nation and its traditions – and in which nations were seen not as the effect of internationalisation and globalisation, but rather as their precondition. Historical research, too, usually concentrates on the internal specifics and characteristics of nationalism; despite all similarities each nationalism is viewed as a phenomenon *sui generis*. The

---

[128] Noiriel, *Tyrannei*, p. 308.
[129] *Ibid.*, pp. 150ff. On bertillonage and other technologies of identification see Vec, *Spur*, esp. pp. 31–46; and Becker, *Verderbnis*.
[130] See Gosewinkel, *Einbürgern*; Fahrmeir, *Citizens*; Torpey, *Invention*; Caplan and Torpey, *Documenting*; and Salter, *Rights*.

question is thus how the demarcation of nation states as a universal process can be reconciled with the idea of the regional specifics of nationalisation.[131]

In an influential monograph, Ernest Gellner has described nationalism as, in the main, a product of global capitalism. Gellner argues that the main function of nation states was to guarantee the mobility of labour that, in the feudal system, was limited by class. Gellner sees many political and social measures, including the codification of formal equality and the standardisation of society, for example in education, as one result of this situation. Nationalism is thus seen as mainly an agent of socio-economic modernisation. This view, however, tends to reduce the formation of nations to its economic function and thus depoliticises it to a large extent. Gellner instead links nationalism to a theory of economic development in the context of which nationalism appears to be a universal phenomenon.[132]

In Benedict Anderson's interpretation the question of specific national features is given more attention. But he, too, bases his ideas on economic development, although this fact has been neglected in the reception of his theory of 'imagined communities'. He postulates a causal link between the development of print capitalism and of national forms of organisation. But, to this reference to a particular stage of economic development, he adds the role of transfer and influence, which were of major importance for the development of nation states. Europe, he argues, was shaped by the development of the nations in the Americas and was itself influential in the spread of nationalism to Asia and Africa. Here, nationalism is seen as the abstract product of both a universal development (as in Gellner's work) and of historically specific contexts.[133]

[131] For the discussion below see the stimulating introduction by Hill, *National History*. See also Buell, *National Culture*.

[132] See Gellner, *Nations*. See also Smith, 'Memory'; Smith, *Nation*; Van den Bossche, 'Nationalism'; and the contributions to Hall, *State*.

[133] See Anderson, *Imagined Communities*. On Anderson's approach see also Kelly, 'Time'. For the constructivist theory of the nation in general see Cubitt, *Imagining Nations*.

However, to a large extent Anderson also glosses over the question of how differences between nationalisms can be explained. For him, differences result from the observation that conditions and constellations were diverse, and hence 'coloured' nationalism differently. In general, it is at this point of the analysis that internal factors are introduced: nationalism is seen as a universal form, and its specific content in a particular case is interpreted as the expression of specific socio-cultural conditions. But can this explain the very fundamental and systematic differences between nationalisms? In the colonised countries, to take one example, the idea of a cultural difference from the West was a constitutive factor for nationalist rhetoric and politics. Where this tendency is explained solely in terms of indigenous traditions, be they Indian, Japanese or Chinese, analysis remains incomplete. The idea of difference played a central role in the spread of nationalism during the nineteenth century. But these differences were themselves embedded in a global context. The demand for national equality, for example, was based on a concept of the world as a system of independent nation states. The specific form that nationalism took in each case can thus be seen not merely as the product of internal conditions but rather as the result of a society's position in the international state system, and the cultural, political and economic world order.[134]

Thus, nationalism as a global discourse for the articulation of local differences varied to the extent that geopolitical positions were transposed into an expression of specific traditions. To return to the concrete example of the Wilhelmine empire: one of the central tropes of German nationalism was the figure of German 'culture' as a third way beyond western 'civilisation' and 'barbarism' in the East. The popularity of this concept grew rapidly in the early years of the twentieth century and peaked during the war years, but it has retained a powerful grip on the German imagination since.[135] It has conventionally been traced back to the Romantic period and to longstanding

---

[134]   On the development of nationalism in a colonial context, see the interesting discussion by Chatterjee, *Nationalist Thought*; and *Nation*, esp. Chapter 2.

[135]   Lepenies, *Seduction of Culture*.

traditions represented by a class of mandarins detached from polit-ics.[136] From the perspective of a history of globalisation, however, the trope can equally be understood as the effect of a distinctive reading of the world political status of the Kaiserreich: Germany as a late-comer when compared to France and Great Britain, both in terms of nation-building and as a global player; and Germany as superior compared to Europe's East, and to the colonial world (the latter being seen as an economically backward world that was not yet organised into nation-state units).

In this context, the concept of 'German work' can also be seen as a specific contribution to the nationalism of the era. Of course, the con-cept of national work was important in other countries too; the idea was not limited to Germany. But there was a widespread belief within the Kaiserreich that German work practice was something unique. This trope was the expression of a quest for uniqueness and an attempt to come to terms with the peculiarities of a nation that could not be defined in terms of its colonial empire (like France or England); had not been shaped by supremacy at sea, capital investment and trade (like England); could not reclaim and colonise an internal border as a resource of seemingly perennial rejuvenation (like the United States); and could not, like Poland and many colonial societies, define its specific characteristics in terms of political domination by a foreign power. In the global context of the turn of the century, the notion of 'German work' can be understood as a typical latecomer discourse, a form of protest against the underprivileged role Germany appeared to play in the international arena.

At the same time, the concept was an expression of pride in Germany's achievements and ambitions. 'German work' was at the heart of the Kaiserreich's attempt to assert the place it deserved, both within Europe and beyond. The concept clearly had an expansionist ring, as is clear from its frequent use to describe colonial settlement, conquest and occupation. At the same time, the slogan was a wake-up call that was intended to mobilise the

---

[136] See Fisch, 'Zivilisation', esp. pp. 760–66; and Pflaum, 'Kultur-Zivilisations-Antithese', pp. 288ff. See also Verhey, *Spirit*; and Flasch, *Mobilmachung*.

population and counteract the danger of slackening, of the possibility of decline or of being overtaken. 'German work' could be interpreted, as I argue in the sixth chapter of this book, as an equivalent to the Protestant work ethic and as the internalised motor of German attempts to become a world power: as a spiritual and cultural resource for *Weltpolitik*. It was a foundational term suggesting that Germany's position in the world was the product of her own efforts and achievements.

Not unlike the development of the German navy, the rhetoric of 'German work' can be read as the expression of an ambivalent mix of pride and minority complex, and it is indicative for the mechanisms through which global contexts were translated into the grammar of nationalism. The afterlife of the trope – the 'soldiers of work' in National Socialism, 'German *Wertarbeit*' as the basis for the economic miracle of the 1950s, and the East German version of a 'state of work' (*Staat der Arbeit*) – attests to the mark it has left on notions of Germanness.

For contemporaries, these exogenous aspects of Wilhelmine nationalism were of only minor importance, and they have not figured much more prominently in scholarly discussions of nationalism. The national-history perspective that is still important in historiography today is itself a result of nationalism and of the development of the nation state in the nineteenth century. In the course of the nationalisation of politics, of economics and of culture, the ordering of knowledge was, from the early nineteenth century onward, restructured within national categories, concepts and academic institutions. The national-history perspective was also a reaction to the victory of the nation state as a sphere of action that shaped and changed the reality of social history. The institutionalisation of the modern humanities took place in a context that was characterised by the political requirements of the developing nation state and the cultural hegemony of national parameters.

The discipline of modern history thus often operated, like sociology, with a view of society that Anthony D. Smith has described as methodological nationalism. By this he does not just mean a narrow parochial view that focuses mainly on events within one's own national society.[137] Rather, in many social sciences, the meth-odological framework actually structured analysis in a manner that took the nation state as the basic unit of investigation. The territorial state was seen as a container for society, and social contacts could, it seemed, only be observed and interpreted within the boundaries of the nation state.[138] Thus, the academic disciplines that developed during the course of the nineteenth century tended to reinforce the assumption that every society must be explained primarily as a result of its internal parameters. Knowledge about the world was thus pre-structured, both discursively and institutionally, in a way that tended to ignore the constitutive role of relationships of exchange.

This national-history perspective has been subjected to fre-quent criticism. In Germany, these criticisms include the world his-tory approaches taken at the turn of the century, for example by Lamprecht's circle in Leipzig.[139] Comparative approaches such as those taken by Otto Hintze and many others after him also took issue with the national-history paradigm. Diverse forms of cultural his-tory and, partially overlapping with these, micro-history have also contributed to questioning the macro-structural assumptions of the national-history mainstream. The discussion below thus picks up on a range of attempts to overcome methodological nationalism within historical studies.

It is important to be aware that this project, to which this book is a contribution, must recognise in part its own impossibility. Given the historical and continued relevance of nation-state institutions, of historiographical traditions and, last but not least, of the way know-ledge is constituted within the nation state – for example in archives and statistics – the project of transnational historiography without an

---

[137] For examples of this tendency, using the example of German historiography, see for example Raphael, 'Sozialgeschichte'; and Osterhammel, 'Außereuropäische Geschichte'.

[138] See Smith, *Nationalism and Modernism*, p. 191. See also Beck, *Globalisierung*, pp. 49ff.; Wallerstein, 'Development'; and Glick Schiller and Wimmer, 'Nationalism'. For criticisms from a systems-theory perspective see Stichweh, 'Theorie'; Wobbe, *Weltgesellschaft*; and, from a post-colonial perspective, Chakrabarty, *Provincializing Europe*.

[139] See for example Middell, *Weltgeschichtsschreibung*.

implicit reference to the unit of nation must remain, in part, an aporetic one: '[a]n impossible "no" to a structure, which one critiques, yet inhabits intimately'.[140] When this attempt is nevertheless made, traces of the national-history 'formatting' of the world are usually still visible. This is the case, for example, in present-day mobility studies and in studies on transnational societies and diasporas, which often tend implicitly to reproduce the national-history paradigm. How far must we travel from our point of departure before we are regarded as mobile? When 'mobility' is under discussion, the overcoming of national boundaries is usually implicitly assumed. Thus the analysis remains focused on the unit of the nation state, as otherwise mobility is barely registered (or treated as a separate category, 'domestic mobility').[141]

In the chapters that follow, I attempt to place national histories in a transnational context while being aware of limits inherent to such an attempt. One of the reasons for these limits is that during the nineteenth century, global interaction and the formation of the idea of the national were not in opposition. Nationalisation and the transnational eradication of boundaries have thus always had an ambiguous relationship – even analytically. In contrast to the utopias of a post-national historiography that aims to free itself from the category of the nation altogether, the chapters below assume that the nationally structured ordering of knowledge and of social practice has not been simply an ideological veil that has hidden the transnational reality but must itself be understood as a reaction to the process of globalisation.[142]

---

[140] Spivak, 'Making', p. 28.
[141] See for example Basch, Blanc-Szanton and Glick Schiller, *Nations*. A similar tendency can be found in Appadurai, *Modernity*; and in Greenblatt, 'Mobility'.
[142] See also Robertson, *Globalization*, pp. 15ff; and Albrow, 'Globalization'.

CHAPTER TWO

'Native policy' in colony and metropole: 'educating to work' in East Africa and eastern Westphalia

It is to be hoped that the possession of colonies with inhabitants far below our race will have an educating influence *on us*.

(Fagus, 1909)[1]

INTRODUCTION

At the opening of the first workers' colony in Wilhelmsdorf in 1882, the Bielefeld pastor Friedrich von Bodelschwingh promised the 'vagabonds' and homeless men who were to be housed there an 'exquisite good, namely work itself'.[2] Regular activity would ensure that these 'people seemingly lost for proper society shall be protected from complete ruin and shall be won back for work and order', as Friedrich, Crown Prince of Prussia, emphasised, when he became patron of Wilhelmsdorf later in the same year.[3] The guiding principle of this project of 'educating to work' was the absence of force: 'We do not want any workers against their will, not for a single hour.' But this educational philosophy only promised long-term success when combined with Christianity: 'Prayer and work combined ... bear blessed fruit for eternity.'[4]

Let us leave the workers' colony for the present and turn to work in the colonies. 'Educating the negro to work' (*Die Erziehung des Negers zur Arbeit*) was one of the main projects of state policy, and especially

---

[1] Quoted in El-Tayeb, *Schwarze Deutsche*, p. 121.
[2] Bodelschwingh, *Ausgewählte Schriften*, p. 431.
[3] Quoted in Gerhardt, *Bodelschwingh*, p. 134.
[4] Bodelschwingh, *Ausgewählte Schriften*, pp. 432, 433.

of church policy, since the acquisition of the first German colonies in 1884. The missions saw it as their task gradually to educate 'the work-shy native to work of his own free will' and 'unobtrusively' to enable him to attain 'an existence fit for human beings'.[5] Here, too, success seemed to depend on avoiding any indication of force, instead appealing to a Christian sense of duty. *Ora et labora* was the motto of missionary policy. And in Africa, too, the 'combination of prayer and labour' was regarded as a precondition for the development of the human individual.[6]

Were these similarities merely accidental? Or was there a link between eastern Westphalia and East Africa that was more than just a coincidence? Was there a link between attempts to return the 'work-shy' on the roads of the German empire to respectable society, and the attempts to raise the members of 'lower races, despite their work-shyness' to a higher level of civilisation?[7] Did the disciplining of the homeless in the German empire have an effect on the simultaneous project of 'civilising the natives' in the empire's African colonies – or perhaps even the reverse? What function did work and educating-to-work play in this regard? After all, these debates were situated in a context in which diverging interests and different logics of social contexts overlapped. For work not only defined the 'moral value' of an individual; it was also commodifiable and thus also determined 'the value or lack of it that the colonies have for our homeland'.[8] The debate about work was part of the dynamics of contemporary globalising capitalism, which was continually undermining boundaries – those between outside and inside and between the colony and the metropole.

These remarks lead us to the question of whether the links between Germany and overseas 'New Germany' may have been closer than is usually supposed. For a long time, the relationship between the Reich and its African colonies was seen as a one-way street: the effects of colonial power, whether seen as civilisation and a cultural mission or as exploitation and destruction, were localised in Africa alone.

---

[5] Berg, *Heidenmission*, p. 293.   [6] Paul, *Mission*, p. 197.
[7] Berg, *Heidenmission*, p. 281.   [8] Buchner, 'Mithilfe', pp. 429, 428.

The German Reich was regarded as an almost completely separate and independent entity.[9] This chapter will challenge this perspective. Following on from approaches taken by post-colonial studies, it will attempt to investigate the metropole and the colony within a single analytic framework.[10] This approach involves asking both about the influences that imperialism had on the colonial periphery and about the effects the imperial project had on the Reich itself. Under the asymmetric conditions of colonial rule, social practices were reciprocally constituted. This chapter attempts to tie colonial experiences together as a method for interpreting the history of the Kaiserreich. The central question is whether Wilhelmine German society was more affected by the colonial experience than contemporaries, and historians in their wake, have made us believe.

THE COLONIAL 'LABOUR QUESTION'

In 1885, just a year after Germany had acquired its first African colonies, the German East Africa Company (*Deutsch-Ostafrikanische Gesellschaft*) in Berlin offered a prize for answers to the question 'How can one best train the Negro for plantation work?'[11] This presentation of the problem already contained an early admission of defeat. During the campaign for the acquisition of colonies, the issues of population and emigration had played a central role. It was hoped that 'settlement colonies' in South America or Africa would be able to redirect the emigratory flows that had been developing since 1880 in the third major wave of emigration that century, and that had been mostly to the United States. Redirecting these flows to the colonies would prevent the 'loss of national energies' and retain the products of 'German work' for the fatherland. In his widely read and influential 1879 volume *Bedarf Deutschland der Kolonien?* (*Does Germany Need Colonies?*), Friedrich Fabri emphasised the important role that colonies could

---

[9] On this topic see Conrad, 'Doppelte Marginalisierung'.
[10] Stoler and Cooper, 'Between Metropole and Colony'. See also Conrad and Randeria, 'Geteilte Geschichten'.
[11] On the competitions, see Markmiller, *Erziehung*, pp. 76ff.

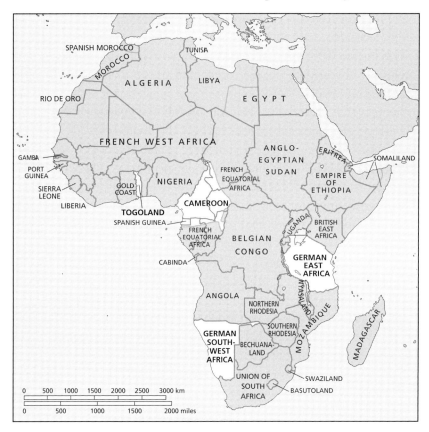

Map 2.1 The German colonial empire in 1914: Togo, Cameroon, German South-West Africa, German East Africa.

play in solving the problem of emigration. 'An understanding and energetic pursuit of a real colonial policy is the only effective way to turn German emigration from a loss of strength into an economic and political gain of strength.'[12] During this era, Malthusian-inspired fears of a population explosion and simultaneous worries about the loss of national substance were widespread.[13] 'For a people that suffers from constant overproduction and every year sends some 200,000 of

---

[12] Fabri, *Bedarf Deutschland*, p. 78. See also Bade, *Fabri*, esp. pp. 84–85.
[13] See Hampe, 'Hintergründe'.

its children to foreign lands, colonisation has become an existential issue', Heinrich von Treitschke argued in 1884.[14]

But during the entire course of German colonisation, emigration to German colonies remained far below the expectations of its propagandists. The tiny principality of Schwarzburg-Sondershausen, with fewer than 90,000 inhabitants, was huge in comparison to the total number of Germans in the colonies, which never exceeded 25,000.[15] There were various reasons for the lack of attractiveness of Germany's African (and Pacific) possessions as 'settlement colonies'. Toward the end of the nineteenth century, the reduction in the birth rate in Europe reducing (the excess of births over deaths) made traditional emigration less important. But the main issue under public discussion at the time was the problem that climate posed for the settlement of the African colonies. Here, the emigration problem was treated as a 'question of acclimatisation'. Rudolf Virchow, the medical expert and anthropologist, believed that Germans were simply not capable of adapting to the climatic conditions in tropical areas and that for this reason permanent settlement in the African colonies would not be possible. In 1886, the German Colonial Association reacted by launching a study that was intended to refute Virchow's theories and to show that Europeans could indeed settle in Africa, Asia and Oceania. But scepticism about the ability of German people to adapt to tropical climates remained.[16]

Against the background of these medical debates, those involved in colonial policy also began to believe that 'Europeans … [were] not suited to physical work in the tropics'. The climatic conditions 'forbid … Europeans any major physical exertion'.[17] This meant that only a small number of emigrants could be expected. Hiring German agricultural workers for temporary periods was no solution, either, given the high wage and transport costs involved.[18] In a

[14] von Treitschke, 'Versuche', p. 670.
[15] See Gann, 'Marginal Colonialism', pp. 1–3.
[16] See for example Leo, 'Arbeiterfrage'. On these debates see Grosse, *Kolonialismus*, pp. 53–95.
[17] Giesebrecht, *Behandlung*, p. 175.
[18] Anton, 'Bedeutung', p. 200.

survey of experts on the problem of how to 'treat natives in German colonies' in 1898, it was agreed that 'given the climatic conditions still prevailing at the moment' – there were actually speculations about the 'possibility of general artificial cooling of houses in the tropics' for the future[19] – 'the black man [would be] the only useful worker in Africa'.[20]

This finding presented the colonial government with a 'labour question', which for many commentators became the vital issue (*Lebensfrage*) for all colonial policies.[21] In fact, the problem of recruiting – and training – suitable workers was the single issue of colonial policy that was discussed in the greatest detail. The abolition of slavery had made it difficult for European plantation economies to obtain native workers. Initially, and despite their abolitionist rhetoric, the German administration in German East Africa continued to tolerate slavery in order to maintain the old pre-colonial economy at local levels. At the turn of the century there were still 400,000 slaves in German East Africa, some 10 per cent of the entire population. Almost all were owned by African elites, while, for legal and other reasons, the colonial plantation economy was able to make only limited use of slaves. The development of a market for labour, therefore, depended on the gradual decline of slavery. After 1900, this set in quickly.[22] The transition from slavery to waged work, however, was not a linear process, as recent research has shown. The use of seasonal

---

[19] Ziemann, *Bevölkerungs- und Rassenproblem*, p. 18.

[20] August Boshart in Giesebrecht, *Behandlung*, p. 42. This was by no means self-evident: in South America and in the Pacific region, contact with Europeans had led to a dramatic reduction in the native population, and the forced labour demanded by Europeans also contributed to the decimation of indigenous inhabitants. In this context it was necessary to 'get used to the idea that the black inhabitants of this continent are … by no means wasting away and disappearing through contact with Europeans' (Merensky, *Wie erzieht man*, p. 3).

[21] Merensky, *Wie erzieht man*, p. 4.

[22] See the detailed account in Deutsch, *Emancipation*. After increasing rapidly around the turn of the century, the number of waged workers in German East Africa in 1913 was around 172,000, of which 140,000 were working for European companies, plantations and missions.

and temporary migrant labour was characteristic of the development of the capitalist system in Africa.[23]

Initially, the shortage of waged workers was a serious problem for German traders and businessmen. In Cameroon and East Africa, especially, 'the circumstances [seemed] ... so ... serious that in these colonies one cannot speak of a labour question but rather of a labour calamity'.[24] At the 1902 German Colonial Congress in Berlin, Major Morgen described the 'labour question' as 'the most important in our colonies; with it stand and fall the tropical colonies at least, but with the colonies, as I also believe, stands and falls the mother country'.[25] The 'labour question' was thus a make-or-break one. Interested observers from the economic, colonial administration and missionary spheres outdid each other with suggestions and possible solutions. Superficially, the problem was that the natives were regarded as lazy. The Africans' 'notorious indolence and laziness' was described, and opinions were given on how to deal with the 'limitless idling and lazy existence' of the new subjects and how to 'target loafers [*Tagedieberei*]'.[26] The pervasive nature of this stereotype indicates that, even at the height of colonial conquest, European colonial power was less than absolute. The continual complaints about 'laziness' revealed the limits to the availability of native subjects. They were also evidence of the resistance, agency and 'obstinacy' of African work, which set its own ideas and interests against the expectations of the colonisers.[27]

Opinions differed on the reasons for the alleged lack of diligence displayed by the subjects of the colonies. There were certainly voices

---

[23] For a general account see Iliffe, *Emergence*. For a more recent account see Berry, *No Condition*, who also shows how little African farmers' access to work was shaped by colonial legislation.

[24] J. Thormählen, in *Verhandlungen des Deutschen Kolonialkongresses 1902*, Berlin, 1903, p. 528.

[25] *Verhandlungen des Deutschen Kolonialkongresses 1902*, Berlin, 1903, p. 538. On this topic see Sunseri, *Vilimani*, especially the chapter on 'Industrialization and the labor question in German East Africa'.

[26] von Byern, *Deutsch-Ostafrika*, p. 13; and Bohner, 'Einführung', pp. 70–71.

[27] See Spittler, *Arbeitswelt*, pp. 1–17; and Gronemeyer, *Der faule Neger*. On the subject in general, see Alatas, *Myth*.

insisting that 'the Negro belongs to a subordinate race' and was thus incapable of intensive work.[28] This was the position taken by vulgar colonialism and essentialising Social Darwinists.[29] The well-known colonial writer Frieda von Bülow, who had a plantation in German East Africa in 1893, no longer believed that mentality and disposition could be changed: 'Hard, disciplined work, our idea of work, is simply not possible for tropical Negroes. That is simply their nature.'[30] But most commentators were convinced that what they saw as the Africans' deficient attitude toward work was a temporary phenomenon. 'Work-shyness' was neither innate nor determined by 'race', but rather by circumstances and environment. The missionary societies, in particular, emphasised that attitudes and views could be moulded. They accepted in principle that the natives were 'capable of civilisation' (*kulturfähig*) and they believed in cultural gradualism.[31] And under the African sun, the question of how to maintain the values of 'German work' seemed no longer so self-evidently vital, even for members of the Reich: 'Put yourself in the position of a Negro and ask yourself: how would my life have looked, under similar circumstances and living conditions? If you are honest you will answer that it would have looked similar to that of the Negro.'[32] The superintendent of the Berlin Mission, Merensky, reminded readers that even 'the ancient Germans, whose menfolk were regarded by the Romans as extremely indolent', only 'became the most industrious people in the world under the influence of Christianity'.[33] The idea that a different way of distributing and organising work might be responsible for the

---

[28] August Boshart, in Giesebrecht, *Behandlung*, p. 45.

[29] See in particular Paul Rohrbach's influential *Deutsche Kolonialwirtschaft*.

[30] Frieda von Bülow, in Giesebrecht, *Behandlung*, pp. 92–93. Frieda von Bülow was the sister of Lieutenant Albrecht von Bülow, who went to East Africa in 1885. She was involved in the Evangelical Mission Society for German East Africa and set up the 'Women's Association for Nursing in the Colonies'. She became well known to a wider public through a number of novels set in East Africa.

[31] See Schneider, *Culturfähigkeit*. See also Vietor, Meinhof and Spieth, *Afrikaner*. See Gründer, *Christliche Mission*, esp. pp. 321–24.

[32] Krämer, 'Einige Gedanken', p. 10.

[33] Merensky, 'Interesse', p. 157. On this debate see also Norris, *Umerziehung*, pp. 76–79.

perception of 'laziness' – in many regions of Africa, work in the fields was the responsibility of women, which made it impossible for men to take jobs as plantation workers, for reasons of status – was only rarely admitted.[34]

'EDUCATING THE NEGRO TO WORK'

Because of this belief that cultural value systems and mentalities could be changed, the problem of 'work-shyness' came to be seen as an issue of education (or upbringing: *Erziehung*, the term generally used, covers both meanings). The priority given to education also harmonised with the ideology of a general cultural mission, which shaped the way most colonial actors saw themselves. The creation of a universal school system was one of the self-imposed duties of the government and in particular of the religious missions, especially after the change in colonial policy in 1907.[35] The concept of 'educating to work' was very much in line with the goal of overall cultural 'improvement'. However, educating to work was more specific and for that reason was also supported by those who had a more sceptical attitude about the possible emancipatory effects of introducing universal education. The demands of business, the government's interest in generating revenue from taxes, and the demands made by the missionaries and the educated classes for cultural 'elevation' in the colonies all combined to ensure that the objective of education to work received broad support. At the 1905 German Colonial Congress in Berlin, the missionary Charles Buchner expressed this overall consensus as follows: '[t]he most important of the problems that present themselves now ... is certainly that of educating the natives and in particular educating them to work'[36] – regardless of whether such measures were 'in the interest of these peoples themselves', as Merensky,

---

[34] Sippel, 'Wie erzieht man', pp. 317–18. See also Groh, *Anthropologische Dimensionen*, pp. 54–113, who attempts to explain the 'natives' preference for idleness' not as 'primitive' but as an appropriate pattern of behaviour in subsistence economies.

[35] On colonial education policy see Weichert, *Schulwesen*; Ansprenger, 'Schulpolitik'; and the contributions to Bade, *Imperialismus und Kolonialmission*.

[36] Buchner, 'Mithilfe', p. 427.

Figure 2.1 African workers on the railway line linking Dar es Salaam and
Morogoro (1907).

another missionary, emphasised.[37] Education to work could also be
for economic reasons, as Bernhard Dernburg, Secretary of State for
the Colonies, pronounced in 1907 in a policy speech: 'Colonising …
means utilising … the people for the benefit of the economy of the
colonising nation.'[38]

It seemed clear to all involved that cultural values and attitudes
could not be changed by order or through friendly persuasion. German
observers believed that the Africans' tendency toward laziness was
mainly a product of their natural environment, or more precisely, of
the climate. By this they meant not (primarily) 'the weakening effects
of the tropical climate',[39] which had made the idea of settling German
workers in the colonies a hopeless venture, but rather, paradoxically,
the extremely favourable climatic conditions there. The problem was,
they believed, that 'the luxuriant tropical countryside often lets the
cornucopia of its fruits fall into [the natives'] lap without costing them

[37] Merensky, 'Interesse', p. 151.
[38] Quoted in Acker, 'Erziehung', p. 123. On the issue of education to work and the
situation of work in general see also Bley, *Kolonialherrschaft*, pp. 263–83; Tetzlaff,
'Koloniale Entwicklung', pp. 233–51; and Rüger, 'Entstehung'.
[39] Mirbt, *Mission*, p. 102.

any serious effort'.[40] Even without working, 'the African ... is thus a rich man'.[41]

Since, as it was generally believed, there could be 'no doubt at all ... that ... the natives in our protectorates will have to learn to work as we understand the term', the issue at the centre of debates about educating to work was identifying the most suitable method(s) of doing so.[42] And since slavery was generally no longer an option for recruiting workers, three main strategies were considered, which – despite the vigorous debates between their supporters – could also be combined. They were: (a) explicitly coercive measures, (b) creating economic incentives and (c) educating the inner person.[43]

(a) It was mainly during the first few years after Germany acquired its African colonies that undisguised calls were made for the introduction of rules making work compulsory for 'these people who have been spoiled by nature'.[44] This position was taken by numerous business owners faced with the problem of finding suitable workers for the plantations. Colonial adventurers such as Carl Peters, himself not known for treating the natives with kid gloves, added their voices to the call for the forcible imposition of labour service. 'The negro was created by God for rough work', he declaimed. 'It would not exactly harm the negro to have to serve the state for a number of years as the German, French and Russian citizens have to do ... Prove to

---

[40] F. Schwager, cited in Markmiller, *Erziehung*, p. 208. See also, for example, Mirbt, *Mission*, p. 102; and Acker, 'Erziehung', p. 120.

[41] Merensky, *Wie erzieht man*, p. 6. See also Warneck, *Evangelische Missionslehre*, p. 68.

[42] Müller, 'Arbeitspflicht', p. 65.

[43] Discussions on 'educating to work' referred to all Germany's African colonies and did not distinguish between the different regions. Only occasionally were differences identified, for example when the 'coastal Negroes of Togo, members of the hard-working Ewes tribe' were judged to be 'on average considerably higher of stature than the coastal Negroes of Cameroon' (Ziemann, *Bevölkerungs- und Rassenproblem*, p. 8). Overall, however, the task of 'educating the Negro to work' was seen as a uniform problem.

[44] *Verhandlungen des Deutschen Kolonialkongresses 1902*, p. 538.

me that it is inhuman to force a lazybones to work.[45] This attitude did persist beyond the early colonial period. As late as 1902, Julius Scharlach issued a demand at the German Colonial Congress in Berlin for state-organised compulsory labour: '[B]ut culture is impossible without work, and for that reason the native is obliged to work from the very first day of occupation by whites. I am not afraid to state that introducing compulsory labour for natives is a moral obligation toward the latter.[46]

However, no statutory period of compulsory labour service was ever introduced. In fact, during the first decade of colonial rule there were no statutory provisions at all on the recruitment or treatment of local workers. Because of the dual legal system used in the colonies, which differentiated according to racial criteria, the labour laws valid in the Kaiserreich did not apply, and no specific regulations governing working relationships for the colonies were issued until 1896. In that legislative vacuum, both the acquisition of workers and working conditions were left to the 'free' interplay of forces. In practice this meant that in the Usambara region of East Africa, for example, the plantation managers looked after their own recruitment and forced the chiefs in the region at gunpoint to provide young men as labourers.[47] Until the turn of the century, at least, the colonial masters in German East Africa rarely questioned the legitimacy of such methods of recruitment.[48] In fact, work under colonial conditions – especially during the early years of colonial power in Africa – could often scarcely be differentiated from indentured labour or forced labour. There was often no clear-cut

---

[45] Peters, *Weltpolitik*, p. 129. Carl Peters (1856–1918) was one of the leading campaigners for a determined campaign of expanding the German empire. He was a proponent of aggressive nationalisam and racist Social Darwinism, and was infamous for his excessive use of corporal punishment. In 1891, after the 'Peters affair' (in which he had had two Africans executed for personal reasons) he was fired from his governmental post as *Kaiserlicher Kommissar* for the Kilimanjaro area.

[46] *Verhandlungen des Deutschen Kolonialkongresses 1902*, p. 534. See also Bauer, 'Arbeitszwang'.

[47] Schroeder, 'Arbeiterverhältnisse', p. 220. On the development of labour law see Schrader, *Arbeiterrecht*; and Wolter and Kaller, 'Deutsches Kolonialrecht'.

[48] Sippel, 'Wie erzieht man', p. 326.

dividing line between slavery and compulsory labour, or between these and paid labour.[49]

The labour regulations introduced in 1896 mainly dealt with working conditions and how workers were to be treated. The main issue was how workers who had run away or were 'careless' (*nach-lässig*) should be punished. During the very early years of German colonial rule, the lack of legal sanctions had meant that corporal punishment was often used, and a decree issued by the Chancellor as late as 1896 confirmed that German employers had the right to use corporal punishment on employees. After a series of scandals emerged and East Africa (and Cameroon) gained the reputation of being 'thrashing colonies', attempts were made to improve the situation. In the meantime, however, the courts in German East Africa had borrowed the concept of the 'parental right to punish' from the German Civil Code and applied it to the natives – 'those great children'[50] – and the changes in the regulations therefore made little difference to the courts' decisions.[51] Instead, detailed debates took place on whether hippopotamus whips or the end of a rope were more humane instruments for punishing workers. 'Educating the negro costs time and – beatings', it was still generally believed.[52] But the use of violent coercive measures and the beating of workers also prompted a growing number of critical reactions. The corporal punishment excesses of arrogant governors and plantation owners led to the first scandals of the young colonial empire. In the German Reichstag, too, resistance began to emerge against the colonial 'culture of beating' (August Bebel).[53]

---

[49] On the German colonies see for example Zimmerer, *Deutsche Herrschaft*, esp. pp. 176–210; and Deutsch, *Emancipation*. Colonial forced labour was explored by historiography especially in the 1970s; Africans were typically described as more or less passive victims of capitalist exploitation. See for example Thomas, 'Forced Labour'; van Onselen, *Chibaro*; and Fall, *Travail forcé*.

[50] Bibo, *Wie erzieht man*, p. 35.

[51] Wolter, 'Deutsches Kolonialrecht', p. 295.

[52] Giesebrecht, *Behandlung*, p. 103.

[53] On the issue in general see Müller, *Kolonien*, pp. 102–8; von Trotha, 'One for the Kaiser'; Tetzlaff, 'Koloniale Entwicklung', pp. 49–51; and Schröder, *Prügelstrafe*.

(b) For that reason, a search for alternatives to the use of force began quite early in the colonial period. There was a widely held view that the population would have to be induced to develop needs that could be satisfied by the market. This would then motivate them to work. Some commentators argued that long-term developments would solve the issue. Siegfried Passarge, a geographer, believed the answer was to 'wait until increases in [the negro] population force them to work'.[54] One institutionalised form of indirect force – taxation – was seen as having great potential. Merensky had already recommended that this step be taken, in an 1885 book awarded a prize by the German East Africa Company. Obliging natives to pay taxes regularly would force them to take up paid work at German plantations. This suggestion was realised in 1897 when a tax on houses and huts was introduced. The regulation stipulated that taxpayers in arrears could be assigned to the administrative authorities or to private plantations in order to work off the taxes they owed. However, this taxation was rejected by the colonised, who reacted with a variety of evasive strategies. In fact, the introduction of the tax on huts must be seen as one of the most important causes of the 1905 Maji-Maji rebellion in German East Africa. Not much tax revenue was raised, in the end, partly because many district heads were afraid of social unrest and thus did not make any concerted attempts to collect the taxes.[55]

(c) These events lent support to the attitude taken by the Christian missions, who had long argued that 'educating the primitive peoples to work in a purely external and mechanical way ... is impossible'. Instead, they believed, a long-term strategy should be used to change the population from the inside. 'Inner changes and inner motives are indispensable if people are really to be educated to work.'[56] The missions' activities thus targeted the entire human being. For them, work was not the goal in itself; it was a means for more general 'civilising' and cultural elevation. The colonised 'should not see work simply as toil and a burden but should love it for itself', with no need for

[54] *Verhandlungen des Deutschen Kolonialkongresses 1902*, p. 540.
[55] Schrader, *Arbeiterrecht*, pp. 32–35; and Sippel, 'Wie erzieht man', pp. 324–25.
[56] Kratzenstein, 'Bemerkungen', pp. 180, 181.

compulsion. Work was not merely a means for attaining economic or fiscal goals; rather, as Carl Mirbt, one of the most important spokesmen for the Protestant missions explained, it should act as a 'criterion of [the native's] moral maturity', as it was indispensable 'for the development of his character'. Even in Africa, work was not a superficial activity, but had to come from within; only by creating an inner work ethic could a 'moral' (and Christian) human being develop.[57]

MISSIONS, WORK AND COLONIALISM

Personal development was seen as an essential prerequisite for regular physical work and was part of the overall civilising mission that the Christian missionary societies felt they were engaged in. Clearly, the two main denominations, and individual missionary societies, had differing views about the objectives and methods of the 'cultural mission'. In addition, there were often conflicts with state institutions and settler groups that were shaped by local conditions. For these reasons it is not possible to discern a single, uniform 'missionary point of view'. However, it is also clear that there were points of convergence. In particular, there was little disagreement, even between Protestant and Catholic missionary societies, about the high value placed on educating the natives to work in actual missionary work.[58]

The overall goal was to Christianise the populations of the colonies. A prerequisite for Christianisation was, it seemed, at least a rudimentary level of education, as Europeans understood the term. 'The savage must first become a human being and then a Christian.'[59] In addition, in the course of the missions' practical work it quickly emerged that attempts at direct conversion had little success, and that almost the only way of maintaining long-term contact with the native communities was to set up schools. So the missions aimed to achieve

[57] Mirbt, *Mission*, pp. 104, 103.
[58] For an overview comparing the German mission societies of both denominations see Gründer, 'Deutsche Missionsgesellschaften'.
[59] According to P. Nachtwey, the Father of the *Oblatenorden*, in *Verhandlungen des Deutschen Kolonialkongresses* 1905, p. 554. For an account from the Protestant viewpoint see for example Warneck, *Beziehungen*.

general cultural 'elevation', but this elevation could not be directly equated with emancipation or modernisation. Usually, the education provided at the missionary schools was limited to instilling obedience and discipline and making students become accustomed to authority. The teaching of cultural subject-matter was reduced to a minimum. There were no ambitions to 'make the blacks fully equal to the whites'. Von Schwartz, a missionary director from Leipzig known for his benevolent stance, saw the idea 'not as a Christian but as a democratic demand' that from the church's point of view might even be counterproductive and might have 'slightly ill-fated results'.[60]

In a more general sense, the cultural mission was a project that broad sections of the German bourgeoisie, petite bourgeoisie and even working class could agree upon. The activity of the missions was thus part of a broader consensus on colonial policy. It is true that there was scathing criticism of colonialism during the Kaiserreich era, focusing mainly on the colonial wars or the numerous colonial scandals, which found public expression mainly in the critical press but also in the Reichstag.[61] But this criticism almost always focused on the appropriate methods, putting the spotlight on colonial policy but not questioning the legitimacy of the colonial project itself. This was also true of the Social Democratic movement. The *Sozialdemokratische Partei Deutschlands* (*SPD*) had initially seen the country's colonial policy as part of the expansion of capitalism and had also fought hard against the way colonialism was used to stabilise the domestic power structures. But the *SPD* was amenable to the ideology of civilisation and in many practical questions it reproduced the assumptions of the cultural mission. This tendency increased after the turn of the century and at the latest with the change in colonial policy in 1907. From this time on, the *SPD*'s criticism was focused on the unviability of the colonies, and a more fundamental criticism of colonialism was rare. Even Bebel, who had long been one of the staunchest critics, now admitted that 'colonial policy … [was] not a crime in itself'; in fact, engaging in colonialism could 'in certain circumstances be a cultural

[60] von Schwartz, *Mission und Kolonisation*, p. 29.
[61] See Schwarz, *Deutsche Kolonialkritik*.

act; the issue is simply *how* colonial policy is pursued'. The attitude taken by Social Democracy – not just by its revisionist wing – was evidence of how the entire political spectrum of the Kaiserreich had internalised the model of European civilisation.[62]

Despite many individual differences, more or less the same philosophy was adopted by the missions. They were an internal part of the colonial project and very rarely expressed any criticism of the fundamental principle. They made use of the state's acquisition of colonies and even helped to promote it, ideologically, allowing colonial policy to become accepted by certain groups who could not have been mobilised without the church's approval. In fact the native populations often saw the missions and the colonial state as a unit. The missions also strongly condemned any resistance to the authority of the state and most missionaries in the field even saw corporal punishment as a necessity. At the same time, the missions imagined themselves the advocates of the 'natives', and in many cases missionaries did actually help to uncover scandals in the colonies. In addition, the missions were involved in the fight against the spread of alcoholic spirits, opium and slavery. The gap between the missions and the colonial state, however, was smaller than between either of them and the local settlers and planters. Both missions and the colonial administration criticised the excesses of the plantation owners and the coercive measures and violence used against workers. The most important issue for the missions was that the use of child labour should be banned, or at least limited, primarily for humanitarian reasons but also because the use of child labour meant considerably lower levels of attendance at the mission schools. Protests against piecework in cotton and coffee plantations did sometimes lead to limits on the employment of small children, but agreement was only reached with the plantation owners because the missions made concessions, reducing the number of days of schooling per week.[63]

---

[62] Cited in Hyrkkänen, *Sozialistische Kolonialpolitik*, p. 224. On the Social-Democratic attitude toward colonialism see also Schröder, *Sozialismus und Imperialismus*; Gollwitzer, *Geschichte*, Vol. II, pp. 274–321; and Fletcher, *Revisionism and Empire*.

[63] See Gründer, *Christliche Mission*, pp. 247–74; Tetzlaff, 'Koloniale Entwicklung', esp. pp. 199–201; Reinhard, 'Christliche Mission'; Norris, *Umerziehung*, pp.

The missions of both denominations emphasised to German set-tlers and commercial plantation owners that the work done on mis-sionary plantations was of a non-extractive and humanitarian nature. According to the rhetoric in the missionary literature, the main objective of this work was to develop the workers' characters. The missions believed that their work was based on an 'unselfish and truly educational standpoint, for the benefit of the natives'.[64] This was also the cause of some discontent among the settlers, who made fun of the missionary slogan of *Ora et labora* and believed that far too little emphasis was placed on the *labora* side of the equation. These mutual stylisations must not blind us to the fact that work in the missions was hard, usually poorly paid, that children were employed on the missions' plantations and that, overall, from a commercial point of view, there was no clear distinction between the missions and other commercial operations.[65]

But there were some differences. In general work at the mission-ary stations was easier and less unpopular than at the plantations. Admittedly, we have only a vague idea how the workers them-selves experienced their treatment. There are few written records by Africans that could provide testimony for the experience of work, whether 'educating to work', forced labour or slavery. In attempting to reconstruct the workers' reactions to the expectations and meas-ures imposed on them, historians must, for the most part, rely on the accounts provided by the missions and the colonial administrators.[66] Individual spaces of agency can only be identified with great difficulty, mainly by reading between the lines in colonial archives.[67] However, some studies have appeared in recent years, based on archival sources

86–106; Brose and von der Heyden, *Kreuz*; and Altena, *Häuflein Christen*, esp. pp. 33–72.

[64] Kratzenstein, 'Bemerkungen', p. 173.

[65] See Gründer, *Christliche Mission*, pp. 239–46.

[66] See Berman, *African Reactions*; and Wright, *German Missions*.

[67] The epistemological and political problem of reconstructing the experiences of the colonised using the texts and discourses of the colonisers has been intensely debated in particular in the context of Indian subaltern studies, leading the histor-ian Gayatri Spivak to talk of the impossibility of making subaltern voices from the past heard. See Spivak, 'Can the Subaltern Speak?'.

of varying quantities, which explore the scope of agency and individual strategies of African workers.[68] The fundamental problems of sources with which any subaltern history in Africa is faced have meant that motives and intentions are read mainly from conflicts and disagreements, from the resistance and protest that are documented in court proceedings and mission files.[69] Thus, the fact that the missions often became refuges for workers who were fleeing forced labour on the plantations can be used to deduce not only local agency but also the implication that conditions in the mission stations were seen as good in comparison. In practice, some stations pursued the objective of helping Africans to become economically independent, while an administrative ban on free economic competition between Europeans and natives remained one of the main demands of the white settlers. In some cases, missions even showed an awareness of the ambivalence involved in education to work, through which 'old orders of life … crumble and waste away'.[70]

Educating to work, understood as a humanitarian act, became the main area of missionary activity. It was regarded as 'the fundamental theorem of native education' although, of course, basic school education, character development and religious instruction also had their place. Missionaries even suggested that 'the Gospel of Christ should be exchanged for the gospel of work' and that 'conversion to Christianity should be abandoned, at least temporarily, as the main purpose of the mission and replaced by educating to work'.[71] It was repeatedly emphasised that the missionaries themselves must set an example and in this way provide instruction in regular work.

How did this self-confidently pronounced project of educating to work look in practice? In the first instance, it required practical work by the converted, in which the means and the end coincided – with

---

[68] See in particular the informative works by Wright, *Strategies*; and Glassman, *Feasts*.

[69] This approach is taken, for example, by Deutsch, *Emancipation*, p. 3 and *passim*; or by Sunseri, *Vilimani*, esp. the introduction.

[70] Carl Mirbt, cited in Norris, *Umerziehung*, p. 86.

[71] Eduard Pechuel-Lösche, 'Das zentralafrikanische Problem', quoted in Warneck, *Evangelische Missionslehre*, p. 67. See also Buchner, 'Mithilfe', p. 430.

the awareness that 'the practical acts and works tend in their turn to give rise to systematic dispositions', as Bourdieu put it a century later.[72] Given the necessity of setting up the missionary stations in the first place, and then of maintaining and financing them, it may seem that this practical work was unavoidable. But it was not immediately evident to all that Christian lessons in work had a charitable purpose only. This ambivalence also resulted in many statements intended to dispel the suspicion that the missions were making monetary profit from their efforts to create cultural elevation.[73] The ambiguity of combining economic rationality with the apparent abjuring of a profit motive was reproduced in a specific 'dialectic between interiority and exteriority'.[74] The real work was based on an inner disposition: the colonised were to 'gain an impression of the *moral value* and the religious *call* for work', if this work was not to remain merely a veneer, an external decoration.[75] On the other hand, the inner life could only be accessed by working on the surface. The surface was thus not just the place where inner change could be seen. Rather, an inner disposition, if not the inner person itself, was to be produced by developing the surface.

Most observers – especially the missionaries of both denominations, but interested business owners, too – agreed that the educative measures must not be limited to work but must include 'elevating the overall way of life'.[76] This usually included a demand for the abolition of polygyny (then usually termed polygamy), which was common in many areas of Africa and was a constant cause of concern to the missionaries and to others. This demand reflected the close links between the issue of work and issues related to gender and sexuality.

---

[72] Bourdieu, *Entwurf*, p. 191.
[73] See for example Mirbt, *Mission*, pp. 112–14. But it was equally often emphasised that commercial profit would by no means get in the way of the missions' activity. Gustav Warneck (1834–1910, founder of the *Allgemeine Missionszeitung*), for example, saw the missions as 'a security guard for world trade that costs the traders nothing'. See *Allgemeine Missionszeitung* 5 (1878), p. 67. For a general account see Tetzlaff, 'Mission'.
[74] Bourdieu, *Entwurf*, p. 164.
[75] Buchner, 'Mithilfe', p. 429. Emphases in original.
[76] Mirbt, *Mission*, p. 120.

Angry remarks about the 'absolutely phenomenally low moral and spiritual level of negro women' have undertones of the mixture of disgust and desire that was characteristic of colonial rhetoric. The context, in terms of social history, was formed by intense debates in the Kaiserreich about 'mixed marriages' which, from 1905 onward, led to a gradual ban on the practice of German men marrying African women.[77]

Polygamy (or *Vielweiberei*), which usually carried connotations of sexual excess, did not correspond to the European family ideal that most self-appointed development workers saw as a precondition for an attitude to work based on regularity.[78] Black women were associated with unbridled promiscuity and permissiveness, and this also suggested that men's energy would be sapped, making them less useful for work. But criticism of local customs was also formulated in terms of work-related issues, not just moral ones. 'The negro', as the Oberinspektor of the Basle mission, Theodor Öhler, stated, 'has not bought a woman in order to work for her. Rather, she is there for him, and must work for him, and the more women he has, the more workers, and thus the less reason he himself has to work.'[79]

Of greater importance than these psychological considerations was the social and gendered division of labour with which the Europeans were faced in many local societies. This applied in particular to 'the custom that indispensable work in the fields is to be done by women'.[80] Across Africa, women had traditionally done a large part of the work in maintaining food supplies. While cattle-herding (where it was practised at all) was reserved for men, agricultural cultivation, which often had religious implications, was usually the responsibility of women.[81] In this context, polygyny released men from the one type

---

[77] Byern, *Deutsch-Ostafrika*, p. 37. See also Gilman, 'Hottentot'. On the heated debates about 'racial mixing' and the legal status of the 'mixed population' see Grosse, *Kolonialismus*, pp. 145–92.

[78] See for example Merensky, 'Interesse'.

[79] Öhler, 'Bemerkungen', p. 166.

[80] Mirbt, *Mission*, p. 102.

[81] On this subject see for example Sheldon, *Pounders of Grain*; and especially the contributions to Davison, *Agriculture*.

of activity that was of importance from a European point of view. To deal with this situation, Alexander Merensky called for the introduction of a marriage tax because 'the easier the women make the African's life the less inclined he is to look for work'.[82] Or at least for the kind of work that missionaries meant. From a European perspective, 'work' meant demanding, physical, male work, not in the private sphere of the home but in the public sphere, in the fields. 'Without an emphatic insistence on monogamy', a contribution to the German Colonial Congress in 1902 stated, 'a people cannot be educated to work'.[83] The social, economic and political contexts of local societies were completely ignored by the project of educating to work.[84] But women were still at the centre of missionary and state efforts; in fact they seemed to have a decisive role in determining whether this educational project would succeed in the long term. 'A new, better race of women must be raised', the missionary Carl Paul emphasised, as 'otherwise no long-term improvement to the life of the African people can be hoped for'.[85]

Educational measures thus had a far-reaching role. With regard to 'educating to work' it was 'imperative to deal with issues that are seemingly only loosely connected to the actual education itself', as Hermann Bibo, a business owner, underlined.[86] Bourdieu would later describe this mechanism as follows: 'The whole trick of pedagogic reason lies precisely in the way it extorts the essential while seeming to demand the insignificant.'[87] Bibo dedicated an entire book to this issue, in which he came up with a broad range of hygiene-related measures, because 'the negro will certainly never … be educated to become a useful worker if his bad habits are not rooted out'. This included washing with cold water in the mornings ('which hardens

---

[82] Merensky, 'Interesse', p. 152.
[83] Schmidt, 'Behandlung', p. 478. See also Öhler, 'Bemerkungen', p. 166. On the same topic see also Grohs, *Stufen*, esp. pp. 72–76, 212–14.
[84] On this topic see particularly Sunseri, *Vilimani*, esp. the chapter '"Wamekwenda Vilimani!": Transformations in Rural Society'.
[85] Paul, *Mission*, p. 12.
[86] Bibo, *Wie erzieht man*, p. 3.
[87] Bourdieu, 'Entwurf', p. 200.

the body'), rules about hairstyle ('short') and clothing ('upper body unclothed'), and the plan for a 'standard house' ('including all requirements relating to ventilation') to guarantee complete 'cleanliness in housing and body'.[88]

From childhood on, children were to be subjected to a detailed schedule, which regulated time of rising, worktimes, mealtimes and bedtimes, 'at the same time for the whole of life'. But 'they must never be left to themselves! A teacher must continuously monitor all their activities.' Working subjects – dependent, thus, on inner dispositions and attitudes – were produced by working on their bodies. The requirements of modernity – educating them 'for plantation work … and simultaneously, for their own benefit, to become civilised and happy people' – were inscribed through engravings on the material surface.[89] Last, but not least, diet and metabolism had to be altered: 'We can only create something approaching history with peoples who eat cereals.'[90] Work, subjects and history – this was the trinity of progress in the colonies, as elsewhere.[91]

In this sense, 'educating to work' was not just an instrument of social discipline but corresponded to the contemporary European belief about the link between work, the development of the subject and modernisation. Those involved in the missions and the colonial administration did not think this necessarily involved depravation or repression. In many cases, the emancipatory rhetoric used was genuinely meant. This viewpoint was sometimes shared by Africans. In retrospect, especially, members of the elite often expressed their esteem for the education provided by the missionary centres. Reactions to the measures taken by the colonial powers thus sometimes differed and also depended on different interests, social status, gender and origins. The self-image of the national movements often included the objective of ingraining modern work habits, and the

---

[88] Bibo, *Wie erzieht man*, pp. 11, 19, 40, 7.
[89] *Ibid.*, pp. 19, 3.
[90] Ziemann, *Bevölkerungs- und Rassenproblem*, p. 25. Ziemann (1865–1939) was a specialist in tropical medicine and a doctor in the colonies.
[91] On this strategy of 'modernisation' see the excellent study by Mitchell, *Colonizing Egypt*, esp. pp. 34–62.

corresponding mentality.[92] This objective also reveals the extent to which the modern western understanding of the modern subject had become hegemonial and even outlasted the end of colonial rule.[93]

The belief that 'educating to work' was ultimately, and regardless of all the coercive measures imposed, in the interest of the colonised was the guiding principle behind all colonial policy. This was 'freedom through force', in accordance with the functionalist view of the logic of modernisation that underpinned Marx's notorious comments on British colonialism in India. This policy received additional legitimation when it was supported by those supposedly affected. One of the most important witnesses for the belief that 'the upward development of the black race' was impossible without a systematic inculcation of modern work ethics was the Afro-American Booker T. Washington. His Tuskegee Institute in Alabama, where the work ethic and work practices were drummed into Afro-American men, was for many German colonial civil servants a model that could be applied for 'educating to work' in Africa too. His concept of the 'New Negro' and his support for western imperialism – Africa, he believed, was backward and would thus have to be 'civilised' through work – met with considerable interest in Germany. Three of his books were translated into German and were read in Germany as user's manuals for Africa, even though they dealt only with the southern states of the USA. 'We are interested in Dr. Washington's book mainly in terms of the possibilities for development for Africans.'[94] In return, Washington believed that the German 'way of treating Negroes in Africa … could be a model for other nations'.[95]

Booker T. Washington's understanding of work was itself a product of the concept of 'civilising', a term that was loaded with beliefs about the differences between 'races' and that by no means stood uncontradicted. Even W. E. B. du Bois, not known as an incisive

---

[92] This is shown in detail by Cooper, *Decolonization*.
[93] On the colonisation of the imagination see for example Nandy, *Intimate Enemy*.
[94] Größer, 'Emporentwicklung', p. 123.
[95] Quoted in Beckert, 'Tuskegee', p. 519. On his support for colonialism see also Adeleke, *UnAfrican Americans*, p. 114; and Harlan, 'White Man's Burden', p. 441.

critic of colonialism, discredited the Tuskegee model as a mixture of 'adjustment and submission' that accepted 'the alleged inferiority of the Negro races'.[96] But for the German authorities this was a reason to see Washington as an ally. This led to a close cooperation between Tuskegee and the Committee for Colonial Economy (*Kolonialwirtschaftliches Komitee*) that culminated in an attempt to apply the structures of Tuskegee in Togo, by modernising its cotton cultivation. Between 1901 and 1909, efforts were made in Togo, in conjunction with the Tuskegee Institute, to intensify cotton production and make the product exportable – for a time with considerable commercial success. This project of creating a 'German Alabama in Africa' is one example of how labour markets and debates about social reform were linked around the globe.[97]

The dispatch of Afro-American graduates of Booker T. Washington's institute was linked to a desire to make the transfer of modern forms of work organisation appear to be in the interest of 'Africans' themselves, rather than something imposed from outside.[98] Despite this, this form of 'educating to work' met with widespread resistance. The reorganisation of cotton production was described by the German authorities as a contribution to strengthening the local native culture (*Volkskultur*) and thus as an alternative to the European-based plantation economy, but from the workers' point of view there was little difference.[99] The introduction of a new way of organising production involved major changes to local methods of cultivation and to local social structures. Many producers insisted on retaining mixed cultivation of a variety of crops and resisted the introduction of a cotton monoculture for the export market. In addition, among the Ewe people in the south of Togo, only women could cultivate and spin cotton. The German and American experts attempted to replace this domestic division of labour, which was linked to the widespread

---

[96] Bois, *Souls*, p. 34. See also Harlan, 'White Man's Burden', p. 442; and Spivey, *Schooling*.

[97] On this topic see especially Zimmerman, 'Alabama'; and West, 'Tuskegee'.

[98] On this experiment see Harlan, *Wizard*; and West, 'Tuskegee Model'. For a global history perspective see Beckert, 'Tuskegee'.

[99] See Sebald, *Togo*, p. 437.

practice of separate households for women and men, by the model of patriarchal labour that seemed to them morally and economically superior. The population's stiff resistance to imposed work structures forced the authorities to resort progressively to coercive measures.[100] The attempts increasingly involved 'unprecedented violence', though often without success.[101] Even the 'cotton school' where children were to be prepared for the new forms of work was attended only by students forced to do so. When, in 1907, two students turned up of their own free will, this was such an extraordinary event that Governor Zech ordered an investigation.[102]

The project of 'educating to work' and transmitting the ideas of freedom and 'civilisation' was often implemented under duress and supported by the power mechanisms of the colonial state. The object of this educational project – which involved refusing to provide higher-level school education – was not 'work' in general but a specific understanding of activity that was loaded with cultural, societal and gender-related beliefs. This form of work was linked to changes in social conditions, created a link between work and the state, and linked production with the world market. If experts inside and outside Africa retrospectively regard the enforcement of this model as unavoidable, this is only on the basis of a formation of the subject that has already taken this now hegemonial link for granted and internalised it.[103]

'WORK-SHYNESS' IN THE GERMAN REICH

Not only was a 'level of work-shyness which by our European standards is not low' seen as a characteristic of the colonies[104] but, during the late nineteenth century, it was also believed to be a serious problem within the German Reich. An unwillingness or inability to carry

---

[100] On this topic see Zimmerman, 'Alabama', pp. 1379ff. See also Cooper, 'Conditions'.

[101] Beckert, 'Tuskegee', p. 534.

[102] See Zimmerman, 'Alabama', p. 1392.

[103] *Ibid.*, p. 1393 and *passim*.

[104] Mirbt, *Mission*, p. 101.

out regular work – usually understood to mean waged employment – was seen as a public nuisance, a personal dilemma for those involved, an illness and occasionally also as a societal problem.[105] Since the foundation of the state, social reformers, legal experts and politicians had been looking for a solution to this problem. When the Prussian 'Work-Shy Act' was finally passed in 1912, this was more than an expression of the unrelenting capitalist logic that made the obligation to work as necessary as the obligation to carry out military service. It was also the result of anxieties about mobility and circulation.

From the mid 1870s in particular, the 'work-shy' – a collective term for the unemployed, homeless, beggars, the wandering poor and 'vagabonds' – had been increasingly seen as a major social problem. Around 1880, about 1 per cent of the population of the country, some 400,000 people, found themselves on the streets on any given day, with no accommodation and in need of assistance. Migration by poor people was not unknown, even at this large scale. In comparison with the peak phase of pauperism during the second third of the century, the size of the vagrant underclasses probably did not increase dramatically. The impression, reflected in the pamphlets and submissions of bourgeois groups, that the issue had become a bigger problem was partly related to the fact that regular work and the stigmatisation of any failure to work had become more important, as Germany was transformed into a society of work. In addition, the migration of the poor was now part of a true explosion in internal mobility and received increased attention in that context. It was only one component of the dramatic increases in mobility that resulted in Reich Statistics 1907 reporting that half of the population no longer lived in their birthplaces. The high level of mobility in the Wilhelmine era was not without precedent in pre-industrial society, but its extent was a new phenomenon. Between 1890 and 1914, especially, mobility became 'a mass phenomenon without precedent in Europe'.[106]

---

[105] On this issue see also Zimmermann, *Constitution du chômage*.

[106] Wehler, *Gesellschaftsgeschichte*, Vol. 1, p. 503. On this topic see Köllmann, *Bevölkerung*; and Langewiesche, 'Wanderungsbewegungen'. The fact that migration was not just directed at large cities is detailed in Hochstadt, *Mobility*, esp. pp. 107–34.

For many, the result was that the experiences of being without a homeplace (*Heimatlosigkeit*) and of suffering poverty became permanent features. The large number of vagrants was partly a general consequence of industrialisation, but it also had more concrete causes. The *Gründerkrise*, the economic crisis of the 1870s after the foundation of the Reich, made more people unemployed. They were soon to be found wandering the roads of the country. Those who were looking for work were picking up on the tradition of wandering journeymen and of mobility as a method of finding it. In the absence of any state labour exchange – these were introduced at a local level in 1880 and for the entire country only after the Labour Exchange Act (*Arbeitsnachweisgesetz*) of 1922 – this was indeed a sensible way of looking for work, in fact an almost unavoidable one. But as mobility had become a permanent phenomenon since the foundation of the Reich, the dividing line between those looking for work and the homeless became blurred – frequently, it was not possible to determine with certainty which category an individual fell into. This blurring of boundaries contributed to the increased attention paid to the issue by philanthropists and social reformers.[107]

As the economic situation worsened and people were spending longer periods without work, begging also became a growing problem. Many anti-begging associations and food stations were set up, especially by bourgeois groups, to prevent door-to-door begging. These charitable efforts were motivated by a combination of welfare concerns and the impression that a crisis of morality was developing. This can be seen in the annual report of the Committee of the 'Association for the Elimination of Street and House Begging in Bochum' for 1880, which included the comment: 'Begging is a decided nuisance for the better-situated; it disturbs him at work and at leisure; it endangers his property; it involves the risk of spreading infectious diseases; it dulls the feeling of heartfelt sympathy, as

[107] On this topic see John, *Wohnsitz*; and 'Vorgeschichte'. On the history of the labour exchange see also Klatt, 'Arbeit'. On the legal dimension, see von Frankenberg and Drechsler, 'Behandlung'.

it is mostly carried on by idlers to make money.'[108] In the same year, 320,548 people were convicted of begging and vagrancy.[109]

The desire for stability and the elimination of vagrancy that is hinted at by anxieties about the spread of germs also marked the statutory provisions on the issue. The Reich Relief Residence Act of 1871 adopted a provision of the Prussian Poor Law of 1842, according to which anyone who left his or her place of residence within a two-year period lost their 'relief residence' and as such their claim on local welfare services. Such persons were described as *landarm* ('land poor'), had to wear an 'L' on their cap, and were sent to an institution for the 'land poor' where they were forced to work. Because factory workers, in particular, but also migrant workers and agricultural seasonal workers, were highly mobile, it was not uncommon for people temporarily to lose their 'relief residence'. Here, the ideology of sedentary life had taken legal form.[110]

THE 'WORKERS' COLONIES'

In 1882, to deal with these problems, a pastor from Bethel, Friedrich von Bodelschwingh, founded the first of his 'workers' colonies' in Wilhelmsdorf, near Bielefeld. Bodelschwingh (1831–1910) had already set up institutions in Bethel for epileptics, in 1867. These were intended to provide a protected and sheltered space for the *Fallsüchtige*. The Bethel centres were a refuge and place of retreat for those rejected by society, but were also intended to provide a sense of meaning to the uprooted individual. The central elements involved were encouragement from the church and practical activity. The most important therapeutic tool was work, especially agricultural work. The idea of setting up an institution for epileptics had come from the Inner Mission (*Innere Mission*) for which Bodelschwingh had worked.

---

[108] Quoted in Scheffler, 'Protestantismus', p. 269.
[109] John, 'Vorgeschichte', p. 14. On this topic see also Evans, 'Dangerous Classes'.
[110] See Ayaß, *Arbeitshaus Breitenau*, pp. 57–62.

He had been sent to Paris as a pastor from 1858 to 1864 to look after Germans abroad, one of the main tasks of the Inner Mission.[111]

The Inner Mission had been created in the context of the *Erweckung* movement, the evangelical revival in Germany during the early nineteenth century. It was a reaction to the perceived decline of a tradition of charitable activities and help for the poor, which was attributed to 'de-Christianization'. The Inner Mission aimed to relieve physical suffering and simultaneously to reinforce faith. The name, apparently paradoxical, also described a project that needs to be understood as the reaction to a situation that was regarded as unnatural. The project of the foreign mission was founded, at base, on the assumption that mankind was clearly divided into Christians and heathens, and that only missionaries (and a small number of colonial administrators) moved between these two separate worlds. But during the first half of the nineteenth century, the situation had changed for good; the people themselves (and not just their spiritual shepherds) were on the move. Spiritual care for Germans abroad was thus soon as much a responsibility of the Inner Mission as converting immigrant population groups such as the Masurians.[112]

But the idea of an Inner Mission was not merely a reaction to the increase in emigration and immigration. It also points to anxiety about another form of circulation, namely domestic migration. Johann Hinrich Wichern had been involved in social/charitable activities in Hamburg as early as 1833 (in the so-called 'Rough House') and believed that the church must not limit its missionary activities to spreading Christian teachings; it should also carry out welfare and social work. 'Love and Faith' was the motto of this pragmatic viewpoint. Wichern was familiar with poverty and knew from his own experience the results of the social upheavals caused by the industrial revolution. These upheavals had resulted in an unprecedented level of mobility, leading to chaotic conditions on the country's highways and in emergency shelters and hostels, and giving the impression that

---

[111]   On Bodelschwingh, see Schmuhl, *Bodelschwingh*. On Wilhelmsdorf, see Benad and Schmuhl, *Bethel–Eckardtsheim*. See also Benad, *Bethels Mission*.

[112]   Gerhardt, *Innere Mission*, p. 273. On the 'Inner Mission', see also Beyreuther, *Geschichte*; and Sachße and Tennstedt, *Geschichte*, pp. 229–32.

barbarity had infected the centre of Christendom. 'He who knows the orgies of the heathens does not yet know what has taken place and is taking place there [in the hostels].'[113] Here, it seemed, missionary work was truly needed, even though it had previously focused on the regions outside the borders of Europe. The field of action for missionary activity was now 'as great as the decline within the Christian world'.[114] The external and the internal seemed almost to be blending into one. In Germany, too, one could now encounter 'the savages, the vagabonds', the strangers in their own land who were capable of things 'with which even the world of the heathens is unfamiliar'.[115]

For Wichern, the consequences of this uncontrolled mobility were clear. The timing of his famous speech to the *Kirchentag* in Wittenberg, regarded as the founding document of the Inner Mission in Germany, was not accidental: it was given in 1848, the year of revolutions. The fear of uprisings by neglected underclasses who had been robbed of their roots and their homeplaces could be felt in every line of Wichern's speech.[116] Here, the spectre that two prescient individuals then saw haunting Europe had become almost tangible. Thus, the Inner Mission was also a project to limit mobility; for Wichern, it was also – after 1789 – a very national project. 'The origins of this aberration are not German. It has come to us from France. The battle that the inner mission is waging against it is therefore a national struggle.'[117]

The 'Hostels for Home' *(Herbergen zur Heimat)* that the Protestant Inner Mission set up across Germany to help control people's mobility[118] were (like the Catholic Kolping houses, which had similar goals) an important model for the workers' colonies that Bodelschwingh set up from the 1880s onward.[119] Bodelschwingh, too, worked on

---

[113] Wichern, 'Verantwortung', p. 52.
[114] Quoted in Gerhardt, *Innere Mission*, p. 238.
[115] Wichern, 'Aufgabe', p. 162.
[116] See especially Wichern, 'Verantwortung', pp. 53–58.
[117] Wichern, 'Aufgabe', p. 163.
[118] On the feudally based societal model on which the *Herbergen zur Heimat* set up by the Inner Mission were founded, see Scheffler, 'Herbergswesen', p. 11.
[119] The workers' colonies were also referring back to other models, especially the local bourgeois anti-begging societies and food stations that had been set up since

the assumption that 'unrestrained freedom of movement must be limited in a compassionate way'.[120] His guiding principle, however, went beyond setting up hostels in which the wandering poor and the homeless could be offered a basic place to sleep and a simple meal to relieve their worst suffering and to prevent their total decline. In fact, he was uneasy about the dominance of this type of charitable activity, which he believed taught the homeless to become passive and to engage in begging. By contrast, and although he was described by Theodor Heuss as the 'most ingenious beggar that Germany has ever seen',[121] Bodelschwingh put work at the centre of his social-reform project. 'Work instead of alms' was the guiding principle in his colonies. 'Educating to work ... is an incomparably greater deed than the piece of bread offered for nothing.'[122]

Only three years after Wilhelmsdorf was opened, there were already thirteen workers' colonies; by 1890 there were twenty-two. They were managed and financed mainly by the Protestant propertied middle and educated classes, but also by some members of the nobility, by government ministries and by the church. The colonies took in homeless people and the unemployed, and gave them food, shelter and clothing for a period of up to four months in return for a daily spell of work. They were paid a small wage and were released, at the end of their period in the colony, into civil life – ideally by taking up a new job. During the first few years, efforts focused on finding work for those capable of it, but soon the colonies began to take on the groups seen as more problematic. In their first quarter of a century, the colonies took in over 200,000 unemployed people. The foundation of the German Hostels Association in 1886 put the care of the poor on a centralised, bureaucratic and professionalised basis; with the 1907 Act on Migrant Workhouses (*Wanderarbeitsstättengesetz*) it was approved by the legislature.[123]

the 1870s, and to ideas of inner colonisation that were linked to the concept of helping those affected to help themselves. See John, 'Vorgeschichte'.

[120] Bodelschwingh, *Wanderarmen*, p. 11.
[121] Heuss, *Deutsche Gestalten*, p. 261.
[122] Quoted in Scheffler, 'Gründungsjahre', p. 28. See also Scheffler, 'Frömmigkeit'.
[123] Scheffler, 'Gründungsjahre'; 'Herbergswesen'; and 'Wandererfürsorge'.

The workers' colonies were not coercive institutions, but were based on the principle of voluntary admission. The unemployed were free to leave the colony at any time (apart from the moral pressure exerted). However, anyone who refused to do the work assigned to them was expelled and sent to the workhouses. Daily activities were scheduled down to the minute. As one observer wrote: 'it is clear that given the character disposition of the colonists … every matter must be regulated down to the last detail'.[124] The workers' colonies were a laboratory of bourgeois society in which the secondary bourgeois virtues could be practised – even if the inmates were not being prepared for a bourgeois existence, but rather for a proletarian one or that of a small farmer. These virtues included, as can be seen in the rules of the Hoffnungstal workers' colony, cleanliness, punctuality and diligence, and abstinence from alcohol. But the rules were not confined to externalities; they were directed at the whole person. 'Admission to the institution creates an obligation of truthfulness.' This project of educating the person was supported by Bodelschwingh's later practice of giving inmates individual rooms instead of the group dormitories that had been the rule in the hostels for the homeless. This innovation was intended not only to make the accommodation more comfortable but also to increase individuation. It was thus 'an important unspoken educational task'.[125]

Days in the colony were filled with work, usually simple manual activities: chopping wood, breaking up stone, digging work for road construction and, above all, agricultural work. It was hoped that horticulture and field work would allow inmates to get back into the routine of an ordered working life and thus 'by means of … a thorough cure' make 'the unfortunates useful members of human society' again.[126] The privileged status assigned to working the land was characteristic of the idealistic view that the conservative aristocrat Bodelschwingh held, of a pre-modern society not contaminated by urbanisation. When, from 1905 onward, he extended his method of

---

[124] Erdlenbruch, *Bedeutung*, p. 52.
[125] Vather Onnasch from Hoffnungstal, quoted in *ibid.*, p. 56.
[126] Citied in Scheffler, 'Gründungsjahre', p. 32.

Figure 2.2 Changing room in the workers' colony Hoffnungstal
in Bernau (1907).

assistance for the unemployed to the city of Berlin, Bodelschwingh
argued that the asylum centres for the homeless should be closed ('a
boil ... and a source of infection for the whole country')[127] and that
colonies should be set up outside the city boundaries, far removed
from the temptations of the metropolis.[128]

[127] Bodelschwingh, *Wer hilft mit?*, p. 9.
[128] Bodelschwingh, *Ausgewählte Schriften*, p. 646.

Bodelschwingh's workers' colonies retained the Christian basis that underlay the Inner Mission. Religious instruction was one of the (unpopular) elements of daily life. 'In our Wilhelmsdorf, the motto shall not only be: Work; here the most important command shall also be: Pray.'[129] This religious indoctrination also made the colonies the target of biting criticism from Social Democrats, who saw them as instruments of patriarchal oppression ('Pray and work but forget your own free will'), not least because those in receipt of the dole lost their right to vote.[130] But all religious admonishment notwithstanding, work was at the centre of all practical activities. 'For thou shalt eat the labour of thine hands: happy shalt thou be, and it shall be well with thee' was the motto that was inscribed on the Wilhelmsdorf building at its formal opening.[131] The objective was indeed to 'educate the wandering poor in industriousness and order', but work was not only an end in itself but also the means, 'an excellent aqua fortis' (*Scheidewasser*, nitric acid), to a higher end: the creation of the individual. Any individuals found without identity papers, for example, were not admitted to the colonies but passed on to the local authorities. However, exposure to hard work could eliminate this deficiency: 'in general after two days of breaking stone … under supervision … the homeless [man] now regains the full rights of a normal destitute wanderer'.[132] Work restored the subject, then, not only morally, but also in legal terms.[133]

SIMILARITY AND DIFFERENCE

Ora et labora as the main activities of the modern individual – this principle linked the educational policies of the overseas colonies and

---

[129] *Ibid.*, p. 433.
[130] *Der Sozialdemokrat* 13 (1883), quoted in Scheffler, 'Gründungsjahre', p. 31.
[131] Bodelschwingh, *Ausgewählte Schriften*, p. 431.
[132] Bodelschwingh, *Wer hilft mit?*, pp. 18–23.
[133] In addition to the workers' colonies, there were other projects that put education to work at the centre of their educational and social reform activities. The main example is the idea of the 'work school' (*Arbeitsschule*), most effectively promoted by Georg Kerschensteiner. On this subject see Gonon, *Arbeitsschule*.

Figure 2.3 Unemployed performing agricultural work in the workers' colony
Hoffnungstal in Bernau, close to Berlin (1907).

of the workers' colonies. In fact, there were very considerable similarities between these two major projects of the bourgeois cultural
mission, even though their areas of activity lay far apart, separated by
state boundaries, oceans and long journeys as well as by the presump-
tion of different 'cultural clusters' (*Kulturkreise*) and racial differences.
In both sites, work was seen as the fundamental basis of personhood
and as the starting-point for the constitution of the subject. Work also
acted as an instrument of cultural 'elevation' and divided the savages from the civilised, or even allowed transcending the boundaries
between the two groups.

How, then, can the relationship between the two spheres,
between the home country and the colony, be analysed? Was it
primarily a form of meeting of civilisations? Contemporaries usually saw it in those terms. Of course, there was frequent mention of the chasm between 'civilised peoples' (*Kulturvölker*) and
'uncivilised' (*kulturlose*) African tribes. But this did not imply that
the latter would gradually adapt and become similar to the former.

Rather, the colonial subjects were seen very much as the Other, simultaneously the subject of fears and the object of a nebulous longing. Despite all the rhetorical annexation of the colonies as 'New Germany', the difference between the German Reich and the 'natives' remained absolute.

Since the 1980s, in particular, scholars have often described conflicts in the age of imperialism and colonialism as elements of 'cultural contacts'. And following the anthropological trend in cultural theory, exchange has usually been interpreted using the terminology of the 'native and the foreign', 'cultural translation' or cultural 'contact zones'.[134] For Tzvetan Todorov, for example, the conquest of the 'New World' is a confrontation of incompatible systems of representation, while Stephen Greenblatt describes the 'discovery' of America as a 'cultural encounter' between societies with differing 'mimetic capital'.[135]

However, the obvious similiarities between the educational projects undertaken within Germany and in Africa would seem to indicate that the relationship between the two regions cannot be understood simply in terms of exoticism and absolute difference. Talk of the 'laziness of the Negro' was more than just an expression of cultural difference. In fact, even the hardworking majority of German society had only been educated into possessing a work ethic – made industrious – during the nineteenth century.[136] In Europe, too, it had long been assumed that most of the population were simply lazy.[137] Does this imply, then, that the educating-to-work project was simply a result in both places of the dictates of economic reason? The debate about contact between cultures would then seem to be an ideological strategy that hides

---

[134] Bachmann-Medick, *Übersetzung*; and Pratt, *Imperial Eyes*. For a critical account see also Schäffner, 'Verwaltung'.

[135] Todorov, *Conquest*; and Greenblatt, *Marvelous Possessions*.

[136] On this topic see Schenda, 'Verfleißigung'; Dreßen, *Pädagogische Maschine*; Helmstetter, 'Austreibung'; Flohr, *Arbeiter*; and Steinert and Treiber, *Fabrikation*. In this context see also the debate initiated by Gerhard Oestreich on 'social disciplining', for example in Jütte, 'Poor Relief'.

[137] Groh, *Anthropologische Dimensionen*, p. 254.

the real process involved. Rudolf Helmstetter has recently said as much: 'Culture', he emphasises, 'would seem in this context to be a decorative context that adorns economic and cultural interests'. In this interpretation there is no difference between the metropole and the African colony; rather '[t]he home country [*Heimat*] *is* the colony, a colony that has for the most part forgotten its own colonisation. Its history includes disciplining and "making diligent" [*Verfleißigung*].'[138]

A post-modern multiplicity of cultures, then, or the monological structure of capital that reveals every perceived cultural difference as 'false consciousness'? Possibly, the truth must be sought, here as elsewhere, between these two extreme positions. In the account below national and cultural boundaries are seen neither as ontological essences nor as veiling superstructures, but rather as the historical product of contingent relationships of exchange. The mobility of people, goods, institutions and ideas is thus seen as a process that runs through both the erection of cultural boundaries and the accumulation of capital. In this interpretation, the difference between the home country and the colony would be neither an unavoidable condition of the 'contact between civilisations' nor a rhetorical trick serving the purposes of global capitalism, but a very real and powerful effect of global circulation.

LIGHT FROM THE WEST

Can we then say that the 'work-shy' were, so to speak, strangers in their own land? In conceptual and rhetorical terms the two groups were certainly close. 'Strangers', 'savages' and 'children' (or 'a mixture of child, clown and rascal')[139] – such were the terms used to describe both vagrants and the 'natives' in Africa. This attitude made it easier to fall back where necessary on coercive measures to ensure the religious instruction of their charges. After all,

---

[138] Helmstetter, 'Neger als Arbeiter', pp. 338–39.
[139] Bibo, *Wie erzieht man*, p. 15.

'[c]hildren need discipline'.[140] In this way the social work carried out by the missions instilled Christian enlightenment and created 'light in the darkness'.[141]

The 'darkness' referred to was both the 'darkness of the metropolis' and the 'dark continent', 'black Africa'.[142] But education through work was not just a question of spiritual illumination; it also made use of metaphors of light in a very material sense. If 'more air' and 'more light' were seen as conditions for the 'elevation' of the working class, then this rhetoric resonated particularly well as around 1900 technical improvements and cost reductions began to make gas lighting affordable in German towns and cities even for poorer sections of society. The enthusiasm with which electric lighting had been greeted since the 1880s contributed to what Wolfgang Schivelbusch has called an 'apotheosis of light' at the turn of the century.[143] In the colonies, too, the aim was 'in the dark forest valley[,] to let the light of eternity stream into the dark hearts'.[144] This 'illuminating effect' of the efforts of the cultural missions was intended to be consecutive and gradual. Initially, the efforts were like 'mere isolated lights' but the objective was 'to turn night into day' in Africa too. Continuous supervision and educational assistance were required to ensure that 'the peoples in our colonies, too … may one day walk in bright light'.[145] Evidence that more than the metaphor of divine light was tapped into is provided by Bodelschwingh's 1897 'Circular on Electric Lighting'. In this document he asks the heads of the German workers' colonies to collect funds for the East Africa missions by levying fines for leaving electric lights on ('a loving penny of punishment'). He suggested that

---

[140] Bodelschwingh, *Briefwechsel*, pp. 455–56; and Erdlenbruch, *Bedeutung*, p. 60.

[141] Göbel, *Dienst*, p. 115.

[142] Bodelschwingh, *Wer hilft mit?*, p. 15. *Light in the Darkness* (*Licht im Dunkel*) was also the title of the quarterly journal published by the Evangelical Mission Society for German East Africa.

[143] Friedrich von Bodelschwingh, quoted in Lehmann, 'Bodelschwingh und Bismarck', p. 619; Krabbe, *Deutsche Stadt*, p. 119; and Schivelbusch, *Lichtblicke*, p. 72.

[144] Bodelschwingh, *Briefwechsel*, p. 292.

[145] Paul, *Mission*, p. 48.

a 'mission negro' be appointed in every German workers' colony to collect this fine and thus 'bring a light to dark Africa'.[146]

The shared phraseology is evidence of the global associative space in which domestic philanthropy was located. The semantic fields in the colony and the metropole frequently overlapped; key metaphors often bore traces of the two seemingly disparate educational projects. However, it is significant that there was little contemporary comment on the 'circulation of social energy'[147] between Africa and the German Reich, between outside and inside. Of course the potency of terms such as the 'savage' or the 'light/dark' contrast was a consequence of the facts that the terminology was overdetermined and the two discussions each reinforced the other. But at the same time, these associations rested on the assumption that there was no direct exchange between the two spheres. For example, the entry in the 1910 *Handwörterbuch für Staatswisschaften* (*Concise Dictionary of Political Science*) on the 'Inner Mission' contains no reference to the conversion of heathens in the colonies. Instead, the existence of separate spheres of activity is suggested; any possible links between the missions at home and abroad are ignored. When, in 1913, Martin Schlunk was considering the relationship between the Inner and the Foreign missions, he admitted that he was entering 'a completely neglected territory'. 'I have not become aware of any account that could have paved the way for me.'[148] The stability of the boundary between the internal and the external was due not least to the fact that the links and transfers between them were rarely discussed.

COLONIAL WORKERS' COLONIES

The parallels between the treatment of the 'work-shy' at home and the 'natives' in the colonies went beyond rhetoric and metaphors. On the level of motives and goals, too, there were similarities between

---

[146] Bodelschwingh, *Ausgewählte Schriften*, p. 413; and Bodelschwingh, *Bodelschwingh*, p. 281.

[147] Greenblatt, *Shakespearean Negotiations*.

[148] Schlunk and Hennig, *Äußere Mission*; Schäfer, 'Innere Mission'. But see also, much earlier, Herdieckerhoff, *Äußere und innere Mission*.

the introduction of workers' colonies and the acquisition of overseas colonies. The missionary impetus that gave both projects some of their dynamism was only one aspect. Another was the fear of social revolution: this fear had prompted both social welfare work and the foundation of the Inner Mission, and was also one of the major motivations for the acquisition of colonies after 1884.[149] And finally, the establishment of colonies was also a reaction to the increase in undirected mobility and migration. While the workers' colonies were intended to curb uncontrolled movements on the roads of Germany, the African colonies were intended to redirect German migration to America toward 'New Germany'.

But the mere identification of common motives does not adequately account for the intertwining of the colony and the homeland. Regardless of the rhetorical barriers between Germany and Africa, between 'here' and 'there', we can see examples of a direct exchange reaching beyond metaphor and ideology. In Bodelschwingh's Bethel centre, for example, the profits from the postage-stamp unit were sent to East Africa to support missionary work there from the mid 1880s onward. This transfer was intended to give even the weakest members of society in Bethel a feeling of being useful to others. This type of cultural work was later tried out on two children from German East Africa, who arrived in Bethel in 1891. However, they proved susceptible to the local climate and soon died, but not without having been baptised (using the Old Testament baptismal motto 'I am black, but comely').[150]

This two-way flow occurred in an era, from the 1880s onward, when enthusiasm for colonialism and fascination with the exotic were on the increase in Germany. Bodelschwingh himself was enthusiastic about the colonial project. He had originally studied theology with the aim of working in the foreign missions after reading a tract on the conversion of heathens that had seemed to him to be a 'call from God'. His social-reform work caused him to abandon this plan and he

---

[149] See Wehler, *Bismarck*, esp. pp. 486–502.
[150] Hellmann, *Bodelschwingh*, pp. 154–55; Jasper, *Werden*, pp. 104–6; and Trittelvitz, *Missionserinnerungen*, pp. 58–66.

never actually made it to the colonies. But his heart still 'beat faster' when Africa was mentioned, and during family evenings in Bethel he was able to report 'so glowingly, so closely, so immediately' about the colonies that visitors assumed he had experienced it all himself.[151]

In this, Friedrich von Bodelschwingh is a typical example of the 'colonial desire'[152] that was characteristic of German society during the Wilhelmine period. The cultural conditions of colonial intervention have become an important topic of recent research. Ideas put forward in post-colonial studies have contributed to an understanding of the acquisition of colonies not (mainly) as political, economic or social-imperialistic strategies, but as the expression of a specific cultural discourse. Issues such as fascination with the foreign, the perception of the 'Other', and the literature of travel have been examined in detail. Susanne Zantop, for example, has studied the 'widespread cult of the colony' in Germany in the century leading up to 1870 – that is, long before the country actually acquired a colonial empire. In her work she describes the colonial imagination that anticipated the actual conquest before it happened: '[i]n the end, reality just caught up with the imagination'.[153] This may be an exaggeration, but Bodelschwingh's letters show us that colonial fantasies were clearly at work. He had set up a little colonial museum in Bethel even before Germany began acquiring colonies in 1884. His own house, too, was home to a missionary box 'in the form of a kneeling negro' which was used to collect funds for religious work in Africa.[154]

Often, post-colonial interpretations went no further than to describe the 'imperialist imagination', without investigating how it was manifested in practice.[155] But colonial desire did not remain limited to propaganda and enthusiasm, and transnational transactions went further than just the profits from the postage-stamp unit. Rather, the colonial fantasy crystallised in direct interventions. An opportunity arose when Bodelschwingh was asked by the Evangelical Mission Society

---

[151] Bodelschwingh, *Bodelschwingh*, pp. 266, 262.
[152] Young, *Colonial Desire.*   [153] Zantop, *Colonial Fantasies*, p. 9.
[154] Bodelschwingh, *Bodelschwingh*, p. 263.
[155] See for example the contributions to Friedrichsmeyer, Lennox and Zantop, *Imperialist Imagination.*

(*Evangelische Missionsgesellschaft*) for German East Africa to work in the colonies himself. He initially rejected the request, but in 1890, when pressed further, agreed that deacons trained in Bethel could be sent to East Africa: 'It is wonderful to look after poor sick white people but yet more wonderful to look after black heathens.' Bodelschwingh's colonial dreams were fed by his preconceptions of the pre-modern utopia that he hoped to find in the 'indescribably different conditions' in Africa. Work among the Negro tribes who were 'completely untouched' by the effects of industrial society seemed in fact to be an idealised model for his rural, idyllic workers' colonies located outside the Moloch of the city. He was looking outside mechanised mass society – without ever having been 'there' – for a sphere of action that was 'as unspoiled as possible by the rotten European civilisation'.[156]

The Evangelical Mission Society, also known as 'Berlin III' to distinguish it from the Berlin and Goßner mission societies, had been set up in 1885 at the height of colonial euphoria. Its most important representative was the infamous colonial activist Carl Peters, who wanted to exploit the mission for his own political and commercial objectives in East Africa. Berlin III had close links with the organised colonial movement. Most of its board members were also members of the German East Africa Company, which at the time held the rights of sovereignty in German East Africa. The established mission societies reacted with scepticism to the new society, about which they had reservations; these reservations were increased by its political character and the involvement of Peters. Because of internal differences in its early years, the new society remained a precarious project. This changed only when Bodelschwingh was coopted onto the board in 1890 and proceeded to take the reins increasingly into his own hands, during the following years. He set up a seminary to which Kaiser Wilhelm II contributed 3,000 marks from his own private budget and organised the dispatch of the missionaries. In 1906, the headquarters of Berlin III was even moved to Bethel.[157]

---

[156] Bodelschwingh, *Ausgewählte Schriften*, p. 522, 647; and *Briefwechsel*, p. 407, 454.
[157] On the history of the Evangelical Mission Society for German East Africa and the relationship between the different missionary societies see Jasper, *Werden*; Niesel,

The other mission societies greeted the gradual assimilation of Berlin III by the Bethel mission with suspicion. Their criticism focused on two main concerns: firstly, the close links between the Bethel mission and the colonial agitators and the German colonial government in East Africa, and secondly, the competition that this missionary 'latecomer' represented; like the German Reich itself, it was now 'claiming its modest place in the sun'.[158] Another problem was that the boundaries between the motherland and the colony were, it seemed, becoming blurred, and the differences between the two spheres were disappearing. 'While for Father all the areas of work on the Earth flowed into one and the boundaries between home [*die Heimat*] and the world of the heathens became blurred', as Bodelschwingh's son Gustav remembered, the critics complained that 'the German protectorates had been placed on the same footing as the German regions'. Bodelschwingh repeatedly had to reject accusations that he was ignoring the differing natures of missionary work abroad and welfare work at home. He replied that he had been 'virtually forced' to take on the colonial mission ('so clear were the signs from God') and had no intention of setting up as a rival to anyone – except perhaps toward the Catholic mission, with its 'large armies'.[159] But he also insisted that the '[I]nner and Foreign missions cannot be separated, either'.[160]

The first deacons were sent out as early as 1890, to the island of Zanzibar. After the German and British governments exchanged the 'kingdom' of Zanzibar for the 'bathtub' of Heligoland later the same year (which met with vigorous protest from the colonial societies), the mission initially set up headquarters in Dar es Salaam. Bodelschwingh, who used the work of the travel writer Oscar Baumann as a source of

'Kolonialverwaltung', pp. 43–46; Paul, *Mission*, pp. 150–212; Gründer, *Christliche Mission*, pp. 36–41; and Gründer, 'Deutsche Missionsgesellschaften'.

[158] Bodelschwingh, *Bodelschwingh*, p. 264.

[159] *Ibid.*, p. 273; Bodelschwingh, quoted in Jasper, *Werden*, p. 33; Bodelschwingh, *Briefwechsel*, p. 292; and Bodelschwingh, *Ausgewählte Schriften*, p. 648.

[160] Cited in Trittelvitz, *Missionserinnerungen*, p. 123. On responses to the criticisms, see also Bodelschwingh, 'Ostafrikanische Mission'; and Trittelvitz, *Missionserinnerungen*, pp. 27–35, 121–27.

reference about local conditions, soon urged that the mission's activities should be moved to the interior of the mountainous Usambara region, one reason being that in the area 'of the great harbours … the people are already suffering too much under the foreign influences'.[161] One by one, mission stations were then set up in the mountains, where the climate was also more tolerable for the German missionaries. The establishment of these subsidiary stations was carried out in close consultation with the German colonial authorities. At times, the Bethel mission acted as an outright agent of colonial expansion. In 1909, for example, Berlin III took possession of the island of Idjwi in Lake Kivu, in Rwanda. The area was under dispute between Belgium and Germany and the occupation served to underline Germany's claim to the region without entering into actual military engagement with Belgium and England. Using the classic language of colonial propaganda, Bodelschwingh justified the occupation with the 'call of four million heathens', seeing himself as their representative: 'Come over and take pity on us for we have never heard a word of the Gospel!'[162] However, these hopes for territorial expansion were soon disappointed: a year later, Idjwi was assigned to the Belgian Congo. A motorboat named 'Bodelschwingh', for which monies had been collected in Bethel, was sent to Rwanda nevertheless.[163]

The mission stations kept in close touch with Bethel and their names have a familiar ring. One of the first was 'Hohenfriedberg', a picture of which hung in Bodelschwingh's study. Others included 'Lobetal', 'Wilhemstal' and, in 1893, an East African 'Bethel'.[164] However, the similarities did not end with the nomenclature. The mission stations were true manifestations of the Bethel motto 'Work instead of alms'. In his regular letters to East Africa, Bodelschwingh himself emphasised the importance of 'educating the dear children of your parish' (*Gemeindekinder*, referring to adults as well as children)

---

[161] Bodelschwingh, *Bodelschwingh*, p. 265.
[162] Bodelschwingh, *Ausgewählte Schriften*, p. 647.
[163] Gründer, *Christliche Mission*, pp. 215–16; and Menzel, *Bethel-Mission*, pp. 200–233.
[164] Most of the mission stations were later given African names, however. See the list in Menzel, *Bethel-Mission*, pp. 165–66.

'in thorough work'; after all, 'no healthy Christendom [was] possible
… on two hours of work'.[165] In Lutindi, one of the showpiece stations
of the Bethel mission, 'more emphasis was placed on work than on
schooling', observers agreed.[166] To the missionary Charles Buchner,
'every mission station seemed like a work station' in any case. It is no
coincidence that it was a missionary from Bethel who had invented
the 'Wilhelmstal work-card system'. This system was used even outside the area of responsibility of the mission stations and obliged all
African men to carry out thirty days' work in every four months at
a private company, for the usual local wages.[167] The workers were
trained for this type of forced labour in the stations of the Bethel
mission. But the mission stations also needed workers themselves,
and thus saw waged work as both an educational objective and an
economic necessity. Life at the mission stations, then, meant 'work
and more work'.[168] It is therefore no surprise that a visitor to Lutindi
remarked: 'My experience was that everything seemed as if I were in
Bethel; the resemblance is striking.'[169]

At first glance, the transfer of a Protestant work ethic rooted in the
bourgeois and petit bourgeois mentalities to the colonies may not seem
surprising. In fact this transfer was not limited to the Bethel missions,
and not even to Protestant missionary activity as a whole. 'Educating

---

[165] Bodelschwingh, *Briefwechsel*, p. 404.
[166] Paul, *Mission*, p. 193. For an almost identical comment see Döring,
Morgendämmerung, p. 73.
[167] On this topic see Pfrank, 'Landarbeiterfrage', p. 144; Iliffe, *History of Tanganyika*,
pp. 153ff.; and Koponen, *Development*, pp. 400–4.
[168] Buchner, *Mission*, pp. 10–12. On the Wilhelmstal work-card system see Gründer,
Christliche Mission, p. 239; Sippel, 'Wie erzieht man', pp. 327–28; and Niesel,
'Kolonialverwaltung', pp. 149–51. In the latter see also pp. 228–32 on work
practices in the mission stations. But the emphasis on the central importance of
work was also a reaction to accusations by planters that the Protestant missions
were neglecting the task of educating natives to work. In fact, there was considerable conflict between the missions and the settlers, especially with regard
to child labour, which removed children from the missions' schools. The missions demanded that children's working hours be limited to three days per week
but were unable to win this argument. On this subject see Gründer, *Christliche
Mission*, pp. 239–46.
[169] Quoted in Menzel, *Bethel-Mission*, p. 114.

Figure 2.4 In 1897, Bodelschwingh's Evangelical Africa Association founded
a hill station for freed slaves in Lutindi in the Usambara mountains. In 1904,
a mental hospital was added that focused its therapy largely on
agricultural work.

to work' was generally a high priority in all missionary work. Indeed,
particular emphasis was placed on it by the Catholic missions. They
proudly cited the 'unanimous verdict by the German colonial civil
servants and officers' who preferred to have Catholic missionaries
sent over: 'The ones they send, they understand how to combine *ora*
and *labora* in a practical and sensible way; they know how to educate
negroes, Kanakas and Chinese to become useful individuals.'[170] The
frequent references to the high level of affinity between the Catholic
mission and the colonial state suggest that Catholicism had partially
adjusted itself to the conditions of the Kaiserreich in the period after
Bismarck's *Kulturkampf*. That adjustment itself was a precondition for
Catholic missions being allowed to work in the German colonies.[171]
So, in fact, the colonial administrators, and even more so the settlers,

[170] Quoted in Hoffmann, 'Katholische Missionsbewegung', p. 40.
[171] On this subject see Morsey, 'Katholiken'; and Gründer, 'Deutsche
Missionsgesellschaften', esp. pp. 87–97.

began to take the view that the Protestant missions placed less emphasis on education to work than on Christian instruction (*Ora et labora*) while the reverse was true for the Catholic missions (*Labora et ora*). In 1890, this issue led to an influential debate between the governor of German East Africa, Reichskommissar von Wißmann, and the leading theoretician on colonial affairs at the Rheinische Mission, Gustav Warneck.[172] In the course of this debate Warneck compared the Catholic mission stations to 'religious plantations' at which 'the mission is the colonist and the purchased black men are the bondsmen'.[173] It is true that the Catholic missions had even fewer scruples about using children in their plantations than the Protestant ones. But overall, the differences between Catholics and Protestants in terms of recruiting and exploiting their charges and educating them to work were only minor. When the Governor of German East Africa, Eduard von Liebert, wrote to Bodelschwingh that 'the Catholic mission … plays into the hands of my civilising efforts everywhere … by creating for me an obedient, easily led people who are willing to work', he could expect that the loyal head of the Bethel centres would not only understand this attitude but would deal with the labour issue in a similar way.[174]

The links between the mission stations in the colonies and the workers' colonies, finally, were not limited to motives and organisation, but also included the transfer of social practices. The missionaries, teachers and deaconesses who had offered to work 'with our black Reich comrades' were trained for their task in Bethel by working with the 'work-shy' and especially with those suffering from epilepsy.[175] The missionary Paul Döring described how he and his colleagues 'received their special training at the Bielefeld centres for the work with the heathens'. One focus of the instruction was on

---

[172] See Markmiller, *Erziehung*, pp. 163–64; and Niesel, 'Kolonialverwaltung', pp. 67–69. The accusation that the Protestant missions had in fact made 'Pray and be idle' their motto was countered with the assertion that, in contrast to their Catholic counterparts, 'Protestant missionaries [had] been educating the negroes to work for 150 years'. See Mueller, *Bete und arbeite!*

[173] Warneck, *Stellung*, p. 48.   [174] Quoted in Gründer, *Christliche Mission*, p. 333.

[175] Bodelschwingh, *Ausgewählte Schriften*, pp. 135, 615, 199.

'becoming simple and natural and practical', as one apparently needed to do in Africa. 'We were to learn here how to work with children … Everything was focused … on working with the heathens, who of course in many respects are like children.'[176]

WORKHOUSES

The treatment of the 'work-shy' in Germany and the cultural 'elevation' of the colonial subjects overlapped, and the two issues influenced each other. 'Is not', Bodelschwingh asked rhetorically, 'the work of the Inner Mission in our modern cities, where so many thousand unbaptised children are growing up, also a foreign mission?'[177] Transfers from Bethel and Berlin to the mission stations in East Africa were gradually professionalised and institutionalised. But conversely, the treatment of vagabonds and beggars, tramps and work-shy wanderers in Germany was loaded with connotations that evoked the colonial experience. For example, the reaping-houses in some workers' colonies were called the 'negro village'.[178] Bodelschwingh even suggested that some African traditions should be adopted, for example that of the 'strangers' monitor' (*Fremdenwart*) 'who is responsible for all strangers travelling through'. Usambara thus could even serve as a model for the vision of a society that was as settled and stable as possible (in highly mobile Wilhelmine Germany 'of course the *Fremdenwart* would not have as easy a job as in Africa').[179]

To be sure, the education of the 'work-shy' and of 'negroes' were not identical projects. Despite all the similarities, there were major differences between the two social reform efforts. Firstly, the inculcation of industrial methods of production and attitudes to work had begun much earlier in Europe than in the colonies. In Germany, educating to work was not a new phenomenon. Educating to work got underway only later in the colonies, partly because German colonialism itself

[176] Döring, *Morgendämmerung*, pp. 172–76.
[177] Bodelschwingh, *Ausgewählte Schriften*, p. 193.
[178] Erdlenbruch, *Bedeutung*, p. 89.
[179] Bodelschwingh, *Ausgewählte Schriften*, p. 135.

was a relatively late development, but also as a result of the different times at which the regions were incorporated into the industrialised world and the world economy.[180] Secondly, the ideas behind educating to work in the colonies were developed in a context of foreign rule and of cultural and ethnic discrimination that was fundamentally different from the situation inside Europe. For this reason, the reality of work in German colonies often bordered on forced labour or in most cases was at the very least a form of semi-free labour. Those involved had few legal protections and very little opportunity to protest about their treatment. In the colonies there was a considerable discrepancy between the normative ideal and the way things worked in practice. The rhetoric of civilisation could thus, in some instances, go hand in hand with aggression and violence.[181] While, in colonial Africa, the cultural mission could in the event of conflict turn into war and destruction, as in the case of the Herero War of 1904, work in Germany on alleviating 'vagabond suffering' through social welfare work and work with the poor was in principle based on the idea of an enlightened and emancipatory, though paternalistic, social reform.

Thirdly, the promises of 'elevation' in the colony and in the metropole were by no means equivalent. In Germany, those willing to work could not, admittedly, expect to rise into the bourgeoisie, but they could be integrated as proletarians into civil society with all the participatory rights that entailed. In the colonies, education to work was always set within the colonial social order. The experience of education at the mission schools could potentially form a basis for social elevation. But it was impossible to overcome the fundamental difference between colonial masters and native subjects, a difference that was legitimised in terms of ethnic origin and legally codified by the introduction of a dual legal system in the colonies.[182] There was no question of natives receiving German citizenship.[183]

---

[180] See for example Thompson, *English Working Class*, which has already become a classic; and Schenda, 'Verfleißigung'.

[181] For the example of German South-West Africa see Zimmerer, *Deutsche Herrschaft*, esp. pp. 176–210.

[182] On this topic see for example Eckert, 'Verwaltung'.

[183] For a detailed account of the naturalisation issue see Nagl, *Grenzfälle*.

Certainly, therefore, there were major differences between the two projects of the civilisatory mission. But it is worth examining whether the differences between the two domains were always as absolute as the Wilhelmine self-view would have suggested. In contemporary Social Democratic criticism, for example, both the African colonies and the workers' colonies in Germany were described as 'an ingenious training centre for human slaves'.[184] The treatment in the workers' colonies could indeed be harsh, even if not all the educational suggestions received ('three days on bread and water and three electric shocks at each meal would work miracles') were put into practice. Bodelschwingh himself ('Discipline is vital') often displayed attitudes typical of a colonial master and 'involuntarily reminded' some visitors of 'Ohm Krüger' (the Boer resistance leader), especially the latter's 'fondness for corporal punishment'.[185]

This phraseology suggests that the treatment of the 'outer Other' could correspond, in public discourse, with the education of marginalised groups within. Just as nation-building presupposed the creation of a stable boundary between the homeland and the colonies regardless of all processes of exchange and transfer, the founding of the 'inner Reich' depended on internal exclusion. That applies not only to the 'work-shy': the groups excluded during the course of the establishment of the Reich included the Poles, especially after the laws on settlement were enacted. In the popular press, the Jews, too, were treated as the 'inner Orient' – although their situation differed from that of the Poles in that governmental policy after 1871 rarely considered actually excluding them from the country.[186] But it is important to recognise that exclusion and marginalisation were not only carried out along ethnic lines. Benedict Anderson, Léon Poliakov, Michel Foucault and others have put forward a variety

---

[184] *Der Sozialdemokrat* 13 (1883), cited in Scheffler, 'Gründungsjahre', p. 31.

[185] Bodelschwingh, 'Drohende Gefahren', p. 197; Bodelschwingh, *Ausgewählte Schriften*, p. 580; and Hyan, 'Arbeiterkolonie', p. 545.

[186] See Wehler, 'Polenpolitik'; and Volkov, *Juden*. In the actual practice of the exclusionary policy, the boundaries between the groups often disappeared, such as in the expulsion of 1885, which affected about 35,000 Poles and Jews. See Neubach, *Ausweisung*.

of theories about whether the idea of social classes developed from an acceptance of the differences between races or whether the genealogy does not, in fact, run the other way around. There is still debate about whether the language of class provided a vocabulary with which to think about issues of ethnicity, or the reverse. Without resolving this issue here, there is no doubt that there was a link between the two strategies of exclusion.[187] At the end of the nineteenth century, ethnic and social forms of marginalisation could not be completely separated, and there was certainly some degree of overlap.[188]

The definition of bourgeois society and western civilisation was based on the distancing from mainstream society of the 'work-shy' and of 'the natives', as two aspects of the same exclusionary social practice. 'The impression of feelings of foreignness towards the poor' that characterised the debate on social reform in Wilhelmine Germany was thus not merely an expression of the 'apocalyptic fears of the bourgeoisie'[189] but also the very precondition for the latter's self-awareness. This was related to the increased importance that 'work' acquired for practices of inclusion and exclusion at the end of the nineteenth century. Social classifications were increasingly linked to work and to an individual's occupation (and not, any longer, to his or her origins). For example, in the modern welfare state, social insurance was directly tied to work. More and more, the boundaries of the community were drawn by reference to the work performed. This becomes apparent in the arrangements for the care of the poor: institutions looking after impoverished migrants (*Wandererfürsorge*), the *Herbergen zur Heimat* and the workers' colonies were in general open only to those willing to work. Indeed, others were not welcome there.

---

[187] See Anderson, *Imagined Communities*, p. 136; Poliakov, *History*; and Foucault, *Society*, pp. 60–63, 178–188. On this topic see also Balibar and Wallerstein, *Race, Nation, Class*.

[188] Ann Laura Stoler has described how in the colonies, too, fear of degeneration referred both to ethnic mixing and social degradation. See Stoler, *Race*, pp. 95–136.

[189] Drude, 'Christliche Wandererfürsorge', p. 154.

'Anyone who refuses the work offered', Bodelschwingh proclaimed, 'must be arrested'.[190]

Anyone who did not want to work or to be educated to work was forcibly admitted to the workhouses. The Prussian 1843 'Act on the Punishment of Vagrants, Beggars and the Work-Shy', most of which was incorporated into the Reich Criminal Code of 1871, stipulated that crimes that were seen as the result of an unwillingness to work (later, prostitution and idleness were added) should be punished by imprisonment in the workhouse. Workhouses were a European institution, invented in the sixteenth century and previously used most widely during the early modern era. But during the late nineteenth century, in the context of industrialisation, they experienced a sudden resurgence. In the early 1880s, more than 20,000 people per year were sent to correctional facilities in the German Reich. As late as 1895, there were forty-seven workhouses in the country, almost all of which had been set up during the nineteenth century.[191]

Of the large numbers of people found guilty of begging, vagrancy or 'work-shyness', between 15 and 20 per cent were sentenced to periods in the workhouse. Initially, Prussian and Reich ministerial decrees regulated workhouse admissions; in 1912, the 'Work-Shy Act' allowed people to be sent there through administrative procedures with no need for a judicial process. Even the charitable workers' colonies were not always able to keep their inmates out of the workhouse. 'Despite all our external successes, real inner success [i.e., changing the inmates' natures] is escaping us', the Central Association of German Workers' Colonies had to admit. The hope of long-term improvement 'unfortunately does not apply to 75 to 90% of our colonists'.[192]

The ideal of 'elevation' that was central to the 'cultural mission' was also typical for the workhouses. In contrast to normal terms of imprisonment, imprisonment here was a means to an end, intended to make 'persons who have given in to inclinations contrary to the

---

[190] Quoted in Scheffler, 'Gründungsjahre', p. 28.
[191] Here and for the account that follows see Ayaß, *Arbeitshaus Breitenau*, pp. 14, 19; and Sachße and Tennstedt, *Geschichte*, pp. 244–56.
[192] Quoted in Scheffler, 'Gründungsjahre', p. 23.

societal order, [accustomed] by means of an ordered way of life ... and especially by strict adherence to continual employment ... to the same and ... fit for the same', and 'to [enable them to] return to human society as useful members'.[193] In everyday practice, this objective, based on ideas about social reform, was translated into many disciplinary rules. The long working hours (roughly twelve a day), the rigid schedules, and the fact that new arrivals had their hair cut short and were made to wear a standard uniform are evidence that in these locations the individual was to be improved by a regime of 'monitoring and punishment'.

A 'DISTANT GERMAN PROVINCE'

Apart from the placement of the work-shy in rural workers' colonies, the workhouses and correctional institutions marked another, even more rigid boundary separating bourgeois society and its 'Other'.[194] But even this exclusion was more than just a domestic issue. Here, too, there were attempts to externalise inner marginalisation. The debate on workhouses bore the traces of global circulation. From the early 1890s on, for example, there were attempts to send the work-shy to the 'foreign colonies' 'where they can no longer become a danger to the Fatherland'. This policy held out the prospect of solving two sets of problems at once: those related to social reform and to colonial policy, and to redirecting 'employment on meaningless local work' to the corrective facilities in the African colonies. 'We are wasting resources [*Kräfte*] in the Fatherland while our colonies lack hands'.[195]

As early as 1885, suggestions had been made in the newsletter *Die Arbeiterkolonie* that, with the expansion of the Reich, 'workers' colonies should be moved immediately to the new overseas colonies'. However, there were fears about the 'moral-educative influence' on the workers, apparently more difficult to guarantee in Africa. Consequently, what was called for were 'no foreign workers'

---

[193] Programm des Arbeitshauses Breitenau, quoted in Ayaß, *Arbeitshaus Breitenau*, p. 178.
[194] This view is shared by Sachße and Tennstedt, *Geschichte*, p. 254.
[195] Bruck, *Gegner*, p. 60; and *Einführung*, p. v.

colonies, but certainly colonies of the deported!'[196] In the following years, the debate focused on the forced transportation of the inmates of workhouses. The most important proponent of the idea to send these 'internal exiles' abroad was Felix Friedrich Bruck, professor of law at the University of Breslau who, in the mid 1890s, wrote many articles arguing for the work-shy to be deported to German South-West Africa. He even drafted a law to provide for this, which he presented at a number of legal conferences, such as the conference of the International Criminal Law Association in Lisbon in 1897. He had also drawn up detailed plans for the implementation of his proposed law. To critics who argued that even transporting some 100,000 of the work-shy would 'entail costs of approximately 20 million marks', he responded with detailed calculations in which he would posit the use of 'decommissioned steam frigates of no use in battle' and oblige the prisoners 'to refund ... the transport costs ... incurred by the Reich'.[197]

Bruck saw penal colonies as a 'valve' by which the Reich could 'be freed of criminal elements'. This was based on a social-imperialist strategy of integrating the working classes into society and pacifying proletarians who had become 'criminals'.[198] He also hoped to increase the value of colonies through the 'cultural work' [*Kulturarbeit*] to be done by the prisoners and the expansion of markets for the products of German industry.[199] In addition, Bruck also attributed an explicitly educational function to deportation. The great distance from home promised greater success in the attempts to educate the 'morally not intact elements' to become civilised individuals. If 'correctly set up' – meaning, for example, the strict separation of men and women (in order 'to prevent ... sexual excesses') – it would certainly be possible

---

[196] Anon., 'Überseeische Arbeiter-Kolonien', pp. 133, 135. See also, fifty years previously, Weidenkeller, *Kolonien*.

[197] Sturm, *Landstreicherei*, p. 92; Bruck, *Gegner*, p. 28; and Bruck, *Einführung*, p. 20. See also Bruck, *Fort mit den Zuchthäusern!*; *Neu-Deutschland*; and *Deportation*. On the debate on deportation see Voigt, 'Deportation'; and Meyer zu Hogrebe, *Strafkolonien*.

[198] Bruck, *Einführung*, p. 31. See also Priester, *Deportation*.

[199] Bruck, *Neu-Deutschland*, p. 42.

to achieve 'the improvement, or more correctly the education of the prisoner'.[200] But this was not merely a project of 'elevation' of individuals. Rather, Bruck believed that the deportation would have social benefits and would contribute to solving social problems. 'Dull, discontented proletarians without any attachment to the fatherland' would, he hoped, 'become happy individuals eager to work and with a patriotic attitude.'[201] In contrast to many of his colonial friends, Bruck was not plagued by the worry that 'the savage tribes … might come to much harm through contact with our German prisoners, who are after all still civilised people [*Kulturmenschen*]'.[202]

The topic was discussed in a variety of contexts. Charitable associations, representatives of the churches and the mission societies, lawyers and prison officers, doctors and those involved in promoting the colonies all took up the issue.[203] Those in favour of deportations included the Pan-German League and the Colonial League, and parts of the bourgeois press.[204] The Reichstag debated the issue in 1898, 1903 and 1908. Some people, such as Leutwein, the governor of German South-West Africa, took quite a favourable view of the proposal at first. But in the Reichstag's budgetary debates, those critical of the idea prevailed.[205] Most political decision-makers rejected the idea. Higher-level civil servants in the colonial administration, especially in the upper echelons of the Colonial Office, eventually rejected the idea 'although of course it would be a welcome development if welfare institutions to help the large number of unemployed people could be set up in our colonies'. But 'the realisation of such a plan [would] meet with insurmountable difficulties'.[206] The issues

---

[200] Bruck, *Einführung*, pp. 23, 27, 22.   [201] Bruck, *Neu-Deutschland*, p. 63.

[202] Bruck, *Gegner*, p. 25.

[203] On this topic see Mittermaier, 'Litteraturbericht'. See also Meyer zu Hogrebe, *Strafkolonien*; and Kundrus, *Imperialisten*, pp. 104–8.

[204] See for example Freund, 'Strafkolonisation'.

[205] See *Stenographische Berichte über die Verhandlungen des Reichstags* (*SBVR*) 159 (1898), pp. 755ff; *SBVR* 160 (1898), pp. 988ff; *SBVR* 187 (1903), pp. 8275ff; and *SBVR* 230 (1908), pp. 3234–3393. See also Bruck, *Gegner*, pp. 67–76.

[206] Reichskolonialamt, 28 December 1909 to the Chairman of the 'Blaukreuz Verein' Braunschweig, in Bundesarchiv (BA) Berlin, R 1001, no. 6286, p. 148.

of transport and financing were not the only problems. Of greater importance were concerns about the revolts and rebellions the prisoners might engage in and fears that the colonial difference would be gradually undermined by the presence of subaltern whites. If natives saw the privileged Europeans as made up not only of colonial administrators and settlers, but also of criminal underclasses, that might undermine the authority of the colonial power. The main concern for all those involved in the administration of the colonies, therefore, was to prevent the emergence of a class of 'white subalterns'.[207] The 'special conditions in our colonies mean that it would not be justified to send any kind of emigrant there indiscriminately'.[208]

These criticisms notwithstanding, a section was set up in the Colonial Office to deal with deportation issues, and in 1909 the young criminologist Robert Heindl was sent to Asia on a fact-finding mission. He visited the penal colonies in New Caledonia ('the island on which the civil dead live'), Australia, the Andaman Islands and China, and studied the prison system and the Chinese practice of deportation. Heindl was sceptical about the idea and, as a result of his experiences, advised against deporting those convicted of criminal offences.[209] His vivid report, published by Ullstein in 1914, was 'discussed eagerly in the press around the world' and is regarded as the model for Kafka's story 'In the Penal Colony'.[210] The extensive reception of his report is evidence of how widespread the debate about deportation had become in late Wilhelmine Germany. But in contrast to Russia, France or Great Britain, such plans were never actually realised in Germany.[211]

---

[207] For similar discussions in British India, see Fischer-Tiné, 'White Women', with further references.

[208] Reichskolonialamt, BA Berlin, R 1001, no. 6286, p. 148. See also Cannstatt, *Kolonisation*.

[209] Heindl, *Reise*, esp. pp. 209–53, 450–53.

[210] Müller-Seidel, *Deportation*, p. 81.

[211] However, plans to deport the unemployed re-emerged in later years, in particular during the world economic crisis of the late 1920s. See Karstedt, *Bekämpfung*, pp. 45ff.

Nevertheless, the debates about transporting prisoners abroad show that internal discrimination and territorial expulsion could overlap. 'There is a relation of reciprocal determination between "class racism" and "ethnic racism"', as Etienne Balibar has described this mechanism, 'and *these two determinations are not independent*. Each produces its effects, to some extent, in the field of the other and under constraints imposed by the other.'[212] The 'work-shy' were not the only social group whose internal marginalisation was associated, in public debate, with the possibility of physically excluding them from the space shared by the community. The early propaganda for colonialism frequently included suggestions about exporting the revolutionary potential of social democracy abroad by setting up penal colonies.[213] Ernst von Weber, who held a *Rittergut* in Saxony, had even demanded 'broad drainage channels' for 'the proletarian masses who become more numerous and dangerous year by year', to ensure that Germany would not move 'with huge steps toward a revolution'.[214] The first suggestions that Jews should be forced to emigrate were also made in this period, and recurred regularly until the Nazi era in the form of the 'Madagascar plan'. In 1885, Paul de Lagarde was the first to suggest the African island as a destination. Over the next few years, there were increasing calls for the 'exclusion of the Jewry [*Judenvolk*] from the federation of Aryan peoples' (the phraseology reveals how fluid the discursive boundary between transport and annihilation had become) and for them to be settled in the colonies.[215]

These strategies of internal and external exclusion were not debated in isolation, but rather overlapped and produced an overdetermined space of both rhetorical and practical exclusion. The mutual entanglements between the German Reich and its colonies are revealed by the ease with which internal conflicts could be externalised without,

---

[212] Balibar and Wallerstein, *Race, Nation, Class*, p. 214. Emphasis in original.
[213] See for example Fabri, *Bedarf Deutschland*, p. 106. See also Meyer zu Hogrebe, *Strafkolonien*, pp. 69–73.
[214] von Weber, *Erweiterung*, pp. 50–51.
[215] Leuss, *Wanzenmittel*, p. 19. Hans Leuss (1861–1920), an anti-Semite and writer, was a member of the Reichstag in 1893/94 for the German Social Reform Party. On this subject see also Brechtken, *Madagaskar*.

however, putting the boundary between 'inside' and 'outside' in question. Ideas and people moved in both directions. For example, there was some discussion during the first decade of the twentieth century about whether the 'masses of people' in Africa could be used to fill the factories in Germany and especially to increase the size of the active army. Germany decided not to create 'black troops', but both Britain and France did recruit for their armies from the colonies. The French *force noire*, made up of some 140,000 soldiers from France's colonies in sub-Saharan Africa, had partly been created in the hope that it would have the 'incomparable power of horrifying the others'. In contrast to the willingness of the French authorities to make use of the 'black hordes' and the 'savage instincts of the negro warriors [*Negersoldateska*]', the nationally minded and pan-German press in Germany saw the Reich as the last refuge of European culture from 'African barbarism'.[216]

German unwillingness to add colonial units to the German army was not just based on demonisation and racist prejudices. It was also a result of the prevailing view that the military should not only be a means of protecting the country abroad, but also of securing it from within. It was to be used to suppress any domestic revolts, but also potentially to prevent the rise of bourgeois or Social Democratic 'elements', as the 1913 debates about increasing the size of the army show.[217] This debate also merged ethnic with social criteria and suggested a circulation between the colony and metropole that was also playing an important role in the project of 'educating to work'. In this sense the Reich and its African colonies were not as far apart as Wilhelmine self-representation suggested. 'German South-West Africa', as Felix Friedrich Bruck commented, in the context of his plans to deport the 'work-shy', 'can be compared to a distant German province'.[218]

---

[216] See Grosse, *Kolonialismus*, pp. 199–209 (where the quotes can also be found). On the sustained effect of fears of the 'black peril' see Campt, Grosse and Lemke-Muniz de Faria, 'Blacks'; and El-Tayeb, *Schwarze Deutsche*, pp. 142–202. On this subject see also Koller, *Wilden*; and Maß, 'Trauma'.

[217] Grosse, *Kolonialismus*, p. 208. See also Förster, *Militarismus*, esp. pp. 247–96.

[218] Bruck, *Gegner*, p. 106.

GERMAN HISTORY IN A COLONIAL CONTEXT

The mutual interaction between colony and metropole was not unique to Germany. In the context of post-colonial studies, many examples have been discussed in recent years that illustrate mutual influence and the formation of social practices in a shared field.[219] In the area of educating to work, too, terminology and rhetorical topoi, governing motifs and capital all circulated, as did actors and elements of educational practice. The influences worked both ways, though not to the same extent. The model of Bethel shaped the everyday life at the missions in German East Africa much more strongly than the other way around. The extent and social relevance of these mutual influences also varied. In Great Britain, with its long imperial tradition and large colonial empire, the impact of interactions was certainly highest. But the issue of transnational entanglements goes beyond a mechanistic understanding of 'reverse effects'. The important point is that ideas, concepts and social practice were transformed within a context that had potentially become global. The deportation projects were just one example.

In addition, colonial entanglement was a European phenomenon, just as German colonialism cannot be described in full without taking its European context into account. German colonial politicians and, even more so, representatives of the colonial administrations, all kept a close eye on developments in other colonies. Great Britain played the most important role, whether as a model (as for Bismarck) or as a competitor and rival (as for Carl Peters), but the administrators also were careful to study developments in the French, Dutch, Belgian and Portuguese colonies. They compared themselves to the others; of even greater importance, however, were the numerous cooperative projects and the role played by experts who were active internationally. Particularly in the area of colonial control and 'native policy', the transfer of ideas and technologies of power between European countries was common practice (the same can be said for the area of social

---

[219] Typical examples are Stoler and Cooper, 'Between Metropole and Colony', esp. p. 4 ; and Sinha, *Colonial Masculinity*.

reform, as British authors took the German workers' colonies and workhouses as a model).[220] Of course, there were some differences. To begin with, each of the European empires was extremely heterogeneous. This was obviously true of the French and British empires, but even in 'New Germany' there were substantial administrative, social and cultural differences between sparsely populated Togo and German East Africa, and even more so between the African colonies and the colony of Jiauzhou, which was managed by the Reich Marine Office. Furthermore, the European colonial empires differed from each other, even if these differences tended to be over-emphasised in national stylisations.[221]

In spite of all the differences, however, colonialism was a cross-European project with many common features and parallels.[222] The ambivalent relationship between a shared 'civilising' mission and the competition between nations is reflected, for example, in the history of the Christian missions, which, on the one hand could operate in areas ruled by foreign governments, but on the other hand tended to develop national rivalries, and increasingly so after the turn of the century.[223] In any case, many of the differences proclaimed with considerable rhetorical effort dissolve when we look at social practice on the ground. It then becomes evident that the variations in forms of rule and in the way the issue of labour was dealt with were much more dependent on local conditions than on the nationality of the colonial administrators. The presence of European settlers, the availability of mineral resources that could be a basis for industrial processes, climatic conditions, population density, local power relationships and the related and highly varying levels of respect accorded to local societies: these were some of the factors that influenced different colonial practice more strongly than membership of one or the other of the European empires.[224] Even educating to work was by no means

---

[220] See for example Dawson, *Vagrancy*, p. 60, 133–78.
[221] The standard works comparing European colonialisms are Reinhard, *Geschichte*; Albertini, *Europäische Kolonialherrschaft*; and Fieldhouse, *Colonialism*.
[222] See the systematic discussion in von Trotha, 'Was war der Kolonialismus?'.
[223] On this topic see Christensen and Hutchison, *Missionary Ideologies*.
[224] On this differentiation, see for example the study by Spittler, *Verwaltung*.

an exclusively German project, although its 'German' character was often emphasised. Very similar rhetoric was used in all the European colonies to give legitimacy to what was hard and often exploitative work.[225] In fact, when the German colonies in western Africa were transferred to French ownership after the First World War, few changes were made to the ways in which workers were recruited, trained and employed.[226]

The overlaps between 'native policy' and philanthropic efforts in European cities were not limited to Germany either. Recent research has teased out the links between these two 'civilising' projects, especially for Great Britain.[227] One fascinating example is the history of the Salvation Army. Its canonical text, *In Darkest England and the Way Out* (1890), an immensely popular book by William Booth, reveals in its allusions to Stanley's *In Darkest Africa* the imperial consciousness that was inherent to this form of social welfare work from its beginnings. The Salvation Army, too, expanded into the colonies in the late nineteenth century, mainly to India. There it looked after not only members of the underclasses who threatened to undermine the colonial difference between the civilised Europeans and the colonial subjects, but also the 'dangerous' elements of Indian society. Experiences in the colonial periphery were shaped by categories and moral standards developed in London, but also played an important reciprocal role in the classification and treatment of the unemployed and vagrants 'at home'.[228] John Marriot has extensively reconstructed the extent to which the beggars and vagrants in London were 'an object of imperial, not merely domestic concern'.[229] The overlaps

---

[225] On the reality of work in colonial Africa see the systematic overview by Eckert, 'Geschichte der Arbeit', esp. pp. 524–30, with an extensive bibliography. For a particularly dramatic example, see the descriptions of the cruelty in the Belgian Congo in Hochschild, Leopold's Ghost.

[226] On this topic see Norris, *Umerʒiehung*, pp. 180, 201.

[227] See the inspiring study by Marriott, *Other Empire*.

[228] See the excellent essay by Fischer-Tiné, 'Global Civil Society'. See also Marriott, *Other Empire*, pp. 130–59.

[229] Marriott, *Other Empire*, p. 221. A similar perspective is taken by Comaroff and Comaroff, 'Hausgemachte Hegemonie'; Thorne, *Missions*; McLaughlin, *Urban Jungle*; and Valverde, 'Dialectic'.

between colony and metropole also involved the mutual reinforcement of social and ethnic categories. Since the late nineteenth century, increasing numbers of social reformers had seen the wretched underclasses as a separate 'race' and argued that the problem should be dealt with by means of sterilisation, marriage bans and other eugenic interventions.[230] These 'reverse imperial effects' contributed to the reconfiguration of society and the mechanisms of social exclusion in India just as in Great Britain. Analysing them gives us insights into the way interdependent spheres of action overlap, insights 'that can disrupt oppositions between metropole and colony and allow us to rethink the … historiographies of national belonging and exclusion'.[231]

Can similar conclusions be drawn for Germany, if perhaps not quite to the same extent? To be sure, the workers' colonies are just one particular example that cannot be generalised. But here, too, we could ask questions about the extent to which ideas about belonging, and practices of exclusion, changed under the influence of colonial globality. Did the overlap between contemporary debates about labour and the colonial experience contribute to the qualitative change that emerged around 1900 in the understanding of work as a criterion of exclusion? To what degree did the traditional understanding of social inequality and class differences become amalgamated with the basic dichotomies that characterised the colonial project, i.e. the essentialisation of difference? Mechanisms of exclusion had of course always existed. Conventional forms of discrimination included the marginalisation of the poor, of the unemployed and of vagrants. However, membership of the groups affected by social stigmatisation was not fixed; education and training, work and leading a 'good' life, had always created opportunities for upward mobility. At the end of the nineteenth century, however, these traditional practices of exclusion became increasingly radicalised – in the workhouses but also in legislation and in the disciplining of the 'work-shy'. The debates about deportations even raised the possibility of physically removing undesirable individuals and groups from the territory of belonging.

---

[230] See Marriott, *Other Empire*, esp. pp. 176–81.
[231] Wilson, 'Introduction', p. 3.

Here, the categories of outside and inside, of class and race, of variable and essentialised difference overlapped. In this context, colonial interaction may have contributed to making absolute some mechanisms of social power and exclusion, mechanisms that already had a long (and internal) history.[232]

In this sense, the radicalisation of the concept of work was not an isolated phenomenon. The history of anti-Semitism in Germany, for example, could be examined from a similar perspective. Anti-Semitism was not an invention of the era; it, too, had a long pre-history. But for the Wilhelmine period we can discern a major change in the strategies of exclusion, with the increasing emphasis on a biological rationale for anti-Semitism. Although this was not a linear development, increasingly it was not individual Jews who were subject to discrimination and polemical attacks, but 'the Jew'. Anti-Semitism also became radicalised, and was ethnicised and reformulated in biological and racial terms during the very era that was shaped by the scramble for Africa, the colonial expansion of the German empire and the first 'racial laws' in the colonies.[233]

Colonialism was founded on the central dichotomy of 'racial differences', which was often treated as absolute. Ann Laura Stoler and Partha Chatterjee, among others, have argued that colonial policy was preoccupied with the idea of preserving this difference. As I have tried to show, this is particularly true of the segregated work in the colonies. As outlined above, debates about work and education to work in Germany and in its African colonies were linked in complex ways and influenced each other (even if in a very asymmetric manner). This means that the understanding of the social question

---

[232] This argument is also put forward by Marriott, *Other Empire*, p. 160: 'The trope of racialization locates shifts in the construction of the poor within the *imperial* formation, and provides a more satisfactory explanation of their chronology and nature than those focusing exclusively on domestic politics and social policy.'

[233] Some examples of the extensive literature on the topic are Berding, *Moderner Antisemitismus*; Bergmann, 'Völkischer Antisemitismus'; Jochmann, *Gesellschaftskritik*, pp. 30–98; Katz, *Vorurteil*; Volkov, 'Antisemitismus'; Volkov, *Juden*; and Zumbini, *Wurzeln*. An important reconstruction of the different types of anti-Semitic views is given in Blaschke, *Katholizismus*. See also the literature reviews by Rahden, 'Ideologie und Gewalt'; and Benz and Bergmann, *Vorurteil*.

in Wilhelmine Germany (the problem of the unemployed, work-shy and vagrant) may have been superimposed with a discourse according to the logic of which exclusion did not just mean discrimination, but could be absolute – could mean physical exclusion. And this happened at precisely the time when the boundaries of social belonging were increasingly being defined through work. The interlinkage of discourses about work suggests that the colonial experience with its Manichean ontology was at least one of the contexts (although not the only one) in which this radicalisation took place.

By the late 1930s, not much was left of the emancipatory ideals of 'education to work'. Anyone found without work or as a vagrant was no longer subjected to measures intended to improve his or her character. Instead, they were now regarded as a 'pest on the German body politic [*Volkskörper*]; the eradication of the adult inferiors' was, according to Wilhelm Polligkeit, a lawyer and the doyen of German welfare, 'a necessity from the point of view of public welfare'.[234] From 1938 onward, the 'work-shy' who were incapable of work were no longer sent to workhouses but, denounced as 'work saboteurs' and 'unreliable elements', to the concentration camps. There, they were forced to wear a black triangle, marking them as 'asocial', and had the highest death rate of any group in the camps.[235] This eliminatory logic was far removed from the educational project of the Kaiserreich. Even plans for deportation during the Wilhelmine era were inspired by the hope of 'elevation', even if the concerns expressed about the possible 'degeneration of the race' resulting from the 'work-shy'[236] indicate that the idea of the biologisation of social difference was beginning to emerge – just as the British colonial administration in India treated the 'criminal tribes' as the product of inbreeding and 'racial' characteristics.[237]

It is important, in this context, to resist the temptation to read the history of the nineteenth century through the lens of its aftermath, as so much of the *Sonderweg* literature depicting Germany's

---

[234] Quoted in Ayaß, 'Wandererfürsorge', p. 275.
[235] Ayaß, *Arbeitshaus Breitenau*, pp. 287–94; see also Ayaß, 'Gebot'.
[236] Bruck, *Gegner*, p. 41.
[237] See Cole, *Suspect Identities*, Chapter 3: 'Native prints'.

deviant path into modernity has tended to do. There was no direct path that can be constructed leading from the shift in notions of work in the Wilhelmine empire to the ideology of *Arbeit macht frei*. Before the First World War, educating to work was a colonial project that Germany shared with other European nations. Likewise, the blending of practices of social exclusion with the notion of colonial difference was not a German peculiarity. In general we can say that modern racism was a European concept in which the transfer of ideas within Europe, especially between France, Great Britain and Germany, was of great importance.[238] Moreover, while not neglecting the criminal acts and atrocities committed overseas, the colonies were for the most part not the site of a politics of genocide. In addition, Wilhelmine anti-Semitism was to an overriding extent not eliminatory in intent. It is probable that the total war launched by Hindenburg, with its radicalisation of the concept of work as a condition of belonging or even of existence – 'He who does not work shall not eat' – marks a sea-change.[239] In any case, the differences between the exclusionary mechanisms used in Wilhelmine Germany, even in its colonial prac-tice, and the 'destruction through work' of the Third Reich, remained substantial.

It remains a puzzle how a few decades would suffice to turn a dis-criminatory discourse into a politics of extermination. It is important to recognise, therefore, that within the social and political projects in imperial Germany some forms of radical exclusion had already become conceivable, even if only by a minority. The debate about deportation of unwanted social groups is an example of this, as are the genocidal fantasies that found their way into colonial warfare.[240] Even if the transformation of practices of exclusion – which, more-over, did not manifest itself in all European countries in the same

---

[238] On this topic see Geulen, *Wahlverwandte*, esp. pp. 42–94; and Fredrickson, *Rassismus*, esp. pp. 53–100.

[239] Ludendorff, *Urkunden*, p. 67. See also Feldman, *Armee*; and Köhler, *Arbeitsdienst*.

[240] This refers to the Herero war that some authors have described as a war of annihi-lation and consequently placed in a line of continuity with the holocaust. See, for example, Jürgen Zimmerer, 'Holocaust und Kolonialismus'. For this debate, see Grosse, 'German Colonialism'; and Malinowski and Gerwarth, 'Holocaust'.

way – cannot directly be derived from the colonial experience, the question nevertheless remains of whether this radicalisation can be understood without taking the colonial context into account.

Why this should have happened in Germany remains an open question. Frantz Fanon once suggested that fascism could to a large extent be understood as a variant of European imperialism turned inward – and which not by coincidence had the greatest effect in Germany, which was robbed of its colonies after 1918.[241] Fanon's hypothesis is equally plausible and difficult to ascertain, and the example of education to work is not sufficient to explore it in detail. True, colonial discourse did influence important dimensions of thought and of social practice. But for the stereotypes and ideas of the Wilhelmine era to become a genocidal policy, developments and factors were required that were not yet at work during the Kaiserreich.

---

[241] See Young, *White Mythologies*, pp. 7–8. The *locus classicus* of the German debate is Arendt, *Elemente*.

CHAPTER THREE

Between the Poles: mobility and nation in Germany's 'real colony'

POLISH SEASONAL WORKERS IN PRUSSIA

In retrospect, the 'disadvantages of employing foreigners' seemed all too obvious. In the summer of 1918, Friedrich Syrup, the first President of the Reich Institute for Labour Exchange (*Reichsanstalt für Arbeitsvermittlung*) in the Weimar Republic, summarised the experiences that had been gained with hiring seasonal workers from Poland as follows: 'The fact that such a large flow of foreign workers involves serious national risks for the German body politic into which it is moving requires no further proof.'[1] In public debates during the Wilhelmine era, Poles in Germany were often seen as a threat to the German nation. This did not necessarily mean that these national considerations could not be set aside – and set aside they were: until the outbreak of the First World War, Polish labour was essential for Prussian agricultural production. At the same time, the admission of Polish immigrants was a thorny issue and was always accompanied and mitigated by restrictions, a search for alternatives and considerable debate.

The 'danger' posed by Polish immigrants was due to the complicated relationships between Germany and Poland which had led, in contemporary discussions, to a differentiation between the 'domestic Poles' (*Inlandspolen*) and 'foreign Poles' (*Auslandspolen*). The Prussian state had included large Polish minorities since the conquest of Silesia, the three divisions of Poland in the late eighteenth century and the reordering of Europe in 1815. At first, after the Congress of

---

[1] Syrup-Stettin, 'Industriearbeiter', p. 295.

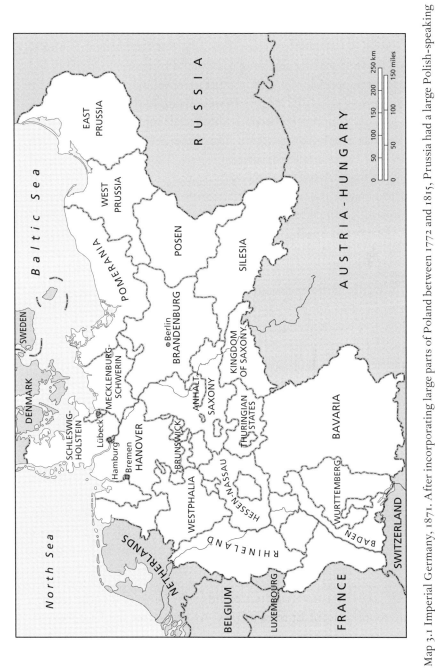

Map 3.1 Imperial Germany, 1871. After incorporating large parts of Poland between 1772 and 1815, Prussia had a large Polish-speaking population. In the province of Posen, for example, about two-thirds of the population declared Polish to be their mother tongue.

Vienna, Prussian policy toward the Polish minorities was guided by the spirit of enlightened absolutism, and issues of linguistic, religious and national equality were taken seriously. For the German national movement, the uprising in Congress Poland in 1830 had actually led to a surge in support for Poland; the Polish rebellion was even seen by them as a proxy struggle. In governmental circles, however – Prussia had pointedly supported Russia – the Polish minority was increasingly seen as a political problem. This view led to the 'new course' taken by the Prussian Oberpräsident Eduard Flotwell. He established a policy of Germanisation, especially in the province of Posen, that aimed to achieve the 'total amalgamation of the two nationalities'.[2] But Flotwell's policy was founded, in essence, on an understanding of power that was based on state dynasties and motivated more by bureaucratic reasons than national concerns; therefore, it aimed not at assimilation, but at political loyalty. A second phase of liberal policy toward the Poles during the *Vormärz* period, under Friedrich Wilhelm IV, was followed, in the course of the 1848 revolution, by a resurgence of national emotions that led to a popularisation of nationalism in Polish regions as well as German ones. From 1848 onward, German and Polish nationalisms were permanently defined in opposition to each other.[3]

The relationships between Germans and Poles therefore already had a long and complicated history when the foundation of the *kleindeutsch* Reich in 1871 marked an important transformation. In particular among the Polish speaking population, the foundation of the nation state was seen as a threat, but the attitude toward minority groups also changed in German nationalist discourse. The Polish minority was the biggest by some margin, numbering 2.4 million people and making up some 10 per cent of the population of Prussia (and 6 per cent of the population of the Reich as a whole). From the foundation of the Reich onward, the 'inner formation of the nation', aimed at reducing ethnic, social, linguistic and religious fragmentation, was

[2] Flottwell quotation taken from Frauendienst, 'Staatsbewußtsein', p. 320.
[3] For an overview of German policy toward Poland see Broszat, *Zweihundert Jahre*; Wehler, 'Polenpolitik'; Eley, 'German Politics'; Hagen, *Germans*; and Blanke, *Prussian Poland*.

seen as one of the most important tasks of the still 'incomplete nation state'.[4]

Policy toward the Polish minority was an important part of this policy of integration. In practice this took the form of a policy of Germanisation, which included the suppression of the Polish nobility and clergy, anti-Polish policies with regard to language and schooling, the anti-Catholic *Kulturkampf*, and finally the 'land struggle' (*Bodenkampf*) in the eastern provinces. To some extent, the policies followed on from those pursued under Flottwell, but there were major differences, since Flottwell had based his policies on the principle of state dynasties. Compared to the Danish and French minorities in Germany, Poles were in a more difficult situation – they had no nation state across the border that could offer them protection or to which they could choose to go in the event of a crisis or emergency. But an independent Polish state remained the political goal of Polish elites, and during the course of the nineteenth century it was increasingly supported by the wider Polish population. For this reason, all Poles in Germany were under suspicion of being involved in nationalist and separatist activities.

The 'domestic Poles' generally had Prussian – and thus, indirectly, German – citizenship, although a range of measures had been introduced to prevent their being treated as equals in legal terms. The main goal of Prussian policy toward the Poles was to assimilate and Germanise them. These attempts provoked considerable resistance. Some, especially the half-million Poles who had immigrated to the industrial cities of the Ruhrgebiet from the 1880s onward, were gradually integrating into German society.[5] The situation was more problematic in the eastern provinces of Prussia, especially in Posen, where most of the population spoke Polish. The aggressive policy of Germanisation introduced after the foundation of the Reich

---

[4] Schieder, *Deutsche Kaiserreich*, p. 39. Serrier, *Entre Allemagne*, p. 45 dates the most important change to 1867 when Prussia moved the German border to the east by setting up the North German Confederation.

[5] On the 'Ruhr Poles' see especially Kleßmann, *Polnische Bergarbeiter*; Murphy, *Gastarbeiter*; and Kulczycki, *Foreign Worker*. An overview of the situation in Berlin is given by Steinert, *Berlin*.

and with the *Kulturkampf*, and which intensified after the mid 1880s, was focused, in principle, on linguistic and cultural homogenisation (although the difference between the nations was upheld in some respects, for example in legal terms).[6]

By contrast, the 'foreign Poles', those living mainly in the western provinces of Russia and in Galicia, then ruled by Austria, were seen by many observers as a danger to the developing German nation state. There were fears that they would gradually infiltrate Prussia and that a broadly based Polish nationalist movement would develop. This fear was based not only on the open campaigning by the politically active nobility and clergy, but also on the cross-border movements of Polish workers. Since the 1850s, with mass emigration to the United States, a gradual labour shortage had developed in Prussian agriculture. The rapidly growing industrial regions in western Germany and the higher wages paid there also attracted workers. As a result, in the eastern Prussian border regions, growing numbers of workers had been recruited from Russian Poland.

From the 1880s onward, in particular, there were increasing public complaints that 'Polonisation is taking place in regions that had already been won for Germanic customs, culture and language'.[7] There was a widespread conviction that Polish immigrants were not merely filling the gaps left by the agricultural workers who had emigrated to western Germany or to the USA, but were in fact 'driving out' the Prussian rural population. As a result of the east–west migration to industrial areas taking place at the time, only part of which was made up of Polish migrants, Germany was gripped by fears of 'flooding' and 'foreign infiltration' (*Überfremdung*). Starting in March 1885, a number of regulations were issued in an attempt to reduce immigration by the 'foreign Poles'. Contravening these regulations could result in expulsion of the persons involved and their families, even where Polish workers were married to German women. In 1885, almost 40,000 Polish and Jewish people who did not hold Prussian citizenship were expelled from the four eastern

---

[6] See Gosewinkel, *Einbürgern*, pp. 211–18.
[7] Quoted in Bade, 'Kulturkampf', p. 128.

Prussian provinces, in spite of vehement protest in the press and in the Reichstag.[8]

From the late 1880s onward, the shortage of Polish seasonal workers to help with harvests became noticeable. Representatives of eastern German agriculture called for Polish seasonal workers to be readmitted, and organisations representing landowners organised a vociferous campaign for limitations on immigration to be suspended. The difference in the wages paid to Polish and to German workers was not the only reason for hiring Polish workers; the demand for mobile workers was also a reaction to the modernisation of agricultural cultivation. Rationalisation and the use of steam threshing machines were speeding up the transition from traditional estate farms to agro-industrial businesses. Another decisive factor was the crisis in German cereals cultivation caused by the pressure of the world market. As a result, many farmers in eastern Prussia switched to growing sugar beet, which was more labour-intensive than wheat. In this sense, their dependence on the cross-border mobility of labour was itself an effect of global economic interlinkages.

Individual reactions to push-and-pull factors cannot adequately explain the extent of Polish migratory movements that were clearly influenced by systemic factors. Between 1870 and 1914, more than 2 million Poles left their homeland for western Europe or the United States. About 90 per cent of those emigrating within Europe, and thus the vast majority of all those emigrating, moved to Germany. In many cases, we cannot differentiate clearly between the three phenomena of urbanisation, seasonal work in Prussia and emigration to the USA. For this reason we must view the migration of some 10 million Polish people during this period (including internal rural–urban migration) in a global context that transcended the bilateral relationship between Germany and the Polish-speaking provinces in central Europe.[9]

---

[8] See *ibid*. On the expulsions see also Neubach, *Ausweisung*; and Mai, *Polenpolitik*. On the immigration of *Ostjuden* see Werthheimer, *Unwelcome Strangers*; and 'Unwanted Element'.

[9] See Morawska, 'Labor Migrations'; and Zarnowska, 'Polnische Arbeiterschaft'.

As the demand for labour grew in Prussian agriculture, the Prussian ministry of agriculture and the Oberpräsidenten of the regions concerned joined the calls for Polish workers to be admitted. The ministry of the interior, however, and, in particular, von Goßler, the Prussian minister of education and cultural affairs, had reservations for national reasons and demanded more effective controls. In late 1890, a compromise was reached that remained in force until the World War. It was intended to deal with the competing economic and political interests. Firstly, Polish workers could be hired only between 1 April and 15 November every year. The workers were obliged to return home for the winter during what was called the 'restricted period' (*Karenzzeit*). This stipulation, introduced to prevent the workers settling permanently and thus altering the ethnic and national balance in eastern Prussia, remained in force in spite of many requests and occasional adjustments to the timing of the limits. Secondly, the use of seasonal workers was restricted to agriculture only, to prevent domestic Polish workers from coming into contact with foreign Polish labourers.[10]

This 1890 regulation, which was modified over the following years, was part of the changes in policy toward Poland under Bismarck's successor Caprivi, who in the early 1890s attempted to find a compromise with Poles as the largest minority group in the Reich. The regulation allowed the German landowners to employ large numbers of seasonal workers; the numbers actually increased each year. By 1913, over 360,000 foreigners were employed in agriculture in Prussia.[11] Almost half of these were women. The high proportion of female workers was partly due to the change toward cultivation of root crops. Work on these crops was mainly carried out in a crouched position (weeding, thinning, hacking, cutting off leaves etc.) and was regarded as women's work. It was believed that 'men, because of their heavy and stiff builds' could do this work 'only ... more slowly and

---

[10]   The starting-point for the history of Polish labour migration remains Nichtweiß, *Saisonarbeiter*. Another central account is Herbert, *Ausländerbeschäftigung*. See also Bade, 'Massenwanderung'; and Barfuß, *Gastarbeiter*.
[11]   For figures on the changes, see Herbert, *Ausländerbeschäftigung*, pp. 25–27.

less thoroughly than ... females and young people'.[12] A gender-based division of labour had become established even before Polish workers began to be employed. But these structures were reinforced by the lower wages paid for women's work. The female Polish workers were generally young and mobile single women. Legal regulations prevented entire families immigrating, just as the 'restricted period' was an attempt to prevent family formation.[13]

This detailed regulation of labour migration and the introduction of an obligation to return home temporarily was unique to Germany; there were no parallels in other European countries. It was complemented by measures introduced early in the twentieth century aiming to establish total state control of labour mobility. The reason for state intervention in the labour market was the existence of many problems that it was thought could not be solved by market forces. The central issue was that of attracting workers. The increase in demand had soon led to a booming trade in workers carried out by private 'human traders' and agents. Soon, there were some 7,000 agents competing for business, who were paid both by the individual workers and by the landowners. Competition between agents led to many conflicts, especially with the workers involved, and public complaints about the agents soon began to be heard.[14]

The landowners, on the other hand, wanted the state to intervene to deal with the problem of 'breaking of contracts'. About 10 per cent of all migrant and seasonal workers did not complete their contracts. In many cases, poor treatment and low wages would lead to workers abandoning one job and looking for a better one. Breaking their contracts was usually the only way that workers could protest against inadequate working conditions. But the landowners and the state agencies had no interest in this expansion of uncontrolled mobility.

In 1905, the German Central Office for Field Workers (*Deutsche Feldarbeiterzentralstelle*) was set up to tackle contract-breaking and

---

[12] Henatsch, *Problem*, p. 8.   [13] On this topic see Roller, *Frauenmigration*.
[14] On labour-market controls see also the following articles (frequently with identical content) by Klaus J. Bade: 'Politik und Ökonomie'; 'Preußengänger'; 'Transnationale Migration'; 'Billig und willig'; and 'Arbeitsmarkt'.

the activities of agents (*Agentenunwesen*), and more fundamentally
to allow immigration to be controlled more closely. The Central
Office was a privately managed association that was supervised by
the Prussian agriculture ministry. It also received financial support from the ministry and gradually took on an increasingly official character. In 1911, it was renamed the *Deutsche Arbeiterzentrale*
(German Workers' Agency). Its task was to take complete control
of the recruitment of foreign seasonal workers. After some initial
difficulties involving competition with private agents, the Central
Office got a monopoly on recruitment in 1908, with the introduction of the *Inlandslegitimierungszwang* (Obligation of Domestic
Legitimisation). At the border stations, each worker was issued with
an identity card that had to be handed over to his or her employer,
making it impossible for workers to change employer without permission. This legitimisation card also allowed the police to keep
tighter controls on those who broke their contracts or entered the
country illegally.[15]

This gradual increase in the powers of the Central Office and
increasing state control over the labour market marked the beginning of state discrimination against foreign workers. It is no coincidence that these measures were introduced in the period following
the Russian revolution in 1905, when the mobility of workers from
eastern Europe was seen as a potentially revolutionary influence. The
obligation to carry identity cards applied only to manual workers, not
to civil servants or white-collar workers. The 'restricted period', on
the other hand, applied only to Polish seasonal workers from Russia
and Austria-Hungary, but not to German migrants or to other foreign
migrant workers. This complex hierarchy of discrimination reveals
the importance that was assigned in Wilhelmine Germany to circulation at its eastern border; to the differentiation between domestic
and foreign Poles; and to the replacement, where possible, of Polish
workers by workers of other nationalities.

---

[15] On the foundation of the Central Office for Field Workers see Nichtweiß,
Saisonarbeiter, pp. 74–186. For a contemporary account see also Becker, *Regelung*.

Figure 3.1 Seasonal agricultural workers in Berlin.

'POLONISATION' – AND 'GERMANISATION'

Germany's eastern border was a central location for the construction of the German nation – in an almost literal sense. Prussian policy toward Poles was at some times, and despite the discrimination that took place, a policy of Germanisation and assimilation. Poles were to become Germans, just as, in Eugen Weber's words, peasants were turned into Frenchmen.[16] But these periods were interspersed with periods during which differences were recognised, and which even saw the granting of institutional concessions such as increases in regional self-administration – for example between 1815 and 1830 and during the 1840s. The interaction between Germans and Poles was also a determining factor in the development of both nations' national identities, identities that were increasingly pitted against each other.[17]

---

[16] Weber, *Peasants into Frenchmen*.
[17] For the period up to the foundation of the Reich, see Böhning, *Nationalpolnische Bewegung*; and Pletzing, *Völkerfrühling*. On the late nineteenth century, see Serrier, *Entre Allemagne*, which focuses on Posen.

This does not mean that the eastern boundary of the Reich was the only, or even the most important, place where national difference was (re)produced. Germany's longstanding, influential and frequently conflict-laden relationship with France, the 'Fatherland of the Enemies', was even more important for the development of the German sense of being different.[18] But less attention has been paid to the country's relationships with eastern areas of Europe, although, as with the Polish-speaking population, these relationships reached far into the Kaiserreich and are capable of undermining the idea that the German Kaiserreich was a nation state.[19] It is also clear that the delimitation between Germans and Poles was not a new development. German fears of 'Polonisation' were based, like the Polish national movement, on existing national discourses. But by the end of the nineteenth century the context of these interactions changed fundamentally. The movements of hundreds of thousands of mobile workers, linked to an increasingly globalised labour market, was a new phenomenon, as was the context of imperialism and colonialism that, as we will see, shaped Germany's relationships with 'the Poles'.

The intensity with which issues of belonging were discussed was partly because it was difficult to draw a clear boundary between 'Germany' and 'Poland'.[20] The fluctuation of Polish seasonal workers played an important role in this regard. When discussing German fears of a national revolution by Poles, reference is usually made to the activities of the Polish nobility and clergy. But for both the wider German public and Prussian bureaucrats, the mobility of Polish workers was an equally unsettling phenomenon and one that, initially, had nothing to do with political propaganda. The opportunities for uncontrolled mobility, border transgressions and infiltration were sources of anxiety for a political system that was paying increasing attention to population issues and to issues of composition.

---

[18] Jeismann, *Vaterland*; Nipperdey, *Deutsche Geschichte 1800–1866*, p. 11; Luys, *Anfänge*, esp. pp. 29ff.; Weber, *Lyrik*, esp. pp. 156ff.; Düding, *Nationalismus*, esp. pp. 28ff.; Buschmann, *Einkreisung*; and Bielefeld, *Nation und Gesellschaft*.

[19] See Ther, 'Deutsche Geschichte'.

[20] See Kopp, 'Contesting Borders', pp. xv–xvi.

Debates about the employment of foreign Poles in Prussian agriculture were shaped by a diffuse fear of gradual 'Polonisation'. Many commentators agreed with the maxim of 'Germany for the Germans', with which the Leipzig national economist Wilhelm Stieda had summarised widespread demands: 'Amalgamation with all these foreign elements can only be fatal for the purity of the Germanic tribes [*Stämme*].'[21] The organs of organised nationalism, for example that of the *Alldeutscher Verband* (Pan-German League), were especially active, using aggressive language to argue for the closure of borders. But approval of anti-Polish slogans extended far beyond the ultranationalist groups. A patriotic commitment to 'keeping foreigners out of the entire German labour market' was widespread, although there were also critical voices.[22]

The comparison between nationalist slogans and hard-nosed economic concerns, between ideology and interests that is customary in the literature[23] does not adequately convey the complexities of the debate about agricultural workers. What is striking, instead, is that economic arguments for the use of Polish workers were also framed within nationalist discourse. Demands for the borders to be opened were justified not with egotistical profit-seeking or references to the laws of the liberal market, but by the overriding national interest in the survival of Prussian agriculture. Those few arguing against the restricted-period policy, too, usually pitched their arguments in a framework of the 'national interest'. For the agricultural economist Friedrich Aereboe, for example, 'amalgamation' (of the populations) was not a real problem, or at least not if the numbers immigrating were fairly limited. He believed that keeping the border closed and enforcing temporary returns home acted to preserve and reinforce Polish nationality, while permanent immigration would make gradual integration possible – and 'defuse' the national issue.[24] In addition, the landowners were conscious of the 'national-political

[21] Stieda, 'Beschäftigung', p. 172.
[22] Knoke, *Ausländische Wanderarbeiter*, p. 105.
[23] See for example Nichtweiß, *Saisonarbeiter*, p. 19; and Herbert, *Ausländerbeschäftigung*, p. 32.
[24] Aereboe, *Ländliche Arbeiterfrage*, pp. 8ff.

risks' of Polish immigration. Even the German Agricultural Council (*Deutsche Landwirtschaftsrat*) insisted that the 'increasing dependence of German agriculture on foreign seasonal workers [must] be reduced and gradually eliminated because of the national and economic dangers it entails'.[25]

This combination of economic necessities and national issues can be identified in most comments and contributions in this heated debate. This even applies to the Catholic church, although it took considerable interest in the day-to-day situation of the migrant workers, most of whom were Catholics, and was thus prepared to criticise some governmental actions.[26] From a Protestant point of view, however, the religion of the migrants was part of the problem – though it was associated with general patriotic concerns about the 'importation of smallpox and trachoma, moral degeneration, tendency towards rebellion' and other aspects of national and cultural infiltration.[27]

It was only the Polish members of the Prussian parliament who openly criticised this nationalist agitation and attempted to counteract the fears of 'Polonisation' by Galician agricultural workers. The Polish members claimed that anyone who was familiar with the 'low mental status' of the Galician workers could not possibly imagine that they would be responsible for political infiltration. 'People like these are not capable of being dangerous, these total political washouts!'[28] The actual measures taken by the Prussian government, and the anti-Polish sentiments the measures expressed, were also regularly criticised by the Social Democrats both in the Reichstag and in their organ *Vorwärts*, which did not mince its words. The obligation to obtain identity cards, in particular, was strongly resisted. This resulted in a 1909 resolution by the Reichstag that was also supported by the Centre party, the Polish representatives and the *Freisinnige* party. But

[25] Deutscher Landwirtschaftsrat, Beschlüsse der 42. Plenarversammlung, 10–13 February 1914, Geheimes Staatsarchiv Berlin (GStA) PK, 1. HA, 87 B, no. 222, p. 153.

[26] See Nichtweiß, *Saisonarbeiter*, pp. 175–86.

[27] *Deutsch-Evangelische Korrespondenz* of 1912, quoted in Wygodzinski, 'Wanderarbeiter', p. 367.

[28] Question by Deputy Szmula, in *Stenographische Berichte über die Verhandlungen des Abgeordnetenhauses*, 15th session, 9 February 1899, p. 431.

opinions were divided even among the Social Democrats. Although many supported the rights of the Polish workers, and even hoped that they would engage in protest action, many voices could be heard to issue warnings about the negative consequences of immigration and describing foreign workers as scabs and strike-breakers.[29]

This close connection between economic and nationalist ideas could be found not only in discussions in the print media but also in the many empirical and academic studies commissioned from the late 1880s onward by interested parties such as the Prussian ministry of agriculture, the Association for Social Policy (*Verein für Sozialpolitik*) and the Federation of Farmers (*Bund der Landwirte*). In addition, a large number of independent studies were carried out at the universities. The reports discussed the whole spectrum of problems related to the 'scarcity of people' in rural Prussia: flight from the land, urbanisation, rural industrialisation and emigration. Most of the commentators reached the conclusion that the flight from the land and the scarcity of workers were mainly the result of the 'displacement' (*Verdrängung*) of German workers by cheaper Polish ones. The most influential argument along these lines was put forward by Max Weber who, in 1893, published a large-scale study on rural work based on a survey by the Association for Social Policy. His warning against recruiting Polish workers from abroad – 'then the displacement of German workers will continue and, along with Germandom [*Deutschtum*] and the capacity of the depopulating East to resist, the human material needed for colonisation will be lost' – was quoted repeatedly in the following years and cited as scientific proof for the necessity of sealing the nation's borders.[30] 'I believe it to be the duty of all the groups involved', Anton Knoke summed up in 1911, explicitly referring to Weber's study, 'to press for a remedy, to counteract migrant labour with all possible force and energy, and if possible to eliminate it altogether'.[31]

[29] On the SPD's position see Nichtweiß, *Saisonarbeiter*, pp. 154–74. A biased account is given in Elsner, 'Deutsche Arbeiterbewegung', p. 91. On the subject in general see also Wehler, *Sozialdemokratie*, pp. 112–64.

[30] Weber, *Landarbeiter*, p. 926.   [31] Knoke, *Ausländische Wanderarbeiter*, p. 86.

The 'displacement thesis' was based mainly on demographic and economic concepts: supply and demand, push-and-pull factors, wage differentials and urbanisation. But the idea of displacement was also seen as disquieting because of its cultural connotations. Polish workers were not only cheaper, but different; as Max Weber emphasised, they were members of a lower 'level of civilisation' (*Kulturstufe*).[32] This belief was not merely widespread; it was almost ubiquitous. It was not new, either, but was based on older stereotypes dating from the first half of the nineteenth century that had already entailed beliefs about dirt and uncleanliness and general social backwardness.[33] Although supporters of immigration cited the Poles' 'undemandingness' and retarded cultural development as positive features, most commentators viewed them as threatening. Ernst von Glasenapp, for example, a Landrat in Marienburg in western Prussia, and a Conservative member of the Prussian parliament, feared an actual 'civilisatory regression' (*Kulturrückschritt*) if Polish mobility was not stopped. 'Anyone who has ever seen these people can really say that extensive treatment with soap and water is needed to bring them to some extent into a condition in which they can work and live together with other people.'[34]

In most cases, it was not economic competition but fears of infiltration and of a 'cultural difference' that were the main reasons for demanding a policy of immigration control. Although a fear of competition from lower Polish labour costs was certainly discussed, the debate was largely conducted in the language of cultural concepts such as the topos of 'German work'. 'There is no work', Knoke emphasised, 'from which the German worker shrinks', and thus there was no need to recruit workers from abroad. In any case, no enrichment could be expected from the Poles ('crawling servility' … 'unhygienic habits') while the 'Germanic worker' ('robust' … 'intelligent') performed 'at least as good work as the foreigners' in any possible area of work.[35] The theme of cultural difference was often accompanied by

---

[32] Weber, *Sozial- und Wirtschaftsgeschichte*, p. 452.
[33] See for example Hofmann, 'Radikale Wandel'.
[34] Von Glasenapp, in *Stenographische Berichte über die Verhandlungen des Abgeordnetenhauses*, 16th session, 10 February 1899, p. 457.
[35] Knoke, *Ausländische Wanderarbeiter*, pp. 62–65.

worries about the values and morals of the German nation, prompted mainly by the mobility of Polish women. From the lack of separate accommodation for men and women to the permissiveness of young single women and the supposedly high number of births outside marriage, the 'national threat' being conjured up was by no means a gender-neutral one.[36]

The administrative response to these problems was to introduce the 'restricted period', the 'forced return' during winter months. But some of those involved also demanded more effective measures, arguing that the Poles should be gradually pushed back and that the eastern border should be sealed off for good. The most important body arguing along these lines was the German Eastern Marches Society (*Deutscher Ostmarkenverein*). This had been founded in 1894 by three nationally minded large landowners in the province of Posen as a reaction to anxiety about the 'Slavic flood', and stood for a fundamentalist policy of 'de-Polonisation' and of cultural and material 'Germanisation'. It focused on attaining a ban on the movement of Polish people to Prussian cities, on the purchasing of Polish land and the settling of Germans there, and on promoting the establishment of the language and culture of the German 'leading culture' (*Leitkultur*). Some of these ideas were based on measures taken during the 1830s, but the policy of Germanisation pursued during the 1880s was far more systematic. By 1914, the association had over 50,000 members. In spite of its sometimes aggressive rhetoric, the Eastern Marches Society had considerable influence on public debate and on the Prussian government.[37]

From the beginning, one of the major concerns raised by the Eastern Marches Society was the influx of Polish seasonal workers. In 1903, the Central Office for Field Workers was set up with the approval of the Prussian ministry of agriculture and the support of

---

[36] See for example the investigations of the 'influence of migrant work [*Wanderarbeit*] on the ethical and moral life of the migrant workers [*Wanderarbeiter*]' in Schmidt, *Wanderarbeiter*, pp. 198–205. See also Roller, *Frauenmigration*, pp. 114–29.

[37] On the *Ostmarkenverein* see Galos, Gentzen and Jakóbczyk, *Hakatisten*; Tims, *Germanizing Prussian Poland*; Grabowski, *Nationalismus*; and Oldenburg, *Ostmarkenverein*.

the Pan-German League. Its task was to prevent the immigration of foreign workers, especially Polish ones. Instead, Polish families from Posen (known as 'domestic Poles') were to be encouraged to emigrate to the United States. At the same time German families from Galicia or Hungary were to be settled on the farms thus freed up. The plans failed because the Austrian authorities rejected them – and because the Pan-German League, which had no interest in reducing the size of German communities abroad, vetoed them.[38]

The second strategy pursued was to hire workers of other nationalities to prevent the 'Polonisation' of Prussian agriculture. 'As soon as the economic situation to some extent allows', an official statement from the Eastern Marches Society declared, 'Slavic immigration is to be pushed back zone by zone … and eventually the border shall be closed completely to Slavic migrant workers'.[39] During its first few years, however, the Central Office was less than successful in its attempts to Germanise rural workers, and it came to public attention mainly because of a number of political scandals and irregularities. In 1904, it had been able to send only around 200 seasonal workers to Germany – at a time when demand ran to hundreds of thousands.

It was only in 1905, when the Prussian ministry of agriculture became more active, providing financial support and placing it on a statutory basis, that the Central Office gradually became an official organisation for recruiting foreign workers. The irony was that an institution that had been founded with the explicit goal of ending the recruitment of foreign workers was now being given the monopoly on the recruitment of such workers. The open and aggressive policy of Germanisation now had to be scaled down, as otherwise it would have been impossible to meet the demand for labour. But the nationalist agenda was not abandoned. The first step taken was to introduce rigid controls on entering and leaving the country and to distinguish clearly 'inside' from 'outside'. One of the first measures organised by

---

[38] See Nichtweiß, *Saisonarbeiter*, pp. 79ff.

[39] Deutscher Ostmarken-Verein, 'Zur Frage der Zulassung russisch-polnischer Arbeiter' (8 December 1900), in GStA PK, I. HA, 87 B, no. 215, p. 9.

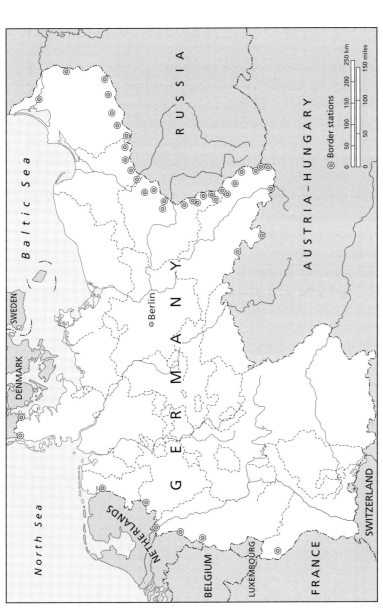

Map 3.2 Between 1907 and 1913, the German Central Office for Field Workers (*Deutsche Feldarbeiterzentralstelle*) set up thirty-nine border stations to control the influx of seasonal workers. Here, the incoming labourers needed to prove that they had a valid contract with a German employer. A medical doctor was attached to each control station and controlled sanitary measures. The border stations were nodal points at which checks on mobility were connected to notions of cultural superiority and hygienic nationalism.

the Central Office for Field Workers was to set up thirty-nine border posts to regulate labour mobility.[40]

The strategy pursued by the Central Office, which increasingly became the official position taken by the Prussian government, was based on a policy of differentiation at a time of fluctuation. Unambiguous and, where possible, permanent distinctions were to be made between 'at home' and 'abroad', Germans and Poles, the domestic and the foreign. The instruments used were the obligation to carry passports, the 'restricted period' and increased staffing for border posts. In a confused situation, 'German work', 'German soil' and Germanisation were to be used to create Germans – and also to create Poles.

Polish and German nationalisms were mutually referential. The setting-up of the German Eastern Marches Society was answered on the Polish side by the setting up of an organisation called *Straż* ('Guard'), which campaigned, like its German equivalent, for seg-regation by nationality (under the motto *Swój do swego*: 'Each to his own').[41] The 'struggle for land' created by the policy of expropriation was also part of a process of nationalisation on both sides, which was reinforced by nationalist groups.[42] As in Germany, migratory move-ments across the boundaries between Prussia and Russia and Austria served to reinforce Polish national feelings.[43] Polish nationalists were afraid that the seasonal workers would bring 'many German charac-teristics' home and could thus cause gradual 'denationalisation'. To guard against this danger, organisations were created to reinforce the national consciousness of the workers entering and leaving.[44] The strategy was often based on that followed in the United States (and in the Ruhrgebiet) where, after arrival, immigrants were welcomed

[40] See Nichtweiß, *Saisonarbeiter*, pp. 93–129, 141.

[41] See Grabowski, *Nationalismus*.

[42] See for example the outline by Schultz, 'Bürger von Birnbaum'.

[43] On the mutual and reciprocal construction of national identity see Serrier, *Entre Allemagne*, esp. pp. 109–168. For an overview of migratory movements see also Bitner-Nowak, 'Nachbarschaft'.

[44] Calendar of the Polish Emigration Association for the year 1914, in GStA PK, I. HA, 87 B, no. 222, p. 289.

by compatriots or clergymen and encouraged to become involved in the church, in voluntary organisations and in Polish cultural life. The result of this patriotic activity in the target regions of migrations was that the Poles, Ruthenians and Jews who usually left together, for example travelling from Galicia, were soon converted into members of different national groups. Emigration contributed to turning neighbours and acquaintances into separate linguistic and ethnic communities.[45] Both in Germany and in Poland, the increase in mobility was accompanied by a policy of nationalisation.[46]

It has become customary for historians to explore the constructed, contingent nature of these processes of forming a nation: invented traditions and imagined communities. This includes paying attention to the gender-specific dimension of ideas of the nation, as in the typical comparison between a female, passive Polish nation (and, frequently, landscape), and a German coloniser imagined in male terms.[47] Yet, in many studies, modern nation states remain the vanishing points of the analysis, and traces of national teleologies have survived even the constructivist turns of historiography. How problematic this is becomes immediately evident if we take a look at those ethnic and religious groupings that during the Wilhelmine era saw themselves neither as simply German nor as definitively Polish, nor, indeed, as national entities at all. Frequently, national assignations were only one, and not always the most important, element of a multi-layered web of religious, linguistic/cultural, social and political identities that seemed to contradict the logic of the nation state.[48] This complexity and multiplicity has often been simplified, not only

[45] On this subject see the classic and still inspirational study by Thomas and Znaniecki, *Polish Peasant*. See also Morawska, 'Labor Migrations'; and Sanders and Morawska, *Polish-American Community Life*, with further references.

[46] This is not just the perspective of those involved; it has remained the historiographical paradigm even in retrospect. Both German and Polish historians have interpreted the contacts, conflicts and debates in divided Poland as contributions to the process of nationalisation. On German and Polish research on the Polish provinces of the German empire in general, see Hackmann, *Ostpreußen*.

[47] For the gender–history dimension of German views of Poland, see Koch, *DruckBilder*.

[48] See the discussion by Smith, 'An Preußens Rändern'.

by the policies of the German Reich and by the Polish national movement, but also by historical research in retrospect. In this way the Masurians, Kashubians, Polish Lithuanians and Ermlanders, and also the Upper Silesians, became 'peoples without a history', as it was only the formation of a nation state (or at least the desire for one, if only as an unfulfilled utopian project) that would allow them to be seen as actors in history.[49] The consolidation of German–Polish identities thus implied the elimination of any possibility of an 'in-between'.

In recent years, since the death of the blocs generated by the Cold War has allowed particularised nationalisms to resurface and the process of European unification has fuelled scepticism about the homogenising policies of the nation state, historians have again been turning their attention to some of these groups. Prussian Upper Silesia, for example, is one of the regions where it was almost impossible to assign the population to clear national categories. In addition to Polish and German nationalisms, which were both loudly propounded by organised interest groups and which were, their representatives believed, mutually exclusive, the population had strong regional ties that persisted for a comparatively long time. From the 1870s onward, there was a politically active Szlonzokian movement that even considered establishing its own written language. Even after the First World War a regional movement developed in Upper Silesia that was based on popular support and that sometimes had the traits of a national movement. The teleological view so characteristic of historiography, which examines 'we'-groups in terms of the development of their nation state (or at least its projected development), tends to neglect the manifold and often complementary identifications that co-existed even during the era of the nation state.[50]

Helmut Walser Smith goes even further in his attempt to reconstruct the complex population constellations in eastern Prussia without falling into the trap of the German–Polish dichotomy. Instead of using regional affinities to relativise and add to the concept of national

---

[49] On the history of these ethnic groups see, among others, Kossert, *Preußen*, *Deutsche oder Polen?*; Blanke, *Polish Speaking Germans?*; and Kamusella, 'Language'.

[50] See Ther, 'Grenzen des Nationalismus'; and Kamusella, 'Language'.

identities, he questions the concept itself. Identity, he argues, is not the correct starting-point for investigations that wish to focus on the multiple links between people without assuming clearly separated communities. For example, religious affinities and practices were used not only to establish boundaries (such as between the Masurians and the Poles) but equally to bridge differences that later, in the era of nationalisms, were seen as absolute. Thus, Dietrichswalde in the Ermland region was, during the 1870s, a place of pilgrimage both for nationalist Poles and for Protestant Masurians – something that is surprising only in retrospect, in our nation-state-coloured view. And the large number of markets and places of exchange in Russian Congress Poland to which Masurians travelled were examples of the way Poles, Jews and Masurians had a shared community life, in a region and era where borders were permeable.[51]

Smith reconstructs a history of experience before that experience was limited by the reduction of individuals' views of themselves to the categories of national identity. This is a history of diminution, loss and impoverishment. It reveals the complexity of social conditions, relations and interactions before the 'tyranny of the national'[52] erected boundaries and physically interrupted these interactions. This is an important contribution to a more complex story but, at the same time, some caution is necessary. This view of a seemingly fuller, more complete history bears traces of a nostalgia that can only understand the victory of modern state-based nationalism as violent suppression. This literature could be read as suggesting that an authentic, truthful experience of human relationships was made impossible by the artificial and limiting ideology of nationalism: the establishment of nation states as a history of alienation.[53]

But this longing for a more ancient form of co-existence is by no means 'innocent'. In fact, it is the product of precisely the development that it wishes to forget or to correct. The dream of pre-national communities is the result of a long history of nationalisation that creates a concept of 'real' traditions as its Other. Thus, the sometimes

[51] See Smith, 'An Preußens Rändern'.   [52] Noiriel, *Tyrannei*.
[53] This is also suggested by Kamusella, 'Language', esp. pp. 69–70.

repressive and homogenising processes of nation-formation create the impression that the pre-national world was peaceful and idyllic. The longing for pre-national completeness should thus be understood more as a symptom of the traumatic, possibly violent, national development of subject formation, not as alienation, which requires a prior condition of completeness. Instead, then, of attempting to reconquer the past – at least in historiography – and to undo the processes of nation-formation, I focus here on these processes of the construction of the national itself. The nationalisation of identities and social relationships should not be 'naturalised' as an organic development, but neither should it be stigmatised as a veil thrown over an earlier, happier age.

THE 'REAL' COLONY

Discussions and debates about the immigration, admission and recruitment of Polish seasonal workers were constantly accompanied by fears of 'Polonisation'. But there were always voices that emphasised the positive aspects of employing Poles. Although they appeared in opposition, the two positions were not necessarily contradictory. Friedrich Syrup, for example, who did not hesitate to list the negative consequences of unmanaged immigration, could not avoid acknowledging the advantages that transferring undemanding, low-cost work to foreign workers would entail. The creation of a sub-class below German workers would mean, he argued, 'a promotion of national energy desirable in terms of hygiene'. By 'elevating' German workers 'to a higher level of civilisation' (*Kulturstufe*), as the Essen Regierungsassessor Bodenstein agreed, it could 'be described as a positive development that foreign workers are available to carry out primitive work'.[54]

Hiring Polish workers for industrial and seasonal work could thus be portrayed as part of a cultural mission that aimed to civilise the German lower orders. Only through recruitment from the East, it was argued, would German workers be able to leave low-level,

---

[54] Syrup-Stettin, 'Industriearbeiter', p. 300; and Bodenstein, *Beschäftigung*, p. 9.

unhygienic and dangerous work behind them. But the importation of workers was not merely a precondition for this 'inner mission'. The relationship was more complex: the cultural mission was interested not only in the German underclasses but also in the Polish workers themselves. 'Thus', the Prussian Oberpräsident of Westphalia, von Studt, noted in a memorandum about the employment of Polish workers, 'a good deed is being done toward the Poles themselves'.[55] The prevailing language of *Hebung* (elevation) rested on a general assumption of superiority that was expressed increasingly in terms of a civilising mission. 'It is to the Prussian rulers that the Polish peasant owes his humane form of existence', as the German-language journal *Lehrer-Zeitung* phrased it in a typical example in 1900, making reference to German work, culture and education as the appropriate means to propel the Polish population into modernity.[56] The hegemony of the discourse of improvement was further corroborated by its appropriation by reform-minded Polish elites, who frequently subscribed to a notion of modernisation in which German culture was a central model.[57]

It is striking to what extent the rhetorical arsenal levelled against the Polish groups was reminiscent of the synchronous attempts to legitimise control in the overseas colonies. When Studt propagated the Germanification of the Polish population in order to improve the 'inferior elements, prone as they are to excesses, and featuring questionable characteristics, in particular among the women', his choice of vocabulary did not differ substantially from the rhetoric of missionaries and governmental 'native policy' in Germany's African colonies: the aim was to have the subject population 'benefit from the economic and moral superiority of Germanness'.[58]

Were these parallels and synchronicities mere coincidence? Or was there a connection between overseas and continental expansion,

---

[55] Quoted in Kleßmann, *Polnische Bergarbeiter*, p. 63.
[56] *Posener Lehrer-Zeitung* (13 December 1900), quoted from Thomas Serrier, *Provinz Posen, Ostmark, Wielkopolska*, p. 114.
[57] *Ibid.*
[58] Quoted in Kleßmann, *Polnische Bergarbeiter*, p. 63. On the concept of the civilising mission in general, see Barth and Osterhammel, *Zivilisierungsmissionen*.

between colonisation, settlement and segregation in Poznan and in Tanzania? Traditionally, these two spheres of imperial projections have been treated in virtual isolation from each other. The literature situates German colonies in Africa and in the South Pacific only, and it assumes that colony and metropole were safely separated by racial difference, cultural incompatibility and the sea. For a long time, historical analysis has eschewed the question of colonialism in Europe. This perspective was supported by general definitions of colonialism, propounded by academics and by the United Nations, that hinge on the assumption of 'structures of dependency vis-à-vis a geographically distant "mother country"'.[59] Possible colonial relations within Europe were thus rendered invisible by conceptual barriers.

In recent years, attempts have been made to correct this view and to bring the notion of colonialism to bear on European history.[60] And on the Kaiserreich. 'The true German counterpart to India or Algeria', David Blackbourn, along with others, has suggested, 'was not Cameroon: it was *Mitteleuropa*'.[61] In the following part of this chapter, I will build on this literature and argue that German encounters with the European East indeed can be read as a form of broadly defined colonialism. It will be important, however, to remain attentive to the particularities and specificities of the situation in central Europe that cannot be equated with the patterns of rule and social hierarchies in the overseas colonies. This is not least because the 'colonial' dimension of Polish Prussia was not only the result of notions of superiority, and of the similarity of discursive tropes. Rather, it must be seen as part and parcel of processes of global integration and the forms of difference it produced between various locations.[62]

---

[59] Osterhammel, *Kolonialismus*, p. 16. On the position taken by the United Nations in a 1960 resolution, see Furber, 'Near as Far', p. 558.

[60] See Broers, 'Cultural Imperialism'; Hechter, *Internal Colonialism*; Brower and Lazzerini, *Russia's Orient*; Dickie, *Darkest Italy*; Schneider, *Italy's Southern Question*; and Feichtinger, Prutsch and Csáky, *Habsburg postcolonial*.

[61] Blackbourn, 'Kaiserreich', p. 322.

[62] For a similar argument see Kopp, 'Contesting Borders', with considerable emphasis on literary history; Charle, *La Crise*; and Ther, 'Deutsche Geschichte'.

In the public consciousness, the colonial dimension of the Prussian East was by no means a new pheonomenon. From approximately the 1830s onward, the German perception of Poland had changed. During this period, the discourse about Poland became reconfigured within national and soon colonial parameters. The colonial overtones of the 'Polish question', and the explicit references to colonisation, were a prominent feature of the discourse of the times. They played a central role in attempts to connect the civilising project of the nineteenth century to longstanding traditions of German settlement in the European East. Accounts of Poznan and Silesia regularly alluded to the 'Drive toward the East' and the expansion of the Teutonic Order. The civilising-mission rhetoric typically appropriated the medieval notion of Germans 'carrying the banner of culture' (*Kulturträgertum*).[63]

Clearly, settler 'colonisation' since the Middle Ages needs to be differentiated from modern colonialism, as it was not tied to an expansionist nation state, not premised on the centrality of national discourse and not predicated on notions of race that were to be crucial for modern forms of colonialism.[64] Even if, in contemporary parlance, there was a strong sense of continuity, it is important to recognise the extent to which the German–Polish encounter had been transformed. Geographic and cultural difference – not necessarily pejorative but also encompassing tropes such as the 'noble Polish folk' – were replaced, from the 1830s onward, by linear concepts of development and hierarchies of progress. In the accounts of German travellers to the Polish provinces, for example, the Poles were no longer primarily strange and different, but increasingly characterised by a language of lack and backwardness.[65] Visits to distant lands were interpreted as travels into the past – this resembles what Johannes Fabian describes as the emergence of a colonising gaze and, in his terms, the 'denial of

---

[63] See Meyer, *Drang nach Osten*; Kaczmarczyk, 'German Colonisation'. See also Wippermann, 'Gen Ostland'; and Wojtczak, *Literatur*, pp. 156–69.

[64] On the medieval colonisation of the East see especially Schlesinger, *Deutsche Ostsiedlung*. See also Wippermann, *Ordensstaat*, esp. pp. 154–96; Wippermann, *Drang nach Osten*, pp. 85–104; Zernack, 'Landesausbau'; and Hackmann, *Ostpreußen*, pp. 102–9.

[65] See Struck, *Nicht West–nicht Ost*. See also his '*Terra Incognita*'.

co-evalness'. Again, therefore, it is instructive to note the synchron-icity of this transformation on the Prussian eastern borders with a general shift toward thinking in developmental stages and concepts of temporality in Europe's relation to the colonial world.[66]

Gustav Freytag's best-selling 1854 novel *Soll und Haben* ('Debit and Credit'), which by 1922 was in its 114th edition, is the best-known example of German colonial consciousness. The Polish population is described as inferior in both cultural and 'racial' terms. Freytag describes the civilisatory 'elevation' and the creation of order in Poland as a German responsibility.[67] The central topos, which com-bines many stereotypes and prejudices about Poles, was the concept of the 'Polish economy' (*polnische Wirtschaft*). This term covered a wide range of negatively connoted characteristics ranging from chaos, recklessness and extravagance to ignorance and, in particular, lack of hygiene. In political, social and economic terms, the 'Polish economy' was a synonym for backwardness and by definition the opposite of 'German work'.[68]

One of the privileged sites where developmentalist tropes were linked to the notion of colonial expansion was the *Ostmarkenroman* (novel of the Eastern Marches). Kristin Kopp has persuasively argued that this literature, originating in the early 1890s, fused tropes from the colonial movement with the *Heimat* idea. It depicted German Poland as a wasteland, as a landscape of colonial conquest, as a 'Wild East' with many parallels to the 'Wild West' in North America. The novels were characterised by rural settings, imbued with traditional social values, and based on a civilising mission rhetoric that also allowed the border between Germans and Poles to be maintained discursively.[69] The texts bespeak a fear of non-identifiability and a

---

[66] Fabian, *Time*; and Osterhammel, *Entzauberung*.

[67] Freytag, *Soll und Haben*. On this topic see also Feindt, 'Polnische Aufstände'; Müller-Seidel, 'Fontane', p. 47.

[68] On this topic see, for examples of the extensive literature on stereotypes, Seepel, *Polenbild*; Zitzewitz, *Polenbild*; Lammich, *Osteuropabild*; Polczynska, *Im polnischen Wind*, pp. 240–49; Orlowski, *Polnische Wirtschaft*, esp. pp. 275–94; and Wojtczak, *Literatur*, pp. 115–30. For a less successful account see Pleitner, *Die 'vernünftige' Nation*. On the context see also Wippermann, 'Antislavismus'.

[69] Kopp, 'Constructing Racial Difference'.

lack of clearly marked boundaries that are typical, as Ann Stoler has argued, for colonial frontiers.[70]

While the discursive appropriation of the European East thus owed much to colonial rhetoric, it is worth remembering that it was employed in a particular situation, as among its backgrounds were the Culture Wars of the 1870s and 1880s. Initially, the *Kulturkampf* in the Polish-speaking areas of Prussia had two separate aims. Primarily, the term implied a challenge to Catholic ultramontanists, at whom the policy of the separation of church and state was directed. But it also entailed a nationalist and anti-Polish component. In this sense the *Kulturkampf* did not end, as is often suggested, in 1887. The anti-Polish provisions in the laws on schooling were not reversed, and even after the turn of the century the relaxation of rules on religious instruction remained an issue of major concern to the Catholic church.[71] Right up until the First World War, German policy toward Poland retained aspects of a *Kulturkampf* in which anti-Catholic measures and ethnic-*völkisch* nationalism were mutually reinforcing. In many cases, too, resistance against the recruitment of Polish seasonal workers seemed to be motivated not primarily by preventing 'the Polish population in the country increasing, but … more by religious issues'.[72] But this contradiction was more apparent than real. In practice, these motivations did not compete, but combined to determine policy toward Polish immigration. The limits on the employment of seasonal workers were thus nothing more than a '"*Kulturkampf*" in the labour market'.[73]

This double thrust of the Culture Wars, however, was complicated by the fact that here, too, a colonial dynamic was at work. As we know, it was Rudolf Virchow, the doctor, anthropologist and liberal politician, who coined the term *Kulturkampf*. What is less known is that, along with its religious dimensions, the term also stood for a change in the understanding of *Kultur* that can only be understood in terms of

[70] Stoler, 'Rethinking Colonial Categories'.
[71] On the link between the *Kulturkampf* and anti-Polish Germanisation policies see Smith, *German Nationalism*; and Trzeciakowski, *Kulturkampf*.
[72] Abgeordneter Graf Strachwitz, in *Stenographische Berichte über die Verhandlungen des Abgeordnetenhauses*, 16th session, 10 February 1899, p. 476.
[73] Bade, 'Kulturkampf'.

the colonial context. While the usual definition of *Kultur* in historiography focused on the concept of humanist education and, in general, took a relativist view of culture, Virchow picked up on what he perceived as the decidedly modern concept of *Kultur* as used by German ethnology, of which he himself was a pioneer. Ethnology posited an insuperable dichotomy between *Natur- und Kulturvölker*: 'natural', or primitive, and 'cultured', or civilised, peoples. As a result only the *Kulturvölker* were capable of development. The *Naturvölker* were truly 'peoples without history' and could be investigated by the discipline of anthropology, using scientific methods.[74]

This definition of *Kultur*, shaped by colonialist concepts of development, made the *Kulturkampf* a debate between pre-modern backwardness and cultural progress. If Constantin Rössler, one of the most vehement anti-Catholic polemicists, hoped that the result of the conflict would be that the German nation would become 'a model for the intellectual life of the *Kulturvölker*', this view included both dimensions of the *Kulturkampf*: Catholicism as difference and also as an earlier stage of development.[75] Virchow, too, saw Catholicism as 'absolutely incompatible with the culture of which we see ourselves the bearers' – but not because it was different, as the historist definition of *Kultur* suggested, but because it had been untouched by historical development. The 'contradiction of Papism and the modern world' was then no longer understood in relativist terms, but rather as diachronic stages of the obsolete followed by the modern.[76] Thus, in complex ways, the three complementing logics of the *Kulturkampf* – a religious but also ethno-national conflict that was reshaped by colonial dichotomies – mutually reinforced each other.

COLONIAL SETTLEMENTS

Yet this appropriation of the Polish-speaking territories as a form of colonial wasteland was more than a discursive event. It was a real

---

[74] On this topic see Zimmerman, *Anthropology*, pp. 38–61.

[75] Rössler, *Deutsche Reich*, p. 439.

[76] Rudolf Virchow, in *Stenographische Berichte über die Verhandlungen des Abgeordnetenhauses*, 64th session, 8 May 1875, Vol. III, pp. 1798, 1800.

element of legal and social practice in the eastern areas of Prussia. In striking synchronicity, indeed, policies of settlement were imposed on overseas colonies such as South-West Africa and on the Polish speaking provinces in eastern Prussia. The redirection of outbound migration to Africa had been one of the *raisons d'être* of the colonial project, and the agitation of the colonial movement aimed at establishing large diaspora communities in 'New Germany'. At virtually the same time, the 'internal colonisation' of Polish Prussia emerged as a central concern in nationalist circles, social science debates and government policies.

In the literature, the settlement policies in the German East are typically seen as part of a long history of Prussian attempts to come to terms with its Polish population. What was called the 'Germanification of the soil' then appeared as the culmination, or escalation, of a politics of homogenisation that assumed a new urgency after unification. Assimilation of linguistic minorities was a central tenet of government policies and can be interpreted both as an element of internal nation-building and of the attempt to repress the Polish nationalist movement. Particular attention was paid to the gradual limitation of the use of the Polish language in schools, churches and political associations. For several decades, intensified by the clash with Catholicism in the 1870s, anti-Polish measures (the so-called *Polenpolitik*) were framed in cultural terms, with a focus on language and religion.

From the mid 1880s, however, the character of intervention changed. The politics of Germanification came to centre on migration and settlement, and included cases of forced expulsion, border control and expropriation of territory. Bismarck spoke of a 'struggle for existence' raging between the Germans and the Poles.[77] Many protagonists, and most historians in their wake, have interpreted these measures as a radicalisation of earlier strategies, since they departed from the hallowed principles of legal equality and benevolent improvement. Indeed, in the Wilhelmian period a form of state-sponsored legal separation was enforced that in many instances

---

[77] Bismarck addresses the Prussian State Ministry, 1 December 1885, quoted from Kohl, *Politischen Reden*, p. 300.

contradicted the principles of the Prussian constitution.[78] At the same time, however, it seems important to understand the broader context of this radicalisation that cannot be understood solely as the continuation of earlier trajectories. What can be observed in these years is a transformation of the logic of intervention whose thrust shifted from culture to demography and biopolitics.

In 1886, the Royal Prussian Colonisation Commission (*Königlich Preußische Ansiedlungskommission*) was established to buy up large Polish estates. It subsequently sold them in smaller plots to German farmers who were lured to the East by state subsidies. The Commission was ideologically supported by the Eastern Marches Society whose members increasingly argued for technologies of population that included the forced movement and relocation of large groups. As the Society was involved in both the settlement of Germans and controls on the admission of Polish seasonal workers, it was one of the most important actors involved in the ethno-'racial' loading of German population policy. In the years leading up to the First World War, its members began to suggest that the 'Polish question' should be solved by resettlement and population movements. These projects have been seen as precursors to later *Lebensraum* ideologies and to Nazi extermination policy.[79] It is more instructive, however, to see the correspondences with similar population policies in the overseas colonies, such as governor Lindequist's call to move 'the whole tribe of Witboois to Samoa' in order to stabilise colonial rule in German South-West Africa. Racial segregation and ethnic separation, and also deportation of large populations after the turn of the century, were common practice in the colonial arena.[80]

On the nationalist fringe, consequently, calls for a politics of segregation and legal separation were frequently voiced. Alfred

---

[78] See Gosewinkel, *Einbürgern*, pp. 211–18, 63–77; Walkenhorst, *Nation–Volk–Rasse*, pp. 252–80; Wehler, *Sozialdemokratie*.

[79] See Wehler, 'Polenpolitik', p. 194. On the *Ostmarkenverein* see Galos, Gentzen and Jakóbczyk, *Hakatisten*; Oldenburg, *Ostmarkenverein*; and Grabowski, *Nationalismus*.

[80] See Mühlhahn, *Herrschaft*, pp. 185–284; Zimmerer, *Deutsche Herrschaft*, pp. 42–55; and Conrad, 'Regimes der Segregation'.

Hugenberg, co-founder of the Pan-German League, demanded in 1902 that 'the German colonists [should be subject] to separate jurisdiction', that schools should be reserved for the German population and that political rights should be restricted to ethnic Germans.[81] Only three years earlier, he had openly envisioned the eventual 'annihilation' of the Polish population.[82] These propositions, as well as the governmental settlement policies, met with fierce criticism, in particular from Social Democrats and the Centre Party.[83] But over the course of time, and in particular during the First World War, the colonialist rhetoric was adopted by ever larger parts of the population. Here, as in other areas, the World War contributed to the radicalisation of ideas that had previously been formulated only occasionally and with no real prospect of being realised. The liberal-conservative historian Friedrich Meinecke, for example, suggested in 1915 that Polish landholdings should be moved to Congress Poland to restore 'the German character of Posen and West Prussia'. In addition, he imagined Courland, after the expulsion of the Latvian population, 'as a land of peasant colonisation'.[84] Poland (and other areas in eastern-central Europe) was widely seen as a colonial tabula rasa suitable for the renewal of the German people, as Meinecke's remarks reveal. These thoughts culminated in the debate on the war objectives during the First World War, when practically no limits were placed on expansionary ambitions, from Naumann's *Mitteleuropa* to the 'Middle Africa Plan' conceived by the German Foreign Office. Friedrich von Schwerin, one of the spokesmen for *völkisch* nationalism, recalled the great 'colonising mission' that was waiting for Germany ('perhaps for the last time in the history of the world') in Poland; it envisaged the 'resettlement of large groups of people'.[85] The demand for colonial lands 'free from people', raised by Heinrich Claß, president of the Pan-German League, was shared by many intellectuals and parts of the

---

[81] Hugenberg, *Streiflichter*, p. 280. [82] *Alldeutsche Blätter* 9 (1899), p. 86.
[83] Wehler, *Sozialdemokratie*, pp. 165–82.
[84] Meinecke to Walter Goetz, in Meinecke, *Briefwechsel*, p. 59.
[85] Quoted in Geiss, *Grenzstreifen*, p. 78.

country's leadership.[86] To ensure that the 'population of foreign origins' within the Reich would not increase further, it was planned that areas annexed during the war 'would be added to the Reich in international law but not in terms of constitutional law' – this was nothing less than the legal definition of a colony.[87]

The politics of settlement in Polish Prussia, then, were framed in colonial terms. This should be seen, however, not as the simple result of rhetorical interference and articulation, but rather as the effect of a common problem. On one level, the politics of settlement was presented as a solution to the problem of mobility and the centrifugal projection of Germans into the world. This was true for overseas expansion motivated by the alleged need to prevent the 'loss of national energies' to the United States and to redirect migration flows to 'New Germany' in Africa. At precisely the same time, the German Eastern Marches Society urged peasants 'not even to think about migrating to the United States' but instead to 'find a new *Heimat* in the East of the German fatherland'.[88]

On a second level, and more importantly, the debate on migration and demography found its ideological structure in the concept of *Lebensraum*. Here, too, territorial acquisitions overseas and in eastern Europe operated within a shared paradigm. As Woodruff Smith has argued, the call for *Lebensraum* emerged as one of the answers to overcome various threats to Germanness, such as immigration from the East, the narrowing of Germany's sphere of economic interests, the closing of the colonial frontier, and the rivalry of the world powers. It was not limited to visions of overseas expansion, as is clear in the case of economist Max Sering, one of the most vociferous protagonists of inner colonisation. Sering's goal was to settle small-scale farmers in the East, with the hope that they would develop the same qualities that overseas colonies were supposed to foster, thus creating a new

---

[86] See Broszat, *Zweihundert Jahre*, p. 184. On this topic see also Basler, *Annexionspolitik*.

[87] 'Denkschrift über die künftige staatsrechtliche und national-politische Gestaltung der von Rußland abzutrennenden östlichen Nachbargebiete des Deutschen Reiches', April 1916, quoted in Oldenburg, *Ostmarkenverein*, p. 231.

[88] Quoted from *ibid.*, p. 147.

social type.[89] The close conceptual linkage between both forms of colonisation was exemplified, at the convention of the Pan-German League in 1905, by a discussion between Theodor Reismann-Grone, advocating the pursuit of *Lebensraum* on the continent, and Eduard von Liebert, former governor of German South-West Africa, who propagated overseas settlements. For Reismann-Grone, inner colonisation was not so much influenced by, but rather a precondition for, subsequent outward expansion. Both positions were clearly part of a common project.[90]

The population politics in eastern Germany, in the end, was not successful, and eventually strengthened, rather than weakened, Polish nationalism in the region. In comparison with the colonial settlements, however, the figures are staggering: more than 120,000 Germans were settled in the Prussian East, more than five times as many as ever lived in the entire colonial empire.[91]

COLONIAL DIFFERENCES: 'RACE' AND 'CULTURE'

To date there has been no systematic investigation of the ideological and political similarities between colonial policies in Africa and central Europe in the nineteenth century.[92] Hannah Arendt has on one occasion put forward some thoughts on the links between 'continental' and 'overseas' imperialism, but very little work has been done to follow up on this idea. However, Arendt, too, emphasises the central difference between the two colonial projects. For Arendt, one of the major differences is that overseas colonialism is characterised by racial difference that has been made absolute, while continental expansion is based on perceptions of a higher level of ethnic similarity and cultural common ground. For Arendt, this differentiation is

---

[89] Smith, *Ideological Origins*, pp. 83–111.
[90] Alldeutscher Verband, *Zwanzig Jahre*.
[91] On the politics of settlement see Balzer, *Polenpolitik*; Broszat, *Zweihundert Jahre*, pp. 142–72; Stepinski, 'Siedlungsbewegung'; and Wehler, 'Polenpolitik'.
[92] See the initial discussion in Ther, 'Deutsche Geschichte'. On the colonial dimension of the Nazis' use of power, see Zimmerer, 'Geburt'; Furber, 'Going East'; and Furber, 'Near as Far'.

important, and it points to one of the main differences between the formal German empire and inner colonisation.[93]

In political practice, this difference was expressed at a number of different levels. The Polish provinces of the German Reich were not administered as colonies. Most importantly, the Polish population had the political and cultural option of assimilating. For a long time, even in the nineteenth century, the German side, especially in the Ruhrgebiet but also in other regions, expressly desired assimilation. Social actors were frequently in a position to articulate different notions of subjecthood, nationality and modernity, and to appropriate them for their own purposes. Moreover, the Polish-speaking inhabitants of the Reich had German citizenship (in contrast to migrants and seasonal workers from Galicia or Russia). There was a basic, fundamental difference between this situation and that of the overseas colonies. The formal colonial empire belonged to Germany in terms of international law, but this did not mean that its inhabitants gained German citizenship. In fact, there were almost no cases of colonial subjects being naturalised.[94]

The practices of separation and segregation, in other words, suggest a different quality of life under colonial conditions, compared with the more conventional forms of prejudices and repression in Prussia's eastern provinces. And indeed, the situations were specific in each case. The argument here, therefore, is not one of sameness, but rather of difference. This is corroborated by the fact that even in the overseas empire, the colonial encounter was by no means uniform. African colonies differed markedly from German rule in Kiaochow (Jiaozhou) in China, where higher education and a university were part of the colonial modernisation project. But even in Africa, social realities were highly heterogeneous: 'There was no singular German approach to colonial governance.'[95] If colonialism was predicated on the 'rule of difference', as Partha Chatterjee has forcefully argued, this difference was not defined by race alone, but rather depended on

[93] Arendt, *Elemente*, esp. pp. 368–94.
[94] On the issue of nationality in the colonies see Nagl, *Grenzfälle*. See also Wagner, *Schutzgebiete*, pp. 249–72.
[95] Steinmetz, *The Devil's Handwriting*, p. 19.

a set of criteria that included regional particularities, affiliation with a 'tribe' or linguistic community, and the import of gender and social status.[96]

Moreover, the impact of racial categories on colonial domination was highly variegated and complex. The French programme of assimilation, in particular in Algeria, aimed at cultural convergence, even though renunciation of Islam was a precondition for citizenship. Integration went even further under Japanese colonialism: the Japanese policy of assimilation (*dôka*) fundamentally treated its colonial subjects in Taiwan and Korea as Japanese citizens. Here, too, the principle of *dôka* did not preclude discrimination and violence, but the imperial ideology rested on the assumption of ethnic affinity and – equally importantly – of the cultural similarity of the eastern Asian countries that were shaped by Confucianism.[97] Thus, colonialism covered a range of different assimilative policies, which could range from integration (often forced integration) to apartheid regimes. But the tension was not only between different forms of colonial policy. More fundamentally, it was an inherent part of the colonial project itself. Technologies of difference and assimilation, in an ambivalent dialectic, mutually reinforced and undermined each other. Thus, the differentiation between the colonisers and the colonised, usually formulated in terms of the discourse of race, was continually negotiated with the cultural-mission ideology of 'elevation' that gave the colonial project its dynamic.

While there is a difference in the way the concept of 'race' was used, we can still identify colonial characteristics in the German relationship with the Polish population. References to the different German and Slavic 'races' were common in Wilhelmine Germany. Anton Wohlfahrt, the German protagonist of Gustav Freytag's novel, saw himself as 'one of the conquerors who, on behalf of free labour and civilisation, have usurped the dominion of the country from a

---

[96] Chatterjee, *Nation*. For an attempt to go beyond Chatterjee's not unproblematic notion of race, see Kolsky, 'Codification'.

[97] For overviews of French and Japanese colonialism see Aldrich, *Greater France*; Beasley, *Imperialism*; and Peattie, *Colonial Empire*.

weaker race'.[98] In the propaganda of the Eastern Marches Society, too, openly racist comments were frequent. As in the overseas colonies, this rhetoric was usually accompanied by genderised issues. The Hakatists (a shorthand for the three founders of the Eastern Marches Society: Hannemann, Kennemann and von Tiedemann) saw Polish women (*Polinnen*) 'in the East' as 'our most effective and most dangerous enemy' because they not only threatened to outnumber German women and the German people by means of their fertility, but sometimes even 'Polonised' upright German Catholic men by marrying them.[99] Here, too, there are noticeable parallels to the contemporaneous fear of hybridisation and 'kaffirisation' in Germany's African colonies. But while concerns about 'mixed marriages' in the eastern provinces of Prussia did not extend beyond rhetoric, the fear of miscegenation was converted into official policy in the overseas colonies. From 1905 onward in the African colonies, and from 1912 in Samoa, it was impossible for a German citizen to marry a native. There was no similar policy in the Polish areas of the eastern Reich, or at least not until the openly racist policies pursued by the Nazis during the Second World War.[100]

The use and implementation of racial categories, then, diverged from colonial practice and were specific to the particular situation in Posen and Silesia. It is equally clear, however, that notions of race increasingly tinted the discourse and practices of belonging. This includes the cases in which Poles and Jews were treated as one group for administrative purposes, for example in issues related to immigration and naturalisation. This change took place in the context of an economic crisis during the 1880s and of intense internal debates about the 'enemies of the Reich', which were interpreted as including Poles and Jews along with Catholics and Socialists. The overlap between anti-Jewish and anti-Polish measures made sense from the

---

[98] Freytag, *Soll und Haben*, Part ii, p. 163. On the topic in general see Kopp, 'Constructing Racial Difference'.

[99] Cited in Drummond, 'Weiblicher Kulturimperialismus', here p. 152.

[100] On the issue of 'mixed marriages' see Grosse, *Kolonialismus*, pp. 145–92; Kundrus, *Imperialisten*; Wildenthal, *German Women*, pp. 79–130; and Becker, 'Kolonialherrschaft'.

administration's perspective because the two migrant groups were often identical. What it also shows, however, is the complex process in which the radicalisation of anti-Semitism and the racialisation of anti-Polish sentiments informed each other.[101]

This trend can be seen clearly in the debates about 'eastern Jews' with which Wilhelmine public opinion was increasingly preoccupied from the 1890s onward.[102] A relatively small number of Jews immigrating from Russia (in total, some 70,000 people) triggered xenophobic fears of a 'flood from the East' that were fed by the topos of cultural backwardness, indeed of 'barbarism'. These heated reactions, which involved cultural prejudices that were often shared by German Jews, were not only based on social fears. They were heightened by the 'through-migration' of much larger numbers of people from eastern and south-eastern Europe. From the early 1880s onward, emigration to America by Jewish and Polish peoples from Russia became a mass phenomenon; between 1880 and 1914, some 5.1 million people (of whom 2 million were Jews) sailed for the United States from German ports. And in the popular imagination eastern European Jews were linked with radicalism, poverty, trafficking in women from eastern Europe, and unhygienic conditions and the importing of infectious diseases, as in the case of the major cholera epidemic of the early 1890s.[103] Anti-Semitic stereotypes were thus reinforced by fears of the 'East' and of 'Asian' influences, and, conversely, the debate about the threat of 'Polonisation' acquired anti-Semitic features. These links were not limited to rhetoric: an example of their real effect is the joint expulsion in 1885 of 40,000 Poles and Jews who

---

[101] On this topic see Gosewinkel, *Einbürgern*, pp. 263–77, who also discusses the differences between the treatment of Poles and that of Jews.

[102] On this topic see Maurer, *Ostjuden*, esp. pp. 122ff., on 'asiatische Eindringlinge oder deutsche Rückwanderer'. An excellent account is Wertheimer, *Unwelcome Strangers*; as well as his 'Unwanted Element'; and Zumbini, *Wurzeln*, pp. 463–562. The most important analysis of the stereotype of the *Ostjuden* is still Aschheim, *Brothers and Strangers*. See also Rahden, *Juden*, pp. 267–99.

[103] See Zumbini, 'Große Migration'. On trafficking in women see Bristow, *Prostitution*; and Kaplan, *Jüdische Frauenbewegung*, esp. pp. 199ff. On the cholera epidemic and the anti-Semitic propaganda that accompanied it see Evans, *Death in Hamburg*; and Kasischke-Wurm, *Antisemitismus*, esp. pp. 133ff.

did not have Prussian nationality. Although this spectacular action remained a one-off and was overtaken by the new regulations on the admission of seasonal workers, discrimination against Poles and Jews as one group continued, for example in the restrictive way naturalisation was managed.[104] Massimo Ferrari Zumbini has argued that in the 1890s there was 'a merging of anti-Slavism and anti-Semitism that was understood in expressly racial terms'.[105]

It is this gradual racialisation of Polishness that rendered conceivable an otherwise entirely unlikely proposal made by a certain Adolf Hentze in 1907 to Bernhard Dernburg, secretary of state of the Colonial Office. Hentze suggested that the 16,000 Herero and Nama who were being held in prisoner-of-war camps in German South-West Africa following the 1904 Herero War should be deployed as agricultural workers in the eastern Prussian provinces. There, they would learn 'morality, the language and how to work the soil', and would be 'educated to work'. From the perspective of the government in Windhoek, this project would have been seen as part of the cultural-missionary task of 'elevating' the colonial subjects while at the same time contributing to security in the colony. But Hentze's initiative went beyond the concrete political context in which it was created. Once in Germany, the prisoners of war would primarily be used to replace immigrant Polish seasonal workers. This initiative only became conceivable because the idea of the difference between Germans and Poles had gradually become radicalised in terms used by the racial discourse at the turn of the century. It was only now that Africans could stand in for, and indeed serve as substitutes for, Polish workers: only now that it could be suggested that the Polish agricultural workers who 'are truly not improving' the German population could be substituted with African 'natives'.[106] Around 1900, racism was by no means a universal discourse. 'Racial' assignments

---

[104] The best account of the expulsions is still Neubach, *Ausweisung*. See also Mai, *Polenpolitik*.

[105] Zumbini, *Wurzeln*, p. 556.

[106] Quotes taken from Zimmerer, *Deutsche Herrschaft*, pp. 52–55. This equating of different racial groups was not unique. Wilhelm Stieda, too, compared the Polish seasonal workers, 'representatives of a second-class working class', with the

and analogies could vary and overlap. Their dynamics were not just determined by biological criteria, but were always embedded in geopolitical contexts.[107]

It is important in this context to recognise, finally, that 'race' could not only be linked to biology, but also to culture. Etienne Balibar, for instance, has forcefully argued that 'culture can also function like a nature, and it can in particular function as a way of locking individuals and groups a priori into a genealogy, into a determination that is immutable and intangible in origin'. In the late nineteenth century, alongside the biological definition of race there emerged a second powerful strand of racialised thinking premised on a system of cultural differences that functions equally as effectively as a means of accounting for social and economic inequality.[108] One of the mechanisms for linking these two paradigms was the reference to Lamarckian notions of the inheritability of acquired characteristics that continued to be influential into the early decades of the twentieth century. The concept of adaptations to the social and cultural environment thus could assume a pivotal position in racial thinking. 'This Lamarckian feature of eugenic thinking', as Ann Laura Stoler has argued, 'was central to colonial discourses that linked racial degeneracy to the sexual transmission of cultural contagions'.[109]

In this context, 'Polonization' could be perceived as a threat equally powerful as the dangers implied by racial mixing in the colonies. To be sure, it was not the same threat. Polish women, for example, were credited with forms of agency that African women – the objects of legal provisions against miscegenation – were not associated with in colonial discourse. Moreover, 'Polonization' was frequently couched in a language of nationalism that at the time was not yet at the disposal of most social actors in the African colonies.[110] But it would be reductionist to assume a global order in which nationalism and

---

'negroes' in the USA, the 'Chinese in California and Australia' and the 'coolies in British West India' ('Beschäftigung', p. 168).

[107] On this topic see Karl, 'Race'.   [108] Balibar, 'Is There a "Neo-Racism"?', p. 22.

[109] Stoler, *Carnal Knowledge*, p. 72.

[110] See Kundrus, review of *Germany's Colonial Pasts*.

colonialism functioned as mutually exclusive forms of discourse and practice. Instead, it is important to recognise that, in an age of high imperialism, differences of nation, culture and class in the Prussian East were increasingly underwritten by, and articulated with, notions of colonial difference.

The colonial dimensions of Germany's appropriation of the 'East' are typically discussed by reconstructing similarities and explaining them in terms of 'repercussions' of the colonial experience. This mode of causation presupposes direct interactions between overseas and continental colonies, linked through flows of people, institutions and discourse. The argument, then, is one of translation from the colonial world to other locations that are then influenced by colonial tropes – and the discussion that ensues focuses on weighing the 'colonial' dimension of social practices against others: nationalism, class difference, gender. This paradigm, however, as the pros and cons that go along with it, rests on a simplified view of the world assuming neatly confined spheres of social experience – that can then influence each other. It rests, ultimately, on a *Schutzgebiete* view of German colonialism. What I have suggested instead is that the 'colonial' character of Polish Prussia can only be grasped by seeing it as part of the global interactions in a world deeply structured – albeit unevenly – by imperialism. It is this larger context that enables colonial dimensions to structure social experience in highly diverse places – without, to be sure, erasing the particularities of the situation in question. Rather than looking at colonial empires as a specific form of territoriality, then, I suggest that Polish Prussia should be understood in the framework of global modernity that was marked by colonialism around the world.[111]

THE INVASION FROM THE EAST: MIGRATION, BATTLE AND DISEASE

One of the effects of this colonial dimension of German population policy in Poland was to make the practice of interaction between

[111] For the concept of global modernity, see Dirlik, *Global Modernity*.

Germans and Poles seem 'unnatural' and to make forms of delimitation more stringent and more absolute.[112] Mobility, not only on the labour market, was increasingly seen as a threat to the nation. These concerns derived further support from the authority of science. This is an issue that has not attracted much attention heretofore in analyses of labour migration and of the *Kulturkampf.* But it is striking to observe that in many popular and scientific publications from the 1880s onward, there was mention of an 'invasion' from the East, of the *'eingeschleppte'* Polish Jews or the 'homeless' from the 'core countries in the Orient'. These concerns often went beyond social competition in labour markets, or patriotic feelings. What was at stake in these debates, instead, was the health of the nation.[113]

In this area, too, Virchow played a leading role. The notion of a 'threat from the East', as Virchow saw it, always involved concerns about imported germs and the invasion of bacteria. These fears were themselves a result of the far-reaching changes in theories of epidemiology during the nineteenth century. When Virchow carried out his famous study on typhus in the Polish provinces in 1848, he still supported the 'geographical school', which believed that climate and social problems created disease-producing miasmas. He had summarised his beliefs into a theory of cellular pathology, which he hoped would supplant the older idea that diseases were caused by pathological imbalances in body fluids ('the humours'). In terms of the history of medicine, this was a major change, but only a few decades later it seemed to have become outdated. By the early 1880s – when Pasteur successfully carried out inoculations and Koch isolated the tubercle bacillus – if not earlier, bacteriology had been established as the most influential paradigm for explaining the spread of disease.[114]

Although today the victory of the contagionist viewpoint seems unsurprising, it was by no means a foregone conclusion at the time. Competing approaches, for example the idea that a disease could

---

[112] For a similar argument see Arendt, *Elemente*, p. 305 and *passim*.

[113] Quotes from the *Deutsche medicinische Wochenschrift*, quoted in Sarasin, 'Infizierte Körper', pp. 226ff.

[114] On Virchow see Goschler, *Virchow*; and Mazzolini, *Analogien*. On the victory of bacteriology see Bulloch, *History*; and Porter, *Benefit*, pp. 429–61.

'grow', or that local conditions were all-important, had not been disproved.[115] Therefore, several factors apart from the scientific evidence established bacteriology as the leading theory. These included the interest of state institutions in a theory that did not blame social conditions for the spread of disease (Virchow had demanded that improvements to infrastructure and local democracy be introduced in Upper Silesia); in fact, bacteriology provided arguments for increasing state intervention.[116] In addition, the use of political metaphors in medicine was of major importance for the popularisation and widespread adoption of immunology.

The triumph of the bacteriological theory could not have happened without the widespread use of topoi and metaphors that picked up on common knowledge and the political rhetoric of the Wilhelmine era. Historians of medicine have focused on the military and war-related aspects of bacteriological language, with the body being seen as the location of a total war between intruders and defenders, 'war' and 'crusades' against disease, and the characterisation of Robert Koch as a 'bacillus killer'.[117] But Philipp Sarasin has pointed out that the discourse was more complex as there were three groups of metaphors that overlapped: along with 'war/struggle for existence', Sarasin speaks of 'poison/purity/self' and 'invasion/migration/foreignness'.[118] In fact it was mainly the reference to migratory processes that helped to link the language of bacteriology with that used in everyday political debate. Since the cholera epidemic in the early 1830s, a belief had become established that epidemics were 'imported' from abroad. The link with the debate about migrant workers and the *Überfremdung* of the eastern provinces is obvious.[119]

But it is important to recognise that influence did not only run one way; rather, the formation of politico-medical metaphors was a two-way process. This implied, for example, that for the immigration

---

[115] See for example Evans, *Tod in Hamburg*, pp. 618–38; and Jahn, *Cholera*.

[116] See for example Göckenjahn, *Kurieren*; Ackerknecht, 'Anticontagionism'; Labisch, *Homo hygienicus*, pp. 133–40; and Evans, *Death in Hamburg*, pp. 343–53.

[117] See Gradmann, 'Bakteriologie'; Gradmann, 'Bazillen'; and Martin, 'Anthropology'.

[118] Sarasin, 'Infizierte Körper', p. 227.   [119] Sarasin, 'Visualisierung'.

authorities, controls on mobility were necessary not only in the interest of 'work' and national delimitation but also for medical reasons. Thus, the director of the Central Office for Field Workers assured the Prussian minister for the interior, in April 1911, that 'at each of the border posts ... a doctor is employed' who 'is responsible for externally examining all foreign workers ... passing through the border post'. This was intended to reduce the 'risk of importing cholera' because if 'the doctor carrying out the investigation misses the disease, still in germ form ... the risk of transporting epidemics becomes infinite'.[120] As early as 1904, a Medical Report by the Prussian ministry for education and culture ('the foreign workers are much more dangerous for the spread of infectious diseases than domestic workers') had created a medical map of contamination that described workers 'originating from Russia and Austria' as possible 'carriers of smallpox, typhus, trachoma, impetigo and scabies, the Italians as spreaders of typhus'.[121]

Beyond the actual medical checks, the mingling of bacteriological rhetoric with migration helped to provide a seemingly scientific basis for reservations and prejudices about the mobility of foreign workers. The anti-Catholic/anti-Polish *Kulturkampf*, the 'battle of resistance' in the labour market and patriotic slogans about the threat of 'Polonisation' thus transported as a subtext the idea of scientific reliability. Diseases and the germs causing them seemed to come 'from outside' and, in the political practice of the Kaiserreich, this meant mainly from the 'East'. The stigmatisation of 'Polish vagabonds' and also of Jews, who were frequently described as 'parasites' from the 1890s onward, linked the debate about human mobility with fears of the movement of micro-organisms. The victory of bacteriology, fears of 'infection' and the preventive immunisation of bodies corresponded to the policy of border controls in the East.

It is interesting to note that in this context, too, there was a colonial dimension at work. At the same time as he became involved in the

---

[120] GStA PK, 87 B, no. 221, letter dated 22 April 1911.
[121] Quoted in Knoke, *Ausländische Wanderarbeiter*, p. 65. In this context see also Maurer, 'Medizinalpolizei'.

Kulturkampf, Virchow adopted the contagionist theory and warned against migration from the East – both of people and of germs. It was no coincidence that he spoke of germs attacking the human organism 'from the outside, like the Sudanese'.[122] In general, attacks by germs were often described as 'colonisation'. At the same time, the idea of foreignness threatening the boundaries of a body or of the state could not be separated from the idea of 'racial' difference.[123] This also applied to the (Russian) Poles.[124] For the eastern European Jews especially, this link between bacteriology, hygiene policy and racism, first created in the 1890s, would prove fatal.[125]

This linking of medical and demographic debates also helped to make the fixing of national boundaries seem natural. The contagionist paradigm replaced fears about the environment and social conditions with an aetiology of infection. In this way, the inside–outside opposition became the central category in diagnosis, prevention and social intervention. The result was a preoccupation with issues of delimitation – initially of individual bodies but soon of collective subjects. At the turn of the century, the national body, the *Volkskörper*, seemed particularly deserving of protection.[126] Sarah Jansen has shown that this change was not limited to human medicine; it also applied to pest control. For example, in the early nineteenth century a pest called *Phylloxera*, which came 'from outside', was seen as causing damage to individual 'trees'. By the early twentieth century the threat was to entire 'cultivated forests' or even to 'Germany'.[127] This paradigm change in the theory of pathogens, which was closely linked to the

---

[122] Virchow, 'Kampf der Zellen', p. 9.

[123] See for example Planert, 'Körper'; Kistner, 'Feind'; and Jansen, 'Männer'. On Virchow's understanding of 'race', see Geulen, 'Blonde bevorzugt'.

[124] Dietrich Geyer has succinctly described the mental map prevalent in Wilhelmine Germany as 'Halbasien begann in Oberschlesien' ('Backward Asia [*Halbasien*] began in Upper Silesia'; 'Ostpolitik', p. 157). See also Klug, 'Rußland'; Lemberg, 'Entstehung'; and Bassin, 'Russia'.

[125] On this topic see Weindling, *Epidemics*, esp. pp. 292–315; Weindling, 'Virulent Strain'; and Weingart, Kroll and Bayertz, *Rasse*. See also Sarasin, 'Visualisierung', esp. pp. 266–74.

[126] See Otis, *Membranes*, esp. pp. 8ff., 23; and Martin, 'Anthropology'.

[127] See Jansen, *'Schädlinge'*, pp. 271–77.

debates about mobility and migration, helped to reinforce the idea that the nation's borders needed to be secured.

These changes were part of the context in which a politically defined 'Polish question' was transformed, around the turn of the century, into a *völkisch*-eugenically defined 'Polish threat'. As an anonymous text addressed to the Prussian minister of state Miquel stated, the Poles were moving west 'like sand dunes', 'burying one centre of Germandom after another underneath them'. Here, mobility and immigration were seen as threats to the *Volkskörper*. The writer believed that the 'highly developed Teutonic people' were already degenerating into 'cultural fertiliser for Slavic peoples'. As a solution, he suggested making use of 'workers drawn from populations that are related by blood'. By this the anonymous author meant the Dutch, Danes, Swedes or Norwegians. In this, he was by no means alone. 'Our nation [*Volk*]', the writer argued, 'has already been permeated with Slavic blood to such an extent that refreshing it with Germanic blood would be very beneficial to it'.[128]

CLUTCHING AT STRAWS: FLEMINGS, ITALIANS, 'GERMANIC BLOOD'

From the start, the gradual, and always partial, opening of the borders to Polish seasonal workers from Russia and Austrian Galicia was accompanied by attempts to replace the Poles by workers of other nationalities. Until about 1905, this substitution was one of the main objectives of the German Eastern Marches Society. Originally, the Hakatists hoped that German emigrants could be encouraged to return and to settle in rural areas of Prussia. German embassies abroad also pleaded for 'the return of Germanic workers to be actively kept in mind'.[129] But occasional successes in these attempts did not come anywhere close to meeting the huge demand for labour. The same was true of the idea of making illegitimate

---

[128] Anon., *Die polnische Gefahr*, pp. 5, 7, 13, in GStA PK, I. HA, 87 B, no. 215, p. 14.
[129] Der Kaiserlich Deutsche Botschafter in Wien von Tschirschky, 1 April 1914, to the Reichskanzler, in GStA PK, I. HA, 87 B, no. 222, p. 274.

children available for the ailing agricultural sector through 'rearing by the state'.[130]

A more promising idea was to promote immigration by 'racially related peoples from abroad', as the German ambassador to Vienna strongly recommended.[131] Between 1892 and 1900, Dutch workers were employed in the construction of the Dortmund–Ems canal, a major state project, but it was very difficult to interest them in agricultural work.[132] Finns, Latvians, Estonians, Ukrainians, Slovakians and Hungarians were considered as possible recruits for an agricultural army – even the Chinese, as outlined below, were considered. But most of these plans were soon shelved. Latvian workers were too demanding, it was believed; recruiting workers in Finland was too expensive, and so forth.[133] Instead, the German embassy in Brussels suggested that Flemish workers, who were capable in every respect of replacing the unwanted Poles, should be used. Every year, some 50,000 Flemish people were employed in France as seasonal workers in agriculture. The plan was to redirect these migratory flows toward Germany. The Flemish were 'rough, but good-natured', as a 1905 report to Chancellor Bülow reported, 'less intelligent and slower, but more honest, more sober and more respectable than the Slavs'. In particular, though, they were 'dogged workers'.[134]

In these reports, the Flemish, 'lower German brothers', seem like a species of 'prehistoric humanity', almost like an earlier variant of the Teutons, who could be trusted to revive the spirit of 'German work', which was in danger of being lost in the 'nationally mixed region' at Germany's eastern border. Consequently, an agricultural expert working for the Foreign Office declaimed, in his 178-page thesis on the subject, that 'Belgium is, more than most other countries of the world, a country of work'. He continued: 'It has to be

[130] See for example the study prepared for the Deutscher Ostmarkenverein: Simon, *Aufzucht.*
[131] Von Tschirschky, in GStA PK, I. HA, 87 B, no. 222, p. 274.
[132] On this topic see Kösters-Kraft, *Großbaustelle.*
[133] On these plans see Nichtweiß, *Saisonarbeiter*, pp. 58–66.
[134] Kaiserlich Deutsche Gesandtschaft Brüssel, 21 December 1905, to Reichskanzler Bülow, in GStA PK, I. HA, 87 B, no. 216, p. 28.

seen to be believed, these Flemish field workers, with their stamina and untiring patience. They are never indifferent about any work, however insignificant.' If only one could say the same of the German rural population; they seemed to have already been spoiled by the trappings of civilisation. But the Flemish still possessed that earthy unspoilt quality in which 'sensory life extends only to the initial forms of psychic experiences' and in which work was still carried out for its own sake.[135] But in the end, the attempt to attract Flemish workers was also doomed to failure, in spite of the support of nationalist groups. The main reasons were economic; an additional factor, however, was the Catholicism of the Flemish people, which was an issue for the *Kulturkampf*-enthusiastic Hakatists.[136]

Most of these plans never got past the stage of mental experiment, memorandum or investigative trips. Italy was the only exception: many workers travelled from Italy to Germany every year, usually temporarily, returning home for the winter. In the years leading up to the First World War, there were usually about 200,000 Italians in Germany. They were mainly employed in industry (especially in southern and western Germany), in brickworks and mining, and last but not least in road construction. In spite of some attempts by interested farmers, by the ministry of agriculture and by the German embassy in Rome, Italians were not employed to work in agriculture. In certain cases this may have been due to cultural differences, which may have led some employers to stop hiring them ('for that reason I had to get rid of the Italians').[137] Fears were regularly expressed that Italian workers were not suited for work in agriculture in the eastern regions, for climatic reasons ('very sensitive to rain')[138] or because of different dietary habits. 'What! What! They want us to use Italians as labourers and field workers, those black, unshaven, ragged, unclean

---

[135] Dr. Julius Frost, 'Belgische Wanderarbeiter, Expertise im Auftrag des Auswärtigen Amtes', in Bundesarchiv (BA) Berlin, R 901, no. 481.

[136] On this topic see Nichtweiß, *Saisonarbeiter*, pp. 83–85.

[137] Graf Ballestrem, in *Stenographische Berichte über die Verhandlungen des Abgeordnetenhauses*, 64th session, 21 April 1898, p. 2108.

[138] Abgeordneter Szmula, Preußisches Haus der Abgeordneten, 15th session, 9 February 1899, p. 429.

brothers that pollute the sides of every road, those lazzaroni, those macaroni-eaters?'[139] But experts on Italy were at pains to dispel these fears. Certain regions of Italy were particularly recommended for recruiting workers. For example, the German consul Theodor Muhr, after travelling through northern Italy, recommended workers from the Lake Garda region and the Adige valley, where one could 'most easily' find 'suitably hardened workers, who have not gone soft, yet have not been brought up too roughly either'. Muhr was particularly impressed by the 'female figures' who, in these regions, 'give a fresh, healthy and happy impression, with slim and yet strong builds'.[140] The fact that very few Italian workers were ever employed in Prussian agriculture was mainly because seasonal work in agriculture was unattractive. In the main, the Italians were attracted by the higher wages and superior working conditions available in western Germany, the very conditions that had created the 'lack of people' in eastern Prussia in the first place.[141]

LIFEBELT: RUTHENIANS

The German Eastern Marches Society believed that it had found a solution to the 'Polish question' precisely where it was believed the problem originated: in Austrian-held Galicia. Polish seasonal workers in Prussia came from two regions: the German-held provinces on the western borders of Russia, and the province of Galicia, held by the Habsburgs. Since the agricultural reforms in 1848, rural conditions in Galicia had become worse and worse. Rural poverty had led to high levels of emigration, mainly to the United States but also,

---

[139] *Deutsche Landwirtschaftliche Presse*, Berlin (20 May 1899), pp. 451–52.

[140] Streng vertraulicher Bericht des kaiserlich deutschen Konsul Theodor Muhr über seine Reise durch Oberitalien an die Landwirtschaftskammer Brandenburg, in GStA PK, 87 B, no. 244, p. 12.

[141] On Italian labour migration see Wennemann, *Arbeit*; Del Fabbro, *Transalpini*; and Trincia, *Migration*. For the global history context, see Gabaccia, *Italy's Many Diasporas*; and Gabaccia and Ottanelli, *Italian Workers*. See also an important older essay, Schäfer, 'Gastarbeiter'; and, of the contemporary literature, Sartorius von Waltershausen, 'Italienischen Wanderarbeiter'; and Meichels-Lindner, 'Arbeiter'.

from the 1890s onward, to Prussia. This applied not only to Galician
Poles but also to Ruthenian peasants who lived in the region with
Poles and Jews. In a census in 1900, about 55 per cent of the 7.3 million inhabitants of Galicia had described themselves as Polish, and 42
per cent as Ruthenians (or Ukrainians).[142]

Nationalist political activities in the province began in the early
nineteenth century, when individual clerics and intellectuals influenced by Romanticism and the pan-Slavic movement contributed to
a cultural renaissance movement. The year1848 marked an important change, which led to more widespread adoption of the national
movement and, not least because of the ending of serfdom, created
the preconditions for the social mobilisation of Ruthenian peasants.
After a period of suppression during the years of neo-absolutism, the
national movement was revived from the 1860s onward and gained
strength toward the end of the century.[143] Both the Polish and the
Ruthenian national movements, then, had older origins, but in Galicia
they increasingly defined themselves in opposition to each other.
Ruthenian nationalism, in which the clergy initially played a major
role, became increasingly anti-Polish in nature – although conflicts
with Jews were also of importance, as was its ambivalent relationship
with Orthodox Ukrainians in southern Russia.[144] This national confrontation was often reinforced by social conflicts. Most major landowners in Galicia were Polish, and the Polish nobility often subjected
Ruthenian peasants to repression and exploitation. This combination
of different concerns contributed to the radicalisation of the national
debates.[145]

Given these tensions, it was not long before the Prussian interior and agriculture ministries had the idea of preventing the dreaded

---

[142] On this topic see Mark, *Galizien*; Schattkowsky, 'Autonomie'; and Daškevyč,
'Ostgalizien'.

[143] See Vulpius, 'Nation'; and Kozik, *National Movement*.

[144] On this topic see Kappeler, Kohut, Sysyn and von Hagen, *Culture*.

[145] On the Ruthenian national movement see Jobst, 'Nationalbewegung'; Jobst,
Nationalismus; Kappeler, 'Nationalbewegung'; Hryniuk, *Peasants*; and Hrycak,
'Genese'. A large amount of material is contained in Himka's social-history study,
Galician Villagers.

'Polonisation' of Prussian agriculture by exploiting the Polish–Ruthenian differences. If Flemings and Scandinavians were not to be had, Ruthenians would have to do. The Central Office for Field Workers launched a campaign to persuade landowners, who were initially hesitant, to employ Ruthenian workers ('a little more lethargic than and not quite as efficient as the Poles').[146] From 1904 onward, large numbers of Ruthenian workers were recruited; during subsequent years, about 100,000 Ruthenians were employed in Prussian agriculture.[147]

In 1904 the willingness of farmers to employ Ruthenians had been increased by fears that the war between Russia and Japan might lead to the closing of the border with Russia, making it impossible to recruit Polish seasonal workers from Russia. But the most important circumstance that was used to encourage employers to hire Ruthenians was that the 'restricted period' rule was discontinued for Ruthenian workers. This was intended to increase their attractiveness to the Prussian landowners; in contrast to their Polish colleagues and competitors, the Ruthenians no longer had to leave Germany in the winter months.

The Ruthenian workers were recruited as an antidote to the 'flooding' and 'Polonisation' of eastern Prussia. This strategy was based on the assumption that a fundamental difference divided the two groups. Von Tiedemann, the President of the Eastern Marches Society, declared 'that there is an unbridgeable chasm between Ruthenians and Poles, deeper than that between fire and water'.[148] This belief referred partly to the regional distribution of the populations: the Poles had settled mainly in western Galicia, where they made up 88 per cent of the population, while east of the river San, the Ruthenians were in the majority, compared to the Poles and the Jews.[149] But the differences went further. The Ruthenians spoke a separate dialect and had a different religious orientation. While the Poles were Roman Catholics, most Ruthenians belonged to the Greek Orthodox church. The most important difference, however, was political. The

---

[146] Landwirtschaftskammer der Provinz Brandenburg, 16 June 1904, to the Deutscher Ostmarkenverein, in GStA PK, I. HA, 87 B, no. 245, p. 50.

[147] On this topic see Nichtweiß, *Saisonarbeiter*, pp. 85–93.

[148] Quoted in *ibid.*, p. 91.   [149] For the figures see Mark, *Galizien*, pp. 80–85.

Ruthenian national committee knew why Ruthenians were attractive to the Prussian government: 'They are hostile to the ... Poles and lean toward Germandom, something that cannot be said of most other Slavic groups.'[150] 'The two nations', Bodenstein, the employers' representative, concluded, 'are fundamentally different'.[151]

The solution to the situation of mobility and fluctuation, then, was a policy of segregation. This strategy was applied not only to the relationship between Germans and foreigners, but to the relationships between the immigrants themselves. 'Divide and conquer', the characteristic of colonial power, became the mode of national population policy in eastern Germany. Just as, at the same time, the United States began to regulate and limit uncontrolled emigration through exclusion and quotas, the authorities at Germany's borders with Austria-Hungary and Russia began to differentiate among immigrants in terms of their nationality. From 1908 onward, differently coloured 'legitimation cards' were issued for each nation: red for Poles, yellow for Ruthenians, blue for Dutch and Flemish workers, brown for Norwegian and Swedish ones, green for Italians, and white for everyone else. Interestingly, it was not nationality in terms of citizenship that was considered the most important criterion for separating immigrants. The classification was based on something more fundamental, the idea of ethnic differences.[152]

It was not just immigration, monitored at specially created border posts, that followed the principle of segregation. The Central Office for Field Workers in Berlin created even more subtle distinctions when acting as an agent for employers. For example, it differentiated between migrant workers from the western Russian border region (bordering on Prussia) and those from the central regions, between Germans from Upper Hungary and Slovakian workers from Upper Hungary, and distinguished both of these groups from migrant workers from southern Hungary. These differentiations corresponded to a

---

[150] Ruthenisches Nationalkomitee to the Minister für Landwirtschaft, 15 December 1904, in GStA PK, I. HA, 87 B, no. 113, p. 276.

[151] Bodenstein, *Beschäftigung*, p. 17.

[152] See the list given in Knoke, *Ausländische Wanderarbeiter*, p. 16.

highly differentiated wage structure, which was then subdivided into rates for men, women, boys, foremen and so forth.[153] Classifying and regulating the workers in this careful way allowed a policy of containment to be imposed, in particular on Polish workers. 'The foreign Poles admitted for employment are to be kept separate from other workers and, except in the case of family groups, to be given separate accommodation for each sex.'[154] Particular attention was paid to differentiating between Poles and Ruthenians who, according to a 1905 decree, could no longer be employed at the same location.

But in practice these attempts at strict separation soon ran into major difficulties. Some of these were diplomatic issues: the Austrian government, for example, protested about the differentiation of its citizens and demanded that they be treated 'uniformly'.[155] An additional source of criticism was that Ruthenian nationalists were involved in recruiting workers for Germany. Politicised clergymen saw labour migration to Germany as part of the national independence campaign. In attracting and selecting workers in Galicia, moreover, the Central Office for Field Workers relied on the Ruthenian national committee, which frequently used the occasion for nationalist agitation. As a result of the protest by the Austrian government, the Prussian government emphasised that there must be no 'externally visible official support' for the Ruthenian cause.[156]

But the main difficulties were inherent to the issue itself, i.e. to the project of cleanly distinguishing and separating populations in a situation of migration and movement. It soon emerged that it was not always possible to distinguish between national groups at a local level as clearly as the ministerial decrees suggested. The Prussian minister of the interior reported that there was often 'great difficulty in distinguishing Poles and Ruthenians'.[157] This may have been due to Poles claiming to be Ruthenians to avoid having to return home during the 'restricted period'. One of the 'most frequently encountered

---

[153] Deutsche Feldarbeiterzentralstelle Berlin, Bedingungen für die Vermittlung, in GStA PK, I. HA, 87 B, no. 221, p. 197.

[154] Bodenstein, *Beschäftigung*, p. 13.

[155] See GStA PK, I. HA, 87 B, no. 222, pp. 217, 274, 372.

[156] *Ibid.*, no. 215, p. 242.   [157] *Ibid.*, no. 221.

falsifications' was to give one's religion as Greek Orthodox to claim membership of the Ruthenian nation.[158] Additional staff had to be hired for the border stations to subject the seasonal workers to a rudimentary language test intended to reveal the truth about their (linguistically defined) identity.

But the real problem was not the falsification and simulation of fixed identities, but rather that such identities were, in many cases, impossible to assign. In 1909, the Central Office for Field Workers reported to the government in Berlin that the 'situation in central Galicia' had become such that 'an unequivocal and really appropriate differentiation between Poles and Ruthenians does not seem feasible'. Or not for the authorities, at least – which does not exclude the possibility that those involved were exploiting these variable assignments and employing them in a strategic fashion. But from the German administration's point of view, cultural and linguistic competencies, social relationships, and religious and national affiliations crossed and overlapped to such an extent that it seemed impossible to draw clear boundaries. Because of the 'long-established co-habitation of the two peoples', clear identities seemed to have disappeared – or, should we say, the invention of national traditions had not yet taken effect? In any case the civil servants had to admit that 'neither racial characteristics nor the otherwise distinct differences in customs and habits' were distinct enough to allow clear differentiation, especially as here, in spite of all the Herderian and cultural-nationalistic assumptions, one 'was let down by the characteristics of religious faith and language'.[159]

As a result, the border posts, Landräte, and Regierungspräsidenten and Oberpräsidenten of the Prussian provinces often sought guidelines on how to deal with a situation in which 'Ruthenians … are often no longer recognisable as a Ruthenian population'.[160] Because

---

[158] Regierungspräsident in Oppeln to Minister des Innern, 30 March 1912, in *ibid.*, no. 221.

[159] Deutsche Feldarbeiterzentralstelle to Minister für Landwirtschaft, Berlin, 7 April 1909, in *ibid.*, no. 219, p. 161.

[160] Der Oberpräsident der Provinz Westpreußen to Minister des Innern, Danzig, 22 August 1910, in GStA PK, I. HA, Rep 77, Tit. 1135, no. 1, Fasz. 7e, p. 4.

of this, the government found itself forced to scale down the regulations about separating seasonal workers by nationality, at least temporarily, and to allow some exceptions. It had emerged that 'a strict implementation of the separation, even if it were actually possible, [would] meet with the strongest resistance from the people themselves'. This was due not least to the fact that the many years during which Poles and Ruthenians had 'lived mixed up together' had led to 'blood mixing', which made it seem questionable whether such priority should be placed on defining people by nationality.[161] And especially among the higher classes, many Greek Orthodox inhabitants of Galicia spoke Polish and identified with Poland and its culture even while simultaneously describing themselves as Ruthenians. In many regions, the Ruthenian language only became dominant (instead of Polish) as a result of nationalist efforts that took place from the 1860s onward.[162] It was obvious to the Prussian ministry of the interior that because of these irregularities, 'establishing nationality [was] in many cases not possible'. The 'contrasts' that were still assumed to exist had 'here become almost completely blurred'.[163]

But this scaling-down of the restrictions did not mean that the principle of separating workers by nation (and by 'race', as was always emphasised) was being abandoned altogether. Instead, the ministry was continually presented with new ideas about how the 'difficult differentiation between Poles and Ruthenians' could be achieved. Technologies of identity-recording and bureaucratic control were put in place. Personal data were recorded and collected, copied and reproduced, placed in alphabetical order, stored and compared. This was supposed to reveal differences and particularities 'in a flawless manner'.[164] Accordingly, the ministry of agriculture protested against

---

[161] Deutsche Feldarbeiterzentralstelle to Minister für Landwirtschaft, Berlin, 7 April 1909, in GStA PK, I. HA, 87 B, no. 219, p. 161.

[162] On this topic see Sereda, 'Public Debates'; and Himka, *Galician Villagers*, pp. 59–104.

[163] Decree issued by the Prussian Minister of the Interior, 31 May 1909, in *Der Arbeitsmarkt: Monatsschrift des Verbandes Deutscher Arbeitsnachweise* 13 (October 1909/September 1910), 54.

[164] Attachment to a letter from the Ministry of Agriculture, 28 May 1907, in GStA PK, I. HA, 87 B, no. 217, p. 143.

the introduction of exceptions and insisted that 'certain contrasts continue to exist' between Ruthenians and Poles. It was still possible, they argued, to assume that the two nations could be separated 'for the most part', a separation which would also 'generally [be] applicable' to the seasonal workers in Germany.[165]

But if the ethno-national order that was assumed could not always be clearly identified, it would have to be reinforced. For this purpose, the Central Office of Field Workers, working with the Ruthenian national committee, created a German–Ruthenian dictionary, which those hired as Ruthenians were obliged to purchase when crossing the border into Germany. The dictionary had the explicit purpose of marking differences and increasing the readers' awareness of national particularities. 'Remember that you are a Ruthenian!' was the most important principle, and it was based, for the most part, on one single condition: 'Never let anyone call you a "Pole"': national identity created from a semiotic of difference.

The pages that followed were full of instructions about preserving Ruthenian traditions and maintaining a distance from the Poles ('never dirty yourself with Poles, neither in faith nor in language'). There were also recommendations on hygiene ('always make sure you are clean and neatly dressed'), on the politically correct manner of finding a job ('go to Prussia for work') and a politicised list of 'ten commandments' (for example: 'You shall recognise no other leader ... except the national committee') which had clearly been composed by the Ruthenian nationalists. The dictionary closed with the 'seven deadly sins' and finally with the 'sins' that were 'screaming to the heavens for revenge' – a catalogue of anti-Polish prejudices and resentments.[166]

In this way, the Prussian hiring of workers was closely linked to the nationalisation of Ruthenian peasants, which it was also meant to promote. Clearly, within the long process of the formation of the Ukrainian nation this was only a marginal event. From the mid 1860s

---

[165] Ministerium für Landwirtschaft, Berlin, 2 May 1911, in *ibid.*, no. 220, p. 288.
[166] Quoted in a transcription of pp. 6–9 of the German–Ruthenian dictionary produced by the *Feldarbeiterzentrale*, in *ibid.*, no. 116, pp. 155–58. Excerpts are also contained in Nichtweiß, *Saisonarbeiter*, pp. 89ff.

onward, the two most important strands of the national movement –
the 'Ukrainophiles' who wanted to achieve a Greater Ukraine (and
who differed from a peripheral Ruthenian strand focusing on the
Habsburg empire) and the 'Russophiles' who wanted the Ruthenians
to be united with the greater Russian nation – had become a broader
movement.[167] This movement was no longer carried by the clergy
alone; it also now involved the growing class of educated laypeople
that had developed during the course of modernisation and the
development of the education system. Both strands set themselves
up in opposition to the Polish majority population, which, after the
Habsburg settlement with the Poles in 1867, had become the politically dominant nation within Galicia.

From the 1880s onward especially, the 'Ukrainophiles', who were
growing in strength and were supported by the Habsburg government, began to attempt to develop a national culture. This included
standardising the Ukrainian language and its script, but also founding
scientific associations, a Ukrainian theatre and a national museum in
Lemberg (Lviv), intensifying ethnological studies, and strengthening
Ukrainian national literature.[168] An example is provided by the reading groups attached to the association for popular education, *Prosvita*,
which by the First World War had 200,000 members. From the start
of the twentieth century, national consciousness had reached large
numbers of the mainly rural Ruthenians.[169] Another important factor
was migration: between 1890 and 1914, some 800,000 Ruthenians/
Ukrainians emigrated from the Habsburg empire, mainly to the
United States and Canada, in addition to those travelling to Prussia
as seasonal workers, and this migration also contributed to the process of nationalisation.

In the event, after a number of protests, the dictionaries had to be
withdrawn because of fears of negative effects on Galician Poles and
on the policy of the Austrian government toward letting its citizens

---

[167] For a comparison of the different national options see Himka, 'Construction'.
[168] On the role of historiography in contributing to the development of Ukrainian
nationalism see Prymak, *Hrushevsky*.
[169] See Moser, 'Entwicklung'; Yekelchyk, 'Body'; Himka, *Galician Villagers*; Himka,
Religion; Mick, 'Ukrainemacher'; and Markovits and Sysyn, *Nationbuilding*.

leave. At the same time, the fact that these dictionaries were compiled and distributed in the first place is evidence of the need felt by the German authorities to be able to distinguish clearly between nationalities, as a reaction to the increase in mobility and fluctuation at Germany's eastern border. The Central Office for Field Workers, too, assessed the situation in identical terms. In a memorandum to the ministry of agriculture, it stated that as a result of 'the migratory movement' relationships that were 'previously rather loose' were now 'especially emphasised'.[170] Mobility and movement produced difference and particularity. 'It is only now', as Bodenstein, the employers' representative fantasised, 'that we … will be able to differentiate cleanly between the foreign workers on the basis of their nationality'.[171] His dream was a vision of bureaucratic controls, a utopia of colonial administration and a longing for clear national identities.[172]

EPILOGUE

In March 1898, a Polish member of the Prussian parliament, Szmula, asked the government 'to tell us whether we have any chance of getting Chinese [people] in the future'. According to the stenographic minutes this question was followed by 'hilarity' among the members. But in this question Szmula was protesting about the many difficulties that were being placed in the way of hiring Polish seasonal workers – and the conservative landowners would have approved. Szmula argued that these restrictions ignored commercial needs. 'We have to have workers, of some kind or another; if they are not to be Poles or Russians you'll have to use Chinese in the end.' Renewed 'hilarity' resulted.[173]

---

[170] Deutsche Feldarbeiterzentralstelle, Berlin, 7 April 1909, in GStA PK, I. HA, 87 B, no. 219, p. 161.

[171] Bodenstein, *Beschäftigung*, p. 23.

[172] This policy was readopted during the Nazi occupation of Poland when the German administration attempted to differentiate between Poles and Ukrainians and to exploit the Ukrainians. See Furber, 'Near as Far', p. 567.

[173] *Stenographische Berichte über die Verhandlungen des Abgeordnetenhauses*, 58th session, 29 March 1898, p. 1941.

But it was a serious issue. The desire for separation and for identity discussed above concealed a deeper fear of mixing and hybridisation. This applied in particular to the Polish immigrants, many of whom adapted rapidly to their host country. In terms of language, culture, appearance and customs, they could barely be distinguished from the indigenous population. The short 'restricted period' during the winter, introduced to ensure that the Polish workers returned home, was little more than a futile gesture. Given the 'racial links [*völkische Verwandtschaft*] with the inhabitants of the border areas' – for example the 'frequent use of Polish-speaking foreigners'[174] – it no longer seemed possible to 'cleanly differentiate' between nationalities.[175] Friedrich Syrup, later President of the Reich Institute for Labour Exchange (*Reichsanstalt für Arbeitsvermittlung*), therefore concluded: 'If a large number of foreigners remain a clearly identified and closed foreign body within the German Reich, this is more tolerable than foreigners being mixed into the German population.'[176]

Max Weber was of a similar opinion. 'In Australia, immigration by the Chinese is forbidden', he warned as early as 1895, 'but the Poles are even more dangerous, because of the possibility of mixing and lowering the German culture'.[177] So were Chinese workers preferable? A 'closed foreign body' with no 'possibility of mixing'? Was it not in fact true that the Chinese had shown 'nothing of national assimilation' regardless of where they had moved to look for work and accommodation? 'Foreign they came and foreign they remained', as a German observer of the Australian situation reported home.[178] In an era of global labour migration, of a transport revolution and of globalisation, it seemed that this could be said only of the Chinese. Was this the solution? Those who wanted irreducible differences seemingly had to turn to the Chinese: 'Not only are they a foreign race, but they remain one.'[179]

[174] Syrup-Stettin, 'Industriearbeiter', p. 296.
[175] Bodenstein, *Beschäftigung*, p. 23.
[176] Syrup-Stettin, 'Industriearbeiter', pp. 295.
[177] Weber, 'Grundlagen der Volkswirtschaft'.
[178] Schenk, 'Chinesische Arbeiter', p. 208.
[179] Paschen, 'Einwanderung', p. 165.

CHAPTER FOUR

The politics of segregation: Chinese workers, global networks and the 'colourless peril'

'THE LONGING FOR CHINAMEN'

In early 1890, von Heppe, Regierungspräsident in Danzig, asked the agricultural societies to submit their assessments of whether it would be advisable to assist the immigration of Chinese workers so as to boost the labour force in western Prussia. The government, landowners and the general public were to revisit this issue on many occasions, with varying intensity, until the outbreak of the First World War. In 1890 a number of large landowners immediately spoke out in support of the project. In the autumn of 1889, demands for the admission of Chinese workers had also been made in Stettin and Greifswald and had been submitted to the Prussian ministry of agriculture. A committee was immediately established, which made contact with the Chinese ambassador to Berlin.[1]

'The longing for Chinamen', as an article in the *Freisinnige Zeitung* wryly termed it, was a direct consequence of the closure of the German–Russian border in 1885, intended by Bismarck to prevent Polish farm workers migrating to Germany. Fears of the 'Polonisation' of eastern Germany, regularly expressed in contemporary rhetoric, had led to a total ban on immigration. But in Prussia, the flight from the land and the intensification of agriculture, together with the increasing cultivation of labour-intensive root crops, had led to a labour shortage that made the issue of foreign seasonal workers a recurrent and dominant topic in Prussian politics. This is the

---

[1] Geheimes Staatsarchiv Berlin (GStA) PK, I. HA, 87 B, no. 211, pp. 2, 3; *ibid.*, Rep 77, Tit. 922 no. 2. See also the short remarks on the issue in Nichtweiß, *Saisonarbeiter*, pp. 38–39; and Herbert, *Ausländerbeschäftigung*, p. 23.

context in which the idea emerged that the problem could be alleviated by importing Chinese workers, who were not seen as posing any national problems.

But public reaction to these plans by no means went along with the idea that importing Chinese workers merely followed the laws of the market. The *Münchener Neueste Nachrichten*, for example, bemoaned the low cultural level of the Chinese workers and predicted that 'competition with them would have the result that in time, the cultural level of the Chinese would become that of the Germans'. Even those opposed to protectionist economic policies could not doubt that because of the Chinese threat, every 'regulation for protecting national work' was appropriate.[2]

The liberal *Freisinnige Zeitung* mocked the way the Junkers, known for anti-liberal Anglophobia, had suddenly developed a love of 'the Chinese': 'German parliamentarism, in particular, is increasingly acquiring a Chinese air', with bureaucratic roles increasing and the influence of the people on politics decreasing. In terms of pomp and rigid social hierarchies, too, the Kaiserreich had 'made considerable progress toward the Chinese [system]', even if 'nobody has yet … come up with the idea of surrounding Germany with a Chinese wall'. The newspaper rejected the idea of importing Chinese workers, as they would be competition for German workers and their presence 'in the country [would have] a demoralising effect in every direction'.[3]

But the Prussian ministry of agriculture was interested enough to ask the general consulate in Batavia to draw up a report on the legal and social situation of Chinese workers on the eastern coast of Sumatra, who had been recruited to work there by the Dutch colonial government. When the report was delivered in the autumn of 1890, however, the reaction from the Prussian landowners was muted. There was no longer much interest in hiring 'coolies', mainly because of the changed situation in Prussia. From November 1890 onward, Polish seasonal workers were once again permitted to enter eastern Prussia, and, a year later, were admitted to the whole state of Prussia.

[2] *Münchener Neueste Nachrichten* (19 January 1890).
[3] *Freisinnige Zeitung* (17 March 1889).

Although there were still limits on Polish immigration, and workers were forced to return home during a 'restricted period' in the winter, the demand for labour had largely dried up, and the calls for Chinese 'coolies' did not resurface for several years.[4]

In the mid 1890s the labour shortage returned. Migration from the farms to the cities had increased; industrial expansion, with its huge demands for labour and the higher wages paid in industrial areas, led to net migration out of agricultural regions that could only be balanced by increased immigration. In 1895, the policy of opening the country's borders with Russia was extended indefinitely, but concerns about the availability of labour remained. Against this backdrop, an eastern Prussian landowner by the name of Schmidt made a submission to the government in December 1894, in which he suggested 'importing Chinese, a sober and hardworking tribe with few needs'.[5] At the same time he sent a letter to Peking asking 'the Imperial Embassy for information about whether Chinese [workers] would be suitable … for eastern Prussia in terms of the climate and the agricultural work to be done'.[6]

In response, the Prussian foreign ministry decided to carry out a detailed evaluation of the issue. The German legation in Peking was asked to supply a detailed report on the practice of emigration by Chinese workers. Practical questions such as transport and wages were the main concerns. But the ambassador responded that, in particular, 'it would probably be very difficult to persuade the inhabitants of northern China, the climatic conditions of which are, while not identical to eastern Prussia, more similar to the latter than those of southern China, to move to a far-distant and completely unknown country'. As a result the foreign ministry announced that 'under these

---

[4] According to the linguistic convention adopted by the Chinese government, the term 'coolie trade' (which was banned) applied only to forced emigration, a form of forced labour. But in the West the term 'coolie' was used to refer to all Chinese workers. The term was also used in contracts with Chinese workers. On the history of the term see Irick, *Ch'ing Policy*, pp. 3ff.

[5] Schmidt quoting himself retrospectively, in the *Illustrierte Landwirtschaftliche Zeitung* (6 January 1897).

[6] GStA PK, 1. HA, 87 B, no. 211, p. 155.

circumstances ... the plan of transferring rural workers of the Chinese race to eastern Prussia [would] have no prospect of success'.[7]

Over the following decade, this remained the position taken by the government every time the issue of Chinese labour was raised. An example was in 1899, when, in the course of a major debate on the admission of Russian-Polish labourers, a member of the Prussian parliament stated that 'in the near future we will probably turn to importing coolies because the use of Galician workers will not be sufficient'.[8] In the Reichstag, the idea of hiring Chinese workers was discussed in 1898, following remarks by August Bebel, and again in the spring of 1900, in connection with the Boxer War. In the meantime, Germany had itself become a colonial power in China, which made it seem more likely that such a plan could be realised. The issue was extensively reported by the press, and as a result the Kaiser asked the agriculture ministry to examine the question. In its answer, the ministry referred to the insights gained four years earlier and stated that the occasional attempts to import 'coolies must be resisted because of the risks to native workers and to our whole civilisation [*Kulturzustand*]'.[9] In 1905, a Stettin businessman, Ernst Rudolf Schuster, who wanted to employ Chinese workers in his factory, was verbally informed that his suggestion was politically impossible.[10]

In late 1906, the issue surfaced again. The plenary assembly of the western Prussian Chamber of Agriculture, presided over by von Oldenburg-Januschau, had decided to deal with the crippling labour shortage in western Prussia by adopting a resolution that stated that, although regrettable for national reasons, the recruitment of Chinese workers was unavoidable. This met with widespread reactions in the national press. Although some organs, such as the *Münchener Post*, were inclined 'to see this note as an early April fool', it soon became clear that 'the western Prussian farmers are deadly serious about their request'. 'The covetous gaze turns to the land of coolies, where the cheapest workers in the world are available en masse.'[11]

[7] *Ibid.*, p. 152.   [8] Haus der Abgeordneten, 17th session, 11 February 1899.
[9] GStA PK, I. HA, 87 B, no. 213, pp. 57, 230, 231.
[10] *Ibid.*, I. HA Rep 77, Tit. 922 no. 2.   [11] *Münchener Post* (6 November 1906).

For most commentators, there was 'no doubt that this issue must have practical consequences ... sooner or later'. The *Deutsche Volkszeitung* saw the plans as a 'resolution with ... fateful implications', which had already been in the pipeline since, for example, Hungary had decided to import 20,000 'coolies': '[i]t was in the air!'. The main organ of the landowners, the *Deutsche Tageszeitung*, attempted to defend the plans. Any criticisms of the project should not focus on the landowners, it wrote, but on those 'who have let it come to this pass' and had failed to employ 'large-scale measures'. What they had in mind were suggestions that the flight from the land and the resulting 'lack of people' in agricultural regions should be prevented by limiting the free movement of the population. Domestic mobility, it argued, created a pull effect that necessarily resulted in cross-border mobility too.[12]

But in general, the idea of recruiting Chinese workers met with objections and sometimes with considerable criticism. Motives differed. For the *Staatszeitung*, for example, the problem was 'that these people are heathens, indeed highly depraved elements' whom one would not like to imagine in the *Abendland*, among other reasons because 'they would bring the custom of infanticide with them'. Other commentators restricted themselves to economic issues and hypothesised about wage and transport costs, the pressure on the labour market, and the situation of German workers. Most of the numerous comments rejected the plan completely and described the 'import of Chinese' as a 'crime against the German Fatherland'.[13]

The suggestion by the western Prussian Chambers of Agriculture was mainly discussed in the press, without any official reaction by government. But during the next year, 1907, landowners increasingly submitted official requests to the Prussian government to be allowed to hire Chinese – and occasionally even Japanese – workers. The reason given was usually 'the general labour shortage in the countryside and the unreliability of the Polish seasonal workers. In contrast

---

[12] *Freisinnige Zeitung* (25 October, 7 December 1906); *Berliner Tageblatt* (7 December 1906); *Deutsche Volkszeitung* (8 December 1906); and *Frankfurter Zeitung* (20 December 1906).

[13] *Staatszeitung* (6, 8 December 1906); *Badische Volkszeitung* (30 December 1906); and *Danziger Allgemeine Zeitung* (9 December 1906).

to these, the Chinese are reputed to be respectable, honest people.' Initially, the ministry of the interior reacted by citing its 1895 rejection of the idea. But 'as the numbers of such applications have increased in recent times', Moltke, the Prussian minister of the interior, asked the Colonial Office and the Navy Office, which was responsible for Kiaochow, to provide 'relevant detailed information'.[14]

The Kiaochow government responded with a report confirming 'that the Chinese are good at farming' and 'are respectable and honest people'. But it did not want to take on the responsibility of such a far-reaching decision and emphasised that 'the behaviour and manner of the Chinese worker in his own country [could] not act as a yardstick for his employment abroad'. Finally, it pointed out the 'not inconsiderable costs of transport' that might prevent the emigration of Chinese rural workers to Prussia. Correspondingly, the Prussian government rejected the idea, stating in its report of September 1908 'that importing Chinese workers to work in agriculture would – apart from more general concerns – involve considerable practical difficulties, especially financial ones'.[15] As far as the government and the civil service were concerned, the matter was now closed. Animated debate about the advantages and disadvantages of 'coolie work' continued in the press for some time, but over the following years there were only occasional suggestions involving concrete plans for importing workers from eastern Asia.[16] Despite years of discussion, the idea of hiring Chinese workers as an officially sanctioned and government-led project never materialised.

'TRADE IN COOLIES' AND THE GLOBAL LABOUR MARKET

The late-nineteenth-century debates about importing Chinese workers were not limited to Germany; they were a global phenomenon. Over the course of the nineteenth century Chinese mobility had

---

[14] GStA PK, I. HA Rep 77, Tit. 922 no. 2.
[15] *Ibid.*   [16] E.g. *ibid.*, pp. 67–70.

vastly increased.[17] It is estimated that between 1840 and 1940, over 19 million Chinese people migrated to other parts of south-eastern Asia and the countries around the Indian Ocean and the southern Pacific. Singapore and the Straits Settlements acted as hubs for these migratory movements, with many people moving there initially and then travelling onward to Dutch India, Borneo, Burma and places further west. A second large migratory flow brought over 30 million Chinese people to Manchuria and Siberia; from the 1890s onward, this was further reinforced by the settlement policies of the Qing Dynasty and by the construction of railways.[18]

The third major Chinese migratory movement, which I shall focus on below, took place in the late nineteenth century and brought some 2.5 million Chinese workers to South Africa, Australia, and North and South America. This so-called 'coolie trade' was generally seen by contemporaries almost as a return to slavery. There were indeed a number of similarities. These included the methods of recruitment, which frequently bordered on kidnapping; the inhuman transport conditions; and the way workers were treated in the sugar plantations and mines to which they were brought, which had high death rates. In fact, where Chinese workers and slaves were both employed in the same plantations, such as in Cuba, there was little difference between the two forms of labour.[19] More recent research has, however, focused on the differences between the various forms of indentured labour, i.e. labour covered by a contract that was entered into for the purposes of transport abroad, and the slave trade.[20] Although the recruitment methods used were certainly drastic, most of those involved were emigrating voluntarily. The high death rates in the plantations and mines have been explained in recent research as caused mainly

[17] For a general account see Pan, *Encyclopedia*. The best study of Chinese migration in the early twentieth century is McKeown, *Migrant Networks*.

[18] See the recent summary in McKeown, 'Global Migration'. See also Segal, *Atlas*; and Zolberg, 'Global Movements'.

[19] On this topic see Emmer, *Colonialism*. Klein, *Slave Trade* provides an excellent overview of research on the Atlantic slave trade.

[20] On the continued existence of unfree labour and its links with global migration see Cohen, *New Helots*.

by disease epidemics and less by maltreatment, though the latter was certainly common.[21]

But even if the migration of Chinese workers cannot be described as slavery, it was closely related to the history of slavery. The recruitment of workers in Asia for Caribbean plantations, for example, increased noticeably as slavery was first restricted and eventually banned in various countries over the course of the nineteenth century: in the USA it was banned in 1865, in Brazil in 1888. The abolition of slavery led to a labour shortage and workers from east and south-east Asia were increasingly hired to fill the gap.[22]

But the dynamics of Chinese labour migration during the latter decades of the nineteenth century cannot be explained by the abolition of slavery alone. A second factor was the change in the international balance of power, the era usually described as 'high imperialism'. Over a few short years, the last non-colonised regions of the planet were claimed by western colonial powers. At the same time, European and American capital, settlers and technology began to conquer the world to a previously unseen extent. This process led to the spread of sugar plantations and thus to increased demand for mobile workers, even in areas where African slavery had been unknown.[23]

These global developments motivated workers from China and other countries to emigrate – including people from Japan, the Philippines and Korea (to Hawaii) and from Java and India (to Canada and in particular to the British colonies in south-east Asia).[24] But a number of internal factors also encouraged the mass exodus from China from the 1850s onward. One interesting aspect of this wave of emigration is that it originated almost entirely in five small regions in the southern Chinese provinces of Fujian and Guangdong (and the island of Hainan). Economic problems, population pressure and a series of natural catastrophes had all combined to make life there more

---

[21] See Engerman, 'Labor'. On the narrow divide between free labour and forced labour in the nineteenth century, see Mann, 'Mär'; Brass and van der Linden, *Labour*; Emmer, *Colonialism*; Steinfeld, *Coercion*; and Eltis, *Migration*.

[22] On this topic see Hu-Dehart, 'Coolie Labour'; and Green, *Emancipation*.

[23] Northrup, *Labor*, pp. 17ff. See also Lai, *Labor*.

[24] See Tinker, *System*.

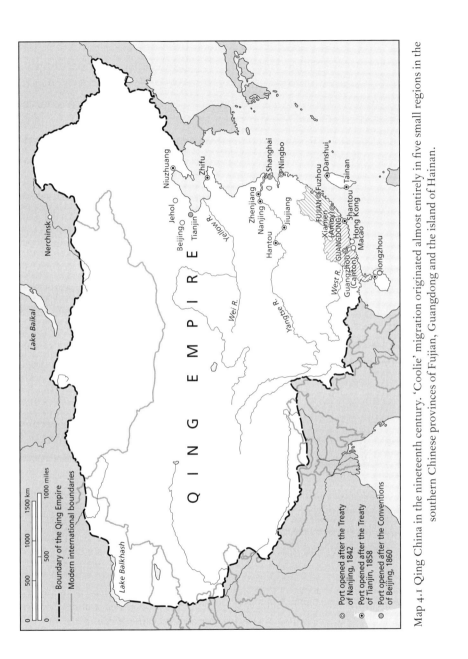

Map 4.1 Qing China in the nineteenth century. 'Coolie' migration originated almost entirely in five small regions in the southern Chinese provinces of Fujian, Guangdong and the island of Hainan.

difficult and made people more prepared to emigrate.[25] Political factors added to the reasons for leaving. In particular the Taiping Rebellion, between 1850 and 1864, devastated central and southern China, left about 20 million people dead and was followed by a period of political and religious oppression. This example itself shows the extent to which internal Chinese affairs had already been affected by contact with the West. Hong Xiuquan, the leader of the Taiping, claimed to be the younger brother of Jesus and preached a variant of the Old-Testament-based Protestant Christianity that had been introduced to China by western missionaries. Hong's rebels believed themselves to be social reformers, aiming to abolish numerous Chinese customs (such as games of chance, opium, foot-binding and prostitution) and replace them with a Chinese version of Christianity. For example, they made contravening any of the Ten Commandments a crime. Western powers were also involved in the suppression of the rebellion, for example with the involvement of Charles 'Chinese' Gordon, an English artillery officer, and his militia of mercenaries, the 'Ever Victorious Army'.[26]

While most studies of Chinese emigration make do with citing such general factors, it is crucial also to take into account, more specifically, the development of Canton (Guangzhou) and the long history of imperialistic engagement with the region by western powers, especially with the province of Guangdong. From 1760, Canton had a monopoly on Chinese foreign trade, as the Chinese empire limited all trade with western countries, especially Britain and/or the East India Company, to this port. Only a few rich merchants were allowed to act as a trading partners; by the end of the period this had been reduced to thirteen firms that formed a guild known as the 'cohong' (gong-hang). Canton thus became the main place of exchange for European ships and wares, and also for people and ideas.[27]

---

[25] On the socio-economic situation in China see the classic study by Wakeman, *Strangers*, which, however, pays very little attention to emigration. See also Faure, *Structure*.

[26] On this topic see Wagner, *Reenacting*; and Gregory, *Great Britain*.

[27] On this topic see Waley-Cohen, *Sextants*, esp. pp. 98–100. On the canton system see Irick, *Ch'ing Policy*, pp. 81–150; and Osterhammel, *China*, pp. 110–17.

With the first Opium War (1839–42) the situation changed. After defeat by Great Britain, China was forced to make a number of concessions that had long-term effects on the development of Canton. They included the opening-up of five ports for international trade, the cession of Hong Kong to Britain, and limits on import taxes. The loss of Canton's trade monopoly resulted in considerable unemployment; domestic industry also suffered through the abolition of imports of English fabrics and textiles. In other words, European imperialist expansion had led to a deterioration of the situation in southern China, and many reacted with flight or migration.[28] During the resumption of hostilities known as the Arrow War or Second Opium War (1858–60), English and French troops occupied Canton for several years. This allowed agents (often operating like slave traders) and people interested in emigrating to avoid the imperial ban on emigration, and it increased the trade in Chinese workers.[29]

Emigration had in fact been strictly banned in China since the start of the Qing period in the seventeenth century. Anyone leaving the country was regarded as either a pariah or a pirate and was seen as having abandoned, even betrayed, civilisation. After a massacre of Chinese people in Batavia in 1740, Emperor Qianlong infamously remarked that these Chinese had abandoned their ancestors for the sake of profit and thus deserved no sympathy. The ban on emigration corresponded to the traditional taboo on leaving one's family and the tombs of one's ancestors. But its main aim was to prevent those loyal to the Ming dynasty, which had been overthrown by the Qing, from resettling outside China. Emigration was thus punishable by death. The imperial government stood by this general ban on emigration and even in the years after the Opium War it refused to recognise the problem of increasing outward mobility. It was only with the British invasion of Peking in 1860 that the government was obliged effectively to accept citizens' right to emigrate. Even so the laws governing emigration were not officially changed until 1893.[30]

---

[28] See Wakeman, *Strangers*, p. 98; and Leong, *Migration*, p. 42.

[29] See Chan, *Asian Americans*, pp. 3–24. On the social upheavals in the region around Canton see also Bastid-Bruguière, 'Currents', esp. pp. 582–86, 591–93; and Lin, *Rural Economy*.

[30] On this topic see the detailed account in Irick, *Ch'ing Policy*.

Wang Gungwu has suggested that various stages and patterns can be identified for Chinese migration, and most authors have adopted his periodisation. According to his account, most migration before 1850 was by merchants and traders (*Huashang*). They, and craftsmen, usually educated and wealthy, settled in foreign port cities and other trading centres. Their lives remained focused on China, and the close personal and professional links between them – and their regular trips home – formed the basis for lucrative trade and commercial success. When outside China they usually lived in discrete Chinese communities, only rarely marrying into the native populations.

The second phase, lasting into the early twentieth century, was marked by 'coolie' migration (*Huagong*) – the migration of impoverished rural and urban underclasses, most of whom returned to China once their contracts had expired. Finally, Wang identifies the start of a third phase (*Huaqiao*) at around 1900. This term referred to all Chinese abroad, regardless of their origins or occupation. It was closely linked to the development of Chinese nationalism and points to the political, legal and cultural transformations in ideas about 'China' and Chineseness.[31]

These references to the history of Chinese migration are important, especially since internal migration, for example to coastal cities, was often a first step on the road toward emigration. When we look at local conditions more closely it also becomes evident that the distinction drawn in historiography between internal migration and emigration was not central to social practice.[32] Thus, most studies on Chinese emigration emphasise the centuries-old tradition of internal Asian migration and trace continuities between nineteenth- and twentieth-century emigration and the north–south migration of the Han Chinese.[33] But this emphasis on continuity runs the risk of overlooking the fundamental change that accompanied the global developments of the era: the end of the slave trade, the new imperialism, the growth of capitalist global trade and the colonial conquest

---

[31] See Wang, *China*, esp. pp. 3–21. See also his 'Perspectives'.
[32] See for example Woon, 'Community', esp. pp. 299–300.
[33] See for example Chan, *Bittersweet Soil*, pp. 7–15.

of China. In addition, the continuity paradigm often involves a perspective – as in Wang Gungwu – that sees merchant migration as the dominant pattern of Chinese emigration. In contrast, I will focus on the mass migration of impoverished workers, which I view as a phenomenon *sui generis* that owed more to the structures of the global economy than to Chinese traditions. The conventional focus on the higher-class but less numerous migrants such as merchants is plausible given their considerable contribution – financial and practical – to the development of Chinese nationalism. In light of the development of global labour markets, however, the emigration of millions of Chinese workers during the second half of the nineteenth century was an equally important process, even if the individual achievements of these workers have rarely found their way into history books.

The overseas transfer of Chinese workers began as early as the beginning of the nineteenth century. In 1810, Chinese workers were being brought to Brazil; from the 1840s onward, 'coolie workers' were being sought in the Caribbean (especially in Cuba). The first transport of Chinese workers to Peru, in 1847, is usually regarded as the start of mass emigration. In 1825, when Peru became independent, 17,000 slaves were liberated, and further imports of slaves were banned. Together with the increasing global demand for guano, a labour-intensive product that was used as a fertiliser, this led to a growing shortage of labour. In 1849, Peru passed a special immigration law to permit the importing of Chinese 'coolies'.[34] Also in Australia, where the deportation of British prisoners ended in 1840, labour shortages, especially in wool production, led to the recruitment of Chinese workers. The first 120 arrived in 1848; by 1852, there were already 2,666.[35]

An important catalyst of Chinese mass emigration was the discovery of gold, firstly in California in 1849, and then in Australia in 1851. The 'gold rush' in both places triggered global migratory flows. In 1852, there were already 20,000 Chinese people in California, who

[34] On migration to Central and South America, see Farley, 'Coolie Trade'; Chang-Rodriguez, 'Labor Migration'; Meagher, 'Introduction'; Helly, *Idéologie*; and Stewart, *Bondage*.

[35] See Yen, *Coolies*, pp. 46–47.

were rapidly employed in a variety of jobs. In Australia, too, the dream of sudden wealth drew people from around the globe, and by 1858 around 40,000 Chinese people had settled there. Other destinations for Chinese emigrants included the goldfields at Fraser River in British Columbia and Klondike in Alaska. But this wave of migration, triggered by the gold rush, was not identical with the so-called 'coolie' trade, which only really took off when workers were hired for plantations and for the construction of railways in the United States. The global mobility of Chinese workers reached a peak only during the third quarter of the century.

The changes in the nature of emigration can be seen in the conditions linked to emigration and the recruitment mechanisms used. These reveal the extent to which Chinese labour had already become a commodity. Emigration to California and Australia had been, on the whole, voluntary. Those who could not afford to pay for the journey undertook to work on arrival to pay off the fare. But with the increasing demand for labour in the plantation economies, forced emigration increased. Until 1859, the Qing administration did not recognise the 'trade in coolies', as emigration was not officially allowed, and simply ignored the phenomenon. From 1860 onward it tolerated voluntary emigration (on the basis of the 'Canton system') but the actual 'coolie trade', defined as a form of forced labour, was banned.

The recruitment of 'coolies' frequently involved abduction. Agents often used false promises to lure young men (in particular) to participate, but then confined them to 'prison-like low barracks'. These mushroomed in the main trading centres such as Hong Kong, Canton, Amoy (Xiamen), Swatow (Shantou) and Macao. In these barracks, 'the coolies [were] housed in a way that can be described without exaggeration as inhuman', as the German consul reported to Berlin in 1902.[36] From there, the inmates were put on ships, which were usually completely overcrowded. The conditions in the barracks and during the voyage were often so intolerable that there were many deaths and even, on several occasions, revolts and

[36] Bundesarchiv (BA) Berlin, R 9208, no. 1532, p. 62.

mutinies.[37] In 1855, England and China passed the British Passenger Act, which laid down minimum standards for transportation of persons on board ship. The USA and Germany soon adopted these rules. The USA even banned the 'coolie trade' overall in 1862, but this legislation only applied if a ship docked at an American port.[38] Over the course of the 1860s there were various attempts to prevent forced emigration, which was increasingly concentrated on Portuguese-administered Macao, where Chinese laws did not apply. International pressure on Portugal to eliminate the 'coolie trade' from Macao finally led to a ban on the trade there in 1874.[39]

This did not mean that the mass emigration of Chinese workers came to an end. In fact, Chinese migration reached its peak during the last three decades of the nineteenth century. By far the largest proportion of Chinese emigrants initially travelled to the Straits Settlements and especially to Singapore, which housed the largest 'coolie market' in eastern Asia.[40] From there, they moved to other south-east Asian countries, especially to Indo-China, the Malay Peninsula and Siam. But the Dutch colonies also recruited workers from the Straits Settlements. The presence of a Chinese population in all of these countries changed the situation there in the long term, to a greater or lesser degree, and led to social problems and conflicts, many of which persist until the present.[41] From the 1860s onward, Chinese workers were hired for sugar-cane plantations in Hawaii. In the USA, they were employed mainly in railroad construction, the Central Pacific Railway Company having been the first to hire Chinese people, in 1865. By the 1870s, about 18,000 Chinese people

---

[37] See for example the eyewitness report of a transport in Gottwaldt, *Auswanderung*, pp. 22ff.

[38] On this topic see Henson, *Commissioners*, pp. 83ff.

[39] See Chan, *Bittersweet Soil*, pp. 22–36; Yen, *Coolies*, pp. 36–71; and Irick, *Ch'ing Policy*, pp. 201–72. See also Wang, *Organization*. A useful case study is contained in Wippich, 'Fanny-Kirchner'.

[40] See Trocki, *Opium and Empire*.

[41] See the summary of overseas Chinese populations in Gottwaldt, *Auswanderung* (chapter entitled 'Die Chinesen im Ausland'). On the development in south-east Asia see Suryadinata, *Ethnic Chinese*; Purcell, *Chinese*; Heidhues, 'Chinese Settlements'; and Wang, *National Identity*.

were entering America every year, before the Chinese Exclusion Act (1882) reduced these numbers dramatically.[42] Finally, after the turn of the century Chinese 'coolies' also found their way to South Africa. As a result of the Boer War, the South African goldmines were in difficulty and the prospect of cutting costs by hiring cheap Chinese labour was attractive. After extended negotiations, the Chinese government finally agreed to the recruitment, and between June 1904 and November 1906, 63,296 'coolies' were brought to the Transvaal. It was the first time that workers had been recruited in northern China, where the combination of natural disasters and the Boxer War had greatly increased people's willingness to emigrate.[43]

GERMAN REACTIONS: A GLOBAL LABOUR MARKET OR A 'YELLOW PERIL'?

The discussions about recruiting Chinese workers for Prussian agriculture that recurred at regular intervals from the 1890s onward took place in the context of this global demand for Chinese labour. We can identify, as ideal types, two major points of view in the German debate, which we can characterise as 'cultural essentialism' on the one hand, and the view of labour as a commodity on the other. In reality, of course, most opinions were located somewhere along this spectrum. On the one hand, there was a belief in the overall, cross-border dynamic of global capitalist trade in goods. In an era of colonialism and colonial goods, of extended trade links and falling transport costs, Chinese workers could be seen as part of this universal mechanism of exchange. The Prussian landowner Schmidt, whose 1894 request had forced the Prussian government to investigate the 'coolie issue' at an official level for the first time, summarised this view of labour as a commodity as follows: 'Surely it makes no difference whether we pay the wages of Russian-Polish workers or of Chinese ones.' And,

---

[42] See Chan, *Bittersweet Soil*, pp. 39ff.

[43] See Yen, *Coolies*, pp. 335–47; Pan, *Sons*, pp. 63–67; Richardson, *Mine Labour*; and Richardson, 'Coolies'. For contemporary accounts see Cooke, *Chinese Labour*; Munro, *Transvaal*; and Payne, *Einführung*.

'our consumers, too, will surely not care who it is who produces our products'.[44]

This type of language was mainly used by landowners, who believed that 'these people are seemingly very hard-working and conscientious' and would thus be suitable workers in Prussia too.[45] Their belief was confirmed by numerous reports by experts on China (often self-appointed ones), most of whom believed in, even raved about, the diligence and stamina of Chinese workers. 'The Chinese is ready for action everywhere and at any time ... always willing, always reliable, content with low wages, with no particular demands', as Max von Brandt, who had been an envoy in China for many years, reported. The geographer Friedrich Ratzel wrote his dissertation on Chinese emigration and also saw the Chinese 'set apart as a people who know how to work hard and manage the fruits of their labour well'. Considerable emphasis was placed on the Chinese workers' agricultural experience and skills, partly because of the suggestions that they should be employed for agricultural work in Prussia.[46]

This was also the view of the German consulates in China, whose reports treat labour almost like any other article for export. Because of the brisk trade in 'coolies' and indentured labourers that was taking place in the southern Chinese port cities, the staff of the consulates were familiar with the practice of global labour migration and did not see it as anything particularly unusual. Inquiries from Prussian ministries and the German government were therefore answered mainly in terms of practical issues – the fundamental idea that labour was a tradeable commodity was taken for granted. The consulates thus emphasised that Chinese workers were in principle suitable for agricultural work, described their wages and diet, and outlined the different roles played by men, women and children. The question of the practicability or otherwise of the 'import of coolies' was discussed in terms of the wage demands and the cost of transporting the workers

---

[44] *Illustrierte Landwirtschaftliche Zeitung* (6 January 1897).
[45] GStA PK, I. HA Rep 77, Tit. 922 no. 2, p. 68.
[46] Von Brandt, *Lande des Zopfes*, p. 10; and Ratzel, 'Auswanderung', quote on p. 803. Also see, for example, Tille, *Wettbewerb*, p. 9; and von Hesse-Wartegg, *China und Japan*, pp. 60–61.

(Shanghai to Bremerhaven: 440 marks for a third-class passage). While the consulates in China generally rejected the idea of importing Chinese workers to Germany, they based this argument mainly on financial reasoning.[47]

This view of Chinese labour as a commodifiable good and as part of global trade links corresponded to the euphoria that was common around the turn of the century about German access to the Chinese market. From 1897 onward, Germany had a colony in northern China in Kiaochow. The colony was under the command of the navy, who intended to develop it systematically as a 'model colony'. Projects included the German Shantung Railway, the Shantung Mining Company and a systematic policy of infrastructural improvements aimed at making the province accessible for commerce.[48] Other areas of China were also the subject of German dreams and aspirations. Even by this early date, some seventy major German companies had opened subsidiaries in Shanghai, and the founding of a German–Asian bank was under discussion. 'Wherever we look', an observer noted, 'we see, in the most important fields, German interests, German capital, German intelligence, German diligence at work spinning the threads that link us and our economy ever more closely with the Celestial Empire'.[49]

The lure of the vast Chinese market thus has a long history.[50] But China's role in this debate was not limited to its function as an export market for German goods. Rather, it seemed indisputable that the global interlinkages of trade and capital flows would result in changes on both sides. Max von Brandt described China as one of the countries 'fated to exert considerable influence on our trade and industry'.[51] Global trade was leading to changes everywhere and influenced all the parties taking part in it, though to different degrees. The idea

[47] See for example GStA PK, I. HA, 87 B, no. 211, p. 152.
[48] See Mühlhahn, *Herrschaft*, esp. pp. 135–49; Stoecker, *Deutschland*; Ratenhof, *Chinapolitik*; Stingl, *Ferne Osten*; and Jung, *Deutschland*.
[49] Etienne, *Deutschlands wirtschaftliche Interessen*, p. 1.
[50] On this topic see the dicussion in Osterhammel and Petersson, 'Jahrhundertwende', pp. 286–93.
[51] Von Brandt, *Lande des Zopfes*, p. 2.

of importing Chinese 'coolies' to Germany fitted into this view of a world whose expansionary logic would increasingly ignore national boundaries and limits. The economist Adolph von Wenckstern, for example, described this vision of the international dynamism of trade policy and *Weltpolitik*, which by 1900 had, he believed, already ensured that 'the theoretical economic boundary of Germany ... is completely abstract from the geographical borders of the Reich'.[52]

This belief that national boundaries were being overcome and a global market was developing was not always greeted with a euphoric or even an enthusiastic response. Even those who assumed that capital and labour were freely transferable sometimes saw the plans to recruit Chinese workers as a threat that had to be resisted. Conservatives protested against the employment of Chinese workers on German ships and against the thoughtless utilitarianism of industry: 'Capital knows no patriotic considerations; whatever is of advantage to it is good.'[53] The Social Democrats also reacted negatively to the idea of hiring Chinese workers. In a major speech to the Reichstag in February 1898, August Bebel spoke of the 'storm of indignation' that 'would erupt ... across the whole German working class' if this plan were to be realised. He saw the 'undemanding, industrious, modest Chinese workers who will put up with anything' as, in the main, 'scabs' (*Lohndrücker*, people putting downward pressure on wages) and as putty in the hands of landowners and business owners, who would use them against the German working class.[54]

The thorny issue of immigration and the conflict between proletarian internationalism and the need to represent the interests of workers at home was hotly debated in Germany and at international socialist congresses. At the 1904 congress in Amsterdam, it became obvious that the relationship between nationalism and internationalism was partly dependent on the actual situation each individual society found itself in. A motion that immigration by 'workers of backward races (such as

[52] BA Berlin, R 8034 II, no. 5801, p. 16.
[53] 'Drohende Chinesen-Einwanderung' (14 June 1889), in GStA PK, I. HA Rep 77, Tit. 922 no. 2.
[54] *Stenographische Berichte über die Verhandlungen des Reichstags* (*SBVR*), 5th session, 8 February 1898, pp. 892–903.

Chinese, negroes etc.)' should be restricted as they would 'prevent the progress and the possible realisation of socialism' triggered a conflict between representatives of the countries from which emigrants were originating (such as Italy, Hungary, Poland and Japan) and those to which they were headed (North and South America, Australia and South Africa). The positions taken by German representatives were ambivalent, as the delegates had to balance their reservations about Chinese workers with their duty to represent the Polish seasonal workers in Prussia. The international congress in Stuttgart in 1907 then rejected the idea of excluding foreign nationalities or 'races', and in the following years the Social Democratic party attempted, at least in principle, to act according to that resolution.[55]

At the other end of the spectrum, the responses employed a vocabulary of peril, contamination and danger. The Chinese were seen as the Other, as a threat to the civilisatory order of the Reich and to western civilisation itself. In cultural terms – insofar as those involved felt the word 'culture' was at all appropriate when speaking of the Chinese – Germans and Chinese people were seen as totally incompatible. This rhetoric formed part of the larger campaign against the 'yellow peril'.[56] Although this form of xenophobic propaganda had a long history in the USA and in Australia, the term only really came into common use in Europe in the 1890s. The phenomenon spanned Europe, though there were important national differences.[57] Many commentators described the different dimensions of this threat, most of them warning against both over-enthusiastic hopes and overly negative fears of racial endangerment. The more extreme positions were typically not held by the experts on China, but found their way into the popular press. At the root of these fears was the belief, influentially framed by the German-Baltic writer Herman von Samson-Himmelstjerna, that Europe was a

---

[55] On this topic see Nichtweiß, *Saisonarbeiter*, pp. 154–74. See also Schippel, 'Konkurrenz'.

[56] See, on the history of this term in general, Gollwitzer, *Gelbe Gefahr*; and Mehnert, *Deutschland*.

[57] On the European dimension and also on the differences, see Gollwitzer, *Gelbe Gefahr*. See also Schwentker, 'Yellow Peril'. On the western image of China in general, see Mackerras, *Western Images*.

'sick culture' that would be forced to capitulate by the health and youthful vitality of the East.[58] The Japanese defeats of China and, especially, Russia, contributed to this *fin de siècle* atmosphere, the belief that the turn of the century marked a 'turning point in world history'. 'The undisputed supremacy of the white man' was coming to its end and Europe was about to experience its own decline and fall.[59]

Two main scenarios contributed to the anxiety about the 'yellow peril'. The first was fear of the growing political and military influence of the 'huge Chinese empire' and, even more so, of Japan. This fear was especially virulent in Australia. But in Germany, too, the theory that 'the yellow race [was preparing] to fight for world dominance' was repeatedly discussed.[60] After 1905, especially, when Japan defeated Russia, fears were often expressed about the Japanese military threat. Seamier publications often used militantly racist rhetoric: 'From the East comes the threat of the new Genghis Khans; sooner or later, they will break over us. Band together, Aryan peoples of Europe, to defend your race and lords [*Herrentum*]; make your preparations before it is too late!'[61] But more influential commentators, too, such as the American naval strategist Alfred Thayer Mahan, warned of a military invasion from eastern Asia. In military terms, the 'yellow peril' was perceived before the First World War mainly as a Japanese threat.[62] This applied in particular to the German Kaiser, the chief propagandist of this stereotype, although his most infamous proclamations, in the so-called 'Hun speech' ('no quarter will be given. Prisoners will not be taken'), referred to China.[63]

---

[58] Von Samson-Himmelstjerna, *Gelbe Gefahr*.

[59] Goltz, *Gelbe Gefahr*, p. iii. On this topic see especially Gollwitzer, *Gelbe Gefahr*, pp. 164ff. On the stereotypes contained in German prejudices about China see Leutner, 'Vorstellungen'. A number of classic texts are reproduced in Hsia, *Deutsche Denker*. Pigulla, *China* reconstructs the academic view. For literature on the topic see Schuster, *China*; Günther, *Aufbruch*; Wei-kui, *Chinabild*; and Changke Li, *China-Roman*.

[60] *Der Reichsbote* (12 December 1906).   [61] Spielmann, *Arier*, p. iv.

[62] See also Mehnert, 'Weltpolitik'.

[63] Mehnert, *Deutschland*, pp. 56–60, 110–19. On the 'Hun speech' see also Sösemann, 'Hunnenrede'. On the Kaiser's role in the context of these debates see Wippich, 'Yellow Peril'.

The second area of concern was economic rather than political, an expression of fears about the economic competition posed by a resurgent China and, after 1895, increasingly by Japan. During the latter half of the 1890s a major economic debate took place in Germany about the industrialisation of eastern Asia and the opportunities and risks this presented for Europe. Economists such as Karl Oldenburg, Gustav Schmoller and Adolf Wagner conjured up an economic 'yellow peril'; they argued that the industrial development of Japan and China would lead to the loss of market share and to the appearance of new competitors in the world market.[64] But this debate was not reflective of German concerns alone; it was the result of widespread fears among existing industrialised states of new economic competitors. As a result, the governments of England, the United States and Germany each sent industrial fact-finding missions to the Far East in 1896 and 1897, each with the task of evaluating the supposed threat.[65] The German team travelled to Japan and China with the support of the Prussian ministry of trade, the Central Association of German Industry, and a number of Chambers of Commerce. Like their British colleagues, however, the experts found that there was no real economic threat.[66] In fact, most of the economic experts were not so much worried about competition as excited by the prospect of huge new markets.[67]

Yet the self-assurance of these experts could not prevent the dangers outlined by the press from generating a considerable response. The overwhelming public reaction to the talk of a 'yellow peril' allowed these fears to be instrumentalised and used for other purposes, such as the construction of a naval fleet or the introduction of protectionist measures.[68] The mass media colourfully described the horrors of the Asian threat. Here, the focus was less on military and economic issues than on fears about mobility and migration. In common parlance and in the popular press, the 'yellow peril' became a demographic threat.

[64] On this topic see Gollwitzer, *Gelbe Gefahr*, pp. 187–92.
[65] See Schultze, *Japan*, pp. 96ff.   [66] See Bueck, *Centralverband*, pp. 61–62.
[67] On this topic see Varg, 'Myth'; McCormick, *China Market*; and Hunt, *Frontier Defense*.
[68] See Mehnert, *Deutschland*, pp. 37ff.

'Like a human plague of locusts', the magazine *Ostasien* prophesied, 'the Chinese, starving and working, will push ever further forward ... until the last free German worker exchanges his bottle of schnapps for an opium pipe in desperation and the last Berlin washerwoman hangs herself on her own washing-line'.[69] There was talk of the 'masses of millions' of Asians who were on the move toward Europe and who would trigger a bitter 'fight for existence between the yellow and the whites ... the horrors of which would be unequalled'.[70] The Catholic social reformer Franz Hitze even predicted 'a clash such as humanity has never seen before ... it will probably not pass off without the "crushing" of entire peoples'.[71]

The central dimension of this fear of Chinese mobility, which was repeatedly expressed in metaphors of waves or floods, was work (*Arbeit*). Chinese workers, it seemed, were threatening to flood Europe. Franz Hitze believed that Germany was about to be 'flooded with "work"'.[72] In these scenarios, economic motives often became mixed with demographic and cultural stereotypes. The 'national competition between white and yellow work', which the Liberal Conservative Alexander Tille (1866–1912), General Secretary of Saarindustrie in Saarbrücken and a member of the Pan-German League, forecasted and investigated in a detailed study, was not seen only as a question of competition but also as a cultural challenge.[73] It was not two interchangeable forms of work and activity that seemed to be colliding, but two ways of understanding work that were incompatible and each of which had cultural overtones. 'German work' was contrasted with Chinese 'slavery', the latter being mechanical and free of all moral force.[74] A 1907 article in the *Neue Gesellschaft* summarised this belief, according to which it was not just jobs that were under threat, but the meaning and dignity of work itself. 'The Chinaman as a worker brings a curse on his area of work ... Wherever the Chinaman appears

---

[69] Quoted in Gollwitzer, *Gelbe Gefahr*, p. 179.   [70] Spielmann, *Arier*, p. 327.
[71] Hitze, *Kapital and Arbeit*, p. 364.   [72] *Ibid.*
[73] Tille, *Wettbewerb*. On Tille see Tille, *Kämpferleben*; and Schungel, *Alexander Tille*.
[74] Abel, *Chinesen*, p. 22.

the white worker can no longer work with the same consciousness of honourable work [*Arbeitsehre*].'[75]

In these phrasings, Chinese work was seen as foreign, as the expression of another culture and 'race'. While those in favour of recruiting Chinese workers assumed that labour was freely exchangeable, in the press a belief in cultural incompatibility prevailed.[76] The landowners and business owners focused on the universal applicability of commodified labour, but in the popular press and nationalist groups the idea of separate 'cultural circles' dominated; exchange between these groups seemed almost impossible unless central beliefs and values were to be abandoned. Reservations about Chinese workers had to do with the work they carried out, which was regarded as of low value, with their modest demands, and with the dirt and sinfulness that they always brought with them.

Reports about the possibility of recruiting Chinese workers regularly commented on the 'incapability of the Chinese coolies', and on the 'inferior workers' to be found there. These comments referred mainly to their supposed slow rate of work; a German observer in Canton reported that 'the Chinaman' carried out 'his work with such slowness and fussiness that your hand itches to watch it'.[77] In addition there were always comments about their distanced and mechanical attitude to work ('he enjoys the mechanical').[78] No fire, no enthusiasm, no engagement: 'Both the Chinese and the Japanese hate intense dedication to their work as nothing has ever been hated', Alexander Tille concluded.[79] In the eyes of many observers, this 'instrumental' attitude to work made Chinese 'coolies' unsuitable for activities that required 'German work'. For this reason the Chinese 'coolie' was 'not usable' for most tasks carried out by German workers (for example in agriculture).[80]

---

[75] Schenk, 'Chinesische Arbeiter', p. 207.
[76] On the concept of cultural difference in the European perception of China see Bitterli, *Wilden*, pp. 54–65.
[77] Quoted in Tille, *Wettbewerb*, p. 12.   [78] *Ibid.*, p. 60.
[79] *Ibid.*, p. 62. The topos of laziness was widespread, especially with reference to Japanese workers. See for example Rathgen, *Japans Volkswirtschaft*, p. 422. On this topos in general see Alatas, *Myth*.
[80] Wolf, *Deutsche Reich*, p. 26.

Paradoxically, this belief in cultural incompatibility, which extended to other areas as well as work, became more prevalent at a time when the actual links and interactions between the societies had already increased. During the eighteenth century, despite the limited amount of direct contact between Europe and China, Chinese institutions and traditions had not been dismissed as exotic and insuperably foreign. In fact, China was often seen as a model, as were many of its institutions (such as the centralised, meritocratic system of examinations that controlled access to a career in the civil service). During the nineteenth century, this willingness to learn from other societies had given way to the paradigm of 'the West and the Rest'[81] that assumed that there was a fundamental difference between modern European societies and non-European cultures, which were now viewed as backward and stagnating.[82]

This process of erasing China from European consciousness took place during an era in which the European presence in eastern Asia was in fact expanding and China was 'opening up' as a result of the 1840 Opium War. By 1900, these contacts (which admittedly were often imposed and asymmetric) had further increased. They included the acquisition by European countries of colonies in China, the Boxer War, the increase in trade, and a European fascination with Chinese art and crafts that was fed by exhibits at the World Fairs. Chinese students travelled to Europe and to the USA. The most important factor was that the migration of millions of Chinese people for work had made China's links with the global capitalism of the turn of the century obvious.

The links themselves, and the effects of this process of exchange, were rarely discussed in the debates about labour migration. Such effects can indeed be described, although little research has been done into the changes in work mentalities and the way work was understood. Some rudimentary analysis has been carried out on how the concept of work developed in China. But there is little question, for example, that the interactions between Chinese society and

---

[81] Hall, 'The West and the Rest'.
[82] See Osterhammel, *Entzauberung*, pp. 72–75, 300–4.

the foreign-owned businesses in Shanghai did indeed have effects on work practices and on attitudes toward work. In 1874, the most important Chinese newspaper, *Shenbao*, described the work practices of foreigners, which were still viewed with amazement as foreign and different, as follows: 'The foreigner … works a [fixed] number of hours every day and, apart from lunch, does not take any breaks. He is simply not capable of working and taking breaks in turn like the Chinese do, with a pipe or cup of tea in between.'[83] Nevertheless, this form of regular work discipline became the rule for Chinese workers employed by Europeans, and soon spread to Chinese factories also. By 1880, the division of the week into six working days and a Sunday for rest had already become so established that it was ironically asked whether all the Chinese had become Christians. The introduction of a fixed day of rest in itself led to the creation of a new industrial sector, manufacturing consumer goods for filling this new leisure time.[84]

Even the Chinese word for work, *laodong*, was a product of the late nineteenth century and the intensive processes of exchange between Europe and eastern Asia. The term was imported, like many other social-science terms, to China from Japan (as a translation of the Japanese term *rôdô*).[85] In Japan, the new term *rôdô* replaced a number of older words that had been used for work activities. The institution of factory work, imported from Europe, entailed a specific type of work discipline and work technique, and also required a change in social context and work relations. In this setting, the terms for 'work' that had been used until then no longer seemed to correspond to the changed realities. The existing words for 'work' all contained meanings relating to the social context in which that work was done. In addition, there were a number of words for work independent of social relations, but these all referred exclusively to the physical aspects of work. Finding a term to describe work within a social context but without the idea of obligation to another person

[83] Quoted in Wagner, 'Concept'.   [84] See *ibid*.

[85] On this topic see Masini, *Formation*. See also Liu, *Translingual Practice*. On the role that China's relationship with Japan played in Chinese modernisation, see Reynolds, 'Golden Decade'; Reynolds, *China*; and Fogel, *Late Qing China*.

proved difficult. None of the existing terms could be used to describe factory work that was based on a voluntary contract between autonomous and equal partners. It was only around the turn of the century that the term still common today, *rôdô*, became established. These terminological changes are evidence of the major changes to the practice of and beliefs about work in Japan and China in response to the intensification of their relations with Europe.[86]

THE 'COLOURLESS PERIL' AND THE JEWS OF ASIA

If, despite their supposedly inferior levels of work, the same Chinese workers whom businessmen and landowners in many parts of the world were happy to employ were seen as a threat, this was because it was perceived that they were undemanding. In the eyes of German workers, the modest level of Chinese demands – in terms of the comfort and standard of living they expected, but also working conditions, working hours, wages and proper treatment – made Chinese workers putty in the employers' hands. The Social Democratic organ *Vorwärts*, which was vehemently opposed to the admission of Chinese workers, believed that the 'coolies' were characterised by 'undemandingness and an apathetic self-sufficiency'. For these 'working machines who live huddled together in the large cities, large-scale capitalist production [was] not an abasement or an affront to their human or personal consciousness'.[87] Ferdinand von Richthofen, the most important German academic authority on China, agreed that the Chinese worker 'could be trained as the perfect machine worker, indeed the perfect machine itself'.[88] Their requirements were so modest that Chinese workers were often regarded as lacking in humanity: 'The coolie is cheap and ready to work; it is impossible to compare him with any other worker, only with a low kind of beast of burden.'[89]

---

[86] See Smith, 'Peasant Time'. See also Lippert, *Entstehung*, pp. 183–86; and Masaaki, *Meiji*, pp. 603–5.

[87] *Vorwärts* (28 January 1898).   [88] Richthofen, *Schantung*, p. 116.

[89] *Badische Volkszeitung* (30 December 1906).

The stereotype of animality was also linked to the belief that the Chinese had animal instincts and customs. These supposed instincts and customs were often brought up when the possibility of Chinese immigration was under discussion. Those involved were not afraid of applying racist clichés ('no orang-utan has ever looked as wild as the Chinese').[90] The Chinese were described as possessing 'a predator-like cruelty' and as being 'inventive in coming up with tortures'.[91] Nationalist commentators warned especially of the almost animalistic habits of the Chinese, their gambling and love of opium. Combined with the Chinese practice observed in the USA of setting up secret societies based on regional and family origins, their use of opium was seen as the greatest 'threat to the rural population' in Germany.[92] Revulsion against all the animalistic practices ascribed to the Chinese usually went hand-in-hand with fascination or even desire, as seen in comments by Otto Kronecker, a *Sanitätsrat* who had spent many years in Kiaochow: 'Through his bee-like industriousness; his unequalled lust for work and joy in work; the strength and flexibility of his attractive, athletically-built body with which he is able to lift and carry the heaviest loads with ease; the Chinaman earns our honest admiration. But as soon as the sun sets, sin takes over everywhere, in the opium dens, in the seedy bars of the port and in the brothels.'[93]

The popular press portrayed the undemanding, animal Chinaman, prone to intoxication and vice, as the incarnation of all that was foreign and 'Other'. While those in favour of 'importing Chinese' argued for the cross-border exchange not only of goods, but also of people and labour, those criticising the free movement of labour operated within a paradigm of cultural incompatibility and insuperable alterity. The angry 'Yellow you are! And yellow you shall remain!', with which Kaiser Wilhelm described the Chinese to his minister Bülow in a marginal note, was an opinion widely shared by his citizens.[94] But the idea that this difference necessarily involved a threat – not

---

[90] Abel, *Chinesen*, p. 12.   [91] *Der Reichsbote* (12 December 1906).
[92] Schenk, 'Chinesische Arbeiter', p. 208.
[93] Kronecker, *15 Jahre Kiautschou*, p. 12.
[94] ('Gelb seid ihr! und gelb bleibt ihr!') Quoted in Mehnert, *Deutschland*, p. 112.

merely the threat of the unknown and foreign but, ironically, the fear that this foreign element might be better able to cope with Germany's own (capitalist) structures – was always inherent in these invectives about the supposedly low demands and requirements of the Chinese workers. In this way, the invocation of the Chinese threat was linked to more general topoi about competition between peoples, of decline and about the 'survival of the fittest' that were linked to contemporary Social Darwinist thought.[95]

At the same time, the comments bespoke apprehensions that this sense of Otherness might be overcome, that boundaries might become blurred. While talk of the 'yellow peril' operated within the notion of absolute difference, it was premised on an even more fundamental anxiety: the fear of the 'colourless peril' of which Hans von Wolzogen, writer and publisher of Richard Wagner's *Bayreuther Blätter*, spoke in 1905, i.e. the fear of 'the blending of races' (*Rassenvermischung*).[96] Incidentally, in the very same year of 1905, the first law banning 'mixed marriages' was passed in a German colony. The debate about the 'blending of races' was carried on in several places: in the colonies, in the Polish regions of Germany and within the Reich itself. The invocation of the 'colourless peril' that recruiting Chinese workers would involve was part of this discourse, which itself was an expression of fears of cross-border mobility and a longing for stable ethnic identities.

The spectre of the 'yellow' and 'white' races intermingling was rarely absent in discussions in the press or, indeed, in the Reichstag, about the risks and problems involved in recruiting Chinese workers.

---

[95] See Hawkins, *Social Darwinism*.

[96] Wolzogen, 'Gefahr', pp. 142–51. Wolzogen, who based his ideas on the racist works of Gobineau and Friedrich Lange, wanted to preserve the racial purity of 'Germandom'; he believed its cultural purity had already been lost, and complained 'that our external civilisation … has become *colourless*, a real mongrel [*Mischlingsprodukt*]' (p. 143; emphasis in original). But the real target of his tirades was the Jewish people. He did not even baulk in principle 'at the future possibility of Euro-Asian mixtures'. But such a policy could not be entertained at that time, as the German 'racial forces' had already been 'threatened', 'weakened' by the 'fundamentally damaging [*urschädliche*]' mixture of German blood with 'semitic-Jewish' blood (p. 146).

The writer Stefan von Kotze foresaw the creation of 'a physically and morally degenerating mixed people [*Mischvolk*]' in Europe if fears about mass immigration became a reality. The Chinaman, he argued, was 'as foreign to us as a Martian and … if he mixes with us, we as a race shall draw the shorter straw'. Such scenarios were regularly invoked, even if the language used was not always as laden with stereotypes as that of von Kotze (a nationalist who felt he must teach the Germans 'the Gospel of race').[97] As Jürgen Osterhammel has observed, '[d]uring the nineteenth century, few things threatened the European self-image as much as the deeply buried fear of being lost among the subjugated millions, of the empire sinking into a world of mulattos and mestizos, as that of the Portuguese had supposedly done'.[98]

Fear of 'racial mixing' brought together the clichés, both cultural (of promiscuity and fertility) and demographic (the 'masses of millions'), that were used to describe China during the era of high imperialism. The discussion was also shaped by the topoi of contemporary debates on national hygiene and eugenics. There were demands for 'racial prophylaxis' and for an Act on Foreigners (*Reichsfremdengesetz*); the spectre that was haunting Germany was variously titled 'racial disimprovement', 'racial humiliation' or a 'mish-mash of peoples' [*Völkerbrei*]. The weekly nationalist journal *Der Reichsbote* concluded that, if the Prussian plans to recruit Chinese workers succeeded, '[t]he poisoning [*Verjauchung*] of our blood would be unavoidable'.[99] When the Reichstag was discussing the German–Japanese trade treaty in a full-scale debate in November 1911, the whole arsenal of concerns was again brought forth. 'Our German people cannot take any disimprovement in the race', the member for Gießen, Dr Werner, commented. 'We cannot take any more of it because only states that can rely on the purity of the blood of their citizens have any prospect of survival.' He, too, demanded a Reich law on foreigners to deal effectively with the 'colourless peril'. 'We must not link economic exchange

---

[97] Kotze, *Gelbe Gefahr*, p. 42.   [98] Osterhammel, 'Forschungsreise', p. 175.
[99] *Der Reichsbote* (12 December 1906).

with human exchange and must not acquire material advantages at the cost of the deterioration of the blood of our people.'[100]

The debate about 'racial mixing' was an expression of the fears that accompanied increases in transcultural interactions. Just as protectionists wanted to limit cross-border trade in goods, those demanding 'racial prophylaxis' wanted to limit the mobility of people. This demand was more than propaganda. It was put forward during debates about how membership of the German nation should be defined in law. During the negotiations, lasting almost twenty years, about a revision of citizenship law (finally passed in 1913), attempts were made to have 'racial' criteria established in law. In the end, administrative difficulties and problems of definition, along with resistance from some members of the Reichstag, resulted in these provisions being excluded from the text of the statute.[101] But attempts to place limits on the movement of people and in particular to prevent ethnic 'mixing' were constant topics of discussion in the areas of anthropology, eugenics, constitutional law and colonial policy.[102]

Apart from the concern for the collective 'national body' expressed in warnings about the 'import of coolies', other bodies were in need of protection from the Chinese: those of German women. The fear 'that blonde-haired fair-skinned girls [would] throw themselves at these Johnny-come-latelys' was a worry to most of the uniformly male commentators on labour and immigration policy.[103] Every time the risks to the population were mentioned, worried eyes turned to German girls and women, presumed to be the primary victims of future Chinese promiscuity. The comments were usually characterised by a paternalistic tone that regarded it as the duty of men to stand up for women's interests.

Fears of the 'sullying' of German women were partly related to the actual history of Chinese migration. During the nineteenth century,

---

[100] *SBVR*, 200th session, 7 November 1911, p. 7695.
[101] See Grosse, *Kolonialismus*, pp. 160–68; Gosewinkel, *Einbürgern*, pp. 310–27; and El-Tayeb, *Schwarze Deutsche*, pp. 60–141.
[102] On the colonial debates see Grosse, *Kolonialismus*, pp. 145–92; and Wildenthal, *German Women*, pp. 79–130.
[103] *SBVR*, 200th session, 7 November 1911, p. 7695.

the emigration of Chinese workers was almost exclusively a male phenomenon. Most of those emigrating were single, and those married men who did migrate usually left their families behind in China and frequently entered into new local relationships, often marrying again.[104] The proportion of women among the emigrants was extremely small. Another factor was that most of the Chinese women who did emigrate worked as prostitutes; estimates differ but some are as high as 85 per cent.[105] Heinrich Gottwaldt, who compiled a detailed study of all aspects of Chinese emigration in 1903, estimated that no more than 1 per cent of Chinese emigrants were married women. As, he believed, it was not 'in the nature of the Chinese … to live in celibacy', Chinese immigration to Germany would be a direct threat to German women.[106]

Similar anxieties were painted in lurid colours by the popular press. The Chinese were regarded as especially prone to unbridled sexuality and sexual excess; 'given their polygamic views', as Robert Schenk warned in a feature for the *Neue Gesellschaft*, based on the Australian experience, any marriage between a Chinese man and German woman would necessarily be a 'disaster for both sides'.[107] The possible details of the Chinese men's sexual approaches were often described in detail in accounts ambiguously shifting between repulsion and desire. Typically, the threat posed to German women was represented as itself taking on female or effeminate features. The Chinaman, one account suggested, 'flirts faun-like with girls and women'; his advances were not male but obsequious ('he crawls and whines like a submissive animal'), obliging and ingratiating: 'a paradise for women … His lustful eyes crawl all over the [woman's] body like hot hands.'[108] These stereotypes were further reinforced by the divisions of the labour market. It was widely believed that the Chinaman was 'an excellent substitute where female assistance is lacking in the home, as a cook, washerman or servant'.[109]

---

[104] On this topic, see the summary by Chen, *Emigrant Communities*, still the best account, esp. pp. 118–45.
[105] See Hirita, 'Free'.   [106] Gottwaldt, *Auswanderung*, p. 49.
[107] Schenk, 'Chinesische Arbeiter', p. 209.   [108] Kotze, *Gelbe Gefahr*, pp. 26–27.
[109] *Illustrierte Landwirtschaftliche Zeitung* (26 June 1907).

For these reasons, Chinese men, 'equipped with all the Asiatic sexual drives and perversions',[110] had to be closely watched. This was regularly demanded by the nationalist press, but the attitude taken by state institutions was in fact similar. This is shown, for example, by an assessment made by the authorities in Bremen. According to their investigations the Chinese men in the city had frequent 'opportunities for sexual intercourse with local women'. As the police officer compiling the report explained, 'this group … mainly targets … young and slimly built women'.[111] Such relationships must, it was believed, result in the unequalled humiliation and degradation of the German women. Stefan von Kotze described the consequences as follows: 'The woman [*Weib*] lies on a pile of stinking blankets in an opium haze, at the mercy of the lust of the whole horrible gang.'[112]

State controls were also needed because women were themselves, apparently, almost incapable of resisting. On numerous occasions we find references to 'the well-known preference of German womanhood for everything foreign and especially for the exotic', making it imperative for state authorities to keep a paternalistic eye on them.[113] Evidently, German women liked Chinese men, as they 'correspond[ed] to the female marriage ideal much better than the German man'.[114] This was because of the supposed pliability and adaptability, the flexible-cooperative, not male-domineering nature of Chinese men. But the essence of the strangers' attractiveness was their erotic appeal and women's sexual desire for the erotic. In this regard particular vigilance by the German male authorities was required. German women ('*Frauenzimmer*'), it was held, were led by 'desire for the perverse sexual secrets of the yellow man'.[115]

This rhetoric is reminiscent of the warnings and precautionary measures that were often deployed when foreigners were being put on show at colonial exhibitions, *Völkerschauen* (ethnographic shows)

---

[110] Kotze, *Gelbe Gefahr*, p. 30.   [111] Quoted in Amenda, 'Vorstellungen'.

[112] Kotze, *Gelbe Gefahr*, p. 28.

[113] According to a Berlin newspaper, which, though independent, did tend to take a nationalist line: *Der Tag* (23 March 1907).

[114] Quoted in Amenda, 'Fremd-Wahrnehmung', p. 84.

[115] Kotze, *Gelbe Gefahr*, p. 27.

and zoological gardens. To limit contacts between German women and the colonial subjects on show, the exhibition areas were usually locked at night and women were expressly forbidden from remaining on the properties. Chinese people living in Germany could not be hermetically sealed off, or subjected to police controls, in the same way as participants in exhibitions and shows. But the authorities did attempt to ensure that an eye was kept on the Chinese workers, and this monitoring extended to their contacts with German women. For example, there is archival evidence of an application by a local woman to the Bremen Senate in 1917 for permission to marry a Chinese worker. After China entered the First World War, in the spring of 1917, Chinese people were 'enemy aliens' and were subject to even closer monitoring than before; however, there was no outright legal ban on marriages with Chinese people. Nevertheless, the authorities refused to give permission for the marriage as it could be expected 'that through the marriage even more children will come and the whole family will later become dependent on the State'.[116]

As these examples show, debates about work and labour were not only ethnically and racially loaded, but were also gendered.[117] The topos of the 'yellow peril' thus overlapped with internal problematics, and the external 'Others' could appear as the double of the inner, domestic 'Others'. The strategies of marginalisation mutually reinforced each other in varied and ambivalent ways, and gender was just one of several dimensions. When, for example, landowners and their representatives in the Prussian regional parliament repeatedly suggested that 'coolies' should be recruited as a way of putting pressure on Social Democrats, the boundaries of race and class clearly overlapped. Immigration by the 'yellow race' was seen as a way of disciplining the lower classes. This fear is also reflected in Bebel's major speech to the Reichstag in 1898: 'The same individuals who are currently talking big as nationalist politicians, as patriots, as men who feel called to create a home for German culture, German education and German customs across the globe – it is mainly these individuals

---

[116] Quoted in Amenda, 'Vorstellungen'.
[117] On the link between 'race' and sexuality see Gilman, *Rasse*.

who believe [that recruiting workers from Galicia, Bohemia and now from China] is compatible with their patriotic German conscience.'[118] From the position of the ruling classes – who saw themselves as the only defenders of a 'healthy race' – it was thus possible to articulate the foreign 'race' and the underprivileged class.[119]

But the most frequently used association was that linking the Chinese with the Jews.[120] In south-eastern Asian trade, it had long been common to refer to Chinese traders as 'the Jews of the East'. In his famous Sinophobic pamphlet of 1914, *The Jews of the East*, the King of Siam reproduced a widely held belief, namely that 'when it comes to money the Chinese know neither morality nor pity'.[121] Similar views were later propounded by the Japanese philosopher Watsuji Tetsurô, who saw the Chinese and the Jews as united in their mercantile spirit and in the privileged status they assigned to money-making. Watsuji described the Chinese as 'more Jewish than the Jews themselves'. If China were to defeat Japan at war, this would be 'a backward step for mankind'.[122] This stigmatisation reinforced a number of forms of discrimination. But it could also be appropriated by the Chinese population themselves, who would claim to be industrious workers or peaceful and apolitical merchants.[123] While in south-eastern Asia and in Japan traditional anti-Chinese stereotypes became linked with elements of European anti-Semitism, which was being spread around the world,[124] the situation in Europe was the

[118] *SBVR*, 5th session, 8 February 1898, p. 902.
[119] On the overlaps between the categories of race and class see Foucault, *Society*, pp. 60–63, 178–188 ; and Balibar and Wallerstein, *Race, Nation, Class*. See also Stoler, 'Rethinking Colonial Categories'.
[120] Little research has been done into the way the practices of exclusion toward these two socially marginal groups overlapped. Even the volume of essays edited by Daniel Chirot and Anthony Reid on Chinese and Jewish people as *Essential Outsiders* remains imprisoned within a comparative approach and does not investigate the effects of translations between the two phenomena. In contrast, see Gabaccia, 'Yellow Peril'.
[121] Quoted in Pan, *Sons*, p. 152. See also Tejapira, 'Imagined Uncommunity'.
[122] Quoted in Oguma, *Genealogy*, p. 275.
[123] On this topic see Mitchell, 'Transnational Subjects'; and Ong, *Flexible Citizenship*, pp. 84–91.
[124] On the role of the image of Jews for the Chinese self-image see Zhou, 'Youtai'.

reverse. In Britain, for example, during the heated debate about limits on immigration the Jews were compared to the Chinese, from whom they differed, it was held, only by degree.[125] Both groups were perceived as being part of mysterious, often conspiratorial transnational networks, and were associated with dirt and contagious disease (especially cholera).[126]

In Germany, too, the comparison was made frequently, owing to the supposed 'innate commercial skill [of the Chinese] which far exceeds anything known to us'.[127] The Chinese seemed mainly to present an economic threat, making them 'a far more dangerous people than the Jews'. But at the same time, fears were voiced that the two marginalised groups might join forces, combining the Jews' entrepreneurial talents with the undemanding willingness of the Chinese for hard work: 'Between these two peoples, the Germans would be in danger of being completely crushed [*zerrieben*].'[128] National rhetoric about exclusion during the Wilhelmine era thus combined anti-Chinese with anti-Jewish metaphors. During the 1890s, when anti-Semitism in Germany was becoming radicalised and was being loaded with biologistic and racial aspects, the topos of the 'yellow peril' may have provided some of the vocabulary that made this ethnicisation possible. The anti-Semitic *Neue Deutsche Volkszeitung*, consequently, saw 'welcome parallels' between 'the North American ban on Chinese immigration and the demands for a ban on Jewish immigration' in Germany.[129] In the course of the debate on immigration by 'eastern Jews', the anti-Semitic press gladly adopted the anti-Chinese rhetoric and applied it to the Jews.[130]

---

[125] See Gainer, *Alien Invasion*, p. 112.
[126] See Zolberg, 'Global Movements', esp. p. 300.　　[127] Kotze, *Gelbe Gefahr*, p. 31.
[128] 'Drohende Chinesen-Einwanderung' (14 June 1889), in GStA PK, I. HA Rep 77, Tit. 922 no. 2.
[129] Quoted in Wawrzinek, *Entstehung*, p. 44.
[130] See Gollwitzer, *Gelbe Gefahr*, p. 174. On the fusion of anti-slavery, anti-Semitism and the 'yellow peril' in *völkisch* thought see Puschner, *Völkische Bewegung*, pp. 102–6. On the overlaps between different racist discourses see the discussion by Gilroy, *Black Atlantic*, pp. 205–12, of the common features of the history of black people and Jews and of their parallel functions in a history of modernity.

CHINESE MIGRATION AND THE ETHNICISATION
OF THE NATIONAL

The discourse of the 'yellow peril' allowed German nationalists to link local themes with global trends. From the beginning of the Chinese project, ideas about recruiting Chinese labour were embedded in the rhetoric of nationalism. The few individuals supporting the project saw it as a means of counteracting the growing Polish nationalism in the Prussian East. For most of those who commented publicly on this topic the 'coolies' themselves represented the real danger to the German nation. What was more, the way anti-Chinese prejudices were articulated with issues of gender, class and anti-Semitism shows us how local problems acquired a wider resonance and were assigned meaning by linking them with global debates.

Because there was little first-hand information or social experience of Chinese workers, the most important arguments were formulated in reference to developments in Australia and in the USA. Reports of anti-foreigner reactions, and the restrictions on immigration that followed, were often used as arguments against recruiting Chinese labour. 'The three major colonial states that have come into contact with the Chinese people, North America and Australia and South Africa, have had terrible experiences with it and are now passionately resisting', as the *Deutsche Volkszeitung* phrased it in 1906, 'the yellow pest'.[131] The fear of the 'yellow peril' as a reaction to Chinese mobility can thus be seen as the expression of a global consciousness linking the development of German nationalism with events in faraway places such as San Francisco or New South Wales.

In fact, from the later decades of the nineteenth century onward, the history of the mobility of Chinese labour became a history of restriction, marginalisation and, eventually, bans on immigration.[132] One of the most important points of reference for the German debate about Chinese immigration was Australia. 'Letters from Australia' were published regularly in the German press warning about the negative

---

[131] Quoted in BA Berlin, R 8034 II, no. 4049.
[132] On this subject in general see Zolberg, 'Great Wall'.

effects immigration from Asia would have on the 'national character' (*Volkscharakter*) and national solidarity. Because of Australia's location and its long history of immigration, issues of race relations and debates about its character as an 'Asian' or 'western' country have always been of considerable importance there. For a long time, and especially in the late nineteenth century, the issue of immigration from China was at the centre of these issues. From the 1880s onward, at the latest, the 'Chinese question' emerged as the most important topic of political, social and cultural discussions, and was instrumental in defining 'white Australia' and the development of an Australian national identity.[133]

The major influx of Chinese was triggered by the gold rush in 1851. At the end of the decade, the Chinese population in Australia was at its height, at 38,742, equalling roughly 9 per cent of the total population. As a reaction to increasing local unrest and conflict, measures of exclusion were introduced. The increasing sensitivity of the Australian public to the Chinese question was combined with concerns that Chinese immigrants would create a bridgehead for a later invasion of Australia by China. Regardless of the plausibility of this idea, these fears contributed to the white population's feeling existentially threatened in the face of Australia's small size and proximity to Asia.[134] After the 'Chinese Crisis' in 1888, ships with Chinese people on board were no longer permitted to enter Australian ports.[135]

Although the political goal of creating a united and independent Australian federation had a long history and was supported by a variety of political and business interests, the reaction against Chinese migration became 'the most important single component of Australian nationalism'.[136] In the process of political unification, the idea of 'White Australia' served as the founding consensus, and the racist overtones of the debate helped to eliminate and to cover over class differences. At the same time, they helped to secure the

---

[133] See Price, *Great White Walls*.   [134] Burke, *Fear of Security*.
[135] See Zubrzycki, 'International Migration'; Matthäus, *Nationsbildung*, esp. pp. 155–91; Markus, *Fear*; and Markus, *Australian Race Relations*.
[136] McQueen, *New Britannia*, p. 41.

necessary consent of the British Crown, whose Secretary of State for the Colonies, Chamberlain, openly expressed his sympathy with 'the determination of the white inhabitants of these Colonies which are in comparatively close proximity to millions and hundreds of millions of Asiatics' to prevent 'an influx of people alien in civilisation, alien in religion [and] alien in customs'.[137]

The most important precedent for anti-Chinese legislation, regularly cited in both the Australian and the German debates on the issue, was the US 'Chinese Exclusion Act' of 1882.[138] In his 1873 book *The Chinese Invasion*, H. J. West had warned the USA of 'an invasion which threatens to overrun it as the great plagues overran Egypt'.[139] Soon, the question was no longer whether a policy of exclusion should be introduced, but what form it should take. Electoral concerns transformed an issue that was initially limited to California into one debated across the entire country, in which fears of economic competition and ethnic stereotypes combined to create a supposed threat to the nation itself. The 1882 Act banned almost all immigration from China for an initial period of ten years and made it impossible for Chinese people to acquire American citizenship.[140] The Act had a huge symbolic effect on the way migration was perceived and dealt with around the world, and the whole issue was followed closely in Europe.[141] From the turn of the century onward, American exclusionary policy was tightened in the face of Japanese immigration, and in 1924 immigration from Asia was banned altogether with the Immigration Act.[142]

The consequences of this policy of exclusion were manifold and complex. It affected the everyday lives of Chinese people in the

---

[137] Quoted in Willard, *History*, p. 112. See also Evans, 'Pigmentia'.

[138] For a comparison of Australian and US nationalisms see Spillman, *Nation*.

[139] Quoted in Mehnert, *Deutschland*, p. 50. See also Rhoads, 'White Labor'. On the history of pre-1870 discrimination see Barth, *Bitter Strength*.

[140] On this topic see Hunt, *Making*; Chan, 'Immigration'; Zo, *Chinese Emigration*; Miller, *Unwelcome Immigrant*; Saxton, *Indispensable Enemy*; Chan, *Entry Denied*, especially chapters 2 and 3; and Salyer, *Laws*. For an overview of the different situations experienced by different Chinese immigrants see Dirlik, *Chinese*.

[141] See Zolberg, 'Migration Policies'.   [142] See Bennett, 'Bitter Fruit'.

USA and impinged on the labour market, urban structures and local commercial businesses. But in addition, the rise of nationalism in the United States as well as among overseas Chinese was intimately connected to the Exclusion Act. Anti-Chinese policies at local and national levels contributed to the establishment of an American nationalism that was increasingly defined by shared ethnic characteristics and that was beginning to accord less importance to civil rights and the ideology of equality and emancipation. From the late nineteenth century onward, immigration law thus became a dynamic site at which concepts of race, immigration, citizenship and nation were transformed. The exclusion of the Chinese, in particular, reflected, produced and reproduced debates about the structure and character of the nation itself.

Of course, ethnic solidarity was only one of many sources for American nationalism; they included the republican tradition and the freedom of citizens, patriotic cosmopolitanism, economic nationalism, and several other issues. It is also important to note that the radicalisation of the idea of belonging and citizenship did not commence with Chinese immigration: it was linked to the long and complex history of race relations within the USA. The merciless wars against the indigenous peoples and the discriminatory rules for Afro-Americans contributed to the development of a racially segregated American society. But from the late nineteenth century on, this long internal history was articulated with a new dynamic. In this sense the 1880s can be seen as an important turning-point in the history of the ethnicisation of American nationalism, now influenced by global mobility.[143] In her analysis of this change from internal marginalisation to external exclusion, Erika Lee describes the Chinese exclusion laws as 'the main catalyst that transformed the United States into a gatekeeping nation'.[144]

There were exclusionary movements in many countries. One of the most pronounced was perhaps that of South Africa where, from the turn of the century on, white workers had been organising themselves

---

[143] See King, *Liberty*. See also his *Making Americans*.
[144] Lee, *America's Gates*, p. 9.

into anti-Chinese societies to prevent further Chinese immigration and make the Transvaal a white state.[145] In many places, the global migration of Chinese workers led to the introduction of exclusionary policies, which were closely linked to the development of a nationalism that increasingly included racial aspects.[146] The effects of Chinese mobility on identity were by no means limited to societies that viewed themselves as mainly 'white'. The discourse of race also acted as a medium for expressing similar fears and worries in regions that had been influenced by Chinese culture for centuries. These links, and the role of the Chinese diaspora in local processes of nation-building, can be observed particularly for south-eastern Asia, which was by far the most significant destination for nineteenth-century Chinese migration.[147]

Chinese migration triggered nationalist reactions in many societies and contributed, in different contexts and different ways, to the formation of modern nationalisms. But the global movement of 'coolies' produced nationalist reactions not only in regions where Chinese immigration was perceived as an ethnic threat, but also within China itself. Here too, to be sure, other factors contributed to the emergence of Chinese nationalism. But historians agree that mobility was a crucial factor.[148]

In the historiography of Chinese nationalism, the contribution of the diaspora Chinese is well known, but the large 'coolie' migration does not play a central role. Instead, the focus is on the social elites and their financial and ideological involvement in the movement.[149] Most accounts pay considerable attention to the merchants and traders who financed Chinese industrialisation and donated large

---

[145] See Yen, *Coolies*, pp. 335–47.
[146] For Canada see the inspiring account by Anderson, *Vancouver's Chinatown*.
[147] On this topic see Keng, *Malaysia*; Purcell, *Chinese*; and Ong, *Flexible Citizenship*. See also Sachsenmaier, 'Identitäten'.
[148] On Chinese nationalism see Karl, *Staging the World*, pp. 3–26; Townsend, 'Chinese Nationalism'; Duara, *Rescuing History*, esp. pp. 17–50; Fitzgerald, *Awakening China*, which is an excellent study but focuses on the 1911–49 period; and Dittmer and Kim, *China's Quest*.
[149] Reid, 'Entrepreneurial Minorities'.

sums to reform-oriented groups.[150] In addition, large numbers of young activists who had fled abroad to avoid imprisonment also made a major contribution to the political history of the national revolution. Sun Yat-sen even described the Chinese communities in south-east Asia as the 'mother of the Chinese revolution' of 1911.[151] Initially, the nationalist ambitions of the overseas Chinese were directed toward achieving broad pan-Asian solidarity or were limited to plans for the independence of Canton. This shows that national identities could go hand-in-hand with transnational ideas, but also that the vocabulary of nationalism could be applied to sub-national entities. From the early twentieth century on, nationalist orthodoxy limited its geopolitical aims to the area of the Chinese empire.[152] Finally, there were Chinese students abroad, in the first instance the intellectual diaspora in Tokyo (where Kang Youwei and Sun Yat-sen, for example, both spent several years). Since the Meiji restoration and especially after the Japanese defeat of China in 1895, Tokyo had become a favoured destination for young Chinese students. At the turn of the century, there were about 9,000 Chinese students in Japan; while there, in addition to their studies they came into contact with nationalist ideas.[153] In other words, in China's national memory the diaspora elite has an important place. But the large-scale mobility of the underprivileged classes has scarcely been investigated in this regard. However, the global displacements of 'coolies', as I would like to argue, were an equally important factor that worked towards the articulation of sentiments of Chinese nationality with broader, global currents.

This applied, firstly, to the emigrants themselves, who usually returned to China after completing several years of contracted work abroad. During their period abroad they came into contact with the idea of a supra-regional unit, a 'mother country'. Even if that country contained unknown peoples who spoke dialects that were frequently incomprehensible, all its citizens were part of one community defined

---

[150] See for example Wang, *China*; Godley, 'Treaty Port Connection'; and Godley, *Mandarin Capitalists*.
[151] Quoted in Yen, *Chinese Overseas*, p. 263. See also Ma, *Revolutionaries*.
[152] See the informative article by Duara, 'Transnationalism'.
[153] See Harrell, *Sowing the Seeds*.

by unalterable links of ethnicity, culture and history. The communication of this idea was often supported by nationalist propaganda. Such ideas were also transported by Chinese language schools (where, often, Mandarin was taught rather than the southern dialects) and by newspapers maintained by nationalist groups. In this way, many emigrants became familiar with nationalist ideas.

This is not to say that individual emigrants, especially those from the higher social classes, did not attempt to adapt to their host society and increasingly identify with it (although this trend only set in in earnest after the Second World War). The effects on the overseas Chinese of the policy of exclusion were not uniformly homogenising. The exceptions in American immigration law, for example for Chinese traders and businessmen, reproduced social conflicts and meant that the main concern for merchants who were arrested by mistake was that they would not be mistaken for their 'uneducated' countrymen. Chinese nationalism was by no means a uniform phenomenon; it differed in the different diaspora communities. It would thus be more appropriate to speak of the development of Chinese nationalisms.[154]

However, these nationalisms shared the belief that the way Chinese workers were treated in each local situation depended on China's global status and prestige. Local exclusions and discrimination seemed a direct result of China's unequal position in the global power system. Another factor was that the constitution of nationality took place in a context in which the concept of race was all-pervasive and affected social practice, not just in the form of rhetoric but in actual discriminatory actions. To cite just one example: when China refused, in 1905, to renew the discriminatory immigration treaty with the USA, merchants in Canton, Shanghai, Xiamen, Tianjin and other states called for a total boycott of American goods. The American government protested, and even though the Emperor was eventually forced to issue a proclamation against the boycott, it did have a significant effect, especially in southern China. Along with anti-colonial excesses such as the 1900 Boxer War, this boycott was one of the most

---

[154] See McKeown, *Chinese Migrant Networks*, pp. 86–99.

important stages in the formation of Chinese nationalism during the latter years of the Qing dynasty.[155] The perception of Chinese nationality was thus usually accompanied by rhetoric about ethnic similarity and China's location in a 'racial' world order.[156] As such, national feelings within the diaspora did not refer to their society of origin alone. They were also situated in a global context.[157]

The mobility of workers thus helped to create a nationalism 'from below', but it also attracted the attention of the governing bureaucrats. While the Chinese empire and its administration had long been negligent of, if not hostile to, the existence of overseas communities, this changed in the latter part of the nineteenth century. The existence of overseas Chinese was now generally recognised by the administration, as was the need to support them. A good example of the changing attitude of the government was the Imperial Delegation that China dispatched in 1873 to investigate into the working conditions of Chinese 'coolies' in Cuba. Several years before the first consulates were established in the United States and Japan in 1878, this delegation is proof of a shift in foreign policy and the scope of international interventions. For the first time, a Chinese government assumed responsibility for workers who had left the sphere of Chinese 'civilisation' and had been treated as criminals only a few years before.[158]

Of course, a number of different traditions contributed to the development of the idea of a Chinese 'nation' toward the end of the Qing dynasty, and labour mobility was just one of many factors. Thinking in national categories replaced earlier ideas of a cosmic and moral order guaranteed by the Emperor and his institutions in Peking and legitimised by a common cultural identity. While the concept of Chinese civilisation retreated, a mental map of the world became established in which China would be just one of many nation states,

---

[155]　On the link between the boycott movement and nationalism see Tsai, 'Reaction'; McKee, *Chinese Exclusion*; Wang, *In Search of Justice*; and Wong, *Boycott Movement*.

[156]　On this topic see Karl, 'Race'. On the concept of race in China see Dikötter, *Discourse of Race*. See also his *Construction*.

[157]　See McKeown, 'Conceptualizing Chinese Diasporas', p. 326.

[158]　On this issue see Duara, 'Nationalists'.

a coherent unit within clearly demarcated borders.[159] Resistance to the attacks of western powers was important here. Kang Youwei's reform movement was just one variant within a broad spectrum of occasionally contradictory national discourses. Some important triggers for Chinese nationalism came from Japan,[160] and cosmopolitan merchants in Shanghai propounded their own version of nationalism, one that was inclusive and based on political rights. Discontent with the rule of the Manchus played a role, just as it has done for the multi-ethnic, state-focused nationalism of the Kuomintang since the 1920s. A different perspective has been offered by Donald Nonini and Aihwa Ong. In an influential book, they have drawn attention to the floating, unfixed identity of the diaspora, an identity that refuses to coincide with conventional categories of territory, region, nationality or ethnicity. They highlight the scope that mobility created and that allowed the three modern regimes of the family, the nation and the factory to be played off against one another, even though they are all embedded in global capitalism. This process, they argue, creates identities that are not predominant or absolute, but rather 'a site of differences'.[161] Overall, it is clear that the formation of a variety of Chinese nationalisms was based on different sources and cultural resources and was the result of complex processes of negotiation and competition.

However, we can state that these ideas about membership of a nation – based on ethnic and cultural boundaries that formed the basis for assigning inalienable rights and responsibilities – developed in a context in which the transnational mobility of Chinese workers played a major role.[162] When analysing the influence of 'coolie'

---

[159] On this topic see the classic study by Levenson, *Liang Ch'i-ch'ao*. Some criticism has been expressed of this theory of the transition from culturalism to nationalism, on which large parts of Chinese historiography rely. See for example Karl, *Staging the World*, pp. 3–26; Townsend, 'Chinese Nationalism'; and Duara, *Rescuing History*, esp. pp. 17–50.

[160] See Harrell, *Sowing the Seeds*; Young, 'Chinese Leaders'; and Reynolds, *China*.

[161] See Nonini and Ong, 'Chinese Transnationalism', p. 25. See also Ong, *Flexible Citizenship*.

[162] See Duara, 'Nationalists'.

mobility, we must take three main issues into account. Firstly, the link with the issue of overseas migration contributed to the popularising of nationalist ideas that had previously been held mainly by small elites. Secondly, the consolidation of social boundaries, which was linked to the contemporary racial discourse, cannot be understood without taking into account the fact that policies of exclusion, whether in California or Australia, were explicitly, and mainly, directed against Chinese workers. Thirdly, the construction of the Chinese nation and the spread of ideas about the nation took place in the context of increased awareness of global relations and colonial links.[163]

CHINESE WORKERS ON GERMAN SHIPS

The frequent references to the situation in Australia and California were evidence of the global consciousness within which these events were discussed. However, to a large extent the debate was fictitious and preventive: the plans to recruit Chinese labour for use in agriculture or industry never led to the actual immigration of Chinese people, partly because of the vehement public protest.

Municipal and state authorities only rarely came into contact with Chinese people, and most cases were in the port cities of Hamburg and Bremen. Forty-three Chinese were registered as residents of Hamburg in 1890; by 1910 this had increased to 207. Most were former sailors. However, the real number of Chinese in the city was considerably higher than this; in addition to those who had settled, there were always Chinese sailors who were temporarily stationed in the ports. By the 1920s, Hamburg was often spoken of as having a 'Chinese quarter', which, for German observers, was as 'mysterious and puzzling as their great mother country in the distant East'.[164]

The presence of Chinese people in German port cities was a result of the changes in transatlantic shipping and the globalisation of the maritime labour market. During the second half of the nineteenth

---

[163] Karl, *Staging the World*.
[164] Ludwig Jürgens, quoted in Amenda, 'Fremd-Wahrnehmung', p. 82.

century, sailing ships were gradually replaced by steamships, which were much larger and faster. These technological changes led to changing demands on the crews. The skills previously required of sailors became less and less important as steamships began to dominate. For work in the engine rooms, a common language, experience, and work traditions were less important. From the 1890s on, many shipping companies began to replace German crews with sailors from China (and to a lesser extent from India and Africa), who were much cheaper.[165]

When steamships were introduced to Chinese waters, German companies, starting with the Norddeutsche Lloyd in 1891, began to employ so-called 'water Chinese' in the engine rooms for coastal shipping in Asia. These workers usually came from Hong Kong; workers from southern China were felt to be less suitable. Soon, the companies began to employ Chinese people on their routes between Europe and eastern Asia. The high level of competition between German shipping companies led to the rapid spread of the practice. Before the end of the century, Chinese sailors were being employed on the other transatlantic routes. By 1900, they made up about 3,000 of the 47,780 seamen registered with the Association of Maritime Occupations (*Seeberufsgenossenschaft*). Their numbers continued to increase until the outbreak of the First World War.[166]

Chinese workers were mainly employed as boilermen and coal trimmers (who brought the coal from the bunkers to the boiler rooms). Over half of non-German workers on German ships were employed in the boiler rooms. However, some Chinese people were also employed as cooks or stewards, and on deck; they were also well regarded as washermen. The main reason for German employers to hire Chinese labour was that the market situation allowed them to pay the Chinese lower wages. Chinese boilermen and coal trimmers received only 50 or 60 per cent of the wages of their German counterparts.[167] In addition, overall wage costs were lower because no social

---

[165] See Rübner, 'Organisationsbedingungen', esp. pp. 1–17.
[166] See *ibid*., pp. 5–7.
[167] See Küttner, *Farbige Seeleute*, pp. 131–33.

Figure 4.1 German officer and Chinese staff on board a ship of the
Norddeutsche Lloyd, *c.* 1910/20.

insurance contributions had to be paid for 'coloured' employees.
Thus, employing Chinese workers often allowed shipping companies to increase their machine-room staff while simultaneously cutting
wage costs. Hiring Chinese workers was made easier by the fact that
the statutory limitations on immigration and residence that regulated
the use of foreign workers in industry and agriculture did not apply
to foreign sailors.[168]

The increasing recruitment of Chinese staff, especially in the
engine rooms, gradually led to German sailors being squeezed out of
the labour market. They could not usually compete with the cut-price
wages accepted by Chinese boilermen. It often happened that German
sailors found themselves laid off in favour of the Chinese workers
when they arrived in Chinese ports, and had to be taken care of by the
local German consulates. This practice led to vehement protests by the
unions and by their representatives in the Reichstag. The Sailors' Union

---

[168] See Rübner, 'Organisationsbedingungen', pp. 7–9.

(*Seemansverband*), in particular, warned of increasing unemployment among German sailors and demanded that 'national work' should be protected. This demand was repeated by Social Democrat members of parliament during a major debate in the Reichstag in 1897. In reaction to these claims, the secretary of state for internal affairs, Posadowsky, requested a national study on the employment of African and Asian sailors, to focus mainly on the effects on wages. But the unions also saw the Chinese as potential scabs who were undermining the sailors' freedom of association. This form of the 'yellow peril' was rhetorically compared to the loyal 'yellow' unions that had been set up by shipping companies from 1907 onward.[169]

Beyond the economic motives, the German shipping companies saw positive advantages in the cultural and ethnic characteristics of the Chinese workers. The employers believed that the Chinese were well suited to the work and diligent; they 'carry out their duties in a conscientious manner, and do not consume alcohol, so that operations proceed from the start of the voyage to its end with the greatest calm and orderliness'.[170] While the employment of foreign crewmen initially led to protests, Chinese, Indian and African staff were soon part of the exotic trimmings expected by passengers on the large passenger ships. They lent the whole experience a colonial air.[171]

But another important reason, and one that was also used to justify the employment of Chinese workers during the Reichstag debates, was of a medical and scientific nature. Asian boilermen and coal trimmers were regarded as highly resistant to heat. 'It is indisputable that the Chinese and Arabs are more usable in tropical climates than European ship crews', the German consul in Rotterdam assured Reich Chancellor Caprivi in 1891.[172] Chinese workers, in particular, were regarded as especially capable of enduring the terrible heat of the boiler room. Firing the ovens, an unpleasant and extremely strenuous

---

[169] On this topic see Küttner, *Farbige Seeleute*, pp. 125–35.
[170] Norddeutsche Lloyd to Handelskammer Bremen, 24 April 1908, quoted in Rübner, 'Organisationsbedingungen', p. 8.
[171] See Küttner, *Farbige Seeleute*, p. 52.
[172] BA Berlin, R 1501, no. 103532, p. 187.

task in itself, was made even more arduous by the high temperatures in the boiler rooms, usually between 40 and 50 °C. In tropical waters the temperature could exceed 70 °C. It was not uncommon for those with weaker constitutions to suffer heatstroke in these conditions, and there was a noticeably high rate of suicide among boilermen.

The higher resistance of the 'coloured races' to heat and tropical climates was a common trope during the colonial era. It was widely believed that, for physiological and 'racial' reasons, Chinese workers were more able to endure high temperatures, and this was confirmed by medical studies. This idea was even successfully deployed in the debate about whether Chinese boilermen should be recruited for the state-subsidised postal steamships (an issue that cropped up in the press at regular intervals): Chinese boilermen were hired, initially for the routes through the Red Sea and the Persian Gulf, which were particularly hot, and eventually for all the transatlantic routes.[173]

But although large numbers of foreign staff were employed, the transatlantic steamships did not become sites of unlimited intercultural encounter and interaction, as feared by some contemporary critics. The Seamen's Union, for example, warned of the risk of plague and cholera that would ensue if the supposedly chronically dirty Chinese workers were let on board. The differences in 'customs and habits' meant that many German sailors felt that co-existence with foreign colleagues on board ship was an affront. They were supported in this view by many German consuls in China, who also believed that having 'Europeans and Chinese live or sleep together in the same constricted rooms must be seen as detrimental to the former in terms of both health and moral issues'. For this reason, they issued orders stating that separate accommodation should be provided for white and coloured crews.[174] In fact, ethnic segregation soon became the rule on the ships even where there were no statutory regulations to that effect. Frequently, spatial segregation extended beyond the sleeping quarters to the working areas: many shipping companies hired different

---

[173] See Küttner, *Farbige Seeleute*, pp. 67–87, 146–55. On the links between the history of medicine and that of colonialism see Eckart, *Medizin*.

[174] Quoted from a letter from the Kaiserliches Konsulat Hongkong dated 29 March 1893, quoted in Rübner, 'Organisationsbedingungen', p. 10.

ethnic groups for different areas of work, with the ethnic differences reflecting the social and economic hierarchies on board.[175]

Segregation increased with the outbreak of the First World War, which converted the graduations of national and ethnic differences into a binary system of 'friend or foe'. This applied, for example, to some 200 Chinese sailors in Bremen who were caught out by the outbreak of war and had to wait out the next few years in the port before being allowed to travel home. They were accommodated not in Bremerhaven, the town attached to the port, but on a ship belonging to the Norddeutsche Lloyd. The sociologist Paul Gilroy has described the ship as the chronotope of modernity because it symbolises its vectoral and diasporic character, but the accommodation on the *Königin Luise* was more like that of a prison. The authorities carried out regular 'Chinese checks', looking for spies and illegally requisitioned foodstuffs. Once China had declared war on the German Reich in August 1917, the Chinese sailors were obliged to report to the police every day. Requests by sailors to break this isolation and settle in Bremerhaven were usually refused. During the last few months of the war, however, when Germany's material supplies were dwindling, a small number of Chinese people were forced to work in armaments production.[176]

But most of the Chinese sailors employed on German ships never set foot in Hamburg or Bremerhaven. Instead, they worked in Asian waters. In the years leading up to 1900, about half of all Asian coastal shipping was run by German-owned companies.[177] Hapag (Hamburg–Amerika-Linie) was the biggest shipping company in the world; the second biggest was the Norddeutsche Lloyd. Kaiser Wilhelm II's enthusiasm for the sea and for everything maritime led him to the view that Germany's future was on the water. Under his rule, the navy was expanded and the growth of merchant shipping was also supported by the state. The country also promoted shipping in eastern Asia by

---

[175] On this topic see Küttner, *Farbige Seeleute*, pp. 37–44.
[176] For a detailed account of the situation of the Chinese population in Germany during the First World War see Amenda, 'Vorstellungen'; *Fremde–Hafen–Stadt*, Chapter 1.1.
[177] On this topic see Seiler, *Ostasienfahrt*.

supporting the *Reichspost* steamship lines. Their profits were meagre, but nationalist and colonialist groups in the Reichstag always managed to ensure that these subsidies were maintained.[178]

For the companies involved, trade *with* China was not the only source of income; they also profited from the trade *in* Chinese workers. For example, large freight ships belonging to the Hamburg–Amerika-Linie and the Norddeutsche Lloyd often called at Amoy (Xiamen) on their return voyage to take Chinese workers to Singapore.[179] Shipping in China and Asia in general was profitable for smaller German companies too. In 1892, 974 German ships were involved in trade between China and foreign countries; 1,042 German ships were involved in Chinese coastal trading, especially in the profitable 'coolie trade'.[180]

The most important destination for Chinese workers was Singapore, where a large Chinese community had developed over the course of the nineteenth century. Singapore soon became the most important place of trans-shipment for Chinese workers; there, jobs could be arranged for them across south-eastern Asia. Even the European colonial powers frequently recruited their Chinese workers in Singapore rather than in China itself.[181] However, it was Europeans who recruited the workers in the Chinese ports and arranged for their transport to the Straits. Prussia had been involved in this trade as early as the 1860s. To assist the German emigration agents and shipping companies active in China, Bismarck's government had accepted the Peking convention of 1866, in which the Chinese government had set down standards for the 'coolie trade'.[182] As steamships became established over the following decades, almost all of the Chinese shipping companies were squeezed out of the market. In 1890, 289 steamships were involved in bringing Chinese workers and emigrants to

[178] On this issue see Reinke-Kunze, *Geschichte.*
[179] As late as 1906, when German involvement had already been considerably reduced, the German consulate in Singapore reported to Chancellor Bülow that from the shipping companies' point of view 'the business of transporting coolies … must still be described as extremely profitable'. See BA Berlin, R 9208, no. 1535, p. 117.
[180] See Brandt, *Lande des Zopfes*, p. 109.   [181] See Trocki, *Opium and Empire.*
[182] BA Berlin, R 9208, no. 1531, documents dating from 1866 and 1867.

Singapore. Only one of them was Chinese (although there were also 44 junks). By this date British shipping companies had gained control of most of the Singapore trade, with the rest shared between German ships and those of other European countries.[183]

Around 1900, the market situation of German shipping companies gradually deteriorated. Some Chinese entrepreneurs who had obtained British citizenship in Singapore were now setting up their own steamship lines under the British flag. As a result of the 'Chinese Immigration Ordinance' introduced in Singapore in 1903, the fees charged to German ships were twice those charged to their British competitors.[184] The German government was no longer interested in supporting German involvement in the 'coolie trade', either; Chancellor Caprivi informed the ambassador to Peking, Max von Brandt, that because of the problems in the target countries, it seemed to him to be 'highly desirable that the … export of coolies stop as soon as possible'. The involvement of German shipping companies was tolerated but there were to be 'no measures … that might create the appearance of its being condoned … by the Imperial Government'.[185]

'COOLIES' FOR THE COLONIES

Hiring Chinese workers and transporting them on German ships was, in the first instance, a business operation for the companies involved. But the presence of Chinese people on German ships at times also brought up issues of constitutional or international law – as for example the question whether, in the event of 'excesses on board German ships' the Chinese citizens accused of contraventions should be 'sent to Germany for sentencing' or handed over to local authorities.[186] But really important issues of legal control and national identity emerged when the 'coolie transports' began to bring Chinese workers into the jurisdiction of the German Reich, instead of just to Singapore and Batavia. From the 1890s onward, at the same time as

---

[183] *Ibid.*, R 1501, no. 103532, p. 183.   [184] *Ibid.*, R 9208, no. 1535, p. 130.
[185] *Ibid.*, R 1501, no. 103532, p. 172.
[186] Gesandtschaft in Peking to the Reichskanzler, 1 April 1890, in *ibid.*, p. 62.

efforts were being made to recruit Chinese workers for agricultural work in Prussia, some of the German colonies began to deal with labour shortages by hiring Chinese workers.[187]

The shortage of suitable workers was the most important problem preventing profits being extracted from the German colonies around the world. When it became clear that the large numbers of German settlers had not materialised in most of the colonies, business owners and the colonial administrations began to attempt to use native labour. These attempts, however, were accompanied by constant complaints about a lack of discipline, low levels of performance and frequent breaches of contract. The large-scale attempts to 'educate' natives to work rarely produced the desired effects either. As a result, initiatives were taken to meet the growing demand for labour by hiring Asian workers. Given the 'reluctance to work that prevents the [natives] from entering into long-term employment', as the Reich Colonial Office reported to the German minister of the interior, the colonial administrations and the business involved felt 'compelled to use foreign labour'.[188] Once slavery, which had been used to meet the demand for labour in South America and the Caribbean for several centuries, had been abolished, demands began to emerge for Chinese 'coolies'.

One model for the use of Chinese labour was the example of the Dutch colonies in the East Indies. The number and size of plantations had been vastly increased, especially in Sumatra, by employing large numbers of foreign workers. The tobacco plantations in Deli, on the eastern coast of Sumatra, employed especially high numbers of Chinese workers, mostly recruited in Singapore. Around the turn of the century, over 100,000 Chinese people were employed there.[189]

The first group to suggest recruiting Chinese workers for German colonies was the German Planters' Association in German East

---

[187] Kiaochow, the German colony in China, was also faced with the problem of a shortage of labour and the necessity to recruit natives. For the politics of labour segregation that ensued, see Mühlhahn, *Herrschaft*, pp. 219–35.

[188] GStA PK, I. HA, 87 B, no. 219, p. 47.

[189] Bericht des Reichskolonialamtes 1914, in BA Berlin, R 1001, no. 6289, p. 222. For more details see Houben *et al.*, *Coolie Labour*.

Africa, in the late 1880s. By 1892, the first Chinese and Javanese workers had arrived in Tanga, and, between 1892 and 1894, about a thousand 'coolies' from China and Java were brought to German East Africa. But the diplomatic effort involved in obtaining these workers was immense. The German government in Berlin gave the project its support and the governor of German East Africa treated the issue as a priority. But the colony's reputation for corporal punishment of workers meant that both China and India banned the export of workers to German East Africa. For this reason, those workers who were hired were recruited not in China but in Singapore. But even there it was not before the British government intervened that the workers were allowed to be shipped out.[190]

The conditions experienced by these workers in East Africa did little to dispel fears. Many of the workers found the harsh climate of the East African coast difficult to cope with, and illness was common. In addition, workers were frequently subjected to arbitrary beatings by plantation owners. Desertion, consequently, was widespread. Nevertheless, as contracts became due to expire, the planters wanted to renew them and to hire additional new workers. But when the first 'coolies' returned to Singapore in 1894 and told of their brutal treatment in German East Africa, Britain refused to allow any further recruitment.[191]

This fiasco brought the chapter of Chinese work in German East Africa to an abrupt end. In subsequent years there were still occasional attempts, supported by the governors of the colony, to recruit workers from China. After 1904, when over 60,000 Chinese workers emigrated to South Africa to work in the goldmines, the topic was again intensively discussed. There were enthusiastic reports of 'competition between negroes and Chinese [to see who could] work faster and longer ... which are always won by the Chinese'.[192] Philipp Holzmann, a construction company mainly involved in railway construction, was among those trying to negotiate directly with

[190] On this topic see Koponen, *Development*, pp. 336–39.
[191] See *ibid.*, p. 338.   [192] BA Berlin, R 9208, no. 1566, p. 237.

Peking about recruiting workers.[193] But none of these attempts was successful.[194]

Instead, the German Pacific colonies in Samoa and New Guinea became the most important site of the debate about Chinese labour. Recruitment of 'coolies' began there after 1899 when the German Reich took over the administration of New Guinea (a German protectorate since 1885) and Samoa. The German governor of New Guinea, Albert Hahl, had, like the business-owners and planters there, reached the conclusion that 'the future development of the protectorate hinges to a great extent ... on importing foreign workers'. A shortage of labour had also become the most important problem for the Pacific colonies. Hahl was even prepared to allow Chinese workers to settle in the colony rather than admitting them only temporarily on work contracts. Unlike his colleagues in German Samoa, where the governor, Solf, feared the creation of a 'mixed race' and prevented Chinese workers from settling or purchasing land, Hahl did not see Chinese immigration as a threat 'because it depends solely on our skill as educators and colonisers [whether we can] obtain by these settlements a people loyal for our purposes'.[195]

Not all of the settlers were quite as convinced as Hahl of the 'necessity of a supply of foreign national elements'. Critics employed stereotypes and fears similar to those brought forward in reaction to the idea of recruiting Chinese workers for agricultural work in Prussia.

---

[193] *Ibid.*, R 1001, no. 6286, p. 41.

[194] While German East Africa was interested in recruiting Chinese workers, similar suggestions by planters and construction companies in German South-West Africa were regularly rejected by the governors there. The Otavi Minen- and Eisenbahngesellschaft (Mines and Railways Company), for example, applied every year from 1907 to 1910 to be allowed to hire Chinese workers, but was always refused. A study by the Colonial Office stated that there was a danger that if the recruitment were permitted 'there could soon be more Chinese people in the country than white ones'. German South-West Africa was 'the country of the white man, including the white tradesman and worker', and for this reason the recruitment of Chinese workers was out of the question. Documentation on 'Arbeiterverhältnisse in den Schutzgebieten: Die Entwicklung der Arbeiterbeschaffungsfrage für tropische Kolonien aus China and Java bis zum Beginn des Krieges 1914', in *ibid.*, no. 6289, p. 153.

[195] *Ibid.*, R 9208, no. 1566, p. 1.

To maintain the cultural, and ethnic, standards of the colony, it was essential 'to prevent our colony being flooded with Chinese'.[196] Also, the import of Chinese workers to Samoa had to be prohibited, some believed, in order to ensure that there would be no mixing of the Samoans, 'the most beautiful people of the world, with the ugliest [people] of the world'.[197] However, given the pressure of economic necessity and the failures of attempts to 'educate' the natives to work, the critics soon became reconciled to the decision 'that we have also resorted to the Chinese'.[198] After the turn of the century, there was general agreement that it would be almost impossible to ensure the economic survival of the Pacific colonies without imported labour.[199]

After 1900, the planters and the colonial governments instigated efforts to recruit Chinese workers for the two German Pacific colonies. In New Guinea, this process had begun a little earlier, and ended in 1902 when the New Guinea company gave up growing tobacco.[200] Chinese workers were hired for phosphate mining on the island of Nauru, which was one of the Marshall Islands but was part of New Guinea for administrative purposes. By 1914, there were 1,377 Chinese (and almost 200 Malays) living in German New Guinea, while the white population numbered only 1,137. The imbalance was even more pronounced in German Samoa: by 1914, there were 600 European (of whom 373 were German) residents, compared with 2,184 Chinese (and around 1,000 Melanesians), most of whom were employed on the plantations.[201]

[196] Tappenbeck, 'Chinesengefahr', p. 167.
[197] Bericht des Reichskolonialamtes, in BA Berlin, R 1001, no. 6289, p. 75.
[198] Tappenbeck, 'Arbeiterverhältnisse', p. 131; and 'Chinesengefahr', p. 167.
[199] See the information provided by the Colonial Office to the Ministry of the Interior in 1909, in GStA PK, I. HA, 87 B, no. 219, p. 47.
[200] The New Guinea Company was founded by Adolph von Hansemann in 1885 and had executed rights of sovereignty, supported by a *Schutzbrief* from the German government, in New Guinea and the Bismarck Archipelago from 1885 onward. However, the hopes for large numbers of emigrants from Germany and for the huge profits to be made from plantations both remained unfulfilled. The company's consistent decline led, in 1899, to the Reich taking over the administration of the colony. See Hiery, *Deutsche Reich*.
[201] See the Colonial Office documentation: BA Berlin, R 1001, no. 6289. On the history of the South Seas colonies in general, see Kennedy and Moses, *Germany*;

During the first few years there were few problems hiring workers in China for the Pacific colonies. Later, this became more difficult. For a considerable time, neither the Chinese public, the Chinese
government nor the administrators of the emigration ports had paid
much attention to labour migration to the South Pacific. From 1905
onward, however, there were increasing numbers of complaints
about the 'barbaric use of beatings' and the tight controls imposed
on Chinese workers in Samoa in particular.[202] In 1908, two Chinese
provinces from which there was large-scale emigration, Guangdong
and Fujian, sent a deputy to Samoa to investigate the situation. His
negative report in 1909 led to a Chinese consul being assigned to Apia
to represent the interests of Chinese workers.[203]

In fact, there had been repeated incidents in Samoa, some of which
were punished by executing some insubordinate workers. The complaints by the Chinese authorities, which were also brought forward
by the Chinese embassy in Berlin, were not just about the draconian
punishments but about the arbitrary and unfair way that workers
were treated in general; legally, they were regarded as equal to the
'natives'. This meant that their wages were paid in German currency
and that they were issued with numbers, which they were obliged to
wear visibly on their person ('something that is only customary in
Europe for cattle and prisoners').[204] A more important issue, however, was the demand that beatings should be eliminated and that
those Chinese workers who wished to settle in the German colonies
after completing their contracts should have the right to do so.

The local German authorities reacted to these complaints with
incomprehension and annoyance. The idea of abolishing beatings was

Hardach, *König Kopra*; Hiery, *Deutsche Reich* (pp. 235–42 give a regional break-
down of the recruitment and treatment of Chinese workers); Christmann,
Hempenstall and Ballendorf, *Karolinen-Inseln*; and Köhler, *Akkulturation*.

[202] Deutsche Gesandtschaft in Kanton to Reichskanzler Bülow, 29 June 1909, in BA
Berlin, R 9208, no. 1566, p. 22.

[203] See the Colonial Office documentation: *ibid.*, R 1001, no. 6289, p. 88. On the labour
issue in the Pacific colonies, see the (extremely detailed) overview by Moses,
'Coolie Labour'; Biskup, 'Foreign Coloured Labour'; and Firth, 'Governors'.

[204] *Note verbale* from the Chinese Embassy to the Foreign Office in Berlin, 1912, in
BA Berlin, R 9208, no. 1570, p. 210.

seen as a serious imposition because 'order and discipline cannot be maintained ... without a certain degree of severity'.[205] Governor Hahl insisted that for New Guinea, 'the low level of education of the ordinary Chinese worker makes strict discipline including the use of corporal punishment absolutely necessary'.[206] In addition, reference was made to the 'Government Decree on Chinese Contract Workers', the provisions of which ensured that Chinese workers would be treated properly. The Decree regulated many aspects of work and everyday life for Chinese workers in detail. They included hygiene ('provision of disinfectant', 'covered latrines, on the wind-sheltered side'), details of the food to be provided ('with the worker's agreement, half the rice can be replaced by three times the quantity of yam, taro, breadfruit or bananas'), a ban on alcohol and exceptions for opium use. But there were also detailed regulations on discipline and punishment. Section 20 stated that 'no person may be beaten with a switch more than once a week' without the approval of a doctor.[207]

Despite the colonists' resistance, the regulations were gradually relaxed; because of the increasing demand for labour, beatings were abolished in Samoa in 1909 (initially 'for a trial period') in the hope that China might agree to the recruitment of Chinese workers. China had made emigration increasingly dependent 'on conditions that in part [were] extremely onerous', and only permitted it on a case-by-case basis.[208] It soon became clear that it would be possible to recruit workers from China only if a bilateral treaty could be signed between Germany and China, similar to that between Great Britain and China in 1904 for the recruitment of workers for the Transvaal. In 1908, the Reich Colonial Office suggested that this idea be pursued; after the opinions of the German embassy and consulates in China had been obtained, a draft treaty was presented to China in 1909.[209]

[205] Anlage 2: Antworten auf die Beschwerdepunkte, Gesandtschaft Kanton to Reichskanzler Bülow, 29 June 1909, in *ibid.*, no. 1566, p. 31.

[206] *Ibid.*, p. 224.

[207] 'Verordnung des Gouvernements Samoa betreffend die chinesischen Kontraktarbeiter 1908', in GStA PK, I. Ha, 87 B, no. 219, p. 53.

[208] Staatssekretär des Reichskolonialamts to Minister des Innern, 1908, in *ibid.*, p. 47.

[209] See the Colonial Office documentation: BA Berlin, R 1001, no. 6289, p. 252.

The main stumbling block was the issue of the legal status of the Chinese workers in Samoa. A 1905 decree by the colonial government stated that Chinese contract workers had the same legal status as 'natives'. When, as frequently happened, Chinese workers were convicted of crimes – in addition to work-related offences these included theft and bodily harm – the punishments imposed often deviated from those outlined in the German Criminal Code, especially with regard to the severity of punishment. From the point of view of the German administration and the colonial courts, this was only natural, as the Criminal Code, they argued, 'was formulated in Germany with a view to the level of civilisation and the development of its inhabitants' sense of law and honour, and obviously cannot apply in punishing offences by natives who, like the defendants, are at a lower cultural level and have grown up with a different outlook'.[210]

The Chinese did not see things in quite these terms, and because of the labour shortage in the Pacific colonies, they had the upper hand. The Chinese ambassador to Berlin sent the German Foreign Office a series of *notes verbales* communicating their wishes and conditions. In particular, they stated, it could not be tolerated that Chinese workers, as 'members of an old civilised people, [should be] placed at the same level as the savages'.[211] In Samoa, the category of 'native' extended beyond the indigenous inhabitants to cover workers from Syria, Goa and Ceylon who had been hired individually. The Chinese government seemed unwilling to accept that its citizens should be 'treated in the same way as these barbaric negro slaves', especially since Japanese people were not to be treated as coloured.[212] The complaints referred to the provisions of international law, according to which, in colonies, distinctions could be drawn between 'whites' and members of recognised states (which included China and, from 1900, Japan) on the one

---

[210] *Ibid*., no. 1568, p. 81. On the legal situation in Samoa see Sack, 'Rechtswesen'.
[211] Kaiserlich Chinesische Gesandtschaft, Berlin, 22 January 1911, in BA Berlin, R 9208, no. 1569, p. 204.
[212] *Ibid*., no. 1568, p. 140. See also Kaiserlich Chinesische Gesandtschaft, Berlin, 22 January 1911, in *ibid*., no. 1569, p. 204.

hand, and 'natives' and other 'coloureds', who were usually treated as 'natives' in legal terms, on the other.[213]

The situation of Chinese workers was complicated by the fact that the Chinese merchants who had already been living in Samoa before the Germans took over had the same legal status as Europeans. The Chinese government claimed the same legal status for the 'coolies', who were also subject to a number of other special regulations. The fact that the German authorities insisted on retaining the existing rules shows that segregation policy was not based solely on the ethnic differences prioritised by the discourse of race. The social difference between merchants and workers was equally important. 'Racial' differences were thus always linked to issues of gender and class, and these could on occasion cut across and undermine the primacy of the race-based order.[214]

Because China was threatening to ban the recruitment of workers for Samoa altogether, the German colonial government decided to compromise. A 1912 regulation classified Chinese workers as 'non-natives'. As such they were under European jurisdiction in terms of criminal and civil law. However, the regulation did not 'intend to grant further concessions, in particular to place the Chinese at an equal level with the Japanese and thus with Europeans', as the Reich Colonial Office made clear. The constitutional limitations on Chinese immigration and settlement remained in force. In contrast to the situation in New Guinea, Chinese workers in Samoa did not gain the right to settle there.[215]

The way the issue of settlement and legal status in Germany's Pacific 'protectorates' was handled was based on the idea of racial differences. After the turn of the century, this idea became increasingly influential for colonial policy. It is important to recognise, however, that segregation along racial lines emerged in the context

---

[213] On this topic see Peters, 'Begriff'; and Mallmann, *Rechte and Pflichten*. See also Wagner, *Schutzgebiete*, pp. 234–72.

[214] On the statutes governing the three Pacific colonies see Hiery, *Deutsche Reich*, pp. 96–136.

[215] Staatssekretär des Reichskolonialamtes, 7 September 1911, in BA Berlin, R 9208, no. 1569, p. 208.

of increasing mobility in the colonies. In German Samoa, to forestall the development of a 'mixed' Chinese-Samoan population, Chinese people were forbidden to purchase land or settle permanently. This policy was part of a general aversion to 'racial mixing'. The governor of the colony, Wilhelm Solf, was incensed by the increasing number of relationships between German men and Samoan women.[216] Yet the Germans' aversion had not prevented the 'half-breeds' significantly outnumbering the Europeans in the country. After his return home from Samoa, when he became a secretary of state, Solf campaigned hard for a ban on 'mixed marriages', which was finally passed in 1912.[217]

Apart from the general issue of the relationship between colonisers and colonised, immigration by Chinese workers created a set of particular problems for the colonial governments. There did not seem to be any danger of the workers 'mixing' with the colonists, as the workers were almost all men and the few German women present were felt to be immune to any advances. But the government did attempt to prevent any intensification of contact between the Chinese and the Samoans. This policy of segregation was defended by asserting that the Germans were politically responsible for protecting what they saw as 'primitive peoples'. This was founded in the image of Samoa as an unspoiled island paradise, an image that was in total opposition to the negative way that Germany's African colonies were perceived. But questions of sexuality and reproduction were not the only issue at stake. Some commentators expressly warned of the 'bad example that the Chinaman gives to the native, whom we undertook to educate [*erziehen*] when we took possession of the country'.[218] The regulations on work thus outlined that the

---

[216] The reverse case, of a German woman wishing to marry a Samoan man, was for Solf unthinkable. He felt that 'for this type of marital blunder … a thrashing for both the intended spouses' would be the suitable response. Quoted in Hiery, 'Verwaltung Samoas', p. 669.

[217] On the debate about the 'ban on mixed marriages' see Grosse, *Kolonialismus*, pp. 145–92; and Wildenthal, *German Women*, pp. 79–130. On the situation in Micronesia see Hardach, *Separate Spheres*.

[218] Tappenbeck, 'Chinesengefahr', p. 168.

'coolies' must be kept under strict control and 'as far as possible kept apart from the remainder of the population'.[219] This policy of segregation extended to almost all areas of social life. Separate hospital barracks were set up, and prison rules stipulated that Chinese and Samoan prisoners could not be housed in the same cell.[220] In the face of the overwhelming population ratios in Samoa, with a handful of Europeans attempting to control a large native (and Chinese) population, a policy of apartheid was one of the tools used by a colonial power reliant on the strategy of divide and conquer. The colonial government certainly believed that these measures had ensured that 'to date any detrimental effects [of Chinese immigration] on the natives in particular have been avoided'.[221]

A similar line was taken in the German colony of New Guinea, although in this case Chinese nationals were in principle permitted to purchase land and settle permanently. But the immigrant workers were kept separate from both the European colonists and the native population. This applied in particular to the island of Nauru, the largest of the Marshall Islands, where large amounts of phosphate had been found around the turn of the century. A German–English joint venture based in London, the Pacific Phosphate Company, was founded in 1901 and began mining phosphate in Nauru in 1906. The company employed only a few native workers; most of its workers came from China and from the neighbouring Caroline Islands. They were kept strictly apart from the native population during working hours and in everyday life. A German police ordinance banned them

---

[219] Reichskolonialamt, Berlin, 6 February 1908, to Minister des Innern, in GStA PK, I. HA, 87 B, no. 219, p. 47.

[220] On this topic see Sack, 'Rechtswesen', p. 681.

[221] Reichskolonialamt, Berlin, 6 February 1908, to Minister des Innern, in GStA PK, I. HA, 87 B, no. 219, p. 47. For a comparison of the situation for Chinese people in Samoa and in the other German South Seas colonies see also Hiery, 'Asiatiques'. On the situation of Chinese people in Samoa in general, see Tom, *Chinese in Western Samoa*. The strategy of *divide et impera* was by no means unique to Germany: in other colonies, too, the Chinese were treated as halfway between the Europeans and the natives and segregation was used. On this topic see Sachsenmaier, 'Identitäten', p. 214. For the discriminatory treatment of Chinese people in Dutch India see Breman, *Coolie Beast*.

from entering native houses or visiting the interior of the island.[222] Concerns about 'mixing' also extended to the English supervisors belonging to the Pacific Phosphate Company. The Reich Colonial Office received complaints that the native 'workers, as a result of their daily interaction with the English, are taking on first the latter's language and then completely English ways'.[223]

To return briefly to the German hopes for a bilateral treaty with China: by 1914, these had still not been fulfilled. After the war began, any attempts to recruit Chinese workers for Prussia came to an abrupt end. In the colonies, too, the issue of hiring Chinese workers was no longer relevant: the war had made recruitment in China and Singapore impossible. In addition, Germany lost its colonies in the early months of the war. Samoa was occupied by New Zealand by August 1914, New Guinea and Micronesia fell into Australian hands a month later, and Kiaochow capitulated to Japanese troops in November of the same year.

However, the colonial question was still part of the debate on Germany's war aims. The most widespread and significant demand was for a cohesive central African colonial empire; Chancellor Bethmann Hollweg included this in his 'September Programme'.[224] Those arguing for a colonial renaissance were also concerned about the issue of labour. In documentation put together by Gustav Bredemann, the agricultural expert of the government of German New Guinea, for the Reich Colonial Office, the issue of labour was given a central role in planning for the post-war period. Bredemann suggested that 'when the war ended, areas with surplus workers [might] be acquired'. These workers could then be used in the tropical and subtropical areas under German control. However, mass recruitment of workers would only be possible from the 'overpopulated parts of China, Java and India'. As the Indian option seemed, even to this optimistic annexationist,

---

[222] See Hiery, *Deutsche Reich*, p. 240. For events in Nauru see Hardach, 'Herrschaft'.

[223] Bericht des Kaiserlichen Bezirksamtes Jaluit, 24 June 1909, in BA Berlin, R 9208, no. 1566, p. 177.

[224] On the colonial debate on German war aims see Fischer, *Griff*; and Stoecker, *Drang nach Afrika*, esp. pp. 229–42.

unlikely to succeed, he concluded by recommending that plans for expansion should concentrate on Java and China.[225]

CONCLUSION

The debates about recruiting Chinese labour for Prussian agriculture and the employment of Chinese workers on German ships and in colonial 'New Germany' are little-explored chapters in the history of the Kaiserreich. In terms of the numbers of people involved, they are insignificant. The number of Chinese workers employed on German ships never exceeded 4,000, and the total figure in the African and Pacific colonies combined was barely higher. The plan of deploying Chinese peasants in Prussian fields never got beyond the drawing-board. Chinese mobility was thus not a major factor in the history of the Kaiserreich.

But there was a little more to the story than this. In the colonies themselves, and especially in German Samoa, the number of Chinese workers after 1900 far exceeded that of the German inhabitants. There, the Chinese presence was by no means marginal. And reducing the debates about 'coolie import' in Prussia to their quantitative result ignores the impact they had. Desires, fears, hopes and projections about identity are rarely driven solely by the extent to which they correspond with a measurable reality. Like the debate in Germany 100 years later about *Kinder statt Inder* ('Children not Indians'), which contrasted the proposal to introduce 'green cards' for foreign IT specialists with the falling German birth rate, the debates around 1900 about Chinese labour must be seen as a reaction to the increasing mobility and connectedness of the era.

The discussions above contribute to our view of Wilhelmine Germany in three ways. Firstly, they link German history with a late-nineteenth-century process that was truly global: that of the global mobility of Chinese workers. Emigration from China was not directed only at their established destinations of Singapore, Australia, South Africa and the USA: Chinese workers also migrated to Cuba

---

[225] Colonial Office documentation in BA Berlin, R 1001, no. 6289, p. 1.

and Peru, and to Samoa, or, as boilermen, to Hamburg. In the era of high imperialism characterised by the expansion of territorial claims by colonial powers and of mobile contract work, the Kaiserreich was involved in the spread of Chinese labour migration, if only at the margins. Its involvement in these global migratory flows was not limited to the recruitment of labour mainly for the Pacific colonies. The agitated debates in the German press and in the Reichstag are evidence that the topic of labour in Germany was framed as part of a global problematic, even if Chinese workers were never actually employed in Prussia. Thus the extent to which the Kaiserreich formed part of late-nineteenth-century globalisation cannot be fully assessed by reference to statistics on imports and exports, immigrants and emigrants. Of equal significance was the awareness of the (possibility of) global interconnectedness that we can observe in the debates about 'imports of Chinese'.

Secondly, this global consciousness involved the possibility of creating links between processes that had previously taken place mainly in a regional context. Increasingly, social and political actors made reference to comparable events in other societies. Social phenomena and economic developments in far-distant societies were now treated as a model and a yardstick. At the same time, there was increasing awareness that distant events would have a local effect. And finally, those involved in politics began to make a link between global structures and local and national problems, 'glocalising' processes that had both universal and specific dimensions.[226] Examples include the overlaying of anti-Semitic prejudices with the transnational rhetoric of the 'yellow peril', or the drawing of analogies between the German situation and the problems of immigration in Australia and the USA. From the point of view of contemporaries, immigration was 'neither a purely local issue nor one purely related to the British empire, but a global question that all white nations have an interest in solving'.[227] Creating this link with transnational processes allowed local actors to claim additional significance for their own concerns, and visions

---

[226] On the concept of 'glocalisation' see Robertson, 'Glokalisierung'.
[227] Paschen, 'Einwanderung', p. 109.

of the nation, by referring to global developments. Of course, these synchronous links did not create nationalism. But the ways in which the nation was seen and the mechanisms of integration and exclusion were treated and practised were influenced, occasionally even transformed, by global references.

Thirdly and finally, the process of the global diffusion of Chinese workers is very informative for an analysis of the links between mobility and identity, and between interaction and delimitation. In many societies, the presence of a Chinese diaspora was one of the factors that contributed to the formation of a national identity and shaped the way it developed. This applies in particular to Australia, where the creation of a separate state independent of Great Britain was formulated and achieved partly by defining the nation's identity in opposition to the small Chinese minority. In South Africa and the USA, too, the processes of nationalisation and ethnicisation underway at the turn of the century were linked to Chinese immigration. And the communities of overseas Chinese played an important role in the development of modern Chinese nationalism. In these cases, nationality and the sense of the nation were by no means pre-existing categories that would necessarily have come into conflict with other nationalisms in the course of migration. Rather, mass migration itself contributed to defining national identities, both in the migrants' regions of origin and in their destinations.

Because Germany was only loosely involved in the global movements of Chinese labour migration, its effects on the development of German nationalism were less intense than in other countries. Apart from a small number of sailors in Bremen and Hamburg, and small groups of merchants and students, there was no Chinese diaspora whose existence could have led to conflicts. But the considerable reaction in the press to the plans to recruit Chinese workers, even where those plans were not completely thought through, reveals the extent to which ideas about the German nation were also the product of fears and longings, anxieties and projections that were linked to global processes – not coincidentally, in an era of *Weltpolitik*. Given the widespread concerns about a 'yellow peril', which increased after the Boxer Rebellion and were promulgated even by the Kaiser himself, the debate about 'importing coolies' into Prussia was more than a marginal issue; it was part of the gradual articulation of German nationalism with categories of ethnicity and race.

EPILOGUE: CHINESE WORKERS ON THE WESTERN FRONT

The warnings about the risk to 'German work' and to the nation's cultural standards had prevailed over any plans to recruit Chinese workers for the Kaiserreich. In this context it seems ironic that, just a few years later, Chinese workers threatened the Reich in a much more real way than the pre-war commentators had ever imagined. From 1916 on, almost 140,000 Chinese workers were sent to the German border – in the service of the French and British armies.

The war economies of the major European nations were highly dependent on foreign workers. In Germany, too, their number increased further after 1914. During the war, some 3 million people from other countries were employed in the country, mainly as a result of forced recruitment in occupied Russian Poland and Belgium. In addition, the increasing labour shortage, particularly in agriculture, was countered by putting almost 2 million prisoners of war to work.[228]

During the war, France and, to a much lesser extent, Great Britain also employed workers who had been recruited from abroad. In France, these were mainly workers from neutral Spain. But in contrast to Germany, both France and Britain recruited labour from their colonial possessions outside Europe. Most commonly, these were soldiers. By the end of the war, the French army had sent over 600,000 soldiers from its colonies to fight in the European battlefields. Britain hired some 1.2 million soldiers from its colonies, but deployed these mainly in Eastern Africa and in the Middle East.[229] But the two countries recruited not only soldiers, but also workers from the colonies,

---

[228] On this topic see Herbert, *Geschichte*, pp. 82–113; Oltmer, *Bäuerliche Ökonomie*.

[229] On the recruitment of soldiers from the colonies see Koller, *Wilden*; and Maß, 'Trauma'.

something that had rarely been done before 1914. Some 200,000 people from Africa and the French colonies in the Pacific were employed in France, 80,000 of those from Algeria alone. They were employed by the *Service d'organisation des travailleurs coloniaux* led by the military, were strictly separated from the native population and had to endure extremely harsh working conditions.[230]

The recruitment of Chinese workers by France and Britain from 1916 onward took place in this context. Both countries negotiated with the Chinese government to be allowed to recruit in northern China. The Chinese president Yuan Shikai had even offered, on several occasions, that China would make a military contribution to the Allied war effort, but as China remained neutral until 1917 this offer was not accepted. Between 1916 and 1918, France recruited almost 40,000 workers from China, and Britain 100,000. Because the British unions were vehemently opposed to the Chinese workers being employed in Britain, all the 'coolies' (as they were officially referred to in the treaties) were put to work in France.[231]

Almost all of these 140,000 Chinese workers had been recruited in the province of Shandong, the province containing the former German colony of Kiaochow. In difficult years, many of these workers would have travelled to Manchuria for seasonal work, so labour migration was in principle nothing new to them. The British authorities preferred to recruit workers from northern China rather than the traditional emigration regions of the south as it was believed that northerners would be better able to cope with the cold European climate.[232] The treaties stipulated that the Chinese workers were not to be involved in military operations. However, they were under the jurisdiction of the military, and their accommodation and the way their work was managed were military in nature. The 'French coolies' were distributed among a large number of French towns and cities, and were also employed in 'civilian' industries. The vast majority,

---

[230] On the situation in France see Horne, 'Immigrant Workers'.

[231] See, here and for the information below, Bailey, 'From Shandong'; Chen, *Chinese Migrations*, esp. pp. 142–58; and Summerskill, *China*.

[232] On the recruitment see Summerskill, *China*, pp. 39–79. For the British point of view see also Jones, *Britain's Search*, pp. 160–92.

however, worked in industries with links to defence, in munitions factories and in shipyards. The 'English' Chinese were put to work on the western coast of France and in particular in north-western France. They were not officially soldiers, but their work served to maintain the front: they dug trenches, transported munitions to the front, repaired gun emplacements, built airfields and buried the dead.[233]

In contrast to its reaction to the 'coolie trade' of the preceding decades, China officially welcomed this recruitment of a large number of workers. The Chinese government presented it as an altruistic contribution to world peace. As a result, local authorities willingly helped the British and French with their recruitment efforts. The government's motivation was both a temporary reduction in unemployment in northern China and an expectation that its contribution to the Allied war effort would be rewarded in the post-war reordering to come. But these hopes were not fulfilled. The Chinese territories in Qingdao claimed by the Japanese were not given back, nor was the British claim on Weihaiwei. And at the Conference of Versailles, the system of unequal treaties that China had hoped would be abolished was in fact reinforced.

While the Chinese authorities had hoped that labour migration would lead to improvements in China's international status, many Chinese intellectuals hoped that it would lead to domestic changes. Here, worker mobility was at the centre of a project in which ideas about work, civilisation and nation overlapped in very complex ways. Chinese reformers hoped that those employed in Europe would, after their return, form the core of a modern, educated Chinese working class. In this utopian view, the unemployed 'coolies' were seen as a proletarian avant-garde; their journey to the West would be not only a metaphor for the nation's journey into the future, but its catalyst.

This project of 'civilising' the Chinese working class was advocated mainly by a group of Francophile intellectuals around Li Shizeng (1881–1973). Li was the son of a Qing court official and had studied in France at the start of the twentieth century. He opened a school in

---

[233] On the reactions in Germany to the recruitment of Chinese workers see Peter, 'Bedeutung', pp. 259–79.

Paris where Chinese workers were to be taught not only French and Chinese, but also science. In addition, the school held courses explicitly designed to cure workers of their 'backward' customs and teach them 'civilised' behaviour. They were encouraged to wipe their shoes before entering a room, to refrain from shouting and gesticulating in public or from spitting long distances in the street, and to read a newspaper regularly on Sundays. In this context 'work' was far more than a means to an economic end; it carried a much wider political and cultural agenda.

This *mission civilisatrice*, which was also supported by a new magazine, was being pursued by other reformers as well. These included Cai Yuanpei, later to become rector of the University of Peking, who was heavily involved in the cultural reform movement of 4 May 1919. The reformers set up a Chinese–French educational institute to build reciprocal relationships; on the French side, intellectuals such as the historian Alphonse Aulard were involved. They also designed programmes of education for Chinese workers and, after the First World War, created the 'Work-Study Movement', which brought some 1,500 Chinese students to France in 1919 and 1920. The goal was not merely to impart to the students the gist of European knowledge. It was also a major social experiment in which students from the upper classes of Chinese society were to interact with the remaining Chinese workers in Europe (after the end of the war some 3,000 Chinese workers stayed in France), overcoming the social divide between the elite and the proletariat and creating an ideal Chinese nation.[234]

This programme of 'civilisatory elevation' was more than a strategy of social discipline. It represented 'technologies of the self' in which many workers enthusiastically participated. The project of developing a national consciousness bore fruit, too. This is shown, for example, by reactions to the news of a disastrous flood in northern China in 1918: many Chinese workers in France sent money or other donations to assist with the national crisis.[235] Chinese nationalism

---

[234] On this topic see Bailey, 'Chinese Work-Study Movement'; and Hayford, *To the People*, esp. pp. 22–31. On Germany see Harnisch, *Chinesische Studenten*.

[235] See Bailey, 'From Shandong', p. 189.

went through profound changes during the period after the First World War and in the context of the May Fourth Movement; the Work-Study Movement was just one of a number of elements. But it reveals how, from the point of view of the reformers, the process of nationalisation was the result of pedagogical interventions intended to transform backward workers with regional identities into modern national subjects. Work, modernisation and nation were the ingredients of a programme intended to catapult China from stagnation into history, or even into the future.[236]

---

[236] On this subject see in particular the excellent study by Fitzgerald, *Awakening China*. See also Wong, *Search*; Unger, *Chinese Nationalism*; and Mitter, *Bitter Revolution*.

CHAPTER FIVE

'Here, the German is not degenerating': Brazil, emigration and the nation's fountain of youth

Ubi bene ibi patria is certainly more correct than *Ubi patria ibi bene*.[1]

The debate about migration and national identity in Germany was shaped to a large extent by the fear of 'intruders'. The metaphorical arsenal of discourses about *Volkstum* from the nineteenth century onward included terms such as the 'flood' of mass immigration from the East, the invasion of 'pests' and 'parasites', and fears of 'mixing' and hybridisation. The treatment of Poles, Danes and Alsatians, of migrant workers from Italy and Holland (and China), of Jews, Sorbs and gypsies was typically shaped by questions such as: who is 'in', who will be allowed entry, and who belongs in the first place?

But for a more complex picture of discourses of Germanness, it is at least equally important to examine ideas about who was to be *kept* within the borders of the nation. Who was to remain a German even if he or she had left the physical nation state behind for good? Who remained within the imaginary boundaries of the nation, whether understood in cultural terms or in terms of the *Volk?* These movements out of the country were of particular importance during the nineteenth century, when emigration reached a level not seen before or since. Between 1820 and 1920, about 6 million Germans left the country, mainly for the Americas. Emigration was a response to hopes and fantasies about overseas destinations as well as a reaction to unsatisfactory conditions at home. But it left its marks in both places. The debates about the advantages and disadvantages of emigration, about

---

[1] Stolze, *Gedanken*, p. 4.

suitable destinations and the possibility of colonisation, about overseas markets and the 'shortage of people' in the agricultural regions,
are central to the history of nineteenth-century Germany.

EMIGRATION, WELTPOLITIK, COLONIALISM

Mass overseas emigration, especially to the United States, was one of
the most dramatic and far-reaching developments in German society
in the nineteenth century. From 1880 to 1893, almost 2 million people
crossed the Atlantic, before emigration slowed to a trickle in the following years. Migration out of Germany became irrelevant in demographic terms, although it remained an important political issue.[2]

From the 1840s onward, emigration was an important topic in
German public debate. Two main phases of discussion can be distinguished here. Until 1870, mass emigration was discussed mainly
in terms of whether it was beneficial or detrimental to the state and
to society and how it should proceed. Critics warned of the loss of
Volkskraft that the outflow of a large number of Germans abroad
would entail. As was characteristic of a late mercantile population
policy, sceptics equated emigration with the loss of 'national energy'.
But those opposed to emigration were in the minority. Most commentators saw emigration as an effective way of reducing social suffering.
It promised to reduce 'overpopulation' and to avoid the Malthusian
trap: an increasing population and stagnating food supplies. In public
perception, emigration was seen as an important way of solving social
problems and of reducing pauperism, although the statistics show
that while many of those who emigrated to America were among the
lower classes, few were members of the very poorest class.[3]

For a long time, government authorities ignored the phenomenon. In 1832, Bremen was the first state to have an active policy of
protection for emigrants. Other states followed gradually. But these
measures were concerned mainly with protecting emigrants: with the

---

[2] The demographic and social history of German emigration to the Americas
is now well researched. For introductions to the extensive literature see Bade,
'Massenauswanderung'; and *Deutsche im Ausland*.

[3] Hansen, 'Die deutsche Auswanderung'.

conditions on ships, or with limiting the activities of agents. They did not yet amount to an active official policy on immigration. Prussia paid no attention to emigrants, and Bismarck's motto, 'a German who has shed his fatherland like an old coat is, for me, no longer a German', shaped emigration policy after the foundation of the Reich too.[4] A national law on emigration was only created in 1897, when high levels of emigration were already a thing of the past.[5]

This law on emigration was passed during the second main phase indicated above, when the debate on emigration was no longer about whether or how it should take place at all, but about which destinations were the most suitable. Of course, there was still some resistance to the phenomenon, especially among major landowners east of the Elbe, who warned of the 'shortage of workers' in agriculture. But in general the debate now focused on the problem of geography and possible target areas. It was part of the wider discussion about *Weltpolitik*, in which Germans abroad were assigned an important function. Germans abroad would play an important role in determining whether Germany would become a world power or was destined for a 'downfall'. They were seen as a lobby group for German interests, as a potential market for German imports, or as a launching pad for colonial ambitions.[6]

Because emigration was generally endorsed, the 1897 Emigration Act did not attempt to restrict individual mobility. Rather, its aims were to 'preserve Germandom [*Deutschtum*] among the emigrants' and, to this end, to 'redirect emigration from unsuitable to suitable destinations'.[7] From the 1870s onwards, the debate about migration policy became a question of geography. It was felt that Germans were assimilating rapidly into their host societies, especially in the United States. There was also a belief that Germany was losing *Volkskraft* that would benefit other, possibly enemy, nations. As a result, the

---

[4] Bismarck, *Reden*, p. 203.
[5] See Joseephy, *Auswanderung*; Mönckmeier, *Auswanderung*; and Bade, 'Massenauswanderung', pp. 297–99.
[6] On this subject see Neitzel, *Weltmacht*. For a contemporary voice see Schmoller, *Handels- und Machtpolitik*, pp. 10ff.
[7] On the 1897 Act and the Announcements see Srbik, *Auswanderungsgesetzgebung*.

debate about emigration in this era focused mainly on redirecting it. Wilhelm Roscher calculated how much 'educational capital' left Germany along with the emigrants (along with the actual cash taken) and the economic loss this entailed.[8] The necessity of redirecting existing emigratory flows toward the areas under the control of the Reich became the most important argument deployed in the debate about the colonies during the 1870s and 1880s.[9]

EMIGRANTS, 'GERMANS ABROAD', AND
'FERTILISERS FOR THE NATION'

The debate about emigration took place within a global context, one shaped by *Weltpolitik* and colonial policy, but it was also a debate about the future of the German nation. In the course of the expansion of capitalism around the world and the spread of imperialism, the territorial order of the world was reshaped, with transformative effects on nations and nation states. The topos of emigration played an important role in this regard. It changed the idea of the German nation and what it meant to be 'German'. Bradley Naranch has shown how this change went hand-in-hand with a change in nomenclature. While German migrants overseas had for a long time been referred to as *Auswanderer* (emigrants), during the last third of the nineteenth century this began to change. Now, the term *Auslandsdeutsche* (Germans abroad, overseas Germans) became hegemonic in the Kaiserreich as its use was extended from German diasporas in Central Europe to overseas migration.[10]

This term is a typical example of what Eric Hobsbawm and Terence Ranger have described as 'invented traditions'. During this period, the debate in the press and politics about whether the country should aim to create a 'greater Germany' (*Großdeutschland*) or 'lesser Germany' (*Kleindeutschland*) was at its height. The promise of

---

[8] Roscher and Jannasch, *Kolonien*, pp. 338ff.

[9] On the pre-1870 debate about colonial policy, see Fenske, 'Auswanderung'; and 'Imperialistische Tendenzen'. For the 1870s, see Gründer, *Geschichte*, esp. pp. 25–50.

[10] For the following see the interesting essay by Naranch, 'Inventing'.

an all-German utopia held out by the proponents of unification competed with numerous regional loyalties that did not want to be taken over by a Reich or to be dominated by Prussia (or by Austria). In this context, the idea of the 'Germans abroad' served as a kind of ersatz national community outside its territorial borders, through which Germans could 'invent' themselves as a nation. This imagined community, although in practice widely dispersed, was part of an integral cultural imagination.[11]

The term *Auslandsdeutsche* was an expression of social and cultural anxieties that had been triggered by increasing mobility and the global expansion of European power. Because the idea of belonging to the German nation was closely linked to the idea of being rooted in the German soil, it was assumed that emigrants must necessarily fear losing their German identity. While the idea of the 'emigrant' placed the centrifugal character of migration in the foreground and assumed permanent removal from the Fatherland, the advent of the term 'Germans abroad' marked an important semantic shift. This terminological change emphasised permanent, stable membership of a German nation, conceived as a cultural and linguistic community. The experience of change and of a deep chasm between home and abroad was connected to the belief that national identity, understood in cultural and, increasingly, in *völkisch* terms, could not be put aside.[12] It is interesting to note, by way of excursion, that the concept of the *Auslandsdeutsche* continued to play a role in political discourse in Germany, even if the rhetoric changed: during the twentieth century, the terms 'border Germans' (*Grenzdeutsche*) and then 'ethnic Germans' (*Volksdeutsche*) came into use, and finally, after 1945, 'returned colonists' (*Aussiedler*). Despite the changes in terminology, each term conveys a fundamental uncertainty and anxiety about the durability of national affiliation.[13]

Woodruff Smith has argued that the debate about emigration and *Auslandsdeutschtum*, and the concept of *Lebensraum* linked to

---

[11] On the links between colonial fantasies and the development of the nation, see Zantop, *Colonial Fantasies*, esp. p. 8.
[12] See Naranch, 'Inventing'.
[13] On the Weimar Republic see Hiden, 'Weimar Republic'.

these terms, should be distinguished typologically from Wilhelmine *Weltpolitik*. These two terms, he argues, represent two differing ways of locating the nation in a globalising world. The concept of *Weltpolitik* referred primarily to the role of the state and its function in promoting Germany's political and economic interests in Europe and abroad; at base it was a project of economic liberalism, though it went hand-in-hand with a nationalist and expansive policy. Imperialism was seen as an opportunity for assisting the economic and social modernisation of the nation and of expanding the economy. In contrast, the concept of *Lebensraum* had originated in the discourse about emigration, even though the term itself was coined only in 1901 (by the geographer Friedrich Ratzel). Inherent to demands for *Lebensraum* was the idea that a people needed to extend the area of their state or else face rapid decline. This belief bore fruit most effectively in the arguments for colonialism from the 1870s onwards. In this context, the focus was less on prospects for new markets and raw materials than on the opportunities for settlement for the German people. While the arguments for *Weltpolitik* can be read as a discourse of modernisation, the rhetoric of *Lebensraum* lent popular expression to concerns about the results of this modernisation, for the people, for 'Germanness', for agriculture and so forth.[14]

But the contrast between these two positions on the expansion of the Kaiserreich's sphere of action was by no means absolute. Generally, the two arguments overlapped; they intersected in colonial policy, which could be motivated by economic or demographic concerns, and in the debate on emigration, to secure foreign markets, or set up German colonies. The changing ideas about the nation at the end of the nineteenth century were linked to this double movement: globalisation, capitalist and diplomatic expansion and the establishment of 'zones of influence' on the one hand, and the global mobility and establishment of diaspora communities on the other.

This expansion was regarded as proof of the vitality of the Reich, of the unlimited energy and youthful and optimistic attitude of the Wilhelmine era. Emigration, and the spread of 'Germanness' that it

---

[14] On this subject see Smith, 'Weltpolitik'; and *Ideological Origins*.

implied, were for that reason also seen, by its promoters, as part of a broader cultural mission. But the debate about 'Germans abroad' was also marked by doubts and fears, by worries that, at the peripheries of the 'civilised' world, German culture would be watered-down and that ethnic homogeneity would be diluted. There was a recurrent and ubiquitous fear of 'racial mixing' (*Rassenmischung*), as it was called. Fears of assimilation presented emigrants not as cultural pioneers but, to use a phrase coined by Heinrich von Treitschke, as potential 'fertilisers for the nations' (*Völkerdünger*), who would serve to reinvigorate foreign nations.

The result was, mainly on the nationalist fringe and among those that reported on the Germans abroad in a booming print culture, a discourse of Germanness and a call for a politics of Germanification in places of German settlement. The fear of rapid assimilation focused on the North American 'melting pot', where German migration was primarily headed. The alleged assimilationist tendencies of the German 'national character', lamentable as they generally were, here were perceived as particularly detrimental against the backdrop of increasing German–US rivalry for a role as a major power and for the leadership of a future global empire.[15]

These concerns eventually led to attempts to redirect the flow of German emigrants elsewhere, in particular to Africa, but also to South America, the Levant and Australia.[16] Here, the reasoning went, Germans did not dissolve into the majority population, but were able to retain and even foster their German national characteristics. The ideology of diaspora Germanness was shaped by these different contexts, but the general thrust of the rhetoric exhibited many similarities.

In the focus of public attention were the settlement projects in the newly acquired African colonies where migration was supported by state subsidies. German South-West Africa, in particular, would, it

---

[15] On the history of German Americans see, of the extensive literature on the subject, Galicich, *German Americans*; Trommler and McVeigh, *America*; Luebke, *Germans*; and Blaschke, 'Deutsch-Amerika'. See also Ermarth, 'Hyphenation'; Fiebig-von Hase, *Lateinamerika*; Fiebig-von Hase, 'United States'; and Gatzke, *Germany*.

[16] See, for example, Fuhrmann, *Traum vom deutschen Orient*.

was planned, become a settler colony, and the first governor Theodor Leutwein initiated a series of measures to establish large planter and settler communities there. The large colonialist associations like the German Colonial Society (*Deutsche Kolonialgesellschaft*) supported these projects, which were fuelled not only by considerations of power politics and international competition, but also by visions of a reconstruction of Germanness. The idea was to found a new Germany that was not riven by internal conflicts of class, region and confession, and thus to go beyond the political unification of the Kaiserreich in 1871, which nationalist and *völkisch* milieux considered incomplete.[17]

Long debates ensued in governmental and colonialist circles in a quest for the ideal settler, who was to be not merely manly and productive but to assume the role of a bearer of German culture. As the recruitment of migrants proved difficult, a number of different schemes was employed, even including attempts to establish tuberculosis sanatoriums in the colony.[18] In the end, however, the policy of colonial settlement proved unsuccessful. Before 1914, the total number of Germans resident in all the overseas possessions combined never exceeded 20,000 – small even in comparison to the tiny German principality of Schwarzburg-Sondershausen.

Instead, the largest diaspora community outside the United States emerged in southern Brazil. 'Unlike any other country in the world', Carl Fabri claimed, 'Brazil was suitable for the accommodation of German immigration'.[19] The most important provisions of the 1897 Emigration Act, consequently, focused on redirecting emigration, and its main, if unspoken, aim was to direct to South America the outflows that were now seen as unavoidable.

EMIGRATION TO SOUTH AMERICA

Throughout the nineteenth century, South America was an important destination for German emigrants, although in terms of numbers

[17] See Walther, *Creating Germans Abroad*. For East Africa, see Söldenwagner, *Spaces of Negotiation*.

[18] Kundrus, *Imperialisten*, pp. 43–119.

[19] Carl Fabri, *Kolonialpolitische Betrachtungen*, p. 19.

it was far less important than the USA: between 1820 and 1930 emigration to South America made up some 5 per cent of the total. Brazil was the most popular destination – by 1930, some 200,000 Germans had emigrated there – followed, to a much lesser extent, by Argentina and southern Chile. Emigration to South America, like that to the USA and Canada, started in 1816. We can identify several different phases during the century.[20]

One important date was 1859. In that year, Prussia banned advertisements for emigration to Brazil, in the decree known as the *von der Heydtsche Reskript*, and the policy was later adopted by several other German states. This did not mean a formal ban on emigration, but the strict prohibition of all forms of recruitment or advertising – which could even include guidebooks or information sessions – made emigration there much more difficult for the remainder of the century. The restrictions had been enacted because of fears about the conditions in which Germans in Brazil were living: partly the climatic conditions in the tropics, but also the confusing situation in the central provinces of Brazil in particular, where it appeared that the legal status of the *Auslandsdeutsche* was unclear. The abolition of slavery had been followed by attempts to replace slave labour with European labourers under the *parceria* system. Many Germans had signed sharecropping contracts that reduced them almost to the status of slaves.[21] Religion also caused complications: because Catholicism was the state religion, there was no provision for civil marriage, and Protestant couples from Germany were therefore regarded as not legally married. Despite many attempts to have it overturned, the *von der Heydtsche Reskript* remained in force until 1896, partly because any attempts to abolish it were bitterly resisted by Prussian landowners.[22]

These factors slowed emigration to Brazil, but could not stop it completely. During the second major wave of German emigration, from the 1860s onward, large numbers of Germans again travelled to South America. The peak came during the Wilhelmine period: in

[20] On this subject see Bernecker and Fischer, 'Deutsche in Lateinamerika'.
[21] On the *parceria* system see Wagner, *Deutsche*.
[22] On the *Reskript* see Sudhaus, *Deutschland*, pp. 108ff.

1885, and again in 1894, a total of 16,000 Germans left for South America. In contrast to the restrictive approach taken by Prussia and most of the other German states, Brazil was actively encouraging immigration and even provided financial support for Europeans who wanted to come. In 1889, the legal status of immigrants was improved by the founding of the Republic of Brazil; all immigrants present in the state were given Brazilian nationality in an event known as the 'great naturalisation'. Along with economic and demographic goals, the Brazilian government saw immigration from Europe as a racial tool, a contribution toward *embranquecimento* (making the population more white).[23]

Nevertheless, when the German Emigration Act was passed in 1897, making emigration to Brazil much easier, the number of Germans emigrating there actually fell instead of rising (as was hoped by those lobbying on behalf of the country, and by the shipping companies). This was partly because the Brazilian central government stopped funding immigration in 1896, passing responsibility instead to the individual states. The main reason, however, was that overall emigration from the Kaiserreich to all countries was now falling as the country became more prosperous. Between 1897 and 1910, only 7,002 Germans settled in Brazil.[24]

As we have seen, emigration from Germany to South America focused on Brazil, Argentina and Chile.[25] There were major differences between these three destinations in terms of local political, social and climatic conditions and in terms of the scale, chronology and social composition of the immigrant flows. Yet we can identify a debate, in Wilhelmine Germany, about 'South America', in which these differences, while not completely ignored, remained in the background. In this chapter, I will focus on Brazil. This corresponds

---

[23] On this subject see Hehl, *Entwicklung*; Skidmore, 'Racial Ideas'; and Stepan, *Hour of Eugenics*, p. 155.

[24] See Brunn, *Deutschland*; Luebke, *Germans*; 'Images'; and 'Patterns'. Figures taken from Bade, *Fabri*, p. 364.

[25] On German emigration to South America in general see Mönckmeier, *Auswanderung*; Bergmann, *Auslandsdeutsche*; a less successful account, Fröschle, *Deutschen in Lateinamerika*; and Illi, *Auswanderung*.

to the contemporary debate, which was focused on the largest cohesive German expatriate community: that in southern Brazil.[26]

Within Brazil, German immigration was concentrated in the three southern provinces of Santa Catarina, Paraná, and Rio Grande do Sul. Santa Catarina was home to some 80,000 German speakers, who made up almost 20 per cent of the population, and was regarded as the most 'Germanised' state in Brazil. Three towns near the coast in the north-east of Santa Catarina – Blumenau, Brusque and Joinville (Dona Francisca) – were inhabited mainly by 'Germans': that is, by first- or second-generation German immigrants. Santa Catarina also saw the only major attempt at concentrated and tightly organised German colonisation in southern Brazil. After the German Emigration Act had been passed, the Hanseatic Colonisation Company purchased an area of over 600,000 hectares for settlement by Germans. But the hopes for mass migration were not fulfilled, and the joint enterprise with the Norddeutsche Lloyd and large export companies resulted in the loss of the capital invested.

By 1914, the southernmost federal state of Rio Grande do Sul, which bordered on Uruguay, had over 150,000 inhabitants of German descent (some 15 per cent of the total population). The main city in the region was Porto Alegre, which was home to a large German community, most of whom worked in the trades and in services: as innkeepers, in transport or as messengers. Rio Grande do Sul was renowned mainly for its settlements of small landholdings in the jungle. They included São Leopoldo, where German emigrant families had settled in the 1820s on landholdings provided by Emperor Pedro I. Over the course of the nineteenth century, German immigration increased and the 'old colonies' became the starting point for the colonisation of the Rio Grande high plateau as far as the Uruguay River.[27] In many respects, Rio Grande do Sul was different from the

---

[26] On the Germans in Argentina see Luetge, Hoffmann and Körner, *Geschichte*; and Ilg, *Deutschtum*. The secondary literature on Germans in Chile is much better: see Young, *Germans*; Hell, 'Deutschland'; and Waldmann, 'Kulturkonflikt'. The most reliable account is Ojeda-Ebert, *Einwanderung*.

[27] On German emigration to Brazil see in particular the good, solid overview in Brunn, *Deutschland*. See also Cunha, *Rio Grande do Sul*; Hell, 'Griff'; Delhaes-

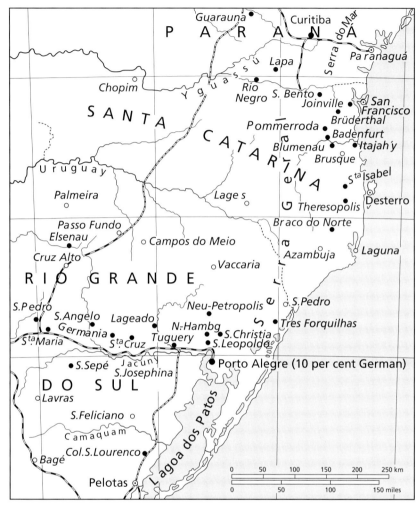

Map 5.1 German Brazil, 1905. Apart from the USA, where more than
90 per cent of German migration went, the largest German overseas
settlements were to be found in the three southern Brazilian states
of Santa Catarina, Paraná and Rio Grande do Sul.

other Brazilian states. In economic terms, it was characterised by settlements of small holdings, with little monoculture and little use of

Guenther, *Industrialisierung*; and Fouquet, *Einwanderer*. More nationalistic in
tone are Oberacker, *Beitrag*; and 'Deutschen'. See also Roche, *Colonisation*; and
Sudhaus, *Deutschland*.

slavery. In political terms, it was different too: the nineteenth- and twentieth-century protests about the dominance of Brazil's central government frequently originated in its southernmost province. A relatively authoritarian regime developed in Rio Grande do Sul and survived the transition of the country to a republic in 1889; the role of the state's parliament was reduced to approving the state budget. In the twentieth century, this special status came to be significant for Brazil as a whole, when a politician from the south, Getúlio Vargas, became President of Brazil and attempted to apply the authoritarian structures (or fascist structures, as they were by then described) of his province to the entire country.[28]

GERMANY'S 'FAR WEST' IN SOUTHERN BRAZIL

Despite the gradual decrease in the numbers of Germans emigrating in general, and in almost inverse proportion to the quantitative dimension of emigration to South America, an intense and noisy debate about emigration to South America set in from the 1880s onward, especially after the Emigration Act was passed in 1897. One of the first to argue in favour of emigration was Friedrich Fabri, who, in his famous volume *Bedarf Deutschland der Kolonien?* (*Does Germany need Colonies?*), had identified South America as a possible region for a targeted emigration policy. Fabri himself was involved in a number of plans to set up colonies, from Paraguay to Argentina. He viewed redirecting the emigratory flows toward the USA to southern Brazil as one of his main goals in life.[29] From the mid 1890s onward, a large number of publications appeared suggesting Brazil as a possible destination for German migration. Many travel reports, written to familiarise those considering emigrating with local conditions in the situation of the German settlements, described the country and the tropical natural world as a place of unlimited possibilities, where all dreams could be fulfilled. August von Eye, a cultural and literary

---

[28] On this subject see Huf, *Entwicklung*, esp. pp. 51ff., 66; Furtado, *Entwicklung*, pp. 140f.; Pietschmann, Bernecker and Zoller, *Geschichte*, pp. 218–19; and Cammack, 'Brasilien'.

[29] On this subject see Bade, *Fabri*, esp. pp. 354–68.

historian, who spent some time in Joinville between 1881 and 1888, told potential new Brazilians that 'you will think you have been transported back to Paradise'.[30]

Brazil promised easy access to land, which settlers could work themselves. Many peasants, it was often emphasised, would find in South America the opportunity to build up their own farms, something that was impossible for them in Germany. 'A man who came over perhaps five or six years ago poor, depressed, from his old Fatherland is now in possession of a considerable piece of land ... *He is his own master on his own land!* To date, every German colonist has attained this goal in southern Brazil.'[31] But along with individual opportunities for development, these geographical descriptions and travel reports also emphasised the Germans' role as bringers of culture. Emigrants who set forth to the 'resigned corner of a dark unknown part of the earth' were regarded as 'brave soldiers of culture [*Cultur*]', who were to propagate the achievements and traditions of 'Germanness'.[32] In this way, emigration also served the German nation; it was viewed as a public duty for the entire nation. Individual migrants were thus connected to the German *Volk*, for whom 'a piece of their future is located here in South America'.[33] South America was regarded as a promising location for German expansion, whether demographic, territorial-colonial, political or economic in nature. The national economist Robert Jannasch demanded that Germans should 'develop the far west of southern Brazil as the Americans have developed their Far West'.[34]

The literature on South America, which was made up of advice for emigrants, texts on geography, local history, letters and travel descriptions, was to a large extent a literature of Germanness. It was frequently a literature of German nationalists, and did not necessarily represent the emigrants themselves. In the towns and cities of Brazil, German groups and the Germanising rhetoric were less important. There, many emigrants integrated into existing social structures,

---

[30] Eye, *Auswanderer*, p. 26.   [31] Breitenbach, *Süd-Brasilien*, pp. 210–11.
[32] Gernhard, *Reise-Bilder*, p. 322.   [33] Vallentin, *Brasilien*, p. 249.
[34] Jannasch, 'Aufgaben', p. 590.

took Brazilian citizenship (though up to 1898, only about a quarter of German Brazilians did so) and identified themselves primarily as Brazilians. Many of the Brazilian Germans may have subscribed to the idea of 'overseas Germanness', but clearly not all.[35]

In any case, the most important target group for most of these writings was not located in Brazil but in Germany. The texts promoting emigration were directed mainly at peasants and the petite bourgeoisie as potential bearers of 'Germanness', while the travel reports were addressed also to the property-owning and educated bourgeoisie. Linking the ideology of agriculture with migration allowed the mobilization of a large part of the population for the emigration project, especially since it did not threaten those benefiting from industrialisation, as it displaced the fulfilment of romantic longings for the rural life to the colonial periphery.[36]

We can identify three groups for whom the plans for the settling of southern Brazil and the preservation of 'Germanness' there were important. The first is the nationalist movement – the Pan-German League, the *Verein für das Deutschtum im Ausland* (Association for Germans Abroad, *VDA*), the German Colonial Society (*Deutsche Kolonialgesellschaft*) etc. – and ideas about South America were also used to support arguments for the expansion of the German navy. Secondly, the settlement project was supported by interested economic groups. Examples are the shipping company Norddeutsche Lloyd, the companies involved in building the North Western Rio Grande Railway, and large exporters. Thirdly, and finally, the churches, who felt it was their role to look after the Germans abroad, also played an important role. The Protestant church in particular, in the form of the Prussian state church and a number of other Protestant societies, worked to preserve the 'Germanness' of the emigrants, providing both funding and staff. These church activities expanded the lobby

---

[35] See Luebke, 'Prelude', p. 3.
[36] On this subject see Smith, *Ideological Origins*, esp. pp. 83–111. In his enlightening (and, in Germany, little known) study, Smith emphasises the liberal origins of the *Lebensraum* concept, which, he argues, was hijacked by nationalists during the Wilhelmine period.

for South America to include groups that had no interest in economic expansion in the narrow sense.[37]

Comparisons with the USA were a defining feature of all the German writings on South America. Every description of the countries, the people and the prospects for the Germans abroad made reference, directly or indirectly, to the situation in North America. For example, when it was said that 'Germans had everywhere provided cultural fertiliser' and had 'dissolved in the foreign nations', 'everywhere' typically meant 'in the United States'. That 'mass grave of Germanness' was contrasted with South America as an enclave of 'Germanness', where the Germans had 'taken care of and preserved their language and their customs, and passed them ... on to their children'.[38] Another reason for the attractiveness of South America was that emigration there would not 'enrich' the population of a political and economic competitor, even a potential enemy; instead it would add a possible area of influence. There was a widespread belief that 'in the whole world the German is offered no greater task than there'.[39]

But some more cautious voices could also be heard. Governmental authorities, in particular, often warned against exaggerated expectations in connection with emigration to South America. They frequently referred to the insecure political situation, in Brazil in particular ('revolutions are commonplace'); the unreliability of the administrative and legal systems ('legal protection is very poor'); and the immense difficulties and hard work that the first few years of settlement entailed.[40] The euphoric tone of the travel reports and the literature for emigrants must not blind us to the fact that outside the colonial movement and the lobby for South America, scepticism about the opportunities provided by emigration prevailed. Most people had reservations about the promises outlined in the travel reports ('Over the decades, we have seen thousands become prosperous, rich, even

---

[37] On this subject see also Fiebig-von Hase, *Lateinamerika*, pp. 207–18.
[38] Giesebrecht, *Deutsche Kolonie*, p. vii.
[39] Benignus, *Deutsche Kraft*, p. 5.
[40] Quotes taken from Meinecke, *Katechismus*, p. 66. See also, for example, Krauel, *Deutsche Interessen*. See also Brunn, *Deutschland*, pp. 124ff.

multimillionaires[41]), and this was reflected in the small number of emigrants from the 1890s onward. And Meinecke's 'catechism' for emigrants confined its comments on the economic outlook for emigrants to a terse remark about there being limits to everything ('es ist dafür gesorgt … daß die Bäume nicht in den Himmel wachsen').[42]

So there were some antidotes to the frequently enthusiastic or even rhapsodic descriptions that were characteristic of turn-of-the-century German writings on South America. In fact, in many circles, scepticism or even criticism of these South American projects prevailed, though they were not so widely publicised. Even the business world was cautious about the issue for a long time, although German settlers were to some extent dependent on their investment. For these reasons, the reports frequently took the form of propaganda. They did not really describe a South American 'reality'. However, their importance does not lie in the extent to which they are depictions of reality. What is interesting about these texts is not so much whether they gave an accurate account of the situation in South America, but what they can tell us about the topoi that were used in the debate about emigration, the arguments deployed to argue either for or against mobility. In these travel descriptions, South America was recreated for Wilhelmine Germany, and the texts are an archive of the discourse about the 'New Germany' overseas.

SUBLIME NATURE

In Wilhelmine Germany, South America emerged as a mythical site for the recreation of the nation. The continent had played this role before, and the turn-of-the-century writings about South America thus built on a long tradition. Examining eighteenth- and early-nineteenth-century German literature, Susanne Zantop has argued that South America acted as a preferred screen onto which national fantasies could be projected. She argues that before the foundation of the

---

[41] Anon., *Deutschen Interessen*, p. 22.
[42] Literally 'care is taken that trees do not grow into the sky'. Meinecke, *Katechismus*, p. 66.

Reich in 1871 made national unification a reality, the German nation had been invented in literature and travel literature about South America as an ersatz space, an imagined nation, long before it became a legal reality.[43]

By 1890, things were different. The ambition of a common nation state had long been realised, in the form of the Kaiserreich, and the 'invention of the nation' was now taking place at home too. At the same time, South America remained an important point of reference and took on a double function in the age of imperialism and *Weltpolitik*. Firstly, South America became a preferred region for German expansion: economic and financial expansion, but also demographic and territorial expansion. Emigration to Brazil was accompanied by beliefs that it could be turned into a zone of influence for the German Reich, or even perhaps a formal colony. These prospects were intensively debated in Wilhelmine Germany. But secondly – and this was more of a subtext – South America was seen not only as a place where the nation could expand to find its place in the new world order, but also as one where it could be reinvigorated from within.

German encounters with South America were also encounters with nature. While emigrants to the United States were confronted with urban structures in a society that in many respects was seen as superior to that at home, one to which they had to adapt and into which they had to assimilate, South America was described in the travel reports as a gigantic tabula rasa. Of course, the descriptions often commenced with the ports and urban centres where emigrants and the writers gained their first impressions of the New World. But these cities were seen more as a place of transition to the 'real' South America: the *pampas*, the tropical hill and mountain regions, the snow-capped peaks and rainforests, the untouched wilderness.

South America was described as a country of luxuriant, almost untamable nature, of mountains, forests and rivers, with an exotic flora and fauna: 'Down at the coast [are] the mythical beauties of subtropical regions, and further up [is] a plateau with grandiose scenery

---

[43] Zantop, *Colonial Fantasies*, p. 7.

that is not equalled by many sub-alpine mountain formations.[44] In particular, the primeval forest (*Urwald*) was viewed as a symbol for the entire continent, one whose 'wild majesty' inspired the fantasies of German visitors – and readers. Almost none of the travel reports failed to describe the primeval forest. Descriptions made use of a shared arsenal of topoi: the lushness and immeasurable fruitfulness, the almost uncontrollable proliferation, the wilderness. An anonymous sketch described 'the luxuriant magic country in its tropical fullness and over-rich fruitfulness' that German colonists would encounter.[45] Wilhelm Lacmann, who published a report on 'Rides and Rest Days in South Brazil' in 1906, spoke of the 'amazing splendour' with which:

the subtropical forest surrounds us. The slender palmito reaches its delicate bouquet of flowers toward the heavens; broad-trunked cedars, tajubas, figueiras, canellas and all the others, the proud giants of the wilderness ... The forest contains a hundred kinds of life. A hundred different voices can be heard, from the croaking squawk of the toucan, the resounding hammering of the woodpeckers and the piercing cries of the parrot to the buzzing and chirping of the tiny hummingbirds who, with the shimmering moths, flutter around the fragrant blossoms. They are a wonderful sight, these colourful creatures.[46]

Such descriptions formed part of a common image of the primeval forest that can be traced back to Alexander von Humboldt's *Reise in die Aequinoktial-Gegenden des Neuen Kontinents* and to the writings of Maximilian Prinz zu Wied-Neuwied, who travelled around the hinterland of Rio de Janeiro between 1815 and 1817. 'This wilderness exceeded everything I could previously imagine in terms of alluring, majestic scenes of nature', Wied admitted, and his successors and imitators adopted his representations of the exotic and reproduced them with many variations. 'Picturesque', 'colossal', 'magnificent' and 'majestic' were the words used to describe the dream of the primeval forest as the sublime.[47]

---

[44] Gernhard, *Reise-Bilder*, p. xxii.   [45] Anon., 'Deutschen in Brasilien', pp. 3–5.
[46] Lacmann, *Ritte und Rasttage*, p. 90.
[47] On the metaphors attached to the primeval forest in general, see Wirz, 'Innerer und äußerer Wald'. The Wied quote is taken from p. 30.

However, most authors did not share the impression of a Garden of Eden that Lacmann's report conjured up. A Catholic priest, Father Leonhardt, stated that, 'if you have to cross it while travelling, the impression you get is not the beauty of well-cared-for German forests with their flowers, trickling streams and the many-feathered song-birds'. There was no trace of happy melodies and a colourful animal kingdom: 'in contrast, here wild majesty reigns in almost complete silence'.[48] The counter-image to that of the idyllic primeval forest was the primeval forest as chaos, as a threat, as danger. This topos was formulated in Henry Morton Stanley's reports from the African rainforest, which were widely read in Germany in translation, and it recurred in a similar form in many reports from South America. Here, the fertility of the tropics became rotting undergrowth, and the primeval forest was regarded as an enemy, rather than an idyll, one that:

offered a view of the most savage struggle for existence in which, as with a disordered human existence, it is by no means always the good or the best that prevails. And where it [the good] has somewhere found a space and is attempting to strive upwards, it is so crowded, sucked out by useless and damaging parasites, that it is usually killed off or dies of neglect, before it has reached half its growth.[49]

The undercurrents of Social Darwinism and the social analogies that could often be found in descriptions of the *Urwald* were not coincidental. They are characteristic of bourgeois ideas about the development of a male subject that would result from conquering nature through cultural achievements. This image of the untouched primeval forest was widespread before 1914 in all colonial societies, and formed part of the colonial ideology, along with the idea that those colonised were without history or culture. The dichotomy between civilisation and nature/lack of culture made travels abroad seem like travels into the infancy of mankind, to the beginning of history. Albert Wirz has said that 'the tropical forest became the mnemotope of the time before and outside history'. For this reason, overcoming the *Urwald*, cutting

[48] Leonhardt, 'Kolonien', p. 18.   [49] Eye, *Auswanderer*, p. 110.

Figure 5.1 A German family near Joinville (Santa Catarina), 1907.
Between 1850 and 1888, Joinville received 17,000 German immigrants,
most of them peasants of Lutheran denomination.

it down and levelling it out, seemed a precondition for any efforts at creating civilisation. It was self-evident that clearing the trees might also entail an inner clearing, which could result in the 'elevation' and civilisation of the indigenous population.[50]

In German literature on South America, which usually contained a chapter describing 'how the *Urwald* becomes cultivated land', this confrontation with the primeval forest was often described as an armed conflict.[51] Cultivation and colonisation were a battle. 'Every step of progress forward had to be painstakingly fought for with a forest knife.' Attempts to create agriculture were 'breaches' and the forest itself a 'fortress'. But resistance by the exotic natural world was futile. Even 'seemingly insurmountable obstacles could not hold these brave men back'. German peasants came as warriors, and this peaceful territorial conquest was by no means a pacifist one. 'Conquest was

---

[50] On this subject see Wirz, 'Innerer und äußerer Wald', p. 29; and Fabian, *Time.*
[51] See Wernicke, *Volkstum*, pp. 97–102.

step-by-step, the men marching one behind the other and keeping in constant contact by calling out to each other frequently.'[52]

COLONIAL FANTASIES

German writings on South America were obsessed with the continent's flora and fauna, with 'virtually impenetrable-seeming areas of primeval forest of truly majestic appearance and immense dimensions', and they treated South America as a continent of landscapes. Encounters with Brazil or Chile were presented as encounters with trees and forests rather than as interactions with people. 'Here', Robert Gernhard wrote of his travels through southern Brazil, 'everything that might remind us of life, namely of human existence, is silent'. In South America, this travel literature made it appear, the German would not encounter any indigenous or colonial inhabitants, but solely pure and untouched nature.[53]

This idea was not new. Mary Louise Pratt has argued that Alexander von Humboldt's writings often combined fervent descriptions of nature with the suggestion of a region almost free from human influence. She describes early travel literature on South America as a part of the commercial and territorial annexation of the continent. Pratt's analysis focuses on Humboldt (because he was so widely read). She argues that in the many volumes communicating his image of South America to Europe, Humboldt 'reinvented' the continent as nature. The titles of his most popular works – from *Views of Nature* to *Cosmos* – reflect his preoccupation with physical geography. In this, he was following in the footsteps of earlier authors from the time of the 'discovery' of the Americas and the first conquests. In their texts, America was often seen as a timeless space inhabited mainly by plants and animals, 'a world', in Pratt's words, 'whose only history was the one about to begin'. The marginalisation of the existing population,

---

[52] Many similar phrasings can be found. These particular quotes are taken from Giesebrecht, *Deutsche Kolonie*, p. 72; Hoerll, 'Kolonisation', p. 32; and Wettstein, *Kolonistenjungenr*, p. 104.

[53] Gernhard, *Reise-Bilder*, pp. xix, 385.

which she calls the 'erasure of the human', was part of an image of South America that could be used to justify colonial intervention.[54]

I will not attempt to assess here whether this is an adequate description of Humboldt's texts, or even intentions.[55] But it is true that the concepts of natural spectacles, of the absence of humans and of virgin territory were central to the reception of his works in Germany. In the colonial movement and in the debate about emigration to South America, Humboldt – a latter-day, less objectionable, more peaceful Columbus – was invoked to justify German involvement with the continent. Humboldt's own awe of Columbus the 'discoverer' contributed to this amalgamation of the two figures.[56]

Even a hundred years after Humboldt's journey and after the large-scale emigratory flows of the nineteenth century, travellers to South America still saw a natural world that was both luxuriant and deserted. 'Here, all is still chaos, all in its natural virginal state.'[57] The naturalness of the continent seemed to go hand-in-hand with the belief that the colonisation of seemingly uninhabited territories was a natural process.

> In the interior of South America are vast lands most lavishly equipped by nature and with a climate suitable for Europeans that, still almost uninhabited, can absorb innumerable millions of hardworking inhabitants. To the people who will one day get a foothold here and develop into a state power through peaceful cultural work [*Kulturarbeit*] – to them belongs the future of this part of the world.[58]

The territorial claims implicit in these words were characteristic of German reports from South America. Susanne Zantop has described the ongoing preoccupation of German literature with Latin America

---

[54] Pratt, *Imperial Eyes*, p. 126.
[55] Pratt does not, I feel, devote enough attention to Humboldt's critical views on colonialism in South America. For more positive assessments of Humboldt, see Raphael, 'Freiheit'; Zeuske and Schröter, *Humboldt*; Ette, *Weltbewußtsein*; Bernecker, *Wiederentdeckung*; Bonnlander, *Imperialismus*; and Osterhammel, 'Humboldt'.
[56] On Humboldt's reception in the nineteenth century see Zantop, *Colonial Fantasies*, pp. 166–72; Rupke, 'Wissenschaftler'; Rupke, 'Popularisierung'; Daum, *Wissenschaftspopularisierung*; and Badenberg, 'Ansichten'.
[57] Gernhard, *Reise-Bilder*, p. 389. [58] Leyer, *Kolonistenleben*, p. 3.

over a period of centuries as an 'imaginary German colonial history', a 'cultural residue of myths' that could be revived when need arose. Zantop is interested less in the campaign, after German reunification, for Germany to acquire colonies, than in the years preceding it, during which, she argues, the absence of German colonies reinforced desires for territorial expansion. Dissociating herself from Said's suggestion that there cannot have been any colonially charged 'Orientalism' in Germany because the existence of a nation state was a precondition for it, Zantop emphasises the virulence of the pre-1871 colonial imagination: 'Imaginary colonialism anticipated actual imperialism, words, actions. In the end, reality just caught up with the imagination.'[59]

Zantop's study, though fascinating, limits itself to analysing literary sources, and it is not always clear how the links between literary production and a colonial disposition worked in practice. She completely fails to examine emigration to South America, even though it started in the early nineteenth century. It was this emigration that created a social group (in both South America and Germany) for whom the colonial imagination went beyond self-referential cultural representation. In Wilhelmine Germany, the literature on South America formed part of the debates about colonialism. This applied to those advertising for emigration to the continent, from Friedrich Fabri to Paul Rohrbach, but also to colonists in South America and to the travelling writers who sent reports home.

This does not mean that there were any formal government plans for colonisation in South America, although enthusiasts often suggested that parts of Brazil or the Chilean island of Chiloé would be suitable places to set up a 'New Germany'. Speculation about possible annexations was most common during the political crisis in Brazil from 1889 to 1893. But most of those arguing for German settlement in southern Brazil agreed that there was no question of these 'colonies' becoming formally linked to the Reich. To protect trade relations with the South American states and to avoid any conflict with the USA, government circles were particularly anxious to avoid giving any

[59] Zantop, *Colonial Fantasies*, pp. 3, 9.

impression that Germany had territorial ambitions in the region.[60]
At the same time, the visions of the radical nationalist groups found
a positive response even in government circles. Although Germany
officially acted with diplomatic caution, then, the project of creating
an informal German empire in South America was indeed seen as an
option by German policy-makers.[61]

The reports by travellers in South America mostly took a defensive, appeasing stance. Rarely were any territorial claims envisaged: in fact, most authors argued that the German emigrants should
take on Brazilian citizenship. But the fact that no demands for formal colonies were made had more to do with other circumstances,
for example the fact that the German Emigration Act had come 'too
late', or the Monroe doctrine and global political issues. The question
of whether the activities of German immigrants to Brazil or Chile
might lead to more far-reaching ambitions was always in the background when the everyday life of the colonists was being described,
although it was usually an unspoken subtext. After all, as the descriptions of the agricultural settlements were intended to demonstrate,
'the German' was 'the best colonist in the world'.[62]

WORK, THE SUBJECT AND CULTURE

The German annexation of South America was not a military one –
Germans saw themselves as following in the footsteps of Humboldt
rather than Columbus – and the movement frequently criticised the
violence and exploitation that had characterised the Spanish conquest.
South America was seen as a place in which 'peaceful work creates victories that are no less important than those of the battlefields'.[63] Work was
central to all the writings of the 'overseas Germans' in South America.
Work was necessary for survival and for gradually building up a modest level of prosperity, and the guidebooks for prospective emigrants
emphasised that a willingness to engage in strenuous physical work was

---

[60] See Mitchell, *Danger*, p. 159.

[61] On this subject see Brunn, *Deutschland*, pp. 119–26; Hell, 'Neudeutschland';
Fiebig-von Hase, *Lateinamerika*, pp. 218–29; Hell, *Griff*; and Katz, 'Grundzüge'.

[62] Benignus, *Deutsche Kraft*, p. 23.   [63] Eye, *Auswanderer*, p. 145.

Figure 5.2 Brazilian-German work: 'The German people can be proud and tranquil, for its sons include heroes of work … They work unceasingly from early to late.' (Niemeyer, 'Deutsche Siedler', p. 384)

a prerequisite for settling in South America. 'There are heroes of the sword and heroes of work', the writer Ernst Niemeyer told his readers. 'The German people can be proud and tranquil, for its sons include heroes of work … They work unceasingly from early to late.'[64]

Overcoming nature, clearing the tropical forest, making the soil cultivable and populating previously uninhabited regions – all these tropes that Pratt has identified as elements of a colonial discourse on South America come together in the concept of work. 'How different the valley would look', Max Beschoren imagined, after travelling through Rio Grande do Sul, 'if it had skilful, intelligent, diligent inhabitants! Nature here gives so much, gives everything, and expects mankind only to provide a little industry and a little activity'. Here, it seems, there were no colonial projects or domineering tendencies,

[64] Niemeyer, 'Deutsche Siedler', p. 384.

just a vacuum needing to be filled – by hard-working hands. 'The only thing missing here is people, skilful workers, skilful German colonists.'[65] Work was seen as the central element of a peaceful conquest by the heirs of Humboldt.

But in the texts of the 'overseas Germans', the subjugation of the tropical forest not only provided legitimation for colonial expansion, i.e. for usurping the Other, but also the point of departure for the development of the individual and collective self. Work (usually meaning agricultural work – small-scale rural industries were rarely mentioned, and commerce or urban industry almost never) made the soil and the land accessible, but also constituted the individual and defined him (or her): as a subject, as a citizen, as a bringer of culture, as a man (and sometimes as a woman too, although male work was in the foreground), as a German.

The *ur*-form of this work was the clearance and cultivation of the tropical forest. The travel reports regularly described it in detail. Most of the German settlements in Rio Grande do Sul and in Santa Catarina were tillage settlements, made up almost exclusively of small farms. Each new arrival was assigned a section of rainforest, which he then had to spend years clearing and preparing for cultivation. Firstly, he had to fell the trees and hack away the undergrowth. This undergrowth, known as *Rossa* (*roça*), was then left on the ground for six to eight weeks and burnt off. The charred remains were then laboriously cleared away until only the tree stumps remained. The first planting could now commence. The land then had to be left fallow for another seven years. During this period, the *capoeira* developed, which was composed of very different vegetation from the former rainforest. This secondary forest then had to be cut down and burnt off in turn before agricultural cultivation proper could begin. The main crops grown were beans, manioc, tobacco and maize, mainly for the planters' own use.[66]

These years of drudgery in the southern Brazilian primeval forest were a form of rite of passage of colonising work, one that promised

---

[65] Beschoren, *Beiträge*, p. 19.
[66] The clearing and planting of the primeval forest were always of central concern in German writings on Brazil. For an example see Lacmann, *Ritte und Rasttage*, pp. 85–90.

to turn the emigrants into German Brazilians. The 'German colonist working unceasingly', who won out despite the difficulties of the climate and the wilderness, who cleared and cultivated the 'virgin soil', was an ideal regularly invoked by the 'overseas Germans' in South America. In this context, 'German work' was contributing not only to the 'development of these lands, whose future is so extremely rich', but also to the transformation of the German colonist himself.[67] As Johann Eduard Wappäus, one of those arguing for emigration to South America during the mid century, put it, '[e]ven work-shy people or those who here are, so to speak, lost to society [could, through hard physical work] in a foreign country gain a kind of energy and feeling that very often turns them into good citizens.'[68]

The idea that a bourgeois subject could be created through hard work was commonplace in Germany as well as at the colonial periphery. In Germany, it had accompanied the process of industrialisation and the rise of bourgeois society. The concept was also based on a belief that people had been 'lazy' during the pre-modern age – especially those in the lower classes – and would have to become gradually accustomed to a proper and industrious life. The disciplining of the proletariat, the establishment of a bourgeois sense of 'achievement' and the overall secular process of valorising work were all parts of this policy of 'making diligent'. During the Wilhelmine period this process also included the debate about tackling 'vagabonds' and vagrancy, and the legal sanctions applied to the 'work-shy'.[69]

These ideas were reproduced at the colonial periphery, though not without some typical differences. In South America, work was mainly taken to mean physical work in agriculture. The term 'German work' as used in Wilhelmine Germany also privileged non-agricultural pre-industrial and manual activities, but in Brazil and Chile, all other types of activity were of no importance compared to the clearing of the unrestrained 'wilderness, which is waiting for hard-working and

---

[67] Benignus, *Deutsche Kraft*, p. 94.   [68] Wappäus, *Auswanderung*, p. 5.
[69] On this subject see Schenda, 'Verfleißigung'; Dreßen, *Maschine*; Flohr, *Arbeiter*; and Steinert and Treiber, *Fabrikation*.

skilled hands to convert it to the condition of culture [*Cultur*]'.[70] Here, the German was seen as a bringer of culture. But in contrast to, for example, North America, this did not primarily mean disseminating German idealism, humanistic ideas and universal visions, but rather the very banal process of the transition to sedentary agriculture. 'Before the German colonies were set up, there was almost nothing in the way of tillage', recalled the publisher Wilhelm Breitenbach, who had spent many years in Brazil and wrote over eighty works about the country and its people. It was only 'German diligence' that was changing the situation: '[A] country of cattle-rearing is being turned into one engaged in tillage; the higher level of culture is replacing the lower one.'[71] History progresses here not on horseback but with the axe and the plough: 'German work' was the embodiment of progress. 'What a contrast between then and now!'[72]

THE GENDER OF WORK

Work was at the centre of all descriptions of Germans and of 'Germanness' in South America. In principle, this implied work by both men and women. Potential emigrants were often warned against setting off across the ocean without a family, and migration to South America was in the main a migration of families. One of the reasons for this advice was the fear of 'racial mixing', although in Brazil the situation in this regard 'was by no means as bad' as in Germany's African colonies, where 'mixed marriages' were banned from 1905 onward.[73] But the main argument for emigrating with the family was simply the need to make use of the labour of women and children, especially in the early years of settling in the rainforest. 'The wife of the German colonist in South Brazil does not know idleness', and even for her, life was 'simply work and more work'.[74]

However, not all work was equal. Work was an imperative for everyone, but the tasks assigned to men and women were different.

---

[70] Eye, *Auswanderer*, p. 139.   [71] Breitenbach, *Deutschthum*, p. 33.
[72] Meyer, 'Geschichte', p. 93.   [73] Gernhard, *Reise-Bilder*, p. 23.
[74] Breitenbach, *Deutschthum*, p. 16.

He, for example, who 'has dared to venture into the loneliness of
the forest', equipped merely with the ability to carry out physical
work, with diligence and with courage, was 'a hero of work'. 'But
an even greater hero is his wife, who has faithfully accompanied him
into the wilderness. His struggle with the forest distracts the man
from any sad thoughts. But at the quiet stove, homesickness creeps
up on the woman's heart.' But female work, too – whereby German
women were always described as wives – could report its own successes: 'And yet, gradually she manages to decorate the house. After
a few years of patient work their first hut has made way for a friendly
stone house.'[75]

These stone houses were a symbol of the progress of the civilisatory standard that had entered the country with German culture.
The stone house was also a symbol of the 'difference between the
German and the Brazilian settlements', which could often be made
out 'in house-building and planting methods'. In colonial rhetoric,
the transition from a wooden hut to stone buildings was one of the
classic topoi of modernisation. This was the case not only in Brazil.
Christian missionaries in southern Africa, for example, believed that
the style and form of their buildings influenced the local people and
introduced square buildings made of permanent stone.[76] When it was
reported from Rio Grande do Sul that 'the German builds solid stone
houses, while his Brazilian neighbour is satisfied with a paltry hut of
tree trunks', the language of architecture had become a language of
progress.[77]

But the interior was equally important. A German house, 'even if
it may be simple', always showed signs of 'striving for a certain level
of comfort in life and of adorning existence'. A house was a home,
it was *Heimat*. 'The Brazilian is quite different!'[78] A German house
created *Gemütlichkeit* (comfort, cosiness), and the task of providing this atmosphere was considered to be one of the most important
duties of the colonist's wife. The man's struggle with nature had its

---

[75] Niemeyer, *Deutsche Siedler*, p. 388.
[76] On this subject see Comaroff and Comaroff, 'Hausgemachte Hegemonie'.
[77] Lacmann, *Ritte und Rasttage*, p. 66.   [78] *Ibid.*

counterpart in the woman's domestic activities: 'The woman looks after the house, creates a home for the man in which he can relax and recover from the worries and effort of work.'[79]

This dichotomy between the public sphere and the area of the home was an essential component of the bourgeois understanding of work in Europe, which regarded the activities of men and women as fundamentally different. Work and leisure, or the absence of work, were all defined in gendered terms. The separation of the home and workplace, which was becoming established in western Europe from the early nineteenth century onward, corresponded to a binary structure in the concept of work, which made the earning of money a male-connoted activity and saw the tasks of domestic reproduction as the task of women alone. This modern discourse of work was part of the integration of the bourgeois family into the capitalist economy as a production unit. It also contributed to the naturalisation of gender identities.[80]

In South America as elsewhere, descriptions of everyday life, of activities and forms of employment in the primeval forest and in the fields, in the villages and in the home, were recurrent themes in the negotiation of gender roles and spheres of action. These roles were codified and modified in social practice and in discussions about social practice. A gendered view of work was common to the 'overseas Germans'. At the same time, discussions about work at the colonial periphery were influenced by two particular areas of concern. Firstly, making new territory accessible was a strenuous task involving considerable privations, and it required the physical labour of everyone in the family. This threatened to even out the differences between the sexes: as described by Frederic Jackson Turner for the USA, the frontier was seen as having an equalising effect. Secondly, the sheer distance between the new settlements and the colonists' homeland risked the loss of traditional social and gender hierarchies.

---

[79] Breitenbach, *Deutschthum*, p. 14.
[80] On this subject see Baron, *Work Engendered*; Hausen, *Geschlechterhierarchie*; Bradley, *Men's Work*; and Knapp, *Frauenarbeit*. See also Lübcke, *Unterschied*, pp. 226ff.

For this reason, the concept of work in South America was mainly formulated using a rhetoric of preservation. 'At home in Germany', as Breitenbach, a veteran of Brazil, explained, 'the woman is the companion, the comrade of the man, and has the same rights and duties in respect of internal family life'. According to this self-view the differences between the genders were limited to the public arena. But this supposedly natural hierarchy could, it seemed, come under threat when the borders of the Kaiserreich had been left behind and Germans were living in a different social context. In North America, Breitenbach claimed, 'as we know, this relationship between man and woman – the only correct one, in our view – has shifted considerably', a shift that was calling into question the patriarchal order 'to the advantage of women'. But this was not the case in Brazil. 'In general, we can say that the German in southern Brazil has remained more or less true to his German family life, insofar as the relationship between man and wife is concerned: in the colonies, by the nature of things, more strictly so than in the towns.'[81] The German enclaves in South America were seen as a haven of traditional gender roles, at a time when this order was gradually being undermined, in Germany as elsewhere, by the women's movement and by the debates about women's education and female suffrage.

'GERMAN WORK'

Work did not just distinguish men from women, it also distinguished Germans from others. We can also identify supposedly 'national' differences in descriptions of female work: Brazilian women 'really do nothing. They spend half the day dreaming in a rocking chair, and require the rest of the day to dress themselves, look out of the window, receive visitors or pay visits.'[82] The reports from South America always describe the Germans living there as separate

---

[81] Breitenbach, *Deutschthum*, pp. 14, 18.   [82] *Ibid.*, p. 15.

from other national groups, and the main way of measuring this distinctness was 'work'.

Descriptions of the natives' lack of enthusiasm for work were a standard feature of the German reports from Brazil. In this context, the reports often referred to the hybridity of the Brazilian population, or, in the commonly used phrase of that time, their 'racial casserole' (*Rassenragout*). 'You have all these tribes of negroes and mulattos, and the mongrels of Indians, negroes and Europeans, each with their own nature and character, and then the descendants of the various Europeans who have immigrated.' For this reason, there was no question of there being such a thing as a uniform Brazilian nation.[83] As a result, the way German settlers distinguished themselves from others also varied. The Luso-Brazilian population, most of whom were white, were characterised in the reports by German visitors as possessing an almost deliberate laziness. A typical feature of these reports was the frequent use of the term *paciência* ('patience. Or to translate it with a full sentence: if you don't come today you'll come tomorrow'). This attitude was also linked to a certain level of sympathy for the easiness of life in the tropics. But the Germans still kept their distance: 'The German language has more suitable words for work, which express the opposite.'[84] The reports suggested that, because of this unwillingness to work hard, Brazilians concentrated on raising cattle and hunting and avoided labour-intensive tillage. For this reason, they were incapable of social or economic progress.

While the deficiencies of 'white' Brazilians were interpreted as social backwardness, German writers distanced themselves more fundamentally when describing the indigenous population and the descendants of African slaves. Black Brazilians, who 'dream and idle' their lives away 'in a kind of undemanding indolence' were believed to possess a form of naive good-naturedness that might make improvement and 'elevation' possible in theory.[85] Of course, the 'negroes'

---

[83] Funke, *Deutsch-Brasilien*, p. 59.
[84] Westermann, *Wie wandere ich nach Südamerika aus?*, p. 61.
[85] Wernicke, *Volkstum*, p. 122.

were, as was often said, 'lazy by nature'. But they could 'become good workers if they have energetic masters'.[86] In these texts, the Germans are seen as patriarchal civilisatory forces, who have a firm hand but good intentions. In addition to the work ethic, the German language was to be important in carrying out this work of 'civilisation'. German visitors often reported encountering Afro-Brazilians who could speak fluent German, who even quoted from *Götz von Berlichingen* 'in a perfect Hunsrück dialect! In truth, here the German peasant had Germanised thoroughly!'[87]

   The text passages dealing with Afro-Brazilians usually had a tone of kindly condescension. In contrast, few spoke in favour of the large 'mixed population'. 'The true, dark-black negro is usually of good-natured character, but the mulatto is a really sneaky type.'[88] This view, and the privileged status accorded to 'purity' compared to any kind of hybrid, was a reflection of deeply held fears about the blurring of ethnic boundaries. These fears were characteristic of all the overseas German communities. The indigenous South American population was described in even more negative terms. The topos of the 'noble savage', which had a long tradition in the ways in which Europeans saw Native Americans, and which had been the dominant model for European descriptions of Indians in the early nineteenth century, now no longer applied.[89] In late-nineteenth-century German reports on South Africa, the native populations are no longer the embodiment of a pre-modern ideal, but are seen as unwanted competitors, as uncivilised animals and even as an enemy. The language used was not always as military in nature as that employed by Wilhelm Lacmann, who described Germans' relationship with the Indian population as 'a situation of war' and as a brutal 'struggle for destruction that the white man must pursue ruthlessly to the finish in the interest of self-preservation'.[90]

---

[86] Funke, *Deutsch-Brasilien*, p. 169.   [87] Lacmann, *Ritte und Rasttage*, p. 164.
[88] Funke, *Deutsch-Brasilien*, p. 169.
[89] On the concept of the 'noble savage' and the development of the idea see Bitterli, *Wilden*; White, 'Noble Savage'; Berkhofer, *White Man's Indian*; and Fludernik, Haslinger and Kaufmann, *Alteritätsdiskurs*.
[90] Lacmann, *Ritte und Rasttage*, p. 93.

This racist language was based not merely on a new image of the native population, but on real social and economic competition. The settlement of German colonists went hand-in-hand with the successive displacement of the indigenous population. In southern Chile, for example, European immigrants were offered 'fiscal lands'. This term referred to lands that had no official owner and were regarded as uninhabited. The establishment of agricultural settlements by German migrants involved the expropriation, usually violently, of the indigenous population. This was partly a result of the Chilean state's policy of settlement, but also of the integration of allegedly unexploited regions into a developing national economy. In southern Brazil, too, indigenous groups were gradually forced back or annihilated by the settlers' advance. On many occasions, murder commandos were deployed to kill the indigenous men and enslave the women and children.[91] German settlers presented these brutal interventions as purely defensive measures, and were backed up by the governments of the federal states of Santa Catarina and Paraná. Nationalists also supported this genocidal policy, making reference to the way Native Americans were being treated in the United States.[92] The settlers described the gradual disappearance of the Native Americans as an unavoidable development.[93] 'Their continued existence alongside German colonists has become impossible, they will have to disappear, just as, gradually, the predatory animals will be eradicated.'[94] In the descriptions by Robert Gernhard, who had travelled to South America, a German sense of superiority and a rhetoric shaped by racism and Social Darwinism overlap with capitalist ideas of productivity and efficiency. 'Culture cannot tolerate such unproductive human beings, its progress and flourishing must as a rule of nature bring about the decline and death of all predatory beings,

[91] See Hemming, *Amazon Frontier*; and 'Indians'.
[92] On this subject see Davis, *Victims*, p. 1.
[93] On attempts by the ethnologist Alberto Vojtech Fric to inform the academic public about the reality of German genocide of the indigenous Brazilian population, see Penny, 'Politics'. On this subject see also Kraus, *Bildungsbürger*.
[94] Gernhard, *Reise-Bilder*, p. 254.

and shall not protect the human animal embodied in the southern Brazilian Indians.'[95]

Differentiating themselves in these ways from the various segments of the native population helped German emigrants to define themselves as a superior group. However, the most important differentiation was that between Europe and South America, or even between the white and the 'coloured' population, without any major differentiation within these two major groups. It was only when the Germans were then differentiated from other European nations that it became clear that the supposed superiority of the 'overseas Germans' was not based solely on the civilisatory advantage of Europeans in general, but specifically on 'German work'.

Assessments by these writers of other European nations and their contribution to the development of the new South American states were careful and refined, much more so than the polemics with which Germans differentiated themselves from the native population. Furthermore, the assessments were not even entirely negative. Often, respect or even admiration was expressed for the cultural contribution made by other countries, for example for the values of the French revolution, which were very influential in the Francophile states of South America. But the idea of German superiority often shone through. German culture was often seen as a reservoir or a synthesis of the achievements of all other peoples. The 'German' represented a true universalism that united the elements of the other European cultures into a harmonic sympathy – a German, non-materialist version of the image of the melting pot.[96]

More usually, however, proof of German superiority was found in a more profane area: in the area of work. Here, too, comparisons and difference were vital for the Germans' self-image. 'Any description of German work and strength in South America would be lacking in detail if the activities of foreign nations were not taken into account.'[97]

---

[95] *Ibid.*
[96] On this subject see Ermarth, 'Hyphenation', pp. 41–42. For examples in the writings on South America see for example Keiper, *Kulturaufgaben*, p. 14.
[97] Benignus, *Deutsche Kraft*, p. 82.

Many overviews described the activities of the English, Americans, French, Spanish and Italians, only then to identify 'German work' as a selfless contribution, and the only long-term one, to the development of South American societies. Only German work, it was held, was not exploitative, extractive or instrumental, but long-lasting and productive. Only 'where the in-flowing German element can exercise its positive influence' could a country prosper, only then would the work be done in a 'non-destructive' manner, 'rather, creating and developing'.[98] All other nationalities were associated with unproductive forms of work. The Americans were associated with imperialistic exploitation, the activities of the British meant that any added value would be extracted from the country through trade and capital investment, and the French represented 'smuggling and buccaneering'.[99] The most fundamental problem was 'the predominance of the Romanic element in this region', the political dominance of nations that 'in the long term cannot maintain the same level as the German one'.[100] These nations were the Spanish, Portuguese, Italians, and even the French. 'These are not the colonists that this grateful country needs.'[101]

The idea of 'German work' gave to tillage privileged status as productive work in contrast to other forms of activity. The pre-industrial ideal of an autarkic agricultural sector corresponded to the forms of existence of the Germans abroad, most of whom were small farmers, at least in the south of Brazil and Chile. But more importantly, it corresponded to the privileged status accorded to agricultural settlements in the travel reports of German visitors. 'While other nationalities such as the English failed completely in the profession of colonists', only the Germans were suited to agricultural activity and would remain 'on the land assigned to them, would battle and fight for their existence'.[102] These accounts also distanced themselves from any understanding of work in instrumental terms in which the soil 'was only an object of exploitation, only a good', and they emphasised

---

[98] Vallentin, *Brasilien*, p. 249.   [99] Benignus, *Deutsche Kraft*, p. 87.
[100] Sievers, *Südamerika*, p. 91.   [101] Wettstein, *Kolonistenjungens*, p. 189.
[102] Hoerll, 'Kolonisation', p. 47.

the 'productive' [*schaffend*], not 'money-grubbing' [*raffend*] character of 'German work'.[103]

The topos of 'German work' was not limited to German texts. National characteristics were not formulated as a monologue, but were frequently reinforced by local actors. Domingo Faustino Sarmiento who later became President of Argentina (1868–74), was particularly influential in this regard. For many years, he argued for and encouraged German immigration to Argentina. In the mid nineteenth century, he found it 'pity-arousing and humiliating' to compare German settlements with those of the natives. In contrast to the industrious settlers ('perpetually in motion and engaged in activity'), the neglected, dirty and wretched villages of the natives, where 'the men lie around on the ground doing nothing', looked like a perfect example of 'barbarism and neglect'.[104] In Chile, too, the government's immigration commissioner Vicente Pérez Rosales spoke of the 'improvement in conditions through activity and work' that German immigration had brought. He saw Chilean towns and villages in less positive terms: 'On the buildings, as on the people's minds, the moss that normally only thrives on the bark of bedraggled and rotting trees can grow in peace.'[105] Similar comments were often heard, especially before 1880, when most of the countries of South America were attempting to attract emigrants from Germany.

The Brazilian government was among those promoting and facilitating immigration from Germany during the nineteenth century.[106] This

[103] Anon., *Deutschen Interessen*, p. 45. This differentiation often included anti-Semitic invective. See for example Eye, *Auswanderer*, p. 139.
[104] Quoted in Hoffmann, 'Deutschen', p. 83. See also Sarmiento's most important volume, *Facundo*, published in 1845, in which he expresses hopes that European and in particular German immigration will have modernising effects on the country. On Sarmiento and his immigration policy see also Shumway, *Invention*, esp. pp. 168–87; and Criscenti, *Sarmiento*, esp. the chapter by Samuel L. Baily.
[105] Quoted in Hoerll, 'Kolonisation', p. 19.
[106] On this subject see Hehl, *Entwicklung*.

policy was backed by intellectuals who, following Gobineau, stressed the advantages of Germans over 'Romans' on racial grounds.[107] For a long time, German settlers were also well regarded by the existing population. But the Italian immigrants were always closer to the Brazilians in both language and culture, and also because the Italian immigrants did not tend to live in separate or isolated settlements to the same extent as the Germans.[108] Away from the ports, in particular, the Germans usually lived among their own compatriots, cut off from the Luso-Brazilian and indigenous populations. For the Pan-German League and other nationalist groups, this was what made southern Brazil attractive and promised to make it easier to define national characteristics. These German perspectives are my main concern in this chapter. But it is important to bear in mind that the Brazilians' relationship with the German immigrants also contributed to the formation of the Brazilian national identity.[109]

This was not least related to the comparative isolation of the German communities, which created a number of conflicts. After the foundation of the Republic in 1889, in particular, the country experienced a wave of nativism, comparable to that in the United States during the same period. Some of the reasons for this were socio-economic, especially in the southern provinces; some historians interpret it as in part a reaction to rapid modernisation. An additional factor was the need for increased immigration from Europe once slavery had been abolished (in 1888). This put the issue of the country's ethnic, cultural and linguistic composition back on the agenda. While acknowledging diversity was part of the Republic's self-image, there were calls during this period for the creation of a new, Brazilian unity. Comtean positivism had a considerable influence in Brazil, and Brazilian nationalism was strongly influenced by the ideology of race, eugenics and the arithmetic of the mixed-race population.[110]

---

[107] See Skidmore, 'Racial Ideas'.
[108] See Freyre, *Order*, pp. 56–57, 123–24, 188–89.
[109] See the general overview in Burns, *Nationalism*.
[110] On this subject see Stepan, *Hour of Eugenics*, esp. pp. 35–62.

In this context, pre-existing prejudices about German Brazilians became accepted more widely. These prejudices were often formulated as a result of social and economic inequality; in the southern provinces of Brazil in particular, many German emigrants had achieved a modest level of prosperity that made them the object of envy. Complaints about the German Brazilians were varied, and had to do with cultural separatism; with their failure to assimilate into Brazilian society in political and social terms or, in many cases, to learn the Portuguese language; with their (in part) Protestant religion; and with their values, some of which were regarded as being specifically German. These values included tolerance of pre-marital sexual relations, regarded with suspicion by the Luso-Brazilians; a tendency toward thrift and saving money; and, last but not least, their specific work ethic.[111]

There were also complaints about the fact that most German Brazilians did not become involved in politics. Because of the restrictive nature of Brazilian voting law and a higher level of literacy among the German population, German Brazilians had a greater entitlement to vote than some sections of the population, but they made little use of this. In Rio Grande do Sul in particular, the German-speaking population often entered into collective voting agreements and exchanged political influence for collective benefits such as the ability to determine their own educational policy. In addition, electoral tactics and the design of constituencies served to reduce German influence even more. Only a small number of Germans became well-known political figures, one of whom was Lauro Müller, later Brazilian Foreign Minister, who was governor of Santa Catarina on several occasions.[112]

However, the main reason for the anti-German feeling was the tendency of German Brazilians to live in closed, isolated settlements, resulting in forms of cultural separatism. From 1900 onward, the protests often focused on the private, Protestant German-language

---

[111] See for example Harms-Baltzer, *Nationalisierung*, pp. 8–14; and Brunn, *Deutschland*, pp. 216ff., 274–82.

[112] See Oberacker, *Beitrag*, esp. pp. 401–5.

schools, in many of which, uniquely in Brazil, Portuguese was not taught. Social and cultural concerns became mixed with political fears: there were anxieties about the colonial ambitions of the Pan-German League and these anxieties were reinforced by Germany's economic activities in South America. During this period, the topos of the 'German peril' (*perigo alemão*) gained currency in Brazil, promoted by individuals like the well-known literary critic Silvio Romero.[113] Political events such as the Panther incident and the Venezuela crisis gave rise to frequent expressions of nationalist propaganda in the popular press.[114] The outbreak of the First World War and Brazil's involvement on the side of the Entente from 1917 onward reinforced anti-German feelings. This led to bans on German publications, schools and German-language religious services, and also to a number of acts of violence. Thus, the development of the Brazilian nation was partly shaped by this conflict with its largest single minority group, the 'overseas Germans'; the conflict acted as a catalyst, bringing the other nationalities in the country together.[115]

'GERMAN WORK' AND THE GLOBAL ECONOMY

The talk of 'German work' was more than rhetorical manoeuvrings by those seeking to preserve Germanness, and more than a strategy of national delimitation in a foreign land. The creation of the idea of the 'overseas Germans' through work was closely linked to the capitalist annexation of South America. For centuries, only the coastal regions of the continent had been affected by Atlantic trade, which focused on the main ports of Buenos Aires, Rio de Janeiro and Valparaiso. It was only during the nineteenth century that the global economy extended to the large agricultural areas of the interior. Several processes contributed to the integration of South America in the world's Atlantic-dominated trade flows: the growth in European settlement,

---

[113] Romero, *Allemanismo*. A similar argument is put forward by Magalhães, 'Germany'.

[114] On this subject see the detailed account by Fiebig-von Hase, *Lateinamerika*.

[115] On this subject see Luebke, 'Images'; and 'Prelude'.

which, around 1900, even took the form of temporary seasonal work; the construction of the railways, which linked the agricultural and raw-materials-producing regions to the ports; and, especially, the huge growth in capital investment, mainly by the USA, Great Britain and Germany. The concept of 'German work' helped to articulate the links between these seemingly anonymous global structures and the actual conditions experienced by overseas German communities.

Firstly, the concept of 'German work' formed part of the creation, or reconfiguration, of a global consciousness around 1900. In the context of global mobility, high imperialism and, in South America, the annexation of the continent by imperialist capital, this was expressed in the form of a Eurocentric and capitalistic teleology. We could describe this as the reinvention of South America in the context of the expansion of northern Europe, especially the expansion of its capital. On an imaginary level, this restructuring of the global consciousness was linked to the idea of the 'real' history of South America, which, as a result of colonialism and capitalist expansion, was now beginning. The frequent references to the uninhabited 'continent of nature' need to be read in this context, as does the frequently expressed belief that it was 'German work' that had allowed development, progress and even history to commence in South America. German emigrants, in this context, were represented as 'the core troops of culture and progress'.[116]

Secondly, 'German work' was seen as a factor in the economic annexation of the continent and in linking the interior to the expanding structures of the world market. The southern Brazilian provinces of Rio Grande do Sul and Santa Catarina only began to be used for agriculture after the arrival of German and Italian immigrants; the same applied to southern Chile, around Valdivia und Osorno, and the so-called *frontera*, north of those regions – the region of Araucanía around Temuco that had formerly been inhabited by the indigenous population. The rural forms of settlement prevalent in these regions corresponded to the emigrants' romantic self-image as farmers, and also corresponded to the expectations of the South American

---

[116] Hoerll, 'Kolonisation', p. 54.

governments, who wanted the rainforest areas to be cultivated and settled. German emigration helped to integrate the southern provinces of Brazil and Chile into the countries' national markets by 1900.[117] 'Integration' may seem a euphemism in some cases, as many of the distant regions were barely accessible, especially in winter. Nevertheless, the German colonists were soon producing goods not only for regional markets, but also for export.[118]

This brings us, thirdly, to the links between emigration and the increases in German trade with South America. The idea that German emigration to South America would act as a catalyst for German exports was an important argument used by those arguing for state promotion of emigration. 'Experience tells us', the Berlin Professor Robert Hoeninger declared at the colonial Congress in 1910, 'that trade follows language and people more than it does the flag'.[119] This was the German counterpart to British free-trade imperialism. Not only was trade with colonies and 'protectorates' believed to be a highly promising venture, but so was trade with the regions where 'overseas Germans' had settled. From the mid 1890s onward, the Foreign Office also promoted emigration to South America, because they had noted that the German colonists there 'retained their national consciousness and become useful consumers for German industry'.[120] The large numbers of Germans emigrating to Brazil triggered hopes for huge new markets for German exports. 'It is clearly evident', as the writer Franz Giesebrecht claimed, 'that we are capable of creating a market for our trade and industry in southern Brazil unequalled by any other we possess in the world'.[121]

German trade with South America increased dramatically during the Wilhelmine era. Before 1900, three-quarters of German imports had come from its European neighbours. This changed after the turn

---

[117] On the integration of Brazil into the global economy see Novy, *Brasilien*, pp. 85–96.
[118] On this subject see the very impressive account by Ojeda-Ebert, *Einwanderung*, pp. 43–76.
[119] Hoeninger, 'Deutschtum', p. 271.
[120] German Foreign Office note dated 2 May 1898, quoted in Hell, 'Griff', p. 133.
[121] Giesebrecht, *Deutsche Kolonie*, p. 34.

of the century, and South America became an important supplier of raw materials and foodstuffs: guano and saltpetre from Chile; wheat, meat and wool from Argentina; and coffee, tobacco and animal hides (and, later, rubber) from Brazil were the most important imports. While South America supplied primary goods, Germany increasingly exported capital goods (mainly machinery and vehicles) and other manufactures, as well as services. For Argentina, Brazil and Chile, Germany took second place, behind Britain, for both imports and exports (except for Brazilian coffee, for which the USA was the main customer).[122] By 1914, Germany was responsible for 17.5 per cent of Brazilian imports, and almost 15 per cent of Brazilian exports. Although Brazil did remain a small market for Germany, German exports to the country grew by over 400 per cent between 1900 and 1910. Capital investment also increased considerably; here, too, Germany was soon the second most important investor after Britain, although still a long way behind.[123] German industry was increasingly focused on exports, and up to 1914 South America was an important market, as it was one of the few still open to Germany, being outside the colonial regions and the British empire.

To what extent was this expansion of German trade with South America a result of German emigration? Writings on emigration and travel in South America rarely doubted that there was a close link between the two. 'In South Brazil', one comment stated, 'Germans want German goods, and in doing so are performing a service for their old fatherland that should not be underestimated'.[124] In this, the observer noted, the Brazilian diaspora differed from German Americans, who did not maintain the same economic links with their homeland. As late as the 1880s, many of the goods and articles needed by the colonists were indeed imported from Germany; contemporaries estimated that German imports made up over 60 per cent of the total. However, it is likely that these figures were exaggerated; the

---

[122] On German trade with South America see Fiebig-von Hase, *Lateinamerika*, pp. 140–77.
[123] On trade with Brazil see Brunn, *Deutschland*, pp. 232–73; Fluck, 'Entwicklung'; and Dettmann, *Aufschwung*.
[124] Breitenbach, *Deutschthum*, p. 32.

direct effects of emigration on the geographic structure of German exports were overestimated for a long time. The general increase in trade that South America experienced in the context of the expansion of the global economy after 1900 greatly reduced the importance of the German settlement areas. While, in 1902, almost 40 per cent of the goods imported into the province of Rio Grande do Sul came from Germany, by 1913 the figure for all three southern provinces together had fallen to only 9 per cent.[125]

'A GNARLED OAK IN THE MIDST OF THE PALM TREES': THE DIASPORA AND THE PROMOTION OF 'GERMANNESS'

The hopes that the German communities abroad would create unlimited markets featured in some of the more utopian ideas expressed in the debate on emigration, although these hopes, like those for a high level of trade with Germany's African colonies, remained unfulfilled. Global mobility promised colonial expansion, increased German influence in global politics, the acquisition of *Lebensraum* and new markets for raw materials and products. But all these hopes were based on the condition that the migrants would not be lost to Germany and would not assimilate in their host countries any more than absolutely necessary. References to the 'overseas Germans' always involved anxieties about alienation and about the phantom pain of national loss.

These fears took institutional form. The Pan-German League and the *VDA* (which by 1890 already had over 350 local groups in South America), provided the organisational structures within which these anxieties about the loss of national strength through mobility and emigration were reinforced. The Pan-German League only had about 18,000 members in total, but it was well established in the educated bourgeoisie and was able to exert considerable political influence through its many publications and connections. Magazines such as *Die Gartenlaube*, *Globus*, *Grenzboten* and *Die Deutsche Erde* reached a

---

[125] On this subject see Ramelow, 'Einfluß'; and *Reiseberichte*; and Brunn, *Deutschland*, p. 242.

larger audience. These magazines reported on the fate of the German communities abroad, on the singing groups and shooting clubs, the beer gardens and panelled living-rooms that acted across the globe as symbols of the spread of the German *Heimat*. From the turn of the century onward, an active German cultural policy was initiated to preserve and maintain these refuges of national culture. Wilhelmine policies to support Germanness abroad included funding German schools, opening consulates and embassies, organising lecture tours and foreign tours by German theatres, and sending impressive warships to visit Brazilian waters.[126]

It was hoped that emigration to South America would help to preserve or even to strengthen 'Germandom' there. The travel reports and many of the descriptions of the German settlements in South America helped to sustain this belief. They generally suggested that '"Germandom" has been more truly preserved here than elsewhere'.[127] It was felt that one of the most important conditions for the preservation of national traditions was that German emigrants should live close together. Only if the dispersal of the 'German element' could be prevented would it be possible for 'Germandom in southern Brazil [to be] preserved in a pure and meaty form ... for many decades'.[128] The half-life of German culture would primarily be determined by the topographical concentration of German emigrants. This view was shared by the South American governments, although their interests were different. Toward the end of the nineteenth century, they increased their attempts to prevent different national groups settling in closed national communities. Their main reason was anxiety about the political influence or even colonial ambitions of the emigrants' 'mother

---

[126] On the Pan-German League, the *VDA* and other institutions involved in promoting Germanness see Puschner, *Völkische Bewegung*; Weidenfeller, *VDA*; Pogge von Strandmann, 'Domestic Origins'; Chickering, *We Men*; Kloosterhuis, *Imperialisten*; Smith, *Ideological Origins*; and Hering, *Konstruierte Nation*. On the discourse of Germanness in *Die Gartenlaube* see Belgum, *Popularizing*, esp. pp. 142–82.

[127] Breitenbach, *Deutschthum*, p. 40. On the policy of promoting Germanness in southern Brazil see the account in Wieser, 'Deutsches Turnen', pp. 252–75; it is, however, very positivistic.

[128] Giesebrecht, *Deutsche Kolonie*, p. ix.

countries'. Another factor was the goal of optimising the 'racial mix' as a strategy of social policy. A report by the Chilean ministry of foreign affairs in 1902 outlined the advantages of an immigration policy that would promote the 'plurality of races'; it would allow Chile 'to make use of the different elements and advantages of civilisation, while simultaneously maintaining an ethnographic balance'.[129]

The effects of the geographic, cultural and linguistic isolation of German emigrants were reinforced by many types of association and an active policy of promoting Germanness. A large number of voluntary associations and societies sprang up in both smaller and larger towns. Singing groups (named 'Harmony' or 'Happiness') and 'German societies' – bowling groups and regular masked balls; gymnastic groups; shooting, rowing and excursion societies; fraternities and charitable groups – helped to create a community and forms of organised sociability, but were also seen as outposts of the national defensive struggle. They were joined by the churches and religious communities. In mostly Catholic South America, the Protestant churches played a major role in defining Germans as different.[130]

The overseas German communities cultivated a specifically bourgeois lifestyle, the 'German' character of which was to be evident even in everyday life. It included a central European form of architecture and 'whitewashed houses and green trees in the extensive farms', explicitly differentiated from the Brazilians' 'clay-built cottages' (*Lehmkaten*).[131] The gardens were carefully laid out with flowerbeds, and the interiors featured Biedermeier furniture, *Kaffee und Kuchen*, painted plates and lace tablecloths. The literary gatherings, social groups and traditional singing groups were also regarded as characteristically German, as were large families, endogamous marriages and a patriarchal order.

The most important indicator of the survival of 'Germanness' was language. Much of the cultural work engaged in by the

---

[129] Quoted in Ojeda-Ebert, *Einwanderung*, p. 32.
[130] On this subject see Wieser, 'Deutsches Turnen'. See also (though it is an equally disappointing account) Messele-Wieser and Wieser, *Heimatland*.
[131] Funke, *Deutsch-Brasilien*, p. 125.

Figure 5.3 The social life in German diaspora communities, such as
here in Blumenau (Santa Catarina), centred around associations and festivities.

Auslandsvereine focused on language policy, including supporting
German schools and newspapers. Almost all of the travel reports
from southern Brazil contained detailed accounts of the condition of the German language there. Usually, visitors were sur-
prised and impressed by the authenticity and purity of the German
spoken by the diaspora. 'The German one hears in Joinville is notably pure despite, or perhaps because of, the fact that the colonists
are a colourful mixture from every part of Germany, Switzerland
and Scandinavia.'[132] However, other opinions could also be heard.
Occasionally, this praise of the cultural conservatism of Germans
abroad was described as propaganda, which had the purpose of
creating 'a blue smoke', to put readers at home into 'a cosily patriotic celebratory frame of mind'. In fact, these authors warned,
the preservation of German traditions did not mean much. It was
notable 'that in Porto Allegre, the German Michel [was] showing

[132] Breitenbach, *Deutschthum*, p. 37.

alarming signs of transforming himself into Miguel'. This was not 'stubborn adherence to Germandom', but adaptation and assimilation.[133] However, these critical and sceptical remarks were mainly directed at the towns and cities, not at the agricultural colonies in the interior of the country. Warnings about the risk of the loss of Germanness usually went hand-in-hand with anti-urban feelings.

Along with language, the reporters were particularly interested in the physical appearance of the emigrants, in the markings of ethnicity. In this regard, too, the rural areas of Brazil and China seemed to be suitable refuges for Germanness, especially since most emigrants came with their families, making intermarriage with locals unusual. Visitors from Germany often described their amazement about 'how pure and unpolluted the Germanic type appears among the population'.[134] Blond, blue-eyed and tall, the Germans abroad were described as the personification of *völkisch* ideals: 'One would think … that the old Teutons [*Germanen*] had come back when one looks at the young race in the German colonies.'[135]

'HERE, THE GERMAN IS NOT DEGENERATING'

The frequent references to the Teutons created a link between the Germans abroad and the 'invented traditions' of the German national imagination, in which the topos of the Teutons had been important from the Romantic era onward.[136] But it was characteristic of descriptions of the German diaspora that here, the legend of the Teutons was used to identify a difference between the diaspora and the Kaiserreich. German settlements in southern Brazil were seen as a 'fountain of youth' and were contrasted with the decadence and excesses of civilisation in the 'ossified old

---

[133] Lacmann, *Ritte und Rasttage*, p. 149. [134] *Ibid.*, p. 158.
[135] Breitenbach, *Deutschthum*, p. 22.
[136] On the myth of Germania and its role in German nationalism see Kloft, 'Germania', which gives further references.

Heimat'.[137] In this way, the German community in South America was claimed to be capable not merely of preventing Germanness 'being assimilated by' (*aufgehen in*) the majority society, but even of recreating Germanness itself. Emigration to South America would both extend the life of national traditions, under the difficult conditions of mobility, and contribute to rejuvenating and purifying them. 'If one wants to come to know and respect the strength rooted in the German nation', Father Leonhardt promised, 'one must follow the German far afield into the swamps and primeval forests of South America'.[138] The areas of German settlement in southern Brazil and in Chile thus not only stayed German longer than other settlements, they were even seen as the more authentic Germany.

This regeneration of Germanness overseas was understood to be primarily the result of natural forces. This belief picked up on the descriptions of South America as a continent of more or less untouched nature. This was 'the country' that 'reforms Germanic characteristics in such a way' that nothing was left of the stupor or artificial refinements of their home country. It was only under the 'glittering sky', 'among the magnificent shapes and colours' of South America that the German could redevelop the characteristics 'that, in the dark and frosty atmosphere of his place of birth, cannot find expression'.[139] Journeys overseas were seen as journeys back to a more original, natural world and as a journey into oneself: only here could 'the human … become a human again'. Nature – and not the state, bureaucracy or society, would 'take on his education'. In his exploration of and battle with nature, the emigrant would discover characteristics and virtues within himself that, in Germany, 'have long since been unknown to him'.[140]

The reports from Brazil were full of euphoric descriptions of the 'national energy' regained. But hopes for the reinvigorating power of overseas Germanness were not limited to their effects on the periphery. The travel reports, which were designed to be read by a wide

---

[137] Wettstein, *Kolonistenjungens*, p. 195.   [138] Leonhardt, 'Kolonien', p. 16.
[139] Eye, *Auswanderer*, p. 145.   [140] Stolze, *Gedanken*, p. 5.

audience, played the role of modern 'Persian letters' targeted at Germany itself. The return to Teutonic nature and the 'rejuvenation of the race'[141] were more than projects for the Brazilian subtropics. 'Our old homeland, too, can learn from these German [*deutsch-völkische*] colonies overseas.'[142] The longing for a return to an unspoilt existence was more than a nostalgic fantasy fed by the exotic nature of the foreign and the attractions of the South American landscape; the counterpart to this pre-industrial society whose focus was on tilling the land was, in fact, the Kaiserreich itself.

In Brazil, demands for new *Lebensraum* for the German people were linked to criticisms of certain aspects of modernity, which was seen as artificial. This criticism created a link between writings about South America and the romantic views about agriculture of the *fin de siècle* era. From the 1890s in particular, with the introduction by Caprivi of new policies on trade and tariffs, and the setting-up, in reaction, of the Farmers' League (*Bund der Landwirte*), conservative groups and parties campaigned for broad rejection of any policy that would see Germany turned into an industrialised country. The agricultural lobby promoted an explicitly anti-industrial and anti-modern ideology, building on the allegedly common interests of large landowners and small-scale farmers. Agriculture, in this view, represented the true, non-partisan national interest, and was free of selfish motives or biases. Cultural nostalgia was combined with anti-urban feelings to create the legend of a primordial agrarian community.[143]

Reservations about the complex structures of an industrial society, about urban conglomerations, and about the division of labour in the economy and society as a whole were also commonplace in *völkisch* groups and in parts of the back-to-nature *Lebensreform* movements in Wilhelmine Germany. Disquiet about the technological and industrial development of the Kaiserreich prompted a number of 'renewal' movements and social utopias during this period. The ideas of the *Lebensreform* had precursors in the 1830s, but the movement began

---

[141] Gernhard, *Reise-Bilder*, p. 100.   [142] Wettstein, *Kolonistenjungens*, p. 195.
[143] On this subject see Linse, *Zurück*, esp. pp. 7–24; Barkin, *Controversy*, pp. 138–85; and Puhle, *Interessenpolitik*, esp. pp. 72–110.

to grow rapidly in the 1880s and reached its zenith around 1900.[144] Almost all of the movements for 'renewal' were based in the towns or cities and most of those involved were members of the bourgeoisie. They shared a rejection of industrial forms of production and the social relations these created; these tendencies were to be countered by a striving for 'naturalness'. One of the most important institutional forms of the *Lebensreform* movement was the rural commune, where one could lead a life that was close to nature, far away from the civilisation of the metropolis or the alienation of industrial society. The discovery of *Heimat*, the longing for a quiet life far from the hectic, heteronomous world of the metropolis, the idyll of rural life and the idealisation of a romantically viewed *Volkstum* were all elements of this concept, seen as a counter-concept to modern industrial society.[145]

There were also differences between the propaganda for South America and the *Lebensreform* movement. The most important was the differing attitude to private ownership of land. Many *Lebensreform*-inspired settlement projects aspired to reject private ownership (although it was not usually fully implemented). The rural and small-town-based German settlements in southern Brazil did not share this rejection of private ownership, although they did supplement private ownership with some communal facilities. Such differences were not very important in practice, however, and there were many similarities. The idea that the countryside could be a 'fountain of youth' for the nation or a harmonious 'area of existence … that [could become] an example for the whole life of the people' corresponded to the rhetoric of 'overseas Germandom'.[146] In addition, the *Lebensreform* movement was also concerned with demographic and population issues. Because most of its adherents had conservative views and did not wish to change the existing ownership situation, land for social projects

---

[144] See Radkau, *Soziale Bewegungen*, p. 44; Krabbe, *Gesellschaftsveränderung*; and Rohkrämer, *Andere Moderne*.

[145] On the life reform movement, see Bergmann, *Agrarromantik*, pp. 38–85; Barlösius, *Lebensführung*; Repp, *Reformers*; and Eley and Retallack, *Wilhelmianism*.

[146] Bergmann, *Agrarromantik*, p. 92.

would have to be found elsewhere, in particular in Germany's eastern provinces or even further afield. This 'inner colonisation', which really meant external colonisation, but within the European continent, took priority over overseas emigration. In fact those leading the movement expressly rejected the idea of Germany acquiring its own overseas colonial empire.[147]

Yet there were close links between the ideas of the *Lebensreform* and the diaspora communities. German settlements overseas, especially those in South America, were often referred to as privileged sites where the societal ideals of *Lebensreform* could be turned into reality. Bruno Wilhelmi, the founder of 'Eden', a vegetarian fruit-growing community, had previously spent two years in Brazil, where, he said, he had been inspired by the '*lebensreformerische* settlement projects'.[148] In many writings, 'Brazil' assumed a metonymic presence and implicitly evoked the promises of authenticity, simplicity and national reawakening. 'I think constantly of Brazil', the young Hermann Hesse confessed in 1895. Hesse, whose father was a teacher with the Basel Mission, had himself decided to emigrate to Brazil. 'The longing for a healthy existence, for a simple culture, for true life, for Brazil, will never sleep in me.'[149] But his plans came to nothing; the realisation of his life-reform impulses had to wait until he spent a period at Monte Verità near Lake Maggiore in 1907, mainly to recover from alcohol addiction. It may not come as a surprise, however, that in 1920, after the Lake Maggiore project had failed, the founder of the resort, Henri Oedenkoven, moved on to Brazil, to establish a vegetarian colony there.

Thus, romantic ideas about agriculture and the *Lebensreform* movement became linked to the *Lebensraum* ideas that were important aspects of settlement imperialism in the German colonial movement. In South America, the concept of 'work' had been the functional core of this alternative utopian vision; it was used to infer the dynamism and youth of 'New Germany'; and it would also, it was hoped, provide the 'fresh blood needed for the social body that has here and

[147] See *ibid.*, pp. 98–99.   [148] Quoted in Radkau, 'Verheißungen', p. 59.
[149] Hesse, *Kindheit*, pp. 10, 67.

there become rotten' at home.[150] The privileged status accorded to agricultural work was linked not only to the ideal of settled lives and peasant rural structures, but also to hopes that the Kaiserreich could regain the virility that it seemed in danger of losing, as the spread of nervous diseases and neurasthenia seemed to demonstrate. Among the Germans abroad, by contrast, Breitenbach found an 'increase in bodily strength and size'; infant mortality was 'in relative terms lower than at home' and the number of children born 'undoubtedly exceeded [that] in the old fatherland'. In short: 'Here, the German is not degenerating.'[151]

'Germandom abroad', Eduard von Liebert, the governor of German East Africa, once said, 'is our most important colony'.[152] This quote illustrates how close colonial territories and settlement colonies had become in nationalist discourse. But ambitions for overseas Germans went further. If the term was not too modernistic we could almost describe the German settlements in South America as a laboratory for the nation. Even though conditions there were hard, often challenging, everything that was failing at home seemed to succeed in South America – or at least, the travellers' reports from South America gave this impression. The conflicts and separations of modern society – religious, regional and even social differences – seemed not to apply; its contradictions and contrasts seemed to have been overcome. The most obvious sign of this was language. In many parts of South America, the differences in spoken German resulting from different regional origins and dialects were smoothed out and replaced by a common standard language; in this respect, the colonists' settlements were like catalysts of national integration. Small groups of emigrants from the Netherlands, Scandinavia and Hungary were rapidly assimilated into the German-speaking communities.[153] Here, the cultural

---

[150] Wettstein, *Kolonistenjungens*. [151] Breitenbach, *Süd-Brasilien*, p. 208.
[152] Quoted in Wettstein, *Brasilien*, p. 1.
[153] This effect of the colonial situation is described in almost all the German reports from South America. On this subject see also Ojeda-Ebert, *Einwanderung*, pp. 139ff. However, some features of certain dialects were preserved; the survival of the Hunsrück dialect in particular has been of interest to linguistics and in research on 'language islands'. An example is Altenhofen, *Hunsrückisch*.

nation had found itself. The 'difference between Germans from the Reich and Germans of other origins' had become blurred: '[i]t disappears behind a common ethnic identity [*Volkstum*]'.[154]

Writings on South America also suggested that social tensions and class conflicts could be smoothed out more easily there than in Europe. Political agitation and conflicts (*Parteiungen*) were little discussed in the reports from the continent, although political and religious conflicts certainly existed.[155] But these social conflicts were not represented in the texts. Instead, there was repeated mention of the 'apolitical Germans'.[156] In this, the emigratory flows around the turn of the century differed greatly from earlier waves in which political issues had played a major role – for example the emigration following the failed 1848 revolution. But in the period around 1900, even those who had left Germany 'as fanatical Social Democrats' soon abandoned their 'sects' and were soon 'anything, but no longer Social Democrats'.[157] Or at least this was the description put forward by those who wanted to see Germans abroad as an organic national community, one that was uniting the different factions in German society.

The diaspora played a similar role in the German national imagination to that of the frontier, as described by the American historian Frederic Jackson Turner in his famous 1893 lecture. Turner asserted that the continual movement westward of the American frontier had allowed the nation to renew itself. The cheap, 'empty' land thus created acted like a safety valve protecting the nation from social unrest and upheavals. And in particular, the difficult nature of life at the frontier, involving battles both with nature and with the indigenous population, had made the disparate immigrant groups into Americans. At the frontier, which was seen as the boundary of civilisation, the immigrants had, Turner argued, set aside their 'European'

---

[154] Hoeninger, 'Deutschtum', p. 264.
[155] On this subject see for example Ojeda-Ebert, *Einwanderung*, pp. 101–4.
[156] See for example Breitenbach, *Deutschthum*, p. 28; and Hoerll, 'Kolonisation', pp. 60ff.
[157] Gernhard, *Reise-Bilder*, p. 114.

characteristics – hierarchical thinking, social classes and decadence – and become free and equal individuals.

The travel reports from South America could be read as suggesting that the overseas German settlements were the German frontier. They involved battles with nature and with Native Americans, the homogenisation of differences, and the abandonment of social differentiation; it was here that the nation was created. There seemed to be no traces left of the 'ossified bureaucratism' that characterised Wilhelmine Germany; there was no need for excessive state interference ('that rigorous administrative apparatus') or party-political manoeuvring ('the pedantic fusspottery that dominates the German Reichstag').[158] Instead, Germans in South America were seen as 'free men on free soil', 'morals and common decency' were highly regarded, robbery and violence were 'extremely rare events', anyone in need could count on 'hearts willing to make sacrifices and helping and generous hands'; Brazil, then, was a utopia where society still meant community. There, it was suggested, 'class differences disappear[ed]' and 'many social problems [found] their own solutions by themselves'.[159] For German nationalists, the communities abroad, in Brazil and elsewhere, served as the location for the transformation of the German nation under conditions of global mobility.

JOURNEYS THROUGH TIME

This nostalgia for a pre-modern, pre-industrial society made South America a realm of fantasy and a realm of the past. In this sense, too, South America was seen as the opposite to the north of the continent, which was imagined as the location of the future. Visits to the United States were seen as 'journeys into the modern world'[160] while travelling to Brazil or Chile meant travelling back in time.

This could also be taken to mean that 'fairly backward conditions' prevailed in the latter countries and that they needed to catch

---

[158] *Ibid.*, pp. 112, 56.   [159] *Ibid.*, pp. 139, 42, 44.
[160] Schmidt, *Reisen in die Moderne*. On this subject see also Kamphausen, *Erfindung*; and Schmidt-Gernig, 'Zukunftsmodell'.

up. German visitors often saw the southern Brazilian provinces as regions that 'in terms of development lie far, far behind our own'.[161] The idea that 'German work' would transmit civilisation and act as a motor for progress in a scarcely industrialised and little-settled country was an important component of all the descriptions about the conquest of these 'virgin' lands. In this sense, descriptions of the continent were always couched in the language of backwardness. It was thus 'no wonder' that in many ways Brazil was 'reminiscent of conditions that at home have long been consigned to the past'.[162]

This temporalisation of difference was a central aspect of the paradigm of progress that was characteristic of nineteenth-century European thought. Together with the adoption of evolutionary theory in the form of Social Darwinism, the paradigm shaped Europeans' understanding of the relationships between civilisations. Johannes Fabian is one of the leading authors who has examined the links between this world-view and global colonisation. The 'denial of coevalness' that the Europeans applied to other societies was both a precondition for, and a justification of, benevolent modernisation under conditions of colonialism. The reordering of the globe was based on this supposed lack of coevalness, which legitimised intervention and 'elevation'. The colonisation of the globe and the transformation of the past into histories of progress each influenced the other.[163]

These colonial connotations were always intrinsic to German descriptions of a South America that was ahistorical or, at the least, backward. But it would be wrong to reduce this idea that different places were at different 'stages' in time to an expansionist ideology. The topos of journeying through time was ambivalent. It served to legitimise colonial rule, but also carried nostalgic implications and made reference to the utopia of an alternative society located not just in another place, but in another time. When, confronted with the Germanness of the South American settlements, visitors from Germany found themselves almost unable to believe that they were 'somewhere in Chile' and 'not in Germany'; it was not Wilhelmine

---

[161] Lacmann, *Ritte und Rasttage*, p. 64.   [162] *Ibid.*
[163] See Fabian, *Time*; and Koselleck, 'Neuzeit'.

Germany they were reminded of, but the Germany 'of fifty or seventy-five years previously'. Here the past did not carry any sense of lacking or backwardness, but abundance: 'prosperity and sufficiency wherever one looks'.[164]

Whether it was fifty, seventy-five or even 'a hundred or more years' ago, the chronometry of 'overseas Germanness' indicated that not only was the real Germany being created at the South American frontier, but that it was an earlier Germany that was meant. Travelling to the periphery meant travelling home and travelling into the past. The further one moved from Europe 'to the peripheral regions', the more one would seem to be 'sinking back into the past'. This journey in time had been made possible because of the revolution in transport infrastructure, with steamships and railways transporting European visitors to every corner of the globe. But distancing oneself from that very infrastructure seemed to be a precondition for experiencing a truly unspoilt, authentic way of life. 'The further from the railway', the symbol of progress and modernity, 'the more antiquated become forms of living'.[165] In fact, life seemed especially 'German', people worked industriously, and the 'sociability of the societies' was most homely where people had 'not yet come into contact with the world [*Weltverkehr*]' and where things were 'still' as they had been before the capitalist economy dominated the world.[166]

These longings for a pre-industrial, settled, rural community, so characteristic of the German South America literature around 1900, were an expression of the settlement imperialism and *Lebensraum* ideology that had become linked to a *völkisch* nationalism. At the same time, this longing was a form of protest or resistance against the globalisation of the age. It was a utopia of stability, of the unchangeable, of immunity against intermingling and hybridity. It represented a desire to make the national unchangeable, and a phobia about contraventions of borders. But paradoxically, this longing

[164] Riesemann, *Süd-Amerika*, p. 60.
[165] Westermann, *Wie wandere ich nach Südamerika aus?*, p. 62.
[166] Giesebrecht, *Deutsche Kolonie*, p. 45.

for a lack of mobility was itself caused by, and made possible only by, the victory of the global mobility it opposed. After all, transatlantic migration and the creation of the 'overseas Germans' on which all these hopes for the preservation and unchangeability of everything German were based were themselves products of contemporary globalisation.

CHAPTER SIX

'German work'

Unchecked movement that ignored national borders: this phenomenon was not only a result of the nineteenth-century revolution in transport, improvements in communications and infrastructure, and the creation of a global market. To a great extent, the international transfer of goods resulted also from the particular characteristics of industrial manufacturing. Standardised manufacturing processes and international standards for industrial production allowed material goods to be exchanged and traded freely with no need for adaptation or translation to national markets. Increasingly, in the world of industrial goods, national differences became irrelevant.

Or so one might think. In fact, the globalisation of markets in goods led to the eradication of boundaries but also to relocalisation; the universalisation of industrial production went hand-in-hand with processes of delimitation and localisation. This was the significance of the British Merchandise Marks Act of 1887, which made it obligatory to identify industrially manufactured goods with their country of origin. The law applied to all countries, but it was easy to see that it was primarily designed to protect British industry from German competition. In Britain, German products were regarded as cheap, shoddy imitations of British goods. In addition, in 1883, Germany had refused to sign an international agreement banning false marks of origin (such as 'Sheffield made'). The Merchandise Marks Act ensured that products claiming to be global, or, worse, British, would be revealed for what they really were: German.

The paradoxical history of the 'Made in Germany' slogan has often been described. Initially, the mark was introduced as, literally, a stigmatisation, intended to be pejorative and to warn against purchasing products that bore it. But gradually, from the mid 1890s onward, 'Made in Germany' came to be seen as a mark of quality and a selling-point. In 1896, Ernest Williams published a book entitled *Made in Germany*, which outlined the danger that German competition presented to British industry and became an immediate bestseller. A year later, the *Saturday Review* published a commentary titled *Germaniam esse delendam* ('Germany must be destroyed'). A strategy of exclusion had become a slogan of threat.[1]

The invention of the expression 'Made in Germany' has been placed in the context of the Great Depression in Great Britain, and historians have debated whether British views of German competition were justified or not.[2] Was the Merchandise Marks Act a protectionist reaction by the home of free trade, a reaction to the 'British decline' of the late nineteenth century? Certainly, it was that. More importantly, however, 'Made in Germany' was a sign of nationalisation in the age of globalisation, a way of assigning identity at the precise moment at which identities were becoming more difficult to distinguish. An item that was 'made in Germany' was represented not as the result of an anonymous, industrialised manufacturing process that could take place anywhere, but as the product of 'German work'.

INTRODUCTION: INTERLINKAGES AND SPECIFICITY

Around the turn of the century, the concept of 'German work' became widely used. Three separate phenomena combined to cause its popularity: the emergence of an increasingly positive connotation assigned to work, a description of Germany as a country of work, and finally an emphasis on a qualitative difference between German work and work done by others. This valorisation of work, firstly, as no longer being

[1] On the history of the 'Made in Germany' mark see Wulf, *Made in Germany*; and Pollard, 'Made in Germany'. Head, *Made in Germany* is less illuminating. See also Williams, *Made in Germany*; and Minchinton and Williams, 'Made in Germany'.
[2] See Pollard, 'Made in Germany'.

associated purely with effort and suffering, itself has a long, European history. The gradual change of attitudes toward work was a secular process that set in during the early days of Christianity. During the nineteenth century, however, positive evaluations of (physical and other) work became more radical, culminating in the widely read 'gospels' of work created by Thomas Carlyle and Samuel Smiles. In these texts, even the lowest forms of work were viewed positively, as ways of constituting individual identity and the collective community. The socialist philosopher Joseph Dietzgen summarised these views by stating that 'work is the saviour of the modern age'. Work became sacred, a replacement for religion; in an age characterised by belief in progress, it was thought that work could 'achieve that which no Redeemer has to date managed to achieve'.[3]

Secondly, toward the end of the nineteenth century, the German-language press became convinced that German society was uniquely characterised by work. This belief was not new. Nor was it original, because it was held in other countries too. But in the Kaiserreich, it was soon a broadly held view. The economist Karl Helfferich was not alone in his belief that 'comparisons with other countries … [make] Germany seem the country of work'. He pointed to 'a very much greater intensity with which work is carried out in Germany', for example in comparison to France.[4] But, thirdly, it was not just a question of intensity, i.e. quantity; rather, the term 'German work' suggested a qualitative difference between the activity practised in other countries and the German way of working.

During the last two or three decades before the First World War, the term 'German work' was commonly used, and became a recurring element in discussions about economic, political and cultural issues. The topos emphasised the special characteristics of German work, which allegedly was different from the mere 'activity' carried out in other countries: German work represented the German nation.

---

[3] Quoted in Hitze, *Kapital und Arbeit*. There is now an extensive literature on the increasing value attached to work. For introductions to this subject see Zorn, 'Arbeit'; Conze, 'Arbeit'; Ehmer and Gutschner, 'Befreiung'; and the contributions to Kocka and Offe, *Geschichte*, which provide further references.

[4] Helfferich, *Volkswohlstand*, pp. 18, 100.

But not only did the term mark Germany as different from the rest of the world; it also suggested a cultural inheritance that had been passed down intact through the centuries, and had even survived the transition to industrial factory work, so that, it seemed, it could now provide a point of reference for modern society too. Thus, the debate about 'German work' could be seen (and has been seen) as an ideological operation through which the rapid and dramatic nature of social change in the nineteenth century was attenuated. In this way, the processes of industrialisation and modernisation were made bearable and made to seem acceptable, since they were following on from existing traditions or even seemed a result of these traditions. The functionalist argument is thus that these references to unchangeable cultural resources allowed social stability to be preserved at a time of major transformation.

But this emphasis on cultural constants was more than an ideology of modernisation. The popularity of the topos of 'German work', I suggest, was not only a product of changes in time, but also of increased entanglements in space. The popularity of the concept at the turn of the century coincided with a previously unknown level of interlinkage in goods and labour markets. Emphasis on the special nature of Germanness coincided with international adaptation and standardisation, with the perception of increased mobility and with cross-border circulation. In this context, the invocation of national specificity can be seen as a reaction to the reality of porous borders, to the growth in imports and exports, and to international labour migration: in other words, to the threatened loss of national characteristics. The rhetoric of 'German work', then, would seem to be a product of turn-of-the-century globalisation.

In this regard, Germany was by no means exceptional. In other countries too, work was being glorified and being equated with the nation; there was nothing unique in a nation terming itself unique. As industrial manufacturing resulted in standardisation and the geographical origins of a product increasingly became irrelevant, the perceived need to mark goods as a national product grew. The homogenisation and internationalisation of industrial production went hand-in-hand with its relocalisation: what Roland Robertson has called 'glocalisation'.[5] In France especially, the idea of *travail national* became common.[6] The World Exhibitions, international forums for labour and its products, provided regular opportunities for identifying national characteristics and differences.[7] The nationalisation of work in the age of globalisation was an overarching phenomenon. For this reason, what is interesting about the idea of 'German work' is not what was unique to it, but rather its representativity, its generality. What was representative about it, however, was the way it emphasised particularity.

'GERMAN WORK'

The concept of German work was by no means new to the Kaiserreich; it had its own prehistory. The concept of national work first appeared in the writings of the French agitator Babeuf and came to Germany in 1848. During the Paulskirche debates in Frankfurt, demands were put forward for a German 'state of work' (*Staat der Arbeit*) that would protect work both at home and abroad. At base, this was a socialist view of the state, one that should include the 'right to work'. But the idea of national, patriotic work was also common in nationally minded and liberal circles, although these did not favour the idea of state involvement. After German unification, the usage of the term spread rapidly.[8]

Because it was so ubiquitous, over the course of time the term began to be used in different ways with different connotations. Initially, 'German work' described economic life, i.e. all the economic activities of a nation state, and this remained its primary meaning. To a large extent, and for a long time, it was used to denote what we would now describe as 'gross national product'. Protecting national work thus meant introducing protectionist measures to benefit the German economy and its products. The term was first widely used in this

[5] Robertson, 'Glokalisierung'.
[6] See for example Blanc, *L'Immigration*. On this subject see Hornbogen, *Travail*.
[7] On this subject see Greenhalgh, *Ephemeral Vistas*, especially pp. 112–41.
[8] On the history of the term see Conze, 'Arbeit', esp. pp. 208–11. See also Sandkühler, 'Arbeit'; and Wiedemann, *Arbeit*.

sense in the debates about free trade from the late 1840s onward. One example was the naming of the 'General German Association for the Protection of Patriotic Work', the *Allgemeiner Deutscher Verein zum Schutze vaterländischer Arbeit*, set up in September 1848.[9]

Although this remained the main meaning for a considerable period, it was only rarely used in a purely technical, economic sense. Firstly, emphasising the national dimension of work could point to the state's responsibility both for work and for capital. 'National work' implied that there was a need to achieve a balance between the interests of industrialists and those of the working class. The policies pursued by the historical school of national economics, by the *Verein für Sozialpolitik* and by Bismarck's social legislation were all based on this principle, which was already inherent to the idea of 'national work'.

But in particular, the term carried cultural meanings, and meant more than the simple expenditure of energy on work. Reports about 'German work' in Asia Minor, in Bolivia or Brazil, which were frequent in the Kaiserreich, did not describe merely the economic activities involved, but also the cultural achievements.[10] Referring to the activities of Germans overseas, they suggested that 'German work' had an expansionary, colonising dimension. Initially, however, it meant that work must not be understood in economic terms alone, but also in intellectual and cultural ones. 'National work', then, was more than the measurable product of work; it represented the cultural and moral core of the people and the nation.[11] In this sense, 'German work' was primarily a nationalistic term. It stood in opposition to both the liberal/market-liberal view of work – work as the origin of property, civil society and liberty, organised through capitalistic market relationships – and the socialist view of work, which aimed to

---

[9] See Finger, 'Schutzzollfrage'; Best, *Interessenpolitik*; Etges, *Wirtschaftsnationalismus*, pp. 97–109; and Hornbogen, *Travail*, pp. 92–97.

[10] Examples of the extensive literature include Menz, *Deutsche Arbeit*; Merensky, *Deutsche Arbeit*; and Wopfner, *Tirols Eroberung*. See also the journal of the *Volksbund für das Deutschtum im Ausland* (first issue 1901), tellingly entitled *Deutsche Arbeit*.

[11] On the concept, see Campbell, *Joy in Work*, pp. 7–15; and Schmieder, 'Arbeitsethos'.

achieve a democratic and collective organisation of production. Over time, though, the concept of 'German work' had an effect far beyond the nationalist milieu.

The starting point and central point of reference for any discussion of 'national work' was the 1861 study compiled by the writer, historian and ethnographer Wilhelm Heinrich Riehl for the Bavarian King Maximilian II. Riehl's book about 'German work' marks the change from a primarily economic and technical use of the term to the cultural connotations that became more and more usual from this time onward. The book was widely read, especially in bourgeois circles. But it became most influential from the 1890s on, when the term 'German work' and its cultural implications became more widely used. By 1918, the book had gone through five editions; during the war, the publisher, Cotta, created a special forces' edition for the moral strengthening of the soldiers in battle. By 1935, the book had gone into its thirteenth edition.[12]

Riehl associated work directly with the nation: 'Each nation works in its own way.' He saw the practice of work and the way society valued work in each individual country as an expression of that country's 'deepest character elements'. For Riehl, the 'soul of the nation' manifested itself in work. The three terms 'work', 'nation' and 'progress' seemed to be almost synonymous. 'It is through *national work* that we assert and develop our national personality.'[13] Furthermore, for Riehl, this general view of the nature of work was combined with the belief that the German nation had a special relationship with work and that Germany should be seen as a country of work.

The actual meaning of the term 'German work' in Riehl remained vague and poorly defined. The most important concept for him was the idea that work was not merely the product of rational activity to a particular end, but the expression of an individual and collective self. Work, in its supposedly German form, was not anonymous and depersonalised or determined by the rationales of the factory or the market; it was 'embedded' and meaningful. 'Soul' and 'moral' were

---

[12] On the book's publication history see Zinnecker, *Romantik*, pp. 333–45.
[13] Riehl, *Deutsche Arbeit*, pp. 1, 49. Emphasis in original.

terms that recurred again and again in discussions about 'German work'. Here, work was seen as a social activity with moral connotations, that the individual could only carry out as part of the community. Every worker should 'be enthused by the consciousness that he is not working just for himself and his family, but also for the nation'. This idea formed part of a reaction against the victory of liberal market mechanisms and was intended to counteract the idea of the independent individual operating in a capitalist labour market.[14]

Riehl believed that this type of work was most often present in peasant life. For him, peasant farmers represented a form of work that was not only close to nature, but also 'moral' and embedded in society. He studied peasant folklore and customs in order to get to the root of the idea of work. His ideal was work that was done for its own sake (and for the nation), or at least not for profit. But in later years, he gradually distanced himself from this romantic view of agriculture. Over the course of the 1870s, the bourgeois citizen gradually replaced the peasant as Riehl's main protagonist; he now believed that the bourgeoisie was the embodiment of the national virtues, while peasants represented only the past. He believed in a natural hierarchy of work, at the apex of which was intellectual work, and he remained ambivalent about the manual work glorified by Socialists.

The increasingly bourgeois nature of Riehl's definition of work went hand-in-hand with an emphasis on men's work. Riehl felt it to be a 'sin against the basic law of the natural division of labour' for women to leave the private area of the bourgeois house in order to become active in the public sphere, the sphere of work. It was not appropriate for women to 'desire those professions that by nature … are assigned to the man'. There should be strict separation between the areas of activity of the two sexes. However, this separation did not mean that women were excluded from 'German work'. Rather, for Riehl, the cultural implications of work included its gender-specific dimensions. Any universalist gender-neutral understanding of work would deny 'the poetry of the female being'.[15] Riehl's *magnum opus* picked up on the misty-eyed anti-capitalist view of work held by the

---

[14] *Ibid.*, p. 107.   [15] *Ibid.*, pp. 240–41.

Romantics, and it emphasised inner values and the ideal of the common good. It must be understood in the context of the post-1848 crisis of liberalism and it also reflected the changes in the experience of work during that era.[16] Industrialisation was revolutionising working conditions and making many traditional professions obsolete. At the same time, work, in the form of industrialised factory work, was threatening to become a mainly standardised and depersonalised activity. Riehl's concept of 'German work', with its emphasis on the substantive and meaningful dimensions of work, had elements of a nostalgic alternative utopia, especially since technology and the capitalist market were barely discussed by him.[17]

At the same time, Riehl's writings were also a product of the Protestant educated bourgeoisie. His ideal was the work ethic of German towns and cities and its carriers were the urban Protestant middle classes. With its anti-Catholic tendencies, Riehl's text needs to be placed in the larger context of the *Kulturkampf*. It was also a counterpoint to the analyses of Karl Marx (despite many similarities, for example between Marx's criticism of alienation and the anti-utilitarian dimensions of 'German work'). Riehl was convinced that there were positive aspects to poverty, and that poverty could be seen as a source of modesty. His plea for a harmonious working existence was in total contrast to – in fact, an antidote to – Marx's idea of the class struggle. For Riehl, the process of proletarianisation could be prevented by means of a healthy family life. In his anti-Socialist concept of society, a hierarchical social order was an ideal, not something to be fought against.[18]

Riehl's concept of work can be contrasted with a number of other concepts that were under discussion during this period. His laissez-faire approach set him apart from the policies of state intervention

---

[16] See Smith, *Politics*, pp. 40–44.
[17] On Riehl, see first and foremost Campbell, *Joy in Work*, esp. pp. 28–46. See also Altenbockum, *Riehl*, esp. pp. 147–99; Steinbach, 'Riehl'; and Lövenich, *Verstaatlichte Sittlichkeit*. On the reception of Riehl's writings see Zinnecker, *Romantik*.
[18] On this subject see Altenbockum, *Riehl*, pp. 188–99; and Campbell, *Joy in Work*, pp. 44–46.

propagated by members of the *Verein für Sozialpolitik* (Association for Social Policy). He was vehemently opposed to the expansion of the bureaucratic state, which he did not see as any solution to the social problems of the day. Another opposing model of work was that put forward by the work sciences and by Taylorism, which had been gaining in popularity from the turn of the century onward. While ergonomists were looking for anthropological constants, Riehl was trying to identify specific national characteristics; while turn-of-the-century studies on fatigue were treating work as a question of bodily physics and the human being as a thermodynamic machine, Riehl was insisting on the moral value of work.[19] The latter was of no interest to Taylorism, which came to Germany during the decade preceding the First World War. 'Through Taylor', as the banker Wilhelm Kochmann declared in 1914, 'man himself is turned into a machine; the worker's intellectual disposition is taken away'.[20] The anonymising strategies of scientific management had nothing in common with the culturally loaded idea of 'German work'.

The nationalist and cultural connotations of the concept of work that we witness in Riehl's text were not new in themselves; they picked up on older ideas. Primarily, these were ideas about a national culture that had become widespread amongst the German bourgeoisie from around 1800 onward. One of the elements of this 'German ideology' was a reference to morality and public-spiritedness: activities of the individual were not seen as something separate from society. Other elements were an emphasis on liberty, both internal and external, which was of major importance in Riehl's concept of work; the issue of uniformity and wholeness, which was contrasted with fragmentation (and the division of labour); and finally a rejection of instrumental rationality and strong anti-utilitarian sentiments. These topoi were part of the growing German nationalist movement of the early nineteenth century and can be identified in a large number of writings of the Classical, Romantic and German Idealist movements.

---

[19] On the work sciences see first and foremost the excellent study by Rabinbach, *Human Motor*, esp. pp. 179–205; and Campbell, *Joy in Work*, pp. 73–106.

[20] Kochmann, 'Taylorsystem', p. 417.

Long before Riehl published his hagiography of 'German work' or before the increase in globalisation in the 1880s, the writings of Hegel, Humboldt and Fichte had framed 'culture', 'occupation' (*Beruf*) and 'education' (*Bildung*) in a similar way and in national terms.[21]

Thus, the concept of 'German work' was vested in a longer tradition, and such references were especially marked in Riehl's work. However, we cannot take this genealogy to mean that the assignment of national significance to work was just a belated adoption of a concept that had already entered other areas of political debate. The popularity of the concept from the 1880s onward cannot be explained solely in terms of continuity with the ideas of major thinkers of the early nineteenth century. Indeed, one characteristic of the turn-of-the-century era was the nationalisation of a term that had not previously been involved in patriotic rhetoric. In addition, its use increased noticeably toward the end of the century; it was only then, and not during the Romantic period or even when Riehl's text was first published, that 'German work' became a popular concept and became 'memorable and indispensable'.[22]

Two developments were necessary for this to take place. Firstly, the process of industrialisation meant that mechanical (and factory-based) work and the division of labour became the norm; in response, nostalgic ideas about self-determined, non-alienated (and usually agricultural) work became more prevalent. Secondly, the global economic interlinkages that entered public debate and the public consciousness from the 1880s onward contributed to the spread of xenophobic sentiments and, as a result, to an insistence on the national character of work. Around 1900, these two processes were often seen as one and the same – for example in the debate about whether Germany should be an 'agricultural or an industrial country', which was the main arena in which Germany's role in the contemporary process of economic globalisation was discussed.[23]

---

[21] On this subject see Vierhaus, 'Bildung'; Assmann, *Arbeit*; Tenbruck, 'Bürgerliche Kultur'; and Koselleck et al., 'Volk'.

[22] Conze, 'Arbeit', p. 210.

[23] On this subject see Barkin, *Controversy*; Steinkühler, *Agrar- oder Industriestaat*; and Harnisch, 'Agrarstaat'.

Thus, references to the cultural-nationalistic ideology of the early nineteenth century and the stereotypes it involved played an important role in the development of the concept of 'German work'. However, these continuities do not explain why the concept became so important around the turn of the century. The fact that traditions are revisited cannot be explained solely in terms of the cultural heritage itself; it must be understood in the social and cultural context of the era at which this reference to prior ideas becomes important for interpreting social reality. This applies to continuities between the Romantic period and the era of globalisation around the turn of the century just as much as it does, for example, to continuities between the Wilhelmine period and the 1930s. After all, social actors are choosing from a multiplicity of possible points of reference and, in doing so, translate their borrowings for the needs of the present, transform them, and link them to the concrete interests at stake. This is what is referred to by the 'invention of traditions', a term that stresses the creativity, frequently retrospective, of constructing genealogies; the process, in other words, cannot be explained in terms of the tradition's own internal dynamics.

From 1870 onward, 'German work' was an element of every major debate on economic or social issues. For example, protecting 'German work' was the major concern in the debate during the 1870s about protective tariffs. The Central Association of German Industrialists (*Zentralverband Deutscher Industrieller*), founded in 1876, which was the most important entity arguing for protective tariffs, used the subtitle 'For the promotion and preservation of national work'.[24] The term also regularly cropped up in debates about the advantages and disadvantages of German emigration, which would result in 'national work' exiting the country. And the discussions about 'educating to work' in the colonies and about the use of Polish seasonal workers in Prussian agriculture also frequently referred to the standards of 'German work'. The term carried so much cultural and national

---

[24] On the debate about protective tariffs see Hornbogen, *Travail*, esp. pp. 144–71; Lambi, *Free Trade*; Rosenberg, *Große Depression*; Ullmann, *Interessenverbände*, pp. 77ff.; Kaelble, *Interessenpolitik*; and Etges, *Wirtschaftsnationalismus*, pp. 252–74.

weight that 'work' could be used to stand in for the collective or the community. Karl Thomas Richter, a professor of *Staatswissenschaften* ('state sciences') in Prague, commented in his report on the Vienna World Exhibition that '*nationality* and *national work* are the same concept'.[25]

The term was most wholeheartedly adopted in conservative and nationalist circles. However, its use was not limited to these groups, even if many Social Democrats were enraged by Riehl's ideas. The term was not necessarily linked to Riehl; it was overdetermined and was used for a variety of different purposes. Elements of the concept turned up in the writings of the *Verein für Sozialpolitik*, for example in their rejections of the commodification of labour. The reconciliation between work and capital that they sought made reference to an understanding of work that went beyond its character as a commodity and, in this sense, overlapped with some of the assumptions that were characteristic to the concept of 'German work'.[26] Overcoming the divide between capital and work was also the motive for the foundation of religious workers' societies.[27] There were points of reference in the Catholic milieu, too. For the democratically minded movements in social Catholicism in particular, hopes that capital and work could be united as fair and equal partners were explained in terms of the 'morality' of work that was to be preserved even in a capitalist industrial society.[28]

In general, the use of the concept 'German work' was based on the idea that the 'cultural condition of a people' could be measured in terms of its attitude to work. For example, Traub, a Dortmund-based pastor, distinguished between three views of work in his discussions about the best 'way toward the nationalisation and idealisation of work'. He distanced himself both from the materialistic desire

---

[25] Richter, *Fortschritte*, p. 2. Emphases in original.

[26] On this subject see Conrad, *Verein*; Campbell, *Joy in Work*, Chapter 4; and Lindenlaub, *Richtungskämpfe*.

[27] On this subject see Mooser, 'Arbeiter', esp. p. 88. On the Catholic labour movement see Denk, *Arbeiterbewegung*; and, on its Protestant equivalent, Feyerabend, *Arbeitervereine*.

[28] See Mergel, *Zwischen Klasse und Konfession*, pp. 227ff.

for profit and from the idealistic apotheosis of work as a purpose in itself put forward by authors like Thomas Carlyle. By contrast, in Germany, he argued, the predominant view of work was the highest possible one, the 'realistic' one: not rationalised for any particular purpose, not a purpose in itself, but 'work as the structured fulfilment of the duties of the community', i.e. embedded in a social context. 'Only in this way is work a cultural factor.'[29]

Frequently, there was no mention of the fact that this idea of work had gender-specific dimensions. But ideas about gender roles were central to beliefs about work in the Kaiserreich and to the concept of 'German work'. This applied, firstly, to the establishment of a gender-specific division of labour that differentiated 'women's work' from the activities of men. In general, this dichotomy was linked to the contrast between public and private domains that had been developing since about 1800.[30]

Secondly, around 1900, beliefs about women's work changed, in the course of debates about the 'national body' (Volkskörper), influenced by ideas of social hygiene, eugenics and social medicine. While, previously, social policy had focused on the material conditions and the 'moral education' of workers, increasing attention was now being paid to the social collective of the German nation. This changed the links between work, reproduction and society and brought policies of social intervention into the foreground. In this way, the nationalisation of 'German work' corresponded with social-hygiene fears about the ability of working women to reproduce.[31]

These concerns about healthy reproduction allowed nationalist and conservative groups to link their ideas about the role of the sexes with the opinions of experts who argued for modern social technologies. 'The woman's passionate desire for economic independence, income and a career', Obermedizinalrat Professor Max von Gruber opined in 1910, 'is so destructive to the racial hygiene because the woman's physical and psychological strength ... is not adequate to bear the

[29] Traub, 'Arbeit', p. 133.
[30] On this subject in general see Hausen, Geschlechterhierarchie; Knapp, Frauenarbeit; and Canning, 'Gender'.
[31] On this subject see Sweeney, 'Work'; Linton, Youth; and Eley, 'Labour'.

huge burden of motherhood along with gainful and professional work'. Gruber believed that Germany's 'future as a world power' would be endangered if female gainful employment and reproductive work continued to be in competition. 'Any standstill in the growth of the population, let alone a reduction in its numbers, means it will vegetate.'[32]

In this context, thirdly, the concept of 'German work' became part of the policies adopted by nationalist women's groups. A large number of institutions were created to counteract, in the national interest, the risks inherent to women's employment. These included advice centres at individual companies for mothers employed there, kindergartens and summer holidays in the countryside for working mothers. In social practice, then, gainful employment by women (going far beyond nursing, an ideal of female employment) was frequently recognised as a reality (and the supposedly negative consequences were counteracted). At an ideological level, however, the 'true essence of German women's work' was still supposed to be 'to serve ... the house and the family'.[33]

The 1882 edition of the German encyclopedia *Brockhaus* shows us how widespread was the understanding of work as national work. In this edition, 'work' is described mainly as a cultural concept, the 'ethical importance' of which is emphasised along with the phenomenon of 'joy in work'. For this reason, work is not the same everywhere, the encyclopedia states, but rather 'very different ... in different countries'. Labour is not seen as something that has become a tradable commodity deployed in the industrial process of manufacture, but as a specific expression of national culture. In this view, the form work takes is determined partly by 'climatic conditions', but more importantly – and this is the very definition of *travail national* – it is

---

[32] Gruber, 'Kommentar', p. 19.
[33] In the war edition of the *Deutsche Handels-Wacht*, the journal of the *Handlungsgehilfen-Verband* (German-National Association of Clerks), quoted in Hess, 'Nation', p. 187. On this subject see also Kleinau and Opitz, *Geschichte*; Planert, *Nation*; Quataert, *Staging Philanthropy*; and Süchting-Hänger, *Gewissen*, esp. pp. 37–44.

shaped by the 'national character, the level of education and culture, customs, and religion'.[34]

Of course, there were competing views. In the internationalism of Social Democrats and the trade unions, work was not seen as something unique to a nation. These movements therefore took a favourable view of the recruitment of foreign workers, at least in principle, although protectionist voices were getting stronger.[35] The *Handwörterbuch der Staatswissenschaften* also defined work in functional and economic terms, with no reference to culture. Where it discussed differences between peoples at all, attitudes to work were not seen as unchangeable; they were the 'consequence of the lack of education' rather than an expression of the nation's character.[36] Nor was the cultural dimension of work of any interest to ergonomists. They were not interested in moral education in work-related values; there were no appeals to the workers' conscience or to work ethics. Instead, work became a question of bodily physics that was managed by the discipline of production itself and by regulating wages and working hours. In ergonomics, debates about the inherent laziness of barbarous tribes and about the moral, intellectual and spiritual value of work were replaced by studies about fatigue.[37]

Thus, the topos of 'German work' did not stand uncontested during the Wilhelmine period. But despite these critical voices and competing perspectives, the concept became more and more widely used. The term was mainly employed for rhetorical effect, frequently with ideological content, to point to the unique aspects of the German work ethic. But it was not a matter of discourse alone. In a study on the wool-processing industry in Britain and Germany, Richard Biernacki has examined the extent to which these ideas actually influenced the reality and practice of work, even of industrial manufacturing. He describes how workers in Britain assumed that their labour

---

[34] Entry on 'Arbeit', *Brockhaus' Conversations-Lexikon*, Vol. I, p. 831.
[35] See Elsner, 'Deutsche Arbeiterbewegung'. A more balanced account is given in Nichtweiß, *Saisonarbeiter*, pp. 154–74. See also Forberg, 'Foreign Labour'.
[36] Harms, 'Arbeit', p. 588.
[37] On this subject see Rabinbach, *Human Motor*; Rabinbach, 'Science of Work'; Rabinbach, 'Ermüdung'; Vatin, 'Arbeit'; and Campbell, *Joy in Work*, pp. 73–106.

was embodied in a saleable object; their focus was not on the production process, but on the finished product. In Germany, however, he argues, the focus lay on the 'work itself'; work was evaluated not in terms of market-ready products but as an activity. These differing connotations of work were not limited to the imagination, but were actually reflected in the material and institutional conditions of factory work: in the way space and working times were organised and control and power exerted. Biernacki shows that even the way workers were disciplined differed in the two countries. In Britain, workers were fined for producing defective goods. In Germany, on the other hand, work itself was monitored and any deviation from work discipline was punished, regardless of whether the products of that work could be sold or not.[38]

This view of work as a cultural activity beyond commodification may have been more widely held in Germany than, for example, in Britain. The most telling expression of this view was the emphasis on 'joy in work'. It was precisely because of the standardised and anonymous nature of industrial work that the issue of joy in work became increasingly important to Wilhelmine discussions about work. Joan Campbell believes that, during this period, the concept of joy in work was more important in Germany than in any other society.[39] The question of how joy in work could be preserved was discussed by Marx, by bourgeois theoreticians, by Catholic authors, by national economists and by work scientists. In general, the issue was based on an assumption that a 'natural', holistic type of work had prevailed in the pre-modern and pre-industrial age, one that had allowed physical and moral/spiritual fulfilment. This nostalgic view of a form of work not contaminated by the development of the modern industrial society found its counterpart in the concept of 'alienation'. This perspective, which has formed the basis for most Marxist approaches throughout the twentieth century, and which can also be identified, for example, in Horkheimer's and Adorno's *Dialectic of Enlightenment*, was essentially based on similar premises to those influencing the idea of 'German work'.

[38] Biernacki, *Fabrication*, esp. pp. 74–78.   [39] Campbell, *Joy in Work*, p. 3.

Many authors linked ideas about work ethics and attitudes to work with concepts of education. It was believed that a common work ethos could serve to overcome social differences. Riehl himself had demanded a 'work school, at a large scale', focused on the social collective. But even at a smaller level, he was concerned 'that children [should be] educated [to possess] the correct spirit of work and the purest work ideal'.[40] In Wilhelmine Germany, there were many competing ideas about educating citizens to work, some of which originated in the ideas of reformist pedagogy; there were also the religiously motivated ideas of the two main confessional denominations. Even the Social Democratic movement was interested in education to work. The *SPD*'s main concern was the establishment of 'child protection commissions' and lobbying for statutory limits to child labour. But it also came up with proposals about how young people could be educated for work. Central to these ideas were 'workers' pride' and 'joy in work', even if it was admitted that these would not directly contribute to any fundamental 'reorganisation of the economic and social order'.[41] Robert Seidel, who published his *Schule der Zukunft, eine Arbeitsschule* ('School of the future, a school of work') in 1908, believed that lessons in work had 'enormous educational value' and expected them to bring about 'far-reaching social and moralising effects'.[42]

But the most important proponent of the idea of educating for work was the Munich city Schulrat Georg Kerschensteiner (1854–1932). He argued for the creation of a separate 'work school' where economic efficiency and a love of work should be instilled. He saw this school as a corrective to the usual text-heavy school practice, 'because it is not the book that is the bearer of culture, but work'. For Kerschensteiner, too, work was defined by its 'morality' (*Sittlichkeit*) and it was embedded in a wider social collective: the objective was to 'educate people' who would 'gratefully dedicate their services [to the state]'.[43] Here,

[40] Riehl, *Deutsche Arbeit*, p. 259.
[41] Quotes taken from Hackel, 'Theorie', pp. 28–31.
[42] Seidel, *Arbeits-Unterricht*, p. 112.
[43] Kerschensteiner, *Grundfragen*, p. 105.

too, the move away from a utilitarian view of work was linked to its nationalisation.[44]

'GERMAN WORK' AND GERMAN STYLE

One example that reveals how influential the topos of 'German work' was is the *Deutsche Werkbund* (German Work Federation). The creation of the *Werkbund* can be seen as a response to the challenges posed by industrialisation and by the standardisation of industrially manufactured products. But the *Werkbund* was also a product of, and a reaction to, the increasing interconnectedness of global markets. The reaction combined a recognition that industrially produced goods were universal and universally tradable with attempts to maintain, if not to create, national specificity. Here as elsewhere, 'German work' was seen as the guarantor of this specificity.

The *Werkbund* was set up in 1907 as an alliance of artists and industrialists who felt themselves to be members of the avant-garde and who wanted to promote the aesthetic value of a functionalist industrial culture. The leaders of the movement were the Belgian architect Henry van de Velde, the architect and art critic Hermann Muthesis, and the liberal politician Friedrich Naumann. By 1914, almost 2,000 artists, art critics and industrialists had become members, and the *Werkbund* was issuing its own annual journal. In that year, it held a major exhibition in Cologne attended by over a million people.[45]

The *Werkbund*'s aesthetic goal was to create a new style for everyday objects, including furniture, everyday consumer goods and even living spaces themselves. In this, the *Werkbund* was picking up on a number of turn-of-the-century reform movements aiming to bring life and art together in a specifically modern way. This reconciliation was based on the idea of combining form and function taking both artistic ambitions and industrial methods of manufacturing into account. This functional industrial style was combined with a

---

[44] On this subject see Gonon, *Arbeitsschule*; Bönkost, *Skizzen*; and Hackel, 'Theorie'.
[45] See the detailed account of the Cologne exhibition in Campbell, *Werkbund*, pp. 73–103.

rejection of the tradition of decoration and a bourgeois differentiation from ornamental forms that were (negatively) viewed as aristocratic. But the *Werkbund*'s relationship with the industrialised world was ambivalent. On the one hand, many of its publications were marked by a longing for the recreation of 'harmonious culture'. This point of view, critical of industrialisation, included movements such as that of the 'garden cities', with its preference for rural styles. On the other hand, the *Werkbund* movement as a whole embraced the modern, industrialised world. It was decidedly modern in its demands for a style that would be influenced by industrial production, and for 'the intellect and the machine' (*Geist und Maschine*) to be brought together; it distanced itself from the romantic view of craftwork taken by the British and American Arts and Crafts movement.[46]

The *Deutscher Werkbund* can thus be seen as an attempt to come to terms with the changes that the industrialised world had brought to the realms of production and of work. But it was also a reaction to contemporary globalisation, and this is where similarities with the concept of 'German work' emerge. The search for a modern style had its roots in the increasing internationalisation of life experiences and of everyday objects. Friedrich Naumann and Hermann Muthesius, in particular, argued for an international industrial culture whose norms and repertoire of forms would become increasingly similar. Muthesius predicted 'a certain uniformity of architectural forms across the entire planet'.[47] Peter Jessen, too, argued that the *Werkbund* should focus its efforts on the new mass-production industries that produced stand-ardised goods for the global market. This vision of homogenisation created by interconnectedness culminated in the foundation in 1917, under wartime conditions, of the Standards Committee of German Industry, based on an American model, to manage the standardisa-tion and mechanisation of industrial production.[48]

But internationalisation was linked not only to homogenisation, but also to the definition of national characteristics and to attempts to

---

[46] On this subject see the concise overview in Hardtwig, 'Identität'; see also Campbell, *Werkbund*, pp. 43–72; and Stern, *Kulturpessimismus*, pp. 213ff.

[47] Muthesius, 'Werkbundarbeit', p. 94.

[48] See Campbell, *Werkbund*, p. 106.

differentiate the nation from others. This is something the *Werkbund* shared with the discourse of 'German work'. The *Werkbund* was a forum for an economically based and internationalist view of art, but also for a national, craftsman-based culture. This national culture had little in common with the semi-official 'German art' promoted by the Kaiser and by people like Anton von Werner, which was explicitly rejected by the *Werkbund*. It rejected the influence of the 'German Gothic' and the 'German Renaissance', and was opposed to paintings and frescoes on important buildings. Even its focus on craftsmanship and the emancipation of the 'lower arts' meant this rejection was inherent to its philosophy.[49] Yet the longing for a national culture was of central importance even for the internationally minded *Werkbund*. The creation of the *Werkbund* can be seen as a reaction to the perceived danger that globalisation and industrialisation would lead to the loss of a national style.[50]

For this reason, the dialectic of interconnectedness and difference was always present in the *Werkbund*'s publications. On the one hand, those involved were attempting to create an international style and aimed for universality. But the search for a modern visual language was also understood as a national project, and the *Werkbund*'s applied art was seen as an expression of a national culture. It was suggested that an industrial functionalism that also aspired to be artistic should be a national project, countering both 'the naked functional style of Americanism' and the 'increasingly decadent classicism of the Latin people'.[51] In contrast, the *Werkbund*'s major exhibition in Cologne led the French press to speak of an 'artistic Sedan' (after the Battle of Sedan in the Franco-Prussian War).[52] Naumann explicitly described the *Werkbund* as 'a national undertaking'.[53] Unsurprisingly, then, Wolfgang Hardtwig has described the *Werkbund* as contributing to the formation of the German nation.[54]

---

[49] See Hardtwig, 'Identität', pp. 521–29.
[50] See Campbell, *Werkbund*, p. 7.
[51] Hoeber, 'Architekturfragen', pp. 1107f.
[52] Quoted in Campbell, *Werkbund*, p. 99.
[53] Naumann, 'Gewerbekunst', p. 285.
[54] Hardtwig, 'Identität', p. 514.

One result of this link between internationalism and an emphasis on national specificity was that ideas developed about a 'cultural mission', in the context of the international competition between nations (initially peaceful and then, after 1914, more robust). Muthesius argued that Germany should take on 'leadership in style formation' in order to achieve 'victory over the world'. He hoped that German stylistic elements and aesthetic standards would 'also become global forms'.[55] From its very beginning, the aims of the *Werkbund* included elements of competitiveness and foreign trade policy: they were linked to national export policy.[56] But this not only involved an economic nationalism whose goal was to secure global markets for German industrial products with an essentially universal use of forms. Although not all of the members of the *Werkbund* shared this national-culture perspective to the same extent, it was still central to the movement's understanding of itself. For Walter Carl Behrendt, an architect employed by the Prussian government and, during the 1920s, editor of the *Werkbund* magazine *Die Form*, the *Werkbund* was 'nothing other' than the 'renewal' of the idea of 'work as a moral act' and an insistence on the 'honour of work' and its 'spiritual [*ideeller*] value'. The rediscovery of national culture was seen as a precondition for economic expansion. For this reason it was 'not a coincidence that, in the fanatic struggle by nations for global markets and the competitive hunt for profit, Germany has been the first to re-emphasise the spiritual [*ideell*] side of work'. Behrendt saw the *Werkbund* not only as a medium for an export drive by industry, but also as the 'preserver of the [German] ideal of culture'.[57]

The *Werkbund*'s discussions, then, substantially overlapped with the discourse on 'German work'. The *Werkbund*'s programme made use of the established elements of this concept, for example when Naumann described 'joy in work' as a precondition for achieving 'artistic leadership' in the global market.[58] In addition, there were often explicit references to everything 'that Wilhelm Riehl has pointed toward in his wonderful book about German work'. Behrendt

---

[55] Muthesius, 'Werkbundarbeit', p. 94.   [56] See Hardtwig, 'Identität', p. 519.
[57] Behrendt, *Kampf*, p. 95.   [58] Naumann, 'Gewerbekunst', p. 275.

suggested that the *Werkbund* stood for 'a more acute awareness of the moral authority and honour of work' that had 'survived, alert and alive, through every epoch of German history'.[59] The *Werkbund*'s products were seen as an expression of a culturally specific form of activity. As such, 'German work' appeared as Germany's most important export. 'What we can ship abroad is our work.' 'German work' had thus become the very core of the nation: 'On it depends our national future.'[60]

During the First World War, the *Werkbund*'s strategies and utterances became increasingly polemical and developed an expansionist tone. Naumann, who argued for Germany to pursue a *Mitteleuropa* policy, even compared the *Werkbund* to the German navy, an 'expression of the way the German spirit has turned to the global economy and to *Weltpolitik*'.[61] During the early months of the war, the *Werkbund*'s Berlin office was engaged in a propaganda campaign for the German government and held a series of exhibitions in Switzerland and Denmark, in close cooperation with the Foreign Office.[62] The architecture critic Fritz Hoeber spoke of the '*Werkbund*'s world mission', a mission that could only be fulfilled with the 'martial victory of *Mitteleuropa*'.[63] Some voices were even more militant: the nationalist press argued that the victory of 'a good German style [should be seen] … as a racial issue'.[64]

'WAR OF WORK'

Any reference to the 'German' character of work always involved an element of competitiveness. As in the case of the *Werkbund*, it was based on the assumption that German work differed from other forms of work in other countries. These competitive aspects of 'German work' were already contained in Riehl's text and sometimes led to

---

[59] Behrendt, *Kampf*, p. 95.
[60] Naumann, 'Gewerbekunst', p. 287. On Naumann's involvement in *Weltpolitik* see Theiner, *Sozialer Liberalismus*; Christ, *Staat*; and Bruch, *Wissenschaft*, with an extensive bibliography on Naumann.
[61] Naumann, 'Gewerbekunst', p. 285.   [62] See Campbell, *Werkbund*, p. 115.
[63] Hoeber, 'Architekturfragen', pp. 1107ff.   [64] Kuh, 'Neue Aufgaben', p. 528.

comments that were extremely militaristic in tone. Riehl stated cat-
egorically that 'lazy peoples will be *worked away* [*hinweggearbeitet*,
emphasis in original] by the more diligent ones'.[65] Work was thus seen
as the subject of a Social Darwinist competition between nations. This
was also the logic behind the World Exhibitions, a kind of Olympic
Games of work. At the exhibitions, work and its products were put
on show, classified by their country of origin; distinguished examples
received gold medals. Germany saw itself in 'competition with the
West', and with the 'national diligence of England and France', as
the official German report on the Vienna World Exhibition of 1873
remarked.[66]

But western Europe was not the only area of competition. Germany
defined itself in opposition to national forms of work ethic by focusing on a variety of different targets. These included workers from
Poland, the Netherlands and Italy, who regularly came to Germany
as seasonal workers for the summer and were seen as being at a lower
'cultural level'. The popularity of the concept of the 'Polish economy'
was an example of the way work done by foreigners in Germany,
which was becoming an everyday occurrence, was differentiated
from German work.[67] 'German work' also played an important role
in areas of national conflict at Germany's borders, for example in
the Italian Alps, where the concept became important in processes
of mutual nationalisation.[68] Sometimes, attention was drawn to the
difference between German work and coolie work. The work carried
out by Chinese, Indian or Javanese workers who had migrated across
the planet was regarded as undemanding and with no moral content.

By contrast, the relationship with work in the United States was
more ambivalent. Some nationalist-minded voices distanced themselves from the supposedly materialistic attitude to work of the North
Americans, carried out in pursuit of 'Mammon'. 'German work' was
something fundamentally different, or at least was not 'such a widely
overexcited pursuit and haste as has become characteristic of the mish-

---

[65] Riehl, *Deutsche Arbeit*, p. 52.   [66] Quoted in Kroker, *Weltausstellungen*, p. 37.
[67] On this subject see in particular Orlowski, *Polnische Wirtschaft*, esp. pp. 275–94.
[68] See Johler, 'Concetto'.

mash of people that have found themselves together at the far side of the ocean'.[69] This kind of polemical criticism of the American focus on profits was common; it often included anti-Semitic elements and stereotypes.[70] But the opposite position, an admiration for America as a 'country of work', was equally common. In 1905, the Gotha-based industrialist Philipp Harjes wrote a report on his 'journey to the country where work is the nobility', a comment with which many observers, not only industrialists, heartily agreed.[71] 'Over there, everyone views the worker with the greatest respect and there are no hierarchies of work because it is self-evident that everyone does the best work he can and in doing so is only doing his duty toward the whole.'[72]

Even the heated debate about the merits and problems of the Taylor system during the decade preceding the First World War made little use of invective about 'American' attitudes to work. Of course, enthusiastic responses, especially by industrialists, were tempered with criticism, which became more pronounced when German industrial companies such as AEG, Siemens, Borsig and Bosch began to implement Taylor's ideas. Union representatives reacted furiously against these methods, which they regarded as 'dehumanising' and degrading; the socialist Kurt Eisner described Taylorism as a 'cultural threat'.[73] But most commentators differentiated between the working methods, seen as 'neutral', and the way they were implemented in the capitalist system. Anti-American responses and denigrations of 'American work' were rare.[74]

At the end of the nineteenth century, then, the concept of 'German work' was a topos that was used widely to describe a unique national characteristic. Over time, however, the term was increasingly adopted

[69] Kuh, 'Neue Aufgaben', p. 524.
[70] On this subject see Klautke, *Möglichkeiten*, Chapter 3. See also Janeck, *Gartenlaube*, pp. 136ff., 310ff.
[71] Harjes, *Reise*.   [72] Unruh, *Amerika*, p. 22.
[73] Eisner, 'Taylorismus', p. 1448.
[74] On the reception of Taylorism in Germany see Homburg, 'Anfänge'; Kocka, 'Management'; Klautke, *Möglichkeiten*, pp. 61–86; and Burchardt, 'Fortschritt'. On the similar reception in France see also Fridenson, 'Tournant taylorien'; and Humphreys, *Taylorism*.

by the nationalist right wing. During this period, biological arguments were used to substantiate it and it became loaded with racist prejudices. In this way, work became part of the 'racial struggle' for *völkisch* nationalism, as a contemporary slogan suggested: 'It is not for himself alone that the individual should work, not even for his family, for his state or for his age; the final result must be that this work is placed in the service of the development of mankind, of the highest race.'[75]

This linking of work with the idea of race also entailed an anti-Semitic dimension; German work was frequently defined as the opposite of Jewish work. Riehl's ideas had already leaned in this direction. He described the Jews as hard-working; this characteristic, he argued, had resulted in the 'more easy-going Christian people' being in some cases actually 'worked off the land'. But he also identified a 'distinct difference in the idea of work honour and work ethic' between 'Semitic and Aryan' work. It was only nineteenth-century emancipation that had allowed Jews access to 'the national forms of work' and had given them 'German ideas about work honour and work ethic'.[76]

Riehl's distinction was still an expression of traditional anti-Jewish prejudices, not a product of the biologically loaded anti-Semitism that developed after 1880.[77] From the late nineteenth century onward, the concept of 'German work' increasingly came to include anti-Semitic connotations. This process adopted the stereotypes of Jewish 'haggling' (*Schacher*) and usury (*Wucher*), and the cliché that Jewish work was 'unproductive' and concentrated on finance and trade. Adolf Stoecker, Kaiser Wilhelm's court chaplain, gave expression to these ideas in his infamous and influential anti-Semitic speeches. He demanded the 'reintroduction of statistics on religious affiliation so that the unequal relationship between Jewish assets and Christian work [could] be identified'. Stoecker maintained that 'modern Jewry' should 'participate in productive work'. The under-representation of Jews in the trades, agriculture and factory work ('the hard and strenuous work') seemed

[75] Kuh, 'Neue Aufgaben', p. 524.   [76] Riehl, *Deutsche Arbeit*, pp. 53–54.
[77] Campbell, *Joy in Work*, p. 39.

to indicate 'that they have no joy in work and no sympathy for the German work ethic'.[78]

This assumption that there was such a thing as 'Jewish work' that could be differentiated from 'German work' was a central element of the anti-Semitic debate of the Kaiserreich and was present in all social milieux.[79] It was not limited to *völkisch* or ultra-national groups. Ideas that 'Jewish work' was inferior were common in Catholic circles too. Anti-capitalist and anti-Semitic prejudices overlapped, and capitalism and Jewishness were often seen as related or even as identical. For that reason the 'struggle against capitalism' that many traditional Catholics saw as a necessity would have to be, 'in the first instance, a struggle against the Jews'.[80] A central aim of this 'struggle' (*Kampf*) was to counteract the way in which Jews supposedly saw work; many Catholics strongly believed that the Jews' view of work was inherently wrong. They criticised the Jews' lack of a work ethic and contrasted Jewish egotism and rapacity with Christian, 'German' work. The *Christlich-Soziale Blätter*, for example, demanded that 'the Jewish people be forced to work and to earn an honest living'.[81]

Social Democrats tended to share these views, although individual members of the *SPD* protested vehemently against popular anti-Semitism, which they saw as an anti-capitalist crisis ideology of bourgeois society.[82] But anti-Jewish stereotypes can even be found in the writings of Marx, and Wilhelmine Social Democrats picked up on these in both private and public utterances.[83] Anti-Semitism had thus become anchored in popular culture, as is evident from the caricatures and narratives in mass-circulation political journals such

---

[78] Stoecker, *Christlich-Sozial*, p. 369. On this subject see also Greschat, 'Antisemitismus'; and Jochmann, 'Stoecker'.

[79] On this subject see Langer, *Vorurteil*; Gerhard, 'Judenfeindschaft'; and Zumbini, *Wurzeln*, esp. Chapter 2.

[80] Hans Rost, in a review of Sombart's book *Die Juden und das Wirtschaftsleben*, quoted in Blaschke, 'Antikapitalismus', p. 119.

[81] Quoted in *ibid.*, p. 126. On Catholic anti-Semitism and the criticisms of 'Jewish work' see also Blaschke, *Katholizismus*, pp. 86–89, 215–17; and Blaschke and Mattioli, *Katholischer Antisemitismus*.

[82] On this subject see Leuschen-Seppel, 'Arbeiterbewegung', pp. 80–90.

[83] On this subject see Silberner, *Sozialisten*.

as *Der wahre Jakob*. Even for August Begel it was 'unquestionable' that Jewish work was generally characterised by 'hucksterism' (by the *Schacher*).[84] From 1890 onward, the critique of capitalism in the popular Social Democratic press became even more markedly anti-Semitic.[85] The anti-Jewish connotations of the concept of 'German work' found an audience across the political and social divides.

This dichotomy between 'parasitic' (*raffend*, literally 'grasping') and 'productive' (*schaffend*) work was, however, more than a rhetorical instrument used by anti-Semitic groups. It was also adopted and adapted by Jewish authors. In particular, the idea of 'Jewish work' played a major role in Zionism.[86] The most important proponent of secular Zionism, Theodor Herzl, predicted that 'the Jews [would] go into their new country under the sign of work'.[87] In his book about the 'Jewish state', Herzl suggested that the Jewish state could be built up using an 'army of labour', which would be made up of unskilled labourers and would be organised along military lines, even including a 'labour marshal'. Much of Herzl's book is occupied with detailing working conditions and how settlements for the first workers to arrive should be organised.[88]

The concept of 'Jewish work' adopted the basic dichotomies inherent in the idea of 'German work'. In particular, it reproduced faithfully the contrast between agricultural work and the non-productive or even 'unhealthy' specialisation in trade and intellectual work of which the Jews were accused. In this, turn-of-the-century Zionism drew on an older tradition. As early as 1862, Moses Hess had demanded the creation of a separate Jewish state in order to promote the 'commendable efforts toward more healthy Jewish working relations'.[89] This pathological view of non-manual work was reproduced in many

---

[84] Quoted in Heid, 'Sozialistischer Internationalismus', p. 113.
[85] On the subject in general see Leuschen-Seppel, *Sozialdemokratie*, esp. pp. 242–80; and Rürup, *Emanzipation*.
[86] On the history of Zionism and the role of the idea of work in the Zionist movement see Brenner, *Geschichte*; Haumann, *Traum von Israel*; Stanislawski, *Zionism*; Laqueur, *History*; and Eloni, *Zionismus*.
[87] Quoted in Schmidt, 'Im Gelobten Land'.
[88] Herzl, *Judenstaat*, pp. 53ff. On this subject see also Gaisbauer, *Davidstern*.
[89] Hess, *Rom und Jerusalem*, p. 111.

Zionist writings, which were thus picking up both on anti-Semitic prejudices and on the *Lebensreform* debate. So while the Zionist debate remained within the theoretical framework of the debate about 'German work', the political position taken was in opposition to it, and 'Jewish work' was defined explicitly as the opposite of 'rapacious' work. Max Nordau, a doctor and writer and a friend of Herzl, called for 'muscular Jews', whose work in developing the Promised Land would eliminate any prejudices about weak ghetto Jews shying away from physical labour.[90] Herzl, too, wanted to 'make many of the current small traders into craftsmen' in order to create the Jewish state on the basis of physical work.[91]

The concept went beyond rhetoric and appeals to the Jewish population. Leo Pinsker, who became well known in the Zionist movement through his 1882 pamphlet on 'auto-emancipation' by Jews, founded a society in Kattowitz in 1884 for the 'promotion of tillage amongst Jews'. The society's aim was to encourage agricultural work as an alternative to 'excessive employment in the area of trade and industry and similar undertakings that are not capable of strengthening the body'.[92] A number of Zionist groups were set up to train Jews in agricultural work. These were often modelled on the Paris-based *Assistance par le travail*, a form of municipal charitable organisation that was also propounded by Herzl. Other groups modelled themselves on the Alsatian *Ecoles de travail*, boarding schools that offered practical vocational training and hoped to contribute to the goal of 'educating to work'.[93]

Finally, the goal of making Jews 'more productive', described by the slogan of the 'conquest of work', was also formulated in the socialist Zionist movement. This applied equally to both the two major socialist parties, *Paole Zion* and *Hapoel Hatzair*, despite the political,

---

[90] Nordau, 'Muskeljudentum'. On this subject see Berkowitz, *Zionist Culture*; Boyarin, *Unheroic Conduct*; Stanislawski, *Zionism*, pp. 91–97; Bechtel, Bourel and Le Rider, *Max Nordau*; and Schulte, *Psychopathologie*.
[91] Herzl, *Judenstaat*, p. 71.   [92] Pinsker, in Gelber, *Kattowitzer Konferenz*, p. 3.
[93] On this subject see the debate at the Fifth Zionist Congress in 1901: *Stenographisches Protokoll der Verhandlungen des V. Zionisten-Kongresses in Basel* (Vienna, 1901), p. 182.

social and theoretical differences between them. They both glorified manual work as an absolute category and as a form of therapy in the process of the national liberation of the Jewish people; agricultural work was believed to be capable of curing almost any social ill. As Labour Zionism had a greater influence on the character of the Zionist movement, and later of the state of Israel, than any other strain, these tendencies remained. The most important theoretician of socialist Zionism, Ber Borochov (1881–1917), linked his hopes for a new revolutionary state in the Near East with a paean to physical work. 'The liberation of the Jewish people', he wrote, 'will be achieved by Jewish work, or it will not be achieved at all'. This statement has expansionist and colonial undertones that were also part of the concept of 'German work'. This became evident, for example, in the settlement of Palestine, when David Ben-Gurion asserted that he did not recognise the Arab population's right to the land, since they were not working it.[94]

The militaristic rhetoric that regularly cropped up in texts about 'German work' culminated in descriptions of relationships between nations as a 'war of work'. And when the Great War finally broke out, it was soon described as a 'war of work' and celebrated as such, especially by the nationalist right wing. In the first edition of the magazine *Deutschlands Erneuerung*, one of the most important organs of the *völkisch* press, launched in 1917, a list of 'new tasks for German work' resulting from the war was outlined.[95] 'The war which everywhere, and with justice, is being called the great teacher, has also made us take a deep look into the essence of work, of our German work.' Germany was once again to be awarded 'the title of the most diligent of all peoples', one that 'not even our most avowed enemies would dare deny us'.[96]

But that was not all: the author of these lines, Felix Kuh, went on to describe the 'mission in world history' that German work was to fulfil. 'We work', he proclaimed, 'to lead humanity "from the darkness into the light"'. As the United States had entered the war earlier

---

[94] See Brenner, *Geschichte*, p. 82; and Laqueur, *Weg*, pp. 285–322.

[95] On the magazine's role, see Mosse, *Revolution*, pp. 240ff.

[96] Kuh, 'Neue Aufgaben', p. 524.

in the same year it may have been unclear to his readers how exactly this was to be achieved. But this cultural view of Germany's 'mission' was in fact reinforced in the face of the country's precarious situation. 'German work' was to be understood as a 'cultural factor for world history'.[97]

These phrases, however, were not alluding to the usual understanding of achievements in high culture that served to stabilise society. During the war years, the idea of work as a 'cultural factor' was assigned a specific meaning that went beyond the usual references to art or to developing domestic society. This was a major turning-point in the history of the idea of 'German work'. The idea of 'cultural work' was gradually transformed, leading to an aggressive, even imperialist understanding of the concept. This dimension was certainly inherent in the competitive element of the concept of 'German work', but it became more and more prominent with the country's military expansion.

Vejas Gabriel Liulevicius has described how the notions of work, 'culture work' (*Kulturarbeit*) and rule became gradually fused in the German-occupied areas of eastern Europe. While German *Kultur* was to be defended on the Western Front against the supposedly superficial western 'civilisation', many saw the campaign in the East as one of German *Kultur* as a civilising element in a region of *Unkultur*. There, 'German work' usually implied appropriation and rule, but also development; *Kulturarbeit* was often used in its original sense of 'agriculture': cultivating and reshaping a land that was seen by most as a tabula rasa. 'A characteristically German kind of work would give German lines and features to the land, putting their stamp on the place ... Foreign land could thus physically 'become' German, with intensive cultivation.'[98]

This was evident, for example, in the administration of 'Ober Ost', as the parts of north-western Russia under the control of the Oberbefehlshaber Ost were known during the occupation. This vast area of over 100,000 square kilometres, which covered the regions

---

[97] *Ibid.*, pp. 526, 536.
[98] See Liulevicius, *War Land*, pp. 29, 46; quotes pp. 45, 46.

Map 6.1 Administrative divisions of Ober Ost.

of Kurland, Lithuania and Bialystok-Grodno, was relatively sparsely inhabited, with an ethnically mixed population of 3 million. Here, the administrators of the Tenth Army, led by Hindenburg and his chief of staff Ludendorff, set out to reshape the face of the land. As a detailed treatise on *Das Land Ober Ost*, published in 1917, made clear, this work of development was seen as a task for 'German work'. This included creating basic infrastructure, ordering its finances, creating a legal system and establishing legal standards, and elements such as introducing a healthcare and sanitation system. Social, medical and technological interventions, the idea of development and modernisation, and colonial rule were thus all combined under the heading of 'German work'.[99]

This allowed the authorities to link the occupation with the long tradition of German colonisation in the East, which was supposed to provide a form of historical legitimacy for the Germans' presence. Cultural relics from the time of the Teutonic Knights were seen as evidence of the German character of this land.[100] An exhibition by the Tenth Army in 1918, intended to document the German influence on art created by the different populations of the region, was thus entitled 'German Work?'. The exhibition text attributed any deviations, or any lower-grade work, to foreign influences. 'With increasing contamination of the guild system by foreign influence, especially Jewish, the quality of work sinks quite considerably.'[101]

The new order that the 'earnestness of constructive [*aufbauende*] German work' had allowed to be created was also a colonial one.[102] Work provided legitimacy for domination or even for annexation. This idea had already been put forward by Gustav Freytag in his 1854 novel *Soll und Haben*, a *locus classicus* of nineteenth-century German bourgeois ideas about work. Its protagonist Anton Wohlfahrt saw Germans in Poland as conquerors who, through 'free work and human *Kultur*', had shown themselves to be superior to the native Poles and had earned the right to 'rule over this soil'. In his view, it was not war and conquest, but 'German work', education and *Kultur*

---

[99] See Oberbefehlshaber Ost, *Land Ober Ost*, esp. pp. 79–154.
[100] On this argument and its effects see Wippermann, *Ordensstaat*, esp. pp. 154–96; and *Drang nach Osten*, pp. 85–104.
[101] Quoted in Liulevicius, *War Land*, p. 132.
[102] Oberbefehlshaber Ost, *Land Ober Ost*, p. ix.

that gave people rights over territories and populations. '[It is] peacefully through our own industry that we have won our own empire over this country.'[103] Gustav Freytag must be regarded as one of the main authors of the concept of 'German work', and from the beginning the term was sometimes invested with an expansionary sense. But it was only during the First World War that ideas like those in Freytag's novel, which were often rather metaphorical in nature, became actual social practice.

This imperialistic dimension of the concept of work developed mainly in the situation of war and occupation. Here, war and work could overlap where they had previously been separate or even opposites. War led to the militarisation of work. This change took administrative form in the Patriotic Auxiliary Service Act (*Gesetz über den Vaterländischen Hilfsdienst*) of 5 December 1916, which obliged all male Germans between the ages of seventeen and sixty not deemed suitable for military service to carry out labour service. It was administered by the 'War Office' that had been set up by the Prussian Ministry of War.[104]

'ARBEIT MACHT FREI'

'We say yes to work [*bejahen die Arbeit*]', Adolf Hitler declared in October 1933 in his Berlin Sportpalast speech, 'as our fathers said yes to it'.[105] 'Work' became a central element of the ideology and social organisation of the Third Reich, the self-appointed 'state of work' in which 'work' stood as an equal alongside 'struggle' (*Kampf*) and 'action' (*Tat*). Konstantin Hierl, later head of the Reich Labour Service (*Reichsarbeitsdienst*), stated that the 'name "worker"' and the respect with which it was endowed by the regime 'shall, like the name "soldier", become an honorary title reminding us of the most noble duties of every German'.[106]

---

[103] Freytag, *Debit and Credit*, pp. 401ff. On Freytag see Bußmann, 'Gustav Freytag'.
[104] For further discussion of labour service after 1919 see Köhler, 'Arbeitsdienst'.
[105] Quoted in Trommler, 'Nationalisierung', p. 102.
[106] Quoted in Brückner, *Arbeit macht frei*, p. 72.

The Nazi concept of work picked up on the earlier debates about 'German work' in a number of ways.[107] But the way the National Socialists used the term, in itself by no means uniform, did not follow directly on from the way it was used in Wilhelmine Germany. The Nazi era brought major changes in terminology and in political practice, major breaks from what went immediately before and, more markedly, from the pre-1914 era. Nazi rhetoric in fact emphasised the differences between Nazi ideas about work and earlier concepts of work.

The Nazi concept of work picked up on the three aspects of 'German work' outlined above, but they were all reinterpreted and radicalised in a particular way. Firstly, the economic aspects of the nineteenth-century debate had focused on demands for protective tariffs in a world dominated by British free trade. Nazi policy went beyond this protectionist policy, adopting economic autarky as a strategic goal.[108] Secondly, in terms of social policy, the debate about 'German work' had been focused on reconciling capital and work, on overcoming the antagonisms between the classes. This issue was also radicalised after 1933 by the *Gleichschaltung* of the unions, the setting-up of the German Labour Front (*Deutsche Arbeitsfront*) and the concept of the *Volksgemeinschaft* or national community. 'Workers and work, as National Socialism understands these words', Martin Heidegger pronounced in 1934, 'do not divide the *Volksgenossen* into classes but bind them together and unite them'.[109] In addition, the Nazis demanded that the division between physical and intellectual work be overcome. Riehl had been concerned with this issue, as had Friedrich Naumann, with his demands for the 'intellectualisation [*Durchgeistigung*] of production'. But in Nazi rhetoric, the separate groups of 'craftsmen [*Handarbeiter*] and brain workers [*Kopfarbeiter*]' became a single 'community of fate'.[110]

---

[107] On these continuities see Lüdtke, 'Honor of Labor'.
[108] See for example Petzina, *Autarkiepolitik*; and Volkmann and Chiari, *Ökonomie und Expansion*.
[109] Heidegger, 'Eröffnung', p. 235. On this subject see also Wege, 'Kult'.
[110] Leonhard Achner (1932) in the national-revolutionary journal *Tat*, quoted in Wege, 'Kult', p. 238.

The cultural dimension was the third aspect. 'Work' was understood to have cultural implications in the Third Reich, too, and this differentiated it clearly from competing ways of seeing work – from both the utilitarian, i.e. instrumental, understanding of work and from the Marxist differentiation between alienating-exploitative (capitalist) and liberating socialist work.[111] In the prevailing Nazi view, work could not be separated from the *Volksgemeinschaft* and was conceivable only within it. The conscious 'nationalisation of the German workers' played a central role in the regime's rhetoric and in its social practice.[112] This social embeddedness opened the way for work to be claimed for use by society, from state intervention through to a duty to work.[113] This appropriation of work by the state also involved its glorification, for example in the *Blut und Boden* rhetoric of Hierl, head of the Reich Labour Service, who saw the Labour Service as, in the first instance, 'work on the soil of the German *Heimat*'.[114] Work had become a service to the fatherland, an obligation to Germany, even a 'prayer for Germany'.[115]

In addition to these differences between the Nazis' concept of work and the 'German work' of the Wilhelmine era, the concept of work was further radicalised during the Third Reich itself. In the main this had to do with its militarisation, something that also picked up on tropes from the First World War. In Nazi rhetoric, work activities and military activities were increasingly regarded as synonymous. During the era of the *Freikorps* and paramilitary groups, Artur Mahraun had demanded a 'liberation war of work'. He was making an explicit link to the medieval German colonisation of eastern Europe; labour service, like military service, implied the creation of a 'dam against the Polish flood', efforts toward 'inner colonisation' and a programme of expansion.[116] This militarisation of work continued

---

[111] See Seifert, *Kulturarbeit*. See also Dudek, *Erziehung*, pp. 67ff.
[112] On this subject see Bons, *Nationalsozialismus*, p. 1; and Heuel, *Stand*.
[113] See Patel, *Soldaten*, pp. 330ff.
[114] Quoted in Brückner, *Arbeit macht frei*, p. 72.
[115] Members of the Reich Labour Service at the *Reichsparteitag* in 1937, quoted in Patel, *Soldaten*, p. 332.
[116] Quoted in Dudek, *Erziehung*, pp. 63ff.

during the Third Reich. As the head of the Committee for Economic Policy in the national headquarters of the Nazi Party proclaimed, '[w]ork and war are basically the same thing'.[117]

Secondly, the polemical and exclusionary aspects of the concept of work were focused mainly on the Jews. Racism and Social Darwinism were central elements of the Nazis' view of work, to a much greater extent than in the Wilhelmine debates about 'German work'. Hitler explicitly differentiated the 'Aryans' moral understanding of work' from the 'egotistical understanding of work' held by the Jews.[118] Hierl saw the Nazi labour camps as 'bulwarks against that Jewish-materialist understanding of work'.[119] Increasingly, this exclusionary function became central to the Nazis' concept of work.

This radicalisation of the anti-Jewish components of 'German work' during the Third Reich went beyond social exclusion, of course, and increasingly took on an annihilatory character. In the concentration camps there was no longer any clear distinction between exploitative forced labour focusing on the economic product of that labour (though with no concern for the workers' lives) and the deliberate extermination of prisoners through work. This applied to the Sinti and Roma and to the 'antisocial' and 'work-shy' prisoners, who were increasingly classified as 'un-German',[120] but the Jews were the largest group held in the concentration camps and work camps, and they were not regarded as 'capable of being educated' (*erziehbar*) through work. The Nazis even spoke of 'annihilation through work' as the consequence of the German understanding of work. 'Principally, Jewish "work" was destruction itself'.[121]

---

[117] Quoted in Patel, *Soldaten*, p. 336. A similar statement was made by Robert Ley: 'Work is just another word for struggle' ('Arbeit ist ja nur ein anderer Ausdruck für Kampf'). Quoted in Schatz and Woeldike, *Freiheit*, p. 83.

[118] Quoted in Phelps, 'Hitlers "grundlegende" Rede', p. 405.

[119] Quoted in Conze, 'Arbeit', p. 214.

[120] On the treatment of the Sinti and Roma see Zimmermann, *Rassenutopie*; and Wippermann, *Zigeuner*. On the Nazis' policy toward 'asocial elements' see Ayaß, '*Asoziale*'; his *Gemeinschaftsfremde*; and Peukert, *Volksgenossen*.

[121] According to Goldhagen, *Hitler's Willing Executioners*, p. 319. A debate has developed among historians about whether 'work' or 'annihilation' was a higher priority in the Nazi camps. Increasingly, the instrumentalist description of 'annihilation

Although the Nazis' use of the concept of work picked up on the debates about 'German work' in a number of ways, then, the concept of 'German work' cannot be directly linked to the *Arbeit macht frei* slogan that encompassed the annihilation of human beings on a massive scale.[122] Here as elsewhere, the importance and the political relevance of the concept cannot be deduced from its history, but must be seen in the real contemporary context, a racially loaded European civil war. In both conceptual and discursive terms, the Nazis' understanding of work differed from the Wilhelmine debate. But in particular, their annihilatory practices differed from the earlier discussions of 'German work', which, while they had contemplated exclusion and segregation, did not extend to the practice of physical annihilation.

EPILOGUE: 'GERMAN WORK' AND THE SPIRIT OF MODERNISATION

Undoubtedly the most important turn-of-the-century text about the role of work in the modern world was Max Weber's *The Protestant Ethic and the Spirit of Capitalism*. In this book, as is well known, Weber examined the link between a religiously motivated work ethic and the development of western capitalism. After the Reformation, he argued, work ethic and the idea of the profession had become increasingly important, which, combined with Calvinist ideas about predestination, had promoted the idea that life as a whole should be organised in methodical and rational terms. This, Weber believed, was not merely compatible with the capitalist mentality, but a prerequisite for it.[123] Weber's study was an attempt to solve a 'problem of universal history'. While the study focused on one historical phenomenon,[124] inherent in Weber's approach was the possibility of

through work' is being seen with a certain amount of scepticism. On this topic see Herbert, 'Arbeit und Vernichtung'; Kaienburg, *Vernichtung*; Zimmermann, 'Arbeit'; Kárný, 'Vernichtung'; and Pohl, 'Holocaust-Forschung'.

[122] On the history of this slogan see Brückner, *Arbeit macht frei*.

[123] The literature on Weber's thesis is now so extensive that it is almost impossible to keep track of it. For a good overview, see Schluchter, 'Religion'. See also Küenzlen, *Religionssoziologie*; and Bily, *Religion*.

[124] Weber, *Religionssoziologie*, p. 1.

historical equivalence, and in his wide-ranging studies on the socio-logy of world religions he examined that possibility in detail. This had little or nothing to do with national specifics, let alone with 'German work'.

Or did it? Weber's text was published in 1904–05, when the rhet-oric of 'German work' was at its height. The term was used in almost every dimension of Wilhelmine society and crossed social and polit-ical boundaries. Can Weber's study have remained uninfluenced by such a dominant discourse of his time? Are no traces of this debate to be found in his work on Protestantism?

In fact, we can identify several areas of overlap between Weber's concept of work and the topos of 'German work'. One of the most important is the transcendental view of work. Appeals to morality and to the moral role of work, above and beyond economic calcu-lations, were an intrinsic part of the debates about 'German work'. For Weber, too, the tireless secular work of the Calvinists was not an end in itself, but loaded with religious connotations and expectations about the next life. Despite many differences in ideas about morality, work became, in both instances, a way of measuring the individual's 'ethical conduct and fate in the secular social order'.[125]

Moral, indeed, but German? Surprisingly, of the many studies and commentaries on Weber's Protestantism theory that have been published over the last hundred years, very few place his 1905 work in the context of his time.[126] And those that do usually focus on the history of the humanities and the exchange of influences and ideas in the work of Knies, Gothein, Jellinek, Sombart or Troeltsch.[127] But no work has been done on the links between his writings and the popular (though admittedly less than scholarly) debate about 'German work'. Yet a 'national' view of economic life was not unusual, as suggested by the term 'national economy' (*Nationalökonomie*). As early as the

---

[125] Weber, *Economy and Society*, p. 1199.
[126] An overview of the reception and discussion of Weber's work, with the relevant literature, is given by MacKinnon, 'Longevity'.
[127] For a detailed account see Takebayashi, *Entstehung*, for example pp. 289–97. See also the contributions to Mommsen and Schwentker, *Max Weber*.

mid nineteenth century, Friedrich List had argued for a national economy – a political economy different in every nation.[128]

But there were also examples of contemporary writings that linked capitalism with a concrete social group, like that identified in *The Protestant Ethic*. These included the writings of Werner Sombart, whose 1912 book *Modern Capitalism*, with its discussion of the 'psychogenesis of capitalism', was one of the leading challenges to Weber's thesis. In 1911, in response to *The Protestant Ethic*, Sombart published a book entitled *The Jews and Economic Life*, in which he identified the Jews as the bearers of the capitalist spirit. As such he was directly contradicting Weber, who had described Jews as proponents of 'pariah capitalism'. Sombart believed that their religion encouraged Jews to deal with money in a rational and, in a capitalistic sense, efficient way. The positions taken by Sombart and Weber on this issue were thus antithetical. Yet there were some parallels. Sombart, who based his work on the 1887 'survey on usury' organised by the *Verein für Sozialpolitik*, reproduced the anti-Semitic differentiation between 'German productive' (*deutsche schaffende*) and parasitic (*raffende*) Jewish work (also setting up a contrast between 'joy in work' and 'determination' to achieve a goal). This is reminiscent of the anti-Jewish tendency of the debate about 'German work'.[129] But we also find echoes of this kind of prejudice in Weber's work when he contrasts Jewish '"adventurer" capitalism' with the Puritan idea of work. Thus Weber, too, reproduced the stereotypical contemporary aversion to trade.[130]

But more important as a starting-point for Weber's work was his examination of Catholicism, not his anti-Semitism. Many commentators have noted that Weber's ideas must be interpreted in the

---

[128] See Tribe, *Strategies*, pp. 32–65; and Winkel, *Nationalökonomie*, Chapters 2 and 3.

[129] Sombart, *Juden*, p. 423; see also p. 420 and *passim*. On this subject see Lehmann, 'Protestantismus', pp. 533ff.; Lehmann, 'Rise'; Raphael, *Judaïsme*; Silbermann, *Was ist jüdischer Geist?*, pp. 27–32; and Eloni, *Zionismus*, pp. 261–69. On Sombart see also Lenger, *Werner Sombart*.

[130] Weber, *Religionssoziologie*, p. 181. On the role of trade in Weber's work see Barkai, 'Judentum', pp. 30ff. For comparisons of Sombart and Weber see also Rehberg, 'Bild'; and Mendes-Flohr, 'Werner Sombart's *The Jews*'.

context of typical views in the Kaiserreich about the role of Catholics in German society. From at least 1870, one of the main elements of liberal politics was a sharp differentiation between Protestantism and Catholicism. Weber's study can also be read (though this idea has not been pursued in any detail) as a product of the *Kulturkampf*.[131] The anti-Catholic element of the liberal view of work was also an element of the debate about 'German work'. Riehl had combined 'work' and 'Protestantism' in the idea of 'German work', and Weber followed in this tradition (although he regarded Lutheranism as 'bound to tradition' and believed that it was Calvinism that had awoken the capitalist spirit).[132] 'It was only on Protestant soil that the new theory of work could step-by-step, during the eighteenth century, take form in a new practice of work', Riehl had stated, in essence preparing the ground for later ideas.[133]

The topos of 'German work' is only contained between the lines in Weber's writings; it is more of a background to his work than the subject of it. Superficially, *The Protestant Ethic* is of course an argument for the autonomy of religious beliefs as separate from national characteristics or a *Volkscharakter*.[134] But nevertheless, elements of nationalism are not entirely absent. Echoes of the debate about German work can be heard most clearly in Weber's large-scale study on *The Condition of Rural Labour in East-Elbian Germany*, which he compiled in 1892 for the *Verein für Sozialpolitik*. This study was a reaction to the increasing 'foreign infiltration' (*Überfremdung*) of the eastern districts of Prussia (the perceived number of 'foreigners' there) and to the emigration of local German workers to the industrial regions of western Germany. It was based on a survey of employers, who were asked about the situation of rural workers; the workers themselves were not interviewed.[135] With this study, Max Weber rapidly became a well-known scholar and in 1894 was appointed a professor of 'national economy' in Freiburg, largely on the strength of this work. But the

---

[131] See Lehmann, 'Protestantismus', p. 536. See also Münch, 'Zusammenhang'; and 'Thesis'.

[132] Weber, *Religionssoziologie*, p. 77.   [133] Riehl, *Deutsche Arbeit*, p. 252.

[134] On this subject see Liebersohn, 'Weber's Historical Concept'.

[135] Weber, *Landarbeiter*.

study was important for him for other reasons too. Its results can be traced 'like a red thread' running through his work.[136]

Weber's detailed study was a contribution to the discussion about the flight from the land and labour mobility, and it contains many analyses of the links between wage structures, the cultivation of root crops and structural change in rural areas, and the 'pushing out' of native workers.[137] But it also reads like an anthropological report from a foreign country. Weber describes in great detail the different elements of society and the social status assigned to each category of rural worker. In addition, he gives a painstaking account of everyday life, from the way pigs and sheep are slaughtered, to living conditions, women's work and sexual relations. Weber's report has marked similarities with the anthropological studies that the German Reich was commissioning during the same period for its African colonies.[138]

I have already discussed the colonial dimension of German policy toward Poland, and this view of Poland as a German colony is also characteristic of Weber's text. The issue that most concerns him is the defence of 'Germany' from immigration by rural labourers from eastern Europe. The 'forcing out of the German labourers' entailed, he argued, the loss of 'Germandom' (*Deutschtum*), of 'defensive strength' (*Wehrkraft*) and of German cultural achievements in the eastern Prussian provinces.[139] In his famous inaugural speech at Freiburg two years later, he outlined his concerns in even more explicit terms. He warned that one should not underestimate the 'role played by physical and psychological racial differences between nationalities in the economic struggle for existence'. For this reason, Weber pleaded for the decisive 'closing of the eastern frontier', but argued that this should be accompanied by an active population policy in the form of 'buying up land' and domestic 'colonisation'. Only

---

[136] According to Käsler, *Max Weber*, p. 74. A similar view is put forward by Radkau, *Max Weber*, p. 133.

[137] On this subject see Herbert, *Ausländerbeschäftigung*, pp. 28ff.

[138] In Africa, the primary function of these studies was to enable 'native law' to be codified, and they were an instrument of colonial rule. See for example Knoll, 'Indigenous Law'.

[139] Weber, *Landarbeiter*, p. 926.

in this way could the 'tide of Slavs' be successfully 'stemmed'.[140] The *Freiburger Zeitung* quoted Weber in 1897 as saying that '[t]he conditions are such that even if a Mongolian were to come to rule Germany … he would have to enforce a German policy in the East'.[141]

In his inaugural address, Weber combined a demand for domestic colonisation with its counterpart – expansion abroad. 'We have to understand the fact', one frequently quoted passage runs, 'that the unification of Germany was a youthful prank carried out by the nation in its old age, and it would have been better, on grounds of expense, to leave it undone if it was to have been the end rather than the beginning of Germany's involvement in world politics'.[142] Just as Friedrich Naumann's *Werkbund* entered into an ideological symbiosis with German naval policy, Weber's defence of German work at the eastern border of the Reich was linked to expansionary imperialist policy. In these remarks, the protection of German culture and 'German work' were intimately linked with anti-Polish elements and a colonial perspective (both at home and abroad).

One could even suggest, and this brings us back to *The Protestant Ethic*, that in his Freiburg address Weber exchanged the focus of Puritan sects on the next world for the imperial vision of the Kaiserreich, for Bülow's 'place in the sun'. In fact, as Hans-Christoph Schröder has pointed out, Weber lamented the lack of any tendency toward worldly asceticism in Wilhelmine Germany. It was regrettable, Weber wrote, 'that our nation has never gone through the school of hard asceticism in *any* form'.[143] It was for that reason that the English and the Americans, and not the Germans, were the 'great working peoples of the earth'.[144] Schröder argues that imperialism seemed to Weber to be a 'kind of replacement' for the lack of Puritan

---

[140] Weber, *Political Writings*, pp. 2, 12. On Weber's Freiburg speech and his nationalism, see Mommsen, *Max Weber und die deutsche Politik*, pp. 37–96; Xenos, 'Nation'; and Anter, *Max Webers Theorie*, pp. 124–46.

[141] Weber, 'Polenthum', p. 823. On Weber's relationship with race theory see Zimmerman, 'Decolonizing Weber'.

[142] Weber, *Political Writings*, p. 26.

[143] Weber to Adolf Harnack in February 1906, in *Briefe*, p. 33. Emphasis in original.

[144] Quoted in Marianne Weber, *Max Weber*, p. 432.

motivation. Visions of *Weltpolitik* had served to prevent the country coming to a sated standstill, resting on what was already achieved, and to allow individual interests to be put aside for the benefit of the greater good – denying oneself in the interests of higher ends, just as the Puritan had worked not for his own material success but to praise God. Schröder suggests that, for Weber, imperialism was not only an 'alternative religion', but the only possible contemporary 'alternative to Puritanism'.[145]

But if the alternative to Puritanism was imperialism, then the Protestant work ethic corresponded to 'German work'. The two concepts overlapped and both helped to link the discussions about work with visions of power politics. With its ambitions of global power, the modern nation state provided a way of avoiding societal stagnation and degeneration and of creating a transcendental vision on which a renewed, modernised form of worldly asceticism could focus: colonial expansion as a motivation for work. Weber's imperialism was an imperialism of work. 'Through our work and our nature', he proclaimed, 'we want to be the forerunners of that future race'.[146] Thus, Weber's *Protestant Ethic* can be seen as part of the broader social debate about 'German work' in the decades before the First World War.

This chapter has suggested that the postulation of national specificity in work corresponded to the increase in global links and references (not least, in the field of work). And, as we have seen, Weber's ideas can be located in the context of imperialism and migration, a context that Weber himself had witnessed in the eastern provinces of Prussia. But there is no mention of these entanglements or of international labour mobility in *The Protestant Ethic*, and this is something else that his study shares with the topos of 'German work'. Instead, Weber's is a decidedly internalist approach. He does not discuss migration across Germany's borders, but internality, internal dispositions and asceticism; not foreign influences, contacts or transfers from abroad, but mechanisms of internalisation. Weber was not interested in external forces, but in the 'subjective appropriation of

---

[145] Schröder, 'Max Weber', p. 476.   [146] Weber, *Political Writings*, p. 15.

ascetic religiosity on the part of the individual'. External structures could force 'external behaviour' but they also paralysed the individual's own driving forces, their inner motivation.[147]

This idea of autopoietic motivation, of development that comes from within rather than being the result of external pressure, has proved to be one of the most enduring elements of Weber's work. Transposed by the 1960s theory of modernisation onto the level of collective subjects, it suggests that development – for individuals, but more especially for societies and nations – is only possible from within. This paradigm has become the dominant approach in historiography, challenged only occasionally by dependency theory or by post-colonial studies. Working within this paradigm, historians have not primarily investigated structures of import and export, military force or cultural interconnectedness, but have localised the resources for successful modernisation within the internal structures of each individual society. In best Weberian tradition, one of the main parameters of this approach has been to inquire about traditional work ethics in each society. Ideas about work have been seen as a privileged storehouse for cultural heritage. For a society to move successfully into the modern age, what was required, this approach suggested, was not interaction and interlinkage, not exchange (even in an asymmetric form) or physical (or systemic) force, but independent development founded on indigenous traditions.[148]

This modernisation theory, which was strongly influenced by Weber's work, has more recently been criticised, but the idea on which it is based, that all modernisations are based on internal developmental forces, has on the whole survived. A perspective that tends to divide history into national units and to analyse the development of nation states in terms of internal developments is still highly influential. This logic of nationalisation is reminiscent of the mechanisms that created the use of the term 'German work': delimitation and

[147] Weber, *Religionssoziologie*, pp. 161ff.

[148] Cf. Turner, *Marx*, p. 10, who notes that Weber's explanation remains 'internalist' as 'he treats the main problems of "backward societies" as a question of certain characteristics *internal* to societies, considered in isolation from any international societal context'.

particularity as reactions to a situation of increasing interconnectedness. Did Weber's project of internal (and inner) causalities adhere to the same logic? Was it itself an (internalising) response to a globalised world? Given the Weberian origins of the concept of modernisation, and the connections between Weber's ideas about work ethics and the topos of 'German work', there could indeed be a direct link. Writing on the development of sociology in the nineteenth century, Roland Robertson has suggested that '[m]uch of social theory is both a product of and an implicit reaction to … the globalization process'.[149] If so, the internalist (Weberian) paradigm that is still influential today would bear the traces of the debate about 'German work', and would itself be a product of an earlier stage of globalisation.

[149] Robertson, *Globalization*, p. 49.

CHAPTER SEVEN

Regimes of territorialisation and the globalisation of the national

THE GLOBALISATION OF THE NATION STATE

The globalisation that was taking place around 1900 did not undermine the institution of the nation state. In fact, the interconnectedness of the world, which had been increasing markedly from about 1880, did not lead to national affiliations becoming diluted, as some contemporaries (and some later historians) believed, but in fact helped to make the idea of the nation more established across the globe. The increase in global interactions took place in a setting shaped by nation states.[1]

The most obvious sign of the nationalisation of the world around 1900, firstly, was the spread of nationalism. In Germany, Great Britain and the Third Republic in France, it became a mass movement from the 1880s onward, and it also became the dominant political concept in some places outside western Europe, for example in the Balkan states, in Egypt and in India. Increasingly, the previously existing, frequently multiple and often vague links within communities gave way to the exclusive concept of national identity. This led, secondly, to the nation state becoming the privileged form of political organisation, as in New Zealand and Australia, in Norway and in Siam. But in Germany, Italy, Japan and the United States too, the 'internal establishment of the nation state' was a product of the late nineteenth century. The big multinational empires – the Ottoman, Habsburg and Russian empires – did manage to survive into the twentieth century. But their ideological foundations had been deeply undermined by

---

[1] But not all the states that claimed to be nation states were homogeneous in national or ethnic terms. On this subject see Connor, *Ethnonationalism*.

nationalist movements, making their collapse as a result of the First World War seem the logical consequence of a long process of decline and dissolution.[2] Thirdly and finally, globalisation around 1900 was linked to the nationalisation of transnational processes – of trade, which was contained within strict protectionist regimes almost everywhere from 1890 onward; of migration, which increasingly came to be controlled by nation states, a process that began with the limiting and abolition of the slave trade and culminated in the quotas of the American immigration laws; and of transnational ideas like racism and religion, which, during the late nineteenth century, were claimed and annexed by nationalist groups.[3]

The spread of nationalism took place during the heyday of imperialism, from 1880 on. Although historians have usually treated the two phenomena as separate, their synchronicity was not a coincidence but an expression of the colonial character of globality at that time. Nationalism made an important contribution to the dynamic of expansion, both in the colonising metropoles, where colonial agitation often took the form of national populism, and at the periphery, for example in Egypt: the British occupation of 1882 (which launched the 'scramble for Africa') was a reaction to the nationalist Urabi Revolt. At the same time, nationalism was not just a cause but also an effect of imperialist domination, and the national movements in India, south-eastern Asia and later in Africa developed under the influence of colonial power.

For this reason, the victory of national structures and ideas outside Europe (and in eastern Europe) was for a long time interpreted as a diffusion of western European models. European discussion centred on Hans Kohn's (and Theodor Schieder's) typology that described the nationalisms of central and eastern Europe as deficient variants of a western model. In this view, the 'normal process' is determined by the liberal (and, in theory, universal) goals of a participatory nationalism

---

[2] See Osterhammel, 'Nationalstaat'. However, the Qing empire remained an imperial nation state even after 1911 and 1919, and the British empire only broke up after 1945.

[3] On this subject see Bayly, *Birth*, pp. 199–243. See also Arrighi, *Long Twentieth Century*, esp. pp. 47–58.

aiming to create an open, democratic society; deviations in eastern Europe (cultural myths, the ideology of a *Volksgemeinschaft*) are seen as deficient and in need of explanation by a theory of modernisation characterised by stages of development and unequal development.[4]

In a similar fashion, national movements at the colonial periphery have been seen primarily as imitations of western European patterns and, simultaneously, as 'delayed' events in terms of global history – as an expression of cultural backwardness. In a highly influential study, Partha Chatterjee subjected this view to scathing criticism, drawing attention instead to the actual conditions in which colonial nationalisms developed. Yet his interpretation tends only to convert the idea of imitation from an empirical problem to a theoretical one. Using the development of Indian nationalism as an example, Chatterjee has suggested that colonial national movements were unable to emancipate themselves from the theoretical dominance of the European model. Even if Indian nationalism was formulated in political terms (which he calls the level of the 'problematic') in opposition to western rule, at an epistemological level (the 'thematic') it remains a 'derivative discourse', one that supports the very power structures it criticises.[5]

This idea that colonial nationalism was temporally (or, in Chatterjee's view, theoretically) subordinate to western nationalism is based on a somewhat restricted interpretation of global interaction as cultural diffusion. Of course, political and cultural models were central to the spread of nationalism. Even nineteenth-century European nationalism was influenced by the newly created Latin American nations.[6] But for the second half of the nineteenth century (at the latest) the idea that the growth of nationalism can be explained as the diffusion and assimilation of 'western' patterns is not an adequate explanation. It ignores the extent to which the growing interconnectedness of the world – and of the process sometimes seen

---

[4] On this subject see Kohn, *Nationalism*; and Schieder, 'Typologie'. For a criticism of Schieder's assumptions see for example von Hirschhausen and Leonhard, 'Nationalismen'. See also Langewiesche, *Nation, Nationalismus, Nationalstaat*.

[5] On this subject see Chatterjee, *Nationalist Thought*.

[6] On this subject see in particular the discussion in Anderson, *Imagined Communities*.

as a 'translation of the West' – itself took place within a global framework.[7] In different ways, an awareness of global links was growing in Europe, in the United States and in Japan, but also in India, China and Egypt: an awareness that went beyond the bilateral focus of colonies on the 'West'.[8]

This has two implications for the way we understand the links between national orders and globalisation. Firstly, it is inadequate to describe the global victory of the nation state and of national categories as 'belated modernisation' or as a derivative of a 'western' discourse. Rather, the dynamics of the Indian, Chinese and Japanese nationalisms were part of a global historical process. The paradigm of local 'reactions' to impulses from Europe and the USA, which dominated interpretations of national movements outside Europe for a long time, is as inadequate as any attempt to explain national movements solely in terms of references to autochthonous cultural traditions. Both views ignore the global context, but around 1900 that global context was increasingly felt and influential in many regions of the world. Thus, the formation of a national consciousness outside the 'West' was not so much a reaction to the global modernity of the era, or even a struggle to resist it, but a central component of it.[9]

Secondly, however, this also means that what we could call the 'globalisation of the national' affected not only regions to which national ideas were new, but also Europe and the USA. Of course, in some parts of the western world we can trace the development of national consciousness and even of a nation state far back into the past, for example in France and England (and in Japan). For these places, it is easy to identify continuities between pre-modern 'ethnic groups' and nineteenth-century nationalism; here, the nation was not just the result of the modern 'invention of traditions' but was itself

---

[7] Howland, *Translating*.

[8] Chatterjee later distanced himself from the concept of the 'derivative discourse'. See primarily Chatterjee, *Nation*.

[9] See the inspiring exploration in Karl, *Staging the World*, esp. pp. 3–26. For a categorisation of turn-of-the-century Asian nationalism, see also Chow, Doak and Fu, *Constructing Nationhood*; Tonesson and Antlöv, *Asian Forms*; and Brook and Schmid, *Nation Work*.

founded on a tradition of the community inventing itself as a nation.[10] And the nation states in Germany, Italy or the USA, too, which took their modern form from the 1860s onward, could also look back on a longer pre-history. Thus, the national order of the late nineteenth century was highly differentiated, and the surge in nationalisation did not affect every society in the same way.

Yet globalisation around 1900 was linked to a process of nation-alisation that was indeed global in extent, and was not limited to the colonial periphery. Of course this did not apply everywhere; just as there were 'old' nation states, there were still regions, in 1914, in which nationalism had barely arrived – parts of the Ottoman and Russian empires, for example, and sub-Saharan Africa. But wherever national affinities and institutions had gained a foothold, the effects that con-temporary globalisation had on this national order could also be felt.

RECAP: GERMANY'S GLOBAL NATIONALISM AROUND 1900

The nationalism of the Wilhelmine era, too, was embedded in global developments that themselves affected the formation of nationalism and the nation state. As the historian and sociologist Otto Hintze described it in 1896, '[t]he nations with which history deals are in no sense natural entities but products of the circumstances of global history'. There was a dialectical relationship, he argued, between global structures and the modes of institutionalisation of particularistic identities: '[t]he great development in world history … is not merely created by the nations; it itself creates nations'. Hintze was convinced that globalisation had 'influenced the national process of development in the most powerful manner … once any interlinkage has taken place'.[11]

Certainly, there was an existing tradition of nationalism in Germany, one that we can trace back at least to the French occupation in the early nineteenth century and the Napoleonic wars. It would be

---

[10] On the concept of the primordial nation, see in particular Smith, *Nationalism and Modernism*. A discussion on the 'tradition of invention' is contained in Suter, 'Nationalstaat'.

[11] Hintze, 'Geschichtsauffassung', p. 67.

interesting to investigate this tradition systematically in terms of its global context. The 'national uprising' of 1813 was part of the surge in nationalisation between 1789 and 1815 that also resulted, for example, in the creation of the new nation states of South America; the 1848 debates about the importance and extent of the nation were linked not only to the revolutionary turmoil in Europe, but also – or so Chris Bayly has argued – to the other major crises of the mid-nineteenth century, the Asian rebellions and the Civil War in the USA; and the foundation of the German state took place in an era during which nation states were taking institutional form around the globe, including the Italian *Risorgimento*, the Japanese Meiji restoration and the 'reconstruction era' in the United States.[12] In Germany, neither the nation state nor nationalism itself were 'inventions' of the late nineteenth century; the nationalism of the era was just one among a number of surges in nationalisation.

Yet we can identify, for the three decades leading up to the First World War, a change in the form of the national. This has been widely described by nationalism research and interpreted as a 'radicalisation'. It took place from the 1880s onward and was founded in the expansion of the social basis of nationalism, the creation of nationalist groups and the establishment of nationalism as a mass phenomenon. A number of the reasons for this expansion were internal or can be found within a strictly European context: among these are the increase in social and political participation, the instrumentalisation of nationalism as an ideology of integration, the growth in mass media, and Germany's anti-British naval policy.

But three aspects of the transformation of the idea of the nation around the turn of the century can be seen as specific products of the contemporary process of globalisation. *Firstly*, the increase in cross-border mobility from, through and into Germany contributed to the stabilisation and consolidation of the physical borders of the nation state. The border checks of the German Central Office for Field Workers (*Feldarbeiterzentrale*), the strengthening of rules

---

[12] See the discussions in Bayly, *Birth*, pp. 148–69; and Geyer and Bright, 'World History'.

on passports, increased checks on individuals, and hygiene-related rules for immigration and through-migration were manifestations of a concern with territorial borders that was characteristic of this era and differentiated it from earlier ones. Most of these rules were created in response to inner-European migration, and especially migration from the Polish regions of Russia and Austria-Hungary. But the increase in such migration, like the huge scale of through-migration from eastern Europe through Germany to the United States, can only be understood in the context of global mobility.

Secondly, a debate developed, in the context of emigration, about modifications to the idea of 'Germanness'. It was primarily the topos of the 'diaspora Germans' (*Auslandsdeutschtum*) that gave expression to new beliefs about the location of the nation and provided the motivation for a policy of promoting 'Germandom' in which both nationalist associations and the state itself were involved. These ideas were not limited to the national diaspora, but involved hopes for the 'rejuvenation' and national re-formation of the Kaiserreich itself. These ideas were more than rhetoric: in fact, the revisions of German citizenship law in 1913 can be read as a direct response to the changes of German notions of belonging under conditions of global migration. While the law of 1870 had stated that citizenship ended ten years after a citizen left the country, this stipulation was revoked in 1913: from now on, citizenship could not expire and was even transferred to descendants. This provision was a reaction to the changing conditions of mobility. During the nineteenth century, the vast majority of emigrants had moved to the United States, presumably for good, and were considered a loss to the national substance. The acquisition of colonies since 1884 was motivated, to a large extent, by a desire to provide emigrants with opportunities without severing their ties to the German nation. In the face of political support for the colonial project, it seemed mandatory to enable Germans to settle in the colonies without risking their legal status. The modification of the durability of citizenship thus was a direct outcome of the debates about global mobility. This was not merely a cosmetic legality, rendered insignificant by the dissolution of the colonial empire just shortly thereafter; rather, it had to do with central dimensions of belonging and participation. It is instructive to note that the effects of this legal adaptation survived the end of empire. When in the 1990s large groups of descendants of former emigrants (*Aussiedler*) 'returned', as it came to be called, from the Soviet Union, they still benefited from this redefinition of Germanness under colonial/global conditions.

Thirdly, the manner in which turn-of-the-century nationalism became overlaid with elements of racial thinking is difficult to explain if we limit our analysis, as is frequently the case, to the history of European thought. The chapters above have explored the extent to which processes of global migration contributed to adding a 'colonial' dimension to categories of belonging and exclusion, both at the level of concepts and stereotypes, and in actual social practice. The topos of the 'yellow peril' is an example of this mechanism. The term was much less important for German policy than it was, for example, in Australia or California. But it suggests that the German debate about exclusion was linked, in the eyes of social actors, to global processes – a connection that could even lead to anticipatory measures. Moreover, the discourse of the 'yellow peril' contributed to the reformulation of notions of belonging by the concept of 'race', providing, for example, some of the vocabulary for the ethnicisation of anti-Semitism.

Processes of global mobility were one factor that helped to anchor the idea of race in Europe. In the chapter on Polish migration, I have shown how German policy toward Poland assumed colonial traits at the same time as Germany was attempting to establish its own African colonies. In a similar vein, the chapter on the ambivalent relationship between the African colony and the European metropole argued that during the late nineteenth century, the concept of work – as an increasingly central category of social inclusion or exclusion – was also affected by transnational mobility. I suggested that the way in which the stigmatisation of those unwilling to work – or the 'work-shy' – became absolute was partly an effect of the addition of concepts of colonial (i.e. essentialised) difference to the discourse of work.

Thus, the surge in globalisation around 1900 contributed to the reconfiguration of the nation and of nationalism in the Kaiserreich. This applied not only to Germany; similar developments can be found in Belgium and Italy too, to say nothing of non-European nationalisms. Within Europe Great Britain, France and the Netherlands, because of their century-long imperial traditions, were probably influenced to a greater extent by colonial and global links than was the Kaiserreich. But in international terms, Germany was still one of the most important entities involved in late-nineteenth-century globalisation. This does not mean that Europe became unimportant to it. In political, economic and cultural terms, Europe remained the Kaiserreich's first point of reference, and its nationalism, too, focused most strongly on France as the nation's 'arch enemy', on Russia and on Great Britain's maritime imperialism. But in addition to these continuities, to the European balance of power, came explicitly global constellations: their effects are vital to explaining the 'racial' loading of German – and indeed European – nationalism. In any case, as the chapters above have shown, any attempt to isolate the Kaiserreich's European references from their global dimension is an artificial one.

One influential reading of German history sees the radicalisation of German nationalism and the adoption of biological criteria of exclusion as part of the genealogy of the Third Reich. Although it is not at the centre of my concerns here, I have suggested that this biologisation of Wilhelmine nationalism did provide the vocabulary and some of the tropes and social practices that the Nazis adopted in their criminal and genocidal policies. It is probable that without the experience of colonial racism around 1900, the history of European racism in the 1930s would have been a different one. But the racism of the Kaiserreich did not lead directly to the holocaust. Despite the eliminatory rhetoric employed, the Kaiserreich's anti-Semitism and its discrimination against the 'work-shy' did not, generally, become violent. For anti-Semitism to become a genocidal policy, national and 'racist' dichotomies had gradually to become seen in absolute terms. The First World War, in particular, and the crisis at the end of the Weimar Republic were two of the stages within which this further radicalisation took place. In addition, and this must not be ignored, the racist aspects of pre-First-World-War nationalism were, despite individual national differences, a cross-European phenomenon. Their transformation into an essentialised category that could determine life or death required additional factors that cannot be derived directly from the history of the Kaiserreich or of its globalisation.

REGIMES OF TERRITORIALISATION

Recent analyses by global historians have occasionally described the far-reaching restructuring of the world during the late nineteenth century as a process of de-territorialisation and re-territorialisation. Leaving aside the semantic field that Deleuze and Guattari associated with these terms, de-territorialisation is usually taken in somewhat vague and general terms to mean a process of dissolution of the world order regulated by nation states, in reaction to mobility and global capitalism.[13] The associative reference to *Mille plateaux* has sometimes infused the concept of de-territorialisation with a spirit of euphoria, connected to an optimistic and utopian reading of globalisation. The undermining of nation states and of a world order based on them is celebrated as an opportunity for overcoming state oppression and the historical forms of imperialism. Thus, the idea of de-territorialisation (and of globalisation) bears positive connotations, while processes of re-territorialisation and of nationalism are, as a result, seen as reactionary and repressive.[14]

But Deleuze and Guattari themselves saw things in a more nuanced manner, and I do not believe such a dichotomisation is a useful way of categorising the complex processes of the reconfiguration of the global order. It would be more useful to speak of regimes of territoriality – changing relationships between the nation and state, between population and infrastructure, between territory and global order. Changes in these regimes resulted from the dissolution of some ties, while other structures and forms of embeddedness became more important. Thus, elements of de-territorialisation have always gone hand-in-hand with processes of re-territorialisation. These structures of territoriality did not affect every region of the world in the same way, and the chronology of their changes also varied. But the

---

[13] See Deleuze and Guattari, *Thousand Plateaus*.
[14] See for example Hardt and Negri, *Empire*.

dynamic of late-nineteenth-century globalisation did mean that both the world order, and the awareness of such an order, became increasingly synchronised.[15]

In a stimulating and influential essay, Charles Maier has sketched the process of territorialisation he has observed for the western world (in particular) from about 1860 onward. For Maier, territorialisation cannot be reduced to marking and delimiting a territory; a preoccupation with borders and with expanding and monitoring them can be traced back into the early modern period. What was new to the nineteenth century was, in particular, the increased attention paid to the development of the area within the borders. This shift, too, looked back to a longer genealogy, especially the infrastructural and population policies of mercantilism. But it was only in the course of industrialisation, and the infrastructural development this involved, that the state and the government began to focus their attention on accessing and activating all of the country's human, energy and material resources. From that point onward, there was no place within the country's borders that would be free from state control. Borders, too, became more important because the state demanded more of its citizens (compulsory military service) and offered them more (social welfare). Territorialisation was concomitant with a centralisation of power and a reorganisation of the economy, with the country's integration into global capitalism as a national economy. Thus, the modern world was governed by an epistemology of separation.[16]

But Maier's interpretation is formulated as a retrospective, as a look back at bygone days. Since about 1960, he believes, different forces have been at work, forces he subsumes under the heading of globalisation. We have been witnesses, he argues, to the dissolution of the paradigm of territoriality.[17] For Maier, too, then, globalisation (from the 1960s onward) and de-territorialisation go hand-in-hand. But this view overlooks the fact that even in the early twentieth century, processes of global interconnectedness played a decisive role in the

---

[15] For an interesting attempt to utilise the concept of re- and de-territorialisation for historical research see Hevia, *English Lessons*.

[16] Maier, 'Consigning'. See also his 'Transformations'.

[17] Maier, 'Consigning', pp. 809, 823ff.

territorial order of the world. And at the same time, it seems too early to announce the end of territoriality: since 2001, if not earlier, the increased stringency of border checks, the introduction of video and biometric technology to register populations, and the use of detention camps have been speaking a different language. Territorialisation and globalisation were not consecutive phenomena. Rather than attempting to identify the beginning, or the end, of an era in which references to borders and territories were central, it seems more fruitful, therefore, to analyse the dynamics of changing regimes of territoriality.

Such a perspective would show more clearly that the world order around 1900 was characterised both by global interconnectedness and also – as a concomitant of this – by nation-state structures; that processes of de- and re-territorialisation were intricately interweaved. The increased focus placed on the nation and on national categories was not just a form of resistance to linkage and interconnectedness, was not merely an expression of xenophobia in the face of a perceived threat posed by seemingly unrestricted mobility, but was itself part of a fundamental process of restructuring at a global scale.

DE- AND RE-TERRITORIALISATION AROUND 1900 AS NATIONALISATION

Late-nineteenth and early-twentieth-century globalisation created a number of structural changes that in many regions (though not everywhere) had a long-lasting effect on relationships between states, their inhabitants and their institutions. It would thus be interesting to explore in conclusion the extent to which investigating regimes of territoriality might be a useful addition to the historiography of the nation and of the nation state. To do so, it would be necessary to distinguish between the different periods in which the idea of the nation changed form. One of these was the consolidation (or occasionally creation) of state rule during the course of the Napoleonic wars, both in Europe and in Latin America. Michael Geyer and Charles Bright identify a second phase between 1840 and 1860, when, for the first time, regional crises in Europe and Asia become linked. These links developed in the context of the territorialisation of power. At the same time, they allowed global regulatory capacities to be created – especially for France and Great Britain; the efforts of Germany, Japan and the United States to achieve autonomy were focused on internal mobilisation.[18] The reconfiguration of the idea of the nation around 1900 in the context of high imperialism and globalisation – the subject of this book – could thus be seen as the third nineteenth-century phase of consolidation of national territorialisation.

Such an attempt would have to identify different levels for the complex relationship between processes of globalisation and changes in the territorial manifestation of the nation. These levels will be outlined here in brief. *Firstly*, the globalisation of nationalism discussed above changed the territorial imagination. For example, the Indian national movement employed a 'mental map' that included 'British India' as well as the states of the independent princes and maharajas; Okinawa, which for centuries had paid tributes both to the Tokugawa-Shoguns and to the Qing Emperor, became a bone of contention and the object of the claims of exclusivity for both Chinese and Japanese nationalisms; the formation of the Siamese nation began, or so Thongchai Winichakul has argued, with cartographic representations, with 'mapping Siam'. These national spaces were to be uniform, homogeneous and 'pure', and for that reason, ethnic enclaves and minorities became a particular problem, whether these were the Chinese in Australia, the United States and Malaya, or the Sorbs and Poles in the Kaiserreich.

But *secondly*, the territorial traces left by globalisation were more than a thing of the imagination. The expansion of infrastructure so instrumental to the global economy, mobility and *Weltpolitik* embedded itself deeply in national landscapes: by the turn of the century railway lines linked the interior of Argentina, Chile and South Africa with the coastal cities, or even, like the South Manchurian Railway, caused actual colonial wars; canals divided countries and brought previously distant regions closer together, as in Panama and Egypt, or, in Germany, in the form of the Kaiser Wilhelm Canal. The expansion of ports, in Europe (for transatlantic trade, migration

---

[18] Geyer and Bright, 'World History'.

or the Reich postal steamers) as in the treaty ports of the informal colonies, changed the coastlines; in China, these became dotted with clock towers and lighthouses and were extended to include three-mile limits. Even the debates about whether German law applied to disputes on German ships between Indian sailors and Chinese boilermen are evidence of how national sovereignty had become geographically displaced.

Thirdly, the increase in interaction and entanglement formed part of the expansion of capitalism around the world, which also contributed to the reorganisation of state boundaries. Customs barriers and protective tariffs, which had already been of importance in the mid century, closed borders again from the 1880s onward, while illegal transfers and smuggling created new routes and new markets. The treaty ports in the Ottoman empire, in Japan and along the Chinese coast were special trade zones and were themselves separated from their hinterlands. While the USA and the European states, with few exceptions, used protectionist policies to reinforce their borders, free trade was established outside Europe through force. Japan was 'opened', only to enforce itself a policy of 'opening' on Korea a short time later; all the major powers were involved in wars in China to ensure that doors to trade were kept open.

High imperialism was a central characteristic of turn-of-the-century globalisation, and the restructuring of the national order was shaped, *fourthly*, by colonialism. In Africa, some borders between states that later found themselves faced with the task of becoming nations were literally 'drawn' by hand on a map; differences between local communities were reified by state boundaries. But the colonial experience was not limited to the colonised; it 'came back' and influenced ideas about the nation 'at home'. The loading of European nationalism with biological and racial categories was part of this process; debates about the status in constitutional law of overseas 'New Germany', the naturalisation of 'natives' and bans on 'mixed marriages' are evidence of a need to redefine the location of the nation in the context of colonial globality.

Regions outside Europe not directly affected by the scramble for colonies did not remain outside this colonial globality. Competition for spheres of influences, favourable terms and trade privileges led to the establishment of numerous informal empires, in South America, in China and in the Ottoman empire. Typical of these links were exterritoriality and foreigner settlements with their own jurisdiction; in the Ottoman empire, the protection of Roman Catholics and Orthodox Christians was institutionalised by France and the Tsars in the 'capitulations'. Land concessions were also typical features – an example is the Baghdad Railway – as were limits on state authority: an example was the foreign administration of Ottoman debts in Constantinople (the Ottoman Public Debt) or, from 1863 onwards, Robert Hart's Imperial Chinese Maritime Customs Service, which by the turn of the century had some 12,000 employees. Such 'synarchic' institutions were an expression of the changed scope (or porosity) of the nation state in the age of informal financial imperialism.

Fifthly, these complex relationships of delimitation and penetration found legal form in the institution of international law, which provided legal legitimacy for the colonial world order. In the Kaiserreich, constitutional law experts debated the reasons for legitimate acquisition of territory; along with cession and 'aggradation' (*Anschwemmung*) these included occupation, annexation or 'taking possession' (*Ersitzung*). International law, which was promulgated by translations of important manuals such as Henry Wheaton's *Elements of International Law* awarded sovereignty only to communities that presented themselves as 'civilised' nations. In this way, the formatting of the world into nation states and the annexation of existing territorial orders in the name of 'civilisation' found legal form. This translation of state intercourse into legal terms also led to the global establishment of the institutions of modern diplomacy, and the eradication of earlier forms, such as kowtowing to the Chinese emperor. Here, too, changed ideas about the extent of national interests became evident: this applied to the consulates that Germany set up in Brazil and in the United States, to the embassies and to the diplomatic quarters where local law did not apply, and to the diplomatic missions that the Qing dynasty began to open in Europe and the USA.

The increase in diplomatic links, and this is a *sixth* dimension of how the idea of the nation was reconfigured, was also a consequence of the increase in cross-border mobility, the most visible manifestation of contemporary globalisation. This had an ambivalent effect on contemporary ways of understanding the re-territorialisation of the nation: on the one hand, mobility was seen as invasion, as a penetration of the national space, and states reacted to this with technologies of stabilisation or even of demobilisation. In the decades before 1914, borders were closed and the laws on asylum and immigration were tightened around the world, most notably in Australia and the USA. Equally, the British 'Aliens Act' of 1905 (which was strengthened after the war) and attempts by the colonial powers to limit the movement of their subjects were part of a process that reduced freedom of movement and that was reflected not only in legal texts, but also in physical changes to national boundaries (or indeed within the national territory, as with the Ruhleben train station in Berlin, which was used as a quarantine station for eastern Europeans travelling through Germany en route to America). The areas of investigation for the new identificatory techniques – bertillonage and fingerprints – that became established to control mobility during this era were dotted along national boundaries in Argentina just as in France or Ellis Island.

But from the authorities' point of view, mobility involved emigration as well as immigration. Laws and bans applied to outward movements, too – like the *von Heydtsche Reskript*, bans on emigration by the Qing court, and laws on emigration passed in Italy, Sweden and Japan. However, more important for the reconceptualisation of nationality were the diaspora communities, whose number, extent and importance increased dramatically toward the end of the nineteenth century. The formation of a Chinese nation is almost impossible to conceive without taking the role of the overseas Chinese into account; Indian migrants in eastern and southern Africa, and Japanese emigrants in Hawaii and California also contributed to nationalisation – both among the migrants themselves, and in the home countries they had left behind.

JEUX D'ÉCHELLES

The reconfiguration of territoriality around 1900 that took place in the context of globalisation was fundamentally linked to the nation state, and the transfers and relationships of exchange – from most-favoured-nation treatment for individual economies and diplomatic contacts to the World Exhibitions and Olympic Games – followed the paradigm of inter-nationality. This context has been the subject of the chapters above. But any more comprehensive theory of the regime of territoriality would have to take into account the fact that the inter-national was not the only level of importance. The nation state was a privileged – but by no means the only – framework for territorial imagination, social practice and policy. It was embedded in a network of corresponding levels that, fundamentally, range from the bodies of individual human beings, which, at a time of increased mobility, increasingly became the object of state interference and inscription, to the utopias of a global state.[19] But these levels were not a rigid matrix; rather, they were mutually constituted through social practices, as Rebecca Karl has shown in the case of Qing China.[20]

In the era under discussion, two levels that have scarcely been mentioned above do deserve particular attention. Firstly, the establishment of nation states was usually concomitant with the production and institutionalisation of the local. Provinces and regions, and the loyalties owed to them, were partly in competition with the project of the 'inner formation' of the nation state and of the infrastructural permeation of the nation's territory. At the same time, local and national affiliations were also compatible in many respects. The 'invention of regions', the institutionalisation of regional history and the popularity of the idea of *Heimat* went hand-in-hand with the creation of nation states, national economies and schemes of social policy. This was a reciprocal process – *Heimat* was also a response to the hegemony of the national but, at the same time, the nation could sometimes be an

[19] On the transformation of individual identity in the context of turn-of-the-century globalisation see Calhoun, 'Nationalism'. On the different levels of reference for identity, see Robertson, *Globalization*, esp. pp. 25–31.

[20] See Karl, 'Creating Asia'.

extension of regional allegiances, as Alon Confino has described for Germany – the 'nation as a local metaphor'.[21] It would be useful to investigate in more detail how globalisation around 1900 not only caused the restructuring of the nation, but also left its traces at the level of the local, and indeed was simultaneously shaped by local developments. This process, discussed in the literature under the rubric of 'glocalisation', could provide an interesting point of departure for a better understanding of the political dynamics of the Kaiserreich.[22]

A similarly ambivalent relationship – a competing yet symbiotic project – characterises the relationship between nations and supranational concepts, which were becoming increasingly important around 1900. The global emergence of a system of nation states and the resultant dissolution or undermining of large empires, as in Austria-Hungary, the Ottoman empire and China, was one of the fundamental processes taking place at the end of the nineteenth century. But from the 1890s onwards, roughly, there was also discussion about political utopias that promised to transcend the nation-based world order. The pan-Islamic movement, for example, hoped to unite all Muslims politically under the aegis of the caliph; supporters of pan-Asianism, most frequently in Japan but also in Annam and India, argued for a kind of Asian Monroe doctrine. The Monroe doctrine of 1823 had become a relevant point of reference for American foreign policy only toward the end of the century, and it also became important for discussions within Europe. The doctrine, and the American model in general, were central to debates about the era to come, in which, many political commentators believed, a small number of global empires would be created by trade blocs, each closed to the others. Germany's plans for *Mitteleuropa*, which gained political importance during the First

[21] Confino, *Nation*. For Germany see also Applegate, *Nation of Provincials*; Green, *Fatherlands*; Umbach, *German Federalism*; Kunz, *Verortete Geschichte*; Weichlein, *Nation*; Lekan, *Imagining the Nation*; and Hardtwig, 'Nation–Region–Stadt'. For Europe, see Applegate, 'Europe'. For eastern Asia, see Wigen, 'Culture'; her *Making*; and Ryûichi, *Furusato*.

[22] On the theoretical debate, see for example Appadurai, *Modernity*, pp. 178–99; Borja and Castells, *Local & Global*; Beauregard, 'Theorizing'; and Robertson, 'Glokalisierung'.

World War, can also be read as an attempt to react to American competition with the foundation of a 'United States of Europe' dominated by Germany. It is obvious that these continental aspirations were a reaction to the challenges posed by contemporary globalisation.

It would be useful to investigate the relationships between these different dimensions of territorial order – dimensions that, while they were in competition, also interacted with each other. The reordering of the national during the period from approximately 1880 to the outbreak of the First World War was also located within these complementary levels of global reconfiguration. This resulted in a change in the form of the nation state, as was also noticed by some contemporaries. The historian Karl Lamprecht, a close friend of the geographer Friedrich Ratzel and, as a member of the Pan-German League, closely involved in the debate about colonial policy, predicted that 'the modern state [will] not at all display the unity of the state of the first half of the nineteenth century and that its powers will have at their disposal an almost unlimited number of modifications of expression and realisation'.[23]

This interpretation was more than just a reaction to emigration and to the creation of German settlements outside the physical borders of the Reich, though such a reaction was common among Lamprecht's fellow Pan-Germans. The demand for an expansion of the nation's scope – 'As far as the German tongue reaches' – corresponded to the logic of *völkisch* nationalism. The definition of the nation as a linguistic and cultural unit that, around 1900, was beginning to challenge the still dominant statist view of the nation, utilised a distinction between the 'residential area' and the 'power area' of a state. 'There is a greater Germany', the Pan-German press argued: 'one that extends far beyond the area of the Reich, flowing apart politically, and completely unlimited in space, but held together by the bonds of the *Volksgemeinschaft*'.[24]

Although traces of this *völkisch* nationalism can be found in Lamprecht's writings, his vision 'of a national society that is no longer limited to the soil' went beyond it. Lamprecht outlined a model of five

---

[23] Lamprecht, *Vergangenheit*, pp. 536ff.   [24] Drews, 'Neue Wege', p. 746.

different complementary forms of territorialisation of the nation. At the centre was the narrowly defined nation state, the 'core of modern Germany' (*Deutschtum*). Around it were grouped, first, a 'ring of other political bodies' and then, as the next level of manifestation of the nation, the German settlements overseas, overseas Germandom. The fourth level in his system was made up of the 'atmospheres of the German industrial … capital investment', and the whole was rounded off with 'clouds of economic exports and scientific and cultural and literary ideas'.[25] The change in the form of the nation state, which Lamprecht described as a 'tentacle state', was thus represented as the result of a double process of expansion. It fused the *völkisch* utopias of *Lebensraum* with the *Weltpolitik* ambitions of the bourgeoisie and the complex ways in which capitalism eroded boundaries.

Inquiring about the change in regimes of territoriality could be a useful starting-point for investigating the break that the globalisation of the period 1880–1914 marks in a (global) history of the nation, nationalism and nation states. Doing so could provide a complement to the dominant dichotomisation of 'good' and 'bad' nationalism, of emancipation and aggression, and could also help to place the 'radicalisation' of nationalism in context. At the same time, such a perspective would suggest that the spatial dimension of nationalisation and the development of nation states must be taken into account. While the history of nations and nationalism is often slotted into a temporal pattern of development, paying attention to processes of territorialisation allows us also to take heed of the synchronicity of processes of nationalisation. There is no doubt that this reconfiguration of the nation was a global event, even if it did not affect every part of the globe to the same extent and, in particular, did not manifest itself everywhere in the same way.

RESCUING HISTORY FROM THE NATION?

Around 1900, the nation was the hegemonial paradigm for social and historical imagination. By this I mean two things. Firstly, nationalism

[25] Lamprecht, *Vergangenheit*, p. 592.

was becoming or had already become the ubiquitous framework of interpretation and political discourse. But secondly, the nation-based world order involved the consolidation of the internalist paradigm of historical knowledge. The dominance of national categories reinforced a way of reading social development essentially as the result of internal dynamics. This axiom of national-history interpretation became all-pervasive in the course of the globalisation of the modern discipline of history. By the end of the nineteenth century, history had been institutionalised in the academy as national history – as in Germany, France, the USA and Japan. But even where this was not yet the case (for example, in India), thinking in national categories went hand-in-hand with a methodological nationalism. The few attempts to overcome national history by deploying a global-history perspective met with strong resistance (as, for example, did Karl Lamprecht's work). Incidentally, Lamprecht himself, when explaining the reasons for the change in form of the nation around 1900, did not refer to the role of influences, transfers or systemic contexts; even this proponent of a 'universal history' was convinced that '[i]n reality, all these upheavals are the most profound product of inner development'.[26] It is almost impossible to find a better illustration of how hegemonial the internalist methodology had become.

These two aspects of the paradigm of national history came together in the concept of 'German work', a national topos that was combined with the idea of something coming 'from within', 'of its own accord'. This is particularly obvious in Max Weber's discussions of the way ideas about work acted as a catalyst for development. In the form of modernisation theory, this figure of thought has remained highly influential right up to the present and has left a long-lasting imprint on historiography. Anyone wishing today to join in an attempt to dissolve or overcome the nation as the sole and given category of analysis is usually occupied, most of the time, in dealing with this inheritance, that of Weber and his interpreters.

One of the most influential and inspiring attempts to 'liberate' history from the grasp of the paradigm of national history has been

---

[26] *Ibid.*, p. 612.

formulated by Prasenjit Duara. Drawing on the examples of India and China, Duara criticises a linear, teleological historiography that defines the nation in terms of the oppositions of tradition–modern, hierarchy–equality or empire–nation. He sees this as a Hegelian narrative that was forced by an imperialist 'West' onto other parts of the world during the course of the nineteenth century. He sees the category of the nation as a repressive instrument of European universalism and identifies its discursive structures as a legitimating basis for the colonial world order. He suggests a number of strategies for undermining these unequal power relationships and hierarchies, and proposes to place more emphasis on local events and the 'disorder' of particular histories than on linear national perspectives.[27]

But, and this is something Duara has in common with some others who also argue against the national-history paradigm, his criticism remains for the most part limited to an argument about discourse and narrative. The dominance of national parameters is seen primarily as a question of representation. But if analysis remains focused on a historiographical criticism of universalist categories, there is a danger that the historical process that rendered these categories predominant in the first place may be sidelined. In other words, rejecting the universalism of the national must not lead us to ignore the historical ubiquity of the nation around 1900 as a cognitive dimension and a space for social practice. Instead of lifting the ideological (or narrative) veil and revealing thinking in terms of nation states to be a form of 'false consciousness', it is more important to analyse the constitution (and reconfiguration) of a national world order in terms of the complex, power-laden and uneven processes for which, around 1900, mobility, colonialism and the specific form of capitalism were the central parameters.[28] Otherwise there would be a danger that pleas for transnationality would merely construct a genealogy for present-day globalisation, one that would make transnational capitalism and the

---

[27] See Duara, *Rescuing History*, esp. pp. 3–50.

[28] For arguments along similar lines, see Dirlik, *Global Modernity*; Geyer, 'Deutschland und Japan'; Karl, *Staging the World*, esp. pp. 17–25; and Goswami, 'Swadeshi'. See also the informative discussion in Hill, *National History*.

development of new empires seem a natural event. Using the perspective of global history thus does not imply abandoning the category of the nation completely for analysing modern history. Admittedly, the nation has served for too long as a *causa prima*, as the final and seemingly autonomous reason, as the cause of all variations in development and difference. What has still to be undertaken is an analysis of national history in a global context, in which the nation is not the starting-point of the investigation but rather the object to be explained within a global context: that is, the *explanandum*.

Bibliography

Abel, Curt, *Chinesen in Deutschland? Eine zeitgemäße Betrachtung*, Berlin, 1890.

Achilles, Fritz W., 'Die Infrastruktur des Reiches', in Volker Plagemann (ed.), *Übersee: Seefahrt und Seemacht im deutschen Kaiserreich*, Munich, 1988, pp. 53–57.

Acker, Amandus, 'Die Erziehung der Eingeborenen zur Arbeit in Deutsch-Ostafrika', *Jahrbuch über die deutschen Kolonien* 1 (1908), 117–24.

Ackerknecht, Erwin H., 'Anticontagionism between 1821 and 1867', *Bulletin of the History of Medicine* 22 (1948), 562–93.

Adas, Michael, 'Contested Hegemony: The Great War and the Afro-Asian Assault on the Civilizing Mission Ideology', *Journal of World History* 15 (2004), 31–64.

Adeleke, Tunde, *UnAfrican Americans: Nineteenth-Century Black Nationalists and the Civilizing Mission*, Lexington, 1988.

Aereboe, Friedrich, *Die ländliche Arbeiterfrage nach dem Kriege*, Berlin, 1918.

Alatas, Syed H., *The Myth of the Lazy Native: A Study of the Image of the Malayas, Filipinos and Javanese from the 16th to the 20th Century and Its Function in the Ideology of Colonial Capitalism*, London, 1977.

Albertini, Rudolf von, *Europäische Kolonialherrschaft 1880–1914*, Zürich, 1987.

Albrecht, Christoph V., *Geopolitik und Geschichtsphilosophie 1748–1798*, Berlin, 1998.

Albrow, Martin, 'Globalization, Knowledge and Society', in Albrow and Elizabeth King (eds.), *Globalization, Knowledge and Society*, London, 1990, pp. 3–13.

Aldenhoff-Hübinger, Rita, *Agrarpolitik und Protektionismus: Deutschland und Frankreich im Vergleich, 1879–1914*, Göttingen, 2002.

Aldrich, Robert, *Greater France: A History of French Overseas Expansion*, New York, 1996.

Alldeutscher Verband, *Zwanzig Jahre alldeutscher Arbeit und Kämpfe*, Berlin, 1910.

Altena, Thorsten, *'Ein Häuflein Christen mitten in der Heidenwelt des dunklen Erdteils': Zum Selbst- und Fremdverständnis protestantischer Missionare im kolonialen Afrika 1884–1918*, Münster, 2003.

Altenbockum, Jasper von, *Wilhelm Heinrich Riehl 1823–1897: Sozialwissenschaft zwischen Kulturgeschichte und Ethnographie*, Cologne, 1994.

Altenhofen, Cléo Vilson, *Hunsrückisch in Rio Grande do Sul: Ein Beitrag zur Beschreibung einer deutschbrasilianischen Dialektvarietät im Kontakt mit dem Portugiesischen*, Stuttgart, 1996.

Alter, Peter, Peter Berghoff and Claus-Ekkehard Bärsch (eds.), *Die Konstruktion der Nation gegen die Juden*, Munich, 1999.

Amenda, Lars, *Fremde–Hafen–Stadt: Chinesische Migration und ihre Wahrnehmung in Hamburg, 1897–1972*, Hamburg, 2006.

'Fremd-Wahrnehmung und Eigen-Sinn: Das "Chinesenviertel" und chinesische Migration in Hamburg, 1910–1960', in Angelika Eder (ed.), *'Wir sind auch da!': Das Leben von und mit Migranten in europäischen Großstädten*, Hamburg, 2003, pp. 73–94.

'Vorstellungen und Nachforschungen: Chinesische Seeleute, deutsche Frauen und bremische Behörden während des Ersten Weltkrieges', in Peter Kuckuk (ed.), *Passagen nach Fernost: Menschen zwischen Bremen und Ostasien*, Bremen, 2004, pp. 184–203.

Anderson, Benedict, *Imagined Communities*, London, 1983.

Anderson, Kay J., *Vancouver's Chinatown: Racial Discourse in Canada 1875–1980*, Bowker, 1995.

Ando, Junko, *Die Entstehung der Meiji-Verfassung: Zur Rolle des deutschen Konstitutionalismus im modernen japanischen Staatswesen*, Munich, 2000.

Anon., 'Die Deutschen in Brasilien', *Das Auswandererproblem* 3 (1912), pp. 3–5.

Die deutschen Interessen in Argentinien, Chile, Bolivien und Peru: Eine der wichtigsten Fragen für Deutschlands Zukunft, Berlin, 1911.

Die polnische Gefahr: Seiner Exzellenz dem Königlich Preußischen Staatsminister a. D. Herrn Dr. v. Miquel aus Verehrung gewidmet vom Verfasser, Leipzig, 1901.

'Überseeische Arbeiter-Kolonien', *Die Arbeiterkolonie* 2 (1885), 133–36.

Ansprenger, Franz, 'Schulpolitik in Deutsch-Ostafrika', in Peter Heine and Ulrich van der Heyden (eds.), *Studien zur Geschichte des deutschen Kolonialismus in Afrika*, Pfaffenweiler, 1995, pp. 43–58.

Anter, Andreas, *Max Webers Theorie des modernen Staates: Herkunft, Struktur und Bedeutung*, Berlin, 1995.

Anton, G. K., 'Die Bedeutung von Zwang und Freiheit: Plantagen- und Volkskulturen für die koloniale Arbeiterfrage', *Koloniale Rundschau* 6 (1914), 196–218.

Appadurai, Arjun, 'Disjuncture and Difference in the Global Cultural Economy', *Public Culture* 2:2 (1990), 1–24.

Modernity at Large: Cultural Dimensions of Globalization, Minneapolis, 1996.

Applegate, Celia, 'A Europe of Regions: Reflections on the Historiography of Sub-National Places in Modern Times', *American Historical Review* 104 (1999), 1157–82.

A Nation of Provincials, Berkeley, 1990.

Arendt, Hannah, *Elemente und Ursprünge totaler Herrschaft*, Frankfurt, 1955.

Arrighi, Giovanni, *The Long Twentieth Century: Money, Power, and the Origins of Our Times*, London, 1994.

Aschheim, Steven E., *Brothers and Strangers: The East European Jew in German and German-Jewish Consciousness, 1800–1923*, Madison, 1982.

Assmann, Aleida, *Arbeit am nationalen Gedächtnis: Eine kurze Geschichte der deutschen Bildungsidee*, Frankfurt, 1993.

Aveni, Anthony, *Empires of Time: Calendars, Clocks, and Cultures*, London, 1990.

Ayaß, Wolfgang, *Das Arbeitshaus Breitenau: Bettler, Landstreicher, Prostituierte, Zuhälter und Fürsorgeempfänger in der Korrektions- und Landarmenanstalt Breitenau (1874–1949)*, Kassel, 1992.

'Asoziale' im Nationalsozialismus, Stuttgart, 1995.

'"Ein Gebot der nationalen Arbeitsdisziplin": Die Aktion "Arbeitsscheu Reich" 1938', *Beiträge zur nationalsozialistischen Gesundheits- und Sozialpolitik* 6 (1988), 43–74.

'Gemeinschaftsfremde': Quellen zur Verfolgung von 'Asozialen' 1933–1945, Koblenz, 1998.

'Die Wandererfürsorge im Nationalsozialismus', in Jürgen Scheffler (ed.), *Bürger und Bettler: Materialien und Dokumente zur Geschichte der Nichtseßhaftenhilfe in der Diakonie*, 2 vols., Vol. 1, Bielefeld, 1987, pp. 275–77.

Aydin, Cemil, 'The Conception of "Civilization" and "Science" in the Journals of Meçmua-i Funun (1862–1867) and Meçmua-i Ulum (1880–1882)', M.A. thesis, Istanbul University, 1995.

The Politics of Anti-Westernism in Asia: Visions of World Order in Pan-Islamic and Pan-Asian Thought (1882–1945), New York, 2007.

Bachmann-Medick, Doris (ed.), *Übersetzung als Repräsentation fremder Kulturen*, Berlin, 1997.

Bade, Klaus J., 'Arbeitsmarkt, Ausländerbeschäftigung und Sicherheitspolitik: Auslandsrekrutierung und Inlandsvermittlung ausländischer Arbeitskräfte in Preußen vor dem Ersten Weltkrieg', in Jochen Oltmer (ed.), *Migration steuern und verwalten: Deutschland vom späten 19. Jahrhundert bis zur Gegenwart*, Göttingen, 2003, pp. 59–84.

'"Billig und willig": die "ausländischen Wanderarbeiter" im kaiserlichen Deutschland', in Bade (ed.), *Deutsche im Ausland: Fremde in Deutschland. Migration in Geschichte und Gegenwart*, Munich, 1992, pp. 311–24.

(ed.), *Deutsche im Ausland-Fremde in Deutschland. Migration in Geschichte und Gegenwart*, Munich, 1992.

'Die deutsche überseeische Massenauswanderung im 19. und frühen 20. Jahrhundert: Bestimmungsfaktoren und Entwicklungsbedingungen', in Bade (ed.), *Auswanderer–Wanderarbeiter–Gastarbeiter*, Ostfildern, 1984, pp. 259–99.

Europa in Bewegung: Migration vom späten 18. Jahrhundert bis zur Gegenwart, Munich, 2000.

Friedrich Fabri und der Imperialismus in der Bismarckzeit: Revolution– Depression–Expansion, Erlangen, 1975.

(ed.), *Imperialismus und Kolonialmission: Kaiserliches Deutschland und koloniales Imperium*, Wiesbaden, 1982.

'"Kulturkampf" auf dem Arbeitsmarkt: Bismarcks "Polenpolitik" 1885– 1890', in Otto Pflanze (ed.), *Innenpolitische Probleme des Bismarck-Reiches*, Munich, 1983, pp. 121–42.

'Massenwanderung und Arbeitsmarkt im deutschen Nordosten von 1880 bis zum Ersten Weltkrieg: Überseeische Auswanderung, interne Abwanderung und kontinentale Zuwanderung', *Archiv für Sozialgeschichte* 20 (1980), 265–325.

'Politik und Ökonomie der Ausländerbeschäftigung im preußischen Osten 1885–1914: Die Internationalisierung des Arbeitsmarkts im "Rahmen der preußischen Abwehrpolitik"', in Hans-Jürgen Puhle and Hans-Ulrich Wehler (eds.), *Preußen im Rückblick*, Göttingen, 1980, pp. 273–99.

'"Preußengänger" und "Abwehrpolitik": Ausländerbeschäftigun, Ausländerpolitik und Ausländerkontrolle auf dem Arbeitsmarkt in Preußen vor dem Ersten Weltkrieg', *Archiv für Sozialgeschichte* 24 (1984), 91–162.

'Transnationale Migration und Arbeitsmarkt im Kaiserreich: Vom Agrarstaat mit starker Industrie zum Industriestaat mit starker agrarischer Basis', in Toni Pierenkemper and Richard H. Tilly (eds.), *Historische Arbeitsmarktforschung: Entstehung, Entwicklung und Probleme der Vermarktung von Arbeitskraft*, Göttingen, 1982, pp. 182–211.

Vom Auswanderungsland zum Einwanderungsland? Bevölkerung, Wirtschaft und Wanderung in Deutschland 1880–1980, Berlin, 1983.

Badenberg, Nana, 'Ansichten des Tropenwaldes: Alexander von Humboldt und die Inszenierung exotischer Landschaft im 19. Jahrhundert', in Michael Flitner (ed.), *Der deutsche Tropenwald: Bilder, Mythen, Politik*, Frankfurt, 2000, pp. 148–73.

Baier, Roland, *Der deutsche Osten als soziale Frage: Eine Studie zur preußischen und deutschen Siedlungs- und Polenpolitik in den Ostprovinzen während des Kaiserreichs und der Weimarer Republik*, Cologne, 1980.

Bailey, Paul, 'The Chinese Work-Study Movement in France', *China Quarterly* 115 (1988), 441–61.

'From Shandong to the Somme: Chinese Indentured Labour in France during World War I', in A. Kershen (ed.), *Language, Labour and Migration*, Aldershot, 2000, pp. 179–96.

Bairoch, Paul, 'Globalization Myths and Realities: One Century of External Trade and Foreign Investment', in Robert Boyer (ed.), *States against Markets: The Limits of Globalization*, London, 1996, pp. 173–92.

Balibar, Etienne, 'Is There a "Neo-Racism"?', in Balibar and Immanuel Wallerstein (eds.), *Race, Nation, Class: Ambiguous Identities*, London, 1991, pp. 17–28.

'The Nation Form', in Balibar and Immanuel Wallerstein (eds.), *Race, Nation, Class: Ambiguous Identities*, London, 1991, pp. 86–106.

Balibar, Etienne and Immanuel Wallerstein (eds.), *Race, Nation, Class: Ambiguous Identities*, London, 1991.

Balzer, Brigitte, *Die preußische Polenpolitik 1894–1908 und die Haltung der deutschen konservativen und liberalen Parteien (unter besonderer Berücksichtigung der Provinz Posen)*, Frankfurt, 1990.

Barber, Benjamin, *Jihad vs. McWorld*, New York, 1995.

Barfuß, Karl Marten, *'Gastarbeiter' in Nordwestdeutschland 1884–1918*, Bremen, 1986.

Barkai, Avraham, 'Judentum, Juden und Kapitalismus: Ökonomische Vorstellungen von Max Weber und Werner Sombart', *Menora: Jahrbuch für deutsch-jüdische Geschichte* 5 (1994), 25–38.

Barkin, Kenneth D., *The Controversy over German Industrialization 1890–1902*, Chicago, 1970.

Barlösius, Eva, *Naturgemäße Lebensführung: Zur Geschichte der Lebensreform um die Jahrhundertwende*, Frankfurt, 1997.

Barlow, Tani E. (ed.), *Formations of Colonial Modernity in East Asia*, Durham, NC, 1997.

Baron, Ava (ed.), *Work Engendered: Toward a New History of American Labor*, Ithaca, NY, 1991.

Barraclough, Geoffrey, *An Introduction to Contemporary History*, Harmondsworth, 1967.

Barth, Boris, *Die deutsche Hochfinanz und die Imperialismen: Banken und Außenpolitik vor 1914*, Stuttgart, 1995.

Barth, Boris and Jürgen Osterhammel (eds.), *Zivilisierungsmissionen: Imperiale Weltverbesserung seit dem 18. Jahrhundert*, Constance, 2005.

Barth, Gunther, *Bitter Strength: A History of the Chinese in the United States*, 1850–1870, Cambridge, MA, 1964.

Basch, Linda, Cristina Blanc-Szanton and Nina Glick Schiller (eds.), *Nations Unbound: Transnational Projects, Postcolonial Predicaments and Deterritorialized Nation-States*, New York, 1994.

Bashford, Alison (ed.), *Medicine at the Border: Disease, Globalization and Security, 1850 to the Present*, London, 2006.

Basler, Werner, *Deutschlands Annexionspolitik in Polen und im Baltikum 1914–1918*, Berlin, 1962.

Bassin, Mark, 'Russia between Europe and Asia: The Ideological Construction of Geography', *Slavic Review* 50 (1991), 1–17.

Bastid-Bruguière, Marianne, 'Currents of Social Change', in Denis Twitchett and John K. Fairbank (eds.), *The Cambridge History of China*, 15 vols., Vol. 11, Cambridge, 1980, pp. 535–602.

Bauer, Adalbert, 'Der Arbeitszwang in Deutsch-Ostafrika', juridical dissertation, University of Würzburg, 1919.

Bauman, Zygmunt, *Globalization: The Human Consequences*, New York, 1998.

Baumgart, Winfried, *Deutschland im Zeitalter des Imperialismus 1890–1914: Grundkräfte, Thesen und Strukturen*, Stuttgart, 1982.

Bausinger, Hermann (ed.), *Reisekultur*, Munich, 1991.

Bayart, Jean-François, *Le Gouvernement du monde: Une critique politique de la globalisation*, Paris, 2004.

Bayly, C. A., *The Birth of the Modern World, 1780–1914*, Oxford, 2004.

Beasley, William G., *Japanese Imperialism 1894–1945*, Oxford, 1987.

Beauregard, Robert A., 'Theorizing the Global-Local Connection', in Paul L. Knox and Peter J. Taylor (eds.), *World Cities in a World System*, Cambridge, 1995, pp. 232–48.

Bebel, August, *Für und wider die Commune: Disputation zwischen den Herren Bebel und Sparig in der 'Tonhalle' zu Leipzig*, Leipzig, 1876.

Bechtel, Delphine, Dominique Bourel and Jacques Le Rider, *Max Nordau (1849–1923): Critique de la dégénérescence, médiateur franco-allemand, père fondateur du sionisme*, Paris, 1996.

Beck, Hanno, *Carl Ritter: Genius der Geographie*, Berlin, 1979.

Beck, Ulrich, *Was ist Globalisierung?*, Frankfurt, 1997.

Becker, Frank, 'Kolonialherrschaft, Rassentrennung und Mission in Deutsch-Südwestafrika', in Becker, Thomas Großbölting, Armin Owzar and Rudolf Schlögl (eds.), *Politische Gewalt in der Moderne*, Münster, 2003, pp. 133–64.

Becker, Otto, *Die Regelung des ausländischen Arbeiterwesens in Deutschland, unter besonderer Berücksichtigung der Anwerbung und Vermittlung*, Berlin, 1918.

Becker, Peter, *Verderbnis und Entartung: Eine Geschichte der Kriminologie des 19. Jahrhunderts als Diskurs und Praxis*, Göttingen, 2002.

Beckert, Sven, 'Von Tuskegee nach Togo: Das Problem der Freiheit im Reich der Baumwolle', *Geschichte und Gesellschaft* 31 (2005), 505–45.

Behrendt, Walter Curt, *Der Kampf um den Stil im Kunstgewerbe und in der Architektur*, Stuttgart, 1920.

Belgum, Kirsten, *Popularizing the Nation: Audience, Representation, and the Production of Identity in* Die Gartenlaube, *1853–1900*, Lincoln, NE, 1998.

Benad, Matthias (ed.), *Bethels Mission. Beiträge zur Geschichte der von Bodelschwinghschen Anstalten Bethel*, 3 vol., Bielefeld, 2001–2003.

Benad, Matthias and Hans-Walter Schmuhl (eds.), *Bethel–Eckardtsheim: Von der Gründung der ersten deutschen Arbeiterkolonie bis zur Auflösung als Teilanstalt (1882–2001)*, Stuttgart, 2006.

Bender, Thomas, *A Nation among Nations: America's Place in World History*, New York, 2006.

(ed.), *Rethinking American History in a Global Age*, Berkeley, 2002.

Benignus, Siegfried, *Deutsche Kraft in Südamerika: Historisch-wirtschaftliche Studie von der Konquista bis zur Gegenwart*, Berlin, 1917.

Bennett, Neville, 'Bitter Fruit: Japanese Migration and Anglo-Saxon Obstacles, 1890–1924', *Transactions of the Asiatic Society of Japan* 8 (1993), 67–83.

Benz, Wolfgang and Werner Bergmann (eds.), *Vorurteil und Völkermord: Entwicklungslinien des Antisemitismus*, Freiburg, 1997.

Berding, Helmut, *Moderner Antisemitismus in Deutschland*, Stuttgart, 1988.

Berg, Ludwig, *Die katholische Heidenmission als Kulturträger*, 2 vols., Vol. I, Aachen, 1923.

Berger, Klaus, *Japonismus in der westlichen Malerei 1860–1920*, Munich, 1980.

Berghahn, Volker, *Der Tirpitz-Plan*, Düsseldorf, 1971.

Berghoff, Hartmut, '"Dem Ziele der Menschheit entgegen": Die Verheißungen der Technik an der Wende zum 20. Jahrhundert', in Ute Frevert (ed.), *Das neue Jahrhundert: Europäische Zeitdiagnosen und Zukunftsentwürfe um 1900*, Göttingen, 2000, pp. 47–78.

Bergmann, Günther J., *Auslandsdeutsche in Paraguay, Brasilien, Argentinien*, Bad Münstereifel, 1994.

Bergmann, Klaus, *Agrarromantik und Großstadtfeindschaft*, Meisenheim, 1970.

Bergmann, Werner, 'Völkischer Antisemitismus im Kaiserreich', in Uwe Puschner, Walter Schmitz and Justus H. Ulbricht (eds.), *Handbuch zur 'Völkischen Bewegung' 1871–1918*, Munich, 1999, pp. 449–63.

Berkhofer, Robert F., *The White Man's Indian: Images of the American Indian from Columbus to the Present*, New York, 1978.

Berkowitz, Michael, *Zionist Culture and West European Jewry before the First World War*, Cambridge, 1993.

Berman, Edward, *African Reactions to Missionary Education*, New York, 1975.

Berman, Nina, *Orientalismus, Kolonialismus und Moderne: Zum Bild des Orients in der deutschsprachigen Literatur um 1900*, Stuttgart, 1996.

Bernecker, Walther L. (ed.), *Die Wiederentdeckung Lateinamerikas: Die Erfahrung des Subkontinents in Reiseberichten des 19. Jahrhunderts*, Frankfurt, 1997.

Bernecker, Walther L. and Thomas Fischer, 'Deutsche in Lateinamerika', in Klaus J. Bade (ed.), *Deutsche im Ausland-Fremde in Deutschland. Migration in Geschichte und Gegenwart*, Munich, 1992, pp. 197–214.

Berry, Sara, *No Condition Is Permanent: The Social Dynamics of Agrarian Change in Sub-Saharan Africa*, Madison, 1993.

Beschoren, Max, *Beiträge zur nähern Kenntnis der brasilianischen Provinz São Pedro do Rio Grande do Sul: Reisen und Beobachtungen während der Jahre 1875–1887*, Gotha, 1889.

Beßlich, Barbara, *Wege in den 'Kulturkrieg': Zivilisationskritik in Deutschland 1890–1914*, Darmstadt, 2000.

Best, Heinrich, *Interessenpolitik und nationale Integration 1848/49: Handelspolitische Konflikte im frühindustriellen Deutschland*, Göttingen, 1980.

Beyreuther, Erich, *Geschichte der Diakonie und Inneren Mission in der Neuzeit*, Berlin, 1983.

Bibo, Hermann, *Wie erzieht man am besten den Neger zur Plantagen-Arbeit? Und welche Ziele müssen wir verfolgen, um unsere Kolonien für Deutschlands Handel und Industrie allgemein nutzbar und segensreich zu gestalten?*, Berlin, 1887.

Bielefeld, Ulrich, *Nation und Gesellschaft: Selbstthematisierungen in Deutschland und Frankreich*, Hamburg, 2003.

Biermann, Werner, *Tanganyika Railways: Carrier of Colonialism. An Account of Economic Indicators and Social Fragments*, Münster, 1995.

Biernacki, Richard, *The Fabrication of Labor: Germany and Britain, 1640–1914*, Berkeley, 1995.

Bily, Lothar, *Die Religion im Denken Max Webers*, St. Ottilien, 1990.

Biskup, Peter, 'Foreign Coloured Labour', *Journal of Pacific History* 5 (1970), 85–107.

Bismarck, Otto von, *Die Reden des Reichskanzlers Fürsten von Bismarck im Deutschen Reichstage 1884–1885*, ed. Horst Kohl, Stuttgart, 1894.

Bitner-Nowak, Anna, 'Die Nachbarschaft der Regionen: Großpolen und Brandenburg im 19. Jahrhundert', in Helga Schultz (ed.), *Preußens Osten – Polens Westen: Das Zerbrechen einer Nachbarschaft*, Berlin, 2001, pp. 39–72.

Bitterli, Urs, *Die 'Wilden' und die 'Zivilisierten': Grundzüge einer Geistes- und Kulturgeschichte der europäisch-überseeischen Begegnung*, Munich, 1976.

Black, Jeremy, *Maps and History: Constructing Images of the Past*, New Haven, 1997.

Blackbourn, David, 'Das Kaiserreich transnational: Eine Skizze', in Sebastian Conrad and Jürgen Osterhammel (eds.), *Das Kaiserreich transnational: Deutschland in der Welt 1871–1914*, Göttingen, 2004, pp. 302–24.

Blaise, Clarke, *Die Zähmung der Zeit: Sir Sandford Fleming und die Erfindung der Weltzeit*, Frankfurt, 2001.

Blanc, Albert, *L'Immigration en France et le travail national*, Lyon, 1901.

Blanke, Richard, *Polish Speaking Germans? Language and National Identity among the Masurians since 1871*, Cologne, 2001.

   Prussian Poland and the German Empire 1871–1900, New York, 1981.

Blaschke, Monika, '"Deutsch-Amerika" in Bedrängnis: Krise und Verfall einer "Bindestrichkultur"', in Klaus J. Bade (ed.), *Deutsche im Ausland-Fremde in Deutschland. Migration in Geschichte und Gegenwart*, Munich, 1992, pp. 170–79.

Blaschke, Olaf, 'Antikapitalismus und Antisemitismus: Die Wirtschaftsmentalität der Katholiken im Wilhelminischen Deutschland', in Johannes Heil and Bernd Wacker (eds.), *Shylock? Zinsverbot und Geldverleih in jüdischer und christlicher Tradition*, Munich, 1997, pp. 113–46.

   Katholizismus und Antisemitismus im deutschen Kaiserreich, Göttingen, 1997.

Blaschke, Olaf and Aram Mattioli (eds.), *Katholischer Antisemitismus im 19. Jahrhundert: Ursachen und Traditionen im internationalen Vergleich*, Zürich, 2000.

Blaut, James M., *The Colonizer's Model of the World: Geographical Diffusionism and Eurocentric History*, New York, 1993.

Bley, Helmut, *Kolonialherrschaft und Sozialstruktur in Deutsch-Südwestafrika 1894–1914*, Hamburg, 1968.

Bloom, William, *Personal Identity, National Identity and International Relations*, Cambridge, 1990.

Bodelschwingh, Friedrich von, *Ausgewählte Schriften*, 3 vols., Vol. II, Bielefeld, 1964.

   Briefwechsel in 9 Bänden, 9 vols., Bethel, 1966–73.

   'Die ostafrikanische Mission und die Bielefelder Anstalten der inneren Mission', *Nachrichten aus der ostafrikanischen Mission* 4 (1890), 135–40, 148–50.

   Die Wanderarmen und die Arbeitslosen, Bielefeld, 1895.

   'Drohende Gefahren für die Zukunft der Arbeiterkolonien', *Die Arbeiterkolonie* 1 (1885), 193–99.

   Wer hilft mit? Ein Wort zur Reorganisation der Berliner Asyle, Berlin, 1904.

Bodelschwingh, Gustav von, *Friedrich von Bodelschwingh: Ein Lebensbild*, Bielefeld, 1922.

Bodenstein, Bernhard, *Die Beschäftigung ausländischer Arbeiter in der Industrie*, Essen, 1908.

Böcker, Anita, Kees Groenendijk, Tetty Havinga and Paul Minderhoud (eds.), *Regulation of Migration: International Experiences*, Amsterdam, 1998.

Böhme, Helmut, *Deutschlands Weg zur Großmacht: Studien zum Verhältnis von Wirtschaft und Staat während der Reichsgründungszeit 1848–1881*, Cologne, 1966.

Bohner, H., 'Die Einführung geregelter Arbeit in Kamerun', *Die deutschen Kolonien* 1 (1902), 67–72.

Böhning, Peter, *Die nationalpolnische Bewegung in Westpreußen, 1815–1871: Ein Beitrag zum Integrationsprozeß der polnischen Nation*, Marburg, 1973.

Bois, W. E. B. du, *The Souls of Black Folk: Essays and Sketches*, Chicago, 1903.

Boli, John and George M. Thomas, *Constructing World Culture: International Nongovernmental Organizations since 1875*, Stanford, 1999.

Bönkost, Klaus Jürgen, *Skizzen zur historischen Entwicklung der Arbeitserziehung und Arbeitslehre*, Bremen, 1995.

Bonnlander, Helene, *Der vermittelte Imperialismus: Der Blick auf außereuropäische Lebenswelten von Alexander von Humboldt zu Heinrich Brugsch*, Frankfurt, 1998.

Bons, Joachim, *Nationalsozialismus und Arbeiterfrage: Zu den Motiven, Inhalten und Wirkungsgründen nationalsozialistischer Arbeiterpolitik vor 1933*, Pfaffenweiler, 1995.

Borchardt, Knut, *Globalisierung in historischer Perspektive*, Munich, 2001.

Borja, Jordi and Manuel Castells, *Local & Global*, London, 1997.

Borscheid, Peter, *Das Tempo-Virus: Eine Kulturgeschichte der Beschleunigung*, Frankfurt, 2004.

Bourdieu, Pierre, *Entwurf einer Theorie der Praxis auf der ethnologischen Grundlage der kabylischen Gesellschaft*, Frankfurt, 1976.

Boyarin, Daniel, *Unheroic Conduct: The Rise of Heterosexuality and the Invention of the Jewish Man*, Berkeley, 1997.

Bradley, Harriet, *Men's Work, Women's Work: A Sociological History of the Sexual Division of Labour in Employment*, Cambridge, 1992.

Brandt, Max von, *Aus dem Lande des Zopfes: Plaudereien eines alten Chinesen*, Leipzig, 1894.

Brass, Tom and Marcel van der Linden (eds.), *Free and Unfree Labour: The Debate Continues*, Bern, 1997.

Brechtken, Magnus, *'Madagaskar für die Juden': Antisemitische Idee und politische Praxis 1885–1945*, Munich, 1997.

Breckenridge, Carol and Arjun Appadurai, 'On Moving Targets', *Public Culture* 1:2 (1989), i–iv.

Breitenbach, Wilhelm, *Aus Süd-Brasilien: Erinnerungen und Aufzeichnungen*, Brackwede, 1913.

Über das Deutschthum in Süd-Brasilien: Eine Studie, Hamburg, 1887.

Breman, Jan, *Taming the Coolie Beast: Plantation Society and the Colonial Order in Southeast Asia*, Delhi, 1989.

Brenner, Michael, *Geschichte des Zionismus*, Munich, 2002.

Bristow, Edward. J., *Prostitution and Prejudice: The Jewish Fight against White Slavery 1870–1939*, New York 1982.

Brockhaus' Conversations-Lexikon: Allgemeine deutsche Real-Enzyklopädie, 13th edn, 17 vols., Leipzig, 1882–87.

Broers, Michael, 'Cultural Imperialism in a European Context? Political Culture and Cultural Politics in Napoleonic Italy', *Past and Present* 170 (2001), 152–80.

Brook, Timothy and Andre Schmid (eds.), *Nation Work: Asian Elites and National Identities*, Ann Arbor, 2000.

Brose, Winfried and Ulrich von der Heyden (eds.), *Mit Kreuz und deutscher Flagge. 100 Jahre Evangelium im Süden Tanzanias: Zum Wirken der Berliner Mission in Ostafrika*, Münster, 1993.

Broszat, Martin, *Zweihundert Jahre deutsche Polenpolitik*, Frankfurt, 1972.

Brower, Daniel R. and Edward J. Lazzerini (eds.), *Russia's Orient: Imperial Borderlands and Peoples 1750–1917*, Bloomington, 1997.

Bruch, Rüdiger vom, *Weltpolitik als Kulturmission: Auswärtige Kulturpolitik und Bildungsbürgertum in Deutschland am Vorabend des Ersten Weltkrieges*, Paderborn, 1982.

Wissenschaft, Politik und öffentliche Meinung: Gelehrtenpolitik im Wilhelminischen Deutschland (1890–1914), Husum, 1980.

Bruck, Felix Friedrich, *Fort mit den Zuchthäusern!*, Breslau, 1894.

Die Gegner der Deportation, Breslau, 1901.

Die gesetzliche Einführung der Deportation im Deutschen Reich, Breslau, 1897.

Neu-Deutschland und seine Pioniere: Ein Beitrag zur Lösung der sozialen Frage, Breslau, 1896.

Noch einmal die Deportation und Deutsch-Südwestafrika, Breslau, 1896.

Brückner, Wolfgang, 'Arbeit macht frei': Herkunft und Hintergrund der KZ-Devise*, Opladen, 1998.

Brugger, Ingried, Johann Georg Prinz von Hohenzollern and Manfred Reuther (eds.), *Emil Nolde und die Südsee*, Munich, 2001.

Brunn, Gerhard, *Deutschland und Brasilien 1889–1914*, Cologne, 1971.

Buchheim, Christoph, 'Deutschland auf dem Weltmarkt am Ende des 19. Jahrhunderts: Erfolgreicher Anbieter von konsumnahen gewerblichen Erzeugnissen', *Vierteljahrschrift für Sozial- und Wirtschaftsgeschichte* 71 (1984), 199–216.

Buchholz, Kai, Rita Latocha, Hilke Peckmann and Klaus Wolbert (eds.), *Die Lebensreform: Entwürfe zur Neugestaltung von Leben und Kunst um 1900*, 2 vols., Vol. I, Darmstadt, 2001.

Buchner, Charles, *Die Mission und ihre Kritiker*, Berlin, 1905.

'Die Mithilfe der Mission bei der Erziehung der Eingeborenen zur Arbeit', in *Verhandlungen des Deutschen Kolonialkongresses 1905 zu Berlin am 5., 6. und 7. Oktober 1905*, ed. Redaktionsausschuß, Berlin, 1906, pp. 427–42.

Bueck, Henry Axel, *Der Centralverband deutscher Industrieller und seine dreißigjährige Arbeit 1876–1906*, Berlin, 1906.

Buell, Frederick, *National Culture and the New Global System*, Baltimore, 1994.

Büttner, Manfred (ed.), *Carl Ritter: Zur europäisch-amerikanischen Geographie an der Wende vom 18. zum 19. Jahrhundert*, Paderborn, 1980.

Bulloch, William, *The History of Bacteriology*, New York, 1960.

Burchardt, Lothar, 'Technischer Fortschritt und sozialer Wandel: Am Beispiel der Taylorismus-Rezeption', in Werner Treue (ed.), *Deutsche Technikgeschichte*, Göttingen, 1977, pp. 52–98.

Burke, Anthony, *Fear of Security: Australia's Invasion Anxiety*, Sydney, 2001.

Burns, E. Bradford, *Nationalism in Brazil*, New York, 1968.

Burton, Antoinette M., 'Civilising Subjects: Metropole and Colony in the English Imagination, 1830–1867', *Victorian Studies* 45 (2003), 699–707.

Buschmann, Nikolaus, *Einkreisung und Waffenbruderschaft: Die öffentliche Deutung von Krieg und Nation in Deutschland 1850–1871*, Göttingen, 2003.

Bußmann, Walter, 'Gustav Freytag: Maßstäbe seiner Zeitkritik', *Archiv für Kulturgeschichte* 34 (1952), 261–87.

Buttmann, Günther, *Friedrich Ratzel: Leben und Werk eines deutschen Geographen*, Stuttgart, 1977.

Byern, Gerhard von, *Deutsch-Ostafrika und seine weißen und schwarzen Bewohner*, Berlin, 1913.

Cain, Peter J., *Economic Foundations of British Overseas Expansion, 1815–1914*, London, 1980

(ed.), *Free Trade and Protection*, Bristol, 1996.

Cain, Peter J. and Anthony G. Hopkins, *British Imperialism 1688–2000*, London, 2002.

Calhoun, Craig, 'Nationalism, Modernism, and their Multiplicities', in Eliezer Ben-Rafael and Yitzak Sternberg (eds.), *Identity, Culture and Globalization*, Leiden, 2001, pp. 445–70.

Cammack, Paul, 'Brasilien', in Walther L. Bernecker, Raymond T. Buve, John R. Fisher, Horst Pietschmann and Hans Werner Tobler (eds.), *Handbuch der Geschichte Lateinamerikas*, 3 vols., Vol. III, Stuttgart, 1996, pp. 1049–1101.

Campbell, Joan, *Der Deutsche Werkbund 1907–1934*, Stuttgart, 1981.

Joy in Work, German Work: The National Debate, 1800–1945, Princeton, 1989.

Campt, Tina, Pascal Grosse and Yara-Colette Lemke-Muniz de Faria, 'Blacks, Germans, and the Politics of Imperial Imagination, 1920–60', in Sara Friedrichsmeyer, Sara Lennox and Susanne Zantop (eds.), *The Imperialist Imagination: German Colonialism and Its Legacy*, Ann Arbor, 1998, pp. 205–29.

Cannadine, David, *Ornamentalism: How the British Saw Their Empire*, Oxford, 2001.

Canning, Kathleen, 'Gender and the Politics of Class Formation: Rethinking German Labor History', *American Historical Review* 97 (1992), 736–68.

Cannstatt, Oscar, *Äußere oder innere Kolonisation? Ein Beitrag zur Frage: Wohin lenken wir unsere Sträflinge?* Hannover, 1903.

Caplan, Jane and John Torpey (eds.), *Documenting Individual Identity: The Development of State Practices in the Modern World*, Princeton, 2002.

Chakrabarty, Dipesh, *Provincializing Europe: Postcolonial Thought and Historical Difference*, Princeton, 2000.

Chan, Sucheng, *Asian Americans: An Interpretive History*, Boston, 1991.

(ed.), *Entry Denied: Exclusion and the Chinese Community in America, 1882–1943*, Philadelphia, 1991.

'European and Asian Immigration into the United States', in Virginia Yans-McLaughlin (ed.), *Immigration Reconsidered*, New York, 1990, pp. 37–75.

This Bittersweet Soil: The Chinese in California Agriculture, 1860–1910, Berkeley, 1986.

Chang-Rodriguez, Eugenio, 'Chinese Labor Migration into Latin America in the Nineteenth Century', *Revista de Historia de America* 46 (1958), 375–97.

Charle, Christophe, *La Crise des sociétés impériales: Allemagne, France, Grande-Bretagne 1900–1940*, Paris, 2001.

Chatterjee, Partha, *The Nation and Its Fragments: Colonial and Postcolonial Histories*, Princeton, 1993.

Nationalist Thought and the Colonial World: A Derivative Discourse, Tokyo, 1986.

Chen, Ta, *Chinese Migrations with Special Reference to Labor Conditions*, Washington, 1923.

Emigrant Communities in South China, New York, 1940.

Chickering, Roger, *We Men who Feel Most German: A Cultural Study of the Pan-German League, 1886–1914*, Boston, MA, 1984.

Ching, Leo T. S., *Becoming 'Japanese': Colonial Taiwan and the Politics of Identity Formation*, Berkeley, 2001.

Chirot, Daniel and Anthony Reid (eds.), *Essential Outsiders: Chinese and Jews in the Modern Transformation of Southeast Asia and Central Europe*, Seattle, 1997.

Chiswick, Barry R. and Timothy J. Hatton, 'International Migration and the Integration of Labor Markets', in Michael D. Bordo, Alan M. Taylor and Jeffrey G. Williamson (eds.), *Globalization in Historical Perspective*, Chicago, 2003, pp. 65–120.

Chow, Kai-Wing, Kevin M. Doak and Poshek Fu (eds.), *Constructing Nationhood in Modern East Asia*, Ann Arbor, 2001.

Christ, Jürgen, *Staat und Staatsräson bei Friedrich Naumann*, Heidelberg, 1969.

Christensen, Torben and William R. Hutchison (eds.), *Missionary Ideologies in the Imperialist Era 1880–1920*, Aarhus, 1982.

Christmann, Helmut, Peter Hempenstall and Dirk Ballendorf, *Die Karolinen-Inseln in deutscher Zeit: Eine kolonialgeschichtliche Fallstudie*, Münster, 1991.

Ciarlo, David M., 'Rasse konsumieren: Von der exotischen zur kolonialen Imagination in der Bildreklame des wilhelminischen Kaiserreichs', in Birthe Kundrus (ed.), *Phantasiereiche: Zur Kulturgeschichte des deutschen Kolonialismus*, Frankfurt, 2003, pp. 135–79.

Clifford, James, 'Introduction: Partial Truths', in George E. Marcus and Clifford (eds.), *Writing Culture: The Poetics and Politics of Ethnography*, Berkeley, 1986, pp. 1–26.

'Mixed Feelings', in Peng Cheah and Bruce Robbins (eds.), *Cosmopolitics: Thinking and Feeling beyond the Nation*, Minnesota, 1989, pp. 362–70.

Routes: Travel and Translation in the Late Twentieth Century, Cambridge, MA, 1997.

'Travelling Cultures', in Lawrence Grossberg, Cary Nelson and Paula Treichler (eds.), *Cultural Studies*, New York, 1992, pp. 96–116.

Cohen, Robin, *The New Helots: Migrants in the International Division of Labour*, Aldershot, 1987.

Cole, Simon A., *Suspect Identities: A History of Fingerprinting and Criminal Identification*, Cambridge, MA, 2001.

Colley, Linda, *Britons: Forging the Nation, 1707–1837*, New Haven, 1992.

Comaroff, John L. and Jean Comaroff, 'Hausgemachte Hegemonie', in Sebastian Conrad and Shalini Randeria (eds.), *Jenseits des Eurozentrismus: Postkoloniale Perspektiven in den Geschichts- und Kulturwissenschaften*, Frankfurt, 2002, pp. 247–82.

Confino, Alon, *Nation as a Local Metaphor: Württemberg, Imperial Germany, and National Memory, 1871–1918*, Chapel Hill, 1997.

Conklin, Alice, *A Mission to Civilize: The Republican Idea of Empire in France and West Africa 1895–1920*, Stanford, 1997.

Connor, Walker, *Ethnonationalism: The Quest for Understanding*, Princeton, 1994.

Conrad, Else, *Der Verein für Sozialpolitik und seine Wirksamkeit auf dem Gebiet der gewerblichen Arbeiterfrage*, Jena, 1906.

Conrad, Sebastian, 'Doppelte Marginalisierung: Plädoyer für eine transnationale Perspektive auf die deutsche Geschichte', *Geschichte und Gesellschaft* 28 (2002), 145–69.

'Regimes der Segregation: Kolonialismus, Recht und Globalisierung', *Rechtsgeschichte* 4 (2004), 187–204.

Conrad, Sebastian and Jürgen Osterhammel (eds.), *Das Kaiserreich transnational: Deutschland in der Welt 1871–1914*, Göttingen, 2004.

Conrad, Sebastian and Shalini Randeria, 'Geteilte Geschichten: Europa in einer postkolonialen Welt', in Conrad and Randeria (eds.), *Jenseits des Eurozentrismus: Postkoloniale Perspektiven in den Geschichts- und Kulturwissenschaften*, Frankfurt, 2002, pp. 9–49.

(eds.), *Jenseits des Eurozentrismus: Postkoloniale Perspektiven in den Geschichts- und Kulturwissenschaften*, Frankfurt, 2002.

Conze, Werner, 'Arbeit', in Otto Brunner, Conze and Reinhart Koselleck (eds.), *Geschichtliche Grundbegriffe: Historisches Lexikon zur politisch-sozialen Sprache in Deutschland*, 8 vols., Vol. 1, Stuttgart, 1972, pp. 154–215.

Conzen, Kathleen Neils, 'Die Assimilierung der Deutschen in Amerika: Zum Stand der Forschung in den Vereinigten Staaten', in Willi Paul Adams (ed.), *Die deutschsprachige Auswanderung in die Vereinigten Staaten: Berichte über Forschungsstand und Quellenbestände*, Berlin, 1980, pp. 33–64.

Cooke, Kinloch, *Chinese Labour in the Transvaal Being a Study of Its Moral, Economic, and Imperial Aspects*, London, 1906.

Cooper, Frederick, 'Conditions Analogous to Slavery: Imperialism and Free Labor Ideology in Africa', in Cooper, Thomas C. Holt and Rebecca J. Scott (eds.), *Beyond Slavery: Explorations of Race, Labor, and Citizenship in Postemancipation Societies*, Chapel Hill, 2000, pp. 106–49.

Decolonization and African Society: The Labor Question in French and British Africa, Cambridge, 1996.

Cooper, Frederick and Randall Packard (eds.), *International Development and the Social Sciences: Essays on the History and Politics of Knowledge*, Berkeley, 1997.

Costello, Peter, *Jules Verne: Inventor of Science Fiction*, London, 1978.

Coulmas, Florian, *Japanische Zeiten: Eine Ethnografie der Vergänglichkeit*, Reinbek, 2000.

Criscenti, Joseph T. (ed.), *Sarmiento and His Argentina*, Boulder, 1993.

Crowe, Sir Eyre, 'Memorandum on the Present State of British Relations with France and Germany, 1.1.1907', in G. P. Gooch and Harold Temperley (eds.), *British Documents on the Origins of the War 1898–1914*, 11 vols., Vol. III, London, 1928.

Cubitt, Geoffrey (ed.), *Imagining Nations*, Manchester, 1998.

Cunha, Jorge Luiz da, *Rio Grande do Sul und die deutsche Kolonisation: Ein Beitrag zur Geschichte der deutsch-brasilianischen Auswanderung und der deutschen Siedlung in Südbrasilien zwischen 1824 und 1914*, Santa Cruz do Sul, 1995.

Dann, Otto, *Nation und Nationalismus in Deutschland*, Munich, 1996.

Daškevyč, Jaroslav, 'Ostgalizien: Ethnische Situation, nationale Mythen und Mentalitäten', in Valeria Heuberger, Arnold Suppan and Elisabeth Vyslonzil (eds.), *Das Bild vom Anderen: Identitäten, Mentalitäten, Mythen und Stereotypen in multiethnischen europäischen Regionen*, Frankfurt, 1998, pp. 93–104.

Daum, Andreas, *Wissenschaftspopularisierung im 19. Jahrhundert: Bürgerliche Kultur, naturwissenschaftliche Bildung und die deutsche Öffentlichkeit, 1848–1914*, Munich, 1998.

Davis, Clarence B., Kenneth E. Wilburn and Ronald E. Robinson (eds.), *Railway Imperialism*, New York, 1991.

Davis, Lance E. and Robert A. Huttenback, *Mammon and the Pursuit of Empire: The Political Economy of British Imperialism 1860–1912*, Cambridge, 1986.

Davis, Shelton H., *Victims of the Miracle: Development and the Indians of Brazil*, Cambridge, 1977.

Davison, Jean (ed.), *Agriculture, Women, and Land: The African Experience*, Boulder, 1988.

Dawson, William H., *The Vagrancy Problem: The Case for Measures of Restraint for Tramps, Loafers, and Unemployables, with a Study of Continental Detention Colonies and Labour Houses*, London, 1910.

de Cecco, Marcello, *The International Gold Standard: Money and Empire*, New York, 1984.

Deist, Wilhelm, *Flottenpolitik und Flottenpropaganda: Das Nachrichtenbureau des Reichsmarineamtes 1897–1914*, Stuttgart, 1976.

Deleuze, Gilles and Félix Guattari, *A Thousand Plateaus: Capitalism and Schizophrenia*, Minneapolis/London, 1993.

Del Fabbro, René, *Transalpini : Italienische Arbeitswanderung nach Süddeutschland im Kaiserreich 1870–1918*, Osnabrück, 1996.

Delhaes-Guenther, Dietrich von, *Industrialisierung in Südbrasilien: Die deutsche Einwanderung und die Anfänge der Industrialisierung in Rio Grande do Sul*, Cologne, 1973.

Denk, Hans D., *Die christliche Arbeiterbewegung in Bayern bis zum Ersten Weltkrieg*, Mainz, 1980.

Dettmann, Eduard, *Brasiliens Aufschwung in deutscher Beleuchtung*, Berlin, 1908.

Deutsch, Jan-Georg, *Emancipation without Abolition in German East-Africa c. 1884–1914*, Oxford, 2006.

Diamond, Jared, *Arm und Reich: Die Schicksale menschlicher Gesellschaften*, Frankfurt, 1998.

Dickie, John, *Darkest Italy: The Nation and Stereotypes of the Mezzogiorno, 1860–1900*, London, 1999.

Diekmann, Irene, Peter Krüger and Julius H. Schoeps (eds.), *Geopolitik: Grenzgänge im Zeitgeist*, 2 vols., Vol. 1: *1890 bis 1945*, Potsdam, 2000.

Dikötter, Frank (ed.), *The Construction of Racial Identities in China and Japan*, Honolulu, 1997.

(ed.), *The Discourse of Race in Modern China*, London, 1992.

Dirlik, Arif (ed.), *Chinese on the American Frontier*, Lanham, 2001.

Global Modernity: Modernity in the Age of Global Capitalism, Boulder, 2007.

'Globalization as the End and the Beginning of History: The Contradictory Implications of a New Paradigm', *Rethinking Marxism* 12:4 (2000), 4–22.

'Is There History after Eurocentrism? Globalism, Postcolonialism, and the Disavowal of History', in Dirlik, *Postmodernity's Histories: The Past as Legacy and Project*, Lanham, 2000, pp. 63–90.

'Modernity as History: Post-Revolutionary China, Globalization and the Question of Modernity', *Social History* 27 (2002), 16–39.

Dittmer, Lowell and Samuel S. Kim (eds.), *China's Quest for National Identity*, Ithaca, NY, 1993.

Dörflinger, Johannes, *Die österreichische Kartographie im 18. und zu Beginn des 19. Jahrhunderts*, Vienna, 1988.

Döring, Paul, *Morgendämmerung in Deutsch-Ostafrika: Ein Rundgang durch die ostafrikanische Mission '(Berlin III)'*, Berlin, 1899.

Doerry, Martin, *Übergangsmenschen: Die Mentalität der Wilhelminer und die Krise des Kaiserreiches*, Munich, 1986.

Dohrn van Rossum, Gerhard, *Die Geschichte der Stunde: Uhren und die moderne Zeitordnung*, Munich, 1992.

Dowrick, Steve and J. Bradford DeLong, 'Globalization and Convergence', in Michael D. Bordo, Alan M. Taylor and Jeffrey G. Williamson (eds.), *Globalization in Historical Perspective*, Chicago, 2003, pp. 191–226.

Dreßen, Wolfgang, *Die pädagogische Maschine: Zur Geschichte des industrial-isierten Bewußtseins in Preußen/Deutschland*, Frankfurt, 1982.

Drews, Curt, 'Neue Wege zur Erhaltung des Deutschtums in Übersee', *Das Deutschtum im Ausland* 15 (1913), 746–54.

Drude, Hartwig, 'Christliche Wandererfürsorge oder die Vollstreckung der bürgerlichen Moral an den Armen', in Jürgen Scheffler (ed.), *Bürger und Bettler: Materialien und Dokumente zur Geschichte der Nichtseßhaftenhilfe in der Diakonie*, 2 vols., Vol. 1, Bielefeld, 1987, pp. 153–57.

Drummond, Elizabeth A., '"Durch Liebe stark, deutsch bis ins Mark": Weiblicher Kulturimperialismus und der deutsche Frauenverein für die Ostmarken', in Ute Planert (ed.), *Nation, Politik und Geschlecht: Frauenbewegungen und Nationalismus in der Moderne*, Frankfurt, 2000, pp. 147–64.

Duara, Prasenjit, 'The Discourse of Civilization and Pan-Asianism', *Journal of World History* 12 (2001), 99–130.

'Nationalists among Transnationals: Overseas Chinese and the Idea of China, 1900–1911', in Donald M. Nonini and Aihwa Ong (eds.), *Ungrounded Empires: The Cultural Politics of Modern Chinese Transnationalism*, London, 1997, pp. 39–60.

Rescuing History from the Nation: Questioning Narratives of Modern China, Chicago, 1995.

'Transnationalism and the Predicament of Sovereignty: China 1900–1945', *American Historical Review* 102 (1997), 1030–51.

Dudek, Peter, *Erziehung durch Arbeit: Arbeitslagerbewegung und freiwilliger Arbeitsdienst 1920–1935*, Opladen, 1988.

Düding, Dieter, *Organisierter gesellschaftlicher Nationalismus in Deutschland (1808–1847): Bedeutung und Funktion der Turner- und Sängervereine für die deutsche Nationalbewegung*, Munich, 1984.

Dumett, Raymond E. (ed.), *Gentlemanly Capitalism and British Imperialism: The New Debate on Empire*, London, 1999.

Eckart, Wolfgang, *Medizin und Kolonialimperialismus: Deutschland 1884–1945*, Paderborn, 1996.

Eckert, Andreas, 'Geschichte der Arbeit und Arbeitergeschichte in Afrika', *Archiv für Sozialgeschichte* 39 (1999), 502–30.

'Verwaltung, Recht und koloniale Praxis in Kamerun 1884–1914', in Rüdiger Voigt and Peter Sack (eds.), *Kolonialisierung des Rechts: Zur kolonialen Rechts- und Verwaltungsordnung*, Baden-Baden, 2001, pp. 167–82.

'Zeit, Arbeit und die Konstruktion von Differenz: Über die koloniale Ordnung in Afrika', *Comparativ* 10:3 (2002), 61–73.

Eckert, Andreas and Albert Wirz, 'Wir nicht, die Anderen auch', in Sebastian Conrad and Shalini Randeria (eds.), *Jenseits des Eurozentrismus: Postkoloniale Perspektiven in den Geschichts- und Kulturwissenschaften*, Frankfurt, 2002, pp. 372–92.

Edelstein, Michael, *Overseas Investment in the Age of High Imperialism: The United Kingdom, 1850–1914*, London, 1982.

Edney, Matthew H., *Mapping an Empire: The Geographical Construction of British India, 1765–1843*, Chicago, 1997.

Ehmer, Josef, 'Die Geschichte der Arbeit als Spannungsfeld von Begriff, Norm und Praxis', in *Bericht über den 23. Österreichischen Historikertag*, Salzburg, 2003, pp. 25–44.

Ehmer, Josef and Peter Gutschner, 'Befreiung und Verkrümmung durch Arbeit', in Richard van Dülmen (ed.), *Erfindung des Menschen: Schöpfungsträume und Körperbilder 1500–2000*, Vienna, 1998, pp. 283–303.

Eichberg, Henning, '"Schneller, höher, stärker"', in Gunter Mann and Rolf Winau (eds.), *Medizin, Naturwissenschaft, Technik und das Zweite Kaiserreich*, Göttingen, 1997, pp. 259–83.

Eisenhart, Karl, *Die Abrechnung mit England*, Munich, 1900.

Eisner, Kurt, 'Taylorismus', *Neue Rundschau* 24 (1913), 1448–53.

Eley, Geoff, 'German Politics and Polish Nationality: The Dialectic of Nation-Forming in the East of Prussia', *East European Quarterly* 18 (1984), 335–64.

'Labour, Women, and the Family in Germany, 1914–1945', *German Politics and Society* 23 (1991), 1–20.

Reshaping the German Right: Radical Nationalism and Political Change after Bismarck, New Haven, 1980.

Eley, Geoff and James N. Retallack (eds.), *Wilhelmianism and Its Legacies: German Modernities, Imperialism, and the Meanings of Reform 1890–1914*, New York, 2003.

Eloni, Yehuda, *Zionismus in Deutschland: Von den Anfängen bis 1914*, Gerlingen, 1987.

Elsner, Lothar, 'Deutsche Arbeiterbewegung und eingewanderte ausländische Arbeiter 1900 bis 1914', in *Internationale Tagung der Historiker der Arbeiterbewegung 1986*, Vienna, 1987, pp. 87–96.

Eltis, David (ed.), *Coerced and Free Migration: Global Perspectives*, Stanford, 2002.

El-Tayeb, Fatima, *Schwarze Deutsche: Der Diskurs um 'Rasse' und nationale Identität 1890–1933*, Frankfurt, 2001.

Emmer, Pieter C. (ed.), *Colonialism and Migration: Indentured Labour before and after Slavery*, Dordrecht, 1986.

Engerman, Stanley, 'Contract Labor, Sugar, and Technology in the Nineteenth Century', *Journal of Economic History* 43 (1983), 635–59.

Epkenhans, Michael, *Die wilhelminische Flottenrüstung, 1908–1914*, Munich, 1991.

Erdmann, Gustav Adolf, *Deutschlands Seeherrschaft im 20. Jahrhundert*, Leipzig, 1900.

Erdlenbruch, Kurt, *Die wirtschaftliche und soziale Bedeutung der deutschen Arbeiterkolonien*, Bethel, 1929.

Ermarth, Michael, 'Hyphenation and Hyper-Americanization: Germans of the Wilhelmine *Reich* View German-Americans, 1890–1914', *Journal of American Ethnic History* 21:2 (2002), 33–58.

Escobar, Arturo, *Encountering Development: The Making and Unmaking of the Third World*, Princeton, 1995.

Esedebe, P. Olisanwuche, *Pan-Africanism: The Idea and Movement, 1776–1991*, Washington, DC, 1994.

Esenbel, Selçuk, 'Japan's Global Claim to Asia and the World of Islam: Transnational Nationalism and World Power, 1900–1945', *American Historical Review* 109 (2004), 1140–70.

Espagne, Michel, 'Sur les limites du comparatisme en histoire culturelle', *Genèses* 17 (1994), 112–21.

Etges, Andreas, *Wirtschaftsnationalismus: USA und Deutschland im Vergleich (1815–1914)*, Frankfurt, 1999.

Etienne, August, *Deutschlands wirtschaftliche Interessen in China: Betrachtungen über die handelspolitische Lage im asiatischen Osten*, Berlin, 1904.

Ette, Ottmar, *Weltbewußtsein: Alexander von Humboldt und das unvollendete Projekt einer anderen Moderne*, Weilerswist, 2002.

Evans, Raymond. '"Pigmentia": Racial Fears and White Australia', in Dirk A. Moses (ed.), *Genocide and Settler Society: Frontier Violence and Stolen Indigenous Children in Australian History*, New York, 2004, pp. 103–124.

Evans, Richard J., 'The "Dangerous Classes" in Germany from the Middle Ages to the Twentieth Century', in Evans (ed.), *The German Underworld: Deviants and Outcasts in German History*, London, 1988, pp. 1–28.

  Death in Hamburg: Society and Politics in the Cholera Years, 1830–1910, Oxford, 1987.

  Tod in Hamburg: Stadt, Gesellschaft und Politik in den Cholera-Jahren 1830–1910, Reinbek, 1996.

Eye, August von, *Der Auswanderer: Winke und Weisungen für Ansiedler in den deutschen Colonien Süd-Brasiliens*, Berlin, 1885.

Faber, Karl-Georg, 'Zur Vorgeschichte der Geopolitik: Staat, Nation und Lebensraum im Denken deutscher Geographen vor 1914', in Heinz Dollinger, Horst Gründer and Alwin Hanschmidt (eds.), *Weltpolitik, Europagedanke, Regionalismus*, Münster, 1982, pp. 389–406.

Fabian, Johannes, *Time and the Other: How Anthropology Makes Its Object*, New York, 1983.

Fabri, Carl, *Kolonialpolitische Betrachtungen zur augenblicklichen Lage Südbrasiliens*, Hamburg, 1894.

Fabri, Friedrich, *Bedarf Deutschland der Colonien? Eine politisch–ökonomische Betrachtung* [1879], Lewiston, 1998.

Fahrmeir, Andreas, *Citizens and Aliens: Foreigners and the Law in Britain and the German States, 1789–1870*, New York, 2000.

'Nineteenth-Century German Citizenships', *Historical Journal* 40 (1997), 721–52.

Fahrmeir, Andreas, Oliver Faron and Patrick Weil (eds.), *Migration Control in the North Atlantic World: The Evolution of State Practices in Europe and the United States from the French Revolution to the Inter-War Period*, Providence, 2003.

Fall, Babacar, *Le Travail forcé en Afrique Occidentale française 1900–1946*, Paris, 1993.

Fanizadeh, Michael, Gerald Hödl and Wolfram Manzenreiter (eds.), *Global Players: Kultur, Ökonomie und Politik des Fußballs*, Frankfurt, 2002.

Farley, M. Foster, 'The Chinese Coolie Trade 1845–1874', *Journal of Asian and African Studies* 3 (1968), 257–70.

Faure, David, *The Structure of Chinese Rural Society*, Hong Kong, 1989.

Febvre, Lucien, 'Zur Entwicklung des Wortes und der Vorstellung von "Civilization"', in Febvre, *Das Gewissen des Historikers*, Berlin 1988, pp. 39–79.

Feichtinger, Johannes, Ursula Prutsch and Moritz Csáky (eds.), *Habsburg post-colonial: Machtstrukturen und kollektives Gedächtnis*, Innsbruck, 2003.

Feindt, Hendrik, 'Dreißig, sechsundvierzig, achtundvierzig, dreiund-sechzig: Polnische Aufstände in drei Romanen von Freytag, Raabe und Schweichel', in Feindt (ed.), *Studien zur Kulturgeschichte des deutschen Polenbildes 1848–1939*, Wiesbaden, 1995, pp. 15–40.

Feldman, Gerald D., *Armee, Industrie und Arbeiterschaft in Deutschland 1914 bis 1918*, Berlin, 1985.

Fenske, Hans, 'Die deutsche Auswanderung in der Mitte des 19. Jahrhunderts: Öffentliche Meinung und amtliche Politik', *Geschichte in Wissenschaft und Unterricht* 24 (1973), 221–36.

'Imperialistische Tendenzen in Deutschland vor 1866: Auswanderung, überseeische Bestrebungen, Weltmachtträume', *Historisches Jahrbuch* 97/98 (1978), 336–83.

Ferenczi, Imre, *Kontinentale Wanderungen und die Annäherung der Völker*, Jena, 1930.

Feyerabend, Bruno, *Die evangelischen Arbeitervereine: Eine Untersuchung über ihre religiösen, geistigen, gesellschaftlichen und politischen Grundlagen und über ihre Entwicklung bis zum ersten Weltkrieg*, Frankfurt, 1955.

Fiebig-von Hase, Ragnhild, *Lateinamerika als Konfliktherd der deutsch-amerikanischen Beziehungen 1890–1903: Vom Beginn der Panamerikapolitik bis zur Venezuelakrise von 1902/03*, 2 vols., Göttingen, 1986.

'The United States and Germany in the World Arena, 1900–1917', in Hans-Jürgen Schröder (ed.), *Confrontation and Cooperation: Germany and the United States in the Era of World War I, 1900–1924*, Providence, 1993, pp. 33–68.

Fieldhouse, David K., *Colonialism 1870–1945: An Introduction*, London, 1981.
Economics and Empire, 1880–1914, London, 1973.

Finger, A., 'Die Schutzzollfrage 1848/49 und der Allgemeine deutsche Verein zum Schutze der vaterländischen Arbeit', Dr. Phil. dissertation, University of Gießen, 1937.

Firth, Stewart, 'Governors versus Settlers: The Dispute over Chinese Labour in German Samoa', *The New Zealand Journal of History* 11 (1977), 155–79.

Fisch, Jörg, 'Zivilisation, Kultur', in Otto Brunner, Werner Conze and Reinhart Koselleck (eds.), *Geschichtliche Grundbegriffe: Historisches Lexikon zur politisch-sozialen Sprache in Deutschland*, 8 vols., Vol. VII, Stuttgart, 1992, pp. 679–774.

Fischer, Fritz, *Griff nach der Weltmacht: Die Kriegszielpolitik des kaiserlichen Deutschland 1914/1918*, Düsseldorf, 1967.

Fischer, Wolfram, *Expansion, Integration, Globalisierung: Studien zur Geschichte der Weltwirtschaft*, Göttingen, 1998.
'Die Ordnung der Weltwirtschaft vor dem Ersten Weltkrieg', *Zeitschrift für Wirtschafts- und Sozialwissenschaften* 19 (1975), 289–304.

Fischer-Tiné, Harald, 'Global Civil Society and the Forces of Empire: The Salvation Army, British Imperialism and the "Pre-History" of NGOs (*ca.* 1880–1920)', in Sebastian Conrad and Dominic Sachsenmaier (eds.), *Competing Visions of World Order: Global Moments and Movements 1880s–1930s*, New York, 2007, pp. 29–67.
'White Women Degrading Themselves to the Lowest Depths: European Networks of Prostitution and Colonial Anxieties in British India *ca.* 1870–1914', *Indian Economic and Social History Review* 40 (2003), 163–190.

Fischer-Tiné, Harald and Michael Mann (eds.), *Colonialism as Civilising Mission: Cultural Ideology in British India*, London, 2004.

Fisher, Lewis R. and Helge W. Nordvik, 'Maritime Transport and the Integration of the North Atlantic Economy, 1850–1914', in Wolfram Fischer, R. Marvin McInnis and Jürgen Schneider (eds.), *The Emergence of a World Economy, 1500–1914*, Stuttgart, 1986, pp. 519–46.

Fitzgerald, John, *Awakening China: Politics, Culture, and Class in the Nationalist Revolution*, Stanford, 1996.

Flasch, Kurt, *Die geistige Mobilmachung: Die deutschen Intellektuellen und der Erste Weltkrieg*, Berlin, 2000.

Fletcher, Roger, *Revisionism and Empire: Socialist Imperialism in Germany, 1897–1914*, London, 1984.

Flohr, Bernd, *Arbeiter nach Maß: Die Disziplinierung der Fabrikarbeiterschaft während der Industrialisierung Deutschlands im Spiegel von Arbeitsordnungen*, Frankfurt, 1981.

Fluck, Julius, 'Die Entwicklung der deutsch-brasilianischen Handelsbeziehungen von 1871–1939, Dr. Phil. dissertation, University of Cologne, 1951.

Fludernik, Monika, Peter Haslinger and Stefan Kaufmann (eds.), *Der Alteritätsdiskurs des Edlen Wilden: Exotismus, Anthropologie und Zivilisationskritik am Beispiel eines europäischen Topos*, Würzburg, 2002.

Förster, Stig, *Der doppelte Militarismus: Die deutsche Heeresrüstungspolitik zwischen Status-Quo-Sicherung und Aggression 1890–1913*, Stuttgart, 1985.

Fogel, Joshua A. (ed.), *Late Qing China and Meiji Japan: Political and Cultural Aspects*, Eastbridge, 2004.

Forberg, Martin, 'Foreign Labour, the State and Trade Unions in Imperial Germany, 1890–1918', in W. Robert Lee and Eve Rosenhaft (eds.), *State, Social Policy and Social Change in Germany 1880–1994*, Oxford, 1997, pp. 102–133.

Foreman-Peck, James (ed.), *Historical Foundations of Globalization*, Cheltenham, 1998.

(ed.), *A History of the World Economy: International Economic Relations since 1850*, London, 1994.

Fortner, Robert S., *International Communication: History, Conflict, and Control of the Global Metropolis*, Belmont, 1994.

Foucault, Michel, *The Order of Things: An Archaelogy of the Human Sciences*, New York, 1970.

'Society Must Be Defended': Lectures at the Collège de France, 1975–76, trans. David Macey, New York, 2003.

Fouquet, Carlos, *Der deutsche Einwanderer und seine Nachkommen in Brasilien, 1808–1824–1974*, São Paulo, 1974.

Frank, Andre Gunder, *ReOrient: Global Economy in the Asian Age*, Berkeley, 1998.

Frank, Andre Gunder and Barry K. Gills, *The World System: Five Hundred Years or Five Thousand?*, London, 1993.

Frankenberg, Hermann von and Dr. Drechsler, 'Die Behandlung der Bettler, Landstreicher und Arbeitsscheuen', in von Frankenberg and Drechsler, *Der Vorentwurf zu einem deutschen Strafgesetzbuch und die Armenpflege*, Leipzig, 1911.

Frauendienst, Werner, 'Preußisches Staatsbewußtsein und polnischer Nationalismus: Preußisch-deutsche Polenpolitik 1815–1890', in Frauendienst, *Das östliche Deutschland*, Würzburg, 1959, pp. 305–59.

Fredrickson, George M., *Rassismus: Ein historischer Abriß*, Hamburg, 2004.

Freund, Fritz, 'Ueber Strafkolonisation und Einrichtung ueberseeischer Strafanstalten', *Preußische Jahrbücher* 81 (1895), 502–37.

Freyre, Gilberto, *Order and Progress: Brazil from Monarchy to Republic*, New York, 1970.

Freytag, Gustav, *Debit and Credit*, trans. L. C. Cummings, New York, 1858.
Soll und Haben: Roman in Sechs Büchern, [1854] Berlin, 1920.

Fridenson, Patrick, 'Un tournant taylorien de la société française' (1904–1918), *Annales* 42 (1987), 1031–60.

Friedemann, Peter and Lucian Hölscher, 'Internationale, International, Internationalismus', in Otto Brunner, Werner Conze and Reinhart Koselleck (eds.), *Geschichtliche Grundbegriffe: Historisches Lexikon zur politisch-sozialen Sprache in Deutschland*, 8 vols., Vol. III, Stuttgart, 1982, pp. 367–97.

Friedrichsmeyer, Sara, Sara Lennox and Susanne Zantop (eds.), *The Imperialist Imagination: German Colonialism and Its Legacy*, Ann Arbor, 1998.

Friedewald, Michael, *Die 'tönenden Funken': Geschichte eines frühen drahtlosen Kommunikationssystems 1905–1914*, Diepholz, 1999.

Fröhlich, Michael, *Imperialismus: Deutsche Kolonial- und Weltpolitik 1880 bis 1914*, Munich, 1994.

Fröschle, Hartmut (ed.), *Die Deutschen in Lateinamerika: Schicksal und Leistung*, Tübingen, 1979.

Fuchs, Eckhardt, 'Das deutsche Reich auf den Weltausstellungen vor dem Ersten Weltkrieg', *Comparativ* 9:5/6 (1999), 61–88.

Fuhrmann, Malte, *Der Traum vom deutschen Orient: Zwei deutsche Kolonien im osmanischen Reich 1851–1914*, Frankfurt, 2006.

Funke, Alfred, *Aus Deutsch-Brasilien: Bilder aus dem Leben der Deutschen im Staate Rio Grande do Sul*, Leipzig, 1902.

Furber, David, '"Going East": Colonialism and German Life in Nazi-Occupied Poland', Ph.D. dissertation, University of New York at Buffalo, 2003.
'Near as Far in the Colonies: The Nazi Occupation of Poland', *International History Review* 26 (2004), 541–581.

Furtado, Celso, *Die wirtschaftliche Entwicklung Brasiliens*, Munich, 1975.

Furuya Tetsuo (ed.), *Gendai Nihon no Ajia ninshiki*, Tokyo, 1994.

Gabaccia, Donna, *Italy's Many Diasporas*, London, 2000.
'Juggling Jargons: "Italians Everywhere", Diaspora or Transnationalism?', *Traverse: Zeitschrift für Geschichte* 12 (2005), 49–64.
'The "Yellow Peril" and the "Chinese of Europe": Global Perspectives on Race and Labor, 1815–1930', in Jan Lucassen and Leo Lucassen (eds.), *Migration, Migration History, History: Old Paradigms and New Perspectives*, New York, 1997, pp. 177–96.

Gabaccia, Donna and Fraser Ottanelli (eds.), *Italian Workers of the World: Labor, Migration and the Making of Multi-Ethnic States*, Urbana, 2001.

Gainer, Bernard, *The Alien Invasion*, London, 1972.

Gaisbauer, Adolf, *Davidstern und Doppeladler: Zionismus und jüdischer Nationalismus in Österreich*, Vienna, 1988.

Galicich, Anne, *The German Americans*, New York, 1989.

Gall, Lothar and Manfred Pohl (eds.), *Die Eisenbahn in Deutschland: Von den Anfängen bis zur Gegenwart*, Munich, 1999.

Gallagher, John and Ronald Robinson, 'The Imperialism of Free Trade', *Economic History Review* 6 (1953), 1–15.

Gallarotti, Giulio M., *The Anatomy of an International Monetary Regime: The Classical Gold Standard, 1880–1914*, New York, 1995.

Galos, Adam, Felix-Heinrich Gentzen and Witold Jakóbczyk, *Die Hakatisten: Der deutsche Ostmarkenverein (1894–1934). Ein Beitrag zur Geschichte der Ostpolitik des deutschen Imperialismus*, Berlin, 1966.

Gandhi, Leela, *Postcolonial Theory*, New York, 1998.

Gann, Lewis, 'Marginal Colonialism: The German Case', in Lewis and Arthur J. Knoll (eds.), *Germans in the Tropics: Essays in German Colonial History*, New York, 1987, pp. 1–18.

Gatzke, Hans Wilhelm, *Germany and the United States: A 'Special Relationship'?* Cambridge, MA, 1980.

Geiss, Immanuel, *Panafrikanismus: Zur Geschichte der Dekolonisation*, Frankfurt, 1968.

  Der polnische Grenzstreifen 1914–1918, Lübeck, 1960.

Gelber, N. M. (ed.), *Die Kattowitzer Konferenz 1884: Protokolle*, Vienna, 1919.

Gellner, Ernest, *Nations and Nationalism*, Oxford, 1983.

Gencer, Mustafa, *Bildungspolitik, Modernisierung und kulturelle Interaktion: Deutsch-türkische Beziehungen (1908–1918)*, Münster, 2002.

Gerhard, Wolfram, 'Die wirtschaftlich argumentierende Judenfeindschaft', in Karl Thieme (ed.), *Judenfeindschaft: Darstellung und Analysen*, Frankfurt, 1963, pp. 80–125.

Gerhardt, Martin, *Friedrich von Bodelschwingh: Ein Lebensbild aus der deutschen Kirchengeschichte*, 2 vols., Vol. II, Bethel, 1952.

  Ein Jahrhundert Innere Mission: Die Geschichte des Central-Ausschusses für die Innere Mission der Deutschen Evangelischen Kirche, 2 vols., Gütersloh, 1948.

Gerlach, H. H., *Deutsche Kolonisation und die deutsche Post in den Kolonien und im Ausland*, Munich, 1985.

Gernhard, Robert, *Reise-Bilder aus Brasilien*, Breslau, 1900.

Gerstenberger, Heide and Ulrich Welke, *Vom Wind zum Dampf: Sozialgeschichte der deutschen Handelsschiffahrt im Zeitalter der Industrialisierung*, Münster, 1996.

Geulen, Christian, 'Blonde bevorzugt. Virchow und Boas: Eine Fallstudie zur Verschränkung von "Rasse" und "Kultur" im ideologischen Feld der Ethnizität um 1900', *Archiv für Sozialgeschichte* 40 (2000), 147–70.

Wahlverwandte: Rassendiskurs und Nationalismus im späten 19. Jahrhundert, Hamburg, 2004.

Geyer, Dietrich, 'Ostpolitik und Geschichtsbewußtsein in Deutschland', *Vierteljahrshefte für Zeitgeschichte* 34 (1986), 147–160.

Geyer, Martin H., 'One Language for the World: The Metric System, International Coinage, Gold Standard, and the Rise of Internationalism, 1850–1900', in Geyer and Johannes Paulmann (eds.), *The Mechanics of Internationalism: Culture, Society, and Politics from the 1840s to the First World War*, Oxford, 2001, pp. 55–92.

Geyer, Martin H. and Johannes Paulmann (eds.), *The Mechanics of Internationalism: Culture, Society, and Politics from the 1840s to the First World War*, Oxford, 2001.

Geyer, Michael, 'Deutschland und Japan im Zeitalter der Globalisierung: Überlegungen zu einer komparativen Geschichte jenseits des Modernisierungs-Paradigmas', in Sebastian Conrad and Jürgen Osterhammel (eds.), *Das Kaiserreich transnational: Deutschland in der Welt, 1871–1914*, Göttingen, 2004, pp. 68–86.

Geyer, Michael and Charles Bright, 'Where in the World Is America? The History of the United States in the Global Age', in Thomas Bender (ed.), *Rethinking American History in a Global Age*, Berkeley, 2002, pp. 63–99.

'World History in a Global Age', *American Historical Review* 100 (1995), 1034–60.

Giddens, Anthony, *The Consequences of Modernity*, Cambridge, 1990.

Giese, Fritz E., *Kleine Geschichte der deutschen Handelsschiffahrt*, Berlin, 1976.

Giesebrecht, Franz (ed.), *Die Behandlung der Eingeborenen in den deutschen Kolonien*, Berlin, 1898.

(ed.), *Die deutsche Kolonie Hansa in Südbrasilien: Reiseerlebnisse aus dem Staate Santa Catharina*, Berlin, 1899.

Gilman, Sander L., 'The Hottentot and the Prostitute: Toward an Iconography of Female Sexuality', in Gilman, *Difference and Pathology: Stereotypes of Sexuality, Race, and Madness*, Ithaca, NY, 1985, pp. 76–108.

Rasse, Sexualität und Seuche: Stereotype aus der Innenwelt der westlichen Kultur, Reinbek, 1992.

Gilroy, Paul, *The Black Atlantic: Modernity and Double Consciousness*, London, 1993.

Glassman, Jonathon, *Feasts and Riots: Revelry, Rebellion, and Popular Consciousness on the Swahili Coast, 1856–1888*, Portsmouth, NH, 1995.

Glick Schiller, Nina and Andreas Wimmer, 'Methodological Nationalism and Beyond: Nation-State Building, Migration and the Social Sciences', *Global Networks* 2 (2002), 301–34.

Godley, Michael, *The Mandarin Capitalists from Nanyang: Overseas Chinese Enterprise in the Modernization of China 1893–1911*, Cambridge, 1982.

  'The Treaty Port Connection: An Essay', *Journal of Southeast Asian Studies* 12 (1981), 249–59.

Göbel, Carl (ed.), *Im Dienst der Liebe: Erlebnisse aus der Arbeit der Inneren Mission*, Bielefeld, 1907.

Göckenjahn, Gert, *Kurieren und Staat machen: Gesundheit und Medizin in der bürgerlichen Welt*, Frankfurt, 1985.

Goldhagen, Daniel Jonah, *Hitler's Willing Executioners: Ordinary Germans and the Holocaust*, New York, 1995.

Gollwitzer, Heinz, '"Für welchen Weltgedanken kämpfen wir?" Bemerkungen zur Dialektik zwischen Identitäts- und Expansionsideologie in der deutschen Geschichte', in Klaus Hildebrand and Reiner Pommerin (eds.), *Deutsche Frage und europäisches Gleichgewicht*, Cologne, 1985, pp. 83–109.

  Die Gelbe Gefahr: Geschichte eines Schlagworts. Studien zum imperialistischen Denken, Göttingen, 1962.

  Geschichte des weltpolitischen Denkens, 2 vols., Göttingen, 1972–82.

  Internationale des Schwertes: Transnationale Beziehungen im Zeitalter der 'vaterländischen' Streitkräfte, Opladen, 1987.

Goltz, Fritz von der, *Die gelbe Gefahr im Licht der Geschichte*, Leipzig, 1907.

Gong, Gerrit W. (ed.), *The Standard of 'Civilization' in International Society*, Oxford, 1984.

Gonon, Philipp, *Arbeitsschule und Qualifikation: Arbeit und Schule im 19. Jahrhundert, Kerschensteiner und die heutigen Debatten zur beruflichen Qualifikation*, Frankfurt, 1992.

Goschler, Constantin, *Rudolf Virchow: Mediziner, Anthropologe, Politiker*, Cologne, 2003.

Gosewinkel, Dieter, *Einbürgern und ausschließen: Die Nationalisierung der Staatsangehörigkeit vom Deutschen Bund bis zur Bundesrepublik Deutschland*, Göttingen, 2001.

Goswami, Manu, 'From Swadeshi to Swaraj: Nation, Economy, Territory in Colonial South Asia, 1870 to 1907', *Comparative Studies in Society and History* 40 (1998), 609–36.

Gottwaldt, Heinrich, *Die überseeische Auswanderung der Chinesen und ihre Einwirkung auf die weiße und gelbe Rasse*, Bremen, 1903.

Grabowski, Sabine, *Deutscher und polnischer Nationalismus: Der deutsche Ostmarkenverein und die polnische Straż 1894–1914*, Marburg, 1998.

Gradmann, Christoph, '"Auf Collegen, zum fröhlichen Krieg". Popularisierte Bakteriologie im Wilhelminischen Zeitalter', *Medizin, Gesellschaft und Geschichte* 13 (1994), 35–54.

'Bazillen, Krankheit und Krieg', *Berichte zur Wissenschaftsgeschichte* 19 (1996), 81–94.

Green, Abigail, *Fatherlands: State-Building and Nationhood in Nineteenth-Century Germany*, Cambridge, 2001.

Green, William A., *British Slave Emancipation: The Sugar Colonies and the Great Experiment*, Oxford, 1976.

Greenaway, Frank, *Science International: A History of the International Council of Scientific Unions*, Cambridge, 1996.

Greenblatt, Stephen (ed.), *Cultural Mobility: A Manifesto*, Cambridge, 2010.

Marvelous Possessions, Chicago, 1991.

Shakespearean Negotiations: The Circulation of Social Energy in Renaissance England, Berkeley, 1988.

Greenhalgh, Paul, *Ephemeral Vistas: The Expositions universelles, Great Exhibitions and World's Fairs, 1851–1939*, Manchester, 1988.

Gregory, John, *Great Britain and the Taiping*, London, 1969.

Greschat, Martin, 'Protestantischer Antisemitismus in Wilhelminischer Zeit: Das Beispiel des Hofpredigers Adolf Stoecker', in Günter Brakelmann and Martin Rosowski (eds.), *Antisemitismus: Von religiöser Judenfeindschaft zur Rassenideologie*, Göttingen, 1989, pp. 27–51.

Groebner, Valentin, *Der Schein der Person: Steckbrief, Ausweis und Kontrolle im Mittelalter*, Munich, 2004.

Groh, Dieter, *Anthropologische Dimensionen der Geschichte*, Frankfurt, 1992.

Grohs, Gerhard, *Stufen afrikanischer Emanzipation: Studien zum Selbstverständnis westafrikanischer Eliten*, Stuttgart, 1967.

Gronemeyer, Reimer (ed.), *Der faule Neger: Vom weißen Kreuzzug gegen den schwarzen Müßiggang*, Reinbek, 1991.

Grosse, Pascal, *Kolonialismus, Eugenik und bürgerliche Gesellschaft in Deutschland 1850–1918*, Frankfurt, 2000.

'What Does German Colonialism Have to Do with National Socialism? A Conceptual Framework', in Eric Ames, Marcia Klotz and Lora Wildenthal (eds.), *Germany's Colonial Pasts*, Lincoln, NE, 2005, pp. 115–134.

Größer, Max, 'Die Emporentwicklung der Neger nach den Methoden des Booker T. Washington', *Zeitschrift für Missionswissenschaft* 8 (1918), 113–30.

Gruber, Max von, 'Kommentar', in Deutsch-Nationaler Handlungsgehilfen-Verband (ed.), *Haushaltsschulen oder Kaufmannsschulen für die weibliche Jugend*, Hamburg, 1913, p. 19.

Gründer, Horst, *Christliche Mission und deutscher Imperialismus 1884–1914*, Paderborn, 1982.

'Deutsche Missionsgesellschaften auf dem Wege zur Kolonialmission', in Klaus Bade (ed.), *Imperialismus und Kolonialmission: Kaiserliches Deutschland und koloniales Imperium*, Wiesbaden, 1982, pp. 68–102.

Geschichte der deutschen Kolonien, Paderborn, 1985.

Gruzinski, Serge, Les Mondes mêlés de la Monarchie catholique et autres "connected histories", *Annales HSS* 56 (2001), 85–117.

Günther, Christiane C., *Aufbruch nach Asien: Kulturelle Fremde in der deutschen Literatur um 1900*, Munich, 1988.

Gugerli, David and Daniel Speich, *Topographien der Nation: Politik, kartografische Ordnung und Landschaft im 19. Jahrhundert*, Zürich, 2002.

Guillén, Mauro F., 'Is Globalization Civilizing, Destructive or Feeble? A Critique of Five Key Debates in the Social Science Literature', *Annual Review of Sociology* 27 (2001), 235–60.

Hackel, Walter, 'Zur Theorie und Praxis der Arbeitserziehung an Volksschulen vor dem ersten Weltkrieg', in Robert Alt and Werner Lemm (eds.), *Zur Geschichte der Arbeitserziehung in Deutschland*, 2 vols., Vol. ii, Berlin, 1971, pp. 9–42.

Hackmann, Jörg, *Ostpreußen und Westpreußen in deutscher und polnischer Sicht*, Wiesbaden, 1996.

Hagen, Antje, *Deutsche Direktinvestitionen in Großbritannien, 1871–1918*, Stuttgart, 1997.

Hagen, William W., *Germans, Poles, and Jews: The Nationality Conflict in the Prussian East, 1772–1914*, Chicago, 1980.

Hall, John A. (ed.), *The State of the Nation: Ernest Gellner and the Theory of Nationalism*, Cambridge, 1998.

Hall, Stuart, 'The West and the Rest: Discourse and Power', in Hall and Bram Gieben (eds.), *Formations of Modernity*, Cambridge, 1992, pp. 275–320.

Hampe, Peter, 'Sozioökonomische und psychische Hintergründe der bildungsbürgerlichen Imperialbegeisterung', in Klaus Vondung (ed.), *Das wilhelminische Bildungsbürgertum: Zur Sozialgeschichte seiner Ideen*, Göttingen, 1976, pp. 67–79.

Hannerz, Ulf, '"Kultur" in einer vernetzten Welt: Zur Revision eines ethnologischen Begriffes', in Wolfgang Kaschuba (ed.), *Kulturen–Identitäten–Diskurse: Perspektiven Europäischer Ethnologie*, Berlin, 1995, pp. 64–84.

Transnational Connections: Culture, People, Places, London, 1996.

Hansen, Christine, 'Die deutsche Auswanderung im 19. Jahrhundert: Ein Mittel zur Lösung sozialer und sozialpolitischer Probleme?', in Günter Moltmann (ed.), *Deutsche Amerikaauswanderung: Sozialgeschichtliche Beiträge*, Stuttgart, 1976, pp. 8–61.

Hardach, Gerd, 'Defining Separate Spheres: German Rule and Colonial Law in Micronesia', in Hermann J. Hiery and John M. MacKenzie (eds.), *European Impact and Pacific Influence: British and German Colonial Policy in the Pacific Islands and the Indigenous Response*, London, 1997, pp. 231–58.

'Die deutsche Herrschaft in Mikronesien', in Hermann Joseph Hiery (ed.), *Die deutsche Südsee 1884–1914: Ein Handbuch*, Paderborn, 2001, pp. 508–34.

König Kopra: Die Marianen unter deutscher Herrschaft 1899–1914, Stuttgart, 1990.

Hardt, Michael and Antonio Negri, *Empire*, Cambridge, MA, 2001.

Hardtwig, Wolfgang, 'Nation–Region–Stadt: Strukturmerkmale des deutschen Nationalismus und lokale Denkmalskulturen', in Gunther Mai (ed.), *Das Kyffhaeuser-Denkmal 1896–1996: Ein nationales Monument im europäischen Kontext*, Cologne, 1997, pp. 54–84.

'Nationale und kulturelle Identität im Kaiserreich und der umkämpfte Weg in die Moderne: Der Deutsche Werkbund', in Helmut Berding (ed.), *Nationales Bewußtsein und kollektive Identität*, Frankfurt, 1994, pp. 507–40.

Nationalismus und Bürgerkultur in Deutschland 1500–1914, Göttingen, 1994.

Harjes, Philipp, *Eine Reise nach dem Lande wo die Arbeit adelt*, Gotha, 1905.

Harlan, Louis R., 'Booker T. Washington and the White Man's Burden', *American Historical Review* 71 (1966), 441–67.

Booker T. Washington: The Wizard of Tuskegee, 1901–1915, New York, 1983.

Harms, Bernhard, 'Arbeit', in *Handwörterbuch der Staatswissenschaften*, 11 vols., Vol I (Jena, 1909), 573–91.

Harms-Baltzer, Käthe, *Die Nationalisierung der deutschen Einwanderer und ihrer Nachkommen in Brasilien als Problem der deutsch-brasilianischen Beziehungen 1930–1938*, Berlin, 1970.

Harnisch, Hartmut, 'Agrarstaat oder Industriestaat: Die Debatte um die Bedeutung der Landwirtschaft in Wirtschaft und Gesellschaft Deutschlands an der Wende vom 19. zum 20. Jahrhundert', in Heinz Reif (ed.), *Ostelbische Agrargesellschaft im Kaiserreich und in der Weimarer Republik: Agrarkrise–junkerliche Interessenpolitik–Modernisierungsstrategien*, Berlin, 1994, pp. 33–50.

Harnisch, Thomas, *Chinesische Studenten in Deutschland: Geschichte und Wirkung ihrer Studienaufenthalte in den Jahren 1860 bis 1945*, Hamburg, 1999.

Harper, T. N., 'Empire, Diaspora and the Languages of Globalism, 1850–1914', in Anthony G. Hopkins (ed.), *Globalization in World History*, London, 2002, pp. 141–66.

Harrell, Paula, *Sowing the Seeds of Change: Chinese Students, Japanese Teachers, 1895–1905*, Stanford, 1992.

Harvey, David, *The Condition of Postmodernity: An Enquiry into the Origins of Cultural Change*, Oxford, 1989.

Haumann, Heiko (ed.), *Der Traum von Israel: Die Ursprünge des modernen Zionismus*, Weinheim, 1998.

Haupt, Heinz-Gerhard and Jürgen Kocka (eds.), *Geschichte und Vergleich: Ansätze und Ergebnisse international vergleichender Geschichtsschreibung*, Frankfurt, 1996.

Haupt, Heinz-Gerhard and Charlotte Tacke, 'Die Kultur des Nationalen: Sozial- und kulturgeschichtliche Ansätze bei der Erforschung des europäischen Nationalismus im 19. und 20. Jahrhundert', in Wolfgang Hardtwig and Hans-Ulrich Wehler (eds.), *Kulturgeschichte heute*, Göttingen, 1996, pp. 255–83.

Hausen, Karin (ed.), *Geschlechterhierarchie und Arbeitsteilung: Zur Geschichte ungleicher Erwerbschancen von Männern und Frauen*, Göttingen, 1993.

Hawkins, Mike, *Social Darwinism in European and American Thought 1860–1945*, Cambridge, 1997.

Hayford, Charles W., *To the People: James Yen and Village China*, New York, 1989.

Head, David, *Made in Germany: The Corporate Identity of a Nation*, London, 1992.

Headrick, Daniel R., *The Invisible Weapon: Telecommunications and International Politics, 1851–1914*, Oxford, 1991.

The Tentacles of Progress: Technology Transfer in the Age of Imperialism, 1840–1914, New York, 1988.

The Tools of Empire: Technology and European Imperialism in the Nineteenth Century, Oxford, 1981.

When Information Came of Age: Technologies of Knowledge in the Age of Reason and Revolution, Oxford, 2000.

Hechter, Michael, *Internal Colonialism: The Celtic Fringe in British National Development 1836–1966*, Berkeley, 1975.

Hehl, R. A., *Die Entwicklung der Einwanderungsgesetzgebung in Brasilien*, Leipzig, 1896.

Heid, Ludger, 'Sozialistischer Internationalismus, sozialistischer Zionismus und sozialistischer Antisemitismus', in Peter Alter, Claus-Ekkehard Bärsch and Peter Berghoff (eds.), *Die Konstruktion der Nation gegen die Juden*, Munich, 1999, pp. 93–118.

Heidegger, Martin, 'Zur Eröffnung der Schulungskurse für die Notstandsarbeiter der Stadt an der Universität', in *Heidegger Gesamtausgabe*, 102 vols., Vol. XVI, Frankfurt, 2000, p. 235.

Heidhues, Mary Somers, 'Chinese Settlements in Rural Southeast Asia', in Anthony Reid (ed.), *Sojourners and Settlers: Histories of Southeast Asia and the Chinese*, Melbourne, 1996, pp. 164–82.

Heindl, Robert, *Meine Reise nach den Strafkolonien*, Berlin, 1914.

Helfferich, Karl, *Deutschlands Volkswohlstand 1888–1913*, Berlin, 1913.

Hell, Jürgen, 'Deutschland und Chile von 1871–1918', in *Wissenschaftliche Zeitschrift der Universität Rostock, gesellschafts- und sprachwissenschaftliche Reihe* 1/2 (1965), 81–104.

'Der Griff nach Südbrasilien: Die Politik des Deutschen Reiches zur Umwandlung Südbrasiliens in ein überseeisches Neudeutschland (1890–1914)', Dr. Phil. dissertation, University of Rostock, 1966.

'Das "südbrasilianische Neudeutschland": Der annexionistische Grundzug der wilhelminischen und nazistischen Brasilienpolitik (1895 bis 1938)', in Heinz Sanke (ed.), *Der deutsche Faschismus in Lateinamerika, 1933–1943*, Berlin, 1966, pp. 102–24.

Hellmann, Manfred, *'Es geht kein Mensch über die Erde, den Gott nicht liebt': Friedrich von Bodelschwingh d. Ä.*, Wuppertal, 1993.

Helly, Denise, *Idéologie et ethnicité: les Chinois Macao à Cuba, 1847–1886*, Montreal, 1979.

Helmstetter, Rudolf, 'Austreibung der Faulheit, Regulierung des Müßiggangs: Arbeit und Freizeit seit der Industrialisierung', in Ulrich Bröckling and Eva Horn (eds.), *Anthropologie der Arbeit*, Tübingen, 2002, pp. 259–79.

'"Der Neger als Arbeiter" und der Arbeiter als "Neger"', in Stefan Rieger, Schamma Schahadat and Manfred Weinberg (eds.), *Interkulturalität: Zwischen Inszenierung und Archiv*, Tübingen, 1999, pp. 333–52.

Hemming, John, *Amazon Frontier: The Defeat of the Brazilian Indians*, Cambridge, MA, 1987.

'Indians and the Frontier', in Leslie Bethell (ed.), *Colonial Brazil*, Cambridge, 1987, pp. 145–89.

Henatsch, Wilhelm Andreas, *Das Problem der ausländischen Wanderarbeiter unter besonderer Berücksichtigung der Zuckerproduktion in der Provinz Pommern*, Greifswald, 1920.

Henson, Curtis T., Jr., *Commissioners and Commodores: The East India Squadron and American Diplomacy in China*, Tuscaloosa, 1982.

Hentschel, Volker, *Die deutschen Freihändler und der volkswirtschaftliche Kongreß, 1858–1885*, Stuttgart, 1975.

Herbert, Ulrich, 'Arbeit und Vernichtung: Ökonomisches Interesse und Primat der "Weltanschauung" im Nationalsozialismus', in Herbert (ed.), *Europa und der 'Reichseinsatz': Ausländische Zivilarbeiter, Kriegsgefangene und KZ-Häftlinge in Deutschland 1938–1945*, Essen, 1991, pp. 384–425.

Geschichte der Ausländerbeschäftigung in Deutschland 1880 bis 1980: Saisonarbeiter, Zwangsarbeiter, Gastarbeiter, Bonn, 1986.

Herdieckerhoff, Otto, *Äußere und innere Mission, ihr Verhältnis zueinander und ihre Bedeutung für die evangelische Kirche*, Leipzig, 1888.

Hering, Rainer, *Konstruierte Nation: Der Alldeutsche Verband 1890 bis 1939*, Hamburg, 2003.

Herren, Madeleine, 'Governmental Internationalism and the Beginning of a New World Order in the Late Nineteenth Century', in Martin H. Geyer and Johannes Paulmann (eds.), *The Mechanics of Internationalism: Culture, Society, and Politics from the 1840s to the First World War*, Oxford, 2001, pp. 121–44.

Hintertüren zur Macht: Internationalismus und modernisierungsorientierte Außenpolitik in Belgien, der Schweiz und den USA 1865–1914, Munich 2000.

Herzl, Theodor, *Der Judenstaat*, Tel Aviv, 1934.

Hess, Christel, 'Nation, Arbeit, Frauen', in Frauen und Geschichte Baden-Württemberg (eds.), *Frauen und Nation*, Tübingen, 1996, pp. 178–189.

Hess, Moses, *Rom und Jerusalem, die letzte Nationalitätsfrage*, Leipzig, 1862.

Hesse, Hermann, *Kindheit und Jugend vor Neunzehnhundert*, 2 vols., Vol. II, Frankfurt, 1978.

Hesse-Wartegg, Ernst von, *China und Japan: Erlebnisse, Studien, Beobachtungen*, Leipzig, 1900.

Heuel, Eberhard, *Der umworbene Stand: Die ideologische Integration der Arbeiter im Nationalsozialismus 1933–1935*, Frankfurt, 1989.

Heuss, Theodor, *Deutsche Gestalten: Studien zum 19. Jahrhundert*, Stuttgart, 1947.

Hevia, James L., *English Lessons: The Pedagogy of Imperialism in Nineteenth-Century China*, Durham, NC, 2003.

Heyden, Ulrich van der and Joachim Zeller (eds.), *Kolonialmetropole Berlin: Eine Spurensuche*, Berlin, 2002.

Hiden, John, 'The Weimar Republic and the Problem of the Auslandsdeutsche', *Journal of Contemporary History* 12 (1977), 273–89.

Hiery, Hermann Joseph, 'Les Asiatiques dans les possessions allemandes du Pacifique 1884–1914', in Paul de Deckker (ed.), *Le Peuplement du Pacifique et de la Nouvelle-Calédonie au XIX siècle (1788–1914)*, Paris, 1994, pp. 275–93.

Das Deutsche Reich in der Südsee 1900–1921, Göttingen 1995.

(ed.), *Die deutsche Südsee 1884–1914: Ein Handbuch*, Paderborn, 2001.

'Die deutsche Verwaltung Samoas 1900–1914', in Hiery (ed.), *Die deutsche Südsee 1884–1914: Ein Handbuch*, Paderborn, 2001, pp. 649–75.

Hildebrand, Klaus, *Das vergangene Reich: Deutsche Außenpolitik von Bismarck bis Hitler*, Stuttgart, 1995.

Hill, Christopher L., 'National Histories and World Systems: Writing Japan, France, and the United States', in Q. Edward Wang and Georg G. Iggers (eds.), *Turning Points in Historiography: A Cross-Cultural Perspective*, Rochester, NY, 2002, pp. 163–84.

National History and the World of Nations: Capital, State and the Rhetoric of History in Japan, France, and the United States, Durham, NC, 2008.

Himka, John-Paul, 'The Construction of Nationality in Galician Rus´: Icarian Flights in Almost All Directions', in Ronald G. Suny and Michael D. Kennedy (eds.), *Intellectuals and the Articulation of the Nation*, Ann Arbor, 1999, pp. 109–64.

Galician Villagers and the Ukrainian National Movement in the Nineteenth Century, Basingstoke, 1988.

Religion and Nationality in Western Ukraine: The Greek Catholic Church and the Ruthenian National Movement in Galicia, 1867–1900, Montreal, 1999.

Hintze, Otto, 'Über individualistische und kollektivistische Geschichtsauffassung', *Historische Zeitschrift* 78 (1897), 60–67.

Hirita, Lucie Cheng, 'Free, Indentured, Enslaved: Chinese Prostitutes in Nineteenth-Century America', *Signs* 5 (1979), 3–29.

Hirschhausen, Ulrike von and Jörn Leonhard, 'Europäische Nationalismen im West-Ost-Vergleich: Von der Typologie zur Differenzbestimmung', in Hirschhausen and Leonhard (eds.), *Nationalismen in Europa: West- und Osteuropa im Vergleich*, Göttingen, 2001, pp. 11–45.

Hitze, Franz, *Kapital und Arbeit und die Reorganisation der Gesellschaft*, Paderborn, 1880.

Hobsbawm, Eric, *Industry and Empire: An Economic History of Britain since 1750*, London, 1968.

Nations and Nationalism since 1780: Program, Myth, Reality, Cambridge, 1995.

Hobsbawm, Eric and Terence Ranger (eds.), *The Invention of Tradition*, Cambridge, 1992.

Hochschild, Adam, *King Leopold's Ghost: A Story of Greed, Terrorism and Heroism in Colonial Africa*, Boston, 1998.

Hochstadt, Steve, *Mobility and Modernity: Migration in Germany, 1820–1989*, Ann Arbor, 2002.

Hodgson, Marshall G. S., *Rethinking World History: Essays on Europe, Islam and World History*, Cambridge, 1993.

Hoeber, Fritz, 'Architekturfragen', *Die neue Rundschau* 29:2 (1918), 1103–8.

Hölscher, Lucian, *Die Entdeckung der Zukunft*, Frankfurt, 1999.

Hoeninger, Robert, 'Das Deutschtum in Übersee', *Das Deutschtum im Ausland* 6 (1910), 261–73.

Hoerder, Dirk, *Cultures in Contact: World Migrations in the Second Millennium*, Durham, NC, 2002.

Hoerder, Dirk and Jörg Nagel (eds.), *People in Transit: German Migrations in Comparative Perspective, 1820–1930*, Cambridge, 1995.

Hoerll, Albert, 'Die deutsche Kolonisation in Chile', in Anon (ed.), *Deutsche Arbeit in Chile: Festschrift des Deutschen Wissenschaftlichen Vereins zu Santiago*, Santiago, 1910, pp. 1–59.

Hoffmann, Lutz, 'Die Konstruktion des Volkes durch seine Feinde', *Jahrbuch für Antisemitismusforschung* 2 (1993), 13–37.

Hoffmann, Robert, 'Die katholische Missionsbewegung in Deutschland vom Anfang des 19. Jahrhunderts bis zum Ende der deutschen Kolonialgeschichte', in Klaus J. Bade (ed.), *Imperialismus und Kolonialmission: Kaiserliches Deutschland und koloniales Imperium*, Wiesbaden, 1982, pp. 29–50.

Hoffmann, Stefan-Ludwig, *Die Politik der Geselligkeit: Freimaurerlogen in der deutschen Bürgergesellschaft 1840–1918*, Göttingen, 2000.

Hoffmann, Werner, 'Die Deutschen in Argentinien', in Hartmut Fröschle (ed.), *Die Deutschen in Lateinamerika: Schicksal und Leistung*, Tübingen, 1979, pp. 40–145.

Hofmann, Tessa, 'Der radikale Wandel: Das deutsche Polenbild zwischen 1772 und 1848', *Zeitschrift für Ostforschung* 42 (1993), 158–90.

Homburg, Heidrun, 'Anfänge des Taylor-Systems in Deutschland', *Geschichte und Gesellschaft* 4 (1978), 170–94.

Honold, Alexander and Klaus R. Scherpe (eds.), *Mit Deutschland um die Welt: Eine Kulturgeschichte des Fremden in der Kolonialzeit*, Stuttgart, 2004.

Honold, Alexander and Oliver Simons (eds.), *Kolonialismus als Kultur: Literatur, Medien, Wissenschaft in der deutschen Gründerzeit des Fremden*, Tübingen, 2002.

Hopkins, Anthony G., 'Back to the Future: From National History to Imperial History', *Past and Present* 164 (1999), 198–243.

'The History of Globalization – and the Globalization of History?', in Hopkins (ed.), *Globalization in World History*, London, 2002, pp. 11–46.

Horkheimer, Max and Theodor W. Adorno, *Dialectic of Enlightenment*, trans. Edmund Jephcott, Stanford, 2002.

Hornbogen, Jens-Peter, *Travail national–nationale Arbeit: Die handelspolitische Gesetzgebung in Frankreich und Deutschland vor dem Hintergrund der Debatte über Freihandel und Schutzzoll 1818–1892*, Berlin, 2002.

Horne, John, 'Immigrant Workers in France during World War I', *French Historical Studies* 14 (1985), 57–88.

Hoskins, Janet, *The Play of Time: Kodi Perspectives on Calendars, History, and Exchange*, Berkeley, 1993.

Houben, Vincent J. H. and Thomas Lindblad, *Coolie Labour in Colonial Indonesia: A Study of Labour Relations in the Outer Islands*, c. 1900–1940, Wiesbaden, 1999.

Howe, Anthony, *Free Trade and Liberal England 1846–1946*, Oxford, 1997.

Howland, Douglas R., *Translating the West: Language and Political Reason in Nineteenth-Century Japan*, Honolulu, 2002.

Howse, Derek, *Greenwich Time and the Discovery of the Longitude*, Oxford, 1980.

Hrycak, Jaroslaw, 'Zur Genese der Idee der politischen Selbständigkeit der Ukraine', *Jahrbuch der Ukrainekunde* 28 (1991), 67–90.

Hryniuk, Stella M., *Peasants with Promise: Ukrainians in Southeastern Galicia 1880–1900*, Edmonton, 1991.

Hsia, Adrian, *Deutsche Denker über China*, Frankfurt, 1985.

Hu-Dehart, Evelyn, 'Chinese Coolie Labour in Cuba in the Nineteenth Century: Free Labour or Neo-Slavery?', *Slavery and Abolition* 14 (1993), 67–86.

Huf, Peter Michael, *Die Entwicklung des bundesstaatlichen Systems in Brasilien*, Frankfurt, 1991.

Hugenberg, Alfred, *Streiflichter aus Vergangenheit und Gegenwart*, Berlin, 1926.

Hugill, Peter J., *Global Communications since 1844: Geopolitics and Technology*, Baltimore, 1999.

Humphreys, George C., *Taylorism in France, 1904–1920: The Impact of Scientific Management on Factory Relations and Society*, New York, 1986.

Hunt, Michael H., *Frontier Defense and Open Door*, New Haven, 1973.

The Making of a Special Relationship: The United States and China to 1914, New York, 1983.

Hyan, Hans, 'Die Arbeiterkolonie Hoffnungstal', *Die Gartenlaube* 26 (1906), 545–48.

Hyrkkänen, Markku, *Sozialistische Kolonialpolitik. Eduard Bernsteins Stellung zur Kolonialpolitik und zum Imperialismus 1882–1914: Ein Beitrag zur Geschichte des Revisionismus*, Helsinki, 1986.

Ilg, Karl, *Das Deutschtum in Chile und Argentinien*, Vienna, 1982.

Iliffe, John, *The Emergence of African Capitalism*, London, 1983.

A Modern History of Tanganyika, Cambridge, 1979.

Illi, Manfred, *Die deutsche Auswanderung nach Lateinamerika: Eine Literaturübersicht*, Munich, 1977.

Irick, Robert L., *Ch'ing Policy toward the Coolie Trade 1847–1878*, Taipei, 1982.

Iriye, Akira, *Cultural Internationalism and World Order*, Baltimore, 1997.

Ishay, Micheline R., *Internationalism and Its Betrayal*, Minneapolis, 1995.

Jahn, Ellen, *Die Cholera in Medizin und Pharmazie im Zeitalter des Hygienikers Max von Pettenkofer*, Stuttgart, 1994.

James, Harold, *The End of Globalization: Lessons from the Great Depression*, Cambridge, MA, 2001.

Janeck, Undine, *Zwischen Gartenlaube und Karl May: Deutsche Amerikarezeption in den Jahren 1871–1913*, Herzogenrath, 2003.

Jannasch, R., 'Die praktischen Aufgaben der deutschen Auswanderungspolitik', in *Verhandlungen des Deutschen Kolonialkongresses 1902*, Berlin, 1903, pp. 586–96.

Jansen, Sarah, 'Männer, Insekten und Krieg: Zur Geschichte der angewandten Entomologie in Deutschland, 1900–1925', in Christoph Meinel and Monika Renneberg (eds.), *Geschlechterverhältnisse in Medizin, Naturwissenschaft und Technik*, Stuttgart, 1996, pp. 170–81.

'Schädlinge': Geschichte eines wissenschaftlichen und politischen Konstrukts 1840–1920, Frankfurt, 2003.

Jasper, Gerhard, *Das Werden der Bethel-Mission*, Bethel, 1936.

Jeismann, Michael, *Das Vaterland der Feinde: Studien zum nationalen Feindbegriff und Selbstverständnis in Deutschland und Frankreich 1792–1918*, Stuttgart, 1992.

Jessen, Ralph and Jakob Vogel (eds.), *Wissenschaft und Nation in der europäischen Geschichte*, Frankfurt, 2002.

Jobst, Kerstin Susanne, 'Die ukrainische Nationalbewegung bis 1917', in Frank Golczewski (ed.), *Geschichte der Ukraine*, Göttingen, 1993, pp. 156–71.

Zwischen Nationalismus und Internationalismus: Die polnische und ukrainische Sozialdemokratie in Galizien von 1890 bis 1914, Hamburg, 1996.

Jochmann, Werner, *Gesellschaftskritik und Judenfeindschaft in Deutschland 1870–1945*, Hamburg, 1988.

'Stoecker als nationalkonservativer Politiker und antisemitischer Agitator', in Günter Brakelmann, Martin Greschat and Jochmann, *Protestantismus und Politik: Werk und Wirkung Adolf Stoeckers*, Hamburg, 1982, pp. 123–92.

Johler, Reinhard, 'Il concetto scientifico di deutsche Arbeit e l'ergologia nell'area alpina', *Annali di San Michele* 8 (1995), 265–86.

John, Wolfgang, *... ohne festen Wohnsitz ... Ursache und Geschichte der Nichtseßhaftigkeit und die Möglichkeiten der Hilfe*, Bielefeld, 1988.

'Die Vorgeschichte der Arbeiterkolonien', in Zentralverband Deutscher Arbeiterkolonien (ed.), *Ein Jahrhundert Arbeiterkolonien: 'Arbeit statt Almosen' – Hilfe für obdachlose Wanderarme 1884–1984*, Bielefeld, 1984, pp. 12–22.

Jones, Larry E. (ed.), *Crossing Boundaries: German and American Experiences with the Exclusion and Inclusion of Minorities*, Providence, 2001.

Jones, A. Philip, *Britain's Search for Chinese Cooperation during the First World War*, London, 1987.

Joseephy, Fritz, *Die deutsche überseeische Auswanderung seit 1871 unter beson-derer Berücksichtigung der Auswanderung nach den Vereinigten Staaten von Amerika: Ein volkswirtschaftlicher Beitrag zur Geschichte der deutschen Auswanderung*, Erlangen, 1912.

Jung, San Su, *Deutschland und das Gelbe Meer: Die deutsche Weltpolitik in Ostasien 1897–1902*, Frankfurt, 1996.

Jütte, Robert, 'Poor Relief and Social Discipline in Sixteenth Century Europe', *European Studies Review* 11 (1981), 25–52.

Just, Michael, *Ost- und Südosteuropäische Amerikawanderung 1881–1914: Transitprobleme in Deutschland und Aufnahme in den Vereinigten Staaten*, Stuttgart, 1988.

Kaczmarczyk, Zdzislaw, 'German Colonisation in Medieval Poland in the Light of the Historiography of Both Nations', *Polish Western Affairs* 11 (1970), 3–40.

Kaelble, Hartmut, *Der historische Vergleich: Eine Einführung zum 19. und 20. Jahrhundert*, Frankfurt, 1999.

Industrielle Interessenpolitik in der wilhelminischen Gesellschaft: Der Centralverband deutscher Industrieller 1867–1919, Berlin, 1967.

Kaienburg, Hermann, *'Vernichtung durch Arbeit': Der Fall Neuengamme*, Bonn, 1991.

Kamphausen, Georg, *Die Erfindung Amerikas in der Kulturkritik der Generation von 1890*, Göttingen, 2002.

Kamusella, Tomasz, 'Language and the Construction of Identity in Upper Silesia during the Long Nineteenth Century', in Kai Struve and Philipp Ther (eds.), *Die Grenzen der Nationen: Identitätenwandel in Oberschlesien in der Neuzeit*, Marburg, 2002, pp. 45–70.

Kaplan, Marion A., *Die jüdische Frauenbewegung in Deutschland: Organisation und Ziele des Jüdischen Frauenbundes 1904–1938*, Hamburg, 1981.

Kappeler, Andreas, 'Die ukrainische Nationalbewegung im Russischen Reich und in Galizien: Ein Vergleich', in Heiner Timmermann (ed.), *Entwicklung der Nationalbewegungen in Europa 1850–1914*, Berlin, 1998, pp. 175–96.

Kappeler, Andreas, Zenon H. Kohut, Frank E. Sysyn and Mark von Hagen (eds.), *Culture, Nation, and Identity: The Ukrainian–Russian Encounter (1600–1945)*, Edmonton, 2003.

Karl, Rebecca, 'Creating Asia: China in the World at the Beginning of the Twentieth Century', *American Historical Review* 103 (1998), 1096–118.

'Race, Ethnos, History in China at the Turn of the Twentieth Century', in Peter Osborne and Stella Sandford (eds.), *Philosophy of Race and Ethnicity*, London, 2002, pp. 97–113.

Staging the World: Chinese Nationalism at the Turn of the Twentieth Century, Durham, NC, 2002.

Kárný, Miroslav, '"Vernichtung durch Arbeit" in Leitmeritz: Die SS-Führungsstäbe in der deutschen Kriegswirtschaft', *1999: Zeitschrift für Sozialgeschichte des 20. und 21. Jahrhunderts* 8:4 (1993), 37–61.

Karstedt, Oskar, *Internationale Bekämpfung der Arbeitslosigkeit durch Erschließung überseeischer Gebiete*, Berlin, 1931.

Kasischke-Wurm, Daniela, *Antisemitismus im Spiegel der Hamburger Presse während des Kaiserreichs (1884–1914)*, Hamburg, 1997.

Käsler, Dirk, *Max Weber: Eine Einführung in Leben, Werk und Wirkung*, Frankfurt, 1995.

Katz, Friedrich, 'Einige Grundzüge der Politik des deutschen Imperialismus in Lateinamerika von 1898 bis 1914', in Heinz Sanke (ed.), *Der deutsche Faschismus in Lateinamerika, 1933–1943*, Berlin, 1966, pp. 9–70.

Katz, Jacob, *Vom Vorurteil bis zur Vernichtung: Der Antisemitismus 1700–1933*, Munich, 1989.

Kayali, Hasan Kayal, *Arabs and Young Turks: Ottomanism, Arabism, and Islamism in the Ottoman Empire, 1908–1918*, Berkeley, 1997.

Keiper, W., *Deutsche Kulturaufgaben in Argentinien*, Berlin, 1914.

Kelly, John D., 'Time and the Global', *Development and Social Change* 29 (1998), 839–71.

Keng, Cheah Boon, *Malaysia: The Making of a Nation*, Singapore, 2002.

Kennedy, Paul M., *The Rise of the Anglo-German Antagonism, 1860–1914*, London, 1980.

Kennedy, Paul M. and John Moses (eds.), *Germany in the Pacific and Far East*, St Lucia, 1977.

Krebs, Diethart and Jürgen Reulecke (eds.), *Handbuch der deutschen Reformbewegungen 1880–1933*, Wuppertal, 1998.

Kern, Stephen, *The Culture of Time and Space 1880–1918*, Cambridge, MA, 1983.

Kerschensteiner, Georg, *Grundfragen der Schulorganisation*, Munich, 1954.

Kindleberger, Charles P., 'The Rise of Free Trade in Western Europe, 1820–1875', *Journal of Economic History* 35 (1975), 20–55.

King, Desmond, *The Liberty of Strangers: Making the American Nation*, Oxford, 2005.

    Making Americans: Immigration, Race and the Origins of the Diverse Democracy, Cambridge, MA, 2000.

Kistner, Ulrike, '"Der Feind im Hause": Nationalismus, Rassismus und bio-politische Seuchenbekämpfung', *metis: Zeitschrift für historische Frauen- und Geschlechterforschung* 6 (1997), 90–105.

Klatt, Ingaburgh, 'Arbeit statt Almosen: Studien zur Geschichte der Arbeitsverwaltung im Deutschen Reich von den Anfängen bis 1933 unter besonderer Berücksichtigung Kiels', Dr. Phil. dissertation, University of Kiel, 1991.

Klautke, Egbert, *Unbegrenzte Möglichkeiten: 'Amerikanisierung' in Deutschland und Frankreich (1900–1933)*, Stuttgart, 2003.

Klein, Herbert S., *The Atlantic Slave Trade*, Cambridge, 1999.

Klein-Arendt, Reinhard, *'Kamina ruft Nauen!' Die Funkstellen in den deutschen Kolonien 1904–1918*, Cologne, 1996.

Kleinau, Elke and Claudia Opitz, *Geschichte der Mädchen- und Frauenarbeit*, 2 vols., Vol. II, Frankfurt, 1996.

Kleßmann, Christoph, *Polnische Bergarbeiter im Ruhrgebiet 1870–1945: Soziale Integration und nationale Subkultur einer Minderheit in der deutschen Industriegesellschaft*, Göttingen, 1978.

Kloft, Hans, 'Die Germania des Tacitus und das Problem eines deutschen Nationalbewußtseins', *Archiv für Kulturgeschichte* 72 (1990), 93–114.

Kloosterhuis, Jürgen, *'Friedliche Imperialisten': Deutsche Auslandsvereine und auswärtige Kulturpolitik, 1906–1918*, 2 vols., Frankfurt, 1994.

Kludas, Arnold, *Die Geschichte der deutschen Passagierschiffahrt*, 5 vols., Hamburg, 1986–90.

Klug, Ekkehard, 'Das "asiatische" Rußland: Über die Entstehung eines europäischen Vorurteils', *Historische Zeitschrift* 245 (1987), 265–89.

Knapp, Ulla, *Frauenarbeit in Deutschland*, 2 vols., Munich, 1984.

Knick-Harley, Charles, 'Late Nineteenth Century Transportation, Trade and Settlement', in Wolfram Fischer, R. Marvin McInnis and Jürgen Schneider (eds.), *The Emergence of a World Economy, 1500–1914*, Stuttgart, 1986, pp. 593–618.

Knoke, Anton, *Ausländische Wanderarbeiter in Deutschland*, Leipzig, 1911.

Knoll, Arthur J., 'An Indigenous Law for the Togolese: The Work of Dr Rudolf Asmis', in Rüdiger Voigt and Peter Sack (eds.), *Kolonialisierung des Rechts: Zur kolonialen Rechts- und Verwaltungsordnung*, Baden-Baden, 2001, pp. 271–92.

Koch, Angela, *DruckBilder: Stereotype und Geschlechtercodes in den antipolnischen Diskursen der 'Gartenlaube' (1870–1930)*, Cologne, 2002.

Kochmann, Wilhelm, 'Das Taylorsystem und seine volkswirtschaftliche Bedeutung', *Archiv für Sozialwissenschaft und Sozialpolitik* 38 (1914), 391–424.

Kocka, Jürgen, *Arbeitsverhältnisse und Arbeiterexistenzen: Grundlagen der Klassenbildung im 19. Jahrhundert*, Bonn, 1990.

  'Industrielles Management: Konzeption und Modelle vor 1914', *Vierteljahrschrift für Sozial- und Wirtschaftsgeschichte* 56 (1969), 332–72.

  Das lange 19. Jahrhundert: Arbeit, Nation und bürgerliche Gesellschaft, Stuttgart, 2001.

  'Sozialgeschichte im Zeitalter der Globalisierung', *Merkur* 60 (2006), 305–16.

Kocka, Jürgen and Claus Offe (eds.), *Geschichte und Zukunft der Arbeit*, Frankfurt, 2000.

Kohl, Horst (ed.), *Die politischen Reden des Fürsten Bismarck 1847–1897*, 14 vols., Vol. XI, Stuttgart, 1894.

Köhler, Henning, *Arbeitsdienst in Deutschland: Pläne und Verwirklichungsformen bis zur Einführung der Arbeitsdienstpflicht im Jahre 1935*, Berlin, 1967.

Köhler, Michael, *Akkulturation in der Südsee: Die Kolonialgeschichte der Karolinen-Inseln im pazifischen Ozean und der Wandel ihrer sozialen Organisation*, Frankfurt, 1982.

Kohn, Hans, *Nationalism, Its Meaning and History*, Princeton, 1965.

Koller, Christian, *'Von Wilden aller Rassen niedergemetzelt': Die Diskussion um die Verwendung von Kolonialtruppen in Europa zwischen Rassismus, Kolonial- und Miltärpolitik (1914–1930)*, Stuttgart, 2001.

Köllmann, Wolfgang, *Bevölkerung in der industriellen Revolution*, Göttingen, 1974.

Kolsky, Elizabeth, 'Codification and the Rule of Colonial Difference: Criminal Procedure in British India', *Law and History Review* 23 (2005), 631–83.

Koponen, Juhani, *Development for Exploitation: German Colonial Policies in Mainland Tanzania, 1884–1914*, Hamburg, 1995.

Kopp, Kristin, 'Constructing Racial Difference in Colonial Poland', in Eric Ames, Marcia Klotz and Lora Wildenthal (eds.), *Germany's Colonial Pasts*, Lincoln, NE, 2005, pp. 76–96.

'Contesting Borders: German Colonial Discourse and the Polish Eastern Territories', Ph.D. dissertation, University of California, Berkeley, 2001.

Korinman, Michel, *Quand l'Allemagne pensait le monde: Grandeur et décadence d'une géopolitique*, Paris, 1990.

Koselleck, Reinhart, 'Fortschritt', in Otto Brunner, Werner Conze and Koselleck (eds.), *Geschichtliche Grundbegriffe: Historisches Lexikon zur politisch-sozialen Sprache in Deutschland*, 8 vols., Vol. II, Stuttgart, 1975, pp. 351–424.

'"Neuzeit": Zur Semantik moderner Bewegungsbegriffe', in Koselleck, *Vergangene Zukunft: Zur Semantik geschichtlicher Zeiten*, Frankfurt, 1979, pp. 300–49.

Vergangene Zukunft: Zur Semantik geschichtlicher Zeiten, Frankfurt, 1979.

Koselleck, Reinhart, Fritz Gschnitzer, Karl Ferdinand Werner and Bernd Schönemann, 'Volk, Nation, Nationalismus, Masse', in Otto Brunner, Werner Conze and Reinhart Koselleck (eds.), *Geschichtliche Grundbegriffe: Historisches Lexikon zur politisch-sozialen Sprache in Deutschland*, 8 vols., Vol. VII, Stuttgart, 1992, pp. 141–431.

Koskenniemi, Martti, *The Gentle Civilizer of Nations: The Rise and Fall of International Law 1870–1960*, Cambridge, 2001.

Kossert, Andreas, *Preußen, Deutsche oder Polen? Die Masuren im Spannungsfeld des ethnischen Nationalismus 1870–1956*, Wiesbaden, 2001.

Kost, Klaus, *Die Einflüsse der Geopolitik auf Forschung und Theorie der politischen Geographie von ihren Anfängen bis 1945*, Bonn, 1988.

Kösters-Kraft, Michael, *Großbaustelle und Arbeitswanderung: Niederländer beim Bau des Dortmund–Ems-Kanals 1892–1900*, Osnabrück, 2000.

Kotze, Stefan von, *Die gelbe Gefahr*, Berlin, 1904.

Kozik, Jan, *The Ukrainian National Movement in Galicia 1815–1849*, Edmonton, 1986.

Krabbe, Wolfgang R., *Die deutsche Stadt im 19. und 20. Jahrhundert*, Göttingen, 1989.

Gesellschaftsveränderung durch Lebensreform: Strukturmerkmale einer sozialreformerischen Bewegung im Deutschland der Industrialisierungsperiode, Göttingen, 1974.

Krämer, 'Einige Gedanken über die Erziehung der Neger zur Arbeit', *Nachrichten aus der ostafrikanischen Mission* 4 (1890), 9–13.

Kratzenstein, Eduard, 'Bemerkungen', *Allgemeine Missions-Zeitschrift* 14 (1887), 169–81.

Krauel, Richard, *Deutsche Interessen in Brasilien*, Hamburg, 1900.

Kraus, Michael, *Bildungsbürger im Urwald: Die deutsche ethnologische Amazonienforschung (1884–1929)*, Marburg, 2004.

Kroeger, Brooke, *Nelly Bly: Daredevil, Reporter, Feminist*, New York, 1994.

Kroker, Evelyn, *Die Weltausstellungen im 19. Jahrhundert: Industrieller Leistungsnachweis, Konkurrenzverhalten und Kommunikationsfunktion unter Berücksichtigung der Montanindustrie des Ruhrgebietes zwischen 1851 und 1880*, Göttingen, 1975.

Kronecker, Franz, *15 Jahre Kiautschou: Eine kolonialmedizinische Studie*, Berlin, 1913.

Küenzlen, Gottfried, *Die Religionssoziologie Max Webers: Eine Darstellung ihrer Entwicklung*, Berlin, 1980.

Kühl, Stefan, *Die Internationale der Rassisten: Aufstieg und Niedergang der internationalen Bewegung für Eugenik und Rassenhygiene im 20. Jahrhundert*, Frankfurt, 1997.

Kuh, Felix, 'Neue Aufgaben der deutschen Arbeit', *Deutschlands Erneuerung* 1 (1917), 524–36.

Kulczycki, John J., *The Foreign Worker and the German Labor Movement: Xenophobia and Solidarity in the Coal Fields of the Ruhr 1871–1914*, Oxford, 1994.

Kumar, Krishan, 'Nation and Empire: English and British National Identity in Comparative Perspective', *Theory and Society* 29 (2000), 575–608.

Kundrus, Birthe, *Moderne Imperialisten: Das Kaiserreich im Spiegel seiner Kolonien*, Cologne, 2003.

(ed.), *Phantasiereiche: Zur Kulturgeschichte des deutschen Kolonialismus*, Frankfurt, 2003.

Review of Eric Ames, Marcia Klotz and Lora Wildenthal, *Germany's Colonial Pasts* (Lincoln, NE, 2005), *H-Soz-u-Kult* (3 January, 2007), http://hsozkult.geschichte.hu-berlin.de/rezensionen/2007-1-006.

Kunz, Georg, *Verortete Geschichte: Regionales Geschichtsbewußtsein in den deutschen historischen Vereinen des 19. Jahrhunderts*, Göttingen, 2000.

Küther, Carsten, *Menschen auf der Straße: Vagierende Unterschichten in Bayern, Franken und Schwaben in der zweiten Hälfte des 18. Jahrhunderts*, Göttingen, 1983.

Küttner, Sibylle, *Farbige Seeleute im Kaiserreich: Asiaten und Afrikaner im Dienst der deutschen Handelsmarine*, Erfurt, 2000.

Laak, Dirk van, *Imperiale Infrastruktur: Deutsche Planungen für eine Erschließung Afrikas 1880 bis 1960*, Paderborn, 2004.

'Kolonien als "Laboratorien der Moderne"?', in Sebastian Conrad and Jürgen Osterhammel (eds.), *Das Kaiserreich transnational: Deutschland in der Welt 1871–1914*, Göttingen, 2004, pp. 257–79.

Labisch, Alfons, *Homo hygienicus: Gesundheit und Medizin in der Neuzeit*, Frankfurt, 1992.

Lacmann, Wilhelm, *Ritte und Rasttage in Südbrasilien: Reisebilder und Studien aus dem Leben der deutschen Siedelungen*, Berlin, 1906.

Lai, Walton Look, *Indentured Labor, Caribbean Sugar: Chinese and Indian Migrants to the British West Indies, 1838–1918*, Baltimore, 1993.

Lambi, Ivo Nikolai, *Free Trade and Protection in Germany 1868–1879*, Wiesbaden, 1963.

The Navy and German Power Politics, 1862–1914, London, 1984.

Lammich, Maria, *Das deutsche Osteuropabild in der Zeit der Reichsgründung*, Boppard, 1978.

Lamprecht, Karl, *Zur jüngsten deutschen Vergangenheit (Deutsche Geschichte, Ergänzungsband 2, zweite Hälfte)*, Berlin [1903], 1921.

Landes, David, *Revolution in Time: Clocks and the Making of the Modern World*, Cambridge, 1983.

The Wealth and Poverty of Nations: Why Some Are So Rich and Some So Poor, New York, 1998.

Langer, Michael, *Zwischen Vorurteil und Aggression: Zum Judenbild in der deutschsprachigen Volksbildung des 19. Jahrhunderts*, Freiburg, 1994.

Langewiesche, Dieter, 'Nation, Nationalismus, Nationalstaat: Forschungsstand und Forschungsperspektiven', *Neue politische Literatur* 40 (1995), 190–236.

Nation, Nationalismus, Nationalstaat in Deutschland und Europa, Munich, 2000.

Nationalismus im 19. und 20. Jahrhundert: Zwischen Partizipation und Aggression, Bonn, 1994.

'Wanderungsbewegungen in der Hochindustrialisierungsepoche: Regionale interstädtische und innerstädtische Mobilität in Deutschland 1880–1914', *Vierteljahrschrift für Sozial- und Wirtschaftsgeschichte* 64 (1977), 1–40.

Langley, J. Ayodele, *Pan-Africanism and Nationalism in West Africa 1900–1945*, Oxford, 1973.

Laqueur, Walter, *A History of Zionism*, New York, 1976.

Der Weg zum Staat Israel: Geschichte des Zionismus, Vienna, 1975.

Lee, Erika, *At America's Gates: The Exclusion Era, 1882–1943*, Chapel Hill, 2003.

Lee, Eun-Jeung, '"Asien" als Projekt: Der Asiendiskurs in China, Japan und Korea', *Leviathan* 31 (2003), 382–400.

Lehmann, Hartmut, 'Asketischer Protestantismus und ökonomischer Rationalismus: Die Weber-These nach zwei Generationen', in Wolfgang Schluchter (ed.), *Max Webers Sicht des okzidentalen Christentums: Interpretation und Kritik*, Frankfurt, 1988, pp. 529–53.

'Bodelschwingh und Bismarck: Christlich-konservative Sozialpolitik im Kaiserreich', *Historische Zeitschrift* 208 (1969), 607–26.

'The Rise of Capitalism: Weber versus Sombart', in Lehmann and Guenther Roth (eds.), *Weber's Protestant Ethic: Origins, Evidence, Contexts*, Cambridge, 1993, pp. 195–208.

Lekan, Thomas M., *Imagining the Nation in Nature: Landscape Preservation and German Identity*, 1885–1945, Cambridge, MA, 2004.

Lemberg, Hans, 'Zur Entstehung des Osteuropabegriffs im 19. Jahrhundert: Vom "Norden" zum "Osten" Europas', *Jahrbuch für Geschichte Osteuropas* 33 (1985), 48–91.

Lenger, Friedrich, *Werner Sombart 1863–1941: Eine Biographie*, Munich, 1994.

Lenz, Karl (ed.), *Carl Ritter: Geltung und Deutung*, Berlin, 1981.

Leo, D., 'Die Arbeiterfrage in unseren afrikanischen Kolonien', *Beiträge zur Kolonialpolitik und Kolonialwirtschaft* 4 (1902/03), 31–34, 44–53.

Leong Sow-Theng, *Migration and Ethnicity in Chinese History: Hakkas, Pengmin, and Their Neighbors*, Stanford, 1997.

Leonhardt, Karl, 'Die deutschen Kolonien im Süden von Chile', *Das Auswandererproblem* 5 (1912), 7–53.

Lepenies, Wolf, *Das Ende der Naturgeschichte: Wandel kultureller Selbstverständlichkeiten in den Wissenschaften des 18. und 19. Jahrhunderts*, Munich, 1976.

The Seduction of Culture in German History, Princeton, 2006.

Leuschen-Seppel, Rosemarie, 'Arbeiterbewegung und Antisemitismus', in Günter Brakelmann and Martin Rosowski (eds.), *Antisemitismus: Von religiöser Judenfeindschaft zur Rassenideologie*, Göttingen, 1989, pp. 77–96.

Sozialdemokratie und Antisemitismus im Kaiserreich: Die Auseinandersetzung der Partei mit den konservativen und völkischen Strömungen des Antisemitismus 1871–1914, Bonn, 1978.

Leuss, Hans, '*Das richtige Wanzenmittel': Ein jüdischer Staat. Ein Vorschlag zur Güte*, Leipzig, 1893.

Leutner, Mechthild, 'Deutsche Vorstellungen über China und Chinesen und über die Rolle der Deutschen in China, 1890–1945', in Kuo Heng-yü (ed.), *Von der Kolonialpolitik zur Kooperation: Studien zur Geschichte der deutsch–chinesischen Beziehungen*, Munich, 1986, pp. 401–43.

Levenson, Joseph, *Liang Ch'i-ch'ao and the Mind of Modern China*, Berkeley, 1959.

Levitt, Harold, 'The Globalization of Markets', *Harvard Business Review* 61 (1983), 92–102.

Leyer, Hermann, *Deutsches Kolonistenleben im Staate Santa Catharina in Süd-Brasilien*, Hamburg, 1900.

Li, Changke, *Der China-Roman in der deutschen Literatur 1890–1930: Tendenzen und Aspekte*, Regensburg, 1992.

Liebersohn, Harry, 'Weber's Historical Concept of National Identity', in Hartmut Lehmann and Guenther Roth (eds.), *Weber's Protestant Ethic: Origins, Evidence, Contexts*, Cambridge, 1993, pp. 123–32.

Lin, Alfred, *The Rural Economy of Guangdong, 1870–1937: A Study of the Agrarian Crisis and Its Origins in Southernmost China*, New York, 1997.

Linden, Marcel van der, 'Die Geschichte der Arbeiterinnen und Arbeiter in der Globalisierung', *Sozial.Geschichte* 18 (2003), 10–40.

Lindenlaub, Dieter, Richtungskämpfe im Verein für Sozialpolitik: Wissenschaft und Sozialpolitik im Kaiserreich vornehmlich vom Beginn des 'Neuen Kurses' bis zum Ausbruch des Ersten Weltkriegs (1890–1914), 2 vols., Wiesbaden, 1967.

Lingelbach, Gabriele, *Klio macht Karriere: Die Institutionalisierung der Geschichtswissenschaft in Frankreich und den USA in der zweiten Hälfte des 19. Jahrhunderts*, Göttingen, 2003.

Linse, Ulrich, *Zurück, o Mensch, zur Mutter Erde: Landkommunen in Deutschland 1890–1933*, Munich, 1983.

Linton, Derek, '*Who Has the Youth, Has the Future': The Campaign to Save Young Workers in Imperial Germany*, Cambridge, 1991.

Lippert, Wolfgang, *Entstehung und Funktion einiger chinesischer marxistischer Termini: Der lexikalisch-begriffliche Aspekt der Rezeption des Marxismus in Japan und China*, Wiesbaden, 1979.

Liu, Lydia H., *Translingual Practice: Literature, National Culture, and Translated Modernity. China, 1900–1937*, Stanford, 1995.

Liulevicius, Vejas Gabriel, *War Land on the Eastern Front: Culture, National Identity and German Occupation in World War I*, Cambridge, 2000.

Lloyd, Jill, *German Expressionism: Primitivism and Modernity*, New Haven, 1991.

Loth, Wilfried and Jürgen Osterhammel (eds.), *Internationale Geschichte: Themen, Ergebnisse, Aussichten*, Munich, 2000.

Love, Joseph L., *Rio Grande do Sul and Brazilian Regionalism, 1882–1930*, Stanford, 1971.

Lövenich, Friedhelm, *Verstaatlichte Sittlichkeit: Die konservative Konstruktion der Lebenswelt in Wilhelm Heinrich Riehls 'Naturgeschichte des Volkes'*, Opladen, 1992.

Lübcke, Alexandra, *"Welch ein Unterschied aber zwischen Europa und hier …": Diskurstheoretische Überlegungen zu Nation, Auswanderung und kultureller Geschlechteridentität anhand von Briefen deutscher Chileauswanderinnen des 19. Jahrhunderts*, Frankfurt, 2003.

Ludendorff, Erich, *Urkunden der Obersten Heeresleitung über ihre Tätigkeit 1916/18*, Berlin, 1921.

Lüdtke, Alf, 'The "Honor of Labor": Industrial Workers and the Power of Symbols under National Socialism', in David F. Crew (ed.), *Nazism and German Society 1933–1945*, London, 1994, pp. 67–109.

Luebke, Frederick C., *Germans in Brazil: A Comparative History of Cultural Conflict during World War I*, Baton Rouge, 1987.

Germans in the New World: Essays in the History of Immigration, Urbana, 1990.

'Images of German Immigrants in the United States and Brazil, 1890–1918: Some Comparisons', in Luebke (ed.), *Germans in the New World: Essays in the History of Immigration*, Urbana, 1990, pp. 110–22.

'Patterns of German Settlement in the US and Brazil, 1830–1930', in Luebke (ed.), *Germans in the New World: Essays in the History of Immigration*, Urbana, 1990, pp. 93–109.

'A Prelude to Conflict: The German Ethnic Group in Brazilian Society, 1890–1917', *Ethnic and Racial Studies* 6 (1983), 1–17.

Luetge, Wilhelm, Werner Hoffmann and Karl-Wilhelm Körner, *Geschichte des Deutschtums in Argentinien*, Buenos Aires, 1955.

Lüsebrink, Hans-Jürgen, 'Civilization', in Daniel Roche and Vincenzo Ferrone (eds.), *Le Monde des Lumières*, Paris, 1999, pp. 169–76.

Luys, Karin, *Die Anfänge der deutschen Nationalbewegung von 1815 bis 1819*, Münster, 1992.

Lyons, Francis S. L., *Internationalism in Europe 1815–1914*, Leiden, 1963.

Ma, L. Eve Armentrout, *Revolutionaries, Monarchists and Chinatowns*, Honolulu, 1990.

MacKenzie, John M., *The Empire of Nature: Hunting, Conservation and British Imperialism*, Manchester, 1997.

MacKenzie, John M. (ed.), *Imperialism and Popular Culture*, Manchester, 1989.

MacKenzie, John M., *Propaganda and Empire: The Manipulation of British Public Opinion 1880–1960*, Manchester, 1986.

Mackerras, Colin, *Western Images of China*, Oxford, 1989.

MacKinnon, Malcolm H., 'The Longevity of the Thesis: A Critique of the Critics', in Hartmut Lehmann and Guenther Roth (eds.), *Weber's Protestant Ethic: Origins, Evidence, Contexts*, Cambridge, 1993, pp. 211–43.

Magalhães, Edgardo de, 'Germany and South America: A Brazilian View', *Nineteenth Century and After* 81 (1917), 67–80.

Mai, Joachim, *Die preußisch–deutsche Polenpolitik, 1885/87*, Berlin, 1962.

Maier, Charles S., 'Consigning the Twentieth Century to History: Alternative Narratives for the Modern Era', *American Historical Review* 105 (2000), 807–31.

'Transformations of Territoriality: 1600–2000', in Gunilla Budde, Sebastian Conrad and Oliver Janz (eds.), *Transnationale Geschichte: Themen, Tendenzen, Theorien*, Göttingen, 2006, pp. 24–36.

Malinowski, Stephan and Robert Gerwarth, 'Der Holocaust als "kolonialer Genozid"? Europäische Kolonialgewalt und nationalsozialistischer Vernichtungskrieg', *Geschichte und Gesellschaft*, 33 (2007), 439–66.

Mallmann, Rudolf, *Rechte und Pflichten in den deutschen Schutzgebieten: Eine Studie über die Rechtsstellung der Bewohner der deutschen Kolonien auf der Grundlage ihrer Staatsangehörigkeit*, Berlin, 1913.

Mann, Michael, 'Die Mär von der freien Lohnarbeit: Menschenhandel und erzwungene Arbeit in der Neuzeit. Ein einleitender Essay', *Comparativ* 13:4 (2003), 7–22.

Manning, Patrick, *Navigating World History: Historians Create a Global Past*, New York, 2003.

Marcus, George, 'Ethnography in/of the World System: The Emergence of Multi-sited Ethnography', *Annual Review of Anthropology* 24 (1995), 95–117.

Ethnography through Thick and Thin, Princeton, 1999.

Mark, Rudolf A., *Galizien unter österreichischer Herrschaft: Verwaltung–Kirche–Bevölkerung*, Marburg, 1994.

Markmiller, Anton, *'Die Erziehung des Negers zur Arbeit': Wie die koloniale Pädagogik afrikanische Gesellschaften in die Abhängigkeit führte*, Berlin, 1995.

Markovits, Andrei S. and Frank E. Sysyn (eds.), *Nationbuilding and the Politics of Nationalism: Essays on Austrian Galicia*, Cambridge, MA, 1982.

Marks, Shula, 'History, the Nation and Empires: Sniping from the Periphery', *History Workshop Journal* 29 (1990), 111–19.

Markus, Andrew, *Australian Race Relations, 1778–1993*, Sydney, 1994.

Fear and Hatred: Purifying Australia and California 1850–1901, Sydney, 1979.

Marriott, John, *The Other Empire: Metropolis, India and Progress in the Colonial Imagination*, Manchester, 2004.

Marrison, Andrew, *Free Trade and Its Reception, 1815–1960*, London, 1998.

Martin, Bernd (ed.), *Japans Weg in die Moderne: Ein Sonderweg nach deutschem Vorbild?*, Frankfurt, 1987.

Martin, Emily, 'Toward an Anthropology of Immunology: The Body as Nation State', *Medical Anthropology Quarterly*, New Series 4 (1990), 410–26.

Marx, Karl and Friedrich Engels, *The Communist Manifesto* [1848], London, 1998.

Masaaki, Sogo (ed.), *Meiji no kotoba jiten*, Tokyo, 1989.

Masini, Federico, *The Formation of Modern Chinese Lexicon and Its Evolution toward a National Language: The Period from 1840 to 1898*, Berkeley, 1993.

Maß, Sandra, 'Das Trauma des weißen Mannes: Afrikanische Kolonialsoldaten in propagandistischen Texten, 1914–1923', *L'Homme* 12 (2001), 11–33.

Mattelart, Armand, *Mapping World Communication: War, Progress, Culture*, trans. Susan Emanuel and James A. Cohen, Minneapolis, 1994.

Networking the World, 1794–2000, Minneapolis, 2001.

Matthäus, Jürgen, *Nationsbildung in Australien von den Anfängen weißer Besiedlung bis zum Ersten Weltkrieg*, Frankfurt, 1993.

Maurer, Trude, 'Medizinalpolizei und Antisemitismus: Die deutsche Politik der Grenzsperre gegen Ostjuden im Ersten Weltkrieg', *Jahrbücher der Geschichte Osteuropas* 33 (1985), 205–30.

Ostjuden in Deutschland, 1918–1933, Hamburg, 1986.

Mazlish, Bruce and Buultjens R. (eds.), *Conceptualizing Global History*, Boulder, 1993.

Mazzolini, Renato G., *Politisch-biologische Analogien im Frühwerk Rudolf Virchows*, Marburg, 1988.

McCormick, Thomas J., *China Market: America's Quest for Informal Empire*, Chicago, 1967.

McKee, Delber, *Chinese Exclusion versus the Open Door Policy 1900–1906*, Detroit, 1977.

McKeown, Adam, *Chinese Migrant Networks and Cultural Change: Peru, Chicago, Hawaii, 1900–1936*, Chicago, 2001.

'Conceptualizing Chinese Diasporas 1842 to 1949', *Journal of Asian Studies* 58 (1999), 306–37.

'Global Migration, 1846–1940', *Journal of World History* 15 (2004), 155–90.

McLaughlin, Joseph, *Writing the Urban Jungle: Reading Empire in London from Doyle to Eliot*, Charlottesville, 2000.

McNeill, William, *The Rise of the West: A History of the Human Community*, Chicago, 1963.

McNeill, William and Ruth S. Adams (eds.), *Human Migration: Patterns and Policies*, Bloomington, 1978.

McQueen, Humphrey, *A New Britannia: An Argument Concerning the Social Origins of Australian Radicalism and Nationalism*, Melbourne, 1970.

Meagher, Arnold, 'The Introduction of Chinese Laborers to Latin America: The "Coolie Trade", 1847–74', Ph.D. dissertation, University of California, Davis, 1975.

Mehl, Margret, *Eine Vergangenheit für die japanische Nation: Die Entstehung des historischen Forschungsinstituts Tôkyô daigaku shiryô hensanjo (1869–1895)*, Frankfurt, 1992.

Mehnert, Ute, 'Deutsche Weltpolitik und amerikanisches Zweifronten-Dilemma: Die 'japanische Gefahr' in den deutsch–amerikanischen Beziehungen 1904–1917', *Historische Zeitschrift* 257 (1993), 647–92.

Deutschland, Amerika und die 'Gelbe Gefahr': Zur Karriere eines Schlagworts in der Großen Politik, 1905–1917, Stuttgart, 1995.

Mehta, Uday Singh, *Liberalism and Empire: A Study in 19th-Century British Liberal Thought*, Chicago, 1999.

Meichels-Lindner, Gisela, 'Die italienischen Arbeiter in Deutschland', *Der Arbeitsmarkt: Monatsschrift des Verbandes Deutscher Arbeitsnachweise* 14 (1911), 102–35.

Meinecke, Friedrich, *Briefwechsel*, Stuttgart, 1962.

Meinecke, Gustav, *Katechismus der Auswanderung: Kompaß für Auswanderer*, Leipzig, 1896.

Mejcher, Helmut, 'Die Bagdadbahn als Instrument deutschen wirtschaftlichen Einflusses im Osmanischen Reich', *Geschichte und Gesellschaft* 1 (1975), 447–81.

Mendes-Flohr, Paul R., 'Werner Sombart's The Jews and Modern Capitalism: An Analysis of Its Ideological Premises', *The Leo Baeck Institute Year Book* 21 (1976), 87–107.

Menz, Reinhold, *Deutsche Arbeit in Kleinasien: Reiseskizze und Wirtschaftsstudie*, Berlin, 1893.

Menzel, Gustav, *Die Bethel-Mission: Aus 100 Jahren Missionsgeschichte*, Bielefeld, 1986.

Merensky, Alexander, *Deutsche Arbeit am Njaßa, Deutsch-Ostafrika*, Berlin, 1894.

'Welches Interesse und welchen Anteil hat die Mission an der Erziehung der Naturvölker zur Arbeit?', *Allgemeine Missions-Zeitschrift* 14 (1887), 147–64.

Wie erzieht man am besten den Neger zur Plantagenarbeit?, Berlin, 1886.

Mergel, Thomas, *Zwischen Klasse und Konfession: Katholisches Bürgertum im Rheinland 1794–1914*, Göttingen, 1994.

Messele-Wieser, Sandra and Lothar Wieser, *Neues Heimatland Brasilien: Texte und Bilder zur kulturellen Entwicklung der deutschbrasilianischen Bevölkerung in Südbrasilien*, Göttingen, 1993.

Metzler, Gabriele, *Großbritannien: Weltmacht in Europa. Handelspolitik im Wandel des europäischen Staatensystems 1856 bis 1871*, Berlin, 1997.

Meyer, Albert, 'Geschichte der Kolonie Contulmo', in Anon. (ed.), *Deutsche Arbeit in Chile: Festschrift des Deutschen Wissenschaftlichen Vereins zu Santiago*, Santiago, 1910, pp. 68–99.

Meyer, Henry Cord, *'Drang nach Osten': Fortunes of a Slogan-Concept in German–Slavic Relations, 1849–1990*, Bern, 1996.

Meyer, John W., John Boli, George Thomas and Francisco Ramirez, 'World Society and the Nation-State, *American Journal of Sociology* 103 (1997), 144–81.

Meyer zu Hogrebe, Cathrin, *Strafkolonien: 'Eine Sache der Volkswohlfahrt'? Die Diskussion um die Einführung der Deportation im Deutschen Kaiserreich*, Münster, 1999.

Meyer-Kalkus, Reinhart, *Weltliteratur in Alexandria*, Berlin, 2004.

Mick, Christoph, 'Die "Ukrainemacher" und ihre Konkurrenten: Strategien der nationalen Vereinnahmung des Landes in Ostgalizien', *Comparativ* 15:2 (2005), 60–76.

Middell, Matthias, 'Kulturtransfer und historische Komparatistik: Thesen zu ihrem Verhältnis', *Comparativ* 10:1 (2000), 7–41.

  Weltgeschichtsschreibung im Zeitalter der Verfachlichung und Professionalisierung: Das Leipziger Institut für Kultur- und Universalgeschichte 1890–1990, Leipzig, 2005.

Mignolo, Walter D., 'Globalization, Civilization Processes, and the Relocation of Languages and Cultures', in Fredric Jameson and Masao Miyoshi (eds.), *The Cultures of Globalization*, Durham, NC, 1998, pp. 32–53.

Miller, Stuart C., *The Unwelcome Immigrant: The American Image of the Chinese, 1785–1882*, Berkeley, 1969.

Minchinton, Walter E. and E. E. Williams, '"Made in Germany" and after', *Vierteljahrschrift für Sozial- und Wirtschaftsgeschichte* 62 (1975), 229–42.

Mirbt, Carl, *Mission und Kolonialpolitik in den deutschen Schutzgebieten*, Tübingen, 1910.

Mitchell, Allan, *The Great Train Race: Railways and the Franco-German Rivalry 1815–1914*, Oxford, 2000.

Mitchell, Katharyne, 'Transnational Subjects: Constituting the Cultural Citizen in the Era of Pacific Rim Capital', in Aihwa Ong and Donald

Nonini (eds.), *Ungrounded Empires: The Cultural Politics of Modern Chinese Transnationalism*, New York, 1997, pp. 228–58.

Mitchell, Nancy, *The Danger of Dreams: German and American Imperialism in Latin America*, Chapel Hill, 1999.

Mitchell, Timothy, *Colonizing Egypt*, Berkeley, 1988.

Mitter, Rana, *A Bitter Revolution: China's Struggle with the Modern World*, Oxford, 2004.

Mittermaier, W., 'Litteraturbericht Deportation', *Zeitschrift für die gesamte Strafrechtswissenschaft* 20 (1900), 613–22.

Moch, Leslie Page, *Moving Europeans: Migration in Western Europe since 1650*, Bloomington, 1992.

Moltmann, Bodo, *Geschichte der deutschen Handelsschiffahrt*, Hamburg, 1981.

Moltmann, Gunter (ed.), *Germans to America: 300 Years of Immigration 1683–1983*, Stuttgart, 1983.

Mommsen, Wolfgang J., *Großmachtstellung und Weltpolitik: Die Außenpolitik des Deutschen Reiches 1870 bis 1914*, Frankfurt, 1993.

Imperialismustheorien: Ein Überblick über die neueren Imperialismusinterpretationen, Göttingen, 1987.

Max Weber und die deutsche Politik 1890–1920, Tübingen, 1974.

Mommsen, Wolfgang J. and Wolfgang Schwentker (eds.), *Max Weber und seine Zeitgenossen*, Göttingen, 1988.

Mönckmeier, Wilhelm, *Die deutsche überseeische Auswanderung*, Jena, 1912.

Mooser, Josef, 'Arbeiter, Bürger und Priester in den konfessionellen Arbeitervereinen im deutschen Kaiserreich 1880–1914', in Jürgen Kocka (ed.), *Arbeiter und Bürgertum im 19. Jahrhundert: Varianten ihres Verhältnisses im europäischen Vergleich*, Munich, 1986, pp. 79–105.

Morawska, Ewa, 'Labor Migrations of Poles in the Atlantic World Economy, 1880–1914', *Comparative Studies in Society and History* 31 (1989), 237–72.

Morsey, Rudolf, 'Die deutschen Katholiken und der Nationalstaat zwischen Kulturkampf und dem Ersten Weltkrieg', *Historisches Jahrbuch* 90 (1970), 31–64.

Moser, Michael, 'Die Entwicklung der ukrainischen Schriftsprache', *Österreichische Osthefte* 42 (2000), 483–96.

Moses, John A., 'The Coolie Labour Question and German Colonial Policy in Samoa, 1900–14', in Paul Kennedy and Moses, *Germany in the Pacific and the Far East*, St Lucia, 1977, pp. 234–61.

Mosse, George, *Die völkische Revolution*, Frankfurt, 1991.

Mueller, Karl Friedrich, *Bete und arbeite! Wie evangelische Missionare schon vor 150 Jahren die Neger zur Arbeit erzogen haben*, Bremen, 1908.

Mühlhahn, Klaus, *Herrschaft und Widerstand in der 'Musterkolonie' Kiautschou: Interaktionen zwischen China und Deutschland, 1897–1914*, Munich, 2000.

Müller, Fritz Ferdinand, *Kolonien unter der Peitsche*, Berlin, 1960.

Müller, Gerhard A., *Friedrich Ratzel (1844–1904): Naturwissenschaftler, Geograph, Gelehrter*, Stuttgart, 1996.

Müller, Gustav P., 'Arbeitspflicht und Arbeitszwang der Eingeborenen', *Die deutschen Kolonien* 1 (1902), 65–66.

Müller-Seidel, Walter, *Die Deportation des Menschen: Kafkas Erzählung 'In der Strafkolonie' im europäischen Kontext*, Stuttgart, 1986.

'Fontane und Polen: Eine Betrachtung zur deutschen Literatur im Zeitalter Bismarcks', in Hendrik Feindt (ed.), *Studien zur Kulturgeschichte des deutschen Polenbildes 1848–1939*, Wiesbaden, 1995, pp. 41–64.

Münch, Paul, 'The Thesis before Weber: An Archaeology', in Hartmut Lehmann and Guenther Roth (eds.), *Weber's Protestant Ethic: Origins, Evidence, Contexts*, Cambridge, 1993, pp. 51–72.

'Welcher Zusammenhang besteht zwischen Konfession und ökonomischem Verhalten? Max Webers These im Lichte der historischen Forschung, *Der Bürger im Staat* 34 (1984), 108–13.

Munro, A. E., *Transvaal (Chinese) Labour Problem*, London, 1906.

Murphy, Craig N., *International Organization and Industrial Change: Global Governance since 1850*, New York, 1994.

Murphy, Richard C., *Gastarbeiter im Deutschen Reich: Polen in Bottrop 1891–1933*, Wuppertal, 1982.

Muthesius, Hermann, 'Die Werkbundarbeit der Zukunft', in Wend Fischer (ed.), *Zwischen Kunst und Industrie: Der Deutsche Werkbund*, Stuttgart, 1989, pp. 85–97.

Nagl, Dominik, *Grenzfälle: Staatsangehörigkeit, Rassismus und nationale Identität unter deutscher Kolonialherrshaft*, Frankfurt, 2007.

Najita, Tetsuo and Harry D. Harootunian, 'Japan's Revolt against the West', in Bob Tadashi Wakabayashi (ed.), *Modern Japanese Thought*, Cambridge, 1998, pp. 207–72.

Nandy, Ashis, *The Intimate Enemy: Loss and Recovery of Self under Colonialism*, Delhi, 1983.

Naranch, Bradley D., 'Inventing the *Auslandsdeutsche*: Emigration, Colonial Fantasy, and German National Identity 1848–71', in Eric Ames, Marcia Klotz and Lora Wildenthal (eds.), *Germany's Colonial Pasts*, Lincoln, NE, 2005, pp. 21–40.

Nassehi, Armin, 'Die "Welt"-Fremdheit der Globalisierungsdebatte', *Soziale Welt* 49 (1998), 151–66.

Naumann, Friedrich, 'Deutsche Gewerbekunst: Eine Arbeit über die Organisation des Deutschen Werkbundes', in Naumann, *Werke*, 6 vols., Vol. vi, Cologne, 1964, pp. 254–89.

Neitzel, Sönke (ed.), *1900: Zukunftsvisionen der Großmächte*, Paderborn, 2002.
    (ed.), *Weltmacht oder Untergang: Die Weltreichslehre im Zeitalter des Imperialismus*, Paderborn, 2000.

Neubach, Helmut, *Die Ausweisung von Polen und Juden aus Preußen 1885/86*, Wiesbaden, 1967.

Neutsch, Cornelius, 'Erste "Nervenstränge des Erdballs": Interkontinentale Seekabelverbindungen vor dem Ersten Weltkrieg', in Neutsch and Hans Jürgen Teuteberg (eds.), *Vom Flügeltelegraphen zum Internet: Geschichte der modernen Telekommunikation*, Stuttgart, 1998, pp. 47–66.

Nichtweiß, Johannes, *Die ausländischen Saisonarbeiter in der Landwirtschaft der östlichen und mittleren Gebiete des Deutschen Reiches: Ein Beitrag zur Geschichte der preußisch-deutschen Politik von 1890 bis 1914*, Berlin, 1959.

Niemeyer, Ernst, 'Deutsche Siedler und Siedelungen im Urwald', *Das Deutschtum im Ausland* 8 (June 1911), 384–93.

Niesel, Hans-Joachim, 'Kolonialverwaltung und Missionen in Deutsch-Ostafrika 1890–1914', Dr. Phil. dissertation, Freie Universität Berlin, 1971.

Nipperdey, Thomas, *Deutsche Geschichte 1800–1866: Bürgerwelt und starker Staat*, Munich, 1983.
    Deutsche Geschichte 1866–1918, 2 vols., Vol. II: *Machtstaat vor der Demokratie*, Munich, 1993.

Nitschke, August, Detlev J. K. Peukert, Gerhard A. Ritter and Rüdiger von Bruch (eds.), *Jahrhundertwende: Der Aufbruch in die Moderne 1880–1930*, 2 vols., Reinbek, 1990.

Noiriel, Gérard, *Die Tyrannei des Nationalen: Sozialgeschichte des Asylrechts in Europa*, Lüneburg, 1994.

Nolan, Michael E., *The Inverted Mirror: Mythologizing the Enemy in France and Germany, 1898–1914*, New York, 2005.

Nolte, Paul, '1900: Das Ende des 19. und der Beginn des 20. Jahrhunderts in sozialgeschichtlicher Perspektive', *Geschichte in Wissenschaft und Unterricht* 47 (1996), 281–300.

Nonini, Donald M. and Aihwa Ong, 'Chinese Transnationalism as an Alternative Modernity', in Nonini and Ong (eds.), *Ungrounded Empires: The Cultural Politics of Modern Chinese Transnationalism*, London, 1997, pp. 3–33.

Nordau, Max, *Entartung*, Berlin, 1892.
    'Muskeljudentum', in Nordau, *Zionistische Schriften*, Cologne, 1909, pp. 379–81.

Norris, Edward Graham, *Die Umerziehung des Afrikaners: Togo 1895–1938*, Munich, 1993.

Northrup, David, *Indentured Labor in the Age of Imperialism, 1834–1922*, Cambridge, 1995.

Novy, Andreas, *Brasilien: Die Unordnung der Peripherie. Von der Sklavenhaltergesellschaft zur Diktatur des Geldes*, Vienna, 2001.

Nugent, Walter, *Crossings: The Great Transatlantic Migrations 1870–1914*, Bloomington, 1992.

Nye, J. V., 'The Myth of Free Trade Britain and Fortress France: Tariffs and Trade in the Nineteenth Century', *Journal of Economic History* 51 (1991), 23–46.

Oberacker, Karl H., *Der deutsche Beitrag zum Aufbau der brasilianischen Nation*, São Paulo, 1955.

   'Die Deutschen in Brasilien', in Hartmut Fröschle (ed.), *Die Deutschen in Südamerika: Schicksal und Leistung*, Tübingen, 1979, pp. 169–300.

Oberbefehlshaber Ost (ed.), *Das Land Ober Ost: Deutsche Arbeit in den Verwaltungsgebieten Kurland, Litauen und Bialystok-Grodno*, Stuttgart, 1917.

O'Brien, Patrick K., *Railways and the Economic Development of Western Europe*, London, 1983.

Obstfeld, Maurice and Alan M. Taylor, 'Globalization and Capital Markets', in Michael D. Bordo, Alan M. Taylor and Jeffrey G. Williamson (eds.), *Globalization in Historical Perspective*, Chicago, 2003, pp. 121–90.

O'Donnell, K. Molly, Renate Bridenthal and Nancy Reagin (eds.), *The Heimat Abroad: The Boundaries of Germanness*, Ann Arbor, 2005.

Oguma, Eiji, *A Genealogy of 'Japanese' Self-Images*, Melbourne, 2002.

Öhler, Theodor, 'Bemerkungen', *Allgemeine Missions-Zeitschrift* 14 (1887), 165–69.

Ohmae, Kenichi, *The Borderless World*, New York, 1990.

Ojeda-Ebert, Gerardo Jorge, *Deutsche Einwanderung und Herausbildung der chilenischen Nation (1846–1920)*, Munich, 1984.

Okada Yoshirô, *Meiji kaireki: 'Toki' no bunmei kaika*, Tokyo, 1994.

Oldenburg, Jens, *Der deutsche Ostmarkenverein 1894–1934*, Berlin, 2002.

Oltmer, Jochen, *Bäuerliche Ökonomie und Arbeitskräftepolitik im Ersten Weltkrieg*, Sögel, 1995.

Ong, Aihwa, *Flexible Citizenship: The Cultural Logics of Transnationality*, Durham, NC, 1999.

Onselen, Charles van, *Chibaro: African Mine Labour in Southern Rhodesia*, London, 1976.

Orlowski, Hubert, *'Polnische Wirtschaft': Zum deutschen Polendiskurs der Neuzeit*, Wiesbaden, 1996.

O'Rourke, Kevin H., 'The European Grain Invasion, 1870–1913', *Journal of European History* 57 (1997), 775–801.

O'Rourke, Kevin H. and Jeffrey G. Williamson, *Globalization and History: The Evolution of a Nineteenth-Century Atlantic Economy*, Cambridge, MA, 1999.

Osterhammel, Jürgen, 'Alexander von Humboldt: Historiker der Gesellschaft, Historiker der Natur', *Archiv für Kulturgeschichte* 81 (1999), 105–31.

'Außereuropäische Geschichte: Eine historische Problemskizze', *Geschichte in Wissenschaft und Unterricht* 46 (1995), 253–76.

China und die Weltgesellschaft: Vom 18. Jahrhundert bis in unsere Zeit, Munich, 1989.

Die Entzauberung Asiens: Europa und die asiatischen Reiche im 18. Jahrhundert, Munich, 1998.

Der europäische Nationalstaat des 20. Jahrhunderts: Eine globalhistorische Annäherung, in Osterhammel, *Geschichtswissenschaft jenseits des Nationalstaats: Studien zu Beziehungsgeschichte und Zivilisationsvergleich*, Göttingen, 2001, pp. 322–41.

'Forschungsreise und Kolonialprogramm: Ferdinand von Richthofen und die Erschließung Chinas im 19. Jahrhundert', *Archiv für Kulturgeschichte* 69 (1987), 150–95.

'Geschichte, Geographie, Geohistorie', in Wolfgang Küttler, Jörn Rüsen and Ernst Schulin (eds.), *Geschichtsdiskurs*, 5 vols., Vol. III, Frankfurt, 1997, pp. 257–71.

'"Höherer Wahnsinn": Universalhistorische Denkstile im 20. Jahrhundert', in Osterhammel, *Geschichtswissenschaft jenseits des Nationalstaats: Studien zu Beziehungsgeschichte und Zivilisationsvergleich*, Göttingen, 2001, pp. 170–82.

Kolonialismus: Geschichte, Formen, Folgen, Munich, 1995.

'On the Spatial Ordering of "Asia Orientale"', in Adriana Boscaro and Maurizio Bossi (eds.), *Firenze, il Giappone e l'Asia Orientale*, Florence, 2001, pp. 3–15.

'"Peoples without History" in British and German Historical Thought', in Benedikt Stuchtey and Peter Wende (eds.), *British and German Historiography 1750–1950: Traditions, Perceptions, and Transfers*, Oxford, 2000, pp. 265–87.

'Raumbeziehungen: Internationale Geschichte, Geopolitik und historische Geographie', in Wilfried Loth and Osterhammel (eds.), *Internationale Geschichte: Themen, Ergebnisse, Aussichten*, Munich, 2000, pp. 287–308.

Raumerfassung und Universalgeschichte, in Osterhammel, *Geschichtswissenschaft jenseits des Nationalstaats: Studien zu Beziehungsgeschichte und Zivilisationsvergleich*, Göttingen, 2001, pp. 151–69.

'Transnationale Gesellschaftsgeschichte: Erweiterung oder Alternative?', *Geschichte und Gesellschaft* 27 (2001), 367–93.

'Die Wiederkehr des Raumes: Geopolitik, Geohistorie und historische Geographie', *Neue politische Literatur* 43 (1998), 374–97.

Osterhammel, Jürgen and Niels P. Petersson, *Geschichte der Globalisierung: Dimensionen, Prozesse, Epochen*, Munich, 2003.

'Ostasiens Jahrhundertwende: Unterwerfung und Erneuerung in west-östlichen Sichtweisen', in Ute Frevert (ed.), *Das neue Jahrhundert: Europäische Zeitdiagnosen und Zukunftsentwürfe um 1900*, Göttingen, 2000, pp. 265–306.

Otis, Laura, *Membranes: Metaphors of Invasion in Nineteenth-Century Literature, Science and Politics*, Baltimore, 1999.

Owen, Roger, *Cotton and the Egyptian Economy: A Study in Trade and Development*, Oxford, 1969.

Pan, Lynn (ed.), *The Encyclopedia of the Chinese Overseas*, Cambridge, MA, 1999.

Sons of the Yellow Emperor: The Story of the Overseas Chinese, London, 1990.

Paschen, W., 'Die asiatische Einwanderung', *Grenzboten* 67 (1908), 109–14, 165–70.

Patel, Kiran Klaus, *Nach der Nationalfixiertheit: Perspektiven einer transnationalen Geschichte*, Berlin, 2004.

'*Soldaten der Arbeit*': *Arbeitsdienste in Deutschland und den USA 1933–1945*, Göttingen, 2003.

'Transatlantische Perspektiven transnationaler Geschichte', *Geschichte und Gesellschaft* 29 (2003), 625–47.

Paul, Carl, *Die Mission in unseren Kolonien*, 2 vols., Dresden, 1898.

Paulmann, Johannes, 'Internationaler Vergleich und interkultureller Transfer: Zwei Forschungsansätze zur europäischen Geschichte des 18. bis 20. Jahrhunderts', *Historische Zeitschrift* 267 (1998), 649–685.

Pomp und Politik: Monarchenbegegnungen in Europa zwischen Ancien Régime und Erstem Weltkrieg, Paderborn, 2000.

Payne, E. George, *Die Einführung der Chinesenarbeit in Südafrika*, Bonn, 1909.

Peattie, Mark (ed.), *The Japanese Colonial Empire 1895–1945*, Princeton, 1984.

Penny, H. Glenn, 'The Politics of Anthropology in the Age of Empire: German Colonists, Brazilian Indians, and the Case of Alberto Vojtech Fric', *Comparative Studies in Society and History* 45 (2003), 240–80.

Peter, Elmar, 'Die Bedeutung Chinas in der deutschen Ostasienpolitik (1911–1917)', Dr. Phil. dissertation, University of Hamburg, 1965.

Peters, Emil, 'Der Begriff sowie die staats- und völkerrechtliche Stellung der Eingeborenen in den deutschen Schutzgebieten nach deutschem Kolonialrechte', juridical dissertation, University of Göttingen, 1906.

Peters, Carl, *Zur Weltpolitik*, Berlin, 1912.

Petersson, Niels P., 'Das Kaiserreich in Prozessen ökonomischer Globalisierung', in Sebastian Conrad and Jürgen Osterhammel (eds.),

Das Kaiserreich transnational: Deutschland in der Welt, 1871–1914, Göttingen, 2004, pp. 49–67.

Petzina, Dieter, *Autarkiepolitik im Dritten Reich: Der nationalsozialistische Vierjahresplan von 1936*, Stuttgart, 1968.

Peukert, Detlev, *Volksgenossen und Gemeinschaftsfremde*, Cologne, 1982.

Pflaum, Georg Michael, 'Die Kultur-Zivilisations-Antithese im Deutschen', in *Europäische Schlüsselwörter: Wortvergleichende und wortgeschichtliche Studien*, 3 vols., Vol. III, Munich 1967.

Pfrank, Christian, 'Die Landarbeiterfrage in Deutsch-Ostafrika', Dr. Phil. dissertation, Friedrich-Wilhelms-Universität Berlin, 1919.

Phelps, Reginald H., 'Hitlers "grundlegende" Rede über den Antisemitismus', *Vierteljahrshefte für Zeitgeschichte* 16 (1968), 390–420.

Pietschmann, Horst, Walther L. Bernecker and Rüdiger Zoller, *Eine kleine Geschichte Brasiliens*, Frankfurt, 2000.

Pigulla, Andreas, *China in der deutschen Weltgeschichtsschreibung vom 18. bis zum 20. Jahrhundert*, Wiesbaden, 1996.

Plagemann, Volker (eds.), *Übersee: Seefahrt und Seemacht im Deutschen Kaiserreich*, Munich, 1988.

Planert, Ute, 'Der dreifache Körper des Volkes: Sexualität, Biopolitik und die Wissenschaft vom Leben', *Geschichte und Gesellschaft* 16 (2000), 539–76.

   (ed.), *Nation, Politik und Geschlecht: Frauenbewegungen und Nationalismus in der Moderne*, Frankfurt, 2000.

Pleitner, Berit, *Die 'vernünftige' Nation: Zur Funktion von Stereotypen über Polen und Franzosen im deutschen nationalen Diskurs 1850–1871*, Frankfurt, 2001.

Plenge, Johann, *Die Zukunft in Amerika*, Berlin, 1912.

Pletzing, Christian, *Vom Völkerfrühling zum nationalen Konflikt: Deutscher und polnischer Nationalismus in Ost- und Westpreußen 1830–1871*, Wiesbaden, 2003.

Plumpe, Gottfried, *Die IG Farbenindustrie 1904–1945*, Berlin, 1990.

Pogge von Strandmann, Hartmut, 'Domestic Origins of Germany's Colonial Expansion under Bismarck', *Past and Present* 42 (1969), 140–59.

Pohl, Dieter, 'Die Holocaust-Forschung und Goldhagens Thesen', *Vierteljahrshefte für Zeitgeschichte* 45 (1997), 1–48.

Pohl, Hans, *Aufbruch der Weltwirtschaft: Geschichte der Weltwirtschaft von der Mitte des 19. Jahrhunderts bis zum Ersten Weltkrieg*, Stuttgart, 1989.

Pohl, Manfred, *Von Stambul nach Bagdad: Die Geschichte einer berühmten Eisenbahn*, Munich, 1999.

Polczynska, Edyta, *'Im polnischen Wind': Beiträge zum deutschen Zeitungswesen, Theaterleben und zur deutschen Literatur im Großherzogtum Posen, 1815–1918*, Poznan, 1988.

Poliakov, Léon, *The History of Antisemitism*, 4 vols., London, 1974.

Pollard, Sidney, '"Made in Germany": Die Angst vor der deutschen Konkurrenz im spätviktorianischen England', *Technikgeschichte* 54 (1987), 183–95.

Pommerin, Reiner, *Der Kaiser und Amerika: Die USA in der Politik der Reichsleitung 1980–1917*, Cologne, 1986.

Pomper, Philip, Richard H. Elphick and Richard T. Vann (eds.), *World History: Ideologies, Structures, and Identities*, Oxford, 1998.

Porter, Bernard, *The Absent-Minded Imperialists: Empire, Society and Culture in Britain*, Oxford, 2004.

Porter, Roy, *The Greatest Benefit to Mankind: A Medical History of Mankind*, London, 1997.

Potts, Lydia, *Weltmarkt für Arbeitskraft: Von der Kolonisation Amerikas bis zu den Migrationen der Gegenwart*, Hamburg, 1988.

Prakash, Gyan, *Another Reason: Science and the Imagination of Modern India*, Princeton, 1999.

Pratt, Mary Louise, *Imperial Eyes: Travel Writing and Transculturation*, London, 1992.

Price, Charles A., *The Great White Walls Are Built: Restrictive Immigration to North America and Australasia, 1838–1888*, Canberra, 1974.

Priester, Oscar, *Die Deportation: Ein modernes Strafmittel*, Berlin, 1899.

Prymak, Thomas M., *Mykhailo Hrushevsky: The Politics of National Culture*, Toronto, 1987.

Puhle, Hans-Jürgen, *Agrarische Interessenpolitik und preußischer Konservatismus im Wilhelminischen Reich, 1893–1914*, Hannover, 1966.

Purcell, Victor, *The Chinese in Southeast Asia*, Kuala Lumpur, 1965.

Puschner, Uwe, *Die völkische Bewegung im wilhelminischen Kaiserreich: Sprache–Rasse–Religion*, Darmstadt, 2001.

Pusey, James R., *China and Charles Darwin*, Cambridge, MA, 1983.

Quataert, Jean H., *Staging Philanthropy: Patriotic Women and the National Imagination in Dynastic Germany, 1813–1916*, Ann Arbor, 2001.

Rabinbach, Anson, 'Ermüdung, Energie und der menschliche Motor', in Philipp Sarasin and Jakob Tanner (eds.), *Physiologie und industrielle Gesellschaft: Studien zur Verwissenschaftlichung des Körpers im 19. und 20. Jahrhundert*, Frankfurt, 1998, pp. 286–312.

'The European Science of Work: The Economy of the Body at the End of the Nineteenth Century', in Steven L. Kaplan and Cynthia J. Koepp (eds.), *Work in France: Representations, Meaning, Organization, and Practice*, Ithaca, NY, 1986, pp. 475–513.

The Human Motor: Energy, Fatigue, and the Origins of Modernity, Berkeley, 1992.

Radkau, Joachim, *Max Weber: Die Leidenschaft des Denkens*, Munich, 2005.

Soziale Bewegungen: Ein historisch-systematischer Grundriß, Frankfurt, 1985.

'Die Verheißungen der Morgenfrühe: Die Lebensreform in der neuen Moderne', in Kai Buchholz, Rita Latocha, Hilke Peckmann and Klaus Wolbert (eds.), *Die Lebensreform: Entwürfe zur Neugestaltung von Leben und Kunst um 1900*, 2 vols., Vol. I, Darmstadt, 2001, pp. 55–60.

Das Zeitalter der Nervosität: Deutschland zwischen Bismarck und Hitler, Munich, 1998.

Rahden, Till van, 'Ideologie und Gewalt: Neuerscheinungen über den Antisemitismus in der deutschen Geschichte des 19. und 20. Jahrhunderts', *Neue politische Literatur* 41 (1996), 11–29.

Juden und andere Breslauer: Die Beziehungen zwischen Juden, Protestanten und Katholiken in einer deutschen Großstadt von 1860 bis 1925, Göttingen, 2000.

Ramelow, Hans, 'Der Einfluß der Auswanderung auf das Wirtschaftsleben des Mutterlandes', in *Verhandlungen des deutschen Kolonialkongresses 1905 zu Berlin am 5., 6. und 7. Oktober 1905*, ed. Redaktionsausschuß, Berlin, 1906, pp. 824–44.

Reiseberichte über Brasilien, für die deutsche Industrie erstattet im Zentralverband deutscher Industrieller, Berlin, 1905.

Randeria, Shalini, 'Geteilte Geschichte und verwobene Moderne', in Jörn Rüsen, Hanna Leitgeb and Norbert Jegelka (eds.), *Zukunftsentwürfe: Ideen für eine Kultur der Veränderung*, Frankfurt, 1999, pp. 87–96.

Raphael, Freddy, *Judaïsme et capitalisme: Essai sur la controverse entre Max Weber et Werner Sombart*, Paris, 1982.

Raphaël, Lutz, 'Freiheit und Wohlstand der Nationen: Alexander von Humboldts Analysen der politischen Zustände Amerikas und das politische Denken seiner Zeit', *Historische Zeitschrift* 260 (1995), 749–76.

'Nationalzentrierte Sozialgeschichte in programmatischer Absicht: Die Zeitschrift *Geschichte und Gesellschaft: Zeitschrift für Historische Sozialwissenschaft* in den ersten 25 Jahren ihres Bestehens', *Geschichte und Gesellschaft* 26 (2000) 5–37.

Ratenhof, Udo, *Die Chinapolitik des Deutschen Reiches 1871–1945: Wirtschaft–Rüstung–Militär*, Boppard, 1987.

Rathgen, Karl, *Japans Volkswirtschaft und Staatshaushalt*, Leipzig, 1891.

Ratzel, Friedrich, 'Die Chinesische Auswanderung', *Das Ausland* 69 (1876), 801–7.

'Die Gesetze des räumlichen Wachstums der Staaten: Ein Beitrag zur wissenschaftlichen politischen Geographie', *Petermanns Mitteilungen* 42 (1896), 97–107.

'Der Lebensraum: Eine biogeographische Studie', in Karl Bücher, Karl Victor Fricker, Franz Xaver Funk, Gustav von Mandry, Georg von

Mayr and Ratzel (eds.), *Festgaben für Alfred Schäffle*, Tübingen, 1901, pp. 101–89.

Politische Geographie, Berlin, 1923.

Rehberg, Karl-Siegbert, 'Das Bild des Judentums in der frühen deutschen Soziologie: "Fremdheit" und "Rationalität" als Typusmerkmale bei Werner Sombart, Max Weber und Georg Simmel', in Hans Otto Horch (ed.), *Judentum, Antisemitismus und europäische Kultur*, Tübingen, 1988, pp. 151–86.

Reid, Anthony, 'Entrepreneurial Minorities, Nationalism, and the State', in Daniel Chirot and Reid (eds.), *Essential Outsiders: Chinese and Jews in the Modern Transformation in Southeast Asia and Central Europe*, Seattle, 1997, pp. 33–74.

Reinhard, Wolfgang, 'Christliche Mission und Dialektik des Kolonialismus', *Historisches Jahrbuch* 109 (1989), 353–70.

Geschichte der europäischen Expansion, 4 vols., Stuttgart, 1983–90.

Reinke-Kunze, Christine, *Die Geschichte der Reichs-Post-Dampfer*, Herford, 1994.

Repp, Kevin, *Reformers, Critics, and the Paths of German Modernity: Anti-Politics and the Search for Alternatives 1890–1914*, Cambridge, MA, 2000.

Reynolds, Douglas R., *China 1898–1912: The Xinzheng Revolution and Japan*, Cambridge, MA, 1993.

'A Golden Decade Forgotten: Japan–China Relations, 1898–1907, *Transactions of the Asiatic Society of Japan* 4:2 (1987), 93–153.

Rhoads, Edward J. M., '"White Labor" vs. "Coolie Labor": The "Chinese Question" in Pennsylvania in the 1870s', *Journal of American Ethnic History* 21 (2002), 3–32.

Richardson, Peter, *Chinese Mine Labour in the Transvaal*, London, 1982.

'Coolies, Peasants, and Proletarians: The Origins of Chinese Indentured Labour in South Africa, 1904–1907', in Shula Marks and Richardson (eds.), *International Labour Migration: Historical Perspectives*, London, 1984, pp. 167–85.

Richet, Charles, 'Dans cent ans', *Revue scientifique* 48 (1891), 737–85.

Richter, Karl Thomas, *Die Fortschritte der Cultur: Einleitung in das Studium der Berichte über die Weltausstellung 1873*, Prague, 1875.

Richthofen, Ferdinand von, *Schantung und seine Eingangspforte Kiautschou*, Berlin, 1898.

Riehl, Wilhelm Heinrich, *Die deutsche Arbeit*, Stuttgart, 1883.

Riesemann, Oskar von, *Rund um Süd-Amerika: Reisebriefe*, Berlin, 1914.

Rippley, La Vern J., *The German-Americans*, Boston, 1976.

Rittenhouse, Mignon, *The Amazing Nelly Bly*, Freeport, 1956.

Ritterberger, Volker, *Internationale Organisationen: Politik und Geschichte*, Opladen, 1994.

Robertson, Roland, *Globalization: Social Theory and Global Culture*, London, 1992.

'Glokalisierung: Homogenität und Heterogenität in Raum und Zeit', in Ulrich Beck (ed.), *Perspektiven der Weltgesellschaft*, Frankfurt, 1998, pp. 192–220.

Roche, Jean, *La Colonisation allemande et le Rio Grande do Sul*, Paris, 1959.

Rohkrämer, Thomas, *Eine andere Moderne? Zivilisationskritik, Natur und Technik in Deutschland 1880–1933*, Paderborn, 1999.

Der Militarismus der 'kleinen Leute': Die Kriegervereine im deutschen Kaiserreich 1871–1914, Munich, 1990.

Rohrbach, Paul, *Deutsche Kolonialwirtschaft: Kulturpolitische Grundsätze für die Rassen- und Missionsfragen*, Berlin, 1909.

Roller, Kathrin, *Frauenmigration und Ausländerpolitik im Deutschen Kaiserreich: Polnische Arbeitsmigrantinnen in Preußen*, Berlin, 1994.

Romero, Silvio, *O allemanismo no Sul do Brasil: Seus perigos e meios de os conjurar*, Rio de Janeiro, 1906.

Roscher, Wilhelm and Robert Jannasch, *Kolonien, Kolonialpolitik und Auswanderung*, Leipzig, 1885.

Rosenberg, Hans, *Große Depression und Bismarckzeit: Wirtschaftsablauf, Gesellschaft und Politik in Mitteleuropa*, Berlin, 1967.

Rössler, Constantin, *Das deutsche Reich und die kirchliche Frage*, Würzburg, 1876.

Rothermund, Dietmar (ed.), *Aneignung und Selbstbehauptung: Antworten auf die europäische Expansion*, Munich, 1999.

Rubin, William (ed.), *Primitivismus in der Kunst des 20. Jahrhunderts*, Munich, 1984.

Rübner, Hartmut, 'Lebens-, Arbeits- und gewerkschaftliche Organisationsbedingungen chinesischer Seeleute in der deutschen Handelsflotte: Der maritime Aspekt der Ausländerbeschäftigung vom Kaiserreich bis in den NS-Staat', *Internationale wissenschaftliche Korrespondenz zur Geschichte der deutschen Arbeiterbewegung* 4 (1997), 1–41.

Rüger, Adolf, 'Die Entstehung und Lage der Arbeiterklasse unter dem deutschen Kolonialregime in Kamerun (1895–1905)', in Helmuth Stoecker (ed.), *Kamerun unter deutscher Kolonialherrschaft*, Berlin, 1960, pp. 149–242.

Rupke, Nicolaas, 'Die Popularisierung Alexander von Humboldts in der europäischen Zeitschriftenliteratur bis zur deutschen Reichsgründung', in Christian Hünemörder, Karin Reich and Gudrun Wolfschmidt (eds.), *Popularisierung der Naturwissenschaften*, Diepholz, 2002, pp. 170–82.

'Der Wissenschaftler als Nationalheld: Die deutsche Alexander von Humboldt-Biographik 1848–1871', in Ralph Jessen and Jakob Vogel (eds.), *Wissenschaft und Nation in der europäischen Geschichte*, Frankfurt, 2002, pp. 168–86.

Rupp, Leila J., *Worlds of Women: The Making of an International Women's Movement*, Princeton, 1997.

Rürup, Reinhard, *Emanzipation und Antisemitismus: Studien zur Judenfrage der bürgerlichen Gesellschaft*, Göttingen, 1975.

Ryûichi, Narita, *'Furusato' to iu monogatari: Toshi kûkan no rekishigaku*, Tokyo, 1998.

Saaler, Sven, 'Pan-Asianismus im Japan der Meiji- und der Taishô-Zeit: Wurzeln, Entstehung und Anwendung einer Ideologie', in Iwo Amelung, Matthias Koch, Joachim Kurtz, Eun-Jeung Lee and Sven Saaler (eds.), *Selbstbehauptungsdiskurse in Asien: China–Japan–Korea*, Munich, 2003, pp. 127–58.

Sachsenmaier, Dominic, 'Die Identitäten der Überseechinesen in Südostasien im 20. Jahrhundert', in Hartmut Kaelble, Martin Kirsch and Alexander Schmidt-Gernig (eds.), *Transnationale Öffentlichkeit und Identitäten im 20. Jahrhundert*, Frankfurt, 2002, pp. 211–35.

Sachße, Christoph and Florian Tennstedt, *Geschichte der Armenfürsorge in Deutschland*, 3 vols., Vol. 1, Stuttgart, 1980.

Sack, Peter, 'Das deutsche Rechtswesen in Polynesien', in Hermann Joseph Hiery (ed.), *Die deutsche Südsee 1884–1914: Ein Handbuch*, Paderborn, 2001, pp. 676–89.

Salter, Mark B., *Rights of Passage: The Passport in International Relations*, Boulder, 2003.

Salyer, Lucy, *Laws Harsh as Tigers: Chinese Immigrants and the Shaping of Modern Immigration Law*, Chapel Hill, 1995.

Samson-Himmelstjerna, Hermann von, *Die Gelbe Gefahr als Moralproblem*, Berlin, 1902.

Sanders, Irwin T. and Ewa T. Morawska, *Polish-American Community Life: A Survey of Research*, New York, 1975.

Sandkühler, Thomas, '"Arbeit" als historische Kategorie im 19. und 20. Jahrhundert', in Horst Walter Blanke, Friedrich Jaeger and Thomas Sandkühler (eds.), *Dimensionen der Historik: Geschichtstheorie, Wissenschaftsgeschichte und Geschichtskultur heute*, Cologne, 1998, pp. 395–406.

Sandner, Gerhard, 'In Search of Identity: German Nationalism and Geography, 1871–1910', in David Hooson (ed.), *Geography and National Identity*, Oxford, 1994, pp. 71–91.

Sarasin, Philipp, 'Infizierte Körper, kontaminierte Sprachen: Metaphern als Gegenstand der Wissenschaftsgeschichte', in Sarasin, *Geschichtswissenschaft und Diskursanalyse*, Frankfurt, 2003, pp. 191–230.

'Die Visualisierung des Feindes: Über metaphorische Technologien der frühen Bakteriologie', *Geschichte und Gesellschaft* 30 (2004), 250–76.

Sarmiento, Domingo Faustino, *Facundo or, Civilization and Barbarism*, London, 1998.

Sartorius von Waltershausen, August, 'Die italienischen Wanderarbeiter', in *Festschrift zu August Sigmund Schultzes siebenzigstem Geburtstag*, Leipzig, 1903, pp. 51–94.

Saxton, Alexander, *The Indispensable Enemy: Labor and the Anti-Chinese Movement in California*, Berkeley, 1971.

Schäbler, Birgit, 'Globale Moderne und die Geburt der Zivilisationsmission an der kulturellen Binnengrenze: Die mission civilisatrice ottomane', *Periplus* 13 (2003), 9–29.

Schäfer, Hermann, 'Italienische "Gastarbeiter" im Deutschen Kaiserreich 1890–1914', *Zeitschrift für Unternehmensgeschichte* 27 (1982), 192–214.

Schäfer, Theodor, 'Innere Mission', in *Handwörterbuch der Staatswissenschaften*, 11 vols., Vol. v, Jena, 1910, pp. 644–51.

Schäffner, Wolfgang, 'Verwaltung der Kultur: Alexander von Humboldts Medien (1799–1834)', in Stefan Rieger, Schamma Schahadat and Manfred Weinberg (eds.), *Interkulturalität: Zwischen Inszenierung und Archiv*, Tübingen, 1999, pp. 353–66.

Schalenberg, Marc, *Humboldt auf Reisen? Die Rezeption des 'deutschen Universitätsmodells' in den französischen und britischen Reformdiskursen (1810–1870)*, Basel, 2002.

(ed.), *Kulturtransfer im 19. Jahrhundert*, Berlin, 1998.

Scharfe, Wolfgang, *Abriß der Kartographie Brandenburgs, 1771–1821*, Berlin, 1972.

Schattkowsky, Ralph, 'Eine Autonomie mit Nachwirkungen: Regionale Identitäten in Galizien 1867–1918', in Philipp Ther and Holm Sundhaussen (eds.), *Regionale Bewegungen und Regionalismen in europäischen Zwischenräumen seit der Mitte des 19. Jahrhunderts*, Marburg, 2003, pp. 43–62.

Schatz, Holger and Andrea Woeldike, *Freiheit und Wahn deutscher Arbeit: Zur historischen Aktualität einer folgenreichen antisemitischen Projektion*, Hamburg, 2001.

Scheffler, Jürgen, 'Frömmigkeit und Fürsorge: Die Gründung der Arbeiterkolonie Wilhelmsdorf und die Wohlfahrtspflege in Westfalen und Lippe um 1880', in Hans Bachmann and Reinhard van Spankeren (eds.), *Diakonie: Geschichte von unten. Christliche Nächstenliebe und kirchliche Sozialarbeit in Westfalen*, Bielefeld, 1995, pp. 117–42.

'Die Gründungsjahre 1883–1913', in Zentralverband Deutscher Arbeiterkolonien (ed.), *Ein Jahrhundert Arbeiterkolonien: 'Arbeit statt Almosen' – Hilfe für obdachlose Wanderarme 1884–1984*, Bielefeld, 1984, pp. 23–35.

'Protestantismus zwischen Vereinswohltätigkeit und verbandlicher Wohlfahrtspflege: Innere Mission und Wandererfürsorge in Westfalen vor dem Ersten Weltkrieg', *Westfälische Forschungen* 39 (1989), 256–82.

Vom Herbergswesen für Handwerksgesellen zur Fürsorge für wandernde Arbeiter: Herbergen zur Heimat im Zeitalter der Industrialisierung, 1854–1914', in Scheffler (ed.), *Bürger und Bettler: Materialien und Dokumente zur Geschichte der Nichtseßhaftenhilfe in der Diakonie*, Bielefeld, 1987, pp. 10–19.

'Die Wandererfürsorge zwischen konfessioneller, kommunaler und staatlicher Wohlfahrtspflege', in Jochen-Christoph Kaiser and Martin Greschat (eds.), *Sozialer Protestantismus und Sozialstaat: Diakonie und Wohlfahrtspflege in Deutschland 1890–1938*, Stuttgart, 1996, pp. 104–17.

Schenda, Rudolf, 'Die Verfleißigung der Deutschen: Materialien zur Indoktrination eines Tugend-Bündels', in Utz Jeggle, Gottfried Korff, Martin Scharfe and Bernd Jürgen Warneken (eds.), *Volkskultur in der Moderne: Probleme und Perspektiven empirischer Kulturforschung*, Reinbek, 1986, pp. 88–108.

Schendel, Willem van, 'Modern Times in Bangladesh', in van Schendel and Henk Schulte Nordholt (eds.), *Time Matters: Global and Local Time in Asian Societies*, Amsterdam, 2001, pp. 37–56.

Schenk, Robert, 'Chinesische Arbeiter und Deutschlands Zukunft', *Die neue Gesellschaft* (30 January 1907), 207–9.

Schieder, Theodor, *Das Deutsche Kaiserreich von 1871 als Nationalstaat*, Köln, 1961.

'Typologie und Erscheinungsformen des Nationalstaats in Europa', in Schieder, *Nationalismus und Nationalstaat: Studien zum nationalen Problem im modernen Europa*, Göttingen, 1992, pp. 65–86.

Schinzinger, Francesca, *Die Kolonien und das Deutsche Reich: Die wirtschaftliche Bedeutung der deutschen Besitzungen in Übersee*, Stuttgart, 1984.

Schippel, Max, 'Die Konkurrenz der fremden Arbeitskräfte: Zur Tagesordnung des Stuttgarter Internationalen Kongresses', *Sozialistische Monatshefte* (1906), 736–44.

Schivelbusch, Wolfgang, *Die Geschichte der Eisenbahnreise: Zur Industrialisierung von Raum und Zeit im 19. Jahrhundert*, Frankfurt, 1984.

Lichtblicke: Zur Geschichte der künstlichen Helligkeit im 19. Jahrhundert, Munich, 1983.

Schlesinger, Walter (ed.), *Die deutsche Ostsiedlung des Mittelalters als Problem der europäischen Geschichte*, Sigmaringen, 1975.

Schlögel, Karl, *Im Raume lesen wir die Zeit: Über Zivilisationsgeschichte und Geopolitik*, Munich, 2003.

Schluchter, Wolfgang, 'Religion, politische Herrschaft, Wirtschaft und bürgerliche Lebensführung: Die okzidentale Sonderentwicklung', in Schluchter (ed.), *Max Webers Sicht des okzidentalen Christentums: Interpretation und Kritik*, Frankfurt, 1988, pp. 11–128.

Schlunk, Martin and Martin Hennig, *Äußere Mission und Innere Mission in ihrer gegenseitigen Beziehung nach Geschichte und Arbeitsweise*, Bremen, 1913.

Schmidt, Alexander, *Reisen in die Moderne: Der Amerika-Diskurs des deutschen Bürgertums vor dem Ersten Weltkrieg im europäischen Vergleich*, Berlin, 1997.

Schmidt, Christopher, 'Im Gelobten Land ist Religion eine Form von Patriotismus. Eine Nation wie alle anderen auch? Die Ideengeber der zionistischen Bewegung', *Frankfurter Allgemeine Zeitung* (2 September 2003), 40.

Schmidt, P. W., 'Die Behandlung der Polygamie in unseren Kolonien', in *Verhandlungen des Deutschen Kolonialkongresses 1902*, Berlin, 1903, pp. 467–77.

Schmidt, Stefan, *Die Wanderarbeiter in der Landwirtschaft der Provinz Sachsen und ihre Beschäftigung im Jahre 1910*, Halle, 1911.

Schmidt, Vera, *Die deutsche Eisenbahnpolitik in Shantung 1898–1914: Ein Beitrag zur Geschichte des deutschen Imperialismus in China*, Wiesbaden, 1976.

Schmidt-Gernig, Alexander, 'Zukunftsmodell Amerika? Das europäische Bürgertum und die amerikanische Herausforderung um 1900', in Ute Frevert (ed.), *Das neue Jahrhundert: Europäische Zeitdiagnosen und Zukunftsentwürfe um 1900*, Göttingen, 2000, pp. 79–112.

Schmieder, Eberhard, 'Arbeitsethos: Eine Einführung in seine Geschichte', *Schmollers Jahrbuch* 79 (1959), 299–337, 429–62.

Schmoller, Gustav (ed.), *Handels- und Machtpolitik: Reden und Aufsätze, im Auftrage der 'Freien Vereinigung für Flottenvorträge'*, 2 vols., Vol. 1, Stuttgart, 1900.

Schmuhl, Hans-Walter, *Friedrich von Bodelschwingh*, Reinbek, 2005.

Schneider, Jane (ed.), *Italy's Southern Question: Orientalism in One Country*, New York, 1998.

Schneider, Wilhelm, *Die Culturfähigkeit des Negers*, Frankfurt, 1885.

Schöllgen, Gregor, *Imperialismus und Gleichgewicht: Deutschland, England und die orientalische Frage 1871–1914*, Munich, 1984.

Scholte, Jan Aart, *Globalization: A Critical Introduction*, Basingstoke, 2000.

Scholz-Hänsel, Michael, *Das exotische Plakat*, Stuttgart, 1987.

Schrader, Rudolf, *Das Arbeiterrecht für Eingeborene in Deutsch- und Britisch-Ostafrika*, Hamburg, 1920.

Schröder, Hans-Christoph, 'Max Weber und der Puritanismus', *Geschichte und Gesellschaft* 21 (1995), 459–78.

Sozialismus und Imperialismus, Bonn, 1975.

Schröder, Iris and Sabine Höhler (eds.), *Welt-Räume: Geschichte, Geographie und Globalisierung seit 1900*, Frankfurt, 2005.

Schröder, Martin, *Prügelstrafe und Züchtigungsrecht in den deutschen Schutzgebieten Schwarzafrikas*, Münster, 1997.

Schroeder, Friedrich, 'Einiges über Arbeiterverhältnisse in Usambara', *Deutsche Kolonialzeitung* 5 (1888), 220–22.

Schröter, Harm G., 'Die Auslandsinvestitionen der deutschen chemischen Industrie 1870 bis 1930', *Zeitschrift für Unternehmensgeschichte* 35 (1990), 1–22.

Schubert, Gunter, *Chinas Kampf um die Nation: Dimensionen nationalistischen Denkens in der VR China, Taiwan und Hongkong an der Jahrtausendwende*, Hamburg, 2002.

Schulte, Christoph, *Psychopathologie des Fin de siècle: Der Kulturkritiker, Arzt und Zionist Max Nordau*, Frankfurt, 1997.

Schulte-Althoff, Franz-Josef, *Studien zur politischen Wissenschaftsgeschichte der deutschen Geographie im Zeitalter des Imperialismus*, Paderborn, 1971.

Schultz, Hans-Dietrich, 'Die deutsche Geographie im 19. Jahrhundert und die Lehre Friedrich Ratzels', in Irene Diekmann, Peter Krüger and Julius H. Schoeps (eds.), *Geopolitik: Grenzgänge im Zeitgeist*, 2 vols., Vol. 1, Potsdam, 2000, pp. 39–84.

Die deutschsprachige Geographie von 1800 bis 1970: Ein Beitrag zur Geschichte ihrer Methodologie, Berlin, 1980.

Die Geographie als Bildungsfach im Kaiserreich, zugleich ein Beitrag zu ihrem Kampf um die preußische höhere Schule von 1870–1914 nebst dessen Vorgeschichte und teilweiser Berücksichtigung anderer deutscher Staaten, Osnabrück, 1989.

Schultz, Helga, 'Die Bürger von Birnbaum', in Schultz (ed.), *Preußens Osten– Polens Westen: Das Zerbrechen einer Nachbarschaft*, Berlin, 2001, pp. 17–38.

Schultze, Ernst, *Japan als Weltindustriemacht*, 2 vols., Stuttgart, 1935.

Schungel, Wilfried, *Alexander Tille (1866–1912): Leben und Ideen eines Sozialdarwinisten*, Husum, 1980.

Schuster, Ingrid, *China und Japan in der deutschen Literatur 1890–1925*, Tübingen, 1977.

Schwartz, Benjamin, *In Search of Wealth and Power: Yen Fu and the West*, Cambridge, MA, 1964.

Schwartz, D. von, *Mission und Kolonisation in ihrem gegenseitigen Verhältnis*, Leipzig, 1912.

Schwarz, Maria-Theresia, *'Je weniger Afrika, desto besser': Die deutsche Kolonialkritik am Ende des 19. Jahrhunderts. Eine Untersuchung zur kolonialen Haltung von Linksliberalismus und Sozialdemokratie*, Frankfurt, 1999.

Schwentker, Wolfgang, *Max Weber in Japan: Eine Untersuchung zur Wirkungsgeschichte 1905–1995*, Tübingen, 1998.

'The "Yellow Peril" Revisited: Western Perceptions of Asia in the Age of Imperialism', in Cedric Brown and Therese Fischer-Seidel (eds.), *Cultural Negotiations: Sichtweisen des Anderen*, Tübingen, 1998, pp. 35–47.

Scott, David, 'Colonial Governmentality', *Social Text* 43 (1995), 191–220.

Sebald, Peter, *Togo 1884–1914: Eine Geschichte der deutschen 'Musterkolonie' auf der Grundlage amtlicher Quellen*, Berlin, 1988.

'Zur imperial-kolonialen Funkstrategie des deutschen Kaiserreichs', *Zeitschrift für Geschichte* 39 (1991), 1112–21.

Seepel, Horst-Joachim, *Das Polenbild der Deutschen: Vom Anfang des 19. Jahrhunderts bis zum Ende der Revolution von 1848*, Kiel, 1967.

Segal, Aaron, *An Atlas of International Migration*, London, 1993.

Seidel, Robert, *Der Arbeits-Unterricht: Eine pädagogische und soziale Notwendigkeit*, Tübingen, 1885.

Seifert, Manfred, *Kulturarbeit im Reichsarbeitsdienst: Theorie und Praxis nationalsozialistischer Kulturpflege im Kontext historisch-politischer, organisatorischer und ideologischer Einflüsse*, Münster, 1996.

Seiler, Otto J., *Hapag-Lloyd: 100 Jahre Linienschiffahrt*, 2 vols., Hamburg, 1986.

Ostasienfahrt: Linienschiffahrt der Hapag-Lloyd AG im Wandel der Zeiten, Herford, 1988.

Sengoopta, Chandak, *Imprint of the Raj: How Fingerprinting was Born in Colonial India*, London, 2003.

Sereda, Ostap, 'Public Debates over the National Identity of the Galician Ruthenians', *Jahrbücher für Geschichte Osteuropas* 49 (2001), 200–12.

Serrier, Thomas, *Entre Allemagne et Pologne: Nations et identités frontalières 1848–1914*, Paris, 2002.

Provinz Posen, Ostmark, Wielkopolska: Eine Grenzregion zwischen Deutschen und Polen, 1848–1914, Marburg, 2005.

Sheldon, Kathleen E. *Pounders of Grain: A History of Women, Work, and Politics in Mozambique*, Portsmouth, NH, 2002.

Shimada, Shingo, *Grenzgänge–Fremdgänge: Japan und Europa im Kulturvergleich*, Frankfurt, 1994.

'Überlegungen zum Konzept "Asien"', in Sefgig Alp Bahadir (ed.), *Kultur und Region im Zeichen der Globalisierung*, Neustadt, 2000, pp. 155–68.

Shumway, Nicolas, *The Invention of Argentina*, Berkeley, 1991.

Sievers, Wilhelm, *Südamerika und die deutschen Interessen*, Stuttgart, 1903.

Silbermann, Alfons, *Was ist jüdischer Geist? Zur Identität der Juden*, Zürich, 1984.

Silberner, Edmund, *Sozialisten zur Judenfrage: Ein Beitrag zur Geschichte des Sozialismus vom Anfang des 19. Jahrhunderts bis 1914*, Berlin, 1962.

Simmel, Georg, 'Das Problem der Soziologie', in Simmel, *Soziologie: Untersuchungen über die Formen der Vergesellschaftung*, Frankfurt, 1992, pp. 13–41.

Simon, Ernst, *Die staatliche Aufzucht unehelicher Kinder als Mittel zur Bekämpfung des Landarbeitermangels im deutschen Osten*, Hohensalza, 1914.

Singha, Radhika, 'Settle, Mobilize, Verify: Identification Practices in Colonial India', *Studies in History* 16 (2000), 151–98.

Sinha, Mrinalini, *Colonial Masculinity: The 'Manly Englishman' and the 'Effeminate Bengali' in the Late Nineteenth Century*, Manchester, 1995.

Sippel, Harald, '"Wie erzieht man am besten den Neger zur Plantagen-Arbeit?" Die Ideologie der Arbeitserziehung und ihre rechtliche Umsetzung in der Kolonie Deutsch-Ostafrika', in Kurt Beck and Gerd Spittler (eds.), *Arbeit in Afrika*, Hamburg, 1996, pp. 311–33.

Skidmore, Thomas E., 'Racial Ideas and Social Policy in Brazil, 1870–1940', in Richard Graham (ed.), *The Idea of Race in Latin America, 1870–1940*, Austin, 1990, pp. 7–36.

Smith, Anthony D., 'Memory and Modernity: Reflections on Ernest Gellner's Theory of Nationalism', *Nations and Nationalism* 2 (1996), 371–88.

The Nation in History: Historiographical Debates about Ethnicity and Nationalism, Cambridge, 2000.

Nationalism and Modernism, London, 1998.

Nationalism in the Twentieth Century, Oxford, 1979.

Smith, Helmut Walser, 'An Preußens Rändern oder: Die Welt, die dem Nationalismus verloren ging', in Sebastian Conrad and Jürgen Osterhammel (eds.), *Das Kaiserreich transnational: Deutschland in der Welt 1871–1914*, Göttingen, 2004, pp. 149–69.

German Nationalism and Religious Conflict: Culture, Ideology, Politics, 1870–1914, Princeton, 1995.

Smith, Neil, *Uneven Development: Nature, Capital, and the Production of Space*, New York, 1984.

Smith, Thomas C., 'Peasant Time and Factory Time in Japan', in Smith, *Native Sources of Japanese Industrialization, 1750–1920*, Berkeley, 1988, pp. 199–235.

Smith, Woodruff D., *The Ideological Origins of Nazi Imperialism*, New York, 1986.

Politics and the Sciences of Culture in Germany, 1840–1920, Oxford, 1991.

'"Weltpolitik" und "Lebensraum"', in Sebastian Conrad and Jürgen Osterhammel (eds.), *Das Kaiserreich transnational: Deutschland in der Welt 1871–1914*, Göttingen, 2004, pp. 29–48.

Snyder, Louis L., *Macro-Nationalisms: A History of the Pan-Movements*, Westport, 1984.

Soja, Edward W., *Postmodern Geographies: The Reassertion of Space in Critical Social Theory*, London, 1988.

Söldenwagner, Philippa, *Spaces of Negotiation: European Settlement and Settlers in German East Africa 1900–1914*, Munich, 2006.

Sombart, Werner, *Die deutsche Volkswirtschaft im 19. Jahrhundert und im Anfang des 20. Jahrhunderts*, Berlin, 1927.

Die Juden und das Wirtschaftsleben, Leipzig, 1911.

Sösemann, Bernd, 'Die sog[enannte] Hunnenrede Wilhelms II: Textkritische und interpretatorische Bemerkungen zur Ansprache des Kaisers vom 27. Juli 1900 in Bremerhaven', *Historische Zeitschrift* 222 (1976), 342–58.

Spengler, Oswald, *Der Untergang des Abendlandes*, Munich, 1998.

Spielmann, Christian, *Arier und Mongolen: Weckruf an die europäischen Kontinentalen unter historischer und politischer Beleuchtung der Gelben Gefahr*, Halle, 1905.

Spiliotis, Susanne-Sophia, 'Das Konzept der Transterritorialität oder: Wo findet Gesellschaft statt?', *Geschichte und Gesellschaft* 27 (2001), 480–88.

Spillman, Lyn, *Nation and Commemoration: Creating National Identities in the United States and Australia*, Cambridge 1997.

Spittler, Gerd, 'Die Arbeitswelt in Agrargesellschaften', *Kölner Zeitschrift für Soziologie und Sozialpsychologie* 43 (1991), 1–17.

Verwaltung in einem afrikanischen Bauernstaat: Das koloniale Französisch-Westafrika, 1919–1939, Stuttgart, 1981.

Spivak, Gayatri Chakravorty, 'Can the Subaltern Speak?', in Cary Nelson and Lawrence Grossberg (eds.), *Marxism and the Interpretation of Culture*, London, 1988, pp. 271–313.

'The Making of Americans, the Teaching of English, the Future of Colonial Studies', *New Literary History* 21 (1990), 781–98.

Spivey, Donald, *Schooling for the New Slavery: Black Industrial Education, 1868–1915*, Westport, 1978.

Spohn, Wilfried, *Weltmarktkonkurrenz und Industrialisierung Deutschlands 1870–1914: Eine Untersuchung zur nationalen und internationalen Geschichte der kapitalistischen Produktionsweise*, Berlin, 1977.

Srbik, Franz von, *Die Auswanderungsgesetzgebung*, 2 vols., Vienna, 1911.

Standage, Tom, *Das viktorianische Internet: Die erstaunliche Geschichte des Telegraphen und der Online-Pioniere des 19. Jahrhunderts*, St Gallen, 1999.

Stanislawski, Michael, *Zionism and the Fin de Siècle: Cosmopolitanism and Nationalism from Nordau to Jabotinsky*, Berkeley, 2001.

Steinbach, Peter, 'Wilhelm Heinrich Riehl', in Hans-Ulrich Wehler (ed.), *Deutsche Historiker*, 9 vols., Vol. VI, Göttingen, 1980, pp. 37–54.

Steinert, Heinz and Hubert Treiber, *Die Fabrikation des zuverlässigen Menschen: Über die Wahlverwandtschaft von Kloster- und Fabrikdisziplin*, Munich, 1980.

Steinert, Oliver, *'Berlin–Polnischer Bahnhof!' Die Berliner Polen: Eine Untersuchung zum Verhältnis von nationaler Selbstbehauptung und sozialem Integrationsbedürfnis einer fremdsprachigen Minderheit in der Hauptstadt des Deutschen Kaiserreichs (1871–1918)*, Hamburg, 2003.

Steinfeld, Robert J., *Coercion, Contract, and Free Labor in the Nineteenth Century*, Cambridge, 2001.

Steinkühler, Martin, *Agrar- oder Industriestaat: Die Auseinandersetzungen um die Getreidehandels- und Zollpolitik des Deutschen Reiches 1879–1914*, Frankfurt, 1992.

Steinmetz, George, *The Devil's Handwriting: Precoloniality and the German Colonial State in Qingdao, Samoa, and Southwest Africa*, Chicago, 2007.

Stepan, Nancy S., *The Hour of Eugenics: Race, Gender, and Nation in Latin America*, Ithaca, NY, 1991.

Stepinski, Wlodzimierz, 'Siedlungsbewegung und landwirtschaftlicher Kredit: Die polnische Forschung zum Verlauf und zu den Folgen der Germanisierungspolitik für die agrarische Modernisierung im preußischen Teilungsgebiet Polens vor 1914', in Heinz Reif (ed.), *Ostelbische Agrargesellschaft im Kaiserreich und in der Weimarer Republik*, Berlin, 1994, pp. 329–43.

Stern, Fritz, *Kulturpessimismus als politische Gefahr: Eine Analyse nationaler Ideologie in Deutschland*, Munich, 1986.

Sternberger, Dolf, 'Das Zauberwort "Entwicklung"', in Sternberger, *Panorama oder Ansichten vom 19. Jahrhundert*, Frankfurt, 1974, pp. 87–121.

Stewart, Watt, *Chinese Bondage in Peru: A History of the Chinese Coolie in Peru 1849–1874*, Westport, 1970.

Stichweh, Rudolf, *Die Weltgesellschaft: Soziologische Analysen*, Frankfurt, 2000.

'Zur Theorie der Weltgesellschaft', *Soziale Systeme* 1 (1995), 29–45.

Stieda, Wilhelm, 'Beschäftigung ausländischer Arbeiter', in *Sten. Bericht des 6. Deutschen Arbeitsnachweiskongresses in Breslau 1910*, Berlin, 1911.

Stingl, Werner, *Der Ferne Osten in der deutschen Politik vor dem Ersten Weltkrieg (1902–1914)*, 2 vols., Frankfurt, 1978.

Stoecker, Adolf, *Christlich-Sozial: Reden und Aufsätze*, Berlin, 1890.

Deutschland und China im 19. Jahrhundert, Berlin, 1958.

Stoecker, Helmuth (ed.), *Drang nach Afrika: Die koloniale Expansionspolitik und Herrschaft des deutschen Imperialismus in Afrika von den Anfängen bis zum Ende des zweiten Weltkrieges*, Berlin, 1977.

Stokes, Gale, 'The Fates of Human Societies: A Review of Recent Macrohistories', *American Historical Review* 106 (2001), 508–25.

Stoler, Ann Laura, *Carnal Knowledge and Imperial Power: Race and the Intimate in Colonial Rule*, Berkeley, 2002.

Race and the Education of Desire: Foucault's History of Sexuality and the Colonial Order of Things, Durham, NC, 1995.

'Rethinking Colonial Categories: European Communities and the Boundaries of Rule', *Comparative Studies in Society and History* 31 (1989), 134–61.

Stoler, Ann Laura and Frederick Cooper, 'Between Metropole and Colony: Rethinking a Research Agenda', in Stoler and Cooper (eds.), *Tensions of Empire: Colonial Cultures in a Bourgeois World*, Berkeley, 1997, pp. 1–56.

Stolze, Georg Adolph, *Gedanken eines Hinterwäldlers Brasiliens über sociale Verhältnisse, besonders in Bezug auf die deutsche Auswanderung nach Brasilien*, Leer, 1895.

Struck, Bernhard, *Nicht West–nicht Ost: Frankreich und Polen in der Wahrnehmung deutscher Reisender zwischen 1750 und 1850*, Göttingen, 2006.

'*Terra Incognita*, European Civilisation and Colonised Land: Poland in Mid-Eighteenth Century to Mid-Nineteenth Century German Travel Accounts', in Hagen Schulz-Forberg (ed.), *Unravelling Civilisation: European Travel and Travel Writing*, Brussels, 2005, pp. 154–79.

Stuchtey, Benedikt, 'Nation und Expansion: Das britische Empire in der neuesten Forschung', *Historische Zeitschrift* 274 (2002), 87–118.

Sturm, Karl, *Die Landstreicherei*, Breslau, 1909.

Subrahmanyam, Sanjay, 'Connected Histories: Toward a Reconfiguration of Early Modern Eurasia', in Victor Lieberman (ed.), *Beyond Binary Histories: Reimagining Eurasia to* c. *1830*, Ann Arbor, 1997, pp. 289–315.

Sudhaus, Fritz, *Deutschland und die Auswanderung nach Brasilien im 19. Jahrhundert*, Hamburg, 1940.

Süchting-Hänger, Andrea, *Das 'Gewissen der Nation': Nationales Engagement und politisches Handeln konservativer Frauenorganisationen 1900 bis 1937*, Düsseldorf, 2002.

Summerskill, Michael, *China on the Western Front*, London, 1982.

Sunseri, Thaddeus, *Vilimani: Labor Migration and Rural Change in Early Colonial Tanzania*, Portsmouth, NH, 2002.

Suryadinata, Leo (ed.), *Ethnic Chinese as Southeast Asians*, London, 1998.

Suter, Andreas, 'Der Nationalstaat und die "Tradition von Erfindung": Die Schweiz, Frankreich und Deutschland im Vergleich', *Geschichte und Gesellschaft* 25 (1999), 138–61.

Sweeney, Dennis, 'Work, Race and the Transformation of Industrial Culture in Wilhelmine Germany', *Social History* 23 (1998), 31–62.

Syrup-Stettin, Friedrich, 'Die ausländischen Industriearbeiter', *Archiv für exakte Wirtschaftsforschung* 9 (1922), 278–301.

Tacke, Charlotte, *Denkmal im sozialen Raum: Nationale Symbole in Deutschland und Frankreich im 19. Jahrhundert*, Göttingen, 1995.

Takebayashi, Shirô, *Die Entstehung der Kapitalismustheorie in der Gründungsphase der deutschen Soziologie: Von der historischen Nationalökonomie zur historischen Soziologie Werner Sombarts und Max Webers*, Berlin, 2003.

Tappenbeck, Ernst, 'Die Arbeiterverhältnisse in Kaiser Wilhelmsland', *Deutsche Kolonialzeitung* 17 (1894), 131–32.

'Die Chinesengefahr in den deutschen Kolonien', *Deutsche Kolonialzeitung* 17 (1894), 166–68.

Tejapira, Kasian, 'Imagined Uncommunity: The *Lookjin* Middle Class and Thai Official Nationalism', in Daniel Chirot and Anthony Reid (eds.), *Essential Outsiders: Chinese and Jews in the Modern Transformation of Southeast Asia and Central Europe*, Seattle, 1997, pp. 75–98.

Teltschik, Walter, *Geschichte der deutschen Großchemie*, Weinheim, 1992.

Tenbruck, Friedrich H., 'Bürgerliche Kultur', *Kölner Zeitschrift für Soziologie und Sozialpsychologie* 27 (1986), 263–85.

'Gesellschaftsgeschichte oder Weltgeschichte?', *Kölner Zeitschrift für Soziologie und Sozialpsychologie* 41 (1989), 417–39.

Tetzlaff, Rainer, 'Koloniale Entwicklung und Ausbeutung: Wirtschafts- und Sozialgeschichte Deutsch-Ostafrikas 1885–1914', Dr. Phil. dissertation, Freie Universität Berlin, 1967.

'Die Mission im Spannungsfeld zwischen kolonialer Herrschaftssicherung und Zivilisierungsanspruch in Deutsch-Ostafrika', in Klaus J. Bade (ed.), *Imperialismus und Kolonialmission: Kaiserliches Deutschland und koloniales Imperium*, Wiesbaden, 1982, pp. 189–204.

Theiner, Peter, '"Mitteleuropa"-Pläne im wilhelminischen Deutschland', in Helmut Berding (ed.), *Wirtschaft und politische Integration in Europa im 19. und 20. Jahrhundert*, Göttingen, 1984, pp. 128–48.

Sozialer Liberalismus und deutsche Weltpolitik: Friedrich Naumann im wilhelminischen Deutschland (1860–1919), Baden-Baden, 1983.

Ther, Philipp, 'Deutsche Geschichte als imperiale Geschichte: Polen, slawophone Minderheiten und das Kaiserreich als kontinentales Empire', in Sebastian Conrad and Jürgen Osterhammel (eds.), *Das Kaiserreich transnational: Deutschland in der Welt 1871–1914*, Göttingen, 2004, pp. 129–48.

'Die Grenzen des Nationalismus: Der Wandel von Identitäten in Oberschlesien von der Mitte des 19. Jahrhunderts bis 1939', in Ulrike von Hirschhausen and Jörn Leonhard (eds.), *Nationalismen in Europa: West- und Osteuropa im Vergleich*, Göttingen, 2001, pp. 322–46.

Thomas, Roger, 'Forced Labour in British West Africa: The Case of the Northern Territories of the Gold Coast, 1906–1927', *Journal of African History* 14 (1973), 79–103.

Thomas, William I. and Florian Znaniecki, *The Polish Peasant in Europe and America*, 5 vols., Boston, MA, 1918–20.

Thompson, Edward P., *The Making of the English Working Class*, London, 1963. 'Time, Work-Discipline, and Industrial Capitalism', *Past and Present* 38 (1967), 56–97.

Thorne, Susan, *Congregational Missions and the Making of an Imperial Culture in Nineteenth-Century England*, Stanford, 1999.

Tille, Alexander, *Der Wettbewerb weißer und gelber Arbeit in der industriellen Produktion*, Berlin, 1904.

Tille, Armin, *Ein Kämpferleben: Alexander Tille 1866–1912*, Gotha, 1916.

Tilly, Richard, *Globalisierung aus historischer Sicht und das Lernen aus der Geschichte*, Cologne, 1999.

Tims, Richard W., *Germanizing Prussian Poland: The HKT-Society and the Struggle for the Eastern Marches in the German Empire 1894–1919*, New York, 1966.

Tinker, Hugh, *A New System of Slavery: The Export of Indian Labour Overseas, 1830–1920*, London, 1974.

Todorov, Tzvetan, *The Conquest of America: The Question of the Other*, trans. Richard Howard, New York, 1984.

Tom, Nancy Y. W., *The Chinese in Western Samoa 1875–1985*, Apia, 1986.

Tonesson, Stein and Hans Antlöv (eds.), *Asian Forms of the Nation*, London, 1996.

Torp, Cornelius, *Die Herausforderung der Globalisierung: Wirtschaft und Politik in Deutschland 1860–1914*, Göttingen, 2005.

Torpey, John, *The Invention of the Passport: Surveillance, Citizenship and the State*, Cambridge, 2001.

Townsend, James, 'Chinese Nationalism', in Jonathan Unger (ed.), *Chinese Nationalism*, New York, 1996, pp. 1–30.

Traub, Gottfried, 'Arbeit und Arbeiterorganisation', in *Festgaben für Friedrich Julius Neumann*, Tübingen, 1905, pp. 127–43.

Treitschke, Heinrich von, 'Die ersten Versuche deutscher Kolonialpolitik', in Treitschke, *Aufsätze, Reden und Briefe*, 5 vols., Vol. IV, ed. K. M. Schiller, Meersburg, 1929, pp. 665–76.

Trentmann, Frank, *Free Trade Nation: Commerce, Consumption, and Civil Society in Modern Britain*, Oxford, 2008.

Treue, Wilhelm, *Eisenbahnen und Industrialisierung: Ein Beitrag zur preußischen Wirtschafts- und Technikgeschichte im 19. Jahrhundert*, Dortmund, 1987.

Tribe, Keith, *Strategies of Economic Order: German Economic Discourse, 1750–1950*, Cambridge, 1995.

Trincia, Luciano, *Migration und Diaspora: Katholische Kirche und italienische Arbeitsmigration nach Deutschland und in die Schweiz vor dem Ersten Weltkrieg*, Freiburg, 1998.

Trittelvitz, Walther, *Nicht so langsam! Missionserinnerungen an Vater Bodelschwingh*, Bethel, 1930.

Trocki, Carl A., *Opium and Empire: Chinese Society in Colonial Singapore, 1800–1910*, Ithaca, NY, 1990.

Trommler, Frank, 'Die Nationalisierung der Arbeit', in Reinhold Grimm and Jost Hermand (eds.), *Arbeit als Thema in der deutschen Literatur vom Mittelalter bis zur Gegenwart*, Königstein, 1979, pp. 102–25.

Trommler, Frank and Joseph McVeigh (eds.), *America and the Germans: An Assessment of a Three-Hundred-Year History*, 2 vols., Philadelphia, 1985.

Trotha, Trutz von, '"One for the Kaiser": Beobachtungen zur politischen Soziologie der Prügelstrafe am Beispiel des "Schutzgebietes Togo"', in Peter Heine and Ulrich van der Heyden (eds.), *Studien zur Geschichte des deutschen Kolonialismus in Afrika*, Pfaffenweiler, 1995, pp. 521–51.

'Was war der Kolonialismus? Einige zusammenfassende Befunde zur Soziologie und Geschichte des Kolonialismus und der Kolonialherrschaft', *Saeculum* 55 (2004), 49–95.

Trzeciakowski, Lech, *The Kulturkampf in Prussian Poland*, New York, 1990.

Tsai, Shih-Shan Henry, 'Reaction to Exclusion: The Boycott of 1905 and Chinese National Awakening', *The Historian* 39 (1976), 95–110.

Turner, B. S., *Marx and the End of Orientalism*, London, 1978.

Ullmann, Hans-Peter, *Interessenverbände in Deutschland*, Frankfurt, 1988.

Umbach, Maiken, *German Federalism: Past, Present, Future*, New York, 2002.

Unger, Jonathan (ed.), *Chinese Nationalism*, New York, 1996.

Unruh, Conrad von, *Amerika noch nicht am Ziele! Transgermanische Reisestudien*, Frankfurt, 1904.

Vallaux, Camille, *Géographie sociale: Le sol et l'état*, Paris, 1911.

Vallentin, Wilhelm, *In Brasilien*, Berlin, 1909.

Valverde, Mariana, 'The Dialectic of the Familiar and the Unfamiliar: "The Jungle" in Early Slum Travel Writing', *Sociology* 30 (1996), 493–509.

Van den Bossche, Geert, 'Is there Nationalism after Ernest Gellner? An Exploration of Methodological Choices', *Nations and Nationalism* 9 (2003), 491–509.

Vance, J. E., *Capturing the Horizon: The Historical Geography of Transportation since the Sixteenth Century*, Baltimore, 1990.

Varg, Paul A., 'The Myth of the China Market, 1890–1914', *American Historical Review* 73 (1967/68), 742–58.

Vatin, François, 'Arbeit und Ermüdung: Entstehung und Scheitern der Psychophysiologie der Arbeit', in Philipp Sarasin and Jakob Tanner (eds.), *Physiologie und industrielle Gesellschaft: Studien zur Verwissenschaftlichung des Körpers im 19. und 20. Jahrhundert*, Frankfurt, 1998, pp. 347–68.

Vec, Miloš, *Die Spur des Täters: Methoden der Identifikation in der Kriminalistik (1879–1933)*, Baden-Baden, 2002.

Verhey, Jeffrey, *The Spirit of 1914: Militarism, Myth, and Mobilization in Germany*, Cambridge, 2000.

Vierhaus, Rudolf, 'Bildung', in Otto Brunner, Werner Conze and Reinhart Koselleck (eds.), *Geschichtliche Grundbegriffe: Historisches Lexikon zur politisch-sozialen Sprache in Deutschland*, 8 vols., Vol. i, Stuttgart, 1972, pp. 508–51.

Vietor, J. K., C. Meinhof and J. Spieth, *Der Afrikaner, seine wirtschaftliche Leistungsfähigkeit, geistige Befähigung, religiöse Veranlagung: Vorträge auf dem II. Deutschen Kolonial-Missionstag zu Cassel*, Bremen, 1912.

Virchow, Rudolf, 'Der Kampf der Zellen und der Bakterien', *Archiv für pathologische Anatomie und Physiologie und für klinische Medicin* 101 (1885), 1–13.

Virilio, Paul, *Revolutionen der Geschwindigkeit*, Berlin, 1993.

Voigt, Johannes H., 'Die Deportation: Ein Thema der deutschen Rechtswissenschaft und Politik im 19. und frühen 20. Jahrhundert', in Andreas Gestrich, Gerhard Hirschfeld and Holger Sonnabend (eds.), *Ausweisung und Deportation: Formen der Zwangsmigration in der Geschichte*, Stuttgart, 1995, pp. 83–101.

Volkmann, Hans-Erich and Bernhard Chiari (eds.), *Ökonomie und Expansion: Grundzüge der NS-Wirtschaftspolitik*, Munich, 2003.

Volkov, Shulamit, 'Antisemitismus als kultureller Code', in Shulamit, *Jüdisches Leben und Antisemitismus im 19. und 20. Jahrhundert*, Munich, 1990, pp. 13–36.

  Die Juden in Deutschland 1780–1918, Munich, 1994.

Vulpius, Ricarda, 'Ukrainische Nation und zwei Konfessionen: Der Klerus und die ukrainische Frage 1861–1921', *Jahrbücher für Geschichte Osteuropas* 49 (2001), 240–56.

Wagner, Norbert Berthold, *Die deutschen Schutzgebiete: Erwerb, Organisation und Verlust aus juristischer Sicht*, Baden-Baden, 2002.

Wagner, Reinhardt W., *Deutsche als Ersatz für Sklaven: Arbeitsmigranten aus Deutschland in der brasilianischen Provinz São Paulo 1847–1914*, Frankfurt, 1995.

Wagner, Rudolf G., 'The Concept of Work/Labor/Arbeit in the Chinese World', in Manfred Bierwisch (ed.), *Die Rolle der Arbeit in verschiedenen Epochen und Kulturen*, Berlin, 2003, pp. 103–36.

  Reenacting the Heavenly Vision: The Role of Religion in the Taiping Rebellion, Berkeley, 1982.

Wakeman, Frederic, *Strangers at the Gate: Social Disorder in South China, 1839–1861*, Berkeley, 1966.

Waldmann, Peter, 'Kulturkonflikt und Anpassungszwang: Ausgangslage und Entwicklung der deutschen Einwanderungskolonien in Südchile', in Justin Stagl (ed.), *Aspekte der Kultursoziologie*, Berlin, 1982, pp. 239–51.

Waley-Cohen, Joanna, *The Sextants of Beijing: Global Currents in Chinese History*, New York, 1999.

Walkenhorst, Peter, *Nation–Volk–Rasse: Radikaler Nationalismus im Deutschen Kaiserreich 1890–1914*, Göttingen, 2007.

Wallerstein, Immanuel, *The Modern World System*, 3 vols., New York, 1974–89.

'Societal Development, or Development of the World-System?', *International Sociology* 1 (1986), 3–17.

Walther, Daniel J., *Creating Germans Abroad: Cultural Policies and National Identity in Namibia*, Athens, 2006.

Wang, Guanhua, *In Search of Justice: The 1905–1906 Chinese Anti-American Boycott*, Cambridge, MA, 2001.

Wang, Gungwu, *China and the Chinese Overseas*, Singapore, 1991.

(ed.), *Global History and Migrations*, Boulder, 1997.

(ed.), 'South China Perspectives on Overseas Chinese', *The Australian Journal of Chinese Affairs* 13 (1985), 69–84.

Wang, Singwu, *The Organization of Chinese Emigration, 1848–1888*, San Francisco, 1978.

Wang, Yeu-Farn, *The National Identity of the Southeast Asian Chinese*, Stockholm, 1994.

Wappäus, Johann Eduard (ed.), *Deutsche Auswanderung und Colonisation*, Leipzig, 1846.

Warneck, Gustav, *Evangelische Missionslehre: Ein missionstheoretischer Versuch*, 3 vols., Vol. III, Part I: *Der Betrieb der Sendung*, Gotha, 1897.

Die gegenseitigen Beziehungen zwischen der modernen Mission und Cultur: Auch eine Kulturkampfstudie, Gütersloh, 1879.

Die Stellung der evangelischen Mission zur Sklavenfrage, geschichtlich und theoretisch erörtert, Gütersloh, 1889.

Wawrzinek, Kurt, *Die Entstehung der deutschen Antisemitenparteien 1873–1890*, Berlin, 1927.

Weber, Ernst, *Lyrik der Befreiungskriege (1812–1815): Gesellschaftspolitische Meinungs- und Willensbildung durch Literatur*, Stuttgart, 1991.

Weber, Ernst von, *Die Erweiterung des deutschen Wirtschaftsgebietes und die Grundlegung zu überseeischen deutschen Staaten*, Leipzig, 1879.

Weber, Eugen, *Peasants into Frenchmen: The Modernization of Rural France, 1880–1914*, Stanford, 1976.

Weber, Marianne, *Max Weber: Ein Lebensbild*, Munich, 1989.

Weber, Max, *Briefe 1906–1908*, ed. Mario R. Lepsius and Wolfgang Mommsen, Tübingen, 1990.

Economy and Society, ed. Guenther Roth and Claus Wittich, Berkeley, 1978.

Gesammelte Aufsätze zur Religionssoziologie, 3 vols., Vol. I, Tübingen, 1920.

Gesammelte Aufsätze zur Sozial- und Wirtschaftsgeschichte, ed. Marianne Weber, Tübingen, 1988.

Die Lage der Landarbeiter im ostelbischen Deutschland: 1892, in Max Weber Gesamtausgabe, 41 vols., Vol. III, Tübingen, 1984.

'Die nationalen Grundlagen der Volkswirtschaft: Vortrag am 12. März 1895 in Frankfurt am Main [Bericht des *Frankfurter Volksboten*]', in *Max Weber Gesamtausgabe*, 41 vols., Vol. IV, Part II, Tübingen, 1993, pp. 726–28.

'Das Polenthum in den deutschen Ostmarken [Bericht der *Freiburger Zeitung*]', in *Max Weber Gesamtausgabe*, 41 vols., Vol. IV, Part II, Tübingen 1993, pp. 821–23.

Political Writings, ed. Peter Lassman, trans. Ronald Speirs, Cambridge Texts in the History of Political Thought, Cambridge, 1994.

Wedlake, G. E. C., *SOS: The Story of Radio Communication*, London, 1973.

Wege, Carl, 'Der Kult der Arbeit: Zu Reden und Schriften von Martin Heidegger und Ernst Jünger aus den Jahren 1932/33', in Ulrich Bröckling and Eva Horn (eds.), *Anthropologie der Arbeit*, Tübingen, 2002, pp. 231–40.

Wehler, Hans-Ulrich, *Bismarck und der Imperialismus*, Cologne, 1969.

Deutsche Gesellschaftsgeschichte, 4 vols., Vol. I: *Vom Feudalismus des Alten Reiches bis zur defensiven Modernisierung der Reformära 1700–1815*, Munich, 1987.

Deutsche Gesellschaftsgeschichte, 4 vols., Vol. III: *Von der 'Deutschen Doppelrevolution' bis zum Ersten Weltkrieg 1849–1914*, Munich, 1995.

'Historische Verbandsforschung: Zur Funktion und Struktur nationaler Kampfverbände in Deutschland', in Wehler, *Historische Sozialwissenschaft und Geschichtsschreibung: Studien zu Aufgaben und Traditionen deutscher Geschichtswissenschaft*, Göttingen, 1980, pp. 151–61.

Nationalismus: Geschichte, Formen, Folgen, Munich, 2001.

'Polenpolitik im Deutschen Kaiserreich', in Wehler, *Krisenherde des Kaiserreichs 1871–1918*, Göttingen, 1979, pp. 184–203.

Sozialdemokratie und Nationalstaat: Die deutsche Sozialdemokratie und die Nationalitätenfrage in Deutschland von Karl Marx bis zum Ausbruch des Ersten Weltkrieges, Würzburg, 1962.

Wei-kui, Fang, *Das Chinabild in der deutschen Literatur, 1871–1933: Ein Beitrag zur komparatistischen Imagologie*, Frankfurt, 1992.

Weichert, Ludwig, *Das Schulwesen deutscher evangelischer Missionsgesellschaften in den deutschen Kolonien*, Berlin, 1914.

Weichlein, Siegfried, *Nation und Region: Integrationsprozesse im Bismarckreich*, Düsseldorf, 2004.

Weidenfeller, Gerhard, *VDA: Verein für das Deutschtum im Auslande*, Bern, 1976.

Weidenkeller, Johann Jacob, *Kolonien als die besten Armenbeschäftigungs- und Versorgungs-Anstalten für alle Staaten Europas: Ein Ruf zur gegenwärtigen Zeit an alle, welchen das Wohl, die Ruhe, Ordnung und Sicherheit ihres Vaterlandes, sowie ihrer Mitmenschen, am Herzen liegt*, Nuremberg, 1848.

Weindling, Paul J., *Epidemics and Genocide in Eastern Europe, 1890–1945*, Oxford, 2000.

    Health, Race, and Politics in Germany between National Unification and Nazism 1870–1945, Oxford, 1989.

    'A Virulent Strain: German Bacteriology as Scientific Racism, 1890–1920', in Bernard Harris and Ernst Waltraud (eds.), *Race, Science, and Medicine, 1700–1960*, London, 1999, pp. 218–34.

Weingart, Peter, Jürgen Kroll and Kurt Bayertz, *Rasse, Blut und Gene: Geschichte der Eugenik und Rassenhygiene in Deutschland*, Frankfurt, 1992.

Welskopp, Thomas, *Banner der Brüderlichkeit: Die deutsche Sozialdemokratie vom Vormärz bis zum Sozialistengesetz*, Bonn, 2000.

Welz, Gisela, 'Moving Targets: Feldforschung unter Mobilitätsdruck', *Zeitschrift für Volkskunde* 94 (1998), 177–94.

Wennemann, Adolf, *Arbeit im Norden: Italiener im Rheinland und Westfalen des späten 19. und frühen 20. Jahrhunderts*, Osnabrück, 1997.

Wenning, Norbert, *Migration in Deutschland: Ein Überblick*, Münster, 1996.

Werner, Michael and Bénédicte Zimmermann, 'Penser l'histoire croisée: Entre empirie et reflexivité', *Annales HSS* 58 (2003), 7–36.

    'Vergleich, Transfer, Verflechtung: Der Ansatz der *Histoire croisée* und die Herausforderung des Transnationalen', *Geschichte und Gesellschaft* 28 (2002), 607–36.

Wernicke, Hugo, *Deutsch-evangelisches Volkstum in Espirito Santo: Eine Reise zu deutschen Kaffeebauern in einem tropischen Staate Brasiliens*, Potsdam, 1910.

Wertheimer, Jack, '"The Unwanted Element": East European Jews in Imperial Germany', *Yearbook of the Leo Baeck Institute* 26 (1981), 23–46.

    Unwelcome Strangers: East European Jews in Imperial Germany, New York, 1987.

Wessel, Horst A., 'Die Rolle des Telefons in der Kommunikationsrevolution des 19. Jahrhunderts', in Michael North (ed.), *Kommunikationsrevolutionen: Die neuen Medien des 16. und 19. Jahrhunderts*, Cologne, 1995, pp. 101–27.

    'Die Verbreitung des Telephons bis zur Gegenwart', in Hans-Jürgen Teuteberg and Cornelius Neutsch (eds.), *Vom Flügeltelegraphen zum Internet: Geschichte der modernen Telekommunikation*, Stuttgart, 1998, pp. 67–112.

West, Michael O., 'The Tuskegee Model of Development in Africa: Another Dimension of the African/African-American Connection', *Diplomatic History* 16 (1992), 371–87.

Westermann, Rudolf, *Wie wandere ich nach Südamerika aus? Teil III: Süd-Brasilien*, Berlin, 1919.

Westney, D. Eleanor, *Imitation and Innovation: The Transfer of Western Organizational Patterns to Meiji Japan*, Cambridge, MA, 1987.

Wettstein, Karl A., *Brasilien und die deutsch-brasilianische Kolonie Blumenau*, Leipzig, 1907.

    Mit deutschen Kolonistenjungens durch den brasilianischen Urwald! Selbsterlebtes: Eine Reise nach und durch Südbrasilien und seine deutsch-völkischen Kolonien, Leipzig, 1910.

Wetzel, Walter, *Naturwissenschaften und chemische Industrie in Deutschland*, Stuttgart, 1991.

White, Hayden, 'The Noble Savage Theme as Fetish', in Fredi Chiappelli, Michael J. B. Allen and Robert Louis Benson (eds.), *First Images of America: The Impact of the New World on the Old*, 2 vols., Vol. 1, Berkeley, 1976, pp. 121–35.

Wichern, Johann Hinrich, 'Um die soziale Verantwortung', in Friedrich Wilhelm Kantzenbach (ed.), *Zeugnis und Zeichen: Reden, Briefe, Dokumente*, Munich, 1964, pp. 48–64.

    'Welches ist die Aufgabe der inneren Mission für die wandernde Bevölkerung?', in Jürgen Scheffler (ed.), *Bürger und Bettler: Materialien und Dokumente zur Geschichte der Nichtseßhaftenhilfe in der Diakonie*, Bielefeld, 1987, pp. 162–64.

Wiedemann, Konrad, *Arbeit und Bürgertum: Die Entwicklung des Arbeitsbegriffs in der Literatur Deutschlands an der Wende zur Neuzeit*, Heidelberg, 1979.

Wieland, Wolfgang, 'Entwicklung, Evolution', in Otto Brunner, Werner Conze and Reinhart Koselleck (eds.), *Geschichtliche Grundbegriffe: Historisches Lexikon zur politisch-sozialen Sprache in Deutschland*, 8 vols., Vol. II, Stuttgart 1975, pp. 199–228.

Wieser, Lothar, 'Deutsches Turnen in Brasilien: Deutsche Auswanderung und die Entwicklung des deutsch-brasilianischen Turnwesens bis zum Jahre 1917', Dr. Phil. dissertation, University of Göttingen, 1990.

Wigen, Kären, 'Culture, Power, and Place: The New Landscapes of East Asian Regionalism', *American Historical Review* 104 (1999), 1183–201.

    The Making of a Japanese Periphery, 1750–1920, Berkeley, 1995.

Wigen, Kären and Martin Lewis, *The Myth of Continents: A Critique of Metageography*, Berkeley, 1998.

Wildenthal, Lora, *German Women for Empire, 1884–1945*, Durham, NC, 2001.

Willard, Myra, *History of the White Australia Policy to 1920*, Melbourne, 1923.

Williams, Ernest Edwin, *Made in Germany* [1896], Brighton, 1973.

Williamson, Jeffrey G., 'The Evolution of Global Labor Markets since 1830: Background Evidence and Hypotheses', *Explorations in Economic History* 32 (1995), 141–96.

'Globalization, Convergence, and History', *Journal of Economic History* 56 (1996), 277–306.

Wilson, Kathleen, 'Introduction: Histories, Empires, Modernities', in Wilson (ed.), *A New Imperial History: Culture, Identity and Modernity in Britain and the Empire 1660–1840*, Cambridge, 2004, pp. 1–26.

Wilson, Ted, *Battles for the Standard: Bimetallism and the Spread of the Gold Standard in the Nineteenth Century*, Aldershot, 2000.

Winkel, Harald, *Die deutsche Nationalökonomie im 19. Jahrhundert*, Darmstadt, 1977.

Winkler, Heinrich A., 'Vom linken zum rechten Nationalismus: Der deutsche Liberalismus in der Krise von 1878/79', *Geschichte und Gesellschaft* 4 (1978), 5–28.

Winzen, Peter, *Bülows Weltmachtkonzept: Untersuchungen zur Frühphase seiner Außenpolitik 1897–1901*, Boppard, 1977.

'Zur Genesis von Weltmachtkonzept und Weltpolitik', in John C. G. Röhl (ed.), *Der Ort Kaiser Wilhelms II. in der deutschen Geschichte*, Munich, 1991, pp. 189–222.

Wippermann, Wolfgang, 'Antislavismus', in Uwe Puschner, Walter Schmitz and Justus H. Ulbricht (eds.), *Handbuch zur 'Völkischen Bewegung' 1871–1918*, Munich, 1996, pp. 512–24.

Der Ordensstaat als Ideologie: Das Bild des Deutschen Ordens in der deutschen Geschichtsschreibung und Publizistik, Berlin, 1979.

Der 'deutsche Drang nach Osten': Ideologie und Wirklichkeit eines politischen Schlagwortes, Darmstadt, 1981.

'"Gen Ostland wollen wir reiten!' Ordensstaat und Ostsiedlung in der historischen Belletristik Deutschlands', in Wolfgang M. Fritze (ed.), *Germania slavica*, Berlin, 1981, pp. 187–235.

Geschichte der Deutsch-Polnischen Beziehungen, Berlin 1992.

Wie die Zigeuner: Antisemitismus und Antiziganismus im Vergleich, Berlin, 1997.

Wippich, Rolf-Harald, 'Die "Fanny-Kirchner"-Affäre 1860: Eine oldenburgische Bank, der chinesische Kulihandel und die internationale Reaktion', *Comparativ* 13:4 (2003), 61–79.

'The Yellow Peril: Strategic and Ideological Implications of Germany's East Asian Policy before World War I: The Case of William II', *Sophia International Review* 18 (1996), 57–65.

Wirz, Albert, 'Für eine transnationale Gesellschaftsgeschichte', *Geschichte und Gesellschaft* 27 (2001), 489–98.

'Innerer und äußerer Wald: Zur moralischen Ökologie der Kolonisierenden', in Michael Flitner (ed.), *Der deutsche Tropenwald: Bilder, Mythen, Politik*, Frankfurt, 2000, pp. 23–48.

Wirz, Albert and Andreas Eckert, 'The Scramble for Africa: Icon and Idiom of Modernity', in Olivier Pétré-Grenouilleau (ed.), *From Slave Trade to Empire: Europe and the Colonisation of Black Africa 1780s–1880s*, London, 2004, pp. 133–53.

Wobbe, Theresa, *Weltgesellschaft*, Bielefeld, 2000.

Wojtczak, Maria, *Literatur der Ostmark: Posener Heimatliteratur (1890–1918)*, Poznan, 1998.

Wolf, Julius, *Das Deutsche Reich und der Weltmarkt*, Jena, 1901.

Wolfe, Patrick, 'History and Imperialism: A Century of Theory, from Marx to Postcolonialism', *American Historical Review* 102 (1997), 388–420.

Wolter, Udo and Paul Kaller, 'Deutsches Kolonialrecht: Ein wenig erforschtes Rechtsgebiet, dargestellt anhand des Arbeitsrechts der Eingeborenen', *Zeitschrift für neuere Rechtsgeschichte* 17 (1995), pp. 201–44.

Wolzogen, Hans von, 'Die farblose Gefahr', in Wolzogen, *Aus deutscher Welt*, Berlin, 1905, pp. 142–51.

Wong, Sin Kiong, *China's Anti-American Boycott Movement in 1905: A Study in Urban Protest*, New York, 2002.

Wong, Young-tsu, *Search for Modern Nationalism: Zhang Binglin and Revolutionary China, 1869–1936*, Oxford, 1989.

Woon, Yuen-fong, 'An Emigrant Community in the Ssu-yi Area, Southeastern China, 1855–1949', *Modern Asian Studies* 18 (1984), 273–308.

Wopfner, Hermann, *Tirols Eroberung durch deutsche Arbeit*, Innsbruck, 1921.

Wright, Marcia, *German Missions in Tanganyika*, Oxford, 1971.

Strategies of Slaves and Women, London, 1993.

Wulf, Julia, *'Made in Germany': Wirtschaftliche Bedeutung und rechtliche Schutzmöglichkeiten*, Frankfurt, 1995.

Wygodzinski, Willy, 'Die ausländischen Wanderarbeiter in der deutschen Landwirtschaft', *Weltwirtschaftliches Archiv* 7 (1916), 351–78.

Wandlungen der deutschen Volkswirtschaft im 19. Jahrhundert, Cologne, 1907.

Xenos, Nicholas, 'Nation, State and Economy: Max Weber's Freiburg Inaugural Lecture', in Marjorie Ringrose and Adam J. Lerner (eds.), *Reimagining the Nation*, Buckingham, 1993, pp. 125–38.

Yekelchyk, Serhy, 'The Body and National Myth: Motifs from the Ukrainian National Revival in the Nineteenth Century', *Australian Slavonic and East European Studies* 7:2 (1993), 31–58.

Yen, Ching-Hwang, *The Chinese Overseas and the 1911 Revolution, with Special Reference to Singapore and Malaya*, Kuala Lumpur, 1976.

Coolies and Mandarins: China's Protection of Overseas Chinese during the Late Ch'ing Period (1851–1911), Singapore, 1985.

Young, Ernest P., 'Chinese Leaders and Japanese Aid in the Early Republic', in Akira Iriye (ed.), *The Chinese and the Japanese: Essays in Political and Cultural Interactions*, Princeton, 1980, pp. 124–39.

Young, George F. W., *The Germans in Chile: Immigration and Colonization, 1849–1914*, New York, 1974.

Young, Michael, *The Metronomic Society: Natural Rhythms and Human Timetables*, Cambridge, MA, 1988.

Young, Robert, *Colonial Desire: Hybridity in Culture, Theory and Race*, London, 1995.

Postcolonialism: An Historical Introduction, Oxford, 2001.

White Mythologies: Writing History and the West, London, 1990.

Zantop, Susanne, *Colonial Fantasies: Conquest, Family, and Nation in Precolonial Germany, 1770–1870*, Durham, NC, 1997.

Zarnowska, Anna, 'Die polnische Arbeiterschaft in der Emigration vor dem 1. Weltkrieg und die Arbeiterbewegung', in *Internationale Tagung der Historiker der Arbeiterbewegung*, Vienna, 1987, pp. 115–22.

Zernack, Klaus, 'Der hochmittelalterliche Landesausbau als Problem der Entwicklung Ostmitteleuropas', in Zernack, *Preußen–Deutschland–Polen: Aufsätze zur Geschichte der deutsch-polnischen Beziehungen*, Berlin, 1991, pp. 185–202.

Zerubavel, Eviatar, *Hidden Rhythms: Schedules and Calendars in Social Life*, Berkeley, 1981.

Zeuske, Michael and Bernd Schröter (eds.), *Alexander von Humboldt und das neue Geschichtsbild von Lateinamerika*, Leipzig, 1992.

Zhou Xun, 'Youtai: The Myth of the "Jew" in Modern China', in Frank Dikötter (ed.), *The Construction of Racial Identities in China and Japan*, Honolulu, 1997, pp. 53–74.

Ziemann, Hans, *Über das Bevölkerungs- und Rassenproblem in den Kolonien (Ein koloniales Programm)*, Berlin, 1913.

Ziegler, Dieter, *Eisenbahnen und Staat im Zeitalter der Industrialisierung: Die Eisenbahnpolitik der deutschen Staaten im Vergleich*, Stuttgart, 1996.

Zimmerer, Jürgen, *Deutsche Herrschaft über Afrikaner: Staatlicher Machtanspruch und Wirklichkeit im kolonialen Namibia*, Münster, 2001.

'Die Geburt des "Ostlandes" aus dem Geiste des Kolonialismus: Die nationalsozialistische Eroberungs- und Beherrschungspolitik in (post–) kolonialer Perspektive', *Sozial.Geschichte* 19 (2004), 10–43.

'Holocaust und Kolonialismus: Beitrag zu einer Genealogie des genozidalen Gedankens', *Zeitschrift für Geschichte* 51 (2003), 1098–1119.

'Kolonialer Genozid? Vom Nutzen und Nachteil einer historischen Kategorie', in Dominik Schaller, Boyadjian Rupen, Hanno Scholtz and Vivianne Berg (eds.), *Enteignet–Vertrieben–Ermordet: Beiträge ʒur Genoʒidforschung*, Zürich, 2004, pp. 109–28.

Zimmerer, Jürgen and Joachim Zeller (eds.), *Völkermord in Deutsch-Südwestafrika: Der Kolonialkrieg (1904–1908) in Namibia und seine Folgen*, Berlin, 2003.

Zimmerman, Andrew, *Anthropology and Antihumanism in Imperial Germany*, Chicago, 2001.

'Decolonizing Weber', *Postcolonial Studies* 9 (2006), 53–79.

'A German Alabama in Africa: The Tuskegee Expedition to German Togo and the Transnational Origins of West African Cotton Growers', *American Historical Review* 110 (2005), 1362–98.

Zimmermann, Bénédicte, *La Constitution du chômage en Allemagne: Entre professions et territoires*, Paris, 2001.

Zimmermann, Michael, 'Arbeit in den Konzentrationslagern: Kommentierende Bemerkungen', in Ulrich Herbert, Karin Orth and Christoph Dieckmann (eds.), *Die nationalsoʒialistischen Konʒentrationslager: Entwicklung und Struktur*, 2 vols., Vol. II, Göttingen, 1998, pp. 730–51.

Rassenutopie und Genoʒid: Die nationalsoʒialistische 'Lösung der Zigeunerfrage', Hamburg, 1996.

Zimmermann, Rainer E., *Das Technikverständnis im Werk von Jules Verne und seine Aufnahme im Frankreich des 19. Jahrhunderts*, Berlin, 1987.

Zinnecker, Andrea, *Romantik, Rock und Kamisol: Volkskunde auf dem Weg ins Dritte Reich – die Riehl-Reʒeption*, Münster, 1996.

Zitzewitz, Hasso von, *Das deutsche Polenbild in der Geschichte: Entstehung, Einflüsse, Auswirkungen*, Cologne, 1991.

Zo, Kil Young, *Chinese Emigration into the United States, 1850–1880*, New York, 1978.

Zolberg, Aristide R., 'Global Movements, Global Walls: Responses to Migration, 1885–1925', in Wang Gungwu (ed.), *Global History and Migrations*, Boulder 1997, pp. 279–307.

'The Great Wall against China: Responses to the First Immigration Crisis, 1885–1925', in Jan Lucassen and Leo Lucassen (eds.), *Migration, Migration History, History: Old Paradigms and New Perspectives*, Bern, 1997, pp. 291–315.

'International Migration Policies in a Changing World System', in William McNeill and Ruth Adams (eds.), *Human Migration*, Bloomington, 1978, pp. 241–86.

Zorn, Wolfgang, 'Arbeit in Europa vom Mittelalter bis ins Industriezeitalter', in Venanz Schubert (ed.), *Der Mensch und seine Arbeit*, St Ottilien, 1986, pp. 181–212.

Zubrzycki, Jerzy, 'International Migration in Australia and the South Pacific', in Mary M. Kritz, Charles B. Keeley and Silvano N. Tomasi (eds.), *Global Trends in Migration*, New York, 1981, pp. 158–80.

Zumbini, Massimo Ferrari, 'Große Migration und Antislawismus: Negative Ostjudenbilder im Kaiserreich', *Jahrbuch für Antisemitismusforschung* 3 (1994), 194–226.

   'Die Wurzeln des Bösen'. Gründerjahre des Antisemitismus: Von der Bismarckzeit zu Hitler, Frankfurt, 2003.

Zweig, Stefan, *Die Welt von Gestern: Erinnerungen eines Europäers*, Frankfurt, 1970.

Index